Routledge History of Philosophy
Volume VII

The nineteenth century was a period of intense intellectual activity with advances being made in the sciences, in mathematics and in psychology which gradually established itself as a discipline independent of philosophy. Philosophical disputes arose about the nature of scientific method and about whether, or to what extent, the understanding of human conduct and human society required the adoption of the methods of observation and experiment common to the natural sciences. Different philosophical theories about the nature of reality, the foundations of knowledge and of morality, and the limits of individual freedom were systematically developed, and many such theories are still very much alive in contemporary philosophical debates.

The philosophers discussed in this volume include those belonging both to the 'analytic' and the 'continental' traditions, as well as the now influential American pragmatists. Each chapter is written by a different author who presents the issues in the context of the period in which they arose, while also keeping an eye on their relevance to current philosophical interests. A few philosophers are discussed in more than one chapter, in different but mutually illuminating contexts.

Each chapter in *The Nineteenth Century* is self-contained and makes a distinctive contribution to a set of philosophical problems. This volume provides a broad, scholarly introduction to nineteenth-century philosophy. It also contains a glossary of philosophical terms and a chronological table of philosophical and cultural events.

C. L. Ten is Visiting Professor of Philosophy at the National University of Singapore and holds a Personal Chair in Philosophy at Monash University, Australia. He has published widely on nineteenth-century philosophy and is a Fellow of the Australian Academy of the Humanities.

Routledge History of Philosophy
General Editors – G. H. R. Parkinson and S. G. Shanker

The *Routledge History of Philosophy* provides a chronological survey of the history of Western philosophy, from its beginnings in the sixth century BC to the present time. It discusses all major philosophical developments in depth. Most space is allocated to those individuals who, by common consent, are regarded as great philosophers. But lesser figures have not been neglected, and together the ten volumes of the *History* include basic and critical information about every significant philosopher of the past and present. These philosophers are clearly situated within the cultural and, in particular, the scientific context of their time.

The *History* is intended not only for the specialist, but also for the student and the general reader. Each chapter is by an acknowledged authority in the field. The chapters are written in an accessible style and a glossary of technical terms is provided in each volume.

Each volume contains 10–15 chapters by different contributors

Routledge History of Philosophy
Volume VII

The Nineteenth Century

EDITED BY
C. L. Ten

London and New York

First published 1994
by Routledge
11 New Fetter Lane London EC4P 4EE

Simultaneously published in the USA and Canada
by Routledge
29 West 35th Street, New York NY 10001

Phototypeset in 10½/12pt Garamond by Intype, London

Printed and bound in Great Britain by
T J Press (Padstow) Ltd, Padstow, Cornwall

British Library Cataloguing in Publication Data

A catalogue record for this book is available from the British Library.

Library of Congress Cataloging in Publication Data

The Nineteenth century / edited by C. L. Ten.
p.   cm.—(Routledge history of philosophy : v. 7)
Includes bibliographical references and index.
1. Philosophy, Modern—19th century.   2. Philosophy, European.
3. Philosophy, American—19th century.   I. Ten, C. L.   II. Series.
B803.N55   1994
190'.9'034—dc20   93-44442

ISBN 0-415-06003-6

Contents

General editors' preface

The history of philosophy, as its name implies, represents a union of two very different disciplines, each of which imposes severe constraints upon the other. As an exercise in the history of ideas, it demands that one acquire a 'period eye': a thorough understanding of how the thinkers whom it studies viewed the problems which they sought to resolve, the conceptual frameworks in which they addressed these issues, their assumptions and objectives, their blind spots and miscues. But as an exercise in philosophy, we are engaged in much more than simply a descriptive task. There is a crucial critical aspect to our efforts: we are looking for the cogency as much as the development of an argument, for its bearing on questions which continue to preoccupy us as much as the impact which it may have had on the evolution of philosophical thought.

The history of philosophy thus requires a delicate balancing act from its practitioners. We read these writings with the full benefit of historical hindsight. We can see why the minor contributions remained minor and where the grand systems broke down: sometimes as a result of internal pressures, sometimes because of a failure to overcome an insuperable obstacle, sometimes because of a dramatic technological or sociological change, and, quite often, because of nothing more than a shift in intellectual fashion or interests. Yet, because of our continuing philosophical concern with many of the same problems, we cannot afford to look dispassionately at these works. We want to know what lessons are to be learned from the inconsequential or the glorious failures; many times we want to plead for a contemporary relevance in the overlooked theory or to consider whether the 'glorious failure' was indeed such or simply ahead of its time: perhaps even ahead of its author.

We find ourselves, therefore, much like the mythical 'radical translator' who has so fascinated modern philosophers, trying to understand an author's ideas in their and their culture's eyes, and, at the same time, in our own. It can be a formidable task. Many times we fail in the historical undertaking because our philosophical interests are so strong, or lose sight of the latter because we are so enthralled by the former. But the nature of philosophy is such that we are compelled to master both techniques. For learning about the history of philosophy is not just a challenging and engaging pastime: it is an essential element in learning about the nature of philosophy – in grasping how philosophy is intimately connected with and yet distinct from both history and science.

The *Routledge History of Philosophy* provides a chronological survey of the history of western philosophy, from its beginnings up to the present time. Its aim is to discuss all major philosophical developments in depth, and, with this in mind, most space has been allocated to those individuals who, by common consent, are regarded as great philosophers. But lesser figures have not been neglected, and it is hoped that the reader will be able to find, in the ten volumes of the *History*, at least basic information about any significant philosopher of the past or present.

Philosophical thinking does not occur in isolation from other human activities, and this *History* tries to situate philosophers within the cultural, and in particular the scientific, context of their time. Some philosophers, indeed, would regard philosophy as merely ancillary to the natural sciences; but even if this view is rejected, it can hardly be denied that the sciences have had a great influence on what is now regarded as philosophy, and it is important that this influence should be set forth clearly. Not that these volumes are intended to provide a mere record of the factors that influenced philosophical thinking; philosophy is a discipline with its own standards of argument, and the presentation of the ways in which these arguments have developed is the main concern of this *History*.

In speaking of 'what is now regarded as philosophy', we may have given the impression that there now exists a single view of what philosophy is. This is certainly not the case; on the contrary, there exist serious differences of opinion, among those who call themselves philosophers, about the nature of their subject. These differences are reflected in the existence at the present time of two main schools of thought, usually described as 'analytic' and 'continental' philosophy. It is not our intention, as general editors of this *History*, to take sides in this dispute. Our attitude is one of tolerance, and our hope is that these volumes will contribute to an understanding of how philosophers have reached the positions which they now occupy.

One final comment. Philosophy has long been a highly technical subject, with its own specialized vocabulary. This *History* is intended not only for the specialist but also for the general reader. To this end, we have tried to ensure that each chapter is written in an accessible style; and since technicalities are unavoidable, a glossary of technical terms is provided in each volume. In this way these volumes will, we hope, contribute to a wider understanding of a subject which is of the highest importance to all thinking people.

G. H. R. Parkinson
S. G. Shanker

Acknowledgements

I wish to thank the following for helping me in one way or another: G. H. R. Parkinson, S. G. Shanker, Rusi Khan, John Bigelow, John Fox, Lloyd Humberstone, Peter Singer, Richard Holton, Rae Langton, Robin Small, Edward Kharmara, Aubrey Townsend, Michael Smith, Gideon Rosen, Tony Coady, Michael James, David Tucker, Knud Haakonssen, Eugene Kamenka, Struan Jacobs, Pang Hee How, Arunasalam Balasubramaniam, Mabel Eickemeyer, David Chan, Chew Mun Yew, Jenny Chan, Rosna bte Buang, Joyce Wong Yuet Yong, Alan Chan, Jamalludin bin Omar, Linda Peach, Chong Kim Chong, and Goh Swee Tiang.

C. L. Ten
October 1993
Singapore

Notes on contributors

Robert Brown has been a member of the History of Ideas Unit of the Australian National University since 1973, is a former editor of the *Australasian Journal of Philosophy*, and has published extensively in philosophical journals and collections. Recently he has contributed a chapter to Blackwell's *A Companion to Contemporary Political Philosophy* (1993) and edited *Classical Political Theories, Plato to Marx* (1990).

C. A. J. Coady is Boyce Gibson Professor of Philosophy and Director of the Centre for Philosophy and Public Issues at the University of Melbourne, Australia. He has numerous academic publications, including his book, *Testimony: a Philosophical Inquiry*. He has an abiding interest in ethical and conceptual problems to do with war and other forms of political violence.

Gerald F. Gaus is Professor of Philosophy and Political Science at the University of Minnesota, Duluth, USA. He was formerly Research Fellow in Philosophy in the Research School of Social Sciences of the Australian National University, and has been Visiting Research Fellow at the University of New England and Visiting Scholar at the Social Philosophy and Policy Center, Bowling Green State University. He is the author of *The Modern Liberal Theory of Man* (1983) and *Value and Justification* (1990). With Stanley Benn, he edited *Public and Private in Social Life* (1983). His latest book is entitled *Justificatory Liberalism*.

Jagdish Hattiangadi is Professor and Chair, Department of Philosophy, and Professor, Division of Natural Science, York University, Toronto, Ontario, Canada. His degrees are B.A. (Bombay 1962), M.A. (L.S.E. 1965), Ph.D. (Princeton 1970). He is the author of *How is Language Possible?* (1987) and numerous journal articles in philosophy and in the history of ideas.

Struan Jacobs lectures in science studies and history of ideas at Deakin University. He has a Ph.D. from the L.S.E., and is the author of *Science and British Liberalism*, and of articles that have appeared in such journals as *History of Philosophy, Canadian Journal of Philosophy*, and *Philosophy of Social Sciences*. His interest in nineteenth-century English thought includes, besides Whewell, Herschel, Whately, and Mill.

R. F. Khan has lectured in philosophy at the University of Singapore and, since 1965, at Monash University, Melbourne, Australia. His main interests are in moral and political philosophy, aesthetics, philosophy of religion and existentialism, and he has published papers in these subjects.

Michael Lessnoff is Reader in Politics in the University of Glasgow, Scotland. He is the author of books on *The Structure of Social Sciences* and *Social Contract*, and of numerous articles on political theory and the philosophy of social science. He has recently completed a book on Max Weber entitled *The Spirit of Capitalism and the Protestant Ethic*.

Cheryl Misak is Associate Professor of Philosophy at Erindale College, University of Toronto, Canada. She is the author of *Truth and the End of Inquiry: a Peircean Account of Truth* and is presently working on a book on verificationism and one on pragmatism and morality.

Edward S. Reed is Associate Professor of Psychology at Franklin & Marshall College, Philadelphia. USA, where he also directs the Interdisciplinary Study of Mind Program. His historical and philosophical studies of psychology have been widely published, including his *James, Gibson and the Psychology of Perception* (Yale University Press, 1989). He is also actively engaged in empirical research on the organization of everyday activities, and is an Associate Editor of the journal *Ecological Psychology*. Dr Reed has been the recipient of fellowships from the (U.S.) National Endowment for the Humanities, the National Science Foundation, and the National Institute on Disability and Rehabilitation Research. He is at present completing a book *Ecologizing Psychology* to be published by Oxford University Press.

John Skorupski studied philosophy and economics at Cambridge University. After lecturing at the University of Glasgow he moved to the Chair of Philosophy at Sheffield University in 1984, and to the Chair of Moral Philosophy at Saint Andrews, Scotland, in 1990. He is the author of *Symbol and Theory* (1975), *John Stuart Mill* (1989), *English-Language Philosophy 1750–1945* (1993).

Robin Small was born in New Zealand, and gained degrees in physics and philosophy at the University of Canterbury, before completing a doctorate at the Australian National University. He is now senior lecturer in philosophy of education at Monash University. His research has been largely in the philosophy of education and the history of ideas.

T. L. S. Sprigge, British philosopher, teaches philosophy as an Endowment Fellow at the University of Edinburgh, Scotland, having taken early retirement from the chair of Logic and Metaphysics. His books include *The Rational Foundations of Ethics* (1987) and *James and Bradley: American Truth and British Reality* (1993). His present research is mainly toward a book on human and animal thought.

John Stillwell was educated at the University of Melbourne and M.I.T. Since 1970 he has been a member of the Mathematics Department at Monash University, Melbourne, Australia, and has written several books, the best known of which is *Mathematics and Its History* (Springer-Verlag 1989).

J. E. Tiles is Professor of Philosophy at the University of Hawaii at Manoa. He is the author of *Dewey* (1988) and *Things that Happen* (1981) and the co-author with Mary Tiles of *An Introduction to Historical Epistemology* (1992).

G. L. Williams lectures in politics at the University of Sheffield. His published work has concentrated mainly on J. S. Mill and the political thought of the nineteenth century. He is the author of *Political Theory in Retrospect* (1991) and is the editor of the Everyman edition of J. S. Mill, *Utilitarianism, On Liberty, Representative Government* (1993).

Chronology

	Politics and religion	The arts
1800		
1801	Newman b.	
1803		
1804	Napoleon becomes Emperor	Johann Strauss (the Elder) b.
1805	Battle of Trafalgar	Wordsworth, *The Prelude*
1806		
1807	Abolition of slave trade in British Empire	
1808		Goethe, *Faust*, part I
1809		Mendelssohn b. Haydn d.
1810		Chopin b. Schumann b.
1811	Luddite riots in England against use of machines in industry	Liszt b. Austen, *Sense and Sensibility*
1812		Dickens b. Wagner b. Verdi b.
1813		Austen, *Pride and Prejudice* P. B. Shelley, 'Queen Mab'
1814	Napoleon abdicates	Austen, *Mansfield Park* Scott, *Waverley*
1815	Battle of Waterloo and defeat of Napoleon	
1816		Charlotte Bronte b. Austen, *Emma* Coleridge, 'Kubla Khan' Scott, *Old Mortality*

Science and technology	Philosophy	
Invention of electric battery by Volta		1800
		1801
Malthus, *An Essay on the Principles of Population* (1st edn 1798)		1803
	Kant d. Feuerbach b.	1804
	Tocqueville b.	1805
	J. S. Mill b.	1806
	Hegel, *The Phenomenology of Mind*	1807
		1808
Charles Darwin b.		1809
		1810
		1811
		1812
	Kierkegaard b.	1813
	Fichte d.	1814
Davy invents the miner's safety lamp		1815
		1816

	Politics and religion	The arts
1817		Austen d. Coleridge, *Biographia Literaria*
1818		Turgenev b. Emily Bronte b. Mary Shelley, *Frankenstein* Austen, *Northanger Abbey* Austen, *Persuasion* Scott, *Heart of Midlothian*
1819		Whitman b. Eliot b. Scott, *Bride of Lammermoor*
1820		Scott, *Ivanhoe* P. B. Shelley, *Prometheus Unbound*
1821		Keats d. Dostoievsky b. Baudelaire b. De Quincey, *Confessions of an English Opium Eater* Scott, *Kenilworth* P. B. Shelley, *Adonais*
1822		P. B. Shelley d. Franck b.
1823		Scott, *Quentin Durward*
1824		Byron d.
1825		Johann Strauss (the Younger) b.
1827		Beethoven d.
1828		Tolstoy b. Schubert d. Goya d.
1829	Catholic Emancipation Act, Britain	Millais b.
1830		Pissarro b.
1831		Goethe, *Faust*, part 2
1832	Reform Act, Britain, extending the franchise to the middle classes	Goethe d. Monet b.
1833	Factory Act, England, prohibiting the employment of children under nine years old in factories Oxford Movement	Brahms b. Carlyle, *Sartor Resartus* (1833–4)
1834		Degas b. Dickens, *Sketches by Boz*

Science and technology	Philosophy	
	Hegel, *The Philosophy of Right*	1817
	Marx b.	1818
	Schopenhauer, *The World as Will and Idea*	1819
Oersted publishes discovery of link between electricity and magnetism	Engels b. James Mill, *Essay on Government*	1820
		1821
Pasteur b.		1822
		1823
		1824
		1825
		1827
	James Mill, *Analysis of the Phenomena of the Human Mind*	1828
Stephenson constructs steam powered railway Lobachevsky, *On the Foundations of Geometry* Thomas Graham, Graham's Law on diffusion of gases		1829
Lyell, *The Principles of Geology*, vol. 1 (vol. 3 1833)	Comte, *Cours de philosophie positive* (1830–42)	1830
Maxwell b. Faraday invents dynamo	Hegel d.	1831
	Bentham d.	1832
Faraday presents the laws of electrolysis	Dilthey b.	1833
		1834

	Politics and religion	The arts
1835		
1836	Beginning of Chartist movement in Britain for extension of the franchise to all adult males	Dickens, *Pickwick Papers* (1836–7)
1837	Victoria becomes Queen of Britain	Pushkin d. Constable d. Dickens, *Oliver Twist* (1837–8)
1838		Bizet b. Dickens, *Nicholas Nickleby* (1838–9)
1839		Cézanne b.
1840		Tchaikovsky b. Rodin b. Dickens, *Old Curiosity Shop*
1841		Renoir b. Dvořák b. Dickens, *Barnaby Rudge*
1842		
1843		Wordsworth becomes Poet Laureate Henry James b. Grieg b. Dickens, *Martin Chuzzlewit* (1843–4) Carlyle, *Past and Present*
1844		
1845		
1846	Potato famine in Ireland. Repeal of Corn Laws in Britain	Dickens, *Dombey and Son* (1846–8)
1847		Mendelssohn d.
1848	Revolutions in Europe. Marx and Engels, *The Communist Manifesto*	Emily Bronte d. Gauguin b. Charlotte Bronte, *Jane Eyre* Thackeray, *Vanity Fair* Emily Bronte, *Wuthering Heights*
1849		Chopin d. Johann Strauss (the Elder) d. Dickens, *David Copperfield*
1850		Wordsworth d. Tennyson becomes Poet Laureate
1851		Turner d.

Science and technology	Philosophy	
	Tocqueville, *Democracy in America*	1835
	James Mill d. Green b.	1836
	Whewell, *History of the Inductive Sciences*	1837
	Sidgwick b. Mach b. Brentano b.	1838
	Peirce b.	1839
	Bosanquet b. Whewell, *The Philosophy of the Inductive Sciences*	1840
	Feuerbach, *The Essence of Christianity*	1841
Discovery of Doppler effect	William James b.	1842
	J. S. Mill, *A System of Logic* Kierkegaard, *Either/Or* Kierkegaard, *Fear and Trembling*	1843
	Nietzsche b. Kierkegaard, *The Concept of Dread* Kierkegaard, *Philosophical Fragments*	1844
Faraday introduces the notion of magnetic field	Whewell, *Elements of Morality, including Polity*	1845
	Bradley b. Kierkegaard, *Concluding Scientific Postscript*	1846
	Boole, *The Mathematical Analysis of Logic*	1847
	J. S. Mill, *The Principles of Political Economy*	1848
	Kierkegaard, *Sickness unto Death*	1849
		1850
Great Exhibition in London	Comte, *Système de politique positive* (1851–4)	1851

	Politics and religion	The arts
1852		Dickens, *Bleak House*
1853		Van Gogh b.
1854		Dickens, *Hard Times*
1855		Charlotte Bronte d. Dickens, *Little Dorrit* (1855–7)
1856		Schumann d.
1857		Elgar b. Charlotte Bronte, *The Professor*
1858		Puccini b.
1859		Dickens, *Tale of Two Cities* Eliot, *Adam Bede*
1860		Chekhov b. Mahler b. Dickens, *Great Expectations* (1860–1) Eliot, *Mill on the Floss*
1861	Abraham Lincoln becomes president of the United States American Civil War starts (ends in 1865)	Eliot, *Silas Marner*
1862	Bismarck becomes Prime Minister of Prussia	Debussy b. Delius b.
1863	Slavery abolished in the United States	Delacroix d. Eliot, *Romola*
1864		Richard Strauss b. Toulouse-Lautrec b. Dickens, *Our Mutual Friend* (1864–5)
1865		Sibelius b. Matthew Arnold, *Essays in Criticism* Carroll, *Alice's Adventures in Wonderland* Dickens, *Our Mutual Friend* Tolstoy, *War and Peace* (1865–9)
1866		Dostoievsky, *Crime and Punishment*
1867	Second Reform Act	Baudelaire d.
1868		George Eliot, *The Spanish Gypsy* Dostoievsky, *The Idiot*
1869		Matthew Arnold, *Culture and Anarchy*

Science and technology	Philosophy	
	Whewell, *Lectures on the History of Moral Philosophy in England*	1852
	Meinong b.	1853
	Boole, *An Investigation of the Laws of Thought*	1854
	Kierkegaard d.	1855
	Freud b.	1856
	Comte d.	1857
		1858
Charles Darwin, *The Origin of Species* Lenoir develops internal combustion engine	J. S. Mill, *On Liberty* Marx, *A Contribution to the Critique of Political Economy* Tocqueville d.	1859
	Schopenhauer d.	1860
	J. S. Mill, *Considerations on Representative Government*	1861
		1862
	J. S. Mill, *Utilitarianism*	1863
Maxwell's equations of electromagnetism		1864
Mendel reports findings on genetics	J. S. Mill elected MP for Westminster	1865
Nobel invents dynamite	Whewell d.	1866
Faraday d.	Marx, *Das Kapital*, vol. 1 (vol. 2 1885, vol. 3 1894)	1867
		1868
F. Galton, *Hereditary Genius: An Inquiry into its Laws and Consequences* Mendeleyev publishes periodic table of elements de Lesseps completes Suez Canal	J. S. Mill, *The Subjection of Women*	1869

	Politics and religion	The arts
1870		Dickens d. Dickens, *Mystery of Edwin Drood*
1871	Britain legalises trade unions Establishment of German Empire	Eliot, *Middlemarch* (1871–2)
1872		
1873		Rachmaninov b.
1874		Schoenberg b.
1875		Bizet d. Ravel b. Tolstoy, *Anna Karenina* (1875–7)
1876		Eliot, *Daniel Deronda*
1877		Henry James, *The American*
1879		Henry James, *Daisy Miller* Dostoievsky, *The Brothers Karamazov* (1879–80)
1880		Eliot d.
1881		Dostoievsky d. Bartók b. Henry James, *Portrait of a Lady*
1882		Stravinsky b.
1883		Turgenev d. Monet d. Wagner d.
1884	Third Reform Act	
1885		
1886		Liszt d. Henry James, *The Bostonians* Stevenson, *Dr Jekyll and Mr Hyde* Stevenson, *Kidnapped*
1887		
1888		
1889		
1890	Newman d.	Van Gogh d. Franck d.
1891		
1892		Whitman d.

Science and technology	Philosophy	
		1870
Darwin, *The Descent of Man*		1871
	Nietzsche, *The Birth of Tragedy* Feuerbach d.	1872
Wundt, *Principles of Physiological Psychology*	J. S. Mill d. J. S. Mill, *Autobiography*	1873
	Sidgwick, *The Methods of Ethics*	1874
		1875
Bell invents the telephone	Bradley, *Ethical Studies*	1876
Edison invents phonograph		1877
Maxwell d.	Frege, *Begriffsschrift*	1879
		1880
		1881
	Green d.	1882
	Dilthey, *Einleitung in die Geisteswissenschaften* Nietzsche, *Thus Spoke Zarathustra* Bradley, *The Principles of Logic* Marx d. Mach, *The Science of Mechanics*	1883
	Frege, *The Foundations of Arithmetic*	1884
Pasteur develops vaccine against rabies		1885
	Nietzsche, *Beyond Good and Evil* Mach, *The Analysis of Sensations*	1886
	Nietzsche, *The Genealogy of Morals*	1887
	Bosanquet, *Logic*	1888
	Nietzsche, *The Twilight of the Idols*	1889
	Green, *Prolegomena to Ethics* William James, *Principles of Psychology*	1890
	Nettleship (ed.), *Works of Thomas Hill Green*, vols. 1–3 (1891–4)	1891
		1892

	Politics and religion	The arts
1893		Tchaikovsky d. Maupassant d.
1894	The Dreyfus Affair in France	
1895		
1896		Millais d.
1897		Brahms d. Henry James, *What Maisie Knew*
1898		Henry James, *The Turn of the Screw*
1899		Johann Strauss (the Younger) d. Henry James, *The Awkward Age*

Science and technology	Philosophy	
	Bradley, *Appearance and Reality*	1893
		1894
Roentgen discovers x-rays Pasteur d.	Nietzsche, *The Antichrist*	1895
		1896
	William James, *The Will to Believe*	1897
		1898
Freud, *The Interpretation of Dreams*	Bosanquet, *Philosophical Theory of the State*	1899

Introduction
C. L. Ten

This volume covers most of the major philosophers of the nineteenth century. The most conspicuous exceptions such as Hegel, Marx, Schopenhauer and Kierkegaard, are included in other, more thematically focused volumes. Of the philosophers considered in this volume, the figure of John Stuart Mill looms large. He made contributions to a wide area of philosophy, although he is best known today for his defence of individual liberty and for his much-maligned attempt to 'prove' the utilitarian principle. The roots of his ethics are to be found in the writings of his father, James Mill, and Jeremy Bentham. None of these was a professional philosopher, unlike many other philosophers of the century. The Mills worked for the East India Company, while Bentham was a man of independent means.

James Mill and Bentham were very concerned with practical issues of changing established social, political and legal institutions, exposing and rooting out the 'sinister interests' behind them. Bentham paid careful attention to language and especially to the language of law. Sinister interests flourish where unclear terms are used. We can make social progress only by trying first to translate the sentences in which these terms occur into equivalent sentences in which the vague terms are replaced by terms referring to entities that are real and perceptible by the senses. We can then be purged of those fictitious entities which cannot in this manner be replaced by real entities. Pleasure and pain are real entities which explain human motivation and also set the end of promoting the greatest happiness which all conduct should aim at. This standard of what we ought to do is the famous principle of utility.

Laws and constitutional arrangements should be framed in accordance with the principle. Bentham and James Mill supported democracy as the system of government that will ensure that the power of the rulers is not abused. But although they argued for the extension of the franchise, James Mill explicitly excluded women from the vote on the ground that their interests would be adequately protected by others. It was left to his son to promote the cause of women in his *The Subjection of Women*.

John Stuart Mill took up many of the concerns of James Mill and Bentham, but there was a distinct shift of emphasis in the way in which he argued for similar causes. The case for representative democracy was presented not just in terms of protecting the interests of the people but also, and perhaps more importantly, as providing the basis for their moral, intellectual and social development through participation in the political process. John Stuart Mill also changed the conception of utility, distinguishing between higher and lower pleasures, and emphasizing the importance of free and active choices between different ways of life. He argued passionately in his essay *On Liberty* for freedom of discussion and for individual liberty to perform acts not harmful to others even though the views expressed, or the acts in question, were those towards which the majority felt repugnance.

Utilitarian theory was developed further by Sidgwick, a professional philosopher in Cambridge. He regarded common-sense morality as a system of rules which tended to promote general happiness. But utilitarianism would systematize and sort out some of the inconsistencies in common-sense morality and give it a rational foundation. Sidgwick recognized a paradox in that the utilitarian goal of promoting happiness may be better served if only a few enlightened people accept utilitarianism. If 'the vulgar' are told the truth that utilitarianism is the ultimate basis for their conduct, then they are likely to produce bad results as they miscalculate the consequences of their actions in an uncertain world. Sidgwick also acknowledged that the utilitarian principle is not the only principle that it is rational to comply with; it is also rational to act on the principle of egoism.

John Stuart Mill developed what he regarded as a refined version of an alternative to intuitionist moral theory in which moral truths are self-evident and known by intuition. One of the targets of Mill's attack was William Whewell. Mill in turn was attacked by the idealist philosophers. Bradley poured scorn on Mill's alleged attempt to show that each person desires the general happiness from the fact that each desires his or her own happiness. Bradley propounded a morality of self-realization to replace the goal of maximizing pleasure, whether it be one's own or the pleasures of all. The two other prominent British idealist philosophers were T. H. Green and Bernard Bosanquet, whose contributions to moral and political philosophy involve the working out of the view that the criterion of reality is coherence. A person's good is identified with the development and integration of his or her capacities into a coherent whole. Social life is necessary for individual perfection, and an account of the common good is developed which involves the harmonious integration of complementary social roles. The sharp and frequent conflicts between the individual good and the social good are absent from this account.

On the continent Nietzsche presented a radical challenge to traditional morality. Declaring 'the death of God', he saw this as undermining the foundations of Christian morality. He distinguished between the 'master morality' of a ruling group and the 'slave morality' of the weak. 'Good' is a term that the ruling group use to refer to themselves and their conduct, and what is common is decreed 'bad'. But the weak have different values, and strength is regarded as 'evil'.

The moral theories of philosophers like John Stuart Mill and Bradley were integrated with their more general philosophical views. Three major types of philosophy were prominent during this period – the empiricism of Mill, the idealism of Bradley and the pragmatism of the American philosophers Peirce and William James.

Major advances were made in mathematics. For example, in the earlier part of the century there were challenges to Euclidean geometry, while the latter part saw Frege's contributions to the understanding of the foundations of mathematics. Similarly, significant scientific discoveries were made, and there was much interest in scientific method, as reflected for example in the dispute between Mill and Whewell on induction and the role of hypothesis in scientific enquiry. Whether, or to what extent, the understanding of human conduct and human society required the adoption of the methods of observation and experiment common to the natural sciences was also a bone of contention. The disagreements were particularly fierce with respect to the nature and status of psychology which gradually established itself as a discipline independent of philosophy.

In France Comte considered himself the founder of the new science of 'sociology', applying scientific method and knowledge to the understanding of social behaviour and to the reconstruction of human societies. His Law of the Three Stages states that there are three stages of intellectual development. In the theological stage, phenomena are explained in terms of the activities of supernatural beings. In the metaphysical stage, explanations appeal to abstract forces. In the third and final positive stage, the human mind seeks the invariable relations of succession and resemblance between phenomena, and explanation is in terms of establishing connections between particular phenomena and some general facts.

In Germany Dilthey rejected the assimilation of the human sciences to the natural sciences. We have internal knowledge of our mental life, a direct understanding different from the external knowledge of an alien, external world. We understand others by analogy with our understanding of our own mental life. Their actions are expressions of human minds, and we understand them by re-living their experiences. This kind of understanding is also applied to other expressions of the human mind – social institutions, literature and works of art. Later Dilthey developed what is now an influential 'science' of hermeneutics which embodies a procedure for interpreting written documents and other expressions of the human mind. Treating these expressions as coherent and unified, the hermeneutic procedure uses the parts of the whole to mutually clarify each other.

Charles Darwin's *The Origin of Species* propounded a contentious theory of evolution. One important issue was the application of evolutionary theory to ethics. Herbert Spencer developed an uncompromising version of Social Darwinism in which the process of natural selection in social life was to be left unhampered, with the weak having to fend for themselves.

The issues mentioned in this brief introduction are among those discussed at much greater length in the various chapters. Some issues and philosophers are discussed in several chapters from different points of view and in different contexts. The styles of the authors of the chapters are different, as are their opinions and philosophical sympathies. But they have all given their own illuminating interpretations of a wide range of philosophical theories.

CHAPTER 1

The early utilitarians
Bentham and James Mill
G. L. Williams

Jeremy Bentham was born in 1748 in London; his prosperous father, a lawyer who became wealthy from property rather than the law, planned out for his son a brilliant legal career. After an early education at Westminster and Oxford he was called to the Bar in 1769. However, instead of mastering the complexities, technicalities, precedents and mysteries of the law in order to carve out a successful career, Bentham's response to such chaos and absurdity was to challenge the whole structure of law and to attempt to replace it with a system as perfect and as rational as it could be. In many ways a typical *philosophe* of the eighteenth century, Bentham at this early stage seized on the possibility of improvement through knowledge, on the supremacy of reason over superstition and of order over chaos. Despite his living and writing into the new age of the nineteenth century – post-revolutionary, industrialized, democratic – this early inspiration that enlightenment would bring about a better world never left him. To help create a world as it might be – as it ought to be – rather than succeed in a world as it was – customary, prejudiced and corrupt – was his constant aim whatever the particular object he pursued within his encyclopaedic interests, and whether the study be abstract and philosophical or detailed and practical. His central concern was the study of legislation, a concern developed from his own disillusionment with the state of English law and his positive response to the works of those like Helvetius and Beccaria who had argued that there must be some general and rational test as to the adequacy of existing law in order to justify its reform. As we shall see, this task involved both expository and censorial elements and the principle of utility which Bentham formulated provided the basis of his life's work.

During the eighteenth century his main approach assumed that the successful achievement of Enlightenment thought would lead to its equally successful application through direct contact and conversion of benevolent despots or at least their influential advisers. In the 1780s he spent two years in Russia with some hope of convincing Catherine the Great, but with his failure to gain influence amongst the powerful, whether over his general ideas or over his detailed projects, he became increasingly convinced that sinister interests – the law, the Church, Parliament – would act as obstacles to Reason and Reform. In which case, politics would have to be reformed – the ruling elite would have to be tamed – before his life's work could be realized. Constitutional law not just civil and criminal law stood in need of drastic reform. The influence of James Mill and later the growth of a school of reformers – the Philosophical Radicals – gave Bentham, now in his sixties, a new zest for work and an added commitment to reforming the law in Russia, America, Spain, Portugal, Greece, Latin America, as well as to reforming all manner of abuses in British public life. Indeed he was as productive in the last twenty years of his life as he had ever been before, if not more, and his belief in the supremacy of his method and his principle as the key to philosophical and practical advancement was as clear and deep as when he first discovered it over sixty years earlier.

The starting point for the whole project which gives meaning and form to these brief biographical points was Bentham's early realization of the importance of language. Not only in the field of law, where falsehoods, absurdities and nonsensities were common, but in many other fields as well, careful definition was sacrificed to vagueness and emotiveness. The dominant and therefore sinister interests in any area – law, morality, politics – maintained a language in which the words were either totally unclear or contained an inherent prejudice or bias in their favour. Unless language could be made clear the truth would be concealed and the possibility of improvement would be lost. Definition is the key and it depends first on distinguishing between real and fictitious entities and then on determining the legitimacy or not of the latter by Bentham's new method – that of paraphrasis.

Nouns can be divided into those which are names of real entities – those things whose existence gives immediate consciousness, which can be directly perceived by the senses, and which are either states of body or states of mind – and fictitious entities which are referred to as if they really exist but need further exposition to give them meaning. In the first category the most basic examples would be pleasure or pain while in the latter the most frequent examples, say in law, would be duty, right or power. These latter are linguistic constructs and as such are 'fictions' but, as those examples show, this does not mean that language could do without them. Although they do not exist in themselves and although they give rise to doubt and confusion this does not mean that they are all meaningless. Fictions then are necessary, but how to distinguish fictions that are legitimate from those which are strictly speaking nonsense – fictional entities from fabulous entities? The key here is a method which while 'translating' fictional entities into real entities at the same time gives a criterion for denying meaning to those fictions incapable of such 'translation'.

The method Bentham discovered was that of paraphrasis, the only mode of exposition for those abstract terms where there was no superior genus to which they belonged and where the Aristotelian method of definition *per genus et differentiam* was thus inapplicable. To define a fictitious entity only by reference to other fictitious entities offered no solution. The clarification needed is in terms of the real and perceptible; Bentham does this not by translating one word by another or one term by its component parts, but by translating one sentence in which the term appears into another which is equivalent but in which the fictitious entity is replaced by a real one. In these two parallel propositions the import would be the same but the device of paraphrasis would give simple clarity to the sentence translated and if such trans- lation into real terms were impossible it would reveal the fabulous or nonsensical nature of the original ([1.5], 495). An example might help here: however much we might classify rights and duties, the general idea of a right or duty can only be explained by paraphrasis – thus a sentence containing those terms would be translated into one explaining for what the law makes us liable to punishment, for doing or not doing, and punishment is then further explained in terms of pain, a real entity. Thus a fiction is made clear by its translation into its relation to the real. Ideas are thus clarified by reference to their context – the sentence; whether or not the sentence can be paraphrased into one which contains real terms is the deciding factor with regard to its sense or nonsense. In a sense the substitute sentence provides the possibility of verifying the original by reference to the world of real entities. Thus if the word 'duty' were used without reference to the pain through punishment which the law laid down then the 'duty' would have no more meaning than an expression of opinion.

In this way the law, by distinguishing between the real and the fictitious and between the fictitious which can be paraphrased or veri- fied and those fictitious entities which cannot be, can be clarified and reformed. The fabulous entities will be purged, the (legitimate) fictional entities will be established on firm – because real – foundations. These real entities are pleasures and pains and where some might refer to 'frugality' and 'thrift' and others to 'meanness' and 'greed' these in the end come down to the pleasures and pains consequent on the action not on any inherent goodness or badness in the motive. The real world must be recognised in this way and all fictions, however necessary, must be referable to them. It is thus important to reform language to give it meaning and so be in a position to change the real world. The slate of confusion, mystery and corruption must be wiped clean and on it written only that which makes sense by being real. Once this is done the process of describing, classifying, quantifying as well as the process of prescribing and reforming can begin – a science of legislation both accurate in detail and conducive to improvement can begin to be formulated. Once vagueness and ambiguity are eliminated and abstract terms are replaced by concrete detail then the way is open for a clear understanding of human nature which will provide the basis for a system of legislation which in turn will be the great instrument for social progress. Bentham's intention was to combine the discovery of new principles with detailed attention to their practical uses; indeed he saw his own genius as lying in the introduction of rigorous detailed investigation to supplement the more traditional concern with general principles. In this he compared his work with that of the natural scientist though in his case the detail came not from observation and experiment but from analysis, classification and division. His belief in the fundamental importance of a clear and accurate vocabulary underlay his early optimism that reason once employed would be the vehicle of both accurate exposition of the law as it was and enlightened criticism of the law as it ought to be.

The *Introduction to the Principles of Morals and Legislation* ([1.5], 11) is Bentham's best known attempt to outline the fruits of this new method by outlining his principle of utility and the structure of law which would result from its adoption and application.

> Nature has placed mankind under the governance of two sovereign masters, *pain* and *pleasure*. It is for them alone to point out what we ought to do, as well as to determine what we shall do. On the one hand the standard of right and wrong, on the other the chain of causes and effects, are fastened to their throne.

This striking though rather compressed summary of his basic philosophy puts forward two distinct claims, though in a manner not altogether without confusion. Following Hume, Bentham was always emphatic that the idea of what is must be kept distinct from the idea of what ought to be, and thus he is here making two claims, a factual or descriptive one and also a normative or prescriptive one. The first is that human beings are so constituted that what they seek is pleasure and the second is that every action is judged right or wrong according to its tendency to augment or diminish such happiness (or pleasures over pains) for the party involved. Thus Bentham is involved in two enquiries – the one into human nature and the other into moral philosophy. Although the second should accord with the first it could not be logically deduced from it; indeed strictly speaking it could not be proved at all. However, that these are two separate statements is important to recognize despite Bentham's linking of them both to Nature. The normative or critical principle indicates what ought to happen, the end, the goal of legislation; the descriptive indicates the material, the limitations imposed on the legislator in achieving those ends. For the project to work these two aspects must be made consistent – the pursuit of pleasure by the individual as a natural activity must be made compatible with the achievement of the happiness of the community over whom the ruler legislates. Only if the two principles are kept separate can the critical one do its work, the work of improvement and reform; indeed only then does it have a role at all. The principle of utility or the 'greatest happiness' principle is meant to be realizable and thus must recognize the natural qualities of human beings, but it has to work on or modify the ensuing conduct in order to achieve its moral end. Whether and how the individual pursuit of pleasure can co-exist with the community's aim of greatest happiness is an issue to be resolved once further exploration of the two claims is completed.

The natural statement – of what is the case – amounts to a form of psychological hedonism, that all action willed by human beings is motivated by the desire to obtain pleasure or avoid pain. This does not necessarily imply psychological egoism, that it is only the agent's own pleasure or pain which acts as the motivating force, though, as we shall see, Bentham sees this as a general rule. However, is the hedonism which Bentham believes in a matter of fact, a matter of definition, or itself also a generalization? Is it an *a priori* axiom or the result of observation? Although Bentham at times seems to incline towards the latter, in that he cites evidence and the results of observation, his enumeration of the great range of motives is entirely in terms of pleasures and pains – not certainly all egoistic – but nevertheless making all human conduct analysable in those terms. Thus the 'facts' of human psychology reflect Bentham's earlier view that the only real entities are pleasures and pains. Such motives can be social, dissocial, or self-regarding but they all correspond to pleasures, even those of goodwill or benevolence. Where all examples can be thus described in terms of pleasure and pain, the original assumption becomes definitional rather than empirical. However, such pleasures are not all self-regarding even if in the final analysis the pleasure sought is the agent's own, for it is still possible to distinguish such pleasures from those more obviously concerned with self-preference. Put differently, while every motive has a corresponding interest this need not strictly speaking be self-interest in a crude egoistic sense.

Nevertheless, having made due allowance for the social motives of sympathy and benevolence, Bentham did not consider them to be of great force and argued that generally self-preference was predominant; certainly it should be the basic assumption for the art of legislation. He argues that such self-preference is the normal state for normal people and that the design of law should reflect this. It is not a definition *a priori* nor a factual truth – the one would be trivial and the other false – but a generalization which is not only true as such but is the only working assumption which a legislator can adopt. In this way all human conduct with all the possible motives influencing it can be reduced to pleasures and pains – real entities experienced by real individuals whose psychology generally puts themselves first. Thus a scientific approach becomes possible in that pleasures and pains become the unit of classification, measurement and comparison. Certainly this will be no easy process, not least because each individual may judge pleasures differently, but the fact that the legislator is dealing with observable conduct which it can be assumed indicates the strength or weakness of the motive opens up the possibility of rational calculation. The evidence of interests, of the pleasures which motivate people, is thus their conduct, and the relative value of such pleasures and pains can be observed. As it is only consequences that count and as these are empirically observable then science can begin its work. The process of analysis and quantification in terms of calculable units offers the opportunity of seeing human conduct with a clarity and precision never before seen.

Although there were a huge variety of pleasures and although exact comparison between the pleasures of different people with different sensibilities and in different circumstances would not be possible, nevertheless from the point of view of the law or policy-maker general calculations were possible. This was to be done through recognizing that pleasures had certain dimensions of value and that the sum of these would give the overall result. Thus intensity and duration were relevant in estimating value as were the degree of certainty and the degree of remoteness of a pleasure, the likelihood of further pleasure following on or the opposite effect occurring. In addition the number of people affected, or the extent of the pleasure, must enter the calculation. Unless this sort of common measure, or currency, were introduced then no comparison would be possible and neither individuals nor legislators could conduct their affairs with any order or rationality or predictive force, those very elements needed for the successful pursuit of the interests which all human beings aimed at.

As well as giving Bentham a fundamental reality by which to describe human behaviour, the idea of pleasure and pain also enters into his moral principle that the only legitimate standard for the individual and the community is utility or the 'greatest happiness principle'.

This is his great critical principle designed to promote reform, not a principle, as with Hume, to explain the rationality of custom and constraint but to emphasize the gulf between what is and what ought to be. It is Bentham's attempt to erect an external standard by which disputes can be resolved by a rational calculation of various options; these options being in turn resolvable down to questions of pleasures and pains. The principle cannot be proved but it is for Bentham the only objective alternative to the mere expression of personal taste. Utility or caprice, reason or mere sound – these are the options and Bentham emphasizes the need for a standard which can be empirically applied. There is no ultimate proof that happiness is better than suffering but, once presented in this way, Bentham is confident that all reasonable people would choose the former and having done so his task is to convert such a principle into a detailed and radical weapon for change.

If happiness is the goal and if moral language is meaningless without reference to this standard then the legislators' task is to create a legal order in which the fictions with which they work are constantly reduced to the real entities of pleasure and pain which should act as their guide in maximizing the community's good. Thus the moral evaluation of a law or a policy proposal comes down in the end to matters of fact, to observation of consequences, to verification. Similarly the tools which the law uses in order to create 'the greatest happiness' are also examples of pleasures and pains, the most notable of course being punishment. The attractiveness of the principle then is that it provides a framework for moral criticism and evaluation which respects the reality of nature and by judicious modification of human behaviour it transforms what could be a life of irrational suffering into one of happy enjoyment. The prescriptive principle is not confused with the descriptive acts; otherwise it would have no role to play. Instead it enables us to become moral actors rather than mere pleasure-seekers, to appreciate our duties and to follow them rather than pursue without restraint the self-preference which our nature inclines us towards. The terms 'duty', 'ought', 'right' and 'good' carry no meaning for Bentham unless they are used of actions which conform to the principle and thus can be translated into statements whose factual elements can be verified. How then are the duties which arise from the moral principle to be reconciled with the pursuit of the self-regarding interests which are posited by the psychological principle? Is the latter, which sees the agent's own happiness as the natural goal of behaviour, compatible with the former, which directs us to act in conformity to the greatest happiness? Could an answer be found which preserved both of the two claims which Bentham is concerned to support? Certainly Bentham did not want to depart from the view that the driving force in society was the individual pursuit of happiness and there is no attempt to replace this with moralistic pleas for altruism or benevolence; equally he holds firm to the principle of utility. Thus duty or conformity to the principle would also have to be something which it was in the interest of the agent to perform. Given the assumption of how people do behave, the society must be so ordered that this behaviour coincides with how they ought to behave. In other words, through the use of sanctions – physical, moral, political and religious – the society would give people an interest in performing their duty. The most powerful influence to bring this about would be punishment, that artificial pain, which would force men to recalculate their happiness and act in accordance with the general well-being. The motives natural to each individual would remain the same but the new threat of pain would deter the anti-social act and create a situation where it would be in an individual's interest to do his or her duty.

It is on the basis of this belief in people as they are and society as it ought to be that Bentham undertakes his massive investigation into the principles of law – constitutional, civil and criminal – and the detailed application of these in all areas of life. And this was a political activity, one geared to bringing about change, not merely an intellectual project aiming at clarity and enlightenment. Bentham was well aware that utility had been a standard held by others in the past; the need now was for it to be applied in detail and through this to be accepted and implemented. Utilitarianism was a theory about the State, government, law, public matters generally, and although Bentham's works published in his own lifetime wander from principle to detail, from general to particular, the total work is a logical and exhaustive – and exhausting – survey of the most general framework of law, the constitutional, down to the most minute detail of actual laws, offences and punishments.

If we turn to the broadest framework of law relevant to the utilitarian aim of reform, Bentham's major work was the *Constitutional Code* [1.6] not begun until he was over seventy and the most developed account of his mature views. In his earlier days he had held a rather naive view that enlightenment – clarity and reason – would itself persuade rulers of the need for legislative reform, but after his adoption of the need for a radical overhaul of the system of government he developed his detailed system of representative government. The *Constitutional Code* was envisaged as the first stage to three other Codes – Procedure, Penal and Civil – which together would make the Pannomion, a complete body of law. It was meant to be a three-volume work but only one was printed in Bentham's own lifetime, a volume which included chapters on the electorate, the legislature, the prime minister and the administration – the whole framework within which the democratic principle would work and where laws would be made according to the principle of utility rather than in response to the sinister interest of those in power. Unless the constitutional arrangements are right then the resulting laws and policies will be likewise flawed. These arrangements must be based on the principle of utility, not on any useless fiction like the original or social contract, a point he had made as early as 1776 in his *Fragment on Government* [1.5]. However, the point is now made in conjunction with his suspicion of sinister interests, and the framework must now be democratic and also contain protection against the tendency of those in power to rule in their own interests. As with human nature in general, interest must be brought into accord with duty, and this is as important a problem in the constitutional arrangements as it is in the spheres of civil and penal law. The possibility of divergent interests between the rulers and the ruled, the few and the many, would not simply disappear with the inauguration of representative democracy but would need rigorous safeguards to prevent it. It is on this issue of making rulers constantly accountable that Bentham is at his most novel and most detailed.

In his own time, Bentham's analysis of democracy was somewhat overshadowed by the more popular and striking writings of James Mill and it is only in recent years that painstaking and illuminating research has brought out the range and quality of Bentham's innovative ideas ([1.6] and [1.50]). The older view of Bentham as someone arguing naively from first principles to their logical and democratic conclusion (people put their own interests first, the rulers do likewise, therefore the people must rule in order to maximize the general interest) is replaced by a much more sophisticated account which combines the empirical approach with the critical utilitarian one. At its heart is a scepticism regarding the ability of institutional arrangements alone to bring about the greatest happiness; they must be subject at all times to the scrutiny of an informed and involved public.

If we turn first to the arguments in favour of representative democracy and then to the extra safeguards to protect against misuse of power we can appreciate most fully Bentham's originality and, it can be argued, also the value of his neglected contribution to democratic thought. Viewing political societies generally, Bentham replaces the traditional concern with discovering their origins in order to define their character, limits and legitimacy with the simpler view that they exist wherever there is a general habit of obedience to a person or assembly. In a democracy the sovereign constitutive authority lies with the people while the legislative authority is omnicompetent within its own domain. It is the people who choose the rulers and who may dismiss them if they fail to serve the greatest happiness; in turn only the rulers have the power to make and execute laws which, because of their representative nature and their accountability to the people, they are likely to do in the common interest.

Looking at the more detailed application of this basic relation between rulers and ruled, we see the state divided into equal districts each electing a member to the legislature while also having its own sub-legislature and forming a judicial district. This model, depending on the size of the State, would be applied also to sub-districts and if necessary to smaller units again. The electorate in each district is based, with few exceptions, on universal manhood suffrage (the world may not yet be ready to grant female suffrage though there is no logical reason to exclude women) and the electors both choose and may dismiss the representatives; mistrust is built into the system and the power of the people preserved. The legislature so elected by secret ballot is a single chamber, normally elected for one year, and comprising full-time and paid members. While this legislative branch is checked by the constitutive branch – through elections and dismissals – it in turn is responsible for the appointment and control over the administrative and judicial branches. The prime minister and justice ministers are elected from outside by the legislature and they in turn appoint ministers from within the legislature and judges respectively. The power to dismiss such appointments lies with the prime minister and justice minister but also with the legislature and the electorate as a whole, such power extending in the latter two cases also to dismissing the prime and justice ministers themselves. Thus the administration and the judiciary, while not being directly elected by the people but chosen for their intellectual and moral qualities, would nevertheless be subject to popular control through the electorate's power of dismissal and if need be punishment. To render this democratic control meaningful, Bentham insists on the open nature of government, administration and judicial affairs, and includes maximum publicity at all stages of the conduct of public affairs. Further, a similar arrangement of elections, legislatures, administration and judiciary is applied at the local level, maximizing at all levels the power of the people and thus the securities against misrule.

In this way, the tendency of those in power to pursue their own interest – one which in an unreformed system sees the wealthy rule at the expense of the poor – must be guarded against even in the reformed constitutional democracy which Bentham outlines and the major anti-dote to the sinister power of government is public opinion. However precise, exact and carefully constructed the constitutional details may be, it is the power of public opinion which is the final guarantee against misuse of power by the rulers. So important was this view to Bentham that he envisages a Public Opinion Tribunal, the voice of the general interest speaking through meetings, speeches, writings and the press, in order to inform, criticize, praise or support the actions of the more formally constituted elements of government. Thus while the people do not themselves rule, their involvement is not restricted to mere elections; they are the guardians as well as the source of power.

More than this, Bentham also believes that his proposed system would protect the individual against abuse of power by the government. Although dismissing any idea of natural rights as nonsense, as fictions which are illegitimate because untranslatable into the real entities of pleasure and pain, he nevertheless pursues a somewhat similar goal of defending the individual, through his concern with securities against misrule. In a sense the whole constitutional system is designed to deter the rulers from abusing their power – through elections, dismissals, publicity, and so on, i.e. through the practice of responsibility and accountability. The system is based on the principle of mistrust and although the legislature is omnicompetent it is limited by the continual scrutiny of the public over its actions as well as by its limited duration. The legislature is essentially dependent on the people and this for Bentham is a greater guarantee of the security and liberty of the citizen than any appeal to rights, whether abstract or legal. In addition, as we shall see, one of the main aims of the law is security, as one of the essential elements of happiness, and for Bentham this security, which it was the duty of the law to maintain, solves those problems traditionally discussed in terms of individual liberty. Constitutionally, however, accountability was the chief means to ensure the security of the individual against oppressive State power through the ability of individuals to control their rulers.

Given this radical overhaul of the system of government it is necessary to see why it has taken place – whatever the source, power and limits of the legislature its function is to create and impose law according to the principle of utility, thus providing an alternative to the traditional view of law as something which grew organically and embodied the wisdom of the past modified by judges in the light of new experience. In many ways this idea of common law was always Bentham's chief target for he saw it as a massive and illegitimate fiction; real law was the expression of the will of the sovereign legislature and should be clear, known and in the general interest not vague, dependent on judges and serving the interest only of lawyers. The law should be the deliberate and rational instrument whereby to create the greatest happiness through the harmony of duty and interest. The test of law should always be its success or failure in making individuals so act as to maximize their own pleasures but in doing so refrain from inflicting pain on others. To attain this end of modifying human behaviour it must be known in advance; otherwise it could not serve its purpose, and Bentham's alternative to the mysteries of the common law was his proposal for the systematic codification of all law. Its validity would be gained from its source, the legislator; its morality from its purpose, utility; but its efficacy from its clear and rational formulation in the form of a code. Such codes would make the law accessible and comprehensible to all through the clear enumeration of offences and the accompanying rationale in terms of utility. It is through the classification of offences and their corresponding punishments that a framework is established such that the good of community can be maintained. Only then would it be known unambiguously what was unlawful, what rights existed, and what punishments were threatened. In this way the unlawful act would be deterred and lawful ones encouraged. The security of the individual would thus be assured.

The key to offences where punishment is involved is their detrimental nature to others; if the offence is entirely self-regarding and involves no other individuals, groups of individuals or the community at large, then the law has no role to play. In this area of an individual's duty to himself or herself, he or she can be left alone to pursue happiness in the way judged best. Punishment being itself a pain is an evil and can be justified only if it prevents the greater evil of the offence under consideration. The threat of punishment should influence the calculation which the individual makes of his or her own interest; it is this fear which acts as the primary deterrent. Punishment looks ahead – it is concerned to prevent future mischief – rather than backwards, as a retaliation for mischief done. Within this perspective there are four further restrictions on the use of punishment (in addition that is to self-regarding conduct): where it is groundless, there being no real mischief to prevent; where it is inefficacious, where it cannot work to prevent mischief; where it is unprofitable, where the cost is too great; and where it is needless, where other means would do as well. At the heart of the perspective is the idea of punishment being used economically – an offence brings a profit and the punishment must threaten a loss sufficient to outweigh the temptation to commit the act.

If Bentham's constitutional reforms were in place and his view of law established, with offences and punishments reflecting the principle of utility, a major question would still remain – would the laws aim at the maximization of aggregate happiness and thus risk the possible sacrifice of individual happiness if and when necessary for the general good, or would the laws work towards the general welfare within the limits of some standards of fair distribution such that individuals would have rights or securities against despotic domination? Is there any connection between Bentham's theory and the liberal desire to protect individual rights against democratic rule or are the two perspectives hopelessly at odds? Should the law aim directly at utility or should it aim to establish rules through which individuals are guaranteed an area in which they pursue their own good in their own way? Is there a framework of rights within which individuals operate or is the general happiness to be pursued and dictated according to the changing judgement of the law and policy-making body? Having established a system of government in which public opinion plays a dominant role, what is there to prevent such opinion operating in a tyrannical way?

In order to answer these questions it is useful to look more closely at the ends at which government ought to aim. As we have noted, the major aim of legislation is security, without which there could be little pleasure or happiness. Unless security of expectation were established no ordered social life would be possible, happiness could never be enjoyed with confidence, long-term pleasures would not be pursued, well-being would be constantly threatened. Although in a general sense pleasure is the only real goal, yet individuals differ on their estimation of what gives them pleasure, and thus the legislator cannot judge on their behalf and thus should not aim to maximize the individual's pleasure but rather provide the basic security, or liberty, by which individuals, judging for themselves, maximize their own happiness. By defining offences and establishing rights, the law created an area free from interference where pleasure could be pursued without harmful consequences to the interests of others. Security is the necessary guarantee of both present and future enjoyment of individual interest, and this is what above all the law provides and provides uniquely. Within this perspective the problem of defining, comparing and calculating pleasures becomes less important, for within the limits laid down by the law the problem passes over to individuals to evaluate and to act as they see fit. This emphasis on individual judgement and control, together with his concern for free elections, free speech and freedom of the press, has led some modern commentators to see Bentham as a liberal utilitarian rather than seeing his utilitarianism as a threat to individual liberty. By seeing security as one of the four main aims into which the general happiness can be divided, it is argued that Bentham's theory avoids the authoritarianism conventionally ascribed to him. Protection against intentional offences was the first priority of law but Bentham also envisaged a fairly wide area of responsibility for the government in preventing a whole range of dangers which could threaten the security of individuals. By thus minimizing pain the individual was free to pursue pleasure in the sphere made secure through the protection of the law.

The second major end involved in the general happiness was subsistence and although in general this could be left to individuals who would naturally seek it, there would nevertheless be circumstances where its attainment would demand government action either by intervention in the economy or through direct provision of relief, involving the limited transfer of means from the rich to the poor. Similarly with the third end, abundance, this would normally be a natural goal best left to individuals. However, the fourth of the subordinate ends, equality, is at once something desirable from a general utilitarian point of view and something threatening from the particular point of view of security.

In Bentham's argument, equality follows from the diminishing marginal utility of wealth or other goods – a pound is worth more in terms of pleasure to a poor man than it is to a rich man; thus redistribution of wealth would maximize aggregate happiness. However, pursuit of this goal appears to threaten the chief object of law which is security of expectation. While equality of rights can be maintained – everyone's security is equally protected – a substantive equality of wealth cannot be guaranteed without undermining people's expectations of future enjoyment. Where the reduction of inequality could occur without damage to security – through various forms of taxation, for example, or through the provision of services to aid the sick, the uneducated or the poor – then this would be justified, but generally Bentham's commitment to political equality does not extend to the material sphere. The primary goal is always security as the framework for the realization of happiness but where suffering and pain can clearly be eliminated through government intervention then this is an obvious responsibility which the government should accept. Indeed much of Bentham's writing is concerned with practical proposals for the reform of prisons, factories, health and safety, education, poor relief and other social institutions.

Although much of Bentham's reputation came from his fierce denunciations of the sinister interests of the ruling establishment of his own day, he was as concerned to construct proposals for future government action as he was to oppose present government action. The test was always utility and, while this might point to action in some cases or inaction in others, it could never justify negligence. In general, nothing could restrict the omnicompetence of the legislature – except utility – and Bentham sees its work not as interventionist or *laissez-faire* in principle but as guided in practice by the general welfare as broken down into its four aims of security, subsistence, abundance and equality. And where utility pointed, Bentham followed – and in great detail. Thus, not content with merely outlining the principles of punishment, he devised in great detail and at great personal expense and over many years a model prison, the Panopticon ([1.12], vol. 4). Similarly in other areas, principles had to be applied and in minute detail to test their possibility and to make utilitarianism a practical reforming creed rather than merely a philosophical rationale. Whether it be the architectural details, the hours of work, the rates of pay, the balance between humanity and economy, the details of the syllabus, the form of record-keeping, whether it be prisons or workhouses, schools or factories, detail was always the test of principle: what ought to be must always be compatible with what could be.

Morality must work with Nature not against it, thus making it a realistic cure for social ills. At times this concern with gathering facts and information can make Bentham appear to value the exercise for its own sake but that would be to forget the inspiration behind his life's work – the desire to do good for a species which ironically he had to assume was itself only concerned with its own good. It was not enough to be a philosopher; his ambition was to be practical, useful and realistic – a critic who could construct as well as demolish, whose goal was both modest and magnificent – to build a system in which people might be happy. And the system as finally devised was one in which the people themselves controlled the system. Indeed one test of the whole enterprise was that once the creation had been completed, the creator was no longer needed.

This movement in Bentham's thinking from reforming the law to reforming the whole structure of political arrangements from which the law would emanate – the movement from adviser of rulers to champion of the people in order to bring about the reign of utility – owed a great deal to the influence of James Mill, who brought to the utilitarian cause not only a sharp, lucid and persuasive style of powerful literary propaganda but also a democratic hostility to the establishment and a rigorous reforming programme in the fields of law, education and political economy based on a foundation of associationist psychology. Often overshadowed in the literature by his friend Bentham and by his son, John Stuart Mill, James Mill was a thinker and active reformer of independent stature. In many ways he was a more dominant figure amongst the radical utilitarians than the master himself.

James Mill was born in 1773 in a small village in Scotland, the son of a shoemaker and a farmer's daughter. After his early education he went to the University of Edinburgh in 1790 and after that studied Divinity and was licensed as a preacher in the Church of Scotland in 1798. Engaged as a tutor by Sir John Stuart he accompanied him to London in 1802, married in 1805 (John Stuart Mill was born a year later), and met Bentham in 1808. From 1806 to 1817, he was busy writing the *History of India* while also writing journal articles and his influential essays for the Supplement to the fifth edition of the *Encyclopaedia Britannica*. Following the publication of his *History of India* in 1818 [1.59], he was appointed to the East India Company where he became Chief Examiner in 1830. He continued to write regularly for radical journals, published his *Analysis of the Phenomena of the Human Mind* [1.54] and his *Fragment on Mackintosh* [1.58]; he died in 1836. His association with Bentham lasted from 1808 until the latter's death in 1832; for some four years he and his family lived with Bentham at Ford Abbey, but his influence on the utilitarian movement was that of someone who brought to it a systematic philosophy already formed rather than that of a mere disciple.

Mill had been educated at Edinburgh and was strongly influenced by the Scottish philosophy of Dugald Stewart and Thomas Reid. From Stewart, amongst other things, he learnt the importance of adding a concern with reform of existing institutions and the development of enlightened legislation to the more traditional concern with explanatory description, a distinction similar to Bentham's between censorial and expository jurisprudence. Thus philosophy must move from the reflective or sceptical to the active and optimistic. In addition, Stewart's lectures introduced Mill to the philosophy of Reid. Reid's philosophy of experience and common sense came down firmly on the side of induction and against deduction, following Bacon and Newton, and although Mill later rejected the Christian underpinning of this philosophy – that we know only because God has given us the power of perception – he held fast to the importance of induction, learning from experience, in order to formulate general laws which in turn would be the basis for deductive reasoning. For Mill the centre of such enquiries into the laws governing human behaviour were the laws of psychology which could be known through observation of the study of mental phenomena. The result was Mill's doctrine of association: the mind perceives the external world by sensations – smell, taste, hearing, touch, sight – and what remain once the sensations cease are ideas. These ideas are copies of the sensations, and just as sensations are associated together, and more strongly the more frequent and vivid the connection, so ideas are associated in the same way. Knowledge is the result of frequency of conjunction; in some cases the frequency and strength is such that the ideas cannot be separated and this is what gives us our belief in the external world. All our mental faculties can be explained by this principle of association as can our behaviour in response to the two ultimate elements of painful and pleasurable sensations. We learn about the world by associating certain actions with certain sensations and thus learn to avoid the one kind and seek the other. Thus the route to the fundamental reality of pleasure and pain which Bentham had discovered through his logical notion of real entities was found by Mill through his notion of the psychological association of ideas as copies of sensations. And just as Bentham's discovery gave him a weapon by which to attempt to change the world so did James Mill's; that their objectives coincided should not blur the differing starting points. It is in pursuing their shared objectives that, at least in a political sense, Mill shows himself the superior.

While Bentham wrote voluminously but published relatively little about the whole range of philosophical, constitutional and legal enquiries, Mill directed his attention to converting the relevant public through concise and clear articles. His *Encyclopaedia* articles were superb examples of a combination of his philosophical views – notably his doctrine of associationism – and his radical political views. They were intended to have an impact and in this they succeeded. His article on 'Education' is probably the clearest example of this attempt to put philosophy into practice. Given that the mind knows only through sensations and their sequences, the object of education is to provide for the constant production of those sequences most conducive to happiness; the individual is virtually what education in the broadest sense makes him or her. If the right associations are made early on in life then education improves not only the intellect but also the moral character. The whole environment has an effect on the progress of the mind, and thus 'education' for Mill encompasses a far wider range than conventionally thought of, and has implications for social and political change. Thus domestic education starts at birth, and associations must be so ordered that the happiness of the individual is the end but one that is bound up also with the happiness of others. After this early formation of character, education in the more normal sense continues to aim at the development of both the intelligence and the moral feelings as the key to happiness. This is supported by the effect of society and government which should provide the environment in which the pursuit of individual happiness harmonizes with general utility. Thus education is a question not simply of the advancement and spread of knowledge to all members of the community but, as importantly, of the development of mutual sympathy and benevolence amongst them. Thus where Bentham had relied on sanctions in order to bring duty and interest into harmony, Mill is more optimistic of the beneficial effects of education in developing the right associations between one's own pleasure and the good of others. To achieve this, early environment as well as school education needs reform within the context of a reformed society led by a reformed government. Only then will individuals pursue their happiness with that degree of self-control which recognizes the importance of the happiness of others.

However, such moderation and harmony cannot be generally expected in an unreformed society and the key to improvement here is to change the system of government. Here Mill's next famous and influential article was his essay on 'Government' [1.56] which highlights the link which Mill forged between utilitarianism and radicalism and which explains his importance to the school of philosophical radicals. His basic argument is that government is necessary in order to protect for each individual the fruits of his own labour. As it is labour not Nature that provides the means for life and happiness and as men, without restraints, would take from each other what they desired and thus undermine the whole enterprise, then a system of government is necessary. Unhappily, however, governments are also composed of men who again, without restraints, would plunder and oppress their fellow men. The laws of human nature are such that the pursuit of pleasure is the primary motive for those within as for those without government, and the main means to such ends are wealth and power. The mere establishment of government, therefore, provides no guarantee that the rulers will follow the general interest rather than their own; indeed it guarantees the very opposite. Hence, the need for government is accompanied by the need to ensure against its oppressive tendencies. Human nature explains the need for government, the dangers of government, and also the key to good government, where the basic problem is one of restraining the power-holders from abusing their role.

Such securities against misrule cannot be found within any of the traditional forms of government. A democratic government – in the literal sense of the whole community gathering together as often as the business of government required – would be near impossible as well as ill-adapted to decision-making. An aristocratic form of rule would naturally pursue its sinister interest against that of the community; so much more so would a monarchical form. Further, any mixture of these three forms is also unable to secure against abuse and thus guarantee the general interest. If there are three powers, two of them will always be able to swallow up the third, and that will mean the monarchical and aristocratic, whose sinister interests are opposed to the people's interests, rendering the community defenceless against its powers. We all desire our pleasures and we all need wealth and power to achieve them; small wonder that the prize of government is so keenly sought by those who want to further their own interests.

From the general viewpoint there is therefore always a tendency for government to be badly conducted, for power to be abused; the antidote lies in a system of checks or securities to prevent such abuse. It is the discovery of representation which makes this possible, where the community's interest in good government acts as a check on the representatives who in turn operate as a check on government. The representatives, while having an identity of interests with the community, have sufficient power to guard against abuse and thus secure good government. Limited terms of office and regular elections would guard against the representatives pursuing their sinister interest and thus destroying the identity which is the rationale of the system. In terms of whose interests should be represented – in crude terms, who should vote – Mill is prepared, at least in this essay which is an argument for parliamentary reform in the 1820s as well as a treatise on the foundations of government, to exclude those whose interests are included in those of others. Thus women and men under forty can all be protected by others and their interests pursued on their behalf. Such a system of representative democracy with an extended franchise could confidently be relied on to pursue the general interest, not least because the dominant part, the middle rank of society, is also the most virtuous and the one whose opinions are most respected by the class of people below them. They are the ones to set the political and social standards which will form the wider educational context for the general improvement of the community. Their influence, combined with that of the law and the formal educational system, will create a culture in which duty and interest go together, not so much as in Bentham because the citizens have an interest – through the various sanctions – in doing their duty but because through the principle of association the pursuit of interest will constantly have the consciousness of others' interests allied to it. Thus with political reform as with educational reform an effect on character will be produced as well as an effect on intelligence and wisdom.

In comparing Mill's case for representative democracy with that of Bentham a curious paradox appears. Mill, the historian of British India, who stressed the need for a close examination of the manners and institutions of that society before recommending any appropriate changes in its organization or government, here adopts a largely abstract deductive method, whereas Bentham, the upholder of that method of logic, appears in the *Constitutional Code* to include much more empirical evidence about the actual practice of societies in order to achieve the end of good government. Thus Mill is optimistic that representation can itself achieve an identity of interests between the rulers and ruled; frequent elections are the key safeguard. Bentham, as we have seen, insists on additional securities against misrule, so that while the legislature remains omnicompetent it is still subject to the power of the people, and much of his evidence in the *Code* is from existing countries rather than from the logic of the situation alone.

In fairness, of course, Mill could claim that the deductive method was one based on a prior and thorough induction giving rise to comprehensive and known principles of human nature. Further, his essay is a brief and direct case for reform rather than a complete study of government. Whatever the case, it is true that it was Mill's method as much as his conclusions which gave rise to fierce criticism at the time. Mill's leading opponent, Macaulay, accused him of assuming certain principles of human nature and then arguing deductively from them, ignoring completely the history and practice of government through the centuries. Even if there were any absolutely true principles of human conduct, no science of government could be deduced from them. Knowledge of politics comes from empirical study and induction, and the generalizations which result will be related always to the context of their discovery ([1.47] 97–129). As already noted, Mill's case, as the utilitarian one generally, was that the original proposition that it is self-interest which is the dominant motive was in fact based on experience. Without any checks, so would men behave, and this need to prevent men from injuring each other in the pursuit of their interests is recognized as the chief function of government. The problem here lies in the status of the original proposition: is it a law of human nature supported by empirical evidence and holding true without exception or is it the only sensible assumption to make in order to organize social and political life? Mill's position seemed to waver between the two – a law that men's actions are governed by their interests, in turn explained by the association of ideas, or a prudential maxim that everyone should be supposed to be acting in their interests; in either case the only safeguard for good government lay through a system of representation to check against the abuse of power. It was this certainty in Mill's thinking, that utilitarianism had to point in a politically radical direction, that helped move Bentham from his original expectation that an enlightened despot or aristocracy would usher in the reign of utility to his mature position that democracy was an essential instrument towards the desired end.

That James Mill's position is more complex than might be assumed from his essay on 'Government' and the deductive method applied there can be seen by examining his further articles in the Supplement to the *Encyclopaedia*. Apart from what seems to be a simple faith in the identity of interest created by regular elections, Mill is aware that for electors to make informed choices and judge their rulers wisely they must have knowledge of their actions and be free to criticize them. Freedom of expression is thus added to the other securities against misrule. His essay on the 'Liberty of the Press' [1.56] attends to this problem. For the government to pursue the greatest happiness, for the system of checks to work, knowledge or the glare of publicity is essential. Democracy as institutionalized mistrust depends on the ruled knowing what the rulers are doing. Truth acts as the great restrainer; a free press is an essential security without which free elections would not serve their purpose.

Having established good government and provided securities against misrule, the question arises as to its responsibilities. As with Bentham, Mill sees the law as providing the framework of organized and secure social life. The law creates offences and these are violations of rights, every infringement of which involves an injury. Utility determines what should be rights and the law should translate these into legal rights. Not all painful acts are to be treated as injuries, for example when they result from people's antipathies to actions which cause no evil, as in the religious hostility to eating or drinking certain types of food or drink, as argued in 'Liberty of the Press' [1.56], 11). Thus while liberty is to be restricted where rights are violated, not every evidence of pain is to count as good reason for legal protection. As with Bentham's four types of case where punishment is not appropriate – because groundless, inefficacious, unprofitable or needless – so Mill excludes intervention where the evil of punishment is not outweighed by some positive good. The law's concern is primarily to deter the commitment of mischievous acts not to compel the individual to seek his or her own happiness in prescribed ways. A duty to oneself is a matter of individual prudence; the law steps in when duty to others is involved. And the moral sanction or public opinion reinforces the force of law in matters where considerations of utility can be objectively shown to be involved. There must be empirical evidence of mischief or injury not merely prejudice or antipathy; with Mill as with Bentham this was what made the principle of utility superior to others. Where there would be no pain without the antipathy, no harm without the dislike, then the case for interference is groundless. Utilitarianism is an external standard capable of being applied empirically. And so the law creates the conditions in which all individuals are allowed to pursue their own conception of happiness secure in the knowledge that fellow individuals will not injure their rights and they likewise are equally secure, equally free to maximize their own good. The individuals' original mistrust of others is replaced by a trust based on the rightness and strength of the law.

Mill is optimistic that democratic reform would lead to utility and rejects the criticism that the poor, once in majority power, would pursue a short-term self-interest which would threaten the security of person and property which it was the law's main business to protect. He believes, on the contrary, that they would act on their long-term interests which involved the maintenance of private property and respect for individual rights. Both the influence of the middle class and the power of education would show people that the rational course demanded such moderation. In such a reformed environment people will indeed successfully pursue their own interests, but in an intelligent, temperate and benevolent manner. In this way Mill injects into utilitarianism a more high-minded tone than generally appears in Bentham, a tone to be accentuated further by his son, John Stuart Mill.

The influence of both Bentham and James Mill is a matter of some controversy, not least because it has to be assessed both philosophically and practically in order to respect their claims that proper understanding could only be tested by practical results. More than this, any practical changes which did occur cannot be unquestionably attributed to the utilitarian philosophy which recommended them. There were many other influences at work. Furthermore, it is difficult to pin-point the exact extent of Bentham's own influence exerted as it was by correspondence, conversation and public discussion as much as by his published work. That much of the reform was in accord with Bentham's thought is not conclusive proof of a connection yet the general atmosphere conducive to reform seems clearly to have been formed at least partly by the activities of Bentham, James Mill and their school of radical utilitarians. Generally speaking the reforms – political, legal, administrative and social – which took place in nineteenth-century Britain were much more modest than Bentham and Mill would have liked and the sinister interests so vehemently attacked by both thinkers were much more powerful and enduring than even they thought possible. Bentham's theory of democracy based on mistrust, accountability and publicity failed to dominate and instead the growth of democracy was attended with deference and secrecy. No written constitution was enacted, the Lords and monarchy survived, as did the Common Law, and the movement Bentham hoped for towards equality of power to challenge the privilege and corruption of the ruling few did not take place. Bentham's faith in the people and his hostility to those in power unless checked by the people was not the faith which motivated democracy; rather a distrust of the people and a reliance on a new ruling elite, more akin to James Mill's version, was the dominant theme in the movement towards democracy. Once Bentham had been converted to the radical cause he was clear that the key to happiness – a life of security, with adequate subsistence, the possibility of abundance, growing equality – lay in a democratic system with accountability as the primary value. In this sense his influence was less than that of James Mill or John Stuart Mill, both in different ways concerned with the quality of the rulers rather than the vitality of the people; this is not of course to say that Bentham's argument was wrong, simply that his radical democracy was overshadowed by a version in which the people ruled only in a distant sense and with little direct involvement or power of supervision.

In the matter of more detailed legislation – parliamentary reform, local government reform, the Poor Law, prison legislation, public health – the growth of government intervention and central administration was influenced by the Benthamites along with humanitarians, philanthropists, working-class radicals and Christian campaigners. The pressure for reform came from many sources but in formulating the detailed proposals and insisting on central control through inspection, in making the new system accountable to government, the Benthamites played a key role.

It is of course in the field of moral philosophy that Bentham is best known largely because of his supposed inferiority to his successor, John Stuart Mill. He has been seen as the proponent of a crude version of utilitarianism which the younger Mill sought to improve. In this way his contributions in the whole field of law and of reform were often seen as suspect, resting as they did on what was seen, following J. S. Mill, as a defective philosophy. Mill's debt to Bentham and to his father was generally concealed behind his somewhat severe criticisms of them. Thus J. S. Mill's *Autobiography*, though giving a distorted picture of his father's character and influence, was regarded as the authorized version, and his critical essays on Bentham were thought to be no more than the master deserved. In consequence, the younger Mill's attempt to defend a new version of utilitarianism, despite later criticisms of it, was thought at least to be an advance on the original. Similarly with J. S. Mill's concern with individual liberty, it was seen as a radical departure from a form of utilitarianism which had no liberal dimension. The influence of Bentham and James Mill was thus cast in terms of an influence from which Mill liberated himself with the aid of new more sensitive, romantic and emotional guides. While there is no doubt that J. S. Mill made important changes to the older version of utilitarianism, the continuities are also important; furthermore the evidence of change does not itself indicate improvement. Given Bentham's ambition to change the world through the power of enlightened law and thus liberate people from the constraints placed on them by the power of sinister interests, and given John Stuart's different agenda to liberate them through the improvement of their characters, perhaps comparison is a misconceived exercise. If it is allowed, who is to say that Bentham's massive but modest practical enterprise is inferior to the grander but more elusive project which animated J. S. Mill? Into this picture James Mill constantly strays, exhibiting at times the practical optimism of Bentham and at other times a sterner pessimism about the possibility of improving character in a world beset with prejudice, ignorance and selfishness. Generally speaking, the older utilitarians took men (and women for Bentham) as they were and looked to laws as they might be, before considering society as it could be. For Bentham, and James Mill to a lesser extent, the strength of his position was that the changes recommended were all possible because tangible; they involved no change in human nature but only in the conditions in which men and women find themselves. All people want a happy life, a life of well-being, and it is politics which can assure them of the right context for such a very human ambition. From this standpoint Bentham never deviates, though James and John Stuart Mill are constantly worried by a more paternalistic concern with evaluating the happiness of the individual, a matter which Bentham is happy to leave to the individual to decide.

In some ways the different interpretations given to utilitarianism were part of its strength as an enduring ethical principle. Thus for those concerned with matters of practical efficiency and reform it offered the possibility of empirical calculation of consequences, while for those concerned with the more spiritual improvement of mankind it offered a standard of qualitative judgement. Thus within the broad utilitarian perspective many versions persisted but all in some ways or other owed much to the classical formulation of Bentham either directly or through its modified transmission by James Mill.

❧ BIBLIOGRAPHY ❧

Bentham: manuscripts

1.1   Bentham Manuscripts in the University College London Library.
1.2   Bentham Manuscripts in the British Library, Add. MSS 33, 537–64.
1.3   Dumont Manuscripts in the Bibliothèque Publique et Universitaire, Geneva.

Editions of Bentham's works

Complete and selected works

The Collected Works of Jeremy Bentham, general eds, J. H. Burns, J. R. Dinwiddy, F. Rosen:
1.4   *Chrestomathia*, ed. M. J. Smith and W. H. Burston, Oxford, 1983.
1.5   *A Comment on the Commentaries and A Fragment on Government*, ed. J. H. Burns and H. L. A. Hart, London, 1977.
1.6   *Constitutional Code*, vol. 1, ed. F. Rosen and J. H. Burns, Oxford, 1983.
1.7   *The Correspondence of Jeremy Bentham*, vols 1–2, ed. T. L. S. Sprigge, London, 1968; vol. 3, ed. I. Christie, London, 1971; vols 4–5, ed. A. T. Milne, London, 1981; vols 6–7, ed. J. R. Dinwiddy, London, 1984; vols 8–9, ed. S. Conway, London, 1988, 1989.
1.8   *Deontology together with A Table of the Springs of Action and Article on Utilitarianism*, ed. A. Goldworth, Oxford, 1983.
1.9   *An Introduction to the Principles of Morals and Legislation*, ed. J. H. Burns and H. L. A. Hart, London, 1970.
1.10 *First Principles Preparatory to Constitutional Code*, ed. P. Schofield, Oxford, 1989.

1.11 *Of Laws in General*, ed. H. L. A. Hart, London, 1970.
1.12 *The Works of Jeremy Bentham*, 11 vols, ed. J. Bowring, Edinburgh, 1838–43.
1.13 *Jeremy Bentham's Economic Writings*, 3 vols, ed. W. Stark, London, 1952–4.
1.14 *Traités de législation, civile et pénale*, 3 vols, ed. E. Dumont, Paris, 1802.
1.15 *Bentham's Theory of Fictions*, ed. C. K. Ogden, London, 1973.
1.16 *Bentham's Political Thought*, ed. B. Parekh, London, 1973.

Separate works

1.17 *An Introduction to the Principles of Morals and Legislation*, ed. J. H. Burns and H. L. A. Hart, London, 1982. Introduction by H. L. A. Hart.
1.18 *A Fragment on Government*, ed. J. H. Burns and H. L. A. Hart, Cambridge, 1988. Introduction by R. Harrison.

Bentham: bibliographies

1.19 *The Bentham Newsletter*, London, 1978–88 and *Utilitas*, Oxford, 1989– .
1.20 *Catalogue of the Manuscripts of Jeremy Bentham in the Library of University College London*, ed. A. T. Milne, London, 1962.

Works on Bentham: general surveys

1.21 Atkinson, C. M. *Jeremy Bentham: His Life and Work*, London, 1905.
1.22 Baumgardt, D. *Bentham and the Ethics of Today*, Princeton, 1952.
1.23 Dinwiddy, J. R. *Bentham*, Oxford, 1989.
1.24 Everett, C. W. *The Education of Jeremy Bentham*, New York, 1931.
1.25 ——*Jeremy Bentham*, London, 1966.
1.26 Halevy, E. *The Growth of Philosophical Radicalism*, trans. M. Morris, London, 1972.
1.27 Harrison, R. *Bentham*, London, 1983.
1.28 Hart, H. L. A. *Essays on Bentham*, Oxford, 1982.
1.29 Himmelfarb, G. 'The haunted house of Jeremy Bentham' in *Victorian Minds*, New York, 1968.
1.30 Hume, L. J. *Bentham and Bureaucracy*, Cambridge, 1981.
1.31 Letwin, S. R. *The Pursuit of Certainty*, Cambridge, 1965.
1.32 Long, D. G. *Bentham on Liberty*, Toronto, 1977.
1.33 Lyons, D, *In the Interest of the Governed*, Oxford, 1973.
1.34 Mack, M. P. *Jeremy Bentham: An Odyssey of Ideas, 1748–1792*, London, 1962.
1.35 Manning, D.J. *The Mind of Jeremy Bentham*, London, 1968.
1.36 Parekh, B. ed. *Jeremy Bentham: Ten Critical Essays*, London, 1974.
1.37 Plamenatz, J. *The English Utilitarians*, Oxford, 1966.
1.38 Steintrager, J. *Bentham*, London, 1977.
1.39 Stephen, L. *The English Utilitarians*, 3 vols., London, 1900.
1.40 Thomas, W. *The Philosophical Radicals*, Oxford, 1979.

Political, moral and legal theory

1.41 Burns, J. H. *The Fabric of Felicity: The Legislator and the Human Condition*, London, 1967.
1.42 Crimmins, J. E. *Secular Utilitarianism*, Oxford, 1990.
1.43 Dicey, A. V. *Lectures on the Relation between Law and Public Opinion during the Nineteenth Century*, London, 1905.
1.44 James, M. H. ed. *Bentham and Legal Theory*, Belfast, 1974.
1.45 Keaton, G. W. and G. Schwartzenberger, eds. *Jeremy Bentham and the Law*, London, 1948.
1.46 Kelly, P. J. *Utilitarianism and Distributive Justice*, Oxford, 1990.
1.47 Lively, J. and J. C. Rees, eds. *Utilitarian Logic and Politics*, Oxford, 1978.
1.48 MacPherson, C. B. *The Life and Times of Liberal Democracy*, Oxford, 1977.
1.49 Postema, G. J. *Bentham and the Common Law Tradition*, Oxford, 1986.
1.50 Rosen, F. *Jeremy Bentham and Representative Democracy*, Oxford, 1983.
1.51 —— *Bentham, Byron and Greece*, Oxford, 1992.
1.52 Waldron, J. *Nonsense upon Stilts: Bentham, Burke and Marx on the Rights of Man*, London, 1987.
1.53 Williford, M. *Jeremy Bentham on Spanish America*, Baton Rouge, 1980.

James Mill: works

1.54 *Analysis of the Phenomena of the Human Mind*, 2 vols. London, 1828; 1869; 1878; New York, 1967.
1.55 *Elements of Political Economy*, London, 1821; 3rd edition, 1826; New York, 1963; Edinburgh, 1966.
1.56 *Essays on Government, Jurisprudence, Liberty of the Press, Prisons and Prison Discipline, Colonies, Law of Nations, Education. Supplement to the Fifth Edition of the Encyclopaedia Britannica*, 1824.
1.57 *An Essay on Government*, ed. C. V. Shields, New York, 1955.
1.58 *A Fragment on Mackintosh*, London, 1835; 1870.
1.59 *The History of India*, 3 vols, London, 1818; 6 vols, 1820; New York, 1968.
1.60 *Utilitarian Logic and Politics*, ed. J. Lively and J. Rees, Oxford, 1978.
1.61 *Selected Economic Writings*, ed. D. Winch, Edinburgh, 1966.

James Mill: bibliographies

1.62 Fenn, R. A. *James Mill's Political Thought*, Appendix II, New York and London, 1987.

Works on James Mill

1.63 Bain, A. *James Mill: A Biography*, London, 1882.

1.64 Burston, W. H. *James Mill on Education*, Cambridge, 1969.

1.65 Davidson, W. L. *Political Thought in England: the Utilitarians from Bentham to J. S. Mill*, London, 1915.

1.66 Halevy, E. *The Growth of Philosophical Radicalism*, London, 1949.

1.67 Hamburger, J. *James Mill and the Art of Revolution*, New Haven, 1963.

1.68 Mazlish, B. *James and John Stuart Mill*, New York, 1975.

1.69 Morley, J. 'The Life of James Mill', *The Fortnightly Review*, n.s. 31, 476–504, 1882.

1.70 Plamenatz, J. P. *The English Utilitarians*, Oxford, 1949.

1.71 Ryan, A. 'Two Concepts of Politics and Democracy: James and John Stuart Mill', in M. Fleisher, ed., *Machiavelli and the Nature of Political Thought*, New York, 1972.

1.72 Stephen, L. *The English Utilitarians*, 3 vols, London, 1900.

1.73 Stokes, E. *The English Utilitarians and India*, Oxford, 1959.

CHAPTER 2

Whewell's philosophy of science and ethics

Struan Jacobs

ON SCIENCE

Introduction

Among the most prodigious of English minds of the nineteenth century, William Whewell (1794–1866) was at various times, and among other things, philosopher, intellectual historian, scientist, educationist, theologian, economist, student of Gothic architecture, classicist. 'Science is his [Whewell's] forte and omniscience his foible', quipped Sidney Smith. Born at Lancaster, son of a master-carpenter, Whewell won in 1812 an exhibition to Cambridge University whose most famous College – Trinity – he went on to serve continuously from 1817, initially as a Fellow then from 1841 as Master, to his untimely death from a riding accident.

Whewell was intellectually eminent in his lifetime, then his reputation went through a long eclipse. Interest in his work has, however, steadily increased over recent decades in an atmosphere more congenial to it, the intellectual shift – displacement of logical empiricism by historically informed philosophy of science – associated with Thomas Kuhn (*The Structure of Scientific Revolutions*) and others. Whewell believed, as now so many scholars believe, that the key to understanding the methods of science and the character of its knowledge lies in history, rather than in formal analysis of propositions and arguments.

Whewellian scholarship has tended to concentrate on those texts that Whewell himself took to be his most important, *The Philosophy of the Inductive Sciences* (1840 [2.3]) and its more concretely detailed companion, *History of the Inductive Sciences* (1837 [2.31]).[1] These were works for whose composition Whewell's extensive interest in science –

crystallography, mineralogy, geology, mathematics, astronomy, physics, biology, tidology, political economy – equipped him superbly.

Historiography

Whewell produced his *History of the Inductive Sciences* concurrently with the *Philosophy*. He envisaged a relation between the two works such that the *History* would, besides providing a chronicle of scientific discoveries, empirically inform the other inquiry. Philosophical study of the methods by which truth in science is discovered requires to be, which to date it has not been Whewell claims, 'based upon a survey of the truths' already known to scientists ([2.1], 1: viii). In this respect Whewell sees the *History* as a work without precedent, as he does also in its 'point of view' or 'plan'.

According to Whewell's broad perspective, development of scientific disciplines typically involves 'preludes', 'inductive epochs', and 'sequels'. Certain disciplinary histories may reveal no epoch at all (thermotics, science of heat, for example); some are exhausted by a single case of the threefold sequence (about Newton's law of universal gravitation revolves the solitary epoch of physical or explanatory astronomy, and round the undulatory theory of Young and Fresnel turns that of physical optics); others show two or more of these cases (formal astronomy, covering astronomical relations as distinct from causes, with epochal figures in Hipparchus, Copernicus and Kepler).

How are inductive epochs, the periods chiefly constitutive of the history of science, identified by Whewell? Their most prominent feature is major intellectual breakthrough, achieved by the inductive method.

No epochal discovery is ever made 'suddenly and without preparation' ([2.1], 1: 10). In the course of preludes, by invention of hypotheses and by analysis, ideas gain in clarity and facts in precision; materials needful for discovery are so prepared. Among 'imperfect, undeveloped, [and] unconfirmed' ([2.1], 2: 370) preludial conjectures, some anticipate and 'touch' the great truths of epochs, as did Descartes' vortex theory relative to Newton's theory of gravity.

In sequels to inductive epochs champions of new theories overcome by argument defenders of traditional beliefs, winning over 'the wider throng of the secondary cultivators' ([2.1], 1: 10). Implications of epochal discoveries are traced out, increasing their evidential support.

Emphasizing 'great discoveries' in the development of disciplines, their concepts and vocabularies undergoing significant change, Whewell may be said to work in the *History* with a concept of *scientific revolutions*. And the term itself is in evidence, Whewell noting the occurrence of 'revolutions' in 'the intellectual world' ([2.1] 1: 9) and of 'revolutions in science' ([2.1], 3: 114).[2] But his use of 'revolution' is attenuated, its connotation including continuity between successive scientific theories, which, with the fact that 'revolution' commonly signifies sudden sweeping change, may explain why Whewell is not at all times comfortable with the word. Discomfort, indeed denial, manifests in his remark that 'earlier truths are not expelled but absorbed, not contradicted but extended; and the history of each science, which may appear like a succession of revolutions, is, in reality, a series of developments' ([2.1], 1: 8). There coexist in the science of Whewell's historiographic depiction an element each of evolution and revolution.[3]

From Whewell's account of scientific development as variations on the theme of prelude, epoch, sequel, one is not to infer it is his view that science has undergone continuous development. He actually finds in the 'history of human speculations' ([2.1], 1: 11) times of stasis when science has languished. Book IV of *History of the Inductive Sciences* presents as the major case the Middle Ages or, in Whewell's phrase, the 'Stationary Period'. From the epoch of Hipparchus virtually to the time of Copernicus, science stood still. Inquiring into why this was so, Whewell notes how often during these one-and-a-half millenniums ideas were left indistinct, and how rarely were theories hauled before the tribunal of facts. These failures were results of deeper tendencies: rigid obeisance to intellectual authority, intolerance of dissent and an 'enthusiastic temper' subjecting 'the mind's operations to ideas altogether distorted and delusive' ([2.1], 1: 81).

Ideas and perception

History of the Inductive Sciences covers one side of the development of science, the observational, *Philosophy of the Inductive Sciences* covering the other, the 'history of the Sciences so far as it depends on *Ideas*' ([2.1], 1: 16). The *Philosophy* commences with a book on 'Ideas in General', books following on each of the better developed sciences: 'Pure Sciences' (mathematics), 'Mechanical Sciences', 'Chemistry', 'Morphology, including Crystallography', and the like. Such sciences impress Whewell as rich storehouses of 'unquestioned truths'. The second – theoretically much the more interesting – part of *Philosophy,* 'Of Knowledge', chiefly consists of Books XI to XIII: 'Of the Construction of Science', 'Review of Opinions on the Nature of Knowledge, and the Method of Seeking It', and 'Of Methods Employed in the Formation of Science'.

It is contended by Whewell that sciences rest on 'fundamental ideas', each science having one idea or some combination of ideas uniquely its own. The 'pure sciences' (of mathematics) are based on ideas of space, time and number; the 'mechanical sciences' on that of cause; 'palaetiological sciences' (historical sciences, including geology and biology) on historical cause. (An implication of this doctrine is denial of disciplinary reductionism. It excludes the possibility of a fundamental bedrock science, of whose laws those of other sciences are functions and from which deducible. Each science is for Whewell *sui generis*.) To the development of each science ideas contribute 'elements of truths'. Elements of another kind also play a part, which dualism is nowhere brought out more clearly by Whewell than in his account of perception. Analysing this will lead us into his philosophy of science.

Perception requires *sensory impressions* of shape, surface, colour, and movement. But there must be in perception materials besides these, for sensations are formless, evanescent, disconnected and without assignable boundaries, whereas perception is of enduring *objects* with specific properties, involved in definite relations. It is inferred by Whewell that mind is greatly involved, informing and fashioning the sensory flux.[4] Perception of objects with properties and in relations – discrete, spatially located, shaped, enduring, numbered, operated on by forces, resembling others – is the synthesis of sensory presentations and mental emanations. Impressions on senses by phenomena without are materials to which form is given by ideas within.[5] Sensations and ideas are one expression of that which Whewell describes as the *'fundamental antithesis'* of knowledge; elements which while mutually dependent are unlike in character and issue from opposite sources.

Innate to the mind and developed over time through its intercourse with the world are powers of forming fundamental ideas (space, time, number, likeness, causality, matter, force, substance, medium, symmetry and design) and of cognate conceptions. To exercise these powers is to organize in definite ways the otherwise shapeless flux of sensations, impregnating it with assumptions. The product of the process is conceptually informed material, sensations and ideas fused in perception.

Whewellian ideas are nothing like the mental images or objects of thought to be found in Descartes and Locke, but are close to Kant's 'forms of sensibility' (space and time). Whewell's account of mind and perception would appear to have been significantly affected by Kant. True, Whewell ([2.6], 334–5) describes his 'main views' as 'very different from Kant's' (instancing Kant's denial of knowledge of noumena or things in themselves), but he admits in the same breath to having 'adopted some of Kant's views, or at least some of his arguments. The chapters ... on the Ideas of Space and Time in the *Philosophy of the Inductive Sciences*, were almost literal translations of chapters in the *Kritik der Reinen Vernunft*'. 'Kant considers that Space and Time are conditions of perception, and hence sources of necessary and universal truth' as indeed – except that he recognizes more of such 'conditions' and 'sources' – does Whewell ([2.6], 336).

Induction

Whewell's philosophy of science builds on the foregoing analysis of perception, elaborating the theme of the fundamental antithesis. The philosophy of science includes among its main components an account of induction as the process of scientific discovery, and standards for measuring which theories are true. The most accessible source of all this is Book XI, 'Of the Construction of Science', forming as Whewell ([2.3], 2: 3–4) puts it the 'main subject' of *Philosophy of the Inductive Sciences*, all earlier chapters being in relation to it 'subordinate and preparatory'.[6]

The materials or 'conditions' of knowledge Whewell in opening his account of it explains are ideas and conceptions emanating from mind and – the other side of the antithesis – facts originating from observation and experiment. Scientific knowledge is expressed in 'exact and universal' propositions. It consists in the application of conceptions or ideas, distinct and 'appropriate' to some science (as is symmetry to morphology, force to mechanics, and vital power to physiology),[7] to numerous facts possessed of clarity and certainty.[8] A *system* of scientific knowledge is said by Whewell ([2.3], 2: 3) to exist 'when, facts being thus included in exact and general propositions, such propositions are, in the same manner, included with equal rigour in propositions of a higher degree of generality; and these again in others of a still wider nature, so as to form a large and systematic whole'.

Necessary for achieving scientific knowledge are a twofold process of preparation – 'explication of conceptions' and 'decomposition of facts' – and a method Whewell distinguishes as 'colligation'. Explication is undertaken to clarify conceptions and to gauge their suitability to research projects. (In the terminology of *History of the Inductive Sciences* it is 'preludial' work.) Controversy is prominent in this process. Vague and unfamiliar, new conceptions are objected to, placing on protagonists the onus of elucidation and integration. It is Whewell's judgement ([2.3], 2: 8), a combination of 'whiggishness' and hindsight, that all controversies respecting scientific conceptions have ended in victory to 'the side on which the truth was found'. Under the broad heading of 'explication' Whewell also includes disclosure of necessary truths as inhering in ideas and functioning as presuppositions of sciences. Ideas must be clear before necessity in axioms can be discerned and their implications be traced out: 'the distinctness of the idea is necessary to a full apprehension of the truth of the axioms' ([2.2], 170).

As conceptions call for 'explication', in the other part of the process of preparing materials for discovery, facts have need of 'decomposition'. Facts properly decomposed are 'definite and certain ... , free from obscurity and doubt' ([2.3], 2: 26). Reduced to simple elements and considered in regard to clear ideas and conceptions, experience may be rid of impurities – the likes of myth, prejudice and emotion. Among the original basis of decomposed facts for astronomy, for example, were the moon's recurrent phases, rising and setting points of the sun, and those regular intervals between which the same stars become visible at the same time of the year.

After explication and decomposition the way is clear for 'colligation' as the really creative work of science. By exercise of imagination, the scientist endeavours to hit upon a conception capable of expressing a 'precise connexion among the phenomena which are presented to our senses' ([2.3], 2: 36). In the case of Kepler's third law, 'Squares of the periodic times of planets are proportional to the cubes of their mean distances from the sun', Whewell finds elementary facts about the planets' solar distances and durations of years colligated (literally, 'bound together') by such conceptions as squares of numbers and proportionality.

Explication, decomposition and, above all, colligation are the constructive elements forming *induction*, from which process Whewell ([2.3], 2: 47) derives all *'real general knowledge'* of the world, by which he believes are discovered all laws of nature. Whewellian induction has little more than its name in common with the process traditionally so called. It is not generalization from facts but invention of an hypothesis using a new conception(s) or an old one(s) transposed from some other context; the hypothesis being superimposed on, so as to bring order to, facts hitherto not perceived as connected. Successful hypotheses depend on suitable conceptions, for invention of which there is no methodological rule, being fruit of sagacity and serendipity.

Whewellian induction also takes in negative testing of hypotheses to strike those out that are false. In coupling colligation with critique, Whewell presages by one hundred years in a most remarkable manner Karl Popper's image of science as 'conjectures and refutations'. Writes Whewell:

> This constant comparison of his [the scientist's] own conceptions and supposition with observed facts under all aspects, forms the leading employment of the discoverer: this candid and simple love of truth, which makes him willing to suppress the most favourite production of his own ingenuity as soon as it appears

to be at variance with realities, constitutes the first characteristic of his temper.

[2.3], 56–7).[9]

There is for scientists a temptation to cling on to hypotheses, setting their faces against empirical violations, and Whewell believes it helps explain the 'obloquy' into which hypotheses 'have fallen' ([2.3], 2: 58). This detraction, and more so the misuse, Whewell regrets. When, however, science proceeds properly, an episode of invention and test continues for as long as it takes for an hypothesis to be framed to bind 'scattered facts into a single rule' ([2.3], 2: 41). Whewell is able to find no clearer illustration of the process in the history of science than Kepler's successive invention and disposal of nineteen hypotheses (oval, combinations of epicycles, etc.) as he struggled to describe the orbit of Mars, which he eventually succeeded in doing through his colligation with the conception of ellipse.

John Stuart Mill, prominent among Whewell's adversaries, critically considered in A System of Logic Whewell's account of the case of Kepler. Mill did this under the heading 'Inductions Improperly So Called', indicating that to his mind what Whewell terms 'colligations' and identifies with inductions are strictly speaking not inductions at all. 'Induction' for Mill ([2.17], 288) 'is the process by which we conclude that what is true of certain individuals of a class is true of the whole class'. It is generalization, the inferring of general propositions, whereas by colligation he ([2.17], 292) understands 'mere description', there occurring no inference from, no going beyond, the facts.

That which Mill ([2.17], 297) identifies as the 'fundamental difference' between Whewell and himself over how Kepler should be interpreted centres on whether the ellipse colligation was logically equivalent to, only a description of, Kepler's experience. Mill ([2.17], 295) demurs to Whewell's suggestion that Kepler 'put what he had conceived into the facts'. In Mill's account, having the concept of ellipse, Kepler considered whether observed positions of Mars were consistent with an elliptical orbit, and realized they were. 'But this fact, which Kepler did not add to, but found in, the motions of the planet . . . was the very fact, the separate parts of which had been separately observed; it was the sum of the different observations' ([2.17], 297).

So far as implications for his own philosophy of science are concerned, Mill, if I may digress to note a most interesting historical fact, devotes undue attention to the lesser of two associated problems. Let us put to one side whether Kepler's third law is no more than a description, and focus on the fact that descriptions do not exhaust Whewell's class of colligations. Universal propositions happen also, even more so, to be included and these, going beyond the facts, are by Mill's standards generalizations not descriptions. Mill ([2.17], 297) unreservedly agrees with Whewell that the 'tentative method' of trying conceptions is 'indispensable as a means to the colligation of facts for purposes of description'. To be true to his inductive philosophy Mill must now restrict Whewell's hypothetical or conjectural method to colligation in the restrictive (Millian) sense, ascribing to induction (generalization) all universal propositions of science. But this he fails consistently to do. Ultimately he wishes also to admit hypothesizing as a further source of general propositions. So it is one finds in Mill's *System of Logic* two philosophies of science: one in essence inductive, the other hypothetical. Of Mill's recognition and comprehension of this second method Whewell, as I have elsewhere argued, was almost certainly an important source ([2.15]; [2.16], 128–32).

Consilience

Whewell considers that scientific hypotheses are susceptible of proof, which is a major difference from Popper in whose view they are falsifiable only. We may conveniently denominate Whewell's conditions of proof as 'static success' and 'progressive success'. Each condition is required, and the two together are sufficient, for proof.

An hypothesis is advanced to explain some property or behaviour of the members of a class of phenomena. The 'static' condition of proof demands of a theory successful predictions of facts of the same nature within its subject class. The condition is minimal and non-definitive, being always satisfied by true, as well as sometimes by false, theories. While the theory of Ptolemy accurately predicted planetary positions along with solar and lunar eclipses, eventually it was judged an inaccurate representation of the structure of the heavens. Is the achievement of any so-far predictively successful theory ever sufficient to insure it against refutation later on? In Whewell's other condition of success lies the answer, and it we see is affirmative.

Whewell notices two forms of 'progressive' explanatory success ('successive generalization' being his term for it). One concerns theories to which hypotheses are added. It may be the case that the hypotheses successively '*tend to simplicity* and harmony; . . . the system . . . [becoming] more coherent as it is further extended'. Observes Whewell ([2.3], 2: 68), 'The elements . . . we require for explaining a new class of facts are already contained in our system', and for him this amounts to an infallible sign of truth. His prize example is the addition to Newton's theory of suppositions of: the sun's *attraction* to satellites to account for the motions of the aphelia and nodes; mutual *attraction* of planets to account for perturbations; *attraction* between earth, sun, and moon to account for tides, for the earth's spheroidal form, and for precession. The pattern is unmistakably that of progressive simplification, says Whewell ([2.3], 2: 70), several hypotheses resolving 'themselves into the single one, of ... universal gravitation'. In cases of the opposite kind, being historically the more numerous, assumptions happen neither to be suggested by nor to be reconcilable with theories to which they are appended. To Descartes' vortex theory were added hypotheses to explain elliptical planetary and lunar orbits, perturbations, and earth's gravitation. But they were independent, arbitrary, and *ad hoc*, and brought the theory into disrepute. By scientists using it to account for weights of chemical compounds, phlogiston theory was supplemented with, to the detriment of its credibility, the barely coherent notion that phlogiston is an element at once heavy and light, which upon entering compounds serves to reduce their weight. *Ad hoc* assumptions are to Whewell a sure sign of false theories.

The other form of 'progressive' success is *'consilience of inductions'*. This is achieved when a theory T ('All Cs have property H'), advanced to causally explain a confirmed generalization $L1$ ('All $P1s$ have property A'), is later discovered also to give a successful explanation of a confirmed law about a class of phenomena, $L2$ ('All $P2s$ have property B'), *different* from that for which it was framed.[10] T is advanced to explain $L1$ on the assumption that $P1s$ are Cs. T's explanation is confirmed if, in testing $P1s$ in various circumstances, H is found to cause property A. This is the 'static' condition above. If – the salient characteristic of consilience of inductions – theory T is successfully applied beyond its intended domain to an (originally) *unintended* domain, such that H is shown to cause property B, it follows that $P2s$, like $P1s$, are members of the class of Cs.

'Static' and 'progressive' success together, Whewell says, 'irresistibly' establish a theory's truth. As Whewell uses the same theories to illustrate both types of 'progressive' explanatory success, the thought occurs that perhaps his 'consilience' and 'progressive simplification' are different names for a single process. In the words of one commentator:

Actually however, Whewell was not that sure that ...
simplification is all that different from a consilience. If we get
a consilience, then one hypothesis is being used to explain facts
from two different classes. And this, in a sense, is what
simplicity is all about, for we are using a minimum to explain a
maximum.

([2.19], 231)

It is clear from what Whewell says that scientists can never hope to induce (generalize) theories and laws from others already established. Conception is unpredictable; imagination strikes out in different directions. Progressive cognitive expansion is none the less suggested. While no one knows in advance how to explain established laws, a new theory is required deductively to so do as a condition of its acceptance. A successful Whewellian scientific discipline resembles in the manner of its growth the construction in layers (theories) of an inverted triangle from apex to base. Explanation is in the opposite direction, deductively descending.

Suffice in closing this section to note that Whewell's paradigm cases of progressive explanatory success – universal gravity and the undulatory theory of light – physicists came in the fullness of time to judge as false. There seems nothing for it but to say Whewell fails to establish a criterion of proof: predictive successes, no matter how outstanding, are no indicator of future performance of theories.

Necessity

Whewell's writings on necessity as a property of (at least some) scientific theories would appear to have given rise to greater interpretative disagreement than has his treatment of any other topic. It will be shown that he theorizes the property in more than one way, which fact, not widely appreciated, may help explain the variety of interpretation. Whewell first addressed necessity in a paper 'On the Nature of the Truth of Laws of Motion' (1834), included later in *Philosophy of the Inductive Sciences*. Focusing on mechanics, science of 'motions as determined by their causes, namely, forces' ([2.3], 2: 574), Whewell identifies three necessary axioms: '*Every change is produced by a cause*'; '*Causes are measured by their effects*'; and '*Action is always accompanied by an equal and opposite Reaction*' ([2.3], 2: 574–6). Newton's laws of motion are respectively related to the axioms, the first axiom applied to motion yielding the first law, 'when no force acts, the properties of the motion [direction and velocity] will be constant' ([2.3], 2: 577), and so on. In the same essay Whewell distinguishes each law of motion into 'necessary' and 'empirical' parts. The first law, continuing here with the same example for ease of exposition, in its necessary part affirms that 'Velocity [as a property of motion] does not change without a cause', the empirical part affirming that 'The time for which a body has already been in motion is not a cause of change of velocity' ([2.3], 2: 591). In what for Whewell consists the 'necessity' of the axioms and laws of motion? He describes the 'necessary' parts of the laws of motion, and, by implication, the axioms from which they derive, as 'inapplicable'. But this adjective, suggesting analytic necessity, is not a happy choice, seeing that Whewell goes on to describe the axioms not only as 'absolutely and universally true' and expressive of

'absolute convictions' but as serving also to regulate *our experience*.
When 'looking at a series of occurrences . . . we inevitably and unconsciously assume' the axioms' truth, for experience we we are unable to
'conceive otherwise' ([2.3], 2: 575).[11]Axioms being necessarily true of,
and indispensable to the reception of, experience, so must be the necessary element in each law of motion. Each such element makes a true,
albeit highly general, assertion about the world. While the first law of
motion *truly asserts* that change of velocity requires a cause, it is silent
on what kind of causation is involved (inherent or extrinsic?) and is on
this level, as Whewell would have it, 'inapplicable'. It is *a posteriori*
that we find out that the causation in question is external, not an inner
power. The kind of necessity of which Whewell ([2.3], 2: 593) here
speaks is instructive and, at the same time, strictly universal (the 'all
possible worlds' variety) for the necessary part of a law of motion
cannot 'be denied without a self-contradiction'. The axioms of mechanics and the non-'empirical' (read non-'contingent') part of each law
of motion appear in Whewell's 1834 essay as synthetic-necessary truths.

In *Philosophy of the Inductive Sciences* the analysis of necessity is
along broadly similar lines except that the doctrine of ideas is now
brought into play. Mechanical sciences in general rest on the idea of
cause and its modes or conceptions of *force* (mechanical cause) and
matter (resistance to force), with the special branch of 'dynamics'
depending on the axioms of cause and the laws of motion. What the
1834 essay presents as axioms *simpliciter* in *Philosophy* appear as axioms
grounded in and expressing the idea of cause. The axioms are described
as 'true independently of experience', meaning *a priori*, and as true
'beyond the limits of experience', meaning necessary and synthetic.
That the truth of axioms is 'necessary' in the robust sense of that word
is evident from the imperative mood of the first axiom: '*Every Event
must have a Cause*' ([2.3], 2: 452). To laws of motion also necessity is
ascribed, yet they are said to have been 'collected from experience'
([2.3], 1: 247; [2.3], 2: 453). The air of contradiction that surrounds this
combination of claims Whewell dispels by noting in each law the
presence of a non-necessary element, the *content* being true but only
contingently so. It is their universality and vocabulary ('cause', 'effect',
'action', 'reaction', etc.), in a word their 'form', in virtue of which the
laws 'exemplify' the corresponding axioms, and in which their necessity
consists. Laws so formed Whewell ([2.3], 1: 249) regards as necessary
in yet another way, drawing attention to an 'indestructible conviction,
belonging to man's speculative nature' that there are laws of motion,
'universal formulae, connecting the causes and effects when motion
takes place'.

Philosophy of the Inductive Sciences, in that part of the third
edition titled *Philosophy of Discovery*, presents knowledge of necessary

truth as 'progressive', Whewell largely devoting himself to making sense of this fact. Part of his explanation is that necessary truth proves accessible only to minds properly prepared. 'To see the truth and necessity of geometrical axioms, we need geometrical culture' ([2.6], 347), just as necessity in axioms of mechanics remains opaque until, their discipline developed, scientists acquire the right culture. While scientific disciplines (mechanics, chemistry, geometry, and the like) could never have been raised other than on the basis of axioms, 'internal conditions' of experience and knowledge as Whewell calls them, the knowledge that axioms are necessary truths is acquired later.

Whewell goes on to claim that in (but not only in) mechanics, his exemplar of excellent physical science, axioms encapsulate 'in a manner' the science in its entirety. 'The whole science of Mechanics is only the development of the Axioms concerning action and reaction, and concerning cause and its measures' ([2.6], 357). For this bold claim Whewell offers no effective support;[12] his present interests not including analysis and defence of his doctrine of necessity.

It has been indicated above that 'Laws of Motion' and *Philosophy of the Inductive Sciences* both treat the axioms of mechanics as wholly necessary and the laws of motion as necessary in form and contingent in content. In that account the laws are not deducible from axioms. By implication, there being in what Whewell says nothing to suggest otherwise, the distinction between necessary and non-necessary truth is an ontological and absolute one, based on objective properties.[13] But *Philosophy of Discovery* presents a different doctrine altogether. As the entire science of mechanics is able to be exfoliated from axioms (once the laws are discovered), the distinction between truths necessary and truths non-necessary in mechanics must in this case be drawn only *relative to* the state of knowledge (level of cultivation), all truths of mechanics in reality being, and eventually recognized as being, necessary.

As noted, Whewell on the subject of necessity in *Philosophy of Discovery* wants specifically to explain the progressiveness of knowledge of necessity: how propositions whose truth is in the first instance known *a posteriori* come to be known *a priori* (as necessarily true). His explanation in its first part revolves around development of disciplines and cultivation of minds. Its second part presents the proposition that structural identity must exist between mind and the world. Ideas exist in God's mind, and these he has impregnated in the human mind as well as constituting the world according to them. Consequences of ideas in the world are laws of nature, which coincide with consquences of ideas in the mind (propositions), consequences of both descriptions being necessary. This same general view Whewell in *Philosophy of Discovery* extends to ethics, postulating the existence of ethical ideas that coincide with ideas in God's mind. We now turn to Whewell's ethical doctrines.

∾ ON ETHICS ∾

Introduction

Whewell has been credited with having revived in the nineteenth century 'the study of moral philosophy at Cambridge', being at the head of an impressive 'line of Cambridge moralists – John Grote, Henry Sidgwick, G. E. Moore, C. D. Broad – whose outlook, despite important differences, is strikingly similar on certain central issues' ([2.21], 109). Their historical importance notwithstanding, Whewell's ethical works have in the twentieth century been almost entirely neglected.[14]

Whewell began publishing on ethics in 1836 with a 'Preface' to James Mackintosh's *Dissertation on The Progress of Ethical Philosophy. On the Foundations of Morals, Four Sermons* appeared in 1837. The following year, appointed Knightbridge Professor of Moral Philosophy (his second chair, that of Mineralogy having been held by him from 1828 to 1832), Whewell delivered twelve lectures which later appeared as *Lectures on the History of Moral Philosophy in England* (1852, [2.5]). Certain themes of these lectures form a backdrop to the *opus magnum* of Whewell the moralist, *Elements of Morality, including Polity* (1845, [2.4]).

The leitmotif of *Lectures on the History of Moral Philosophy in England* is the history of conflicting understandings of the foundations of morals, the basic principles of duty or right conduct. Theories of one class, distinguished by Whewell as 'high' or 'independent', explain conduct as moral or immoral *per se*, right and wrong being independent (inherent) qualities of actions. According on the other hand to the theories Whewell designates as 'low' (the adjective serving to make plain his antipathy), morality is reducible to facts more fundamental and real. The facts in question are consequences of actions, notably pleasure and pain. The debate between theorists of these two proclivities arose in ancient Greece, Stoics pitted against Epicureans. Woven through Christian moralizing, the independent perspective was long ascendant, up to the seventeenth century in fact. Then, at the same time as Hobbes and Locke were forcefully asserting the low view of morality, developments in science and metaphysics were straining and breaking the web of traditional belief. The high position began to look anachronistic, fewer people found it credible. For a new age, in a new climate of opinion, the independent doctrine had to be appropriately reformulated. And while attempts have been made to adapt it to the altered circumstances, they have only been partial and never really satisfactory. So far as Whewell is concerned, the real work of reconstruction remains to be done.

From the early eighteenth century, in England generally and at Cambridge University in particular, dependent theorizing on morality formed 'the general tendency' ([2.5], 165). Since the middle of that century, the successive main sources of the ethical instruction given at Cambridge have been Gay, Rutherforth and William Paley. Gay's *Dissertation* (1732) affirms God's will as the determinant of virtue, and human happiness the measure. On any occasion the action productive of greatest happiness is that which God would have us perform. In *Essay on the Nature and Obligations of Virtue* (1744) Rutherforth attempts to show that happiness as the ultimate end of action is a teaching of reason, with revelation the source of our knowledge that God will reward with happiness in the next life right conduct towards others in this. The major production of Paley was *Principles of Morals and Politics* (1785). Such has been its intellectual impact, Whewell puts it in another league altogether from the last mentioned works. Radiating influence far beyond the walls of Cambridge colleges, Paley affected 'the habits of thinking, reasoning and expression' of English people 'to at least as great an extent as any previous moral doctrine has ever done' ([2.5], 176–7). The central teaching of Paley is that happiness for humanity is desired by God, by whom those of our actions that conduce to happiness are deemed right and to whom they prove agreeable. We may know God's will so Paley reasons, and reasoning thus he is close to Gay, by determining which actions achieve most happiness for all concerned. There is for Whewell sad irony about Paley's labours; of noble intentions and impeccable religiosity, his thought was a major antecedent of secularized utilitarianism. Little did he, and profoundly would it have aggrieved him to, know that his writings would in time 'lead to dangerous and immoral tenets' and 'produce ... evil' ([2.5], 178). Whewell expresses in *History of Moral Philosophy* a resolve to deal with the problem as he recognizes it, seeking reform of the Cambridge curriculum. The 'system of [Paleyian] morals which is now taught among us is unworthy of our descent and office; and it will be my endeavour in future years ... further to point out, and, if possible, to remedy the defects which I lament' ([2.5], 184). He was as good as his word. Whewell's ethical 'writings became text-books at Cambridge, and were naturally studied by young men reading for Trinity fellowships' ([2.24], 1371).

The reader of *History of Moral Philosophy* catches glimpses of some of the likely sources of influence on Whewell's constructive ethical thought. Grotius, Pufendorf and Cumberland are approved of for having recognized in human nature principles besides self-interest. He accepts Butler's proposition that 'The proper office of each of the principles of our nature assists us ... to determine their limits, and to lay down rules for their direction, control, or restraint', rules that is for framing 'special moral duties', although he can nowhere find in Butler a satisfactory 'classification of the faculties and operations of the human mind' ([2.5], 112). And with Paley, Whewell ([2.5], 166) is able to agree on at least this: the task of the moralist must include deductive ordering of 'the commonly-received rules of morality'. This leads on to Whewell's constructive doctrine.

Rational morality in context

The diverse materials of *Elements of Morality* are sorted into six books: '*Introduction*. Elementary Notions and Definitions', '*Morality*. Of Virtues and Duties', '*Religion*. Of Divine Laws and their Sanction', '*Jus*. Of Rights and Obligations', '*Polity*. The Duties of the State' ('*Jus*' treating law as it is, '*Polity*' law as it ought to be), and '*International Jus*. Rights and Obligations Between States'. In its final (fourth) edition, the main body of the work runs to around 550 pages, with its longer books, '*Morality*' and '*Polity*', in the order of 200 and 130 pages respectively. There are two senses of 'morality' to be noticed in the titles. In that of the volume it connotes the five provinces of human conduct and rules, of which each, while 'intimately connected', has its own questions and modes of answering them. In the case of reasoned 'Virtues and Duties' (Book II), 'morality' signifies the primary part of the whole.

Elements of Morality is a work of conservative intent. It is not designed to add to the first-order ethical knowledge we have already (which Whewell takes to be considerable), nor to inquire into how such knowledge is obtained – Whewell supposing himself to keep to the bare essentials. Whewell ([24], x) wrote the *Elements* principally to bring method to bear on what we know about how we ought to act, 'to construct a [moral] *system*'.[15] Our knowledge of rules, duties and virtues is seen as demonstrable by stepwise deductions. The purely ethical part of the system, rational morality comprising Book II, is based by Whewell on the supreme rule of human action or of 'human nature', which notion, as 'universal standard' of right, is redolent of natural law. From this supreme rule of reason lesser moral rules are drawn, each conveying some part of its content.

'Moral Rules Exist Necessarily' Whewell titles one of the chapters in the first book of the *Elements*, and it is a statement that underlies his explication of basic concepts. The predicate 'right' describes conformity of action to rule. Rules indicate by what actions objects of designated classes may be properly attained. 'Labour, that you may gain money' prescribes labouring as 'the *right* way to gain' that object ([2.4], 48). Rules gain validity, and objects value, from superior cases. 'The Rule, *to labour*, derives its force from the Rule, *to seek gain*' ([2.4], 48). In the same way, it is suggested, rules receive reasons: Why should I labour? To earn income to maintain myself and dependants. Climbing the scale eventually one comes upon an object of intrinsic value, source of value in all other objects. The chain of reasons must if valid likewise have a terminus, one rule exerting sway. So it is that Whewell settles to his own satisfaction the existence of the supreme rule and supreme good.

In utilitarianism is recognized by Whewell the main alternative interpretation of 'right' and cognate moral terms. He argues against it that pursuit of rightness is distinct from and apt to conflict with wanting to maximize pleasure, and in cases of conflict it is rightness every time that makes the stronger claim on us. To assess an action accurately as right is to provide for its performance a reason, writes Whewell: '*paramount* to all other considerations. If the action be right, it is no valid reason against doing it, that it is unpleasant or dangerous. We are not to do what is pleasant and wrong. We are to do what is unpleasant if it be right' ([2.4], 6). 'Right' is in ethics an absolute term implying a supreme rule as the ultimate reason for action: above all we are to act rightly.[16]

Whewell's supreme rule extends beyond morality in the ordinary acceptation of the word. All feelings and conduct are regulated by it, 'all intercourse of men, all institutions of society' ([2.4], 77). Rules acquire the property of rightness from expressing portions of the supreme rule of action, but whether Whewell regards as its components all rules that have a defensible claim on conduct is uncertain. He distinguishes moral rules from prudential, but by his ([2.4], 139) description of the latter as 'not directly moral' a connection with the supreme rule is not necessarily excluded. What is clear however and for Whewell's purposes more important is that *laws* are part of the supreme rule's content no less than are moral precepts. These are respectively characterized as 'Rules of external [bodily] action' and rules of internal action or events – 'Will and Intention, ... Desires and Affections' ([2.4] 68) – which form 'the only really human part of actions' ([2.4], 66).[17] Laws create rights and correlative obligations; precepts impose duties.

While 'Every thing is *right* which is conformable to the Supreme Rule of human action' ([2.4], 54), on another level there exist what Whewell identifies as 'national' moralities. 'Nations and communities ... have their Standards of right and wrong', including positive laws and 'current moral Precepts and Rules' ([2.4], 199).

From so devout a Christian as was Whewell (Anglican clergyman, doctor of divinity and theologian) it comes as no surprise to learn that ethics is religiously embedded. Natural religion furnishes the idea of the course of nature as in harmony with, as subject to, divine moral government. God governs by laws he wills, that of which in human affairs is foremost being the selfsame supreme rule. Endowed with reason as part of the divine providence individuals are able to, and of course should, act conformably to the divine laws.

> The Supreme Rule of Human Action derives its Real Authority, and its actual force, from its being the Law of God, the Creator of Man. The Reason for doing what is absolutely right, is, that it is the Will of God, through which the condition and destination of man are what they are.

([2.4], 141)

By God's appointment, violation of his moral laws is punishable by misery, and conformity rewardable with happiness. The apportionment, taking place in the next life, serves to complete the divine 'moral government', God determining the final, eternal condition of the soul according to the level of its moral progress when embodied.

The 'history of the world' recorded in the Scriptures Whewell presumes to be the 'fact' corresponding to the 'idea' just noted. The part of the Scriptural record of chief importance concerns God's trans-actions with humanity, 'Revelations of the Commands and Promises of God, and of the Methods by which men are to be enabled to obey these Commands, and to receive the benefit of these promises' ([2.4], 257). The revelation made through Jesus Christ confirms the claims of natural theology.

Through the addition of Christian precepts and doctrines to those of rational ethics we are offered, Whewell believes, a more complete picture of the grounds of duty, providing for virtue's more effective pursuit. Christ embodied in human form the moral perfection we conceive in God, and Christian morality presents this 'Image of God in Christ' as the 'summit of the Moral Progress, which it is our Duty to pursue' ([2.4], 258). It is important to our hopes and aspirations, and to the way we conduct our lives, that we know whether sinners may be saved from eternal punishment. The answer, to be found in revealed Christian doctrine, is that Christ's crucifixion, burial and ascent into heaven formed a divine interposition to save humanity from 'infliction of merited punishment' ([2.4], 259). Conditions are revealed as necessary to fit the soul for future life: belief in Christ ensures participation in the Holy Spirit, and united with Christ the soul receives its aliment.

Law and morality

Leslie Stephen ([2.24], 1372) has described as 'The most curious characteristic' of Whewell's ethical writings 'the prominence given to positive law in the deduction of moral principles'. It is possible to understand Whewell's ethics only after studying how he relates law to morality, and this requires the disentanglement of a number of threads in his work.

Of Whewell's claims on this subject perhaps the most prominent is that *morality depends on law*. He opens with an argument that mental desires, our 'most powerful' springs of action, can be gratified only if regulated, and on their gratification preservation of the fabric of society depends. Whewell ([2.4], 45–6) in the first instance describes these rules as 'moral'. This it may be thought is in conflict with the basic dependence relation: '*that Moral Rules may exist, Men must have Rights*', where 'rights' signifies abstract conceptions assigned to people by positive laws that are 'subordinate to the Supreme Rule' ([2.4], 51). But upon inspection the conflict turns out to be verbal only, apparent rather than real. 'Moral' is in the first sense inclusive of, and used in such a way as to highlight, laws as a type of moral rules, having in the second its usual, more restricted, meaning. At least three claims may be distinguished. There is a thesis, call it 'causal', about the possibility of moral conduct: people cannot act morally unless already they obey positive laws. Moral conduct and character presuppose legally ordered society. There is a closely related ontological claim about the possibility of moral rules: 'We must suppose the Rights of Property, and the Laws of Property, before we can lay down the Moral Rules, Do not steal, or Do not covet another man's Property', etc. ([2.4], 55). A further claim, this made in regard to morality's vocabulary, is that 'Desires and Intentions cannot be defined or described in any way, without some reference to Things and Actions; and therefore, cannot supply a basis of Morality independent of Law' ([2.4], 201). Without him saying it in so many words, the precedence of law for Whewell really boils down to it enabling mental desires to be satisfied. More than moral rules, suggests Whewell, laws are directly concerned with constraining conduct and, being enforced, usually succeed in this.

Whewell's follow-up to this is a rather more informative statement that duties (morality) depend upon rights, not in general but of a *specific class*. What 'Rights must exist' are determined by – a common expression in eighteenth- and nineteenth-century philosophical writing – *springs of action* ([2.4], vii).[18]

Acts Whewell believes are properly ours when reason directs the will. Through the faculty of reason we discover truth and falsehood, conceive of general rules, recognize actions as cases of rules, and discriminate right from wrong.[19]

Will represents the final step of intention (purpose), a process of internal motion as Whewell conceives it, produced by springs of action. Springs of action he distinguishes by their ends. Bodily desires for physical objects are *appetites*, primordial among which are 'natural wants' (hunger, thirst). Satisfaction of wants is a source of enjoyment, giving rise to the desire of *pleasures of sense*. Employment of art to satisfy appetites stimulates *artificial wants*. As appetites are directed to things, *affections* (love and anger) tend to people. Most 'universal and most powerful' ([2.4], 32) among springs of action are *mental desires* for abstract conceptions of physical safety, private property, companionship of family and membership of civil society, kept promises and respected agreements ('mutual understanding'), 'superiority' (skill, strength, wealth, or power), and 'knowledge' or reason. *Moral sentiments* (approval, esteem, and their opposites) accompany moral evaluations of actions, disposing us to treat people 'as we approve or disapprove their actions' ([2.4], 41). *Reflex sentiments* are the desire that others would love and esteem us; and desire of honour, fame and self-approval.

From mental desires as the predominant springs of action Whewell derives fundamental rights. To have a satisfactory life each person is in need of: protection from assault (right of person), control over physical objects (right of property), dependable conduct from others (right of contract), exclusive relations with certain others (family rights), and an organization to establish rights (rights of government). The rights are to objects of mental desires. (In *'Jus'*, Book IV of the *Elements*, rights in Roman and English systems of law receive extensive classification under the foregoing heads.)

These 'primary and universal' rights Whewell respects as absolutely valid, imperatives in all societies. They are rights that *must be*. 'Family Rights', as a case in point, 'necessarily exist'; while society without 'Rights of Government... loses its social character; and the moral character of man cannot find its sphere of action', and so on ([2.4], 52). The most important objects in our lives, those of primary (mental) desires, cannot be secured outside a framework of law. Rights respected are realities; abstract conceptions as objects are thus realized.

As we have so far understood Whewell in this part of his thought, his essential theses are two. There is a set of *ideal* rights corresponding to springs of action. The same rights serve in *fact* as the indispensable conditions of social order and morality.

To this conjunction an objection immediately suggests itself: Is not the proposition that ideal rights necessarily exist contradicted by the variety of laws and rights found both within (temporally) and between societies? The objection is one that Whewell ([2.4], 59) himself anticipates in order to obviate, claiming the positions to be 'reconcilable'. In this reconcilableness he sees a further case of the fundamental antithesis or distinction between *ideas* (conceptions) and *facts*. Ideas of the primary rights are derivations from human nature. There can be no conceiving of people as members of society nor as moral agents except in so far as they have the (ideal) rights to personal safety, property, etc. That said, ideas of rights must be in society as facts. By positive laws the forms so to speak are specifically defined and, on account of being historically conditioned, the definitions of ideas of rights differ between societies. The traveller whom law in one society permits to 'pluck the fruits of the earth as he passes' finds such fruits are in another society 'the Property of him on whose field they grew'. Explains Whewell ([2.4], 59), the 'Precept, *Do not steal*' is absolutely moral and 'universal', a corollary of primary rights, whereas 'the Law, *To pluck is to steal*', is historically contingent or 'partial'. According to the present thesis *actual rights (in 'national moralities') are in all cases definitions of, and consistent with, the rights identified as ideal.*

Appearing in *Elements of Morality* is a further account of rights positive in relation to rights ideal, almost certainly contradicting the account above. In a passage that merits quoting at length we have Whewell (1864: 68) saying:

> positive definitions of Rights for the moment, may be themselves
> immoral. Rights, as we have described them ... , are
> arrangements not only historically established, but also
> established in conformity with the supreme Rule; that is, they
> are such as are right. The actual definitions of Rights at any
> moment, that is, the state of the Law, may need improvement
> and reform: but in general, the Law gives, for the moment, the
> definitions of Rights upon which Morality must proceed.[20]

Actual rights may be immoral, contradicting ideal rights. So, while *positive rights* should, the fact is they *do not, in all cases assign definite shape to some part or other of the content of ideal rights.*[21]

From his case for morality requiring a specific set of rights Whewell has veered away, apparently unaware of how damaging to his basic doctrine are the implications of such change. Societies may produce, and their 'national' moralities may exist on, immoral rights, conflicting with the ideal or 'primary' rights and failing to gratify primary desires.

Closing coverage of this part of *Elements of Morality* it may be commented that Whewell's procedure – grounding ideal rights in human nature – appears strange given his inclusion of the same rights in the supreme rule. To this, the first and fundamental principle of morality, he might have been expected to go and exfoliate the ideal rights directly.[22]

Rational morality

In '*Morality*. Of Virtues and Duties' we confront the longest and most important of the *Elements'* six books. The core of this as of the other parts of Whewell's ethical thought is the 'supreme rule' coupled with the 'supreme object'. These points have been noted. Whewell early in Book II equates the idea of the supreme object with moral goodness, to which he otherwise refers as virtue or rightness in the soul. The soul attains this state when the faculties (consciousness, reason, will, imagination, and affections) are regulated by virtue and habituated to duty. The supreme object – goodness or virtue – Whewell ([2.4], 241) also designates as happiness, which he specifically says stands for 'the Supreme Object of our Desires' and is 'identical with ... the Ultimate and Supreme Guide of our Intentions'. Utilitarians have commonly equated happiness with pleasure, demonstrating to Whewell ([2.4], 254) how confused they are, for in happiness is a compound of 'all other objects', whereas pleasure is only that *simple* state we experience upon the satisfaction of our physical desires. The doctrine of absolutely right action (as action in accordance with the supreme rule) denies that pleasure can be, while confirming that happiness is, the ultimate desire and end.

> The Desire of Happiness is the Supreme Desire. All other
> Desires, of Pleasure, Wealth, Power, Fame, are included in this,
> and are subordinate to it. We may make other objects our
> ultimate objects; but we can do so, only by identifying them
> with this.
>
> ([2.4], 241)[23]

No doubt some utilitarians would approve of this, and imagine that Whewell on account of it might be counted as one of them. But although Whewell takes it as true that happiness ought to be increased, he goes on to suggest that there is no possibility of anyone knowing how to go about it. A basket, or if you like an umbrella, concept, no 'special element' is implied in happiness while 'all ... objects' and 'all good' are ([2.4], 243). As happiness, Whewell says, is too complex and indeterminate to be measurable, rules for attaining it are out of the question. Whereupon the possibility of Whewell's project of arranging existing rules-and-objects hierarchically boils down to this: there must be some other way, more fertile of implications, in which to envisage the supreme object.

Whewell for his part typically discusses this object with reference to, and in such a way as to identify it with, 'goodness', reducing it to five terms – benevolence, justice, truth, purity and order – each with subjective and objective denotations. Subjectively they refer to classes of dispositions or 'cardinal virtues', and objectively to 'abstract mental Objects or Ideas' ([2.4], 75–6) to which dispositional desires and affections are directed. *Benevolence* as virtue is the sum of all affections that bring together people, and the absence of feelings that divide; of which the corresponding idea, 'humanity', is of the good or well-being of all people.[24] *Justice* as virtue is 'the Desire that each person should have his own' ([2.4], 73), and as idea or object is 'the Rule, To each his own' ([2.4], 76). *Truth* as virtue or disposition has as its idea *'Objective Truth*, the agreement between the reality of things and our expressed conceptions of them' ([2.4], 76). In the state of *purity* reason and moral sentiments govern bodily desires, the objective counterpart consisting in the idea of human nature 'free from ... mere desire' ([2.4], 76). *Order* denotes the disposition to conform willingly to positive laws and moral rules and, objectively, the idea of obedience.

Goodness or virtue is the supreme object of action and of rules, subordinate objects all taking their moral value from it. Enjoining us to love virtue (benevolence, justice, etc.) and to seek it 'as the ultimate and only real object of action' ([2.4], 77), the supreme rule directs our 'Affections and Intentions to their proper objects' ([2.4], 96). Conforming to this rule, *character* is virtuous and *action* dutiful, the twin elements serving to make a person good. The supreme rule is possessed of a structure which for the most part reflects its (supreme) object, with matching pairs – objective and subjective – of component rules. Conveying aspects of the supreme rule's content, *express* (objective) moral principles have objects in the form of ideas. The principles are those of humanity, *'Man is to be loved as Man'*; justice, *'Each Man is to have his own'*; truth, *'We must conform to the Universal Understanding among men which the use of Language implies'*, desisting from lying; purity, *'The Lower parts of our Nature are to be governed by, and subservient to, the Higher'*; and order, *'positive Laws [are to be obeyed] as the necessary Conditions of Morality'* ([2.4], 95–6). Completing the list of express principles are: earnestness, *'The Affections and Intentions must not only be rightly directed, but energetic'*; and moral purpose, *'Things are to be sought universally*, not only in subservience to moral rules, but *as means to moral ends'* ([2.4], 96). The supreme rule's other set of principles Whewell distinguishes as 'operative'. These have to be cultivated; express principles being incorporated into the character of an individual habitually to guide affections and purposes, functioning as springs of action.

Specific virtues and duties, the bulk of the materials of rational morality, Whewell explicates in terms of, and distributes according to, the plan above. Virtues are a sub-class – those that are desirable – of the habits or dispositions of inner states (desires, affections and volitions), combining to form an agent's moral character. Duties are right actions, the ways in which we ought to conduct ourselves. Virtues exist and operate unconsciously, while duties are conscious. Between the two Whewell finds a relation approaching to concomitance. Duties need not issue from virtues (motives to right actions may be amoral, even immoral), but virtues are manifested in and developed by performance of duties, and by cultivation of virtues performance of corresponding duties is made more likely. 'Acts of Duty are both the most natural operation of virtuous Dispositions, and the most effectual mode of forming virtuous Habits' ([2.4], 97).

Distinguishing duties in relation to objects, Whewell's basic categorization of them is similar to that of cardinal virtues, with duties of affections (benevolence), property, truth, purity, and order. A duty of cultivating the affections is also recognized, reducible to which is a duty of the affections: the 'Duty of thus cultivating these Affections includes the Duty of possessing such affections' ([2.4], 115). It is unclear whether Whewell believes all duties owed to other people involve the duty of affection, but at least those of justice and truth in his view do.

From these primary duties, enjoined by the 'express' principles of morality, Whewell goes on to deduct rationally many specific rules of duty, but their enumeration shall not detain us. The general classification of duties reappears to shape discussion in other parts of Elements. The book 'Polity' has chapters on the State's duties of 'Justice and Truth', 'Humanity', 'Purity' and 'Order'. Explicating religious ethics, Christian precepts are arranged by Whewell under such headings as 'Duties of the Affections', 'Property', 'Truth', 'Purity', 'Obedience and Command'.

One further duty to be noted is that of moral progress, incumbent on States and individuals alike. The State must be recognized as an agent given that it, among other things, 'makes war and peace, which it may do justly or unjustly; keeps Treaties, or breaks them; educates its children, or neglects them' ([2.4], 208). Continuously existing, purposive and active, States are moral beings endowed with life, and 'During this Life, it is their Duty to conform their being more and more to the Moral Ideas' ([2.4], 208). By its duty of moral progress the State is obliged to acquire more virtue and to perform its duties better. It must become more just and act more justly (observe treaties with, and respect possessions of, other States; make laws that remedy inequalities from the past), become more benevolent and act more benevolently (liberate slaves, relieve poverty), and so on. What meaning is to be given to Whewell's talk of the State as a subject of virtue, and of it being by the enhancement of its own virtue disposed to perform duties better? It seems probable he regards this virtue and its increase as a function of citizens:

> And, as the condition of other Duties being performed, the moral Education of its citizens, *and consequently of itself*, is a Duty of the State. It is its Duty to establish in the minds of its children, and to unfold more and more into constant and progressive operation, the Moral Ideas of Benevolence, Justice, Truth, Purity, and Order.
>
> ([2.4.], 208, emphasis added)

Correspondingly, to the individual is ascribed a 'reflex' duty of moral progress or of moral self-culture. The character should according to this duty be developed as far as possible towards the ideal centre of morality at which, the point of goodness, cardinal virtues represent tendencies ('operative principles') of conduct so firmly established that no duty can ever be transgressed. Among the requirements of this duty, *benevolent affections* of gratitude to benefactors, compassion to the afflicted and love between family members are to be made steadier and more earnest; the *malevolent feelings* of violent anger, peevishness and captiousness are to be suppressed. *Justice* is to be developed as an operative principle, the character being cleansed of stains of greed, covetousness, and partiality; the agent desiring only possessions to which she or he is entitled and only for moral purposes. The individual is likewise called on to foster the other virtues – truth, purity, order – while eliminating desires running contrary to them. 'We have to form our character, so that these principles [benevolence, justice, truth, purity, and order] are its predominant features. We have to seek not only to *do*, but to *be*; not only to perform acts of Duty, but to become virtuous' ([2.4], 142). The duty of moral progress is itself performed, just as the several virtues are most effectively cultivated, by performance of the other, more particular, duties. And in opposite fashion whenever temptations are succumbed to and rules of duty transgressed, when affections are malevolent and intentions fraudulent, moral progress ceases and the character goes down 'a retrograde moral course' ([2.4], 143).

While the present study of Whewell's view of ethics has concentrated on that which he labels 'rational morality' as the truly distinctive, striking and substantial part of his teaching, it is as well to remind ourselves that this department depends for him in a most fundamental manner on religion. The cardinal virtues, as noted, are conceived of by

Whewell as perfectly realized in God and as having had embodiment in human form in Christ. The supreme rule of rational morality is the rule of God which fact in conjunction with his imposition of sanctions provides the compelling reason for obeying it. The supreme rule as understood by Whewell

> derives its Real Authority, and its actual force, from its being the Law of God, the Creator of Man. The Reason for doing what is absolutely right, is, that it is the Will of God, through which the condition and destination of man are what they are.
>
> ([2.4], 141)

The rule commends to us, and commands us to emulate, the character of Jesus, moral progress having the goal of 'a godlike being and a heavenly life' ([2.4], x). On our success in following the supreme law and in making moral progress depends our prospect of happiness in this life and, more so, the next.

Postscript

It is natural to ask whether in its structure and method Whewell's analysis of morality resembles his philosophy of science. There is a difficulty to be faced, however, before answering this, the two main works in question, *Philosophy of the Inductive Sciences* and *Elements of Morality, including Polity*, each being predominantly on a different level from the other. Rehearsal of some basic distinctions will enable us to identify more clearly the source of the difficulty. Concerning the subject-matter of physical objects and processes (level 1), scientists advance propositional laws and theories (level 2), with philosophers theorizing scientific practice and products (level 3). Whewell's *Philosophy* is a contribution on the third of these levels. The corresponding levels of ethics put simply are: human agents and actions, rules dictating how agents ought to conduct themselves, and meta-ethical theories of the discovery and evaluation of right rules. Most of *Elements of Morality* occupies the second level, systematizing occurrent rules, duties and virtues. Philosophical analysis of ethical knowledge and its methods is not its major concern. We are not altogether without material for comparison, Whewell producing some philosophy in the *Elements*, but for comparison to be full and rigorous more of such matter would be needed. We proceed bearing in mind this caveat.

Whewell himself ([2.5], 168) speaks confidently of the 'analogy between the progress of the science of Morals and other sciences'. Concepts and knowledge in both subjects form part of the flux of history. In *Elements of Morality* ([2.4], 202), for example, it is observed generally that 'As the intellectual culture of the nation proceeds, abstract words are used with more precision; and in consequence, the conceptions, designated by such words, grow clearer in men's minds'.

Whereas progress of scientific theories turns for Whewell on wider colligations, that of ethical rules is accounted for by him differently,[25] the key apparently being morality's interaction with law. Definitions that laws give of rights vary socially and historically, and the virtues and duties supported in society depend upon its laws. At the same time morality exercises authority over law and, as a nation's morality improves, laws should be and, Whewell it would appear believes, typically are brought into line. Exactly how improvement in morality is effected and how people have in the past been able to tell that morality was changing to the good are matters which in Whewell remain obscure. Perhaps Christianity's revealed morality has acted as both inspiration for and criterion of improvement in national moralities. But whether (as I am inclined to believe) or not this speculation constitutes Whewell's opinion on the matter, the main point at the moment is that *Elements of Morality* has no doctrine corresponding to that of colligatory trial and error.

Whewell as explained sees a corpus of real moral knowledge having formed through history. It is to this knowledge, expressed in rules, that under the rubric of 'rational morality' he imparts systematic shape. The axioms employed by him to this end are, like those he locates in science, understood by Whewell to be presuppositions of knowledge, embedded in ideas. Yet their roles are appreciably different: axioms are in rational ethics used for *proving* claims to knowledge (whether rules are right), which in science falls to the lot of the *a posteriori* test of consilience, axioms transmitting necessity to, and assisting deductive ordering of, propositions less general.

The presence in science and ethics of the 'fundamental antithesis' provides what is for Whewell perhaps their most striking similarity. The antithesis is recognized in *Philosophy of the Inductive Sciences* in its second edition ([2.3], x) as 'suited to throw light upon Moral and Political Philosophy, no less than upon Physical'. Now without in any way gainsaying that Whewell often employs the terms 'idea' and 'fact' in *Elements of Morality*, one does find that phenomena to which he applies them are in their natures most diverse. He for example writes of ideas and conceptions of primary rights, and of their 'definitions' by positive laws as facts. In another part of the work, as already we have had cause to comment, he finds in natural religion the idea 'of the course of the World', whose corresponding fact is God's manifestations in history (revealed religion). But Whewell's principal usage, of 'idea' at any rate (for he is silent on what the term 'fact' might in this case mean),[26] is that which we find in his explication of rational morality. And the way in which he understands ideas here is nothing like how he understands them in his philosophy of science. Whewellian ideas in rational ethics are *ideals* forming *subjects* of inquiry. To know their content is to have moral knowledge about what rules are right. In science, by contrast, ideas are conditions of and materials for knowledge, of which *physical reality* is the *subject*. Gaining knowledge of that reality, a scientist at the same time gains knowledge of ideas, but the latter is more properly regarded as a secondary effect of enquiry rather than as its purpose.

Whewell has been described as having 'written with an explicit view not merely to embrace the world of learning but to synthesize it and render it a unified intellectual whole' (Fisch [2.13], 31), and this may well be true. But if he so sought synthesis and unification, what has been said in this paper must cast doubts on whether he attained them.

❧ NOTES ❧

A significant portion of the research for this study was undertaken in 1992 during a Visiting Fellowship at The Australian National University's Research School of Social Sciences. The author gratefully acknowledges the support of Professor Geoffrey Brennan, the School's Director, and that of Professor Eugene Kamenka, chair of the Research School's History of Ideas Unit. For helpful comments on draft versions of the paper he thanks: Mr Kerry Cardell, Professor David Walker, Dr George Zollschan, and Dr Frank Maher.

1 'Whewell himself regarded his *History of the Inductive Sciences* ... and *Philosophy of the Inductive Sciences* ... as both the crowning achievement of his career and the unifying "hard core" of his entire system of thought' ([2.12], 2). I shall in what follows also refer to these works simply as *History* and *Philosophy*. References unless otherwise indicated are to the reprint editions (1967).

2 Cohen ([2.7], 528ff.) is illuminating on Whewell's notion of revolution.

3 Schipper ([2.20], 49), after noting several respects in which Whewell's historiography of science anticipates that unfolded by Kuhn in *The Structure of Scientific Revolutions*, argues that in this – cognitive continuity (Whewell) as against discontinuity (Kuhn) – consists their major difference. This leads on to a further difference: science from Kuhn's standpoint is ultimately aimless while Whewell ascribes to it the aim of truth.

4 As Richard Gregory ([2.14], 219), distinguished psychologist of perception, states: 'objects have a host of characteristics *beyond their sensory features*. They have pasts and futures; they change and influence each other, and have hidden aspects which emerge under different conditions' (emphasis added). Whewell's account of perception (and of facts) has a readily discernible counterpart – 'theory-dependence of observation' – in writings of such twentieth-century figures as Karl Popper, N. R. Hanson, and Kuhn.

5 As explicitly defined, '*ideas*' refers 'to certain comprehensive forms of thought, – as *space, number*, . . . – which we apply to the phenomena which we contemplate'. Whewell ([2.3], 2: 5–6) then proceeds to define the important related term – '*conceptions*' – as 'special modifications of these ideas', giving as examples '*a circle, a square number, an accelerating force, a neutral combination* of elements'.

6 A fine-grained, more technical and more manifestly prescriptive rendering by Whewell of scientific methods is in Book XIII of the *Philosophy*. Ducasse ([2.9], 183–217) digests this particular book; Todhunter ([2.25], 139–42) detects several discrepancies between its structure and that of Book XI.

7 With reference to their disregard of this condition Whewell explains the Greeks' failure fully to cultivate science, whereas in the 'Stationary Period', as noted, the accent was the opposite, on ideas at the expense of facts.

8 This suggests that facts are reports of perceptions of concrete objects and events. 'Fact' for Whewell may also cover theories or inductions as candidates for explanation. In the latter distinction theories and facts are of the same nature, have the same properties, the distinction being time-dependent and relative.

9 Niiniluoto [2.18] deals at length, in most interesting fashion, with this and other similarities between the images of science of Whewell and Popper.

10 This explication of consilience owes a great deal to that of Fisch [2.11].

11 According to Fisch ([2.10], 287; [2.12], 158) Whewell's axioms are true only of ideas. But if, as quite clearly Whewell maintains, axioms are true 'beyond . . . experience' they must also be true within and of it. He is to be understood as saying that axioms (1) express the content of ideas, and (2) are propositions about physical reality.

12 Some would say (e.g. Fisch [2.10]; [2.12]) that Whewell's *Mechanical Euclid* provides ample evidence for this claim. But Whewell there on my reading presents the distinction between inductive (non-necessary) and non-inductive (necessary) truths in mechanics as absolute rather than as epistemologically relative (to the state of knowledge). So no matter what he may say or suggest to the contrary, on his account of it in that work, the non-necessary truths cannot and can never be logical derivatives of the necessary. That which *is* true (but could be false) is not among the implications of that which *must* be true.

13 Again, aside from those passages already referred to, Whewell should be seen as operating with just such a distinction in his opening account of necessity in *Philosophy of the Inductive Sciences* ([2.1], 54–73).

14 The paucity of exceptions serving to prove this rule are Schneewind ([2.21] and [2.22], 101–17) and Donagan [2.8].

15 About this Whewell is clearest in the preface of the first edition. See also the letter in Stair Douglas ([2.23], 326), and the preface of the fourth edition ([2.4], 3 and 6).

16 For further discussion of happiness and of utilitarianism see Whewell [2.5], x, 170ff., 174ff., and 188ff.; [2.4], 125–6, 254ff.

17 Not always faithful to this characterization, Whewell ([2.4], 244) may on occasion subsume external action under precepts.

18 The language of necessity ('must'), freely employed in the *Elements*, is ambiguous in signifying what ought to be (ideal morality), or else what cannot but exist (in 'national' moralities) in that human nature demands and cannot survive

without it. Arguing that certain rights 'must' exist, Whewell conflates both senses.

19 For extensive enumeration of the operations of the faculty of reason see Whewell [2.4], 23–4.

20 Other relations between rights and morality are delineated later in the work ([2.4], 201f., 229ff., 337ff.).

21 The same contradiction between this and his doctrine about necessary rights is latent in a note in the second and subsequent editions ([2.4], 62).

22 This calls into question the categorization of Whewell as an 'intuitionist'. Tracing rights from human nature his method is a combination of empiricism and deduction.

23 This embracing conception of happiness is noteworthy for being akin to that which one finds in John Stuart Mill's 'utilitarianism'.

24 Not the least of the difficulties facing the reader of *Elements* is that a number of key terms have different denotations which Whewell fails to mark. 'Ideas' is a case in point: usually referring to a select class of ideals or objects of action, Whewell ([2.4], 94–5) may also apply it to dispositions to seek those objects.

25 Similarity of methods is suggested, it is true, in the *Lectures* ([2.5], 168) but not shown, and careful examination of the texts uncovers no evidence of it.

26 Schneewind ([2.21], 120) speaks in this context of 'Human Nature' as the corresponding 'fact', but he provides no evidential support to show Whewell has this in mind and, so far as this author can ascertain, none exists.

❧ BIBLIOGRAPHY ❧

Works by Whewell

2.1 —— *History of the Inductive Sciences*, London: Parker, 3 vols, 1st edn, 1837, 2nd edn, 1847, 3rd edn, 1857; 3rd edn, reprinted by Cass, London, 1967.

2.2 —— *The Mechanical Euclid*, London: Parker, 1837.

2.3 —— *The Philosophy of the Inductive Sciences, Founded Upon Their History*, London: Parker, 1st edn, 2 vols, 1840, 2nd edn, 1847, 3rd edn, 3 vols, 1856–60; 2nd edn, reprinted by Cass, London, 1967.

2.4 —— *The Elements of Morality, including Polity*, London: Parker, 1st edn, 2 vols, 1845, 2nd edn, 1848, 3rd edn, 1854, 4th edn, 1 vol., 1864.

2.5 —— *Lectures on The History of Moral Philosophy in England*, London: Parker, 1852; reprinted by Thoemmes, Bristol, 1990.

2.6 —— *On the Philosophy of Discovery*, London: Parker, 1860; reprinted New York, Burt Franklin, 1971 (vol. 3 of 3rd edn, *Philosophy of the Inductive Sciences*).

Other works cited

2.7   Cohen, I. *Revolution in Science*, Cambridge, Mass.: Belknap Press, 1985.

2.8   Donagan, A. 'Whewell's *Elements of Morality*', *The Journal of Philosophy*, 71 (1974): 724–36.

2.9   Ducasse, C. 'William Whewell's Philosophy of Scientific Discovery', in E. Madden (ed.), *Theories of Scientific Method: The Renaissance through the Nineteenth Century*, New York: Gordon and Breach, 1989, 183–217.

2.10 Fisch, M. 'Necessary and Contingent Truth in William Whewell's Antithetical Theory of Knowledge', *Studies in History and Philosophy of Science*, 16 (1985): 275–314.

2.11 —— 'Whewell's Consilience of Inductions: An Evaluation', *Philosophy of Science*, 52 (1985): 239–55.

2.12 —— *William Whewell Philosopher of Science*, Oxford, Clarendon Press, 1991.

2.13 —— 'A Philosopher's Coming of Age: A Study in Erotetic Intellectual History', in M. Fisch and S. Schaffer (eds) *William Whewell: A Composite Portrait*, Oxford: Clarendon Press, 1991, 31–66.

2.14 Gregory, R. *Eye and Brain*, New York: McGraw-Hill, 1981.

2.15 Jacobs, S. 'John Stuart Mill on Induction and Hypotheses', *Journal of the History of Philosophy*, 29 (1991): 69–83.

2.16 —— *Science and British Liberalism*, Aldershot: Avebury, 1991.

2.17 Mill, J. *A System of Logic Ratiocinative and Inductive*, Toronto: University of Toronto Press, 1981.

2.18 Niiniluoto, I. 'Notes on Popper as Follower of Whewell and Peirce' in I. Niiniluoto (ed.), *Is Science Progressive?*, Dordrecht: Reidel, 1984, 18–60.

2.19 Ruse, M. 'The Scientific Methodology of William Whewell', *Centaurus*, 20 (1976): 227–57.

2.20 Schipper, F. 'William Whewell's Conception of Scientific Revolutions', *Studies in History and Philosophy of Science*, 19 (1988): 43–53.

2.21 Schneewind, J. 'Whewell's Ethics' in N. Rescher (ed.), *Studies in Moral Philosophy*, Oxford: Blackwell, 1968, 108–41.

2.22 Schneewind, J. *Sidgwick's Ethics and Victorian Moral Philosophy*, Oxford: Clarendon Press, 1986.

2.23 Stair Douglas, J. *The Life Selections from the Correspondence of William Whewell, D.D*, London: Kegan Paul, 1881. Reprinted Bristol: Thoemmes, 1991.

2.24 Stephen, L. 'Whewell, William', *The Dictionary of National Biography*, London: Oxford University Press, vol. 20, 1967–8, 1365–74.

2.25 Todhunter, I. *William Whewell, D.D. Master of Trinity College Cambridge: An Account of his Writings with Selections from his Literary and Scientific Correspondence*, London: Macmillan, vol. 1, 1876.

CHAPTER 3

J. S. Mill
Ethics and politics
R. F. Khan

❦ ON LIBERTY ❦

John Stuart Mill's mature views on ethics and politics are to be found in *On Liberty* (published in 1859), *Utilitarianism* (1861), *Considerations on Representative Government* (1861) and *The Subjection of Women* (written in 1861–2 but published in 1869). Of these, *Liberty* is the centrepiece, detailing the doctrines and themes which govern most of the discussion in the other works. It is also the work by which Mill will be most remembered. He himself picked it out as 'likely to survive longer than anything else' that he had written.[1] It has aroused more controversy than any other of his writings, and the essay *On Liberty* has been taken by many of Mill's critics as well as his supporters to be the most distinctive if not authoritative statement of the liberal position.[2]

In Mill's words, the subject of the essay is 'moral, social, and intellectual liberty asserted against the despotism of society whether exercised by governments or by public opinion' (15: 581). From the outset, Mill emphasizes the threat to individual liberty posed by 'the tyranny of the majority' exercised either by a democratically elected government or through the non-legal pressure of public opinion (219–20).[3] This was a concern that Mill had expressed in earlier writings, notably in the article on *Bentham*[4] and in his reviews of Alexis de Tocqueville's *Democracy in America*.[5] In *Liberty* the main threat to individual independence is portrayed as coming from majority rule. This is because Mill believed that, at least in the western world, democracy based on universal suffrage was the inevitable next stage of history (218).[6] But it makes little difference to his main arguments whether the threat to individual liberty comes from a majority dominated government and society or from non-democratic or less democratic social and political organization.

In order to draw the dividing line between the area of individual independence and social control, Mill appeals to a 'very simple principle' initially stated and elucidated as follows:

> the sole end for which mankind are warranted, individually or collectively, in interfering with the liberty of action of any of their number, is self-protection. . . . [T]he only purpose for which power can be rightfully exercised over any member of a civilized community, against his will, is to prevent harm to others. His own good, either physical or moral, is not a sufficient warrant. He cannot rightfully be compelled to do or forbear because it will be better for him to do so, because it will make him happier, because, in the opinions of others, to do so would be wise, or even right. These are good reasons for remonstrating with him, or reasoning with him, or persuading him, or entreating him, but not for compelling him, or visiting him with any evil in case he do otherwise. To justify that, the conduct from which it is desired to deter him, must be calculated to produce evil to some one else. The only part of the conduct of any one, for which he is amenable to society, is that which concerns others. In the part which merely concerns himself, his independence is, of right, absolute. Over himself, over his own body and mind, the individual is sovereign. (223–4).

Two points fundamental to Mill's doctrine are affirmed here. Firstly, the self-protection principle, invoked to justify social and other external restrictions on individual independence, appeals to the distinction between conduct that only 'concerns the individual' and that which also 'concerns others'. This distinction, commonly referred to as that between 'self-regarding' and 'other-regarding' actions,[7] has often been the target of Mill's critics. They have sought, by challenging the validity of the distinction, to undermine Mill's entire case for individual liberty. The standard objection has consisted in denying that there is, or can be, any such thing as purely self-regarding conduct. James Fitzjames Stephen, a younger contemporary of Mill and a most vehement critic, declared that 'every act that we do either does or may affect both ourselves and others', consequently the distinction between self-regarding and other-regarding actions is 'altogether fallacious and unfounded'.[8] And in spite of the fact that what Mill says in further elaboration of the distinction is enough to rebut this objection, it has been echoed by other commentators.

The second feature of Mill's doctrine that is emphasized in the passage quoted above is the rejection of paternalism – the view that society is justified in preventing otherwise fully responsible people from hurting or injuring themselves. The individual's own good or simply the perceived wrongness of his or her conduct is never 'a sufficient warrant' for any kind of coercive interference on the part of society or anyone else. Mill's uncompromising stand against paternalism has provoked much criticism and has found little favour even amongst many of those who claim to support his other views and his general outlook.[9]

Mill claims that his case for individual liberty is based on utilitarian grounds: 'I forego any advantage which could be derived from the idea of abstract right, as a thing independent of utility. I regard utility as the ultimate appeal on all ethical questions; but it must be utility in the largest sense, grounded on the permanent interests of man as a progressive being' (224). However, this qualification of the principle of utility, particularly as Mill presents it in the detail of his argument, has led some commentators to hold that Mill has abandoned utilitarianism,[10] and many others to assign to him doctrines which are more or less radically modified versions of classical or Benthamite utilitarianism.[11] Whether, and to what extent, this is true constitutes an area of continuing interest in Mill's moral and political philosophy.

The view that self-regarding conduct should be protected from external coercive interference implies, as Mill points out, the freedom to frame and pursue our plan of life so long as what we do does not harm others; and also the freedom to associate with others for purely self-regarding purposes. Mill also specifies as a necessary feature of a free society: 'liberty of conscience, in the most comprehensive sense; liberty of thought and feeling; absolute freedom of opinion and sentiment on all subjects, practical or speculative, scientific, moral, or theological' (225). However, Mill does not justify freedom of speech on the grounds of a simple appeal to the self-protection principle. Although expressions of opinion may be said to be a species of other-regarding conduct, the question of their permissibility or otherwise is not to be decided on the basis of how they affect others – because 'The liberty of expressing and publishing opinion ... being almost of as much importance as the liberty of thought itself, and resting in great part on the same reasons, is practically inseparable from it' (225–6). Mill's concern is to defend freedom of speech regarding only the subjects he specifically mentions, thus excluding matters pertaining to a person's private affairs. It is with respect to this specified area of thought that he supports absolute or unrestricted freedom of expression,[12] and seeks to justify it on grounds other than those based on the distinction between self-regarding and other-regarding conduct.

The essential ideas which constitute or underpin Mill's defence of individual freedom are the distinction between self- and other-regarding conduct, the rejection of paternalism, the unrestricted right to freedom of expression, and the ethical doctrine to which he appeals. These are the theses that his critics have challenged ever since the publication of *Liberty*. And the fact that they are still being questioned speaks not only for the central character of the issues Mill addresses but also for the strength of the arguments that can be mounted in defence of his answer.

∾ FREEDOM OF EXPRESSION ∾

Chapter 1 of *Liberty*, which sets out Mill's general position, is followed by his defence of freedom of expression. Almost a third of the book is devoted to this subject and it is clear that Mill regards the arguments and considerations that he advanced in support of free speech to have special significance for individual liberty.

The central argument[13] that Mill cites against censorship is epitomized in the statement that 'All silencing of discussion is an assumption of infallibility' and, therefore, unjustified since any such assumption must be unfounded (229–30).[14] The argument proceeds on the basis that 'Complete liberty of contradicting and disproving an opinion, is the very condition which justifies us in assuming its truth ... ; and on no other terms can a being with human faculties have any rational assurance of being right' (231).[15] This is a logical claim regarding the rationality of beliefs or the basis for the assignment of truth-values to beliefs. Mill's contention is that we are entitled to hold a belief or declare it to be true only if it is open to criticism and survives attempted refutations. Consequently, if discussion and criticism of an opinion are prevented by legal or social restrictions, then there can be no rational basis for taking it to be true or false.

This principle of the rationality of beliefs is explicitly acknowledged in the following passage:

> The beliefs which we have most warrant for, have no safeguard to rest on, but a standing invitation to the whole world to prove them unfounded. If the challenge is not accepted, or is accepted and the attempt fails, we are far enough from certainty still; but we have done the best that the existing state of human reason admits of; we have neglected nothing that could give the truth a chance of reaching us: if the lists are kept open, we may hope that if there be a better truth, it will be found when the human mind is capable of receiving it; and in the meantime we may rely on having attained such approach to truth, as is possible in our own day. This is the amount of certainty

attainable by a fallible being, and this the sole way of attaining
it. (232)[16]

The passage also indicates that in Mill's view there are no absolutely
certain beliefs and that all claims to truth are provisional in so far as
subsequent criticism may overthrow them.[17] Of course, as Isaiah Berlin
points out, those who maintain that it is possible to ascertain and affirm
absolute truths will not accept Mill's account of the logical foundation
of beliefs.[18] On the other hand, those who claim that we can get hold of
absolute truth, particularly in the area of human affairs, will need to
show that we can still have a viable conception of rationality, and it is
Mill's contention that this is not possible.[19]

Fitzjames Stephen, who recognized the real (logical) character
of the argument from infallibility,[20] challenged it on the grounds of
irrelevance to the question of censorship. He pointed out that censorship may be, and commonly is, justified not because the suppressed
opinion or doctrine is considered to be false but because 'it is not
considered desirable that it should be discussed' ([3.30], 77). Mill anticipates such a move which, as he puts it, seeks to make 'the justification
of restraints on discussion not a question of the truth of doctrines,
but of their usefulness; and flatters itself by that means to escape the
responsibility of claiming to be an infallible judge of opinions' (233).[21]
He rejects the move on the grounds that 'no belief which is contrary
to truth can be really useful' in that no one can genuinely hold a belief
unless it is taken to be true. And as the usefulness of a belief requires
that it should be subscribed to, it follows that its utility would also
require it to be regarded as true.[22] What Mill is maintaining here is not
to be questioned on the grounds that many useful beliefs happen to be
false. What, in his view, is necessary is that when these beliefs are held
they are subjectively taken to be true. Consequently, beliefs protected
from criticism on the basis of their utility must also be viewed as true,
and those contrary to them as false, thus exposing such a move to the
original charge of irrationality. No doubt those who protect a belief
because of its utility – the censors – need not take it to be true and
may even regard it as false. But they cannot avoid *declaring* it to be
true in so far as they want to promote subscription to it. And as they
must declare it to be true without permitting it to be criticized,
they present themselves as infallible.[23]

In the second part of his case against censorship Mill proceeds as
if he concedes for the sake of argument that truth is not logically tied
to scrutiny and discussion.[24] We may then take an opinion to be true
independently of any critical assessment of it. But, Mill declares, this
still does not justify protecting it from criticism because such a move
reduces the belief in question to 'a dead dogma', – 'held in the manner

of a prejudice ... deprived of its vital effect on the character and conduct, ... as a mere formal profession' (243, 258). If beliefs are to function as living truths governing the conduct and affairs of those who hold them, they need to be fully and frequently put to the test of critical discussion. Mill suggests that where there is a natural and general consensus in favour of some view, it may be necessary to introduce artificially a programme of dissent and criticism in order to vitalize it (251).[25]

It is not clear why, and consequently in what sense, opinions in the absence of discussion turn into 'dead dogma'. On the one hand, we are told that they have no effect on character and conduct in that they involve only a verbal adherence.[26] Those who hold a belief or subscribe to a doctrine in the absence of discussion do not in any proper sense of the word know what they profess, the very meaning of the belief is lost or seriously distorted (247, 258);[27] consequently, it cannot have any significant impact on character and conduct. On the other hand, the protected beliefs are said to be held as mere prejudice, without any rational consideration of their grounds (244). But as we all know, prejudice serves very effectively as a determinant of dispositions and actions. Moreover, the examples that Mill gives of 'dead' beliefs do little to clarify the conception. He points out that 'the maxims and precepts contained in the New Testament', which constitute the central doctrines of the faith, were accepted as 'living truths' by the early Christians because they were held in the face of active and hostile criticism. These same doctrines have become 'dead dogmas' because in the modern era Christianity is protected from critical dissent. With hardly any exception, latter-day Christians merely verbally acknowledge that one should love one's neighbours as oneself or take no thought for the morrow, or that it is doubtful that the rich can enter the kingdom of heaven, etc. without acting on these beliefs (248–50). But clearly the case that Mill draws attention to is open to a different and more reasonable interpretation. The beliefs he mentions are those whose content essentially spills over into conduct, so that in the consistent absence of relevant actions we may well deny that they are held at all by those who profess them. What we would have then would be cases of hypocrisy and not, as Mill claims, failure to grasp the meaning of these propositions.

This is the least satisfactory part of Mill's case for freedom of expression. Even if we grant that protecting a belief from criticism implies ignorance of its grounds,[28] it does not follow from this that one does not know the meaning of what one believes.[29] The view that a racial group is inferior in specified respects may be protected from criticism without any loss in meaning to those who subscribe to it.[30] Propaganda and other forms of indoctrination by their very nature exclude criticism and rational discussion but they still succeed in promoting the desired beliefs. And, as history shows, there is no reason to hold that such protected beliefs have little or no direct influence on conduct.

The strength of Mill's case against censorship lies in his central contention that the very idea of rationality regarding beliefs and attitudes depends on the possibility of critical assessment. The value of freedom of expression then consists in the fact that its provision makes it possible for us to be rational. Where the life of a community is concerned, freedom of discussion is indispensable for 'great thinkers' to pursue bold and novel lines of thought, and much more so for 'average human beings to attain the mental stature they are capable of' (243).[31] In other words, since our mental well-being depends on our being rational, freedom of discussion is necessary for our mental well-being (on which all other well-being depends) (257–8).

∾ SELF-REGARDING CONDUCT AND ∾ INDIVIDUALITY

The line dividing the area of individual freedom from that of legitimate social control is identical to that separating self-regarding from other-regarding conduct. Mill indicates from the start that the boundaries of these regions are not to be drawn simply on the basis of determining whether or not a causal connection exists between the individual's actions and specified effects suffered by others. Rather, he makes it abundantly clear that we need to appeal to a normative criterion in order to demarcate between self-regarding and other-regarding conduct. Thus, in the opening chapter of *Liberty*, Mill describes the area of self-regarding action as 'comprehending all that portion of a person's life and conduct which affects only himself, or if it affects others, only with their free, voluntary and undeceived consent and participation' (225).[32] This statement is immediately qualified: 'When I say only himself, I mean directly and in the first instance; for whatever affects himself may affect others through himself; and the objection that may be grounded on this contingency will receive consideration in the sequel' (225). In the 'sequel', i.e. chapter 4 of *Liberty*, Mill concedes that

> the mischief which a person does to himself may seriously affect, both through their sympathies and their interests, those nearly connected with him, and in a minor degree, society at large. When, by conduct of this sort, a person is led to violate a distinct and assignable obligation to any other person or persons,

the case is taken out of the self-regarding class, and becomes amenable to moral disapprobation in the proper sense of the term ... Whoever fails in the consideration generally due to the interests and feelings of others, not being compelled by some more imperative duty, or justified by allowable self-preference, is a subject of moral disapprobation for that failure, but not for the cause of it, nor for the errors merely personal to himself, which may have remotely led to it. In like manner, when a person disables himself, by conduct purely self-regarding, from the performance of some definite duty incumbent on him to the public, he is guilty of a social offence ... Whenever ... there is a definite damage, or a definite risk of damage, either to an individual or to the public, the case is taken out of the province of liberty and placed in that of morality or law ... But with regard to the merely contingent, or ... constructive injury which a person causes to society, by conduct which neither violates any specific duty to the public, nor occasions perceptible hurt to any assignable individual except himself; the inconvenience is one which society can afford to bear, for the sake of the greater good of human freedom. (281–2)[33]

Although, in these statements, Mill seems to be specifying two necessary conditions of self-regarding conduct – that it does not involve the breach of a specific duty and also that it is not the cause of perceptible hurt to an assignable individual – further consideration shows that the second condition should be regarded as subordinate to the first. The cases of contingent injury that Mill specifies are of the following four kinds: (1) An individual through some form of self-indulgence harms himself ('deteriorates his bodily or mental faculties') with the result that he is unable to use his abilities for the benefit of society, e.g. he cannot be, or any longer function as, a doctor (280).[34] (2) Similar conduct on the part of an individual that affects others adversely by serving as a bad example which they follow (280). (3) An act (e.g. not observing the Sabbath) which causes pain and distress to others because it goes against their views and practice (283ff.).[35] (4) An individual's success in a competitive examination, or the competitive selection of candidates for a job, causes loss and pain to those who, as a consequence, are not preferred (292–3). The injury caused in these and other cases may be perceptible enough and may clearly affect assignable individuals. For example, selling or renting a house to a black family in a white neighbourhood may bring about a fall in the value of adjacent properties, so that other house-owners suffer serious financial loss. Or the knowledge that the next-door neighbours are atheists may cause a religious person's feelings to be outraged to the extent of bringing on a serious illness. What would make these injuries 'merely contingent' is not the fact that they are 'non-perceptible' nor the fact that they do not affect an assignable individual – for in these two cases we can specify precisely those who suffer a clear injury – but the fact that the individual concerned is not violating any specific public duty or any distinct obligation to the other persons concerned. No one, it might be said, is under an obligation not to sell or rent a house to a black family, or to be religious.

It is along these lines that Mill responds to the kind of cases he mentions. With regard to (1) above, he points out that society has no right to exact any socially beneficial exercise of the talents and capacities which individual members of it may possess, so that the individual has no such corresponding duty (282).[36] In connection with (4), he states that 'society admits no right, either legal or moral, in the disappointed competitors to immunity from this kind of suffering', i.e. no one owes a duty to another to ensure that such pain and loss does not occur (293). With regard to (3), the actions complained of cause pain and distress to others only because they are believed to be wrong, so that the injury in question would not exist independently of these beliefs.[37] Mill takes this fact to imply that the so-called injured parties in such cases have no right to expect those whose conduct is found to be offensive to act differently.[38] Mill's notion of self-regarding conduct then depends on the existence and nature of the duties the individual owes either to society at large or to other persons. If an action is not a violation of such a duty then it is to be classified as self-regarding and any injury it causes to others taken to be merely contingent.

How should we determine the existence and nature of these duties which serve to mark out self-regarding from other-regarding conduct? It is as a utilitarian that Mill claims to answer this question. The ultimate appeal on all ethical questions should be to utility, provided that we take it to be 'grounded on the permanent interests of man as a progressive being' (224). This qualification is explained in chapter 3 of *Liberty* where Mill specifies *individuality* to be 'one of the principal ingredients of human happiness', 'one of the leading essentials of well-being' (261). What he has centrally in mind when he speaks of 'individuality', in particular 'the free development of individuality' or 'individual spontaneity', is the development of a certain kind of character or person. The favoured kind of person is one who does not do things just because it is customary or because it conforms to someone's views. This does not mean that such a person ignores general preferences and other people's views but only that this 'recorded experience' when available is used and interpreted in the individual's 'own way', in so far as it is deemed to be 'properly applicable to [the individual's] own circumstances and character' (262). What Mill values here is the nature or character of the individual's choice, of the reasons for which a course or policy of action or plan of life is chosen. The desirable kind of choice is that where the grounds on which it is made and justified are the product of the individual's own reasoning and judgement taking into account his or her own beliefs and desires, and not something derived mechanically from an external source ignoring 'the opinions and feelings of home growth' (264–5). Mill insists that such a choice should be based on the individual's 'own impulses and desires', which he identifies in terms of the distinction drawn between a deliberately made person whose character has been fashioned on the lines of a model hostile to natural endowment and one whose development has been allowed to occur 'naturally' within the unavoidable framework of a particular social and cultural environment.[39] It is only the latter kind of person whose desires can be said to be their own, it is only of such individuals that we can predicate true 'individuality of desires and impulses' and, accordingly, what we might call autonomous or genuine choice (264).[40]

Mill declares that it is only by making autonomous choices that one exercises and develops the essential human faculties of 'perception, judgement, discriminative feeling, mental activity, and even moral preference' (262), whereas those who fail to operate autonomously fail to make a choice in the proper sense of the word.[41] If choosing non-autonomously is not to choose at all, then we can say that what Mill wants to secure is freedom in a substantial or positive sense of the term – not simply freedom from external interference which allows the translation of prevailing desires into action but which also consists in being moved by reasons which are, in the sense specified, one's own and in realizing one's own purposes and goals.[42]

If it is only the individually spontaneous person who is a human being in the full sense of the term – in that we have with such a person the development of distinctive human endowments – then we can see what Mill means when he declares individuality to be one of the principal ingredients of human happiness and, therefore, desirable in itself. In so far as we aim to bring about happiness, we must find place in this final end for the happiness of those who have developed their individuality. And if we measure happiness in terms of pleasure or the satisfaction of desires and preferences, then we can point out on Mill's behalf that individually spontaneous persons will gain pleasure or satisfaction from the fact that they act and live in accordance with their true nature, i.e. in being what they are. In addition, Mill holds out other avenues of satisfaction available to autonomous persons if they develop their capacities to the full – the satisfaction of having achieved a distinct wholeness of being which translates into the pattern of their lives.[43]

The values placed on the development of individuality can be carried over to the pleasure or satisfaction associated with it. However, this does not mean that we can detach the pleasure or satisfaction from the exercise of individuality – it has value as part of happiness only because it is related to individual spontaneity. Mill's qualified appeal to the principle of utility on the basis of taking into account 'the permanent interests of man as a progressive being' amounts to assigning an independent intrinsic value to the development of individuality ([3.31], 73–5). Again, the modified view is not an aggregative doctrine ([3.31], 78–9). Neither the development of individuality nor the attendant satisfaction can be traded off against a greater degree of it in some other case or against a nett increase in the total amount.

If individuality is recognized to be desirable in itself then each of us will have a right to its promotion provided that what we do does not prevent others from pursuing it.[44] Consequently, there will exist a general duty to refrain from acting in ways that prevent others from being individually spontaneous and, in this sense, to refrain from harming or hurting them. The boundaries of self-regarding conduct in specific situations will be marked out on the basis of respecting the rights of others, and acknowledging corresponding duties, regarding the development of individuality.

We also need to consider the other components of happiness in order to determine rights and duties, and by reference to these the boundaries of individual freedom. In *Utilitarianism* Mill takes observance of the 'rules of justice', i.e. the moral rules which fall under the category of justice, to be part of 'the essentials of human well-being' and thus as the grounds, in given situations, of specific duties to others.[45] Examples of such duties, whose violation constitutes harm done to others, and determines the conduct to be other-regarding, are the obligation to keep one's promises or carry out the requirements of a commitment that one has voluntarily entered into (10: 242–3). It is on this basis that in *Liberty* Mill declares that a man may be legally coerced into providing education for his children, and that it would not be a violation of liberty to legally forbid marriage unless the parties concerned can show that they have the means of supporting a family (300–4). In addition, there are duties which we owe to the society to which we belong and whose object is to ensure its continued viability – for example, to give evidence in a court of law, to share in the common defence of the country, etc. (224–5). Our obligations to the community and to others will need to be restricted to the minimum required for a viable society to exist in order to provide for a sufficiently large area of self-regarding conduct and of individual freedom. But this will be secured by the great intrinsic value placed on individual spontaneity.

As a component element of happiness or well-being, individuality is regarded as a greater good than the other elements. Its higher value is justified on the grounds that it is a necessary condition of other components of happiness: 'it is not only a co-ordinate element with all that is designated by the terms civilization, instruction, education, culture, but is itself a necessary part and condition of all those things'.[46] Without individual spontaneity these other ends will lose their value – for what can be the worth of education and culture if those involved in their pursuit are incapable of thinking and deciding for themselves? The classical utilitarian ends of pleasure and freedom from pain will also form part of happiness, and they may be partly accommodated under 'the obligations of justice' which provide security for the individual in various respects (10: 251). Otherwise they are to be regarded as goods which are less valuable than the other components of happiness: paternalistic control may promote people's welfare or keep them out of harm's way, but the comparative worth of such an undertaking will be much less than individuals determining their own affairs (263).

Mill concedes that some, possibly many, may not want to lead an individually spontaneous life because they do not recognize its intrinsic value (261, 267). To these one can point out that a society which permits and encourages the free development of individuality will benefit in that such a move will introduce 'originality' in its affairs. The value of originality is said to consist in the discovery by 'persons of genius' of 'new truths' and 'new practices' which may prove beneficial to others in the community. In addition, we may expect the free development of individuality to promote the existence of 'a succession of persons whose ever-recurring originality', by insisting on an independent and rational scrutiny of the grounds of generally accepted beliefs and practices, will help to prevent merely mechanical and unthinking acceptance of these on the part of the rest of society (267). Clearly, in the latter sense of 'original', the belief or practice that is supported need not be novel, and all that is required is that its truth or desirability is affirmed or defended independently by the individual.[47] Mill admits that geniuses are likely to be few in number, so that it is originality in the sense of independence of thought that may be held out as being within the reach of the generality of humankind and as a necessary feature of a free society. Far from advocating the control of a community by an elite or 'the strong man of genius', it is originality in the sense of independence of thought that Mill emphasizes: 'If a person possesses any tolerable amount of common sense and experience, his own mode of laying out his existence is the best, not because it is the best in itself, but because it is his own mode' (270).[48]

❧ PATERNALISM ❧

The intrinsic value placed on individuality rules out, with exceptions, paternalism, i.e. the entitlement to coerce people for their own good, for example, prevent them from hurting themselves. One class of exceptions Mill stipulates is children and persons below the legal age of adulthood as well as 'those backward states of society in which the race itself may be considered as in its nonage' (224). In the case of the latter, benevolent despotism, which seeks to improve the condition of the people, is justified until they have become 'capable of being improved by free and equal discussion . . ., of being guided to their own improvement by conviction or persuasion' (224). It is very likely that Mill had in mind not only ancient communities but also contemporary societies judged not to be developed enough for the application of libertarian principles. His view may be challenged on the grounds that he is mistaken about the existence of such societies anywhere whose members are generally incapable of being moved by rational discussion and persuasion. But by convicting Mill of any such factual error we do not invalidate his case against paternalism.[49]

The other kind of exception mentioned by Mill is that where we are justified in forcibly preventing people from injuring themselves because it is clear that they are not aware of what they are doing – e.g. physically preventing someone from crossing an unsafe bridge when they are ignorant of its condition and there is no way of warning them (294). Ignorance of the particular circumstances of the action in such a case vitiates the decision to perform it.[50] But where there is no reason to doubt the voluntary character of the individual's choice then there is no basis for any kind of paternalistic interference, however undesirable or harmful the consequences of the action may be for the agent concerned.[51]

To abandon coercion in such cases is not to give up attempts to influence the individual to modify his conduct. We may, and in certain circumstances should, try to deflect someone from harming himself or herself by means of advice, persuasion or entreaty. And where self-regarding conduct exhibits folly or some other defect it may, according to Mill, properly become the object of distaste and even of contempt on the part of others. Such adverse judgements of individuals' self-regarding deficiencies may carry further penalties in the form of avoidance of their society or cautioning others about them, etc. Such penalties are not to be seen as specially designed forms of punishment – they are the natural outcome of the individual's self-regarding faults in that the restrictions they bring are 'strictly inseparable from the unfavourable judgement of others'. If we feel contempt regarding a person's conduct then it is natural (to be logically expected) that, unless there is some special reason for explanation, we will avoid the individual's company. Mill emphasizes the difference between adverse judgements of self-regarding faults and moral denunciations of harmful other-regarding actions. In the latter case, the conduct is regarded as the proper object of 'moral reprobation, and, in grave cases, of moral retribution and punishment'. Moreover, the penalties suffered in such cases are purposely inflicted in order to punish the individual. Self-regarding faults 'are not properly immoralities, and ... do not constitute wickedness'. What they reveal is folly, imprudence and absence of self-respect and, as such, deserve 'lack of consideration' but not 'reprobation'; consequently, they do not call for any kind of coercive interference in the individual's affairs (278–80).[52]

Referring to Mill's views on paternalism, H. L. A. Hart states that he

> carried his protests ... to lengths that may now appear to us as
> fantastic. He cites the example of restrictions of the sale of
> drugs, and criticizes them as interferences with the liberty of the
> would-be purchaser rather than with that of the seller. No
> doubt if we no longer sympathise with this criticism this is due,
> in part, to a general decline in the belief that individuals know
> their own interests best, and to an increased awareness of a great
> range of factors which diminish the significance to be attached
> to an apparently free choice or to consent. Choices may be made
> or consent given without adequate reflection or appreciation
> of the consequences; or in pursuit of merely transitory desires;
> or in various predicaments when the judgement is likely to be
> clouded; or under inner psychological compulsion; or under
> pressure by others of a kind too subtle to be susceptible in a
> law court. Underlying Mill's extreme fear of paternalism there
> perhaps is a conception of what a normal human being is like
> which now seems not to correspond to the facts. Mill, in fact,
> endows him with too much of the psychology of a middle-
> aged man whose desires are relatively fixed, not liable to be
> artificially stimulated by external influences; who knows what
> he wants and what gives him satisfaction or happiness; and who
> pursues these things when he can.[53]

Part of this criticism, in so far as it depends on the defective character of the individual's choice, will fall under the exceptions Mill cites to his rejection of paternalistic interference. And where the impairment of the individual's choice is due to the activities of others (for example the use of various kinds of subtle pressure), the coercive interference, even if not provable in a court of law, will still invoke the self-protection principle. If the impairment of individual choice is said to be substantial, then, besides enlarging the area of paternalistic direction, we will need to bring about other more radical institutional changes, e.g. exclude at least the ordinary person from serving on juries or electing a legislature etc. If we are not prepared to support such moves then, to that extent, we cannot support Hart's general doubts regarding the authenticity of individual choice.

The other common objection to Mill's rejection of paternalism, which Hart also mentions, is that it is doubtful that individuals know their own interests best. However, it is not Mill's contention that individuals can always or mostly be relied on to know where their real good lies but only that others are unlikely to do so. This is because estimates of the individual's interests made by others are arrived at from the outside, so to speak, and they fail to capture the intimate view which the person actually affected by the situation normally has. In contrast, the individual's own assessments of what constitutes his or her good are more reliable because 'with respect to his own feelings and circumstances, the most ordinary man or woman has means of knowledge immeasurably surpassing those that can be possessed by any one else' (277). Whereas the individual's knowledge is based on immediate acquaintance with what happens to and around, those who seek to direct his or her life from the outside can proceed only on the basis of 'general presumptions ... which may be altogether wrong, and even if right, are as likely as not to be misapplied to individual cases' (277).[54]

William James, discussing the special case of appreciating the way of life of those who are significantly different from us, distinguishes (as Mill does) between how things appear from the external standpoint and the assessments made from the point of view of the individual concerned: 'The spectator's judgement is sure to miss the root of the matter, and to possess no truth. The subject judged knows a part of the world of reality which the judging spectator fails to see, knows more while the spectator knows less'. In James's view, the greater the difference in lifestyles between 'the judging spectator' and 'the subject judged', the greater the chances of the former's judgement being distorted ([3.16], 1–2). Mill (and also James) sometimes talks as if it was impossible for anyone to see and estimate things accurately enough on behalf of another person. But it is not necessary, even if it is possible, to hold this extreme view. We may concede that there may be occasions where one may understand and follow the 'mechanisms of the mind' of some people well enough. But we may still be justified in doubting that this happens, or is likely to happen, often or normally or typically. That should provide sufficient grounds to challenge the reasonableness of a policy which seeks, in the likely absence of relevant knowledge, to manage the lives of people in order to promote their real good.

Mill's objections to paternalism gain support from the additional fact that the inability to see and assess matters from the standpoint of the individual whose interests are to be promoted may lead, possibly unwittingly, to the imposition of values held by those engaged in carrying out the undertaking. Paternalism then will collapse into an attempt to bring about conformity with values held by others and the good sought on behalf of the individual misidentified in terms of a set of alien norms.[55] But, apart from all these considerations, we cannot expect external control and direction normally to promote the individual's interests because it is a central part of the individual's good that he or she should be free from any such direction. As Mill points out, 'All errors which he is likely to commit against advice and warning are far outweighed by the evil of allowing others to constrain him to what they deem is his good' (277). If the removal of tutelage and the exercise of individuality is the most essential part of a person's wellbeing then how can paternalism, which consists in imposing tutelage, contribute to it?

∾∾ UTILITARIANISM ∾∾

In one of his earlier letters to Carlyle, Mill states that he is 'still, and likely to remain a utilitarian – but having scarcely any secondary premisses in common with those picked out as Utilitarians; and a utilitarian in a sense which no one else would regard as one' (12: 207–8). Originally intended to deflect Carlyle's hostility to utility as the foundation of morals, the statement indicates well enough the final direction of his thought. There is a sense in which Mill never gave up utilitarianism but his views, in spite of his efforts to hold on to their original character, would not have been acknowledged by those professing the Benthamite and hedonistic version of the doctrine. In *Liberty*, the modified account of utilitarianism that Mill appeals to consists in specifying individual spontaneity to be both desirable in itself and a greater good than the other elements of happiness. *Utilitarianism*, which is meant to be both a defence of utilitarian doctrine and also an account of his own ethical theory, re-affirms this conception of happiness as comprising a plurality of ends some of which are more valuable than others. The 'utilitarian formula' is said to be 'a comprehensive formula, including all things which are in themselves good' (10: 208) and happiness is characterized as 'a concrete whole' whose constituents or 'parts' are such things as health, virtue etc. (10: 236). And although Mill declares that 'the theory of life' on which his moral views are founded is still the orthodox belief that 'pleasure and freedom from pain are the only things desirable as ends' (10: 210), his further characterization of the ideas of pleasure and pain as well as the role he assigns to this central belief in our moral thinking leaves little room for the original hedonistic character of the doctrine.

Two kinds of pleasure are distinguished – that associated with the exercise of our higher faculties and the one involved in the operation of our bodily nature and the satisfaction of the animal appetites. The 'pleasures of the intellect, of the feelings and imagination, and of the moral sentiments' – of the capacities specified in *Liberty* as the distinctive endowments of a human being – are declared to have 'a much higher value, as pleasures than ... those of mere sensation' (10: 211). Since the difference between the two is qualitative, the higher kind of pleasure is said to be more desirable than any amount of the lesser variety (10: 211). Mill leaves the difference in quality between the two kinds of pleasure to be indicated by the expressed preference (in judgement and action) of those who have had actual experience of both. No further description is given, or even considered to be possible, of the qualities which are supposed to distinguish the two kinds (10: 213). This is understandable in that whether we take 'pleasure' to stand for a psychological state or experience, or construe it in terms of enjoyment or of the satisfaction of desires, no reasonable candidate for any such distinguishing quality is available. Quantitative differences may be readily specified: the pleasure or enjoyment or gratification that attends the operation of the higher faculties may be deeper or longer lasting or superior in terms of fecundity and, on this basis, one may prefer to engage in intellectual pursuits as against the satisfaction of bodily appetites. But what other, non-quantitative, considerations can one mention here except the character of the goals pursued and activities engaged in? And it is on this basis that Mill himself promotes the distinction: the one kind of pleasure is superior to the other because the activities and pursuits it is associated with are more valuable. He speaks of opting for the higher kind of pleasure as equivalent to preferring 'the manner of existence which employs [the] higher faculties' (10: 211). And he remarks on our general unwillingness 'to sink into ... a lower grade of existence' because it offends 'the sense of dignity which all human beings possess in ... proportion to their higher faculties ... It is better to be a human being dissatisfied than a pig satisfied; better to be Socrates dissatisfied than a fool satisfied' (10: 212).

If a human life, in spite of its many dissatisfactions,[56] is to be preferred to the contented life of a pig, then what makes it more valuable is its character, the kind of life it is. Mill, however, also wants to maintain that such a life, in spite of the imperfections and disappointments it is likely to contain, will still be productive of pleasure in that human beings will want to pursue it and desiring something is necessarily to find it to be pleasant.[57] In order, then, to hold on to hedonism, he falls back on a version of the doctrine according to which the pursuit of pleasure as an end turns out to be the pursuit of anything that we may desire as such. Moreover, Mill allows that we may intentionally aim at ends other than pleasure and even persist in such conduct when it is productive of pain – but in such cases it is still true that the conduct in question was originally ('in the beginning') followed because it was a source of pleasure or served to avert pain.[58] Finally, what is valued as a means to happiness (because it is externally productive of pleasure or instrumental in the satisfaction of desires) may, we are told, become *part* of it and valued for itself (for the pleasure directly associated with it).[59] It is in this way that wealth, power, fame and virtue can become parts or constituent elements of happiness. The unrestricted pursuit of some of these ends, such as power or wealth, may have a negative effect on the general welfare, but there need be no limit placed, in this regard, on the disinterested pursuit of virtue: 'Utilitarianism ... could only obtain its end by the general cultivation of nobleness of character' (10: 213–14), hence 'the utilitarian standard ... enjoys and requires the cultivation of the love of virtue up to the greatest strength possible, as being above all things important to the general happiness' (10: 237).

Mill remains a utilitarian to the extent that his moral theory appeals to *consequences* as the test of right and wrong. In this he sees himself to be following Bentham and the other classical utilitarians in holding that a necessary condition of an acceptable morality is that it appeals to an 'external standard' and is not based simply on 'internal convictions' or feelings (10: 111, 179). But the consequences that Mill specifies are not restricted to pleasure and the avoidance of pain in the ordinary sense of these terms. He includes other items in his conception of happiness as the ultimate end. And he tries to preserve the hedonistic character of these items, such as the cultivation of virtue, by (1) postulating a necessary connection between desiring something and getting pleasure from it; and (2) appealing to the empirical hypothesis that it is only by way of an original means–end relationship to pleasure that any other element of happiness comes to be valued in itself. But the first move is dubious unless we dilute 'pleasure' to mean no more than being pleased to do what one intentionally does or wants to do. And the second is equally doubtful as an account of why we come to value such things as virtue. We may get pleasure from being virtuous and perhaps, as Aristotle states, if we are truly virtuous then we must 'delight' in being so (*Nicomachean Ethics* 1104b 4–8), but this does not mean that we initially or otherwise come to value virtue for the pleasure it brings. Mill takes the main difference between his version of utilitarianism and the original Benthamite doctrine to lie in the 'secondary premises' which his own view supports and highlights. He tries to play down the difference by claiming a hedonistic foundation for these secondary rules along the lines mentioned above. Consequently, if we reject this attempt to re-introduce hedonism then some of the secondary premisses will effectively govern interests or pick out ends other than pleasure and the avoidance of pain, such as the free development of individuality, the exercise and fulfilment of the higher human capacities, the cultivation of virtuous dispositions, etc.

The different items in Mill's conception of happiness will need to be ranked and he seems to provide for this partly by way of the distinction between higher and lower kinds of pleasure, so that those elements associated with the higher kind of pleasure may be said to be more valuable. And partly the ranking is made to depend on the extent to which an element of happiness, though valuable in itself, is also valued as a necessary ingredient of other component ends – for example the free development of individuality is valuable not only in itself but also as a necessary feature of significant achievement in education and the promotion of culture (261).[60] On this basis, 'the standard of morality' will ensure the 'happiness' (i.e. serve and advance the interests) of human beings as creatures essentially endowed with the higher faculties and capable of freely developing their individuality. This in effect is the criterion characterized by Mill in *Liberty* as the appeal to 'utility grounded on the permanent interests of man as a progressive being'.

In *Utilitarianism* Mill gives a proof of the principle of utility which has achieved notoriety because of the fallacies it is supposed to involve. The first part of the proof where these fallacies are located runs:

> [T]he only proof capable of being given that an object is visible, is that people actually see it. The only proof that a sound is audible, is that people hear it . . . In like manner . . . the sole evidence it is possible to produce that anything is desirable, is that people do actually desire it. If the end which the utilitarian doctrine proposes to itself were not, in theory and practice, acknowledged to be an end, nothing could ever convince any person that it was so. No reason can be given why the general happiness is desirable, except that each person . . . desires his own happiness. This, however, being a fact, we have not only all the proof which the case admits of, but all which it is possible to require, that, happiness is a good: that each person's happiness is a good to that person, and the general happiness, therefore, a good to the aggregate of all persons. Happiness has made out its title as *one* of the ends of conduct and consequently one of the criteria of morality.
>
> (10: 234)

The inference from something being seen to its being visible is justified because it is part of the meaning of 'visible' that the thing in question is capable of being seen. But no such conceptual rule links 'desired' with 'desirable', hence what is actually desired may not be desirable (or worthy of being desired) at all. If it is Mill's purpose to base his case for utilitarianism on a strict analogy between 'visible' and 'desirable', then clearly he is guilty of arguing fallaciously. But it is open to us to take the offending statements in the proof to be no more than a bad rhetorical flourish. In the introductory chapter of *Utilitarianism*, Mill declares that ultimate moral principles cannot be justified by means of strictly deductive reasoning: 'Questions of ultimate ends are not amenable to direct proof', consequently the utilitarian theory cannot be the 'subject of what is commonly understood by proof' (10: 207–8). But such issues still fall within the scope of rational inquiry in that 'Considerations may be presented capable of determining the intellect either to give or withhold its assent ... and this is equivalent to proof' – so that we are to consider whether and 'what rational grounds ... can be given for accepting or rejecting the utilitarian formula' (10: 208). We can then ignore the unjustified analogy and take Mill's point to be that a central reason for regarding happiness as desirable is the fact that it is generally desired.[61] We must take happiness in this connection as comprising the constituent elements Mill assigns to it and its more or less general pursuit to be the product of experience and reflection.[62]

The further inference from each person's happiness being a good to that person to the general happiness being a good to the aggregate of all persons should also be interpreted in the light of Mill's reservations here about strict deductive proofs. What we must consider is whether there are good reasons in favour of the principle of utility, and although Mill does not canvass these reasons in the context of his proof we can specify them as they are mentioned elsewhere in his account. The consideration that seems to be most central is discussed in the chapter preceding the statement of the proof: Mill maintains that we naturally see ourselves as social beings,[63] so that whatever is thought to be necessary for the continued existence of the society to which we belong comes to be regarded as essential to human (including our own individual) existence. The movement of history is towards a state of human society where more and more people regard themselves as equal. And since social relations between equals can survive only if the interests of all concerned are considered equally, individuals in these circumstances come to recognize the interests of others as their own: 'The [individual] comes, as though instinctively, to be conscious of himself as a being who *of course* pays regard to others. The good of others becomes to him a thing naturally and necessarily to be attended to, like any of the physical conditions of our existence' (10: 232). In this way the good of others forms part of the individual's own good and the greatest good or happiness of others part of the individual's greatest happiness.[64] An additional consideration that Mill seems to rely on is that ethical doctrines opposed to utilitarianism not only acknowledge the duty to pursue the general good but also assign to it a pronounced importance (10: 230).[65] These opposing moralities differ from utilitarianism in that they also support the pursuit of other ends besides happiness and the second part of the proof is designed to show that they are mistaken in this regard as happiness (in the form of promotion of pleasure and avoidance of pain) is the only end desired.

But, as we have seen, Mill reaches this conclusion on the basis of doubtful moves, so that we are left with an unreduced plurality of ends – both with regard to the opposing moralities and with regard to his own doctrine. We may, of course, group these different ends under 'happiness' as an inclusive ultimate end. One of the elements of this inclusive end will be the general well-being or the good of the society or collective to which the individual belongs. And although the general good is conceived to be the sum of the good of individuals,[66] it will function as just one of a plurality of ends and not as the overriding goal of orthodox utilitarianism.[67]

❧ REPRESENTATIVE GOVERNMENT AND ❧ THE SUBJECTION OF WOMEN

Much of the discussion in *Representative Government* is about practical proposals regarding the mode of operation of a parliamentary government, particularly the method of electing members of parliament.[68] The theoretical issues considered relate to the value of parliamentary democracy and take up Mill's concerns regarding the dangers inherent in government by the majority.[69] Mill gives two main reasons why parliamentary democracy based on universal suffrage is to be preferred to other forms of government. Firstly, it enables every member of society to assert and defend their own rights and interests and, consequently, prevent them from being disregarded.[70] And, secondly, a democratic society, by giving citizens a voice in its affairs and letting them take part in the business of government, promotes those qualities of mind and character which make for excellence in intellectual, practical and moral capacity (19: 407). The outcome of this process of education is the development in such a society of active and energetic individuals with a real desire to pursue the public good and the capacity to do so (19: 408–12). The idea of individual development canvassed here is the same as that supported in *Liberty* and *Utilitarianism*;[71] hence we may take Mill's defence of representative democracy to appeal to the same conception of utility as that proposed in these works.

As regards the danger inherent in a parliamentary democracy based on universal (or fairly extensive) suffrage, Mill holds the greatest to be that of 'class legislation: of government intended for... the immediate benefit of the dominant class' made up of the numerical majority (19: 446). This is the threat posed by 'the tyranny of the majority' which Bentham and the other utilitarians had ignored and which de Tocqueville had emphasized. The other defect of representative government based on majority support is the likelihood of 'general ignorance and incapacity, ... insufficient mental qualifications' in those who make up the legislative body (19: 436). Mill thinks that both these deficiencies can be overcome by the adoption of an electoral system such as the one proposed by Thomas Hare involving the representation of minorities in proportion to their size. This would allow minority points of view to be represented in the deliberations of parliament and thus prevent minority interests from being disregarded (19: 449). The scheme would also allow people of merit and independent views to be elected, thus raising the intellectual level of the assembly and serving to counter the tendency of all universal democracies towards 'collective mediocrity' (19: 456-7). Mill is so concerned about the ignorance and stupidity of the electors rubbing off on those they elect, and thus lowering the intellectual standard of parliament, that he proposes minimum educational qualification for all voters.[72] And he also recommends, if it is possible to overcome practical difficulties, additional votes given to those who are intellectually qualified or more intelligent (19: 476-9).

The presence in parliament of people representing points of view different from that of the majority, and of people who are intellectually superior, will provide a public centre of opposition and dissent where, whenever necessary, majority opinion may be challenged and minority views defended. Parliament so constituted will then perform an important social function ('the function of Antagonism') without which the community living under the unchallenged influence of the majority is likely to stagnate or decline (19: 458-9). It is not too implausible to trace a connection with *Liberty* here: just as beliefs in the absence of criticism are supposed to turn into dead dogmas, so too are societies existing under the direction of unchallenged power fated to end in stagnation and decay. Conflict and collision are the foundation both of truth and social progress.

The Subjection of Women is designed to show that the social and legal disabilities suffered by women (for instance in nineteenth-century England) are unjustified and that the relations between the two sexes should be governed by a 'principle of perfect equality, admitting no power or privilege on the one side, nor disability on the other'

(21: 261). Pointing out that he has held this view from his earliest days, Mill concedes the difficulty involved in the enterprise – not because of 'the insufficiency or obscurity of the ground of reason on which [the] conviction rests' but because the contrary beliefs are embedded in 'a mass of feeling' against which rational argument is ineffectual (21: 261).[73] Consequently, much of what he has to say against the subordination of women takes on the character of tracing these 'feelings' to their source or revealing their influence when they are dressed up as 'reason'. Mill does recognize that the disabilities suffered by women, particularly their disenfranchisement and exclusion from the political process, their status in the marriage contract and relation ('the assimilation of the wife to the slave' (21: 286)) and the denial of entry to the professions and educational institutions, are unjustified in terms of the principles asserted in *Liberty* and *Representative Government*. Thus, he invokes the doctrine of *Liberty* when he declares that refusing women entry into the professions and various occupations for their own good constitutes denying them 'the equal moral right of all human beings to choose their occupation (short of injury to others) according to their own preferences, at their own risk' (21: 300). And he argues that given the value of 'personal independence as an element of happiness', the subordination of women, in so far as it denies them freedom as individuals, contributes to their (and to the general) unhappiness (21: 336–40).[74] Again, he justifies giving women the right to vote because it is 'a means of self-protection due to every one' (21: 301), appealing to what for him is an essential feature of representative democracy.[75]

However, the greater part of the discussion consists of an examination of various arguments purporting to defend the subordinate status of women. Many of these arguments are manifestly weak[76] but Mill still takes them seriously and considers them at length, possibly because he wants to reveal the underlying irrational basis in 'feeling' and, perhaps, also because 'such things do affect people's minds' (21: 303).[77] Referring to the general practice of distinguishing the sexes in terms of their different '*natural*' capacities and inclinations – so that women's disabilities (and male privileges) are seen to be natural and attempts to remove them unnatural – Mill points out that what is taken to be natural in this case can easily be shown to be the product of historical and social circumstances: 'What is now called the nature of woman is an eminently artificial thing – the result of forced repression in some directions, unnatural stimulation in others', the product of 'a hot-house and stove cultivation . . . for the benefit and pleasure of their masters' (21: 276).[78]

Mill's account is particularly significant in that he tries to show how women become the product of the system which oppresses them, so that they may appear to justify the discrimination and may even need to be convinced of their oppression.[79] His psychological insights in this regard and in his characterization of the effects of the legal and social subordination of women on the male psyche have been singled out for praise.[80] And in general his views, and sometimes even the language in which he presents them, are well ahead of his times and more appropriate to our contemporary scene.[81] But it is the classic doctrine of *Liberty* that gives shape to most of the views expressed in the other works, so that we can see them as part of a conception of human affairs centred on the supreme value of individual freedom and autonomy.

❧ NOTES ❧

All references to Mill's writings unless otherwise indicated are to *The Collected Works of John Stuart Mill* cited by volume and page. References to *On Liberty* in volume 18 are by page number only.

1 '(with the possible exception of the *Logic*)' (1: 259) But the parenthetical quali-fication has not been borne out by time. *Liberty* has continued to be the subject of discussion and controversy as much (if not more) in our times as in the years immediately following its publication. In the last two or three decades alone there have been, in English, nearly thirty studies of it and of Mill's views on ethics and politics. There is nothing comparable to this with regard to the *Logic*.

2 In the *Autobiography* Mill states that *Liberty* was revised many times (jointly by his wife Harriet and himself) – 'there was not a sentence of it that was not several times gone through by us together, turned over in many ways, and carefully weeded of any faults, either in thought and expression, that we detected in it' (1: 258–9). This fact seems to have escaped the notice of many of his critics, particularly those who claim to have found the most obvious inconsistencies and defects in his argument. A close reading of the text much more often than not reveals Mill's awareness of these objections and a sufficient response to them.

3 Mill often talks as if the greater threat to individual liberty exists in the coercion exercised through the medium of public opinion than in the form of legal or government interference. However, this is not meant to be taken as anything more than a contingent fact regarding English political life: 'The majority have not yet learnt to feel that power of the government their power, or its opinions their opinions. When they do so, individual liberty will probably be as much exposed to invasion from the government, as it already is from public opinion' (223).

4 According to Mill, a major defect of Bentham's political philosophy is that 'not content with enthroning the majority as sovereign, by means of universal suf-frage without king or house of lords, he exhausted all the resources of ingenuity in devising means for riveting the yoke of public opinion closer and closer round the necks of all public functionaries, and excluding every possibility of

the exercise of the slightest or most temporary influence either by a minority, or by the functionary's own notions of right.' Conceding that it is best (because less unjust than any other arrangement) that power should be vested in the majority, Mill proposed as a corrective institutional provisions (left unspecified) for the protection of 'freedom of thought and individuality of character, a perpetual and standing opposition to the will of the majority' (10: 106–8).

5 'De Tocqueville on Democracy in America' I (1835) and II (1840) (CW, vol. 18). In the *Autobiography* Mill acknowledges his debt to de Tocqueville's 'masterly analysis [of] the specific dangers which beset *Democracy* considered as the government of the numerical majority'.

6 Mill accepts de Tocqueville's contention that the civilized world shows clear signs of an inevitable progress to democracy.

7 Mill speaks only of 'self-regarding' conduct etc. (226 and 276ff.); the expression 'other-regarding' has been supplied by commentators.

8 Stephen [3.30], 28. Fitzjames Stephen originally saw himself as Mill's disciple. And it was as a classical or Benthamite utilitarian, determined to rescue Mill from his heretical abandonment of the doctrine, that he attacked the views expressed in *Liberty* ([3.30], 2, 11–12). Mill's comment that he 'does not know what he is arguing against' is, in general, not an unjust assessment of Stephen's passionate but often misguided critique ([3.2], 111).

9 An example of a friendly or liberal critic of Mill on this point is H. L. A. Hart who holds that 'Mill carried his protests against paternalism to lengths that may now appear to us as fantastic', hence 'a modification in Mill's principle is required' ([3.11], 32–3). At the other extreme, we have Fitzjames Stephen in whose view the ignorant and stupid, who will always exist in number in any society, clearly ought to be coerced into pursuing their own good ([3.30], 65ff.). Carlyle held similar beliefs: 'The immense mass of men he believed to be poor creatures, poor in heart and poor in intellect, incapable of making any progress at all if left to their own devices ... Every advance which humanity had made was due to special individuals supremely gifted in mind and character. It was not true ... that men were equal. They were infinitely unequal ... in intelligence, and still more ... in moral purpose. So far from being able to guide or govern themselves, their one chance of improvement lay in their submitting to their natural superiors, either by their free-will or else by compulsion' (Froude [3.6], 386–7).

10 For example Isaiah Berlin in 'John Stuart Mill and the Ends of Life' declares that Mill's version of utilitarianism stretches the meaning of utility or happiness 'to the point of vacuity' ([3.4], 181).

11 Compare Ten [3.31], [3.32], Gray [3.7], Berger [3.3], Donner [3.5], etc.

12 Mill distinguishes between the formation of beliefs or opinions and the expression of beliefs or opinions. We may then take the reference to absolute freedom of opinion to apply to the former, which would make the freedom to express opinions nearly but not entirely absolute. This would allow restrictions on freedom of speech mentioned or implied by Mill in the subsequent discussion. On the other hand, it seems reasonable to hold that in *Liberty* Mill had in mind only opinions having to do with the range of subjects he specifically mentions – 'practical or speculative, scientific, moral, or theological'. If we take 'practical' to cover social, political and general human affairs, then the specified

range of topics will rule out personal and private matters. Although he did not explicitly canvass it in *Liberty*, Mill did have a notion of privacy in so far as he held that there was no general right on the part of others to enquire into the personal aspects of an individual's life and affairs. During the period of his election to Parliament in 1865, he refused to give any information regarding his religious beliefs on the grounds that 'no one has any right to question another on his religious opinions' (*Later Letters*, *CW*, vol. 16, no. 834; also cf. no. 1324 and the *Autobiography*, 1: 274). In 1834, in response to Daniel O'Connell's proposal in his bill regarding freedom of the press that truth should be a justification, Mill declared that 'there are insuperable objections to allowing the details of a person's private conduct' to be aired in public and, in a libel action, made the subject of judicial investigation in order to determine its truth (6: 166–7; cf. *Earlier Letters*, *CW* vol. 12, no. 99). The fact that Mill's discussion of the right to free speech in *Liberty* makes no mention of the laws of libel also indicates the exclusion of an area of privacy from the scope of this right.

In *Liberty*, Mill holds that 'opinions lose their immunity, when the circumstances in which they are expressed are such as to constitute their expression a positive instigation to a mischievous act', for example denouncing corn-dealers as oppressors of the poor to an excited mob before a corn-dealer's house (260). Clearly the exclusion here is only nominal in that the case specified is such that the so-called expression of opinion really constitutes an action designed to incite or get others to hurt someone, like throwing the first stone (cf. Ten [3.31], 131ff. and Monro [3.21], 239–40). In 'Law of Libel and Liberty of the Press', one of his earlier publications in the *Westminster Review*, Mill quotes a passage from Montesquieu's *De l'Espirit des Lois* which specifically refers to cases where words, or what is said, by participating in an action take on the character of an action (21: 5).

13 Mill divides his case into three parts: where the suppressed opinion is true (and the protected opinion false), where it is false (and the protected opinion true) and where the truth is shared between the conflicting opinions; and he cites different objections to censorship under this division. However, what I have called his central argument clearly covers all these cases and governs in each case the assignment of truth-values to both the protected and the suppressed beliefs.

14 According to C. L. Ten, the assumption of infallibility argument is ambiguous in that Mill sometimes uses it to affirm the necessity of freedom of expression for the actual discovery of true beliefs and sometimes as a condition of rational beliefs ([3.31], 124–6). Perhaps one can say, in Mill's defence, that if there is an ambiguity here it is not significant since, for him, it is only on the basis of the principle of the rationality of beliefs that truth-values are to be assigned in particular cases.

15 Bain points out that Mill's view on freedom of discussion 'works round a central idea ... namely, the necessity of taking account of the *negative* to every positive affirmation; of laying down, side by side with every proposition, the counter-proposition' ([3.2], 104).

16 Although Mill generally speaks in terms of the truth or falsity of beliefs and opinions, his central argument applies even in those cases where we may use

other (cognate) notions such as 'justified'/'unjustified', 'reasonable'/'unreasonable' etc.

17 This brings to mind Sir Karl Popper's views concerning the character of scientific theories, according to which tests of such theories are to be regarded as attempts to refute them; and a successful test (where such an attempt fails) can only temporarily support the theory since future tests may produce a negative result ([3.25], chapters 1 and 10). It is interesting to find the arch-inductivist invoking elements of the hypothetico-deductive account of knowledge. Still it should be noted that the strength of Mill's defence of freedom of expression is that it presents more or less the same line of thought as what many would regard as an illuminating and fruitful view of the structure of scientific inquiry (cf. Ryan [3.27], 136ff.).

18 Berlin holds that Mill's account follows from his general empiricist outlook: 'he believed that no truths are – or could be – rationally established except on the evidence of observation. New observations could in principle always upset a conclusion founded on earlier ones' ([3.4], 187).

19 Berlin takes Mill as no more than contemptuously dismissing his opponents here ([3.4], 187). It seems to me that it is more reasonable to take the discussion on pp. 230–43 of Liberty as partly constituting an attempted rebuttal of absolutism on these lines. Mill uses historical examples to support his case.

20 [3.30], 76. Other commentators were less discerning. John Morley in an article in The Fortnightly Review of August 1873 takes the argument to make the same point as Milton in Areopagitica ([3.22], III). But Milton's point is very different from Mill's. Milton's contention is that if censorship is justified on the grounds of protecting people from 'Vice and Error', then how can those who do the censoring avoid these calamities unless it is assumed that they are proof against deception and corruption: 'how shall the licensers themselves be confided in, unless we can confer upon them, or they assume above all others in the land, the grace of infallibility and uncorruptedness?' ([3.20], 73). Another misinterpretation is that by John Plamenatz who takes Mill's point to be that those engaged in the business of censorship actually come to believe that they are infallible. He thinks Mill is wrong about this: 'It may be true that men who often silence discussion come, in the end, to believe that they are always right ... But this is not nearly enough to establish Mill's point. It does not prove that those who exercise the power only occasionally and under the guidance of a powerful tradition make any such assumption' ([3.24], 127).

21 What Mill had in mind was the prevailing and popular view regarding the social utility of religion. In the Autobiography he refers to the 'examination not of the truth, but of the usefulness of religious belief ... which, of all the parts of the discussion concerning religion, is the most important in this age, in which real belief in any religious doctrine is feeble and precarious, but the opinion of its necessity for moral and social purposes almost universal' (1: 73).

22 Mill's argument, which is not stated too clearly, is to be found on pp. 233–4 of Liberty.

23 I take Mill's statement 'it is not the feeling sure of a doctrine ... which I call an assumption of infallibility. It is the undertaking to decide that question for others without allowing them to hear what can be said on the contrary side' (234) to have this contextual relevance.

24 Or we may take Mill's argument here as addressed to those who do not accept the proposed principle of rationality.

25 The proposal is to be taken seriously in that we can envisage such cases in terms of Mill's non-absolutist conception of truth, namely where beliefs, though open to scrutiny, are not as a matter of fact challenged or discussed.

26 'The words which convey it cease to suggest ideas, or suggest only a small portion of those they were originally employed to communicate' (249). This is the same notion as Locke's 'bare sounds' without any ideas or mental significata annexed to them (*Essay Concerning Human Understanding*, III. 10.26 etc.). The absence of the corresponding ideas is supposed to exclude the so-called belief from the causal or associative mental chains leading to the adoption of attitudes and to action.

27 Mill's view is that it is only by defending the belief and criticizing opposing beliefs that one really grasps its content and meaning.

28 Because its grounds involve the refutation of other opposing beliefs from which it is protected (244–5).

29 Mill is quite vague here: 'Instead of a vivid conception and a living belief, there only remain a few phrases retained by rote; or, if any part, the shell and husk only of the meaning is retained, the finer essence being lost' (247).

30 I am not implying that such a belief is true. Mill's contention that absence of criticism turns a belief into a 'dead dogma' will apply also to the adoption of beliefs which are false.

31 Mill makes it quite clear that it is not only for an elite that he advocates freedom of discussion: 'There have been, and may again be, great individual thinkers in a general atmosphere of mental slavery. But there never have been, nor ever will be, in that atmosphere, an intellectually active people' (243).

32 The normative character of the criterion is brought out by the fact that *consent* on the part of the affected parties is meant to ensure the self-regarding nature of the relevant actions.

33 Mill is here primarily concerned about the liability of 'personal errors' such as intemperance or extravagance to legal and moral penalties. However, the discussion naturally leads him to specify the criteria of self-regarding and other-regarding conduct.

34 The example is not Mill's. A parallel case he mentions is where someone by damaging his own property supposedly 'diminishes ... the general resources of the community' (280).

35 Mill's examples refer to the prohibition on the eating of pork in a Muslim society and of Protestant forms of worship in a Catholic country. Mill does discuss sabbatarian legislation and restrictions but not in relation to contingent injury.

36 (2) calls for a similar response. But Mill does not adopt it because he takes the view that where individuals directly harm themselves by some form of self-indulgence, the example is likely to make others avoid that kind of conduct because 'it displays ... the painful or degrading consequences ... attendant on it' (283).

37 For a fuller discussion of this feature of self-regarding conduct see Wollheim [3.35] and Ten [3.31], 19ff. Honderich argues that there is no basis for assigning this idea to *Liberty*.

38 'There are many who consider as an injury to themselves any conduct which they have a distaste for, and resent it as an outrage to their feelings; as a religious bigot, when charged with disregarding the feelings of others, has been known to retort that they disregarded his feelings, by persisting in their abominable worship or creed. But there is no parity between the feeling of a person for his own opinion, and the feeling of another who is offended at his holding it; no more than between the desire of a thief to take a purse, and the desire of the right owner to keep it' (283). Ten [3.31] takes this passage to refer to the idea of morality-dependent harm. Honderich [3.14] finds only the last sentence to give off no more than a ring in support of Ten. I draw attention to the passage also because of the implicit reference to rights and duties.

39 Compare 'Human nature is not a machine to be built after a model, and set to do exactly the work prescribed for it, but a tree, which requires to grow and develop itself on all sides, according to the tendency of the inward forces which make it a living thing' (263). And: 'A person whose desires and impulses are his own – are the expression of his own nature, as it has been developed and modified by his own culture – is said to have a character. One whose desires and impulses are not his own, has no character; no more than a steam-engine has a character' (264). Also compare Mill's critique of the Calvinistic 'conception of humanity' which takes its nature to be bestowed on it for no other purpose than 'merely to be abnegated' (265–6). Gertrude Himmelfarb points out that Mill assumed that a larger amount of 'the raw material of human nature' meant that though there was a greater potential for evil, there was also a greater potential for good ([3.12], 63).

40 I use 'autonomous' to refer to nothing more than the kind of choice (and life) that Mill assigns to the 'individually spontaneous' person.

41 'He who does anything because it is the custom, makes no choice' (262).

42 For the distinction between the positive and the negative sense of freedom, see Isaiah Berlin, 'Two Concepts of Liberty', [3.4], 122ff. When Mill refers to freedom of speech it is wholly in the negative sense of freedom from external coercive barriers to expression and discussion of opinion. But where action is concerned, he adds the *further* requirement regarding the character of the choice determining it. Unlike Rousseau and the Hegelian idealists, he does not abandon 'negative freedom' in favour of a positive conception.

43 Compare 'Such are the differences among human beings in their sources of pleasure, their susceptibilities of pain, and the operation on them of different physical and moral agencies, that unless there is a corresponding diversity in their modes of life, they neither obtain their fair share of happiness, nor grow up to the mental, moral, and aesthetic stature of which their nature is capable' (270). And: 'In proportion to the development of his individuality, each person becomes more valuable to himself.... There is a greater fullness of life about his own existence' (266). Also compare Wilhelm von Humboldt's views in *The Sphere and Duties of Government* – which Mill quotes with approval: 'the end of man ... is the highest and most harmonious development of his powers to a complete and consistent whole' (261). Humboldt contrasts the partial and one-sided development of the individual's separate human capacities with 'harmoniously combining them' so as to achieve an organic unity of life, a 'union of the past and the future with the present' ([3.15], 16–17). Cf. Ten [3.31], 73.

44 In *Liberty* Mill refers to 'the limits imposed by the rights and interests of others' on freedom of action (266) and speaks of 'certain interests which either by express legal provision or by tacit understanding ought to be considered as rights' (276). In the *Autobiography* he assigns to *Liberty* as its 'leading thought', 'the doctrine of the rights of individuality' (1: 260). Cf. Berger [3.3], 229; Donner [3.5], 190–1.

45 'Justice is a name for certain classes of moral rules, which concern the essentials of human well-being more nearly, and are therefore of more absolute obligation, than any other rules for the guidance of life; and the notion which we have found to be of the essence of the idea of justice, that of a right residing in an individual implies and testifies to this more binding obligation . . . The moral rules which forbid mankind to hurt one another (in which we must . . . include, wrongful interference with each other's freedom) are more vital to human well-being than any maxims . . . which only point out the best mode of managing some department of human affairs' (10: 255). J. C. Rees distinguishes self-regarding from other-regarding conduct in terms of actions which *merely affect* others from those which also adversely affect the *interests* of others; and he takes the 'rules of justice' to pick out essential or vital human interests ([3.26], chapters 5 and 6).

46 Cf. Berger [3.3], 233; and Donner [3.5], 125 – Aristotle conceives of 'happiness' or *eudaimonia*, 'the most final end', as made up of several elements, each of which is necessary for achieving it, but some of which are more valuable than others; for example, *moral virtue* because while those who possess it may miss out on happiness, still they can never become 'miserable' (*Nicomachean Ethics*, I, 7–10). For a discussion of Aristotle's conception of eudaimonia as an inclusive end see Hardie ([3.10], chapter 2) and Ackrill [3.7].

47 'Original' here means 'underived, independent, proceeding from the person directly'. Cf. *The Subjection of Women*, 21: 314.

48 Mill's plea that 'exceptional individuals should be encouraged in acting differently from the mass' because 'in this age, the mere example of nonconformity, the mere refusal to bend the knee to custom, is itself a service' (269) surely covers the exercise of originality in both senses of the term. One can act differently from the mass, and refuse to bend the knee to custom not only by supporting novel beliefs and practices but also by subscribing to beliefs and practices, whether novel or not, only on the basis of one's own rational assessment: the manifestation of nonconformity can also be seen as the refusal to follow custom just because it is custom or subscribe to opinions just because they are generally acknowledged.

49 Cf. Donner [3.5], 170–1. Fitzjames Stephen asks: 'Was there ever a time or place at which no men could be improved on any point by free discussion?' But he goes on to support a more restrictive interpretation of Mill's criterion which justifies paternalistic intervention in every society ([3.30], 69).

50 Cf. Ten [3.31], 110; and chapter 7 for a full and valuable discussion of Mill's rejection of paternalism.

51 Mill declares that people should not be allowed to sell themselves as slaves, or otherwise contract to become someone's slave (299–300). This is sometimes said to be inconsistent with his rejection of paternalism. But we need not take the prevention of people selling themselves into slavery as justified on paternalistic

grounds. Mill advocates making any such engagement 'null and void', i.e. not enforceable by law or the pressure of public opinion. Clearly what this is meant to achieve is to prevent anyone else from coercing the individual to act as their slave on the basis of such a contract. The rejection of such contracts then can be taken to fall under the self-protection principle. At the same time, the exclusion of formal slavery contracts does not mean that we should also prevent someone from actually acting and living as another's 'slave' of his or her own free choice (cf. Ten [3.31], 117–19).

52 The distinction Mill seeks to make here, and which he stresses is not 'merely nominal', is designed to show that protecting the area of self-regarding actions from coercive intervention does not preclude us from being concerned with such conduct on the part of others and from judging its worth. The doctrine of *Liberty*, Mill points out, is not one of 'selfish indifference', unconcerned about what happens to others unless one's own interests are involved. Rather, it allows full scope for 'disinterested exertion to promote the good of others. But disinterested benevolence can find other instruments to persuade people to their good, than whips and scourges, either of the literal or the benevolent sort' (276–7) (also cf. 10: 246).

53 [3.11], 32–3. With regard to restrictions on the sale of poisons, Mill is concerned about the liberty of the purchaser because some regulations would effectively prevent their purchase: 'to require in all cases the certificate of a medical practitioner, would make it sometimes impossible, always expensive, to obtain the article for legitimate uses' (294). He is not against requiring purchasers to give their name and address and specify the proposed use of the substance, and even when there is no medical prescription to require the presence of a third person to attest to the sale. Mill acknowledges the 'right inherent in society to ward off crimes against itself by antecedent precautions' (295). But he is also concerned that this 'preventive function of government' may be abused 'for there is hardly any part of the legitimate freedom of action of a human being which would not admit of being represented, and fairly too, as increasing the facilities for some form or other of delinquency' (294). It should be noted that Mill is here offering 'not so much applications, as specimens of applications' designed to illustrate the relevant kinds of reasoning entailed by his doctrine (292).

54 The 'general presumptions' Mill has in mind are beliefs of the form 'Most people would or would not want ...', 'No one wants ...' etc.

55 Cf. Ten [3.31], 116–17; Khan [3.17], 61–5.

56 And, according to Mill, it is only in order to escape from *extreme unhappiness* that one would prefer to abandon a distinctive human existence (10: 211).

57 Cf. 'desiring a thing and finding it pleasant, aversion to it and thinking of it as painful, are phenomena entirely inseparable, or rather two parts of the same phenomenon; in strictness of language, two different modes of naming the same psychological fact' (10: 237). Mill justifies the claim on factual grounds; however it should be noted that for him all truths, even those of mathematics, are empirical; and that he goes on to say that 'to desire anything, except in proportion as the idea of it is pleasant, is a physical and metaphysical impossibility' (10: 238).

58 According to Mill, the *will* or 'conscious volition ... which has become habitual'

is to be distinguished from *desire*, and may be directed to ends other than pleasure. But it is still the case that 'will, in the beginning is entirely produced by desire; including in that term the repelling influence of pain as well as the attractive one of pleasure' (10: 238–9). (Also cf. *Logic*, 8: 842–3).

59 Cf. 'What was once desired as an instrument for the attainment of happiness, has come to be desired for its own sake ... as *part* of happiness. The person is made, or thinks he would be made, happy by its mere possession; and is made unhappy by failure to obtain it' (10: 236). And: 'Those who desire virtue for its own sake, desire it either because the consciousness of it is a pleasure, or because the consciousness of being without it is a pain, or for both reasons united' (10: 237).

60 Another such element is the provision of a sense of security as the outcome of a general acknowledgement and society's protection of individual rights (picked out by the 'rules of justice' – for example protecting people from unjustified infliction of injury and wrongful interference with their freedom). Without security no good can be pursued or enjoyed and no evil confidently averted. For this reason, Mill takes the claim for security to assume a 'character of absoluteness' so that 'indispensability becomes a moral necessity' (10: 251). Berger divides the essential elements in Mill's conception of happiness into two basic categories: (1) 'the constituents and requirements for an individual's sense of being his or her own person, of developing one's life as one chooses – a sense of freedom, power, excitement', and 'whatever is necessary to maintain human dignity'. And (2) 'those things requisite for a sense of security, the prime ones being the fulfilment by others of the rules of justice, and their respect for our rights' ([3.3], 40–2). I am greatly indebted here and elsewhere to the late Professor Berger's account of Mill's moral and political views and, in particular, of Mill's concept of happiness. For a discussion of Berger's views see Hoag [3.13] and Ten [3.32].

61 In a letter to Gomperz, the translator of the German edition of *Utilitarianism*, Mill refers to 'the real argument' behind his misleading statement of it and seems to accept the need for dropping the offending analogy (10: cxxvi; and 16: 1413–14).

62 Cf. Skorupski [3.29], 286–7. It seems to be Mill's view that the evidence we are supposed to cite in favour of the desirability of happiness is that it is consistently and generally desired or pursued as an end and also acknowledged or accepted as such on the basis of reflection and rational consideration. If this were the case then, in the absence of a countervailing explanation, we would have a strong argument in favour of the principle of utility.

63 He declares that 'the social feelings of mankind' involve 'the desire to be in unity with our fellow creatures ... The social state is at once so natural, so necessary, and so habitual to man, that, except in some unusual circumstances or by an effort of voluntary abstraction, he never conceives himself otherwise than as a member of a body' (10: 231). (Cf. Berger [3.3], 44 and 59–61 for a fuller discussion of this aspect of Mill's views.)

64 The argument proceeds on the basis that social life is requisite for the individual's own happiness and a requisite of social life is a concern for the general welfare ([3.3], 59).

65 According to Berger, the proof is addressed to intuitionists who held that our

moral *feelings* are the sole foundation of moral obligations and judgements ([3.3], 53–4).

66 But, as Skorupski points out, this is not enough. We need to know on what principles the good of individuals is to be incorporated into the general good ([3.29], 287). (For a discussion of this and related issues see chapter 9.)

67 Referring to Mill's proof, Berger writes: 'It is tempting... to say that there is a missing premise or assumption here, namely, that Mill believed there is a strong connection between the individual's welfare and the general welfare. Each individual's welfare is *included in* the general welfare, so, if a person desires that person's own welfare, and it is therefore a good to them, the general welfare is also a good to them. Of course, it does not follow that they *desire* the general welfare, because *they* may not see the connection; yet, it will be true that the general welfare is good for them. Moreover, they can come to desire the general welfare when made aware of the connection, especially if social life is requisite for their happiness, and a requisite of social life is a regard for the general welfare' ([3.3], 59). This would make it possible, at least technically, to hold on to the general welfare or happiness as a necessary feature of the moral standard.

68 Part of what Mill says concerning the mechanism of parliamentary government is also to be found in two other essays published in 1859 – *Thoughts on Parliamentary Reform* and *Recent Writers on Reform* (19: 311ff.). The latter contains a review of Thomas Hare's *A Treatise on the Election of Representatives* (1859) containing the proposal for an electoral system based on proportional representation involving a national quota of votes for entry to parliament together with preferential voting, a scheme that Mill enthusiastically supported. Having, as he thinks, answered objections brought against the scheme, he predicts that its implementation will usher in a new era of parliamentary government (19: 453–65). But he does not consider the standard objection that such a system is likely to introduce political instability and allow minorities to wield power out of proportion to their size or importance.

69 He also discusses other matters which cut across this division, such as the forms of government best suited to the rule of colonies by a democracy (19: 562ff.).

70 He refers to this as the power of 'self-protection' (19: 404, 21: 301). However, this feature of democracy has no relation to the self-protection principle mentioned in *Liberty*.

71 See 19: 399–403, 467–9, etc.

72 He wants minimum proficiency in the three R's: the voter should be able to 'copy a sentence from an English book, and perform a sum in the rule of three' (19: 471). He also stipulates that every voter should be a taxpayer, so that those who elect legislatures will have a special interest in keeping expenditure and taxes down. But to allow most people to qualify under this rule, he recommends that a direct tax in lieu of some existing indirect taxes should be levied on all adults. Other categories of exclusion are undischarged bankruptcy and non-payment of taxes, and 'the receipt of parish relief' (19: 472).

73 'So long as an opinion is strongly rooted in the feelings, it gains rather than loses in stability by having a preponderating weight of argument against it... ; the worse it fares in argumentative contest, the more persuaded its adherents are that their feeling must have some deeper ground, which the

arguments do not reach; and while the feeling remains, it is always throwing up fresh entrenchments of arguments to repair any breach made in the old' (21: 261).

74 Also cf. 21: 273, 280; *Liberty* 301, and *Papers on Women's Rights*, the joint product of Mill and his wife, Harriet, 21: 386.

75 Also cf. *Representative Government*, 19: 479–81; and 21: 386–7.

76 For example, the contention that women's 'greater nervous susceptibility' makes them too impulsive and changeable, incapable of perseverance, uncertain, etc. so that they are not fit for anything but raising a family! Or the view that men are superior to women in mental capacity because they have a larger brain (21: 307–12).

77 Another reason for Mill to review these arguments might be the fact that they were commonly used in public debate and he wants to provide opponents of discrimination with the details regarding their refutation. It should be recognized that Mill saw *The Subjection of Women* to be a manifesto for legal and social reform – as he said in a letter to Bain, he wanted 'to stir up the zeal of women themselves . . . , excite the enthusiasm in women which is necessary to break down the old barriers' (17: 1623).

78 Also cf. 21: 302. As part of the social forces which are said to produce female character traits and mental capacities, Mill assigns a central function to 'the education given to women – an education of the sentiments rather than of the understanding and the habits which are the outcome of their restricted life-styles' (21: 330). Mill does not deny that the subordination of women may seem to be natural, for: 'unnatural generally means only uncustomary, and . . . everything that is usual appears natural. The subjection of women to men being a universal custom, any departure from it quite naturally appears unnatural' (21: 270).

79 Women, according to Mill, are indoctrinated to be submissive and obedient 'by representing to them meekness, submissiveness and resignation of all individual will, into the hands of a man, as an essential part of sexual attractiveness' (21: 272). This is reflected in the work of women writers, so that the 'greater part of what women write about women is mere sycophancy to men' (21: 279).

80 'its psychological contribution is the book's great achievement: Mill's psychology is grounded in a more lucid distinction between prescription and description than one encounters in Freud, and a far more intelligent grasp of the effects of environment and circumstance. Mill is also sensitive to the mechanisms by which conservative thought construes the status quo into the inevitable' (Millett [3.19], 96). Kate Millett's account of Mill's views as contrasted with those of Ruskin is an important contribution to our understanding of the issues involved ([3.19], 88–108).

81 For example, the 1852 edition of the *Logic* carried a footnote which deplored the common use of the pronoun 'he' to refer to human beings in general, and went on to point out that this was 'more than a defect in language; tending greatly to prolong the almost universal habit, of thinking and speaking of half the human species as the whole'. Although the footnote was deleted in later editions, its existence indicates an awareness on Mill's part of the 'gender-bias' attaching to language ([3.34], 136).

❧ BIBLIOGRAPHY ❧

This bibliography contains works cited in the text together with a few other items of interest.

3.1 Ackrill, J. L. 'Aristotle on *Eudaimonia*', *Proceedings of the British Academy* 60 (1974): 339–59.

3.2 Bain, A. *John Stuart Mill: with Personal Recollections*, London: Longmans Green, 1882.

3.3 Berger, F. R. *Happiness, Justice and Freedom: The Moral and Political Philosophy of John Stuart Mill*, Berkeley: University of California Press, 1984.

3.4 Berlin, I. 'Two Concepts of Liberty', 'John Stuart Mill and the Ends of Life', in *Four Essays on Liberty*, London: Oxford University Press, 1969.

3.5 Donner, W. *The Liberal Self: John Stuart Mill's Moral and Political Philosophy*, Ithaca and London: Cornell University Press, 1991.

3.6 Froude, J. A. *Life of Carlyle*, abridged and ed. by J. Clubbe, London: John Murray, 1979.

3.7 Gray, J. *Mill on Liberty: A Defence*, London: Routledge & Kegan Paul, 1983.

3.8 —— (1991) *Liberalisms: Essays in Political Philosophy*, London, Routledge, 1991.

3.9 Gorovitz, S. ed. *Mill's Utilitarianism*, Indianapolis: Bobbs Merrill, 1971.

3.10 Hardie, W. F. R. *Aristotle's Ethical Theory*, 2nd edn, Oxford: Clarendon Press, 1980.

3.11 Hart, H. L. A. *Law, Liberty and Morality*, London: Oxford University Press, 1964.

3.12 Himmelfarb, G. *On Liberty and Liberalism: The Case of John Stuart Mill*, New York: Alfred Knopf, 1974.

3.13 Hoag, R. W. 'Happiness and Freedom: Recent Work on John Stuart Mill', *Philosophy & Public Affairs* 15 (1986): 188–99.

3.14 Honderich, T. '*On Liberty* and Morality-dependent Harms', *Political Studies*, 30 (1982): 504–14.

3.15 Humboldt, W. von *The Limits of State Action*, ed. by J. W. Burrow, Cambridge: Cambridge University Press, 1969.

3.16 James, W. 'On a Certain Blindness in Human Beings', in *Selected Papers on Philosophy*, London, J. M. Dent, 1961.

3.17 Khan, R. F. 'Mental Retardation and Paternalistic Control', in R. S. Laura and A. F. Ashman, eds, *Moral Issues in Mental Retardation*, London: Croom Helm, 1985.

3.18 Mill, J. S. *Collected Works*, 33 vols, ed. by J. M. Robson, Toronto and London: University of Toronto Press, and Routledge & Kegan Paul, 1963–91.

3.19 Millett, K. *Sexual Politics*, London, Virago Press, 1983.

3.20 Milton, J. *Areopagitica: A Speech to the Parliament of England for the Liberty of Unlicensed Printing*, London, Hunter & Stevens, 1819.

3.21 Monro, D. H. 'Liberty of Expression: Its Grounds and Limits II', *Inquiry*, 13 (1970): 238–53.

3.22 Morley, J. 'Mr Mill's Doctrine of Liberty' in P. Stansky, ed., *John Morley:*

Nineteenth Century Essays, Chicago and London: University of Chicago Press, 1970.

3.23 Packe, M. St. J. *The Life of John Stuart Mill*, London: Secker & Warburg, 1954.

3.24 Plamenatz, J. *The English Utilitarians*, 2nd edn, Oxford: Basil Blackwell, 1958.

3.25 Popper, K. R. *The Logic of Scientific Discovery*, London: Hutchinson, 1959.

3.26 Rees, J. C. *John Stuart Mill's On Liberty*, Oxford: Clarendon Press, 1985.

3.27 Ryan, A. *J. S. Mill*, London: Routledge & Kegan Paul, 1974.

3.28 Schneewind, J. B. ed. *Mill: A Collection of Critical Essays*, New York: Doubleday, 1968.

3.29 Skorupski, J. *John Stuart Mill*, London: Routledge, 1989.

3.30 Stephen, J. F. *Liberty, Equality, Fraternity* ed. by R. J. White, Cambridge: Cambridge University Press, 1967.

3.31 Ten, C. L. *Mill on Liberty*, Oxford: Clarendon Press, 1980.

3.32 —— 'Mill's Defence of Liberty', in K. Haakonssen, ed., *Traditions of Liberalism: Essays on John Locke, Adam Smith and John Stuart Mill*, Sydney: Centre for Independent Studies, 1988.

3.33 Thompson, D. F. *John Stuart Mill and Representative Government*, Princeton: Princeton University Press, 1976.

3.34 Tulloch, G. *Mill and Sexual Equality*, Hemel Hempstead: Harvester Wheatsheaf, 1989.

3.35 Wollheim, R. 'John Stuart Mill and the Limits of State Action', *Social Research* 40 (1973): 1–30.

3.36 Wood, J. C., ed. *John Stuart Mill: Critical Assessment*, vol. I, London: Croom Helm, 1987.

CHAPTER 4

J. S. Mill
Logic and metaphysics
John Skorupski

ᕀᕀ ENLIGHTENMENT AND ROMANTICISM ᕀᕀ IN MILL'S PHILOSOPHY

Mill's importance as one of the major figures of nineteenth-century politics and culture, and the current interest in him as a moral and political philosopher, are both so great that they make it hard to see him in another aspect – as a leading contributor to the British tradition of epistemology and metaphysics. Yet it was the *System of Logic* (1843) that first established his reputation; and his views in this field remain as interesting and relevant as his better known views in ethics and politics.

Throughout his intellectual life Mill sought to weave together the insights of enlightenment and Romanticism. He applied Romantic idealism's moral understanding to utilitarianism's concepts of character, imagination and purpose, freedom and reason, human good. To German Romanticism he owes one of his master themes – that of the culture of human nature as a whole, both in its diverse spontaneity and in its rational autonomy. But the metaphysical and psychological foundations of his thought lie securely in the naturalistic empiricism of the British school – and, moreover, in its radical and associationist, rather than its conservative and innatist, wing. Thus the deepest questions about Mill's philosophical success turn on the possibility of such a synthesis, and on how far he achieved it.

Reasons for doubt centre on two great issues, which at bottom are linked. Must not naturalism subvert reason, as Kant thought? And must not a natural science of man – a scientific psychology – subvert the understanding from within, the *moral* psychology of autonomy and expressive spontaneity, which Mill shares with the 'Germano-Coleridgeans' (as he called them)? Both questions lead us to the *System of Logic*: the first to its analysis of deductive and inductive reasoning, the second to its treatment of freedom and determinism. They remain important issues in contemporary philosophy. Beyond these two questions about the coherence of Mill's thought, there is a third – whether his associationist psychology can be reconciled with the idea of determinate human potentiality he requires for his account of 'man as a progressive being'. But this question does not have the direct contemporary significance that the other two have and will not be discussed here.

➤➤ NATURALISM AND SCEPTICISM ➤➤

Naturalism is the view that the mind is an entirely natural entity – a part of the natural order. But if the mind is only a part of nature, it seems that no real knowledge of the natural world can be *a priori*. Either all real knowledge is *a posteriori*, grounded in experience, or there is no real knowledge. That this consequence genuinely follows from naturalism Mill and Kant would have agreed. The difference between them was that Mill, unlike Kant, thought that knowledge could be grounded on such a basis. Thus the purpose of the *System of Logic* was, firstly, to spell out the full extent of epistemological empiricism – that is, of the view that all knowledge is *a posteriori* – and, secondly, to show how knowledge is possible on that basis. Its greatest achievement is the radicalism and the rigour with which it presses through to the first of these objectives.

Before we examine the *System* it will be useful to draw some further broad contrasts between Mill, Kant, David Hume and Thomas Reid. Unlike Hume, Kant or even Reid, Mill shows no interest at all in scepticism. He agrees with Kant that naturalism must remove *a priori* grounding from the common-sense principles which Reid presents. He does not agree with Reid that those principles are 'innate', but he also sees – though with less clarity, as we shall see – that even if they were, that would not give them an epistemological, as against a merely psychological, independence of experience. Yet he does not unleash a sceptical attack on reason as Hume does, nor does he see any need to defend reason against such an attack. In fact he sees no crisis of reason, and it is this that sets him apart most fundamentally from the Critical legacy of Kant.

Here he is loyal to his Benthamite inheritance. The Benthamites wished to distance themselves from Hume's scepticism just as firmly as the Scottish common-sensists did – unlike the latter, though, they felt no call to respond systematically to it. Mill agreed with them: in this respect his attitude was English rather than Scottish. More broadly, however, both Mill and Reid belong in that British naturalistic camp which believes that no serious philosophical lesson can be drawn from scepticism. For neither of them thinks – as Hume did – that sceptical arguments are sound and significant, that they show something of negative importance about reason. The difference between them is rather that Reid believes that scepticism stems solely from an erroneous theory of mind, and can be entirely defused by denying the existence of the objects postulated by that theory – ideas – while Mill in contrast never engages with scepticism at all.

If one thinks that scepticism is both unanswerable and unserious this may be the true philosophic wisdom. Whether it is wisdom or evasion is a question which keeps on returning in philosophy. But whatever view one takes on it one will misunderstand the *System of Logic* if one does not grasp that it is a work of what a contemporary philosopher in the same tradition, W. V. O. Quine, has called 'naturalized epistemology'. One of the ways in which it is, is precisely this: that it neither raises nor seeks to answer sceptical questions.

THE ANALYSIS OF LANGUAGE: ❧ LOGIC AND MATHEMATICS ❧ CONTAIN REAL INFERENCES

Fundamental to the *System* is a distinction Mill draws between 'verbal' and 'real' propositions, and correspondingly, between 'merely apparent' and 'real' inferences. He applies it with greater strictness, and addresses his thesis, that merely apparent inferences have no genuine cognitive content, with greater resolution, than anyone had done before.

We can best reconstruct it by starting with the notion of a merely apparent inference. An inference is merely apparent when no real inferential move has been made. For this to be so, the conclusion must literally have been asserted in the premises. In such a case, there can be no epistemological problem about justifying the apparent inference – there *is* nothing to justify. A verbal proposition can now be defined as a conditional proposition corresponding to a merely apparent inference. (This is not the whole of Mill's distinction, for he also counts elementary inferences and propositions concerning identity as verbal; but we can ignore that for the moment.)

The distinction corresponds, as Mill himself notes, to that which Kant makes between 'analytic' and 'synthetic'. (Kant formulates it for affirmative predicative propositions, and so does Mill, but the version given in the previous paragraph can be used to avoid this limitation.) But there is also a broader notion of analyticity, which has been influential in this century and which may also be thought to be implicit in some, though not all, of Kant's formulations. It defines an analytic truth as one from whose negation a contradiction can be deduced, with the help, where necessary, of definitional transformations, and using principles of logic alone. In the broad sense of 'analytic', it becomes a trivial truth that logical principles are analytic. But what is then no longer trivial is the crucial thesis that analytic propositions have no genuine cognitive content, and hence pose no epistemological problem.

If we keep to Mill's understanding of the distinction between 'verbal' and 'real', which corresponds to the narrower Kantian notion of analyticity, pure mathematics, and logic itself, contain 'real' propositions and inferences with genuine cognitive content. The clear recognition of this fact is the chief philosophical achievement of the *System of Logic*. For if Mill is also right in holding that naturalism entails that no real proposition is *a priori*, then he has shown the implications of naturalism to be radical indeed. Not only mathematics but logic itself will be empirical.

To demonstrate that logic and mathematics contain real propositions Mill has to embark on an extensive semantic analysis of sentences and terms (he calls them 'names'), of syllogistic logic, and of the so-called 'Laws of Thought'. His analysis has many imperfections and he never unifies it in a fully general account. But he does supply the foundations of such an account, and in doing so takes the empiricist epistemology of logic and mathematics to a wholly new level.

The starting point is a distinction between the denotation and connotation of names. Names, which may be general or singular, denote objects and connote attributes of objects. (Attributes may themselves be denoted by 'abstract' names, though the term is misleading, for Mill conceives attributes nominalistically). A general name connotes attributes and denotes each object which has those attributes. Most singular names also connote attributes, but their grammatical construction indicates that they denote just one object if they denote at all.

There is however an important class of singular names – 'proper names' in the ordinary sense, such as 'Dartmouth' – which denote an object without connoting any property. Identity propositions which contain only such non-connotative names, as 'Tully is Cicero', are in Mill's view verbal. They lack content in the sense that, according to Mill, the only information conveyed is about the names themselves: 'Tully' denotes the same object as 'Cicero' does. Mill's point is that there is no fact in the world to which 'Cicero is Tully' corresponds; a thought similar to that which inspired Wittgenstein's treatment of identity in the *Tractatus*. The obvious difficulty about assimilating them to verbal propositions on this basis is that knowledge that Cicero is Tully is not *a priori*. We cannot know the proposition to be true just by reflecting on the meaning of the names – whereas Mill's overall intention is that the class of verbal propositions should be identical with the class of propositions which are innocuously *a priori because* empty of content. He does not seem to notice this difficulty.

The meaning of a declarative sentence – 'the import of a proposition' – is determined by the connotation, not the denotation, of its constituent names; the sole exception being connotationless proper names, where meaning is determined by denotation. (Again there is something puzzling here, for it needs to be explained how this thesis about the meaning of proper names is to be reconciled with the aposteriority of 'Cicero is Tully'.) Mill proceeds to show how the various syntactic forms identified by syllogistic theory yield conditions of truth for sentences of those forms, when the connotation of their constituent names is given.

Armed with this analysis he argues that logic contains real inferences and propositions. (He assumes that to assert a conjunction, *A and B*, is simply to assert *A* and to assert *B*. He defines *A or B* as 'If not *A*, then *B*, and if not *B*, then *A*'. 'If *A* then *B*' means, he thinks, 'The proposition *B* is a legitimate inference from the proposition *A*'.)

His strategy is an admirably forceful pincer movement. One pincer is an indirect argument. If logic did not contain real inferences, all deductive reasoning would be a *petitio principii*, a begging of the question – it could produce no new knowledge. Yet clearly it does produce new knowledge. So logic must contain real inferences. The other pincer is a direct semantic analysis of the supposed 'axioms' of syllogistic reasoning and of the laws of thought. It shows them to be real and not merely verbal.

The execution of this strategy is flawed, because Mill mixes it up with an interesting but distinct objective. He wants to show that 'all inference is from particulars to particulars'. The point is to demystify the role general propositions play in thought. He argues that in principle they add nothing to the force of an argument; particular conclusions could always be derived inductively direct from particular premisses. Their value is psychological. They play the role of 'memoranda', summary records of the inductive potential of all that we have observed, and they facilitate 'trains of reasoning' (as e.g. in 'This is *A*, all *A*s are *B*s, no *B*s are *C*s, so this is not *C*'). Psychologically they greatly increase our memory and reasoning power, but epistemologically they are dispensable.

As Mill presents it, this thesis is tied in with his rejection of 'intuitive' knowledge of general truths and with his inductivism (which we shall come to shortly). For it assumes the illegitimacy of *hypothesizing* general propositions, as against generalizing to them from observation of singular conjunctions. Beneath this, however, there lies a deeper and obscurer sense in which a radical empiricist must hold that all inference is from particulars to particulars. For consider the inference from 'Everything is F' to 'a is F'. Is it a real or merely apparent inference? It is impossible to hold it real if one also wishes to argue that real inferences are *a posteriori*. But the only way of treating it as verbal which is open to Mill is to treat the premiss as a conjunction: 'a is F and b is F and ...' If that approach is precluded then all that remains is to deny that 'Everything is F' is propositional – it must, rather, express an inferential commitment.

Both approaches are very close to the surface in Mill's discussion of the syllogism, and he comes closest to the latter when he emphasizes that a general proposition is 'a memorandum of the nature of the conclusions which we are prepared to prove'. But these issues about generality (and about conditional propositions) do not emerge clearly in his analysis; like his treatment of proper names and of identity, they were destined to make a decisive appearance on the agenda of philosophical logic only later, in the twentieth century.

❧ MILL'S EMPIRICIST VIEW OF LOGIC, ❧ GEOMETRY AND ARITHMETIC

Though Mill's treatment of generality and the syllogism is somewhat confused and opaque, he is quite clear cut in holding the laws of contradiction and excluded middle to be real – and therefore *a posteriori* – propositions. He takes it that 'not P' is equivalent in meaning to 'it is false that P'; if we further assume the equivalence in meaning of P and 'It is true that P', the principle of contradiction becomes, as he puts it, 'the same proposition cannot at the same time be false and true'. 'I cannot look upon this' he says 'as a merely verbal proposition. I consider it to be, like other axioms, one of our first and most familiar generalizations from experience.' He makes analogous remarks about excluded middle, which turns – on these definitions – into the principle of bivalence, 'Either it is true that P or it is false that P'.

A truly radical empiricism! After this it is not surprising to find the same broad strategy applied to mathematics. If it was merely verbal, mathematical reasoning would be a *petitio principii*. Moreover a detailed semantic analysis shows that it does contain real propositions.

Mill provides brief but insightful empiricist sketches of geometry and arithmetic. On geometry he is particularly good. The theorems of geometry are deduced from premisses which are real propositions inductively established. (Deduction is itself of course a process of real inference.) These premisses, where they are not straightforwardly true of physical space, are true in the limit. Geometrical objects – points, lines, planes – are ideal or 'fictional' limits of ideally constructible material entities. Thus the real empirical assertion underlying an axiom such as 'Two straight lines cannot enclose a space' is something like 'The more closely two lines approach absolute breadthlessness and straightness, the smaller the space they enclose'.

Mill applies his distinction between denotation and connotation to show that arithmetical identities such as 'Two plus one equals three' are real propositions. Number terms denote 'aggregates' and connote certain attributes of aggregates. (He does not say that they denote those attributes of the aggregates, though perhaps he should have done.) 'Aggregates' are natural not abstract entities – 'collections' or 'agglomerations' individuated by a principle of aggregation. This theory escapes some of the famous but rather unfair criticisms Frege later made of it, but its viability none the less remains extremely doubtful. The trouble is that the respects in which aggregates have to differ from *sets* if they are to be credibly natural, and not abstract, entities are precisely those in which they seem to fail to produce a fully adequate ontology for arithmetic. (One can for example number numbers, but can there be aggregates of aggregates, or of attributes of aggregates, if aggregates are natural entities?)

However this may be, Mill's philosophical programme is clear. Arithmetic, like logic and geometry, is a natural science, concerning a particular department of the laws of nature – those concerning the compositional properties of aggregates. The upshot is that the fundamental principles of arithmetic and geometry, as well as of logic itself, are real. Given epistemological empiricism, it follows that deductive reasoning, 'ratiocination', is empirical. Mill has provided the first thoroughly naturalistic analysis of meaning and of deductive reasoning itself.

He distinguishes his own view from three others – 'conceptualism', 'nominalism' and 'realism'.

'Conceptualism' is his name for the view which takes the objects studied by logic to be psychological states or acts. It holds that names stand for 'ideas' which make up judgements and that 'a proposition is the expression of a relation between two ideas'. It confuses logic and psychology by assimilating propositions to judgements and attributes of objects to ideas. Against this doctrine Mill insists that

> All language recognises a difference between a doctrine or
> opinion, and the fact of entertaining the opinion; between
> assent, and what is assented to ... Logic, according to the
> conception here formed of it, has no concern with the nature of
> the act of judging or believing; the consideration of that act, as
> a phenomenon of the mind, belongs to another science.

(7: 87)

He traces conceptualism to the seventeenth century: it was introduced by Descartes, fostered by Leibniz and Locke, and has obscured the true status of logic – which is simply 'the Science of Science' – ever since.

The nominalists – Mill cites Hobbes – hold that logic and mathematics are entirely verbal. Mill takes this position much more seriously than conceptualism and seeks to refute it in detail. His main point is that nominalists are able to maintain their view only because they fail to distinguish between the denotation and the connotation of names, 'seeking for their meaning exclusively in what they denote' (7: 91).

Nominalists and conceptualists both hold that logic and mathematic can be known non-empirically, while yet retaining the view that no real proposition about the mind-independent world can be so known – but both are confused. But what if one abandons the thesis that no real proposition about the mind-independent world can be known *a priori*? The realists do that – they hold that logical and mathematical knowledge is knowledge of universals existing in an abstract Platonic domain; the terms that make up sentences being signs that stand for such universals. This is the view Mill takes least seriously – but versions of it were destined to stage a major revival in philosophy, and semantic analysis would be their main source.

In fact in the contemporary use of the term, Mill is himself a nominalist – he rejects abstract entities. That is why he treats aggregates as concrete objects, and attributes as natural properties rather than universals. But, just as severe difficulties lie in the way of treating the ontology of arithmetic in terms of aggregates rather than classes, so there are severe difficulties in the way of treating the ontology of general semantics without appealing to universals and classes, as well as to natural properties and objects. We can have no clear view of how Mill would have responded to these difficulties had they been made evident to him. But we can I think be fairly sure that he would have sought to maintain his nominalism.

However, the central target of Mill's attack is the doctrine that there are real *a priori* propositions. What, he asks, in practice goes on, when we hold a real proposition to be true *a priori*? We find its negation inconceivable, or that it is derived, by principles whose unsoundness we find inconceivable, from premises whose negation we find inconceivable. Mill is not offering a definition of what is meant by such terms as '*a priori*', or 'self-evident'; his point is that facts about what we find inconceivable are all that lends colour to the use of these terms.

They are facts about the limits, felt by us from the inside, on what we can imagine perceiving. Mill thought he could explain these facts about unthinkability, or imaginative unrepresentability, in associationist terms, and spent many pages claiming to do so. They are not very convincing pages, but that does not affect his essential point, which is this: the step from our inability to represent to ourselves the negation of a proposition, to acceptance of its truth, calls for justification. Moreover, the justification *itself* must be *a priori* if it is to show that the proposition is known *a priori*. (Thus Mill is prepared for example to concede the reliability of geometrical intuition: but he stresses that its reliability is an empirical fact, itself known inductively.)

At this point, Kant could agree. To vindicate the possibility of synthetic *a priori* knowledge calls, he claims, for nothing less than transcendental idealism. But without synthetic *a priori* knowledge, knowledge as such becomes impossible. The very possibility of knowledge requires that there be *a priori* elements in our knowledge.

❧ THE METHODS OF INDUCTION ❧ AND THEIR STATUS

The *System of Logic* in contrast sets out to vindicate in general terms the possibility of a scheme of scientific knowledge which appeals at no point whatever to an *a priori* principle. One point in the opposition between *Critical* and *naturalistic* epistemology, as we have noticed, is the latter's refusal to take seriously pure sceptical arguments; but naturalistic epistemology also has two other ingredients – an appeal to a natural, or in Mill's word 'spontaneous', agreement in propensities to reason, and what may be called an 'internal' vindication of these fundamental reasoning propensities. All three ingredients are present in the *System of Logic*.

For Mill, the basic form of reasoning – epistemologically, historically and psychologically – is enumerative induction, simple generalization from experience. This is the diposition to infer to the conclusion that all As are B from observation of a number of As which are all B. (Or to the conclusion that a given percentage of all As are B from observation of that percentage of Bs among a number of As.) We spontaneously agree in reasoning that way, and in holding that way of reasoning to be sound. The proposition 'Enumerative induction is rational' is not a verbal proposition. But nor is it grounded in an *a priori* intuition. All that Mill will say for it is that people in general, and the reader in particular, in fact agree on reflection in accepting it. It is on that basis alone that he rests its claim.

Mill's problem of induction, the problem *he* wants to solve, is not Hume's. In sidestepping the purely sceptical question about induction, Mill uses the analogy of a telescope which Thomas Reid had also used in a similar context – though in Reid the telescope is Reason as against Common Sense, while in Mill it is Scientific as against spontaneous induction:

> Assuredly, if induction by simple enumeration were an invalid process, no process grounded on it would be valid; just as no reliance could be placed on telescopes, if we could not trust our eyes. But though a valid process, it is a fallible one, and fallible in very different degrees: if therefore we can substitute for the more fallible forms of the process, an operation grounded on the same process in a less fallible form, we shall have effected a very material improvement. And this is what scientific induction does.
>
> (7: 567–8)

Mill's aim is to provide the telescope. The problem he starts from is not a sceptical but an internal one – why is it that some inductions are more trustworthy than others?

> Why is a single instance, in some cases, sufficient for a complete induction, while in others, myriads of concurring instances, without a single exception known or presumed, go such a very little way towards establishing a universal proposition?
> Whoever can answer this question . . . has solved the problem of induction.
>
> (7: 314)

Mill's answer takes the form of a natural history of the 'inductive process'. The point is to show how that process is internally vindicated by its actual success in establishing regularities, and how it eventually gives rise to more searching methods of investigation.

Mankind begins with 'spontaneous' and 'unscientific' inductions about particular unconnected natural phenomena or aspects of experience. Generalizations accumulate, interweave and are found to stand the test of time: they are not disconfirmed by further experience. As they accumulate and interweave, they justify the second-order inductive conclusion that *all* phenomena are subject to uniformity, and, more specifically, that all have discoverable sufficient conditions. In this less vague form, the principle of general uniformity becomes, given Mill's analysis of causation, the Law of Universal Causation. This conclusion in turn provides (Mill believes) the grounding assumption for a new style of reasoning about nature – eliminative induction.

In this type of reasoning, the assumption that a type of phenomenon has uniform causes, together with a (revisable) assumption about what its possible causes are, initiates a comparative inquiry in which the actual cause is identified by elimination. Mill formulates the logic of this eliminative reasoning in his well-known 'Methods of Empirical Inquiry'. His exposition is rather garbled but he was right to be proud of it, for it did show how effective eliminative reasoning can be. His picture of the interplay between enumerative and eliminative reasoning, and of the way it entrenches, from within, our rational confidence in the inductive process, is elegant and penetrating.

The improved scientific induction which results from this new style of reasoning spills back on to the principle of Universal Causation on which it rests, and raises its certainty to a new level. That in turn raises our confidence in the totality of particular enumerative inductions from which the principle is derived. In short, the amount of confidence with which one can rely on the 'inductive process' as a whole depends on the point which has been reached in its natural history – though the confidence to be attached to particular inductions always remains variable.

The fundamental norm of scientific reasoning, enumerative induction, is not a merely verbal principle. But what can it mean to deny that it is *a priori*? Mill says that we learn 'the laws of our rational faculty, like those of every other natural agency', only by 'seeing the agent at work'. He is quite right: we can find out what our most basic reasoning dispositions are, only by critical reflection on our practice. This reflective scrutiny of practice is, in a *certain* sense, an *a posteriori* process. It examines dispositions which we have before we examine them. Having examined our dispositions, we reach a reflective equilibrium in which we endorse some – and perhaps reject others. We endorse them as sound norms of reasoning.

But at this point the sceptic will ask by what right we do so – and Mill rules his question out of order. So denying that the fundamental principle of induction is *a priori* comes down, it seems, to just that ruling. Might it not just as well have been said that the principle is *a priori*? But that would suggest that there was some further story, Platonic or transcendental, to be had, which explained and legitimated our reasoning practice, and *this* is what Mill denies.

So too does the sceptic: the fact that the sceptic and the naturalist agree on that hardly shows why it is all right to rule the sceptic's question out of order. It seemed obvious to Mill's epistemological critics, whether they were realists or post-Kantian idealists, that this was evasive: naturalism could seem to differ from scepticism only by being uncritical.

Where Hume launches a sceptical assault on reason, Mill opens up *all* our beliefs to an empirical audit. Hume takes deduction for granted and raises sceptical questions about induction. Mill takes the legitimacy of natural reasoning propensities for granted, but he questions the aprioricity of deduction. Hume and Mill are both naturalistic radicals – but in quite different ways. Mill leaves no real principle of deduction, no common-sense belief entrenched – with one telling exception. The exception is our disposition to rely on the deliverances of memory, which he acknowledges, in the manner of Thomas Reid, to be 'ultimate'. But, with this exception, the only ultimate principle that survives in Mill's science of science is enumerative induction. The whole of science, he thinks, can be built by this single instrument.

❧ HYPOTHESIS ❧

This is Mill's *inductivism* – the view that enumerative induction is the only *ultimate* method of inference which puts us in possession of new truths. Is he right in thinking it to be so? The question produced an important, if confused, controversy between him and William Whewell (1794–1866). Their disagreement concerned the role of hypotheses. Whewell argued that the Hypothetical Method was fundamental in scientific inquiry: the method in which one argues to the truth of an hypothesis from the fact that it would explain observed phenomena.

Mill had read Whewell's *History of the Inductive Sciences* (1837), and he could hardly fail to be aware of the pervasiveness of hypotheses in the actual process of inquiry, or of their indispensableness in supplying working assumptions – their 'heuristic' value, Whewell called it. The same point – the indispensableness of hypotheses in providing lines of inquiry – had been emphasized by the Frenchman Auguste Comte, with whose *Cours de philosophie positive* (which began to appear in 1830) Mill was also familiar. But what Mill could not accept was that the mere fact that an hypothesis accounted for the data *in itself* provided a reason for thinking it true. He denied that the Hypothetical Method constituted, in its own right, a method of arriving at new truths from experience.

Yet Whewell's appeal was to the actual practice of scientific reasoning, as observed in the history of science. An appeal of that kind was precisely what Mill, on his own naturalistic principles, could not ignore. The disposition to hypothesize is spontaneous, so why should it not be recognized as a fundamental method of reasoning to truth, as enumerative induction is?

Mill's refusal to recognize it is not arbitrary. The essential point underlying it is a powerful one: it is the possibility that a body of data may be explained equally well by more than one hypothesis. What justifies us in concluding, from the fact that a particular story would, if true, explain the data, that it is a true story? Other stories may equally explain the data.

Mill places great emphasis on the increasingly deductive and mathematical organization of science – that is quite compatible with his inductivism, and indeed central to it. But he takes the 'Deductive Method' of science to involve three steps: 'induction', 'ratiocination', and 'verification'. A paradigm, in his view, is Newton's explanation of Kepler's laws of planetary motion. Induction establishes causal laws of motion and attraction, ratiocination deduces lower level regularities from them in conjunction with observed conditions, and verification tests these deduced propositions against observation. (Though this was not, and did not need to be, the historical order of inquiry.) But

> the Hypothetical Method suppresses the first of the three steps, the induction to ascertain the law; and contents itself with the other two operations, ratiocination and verification; the law which is reasoned from being assumed, instead of proved.
>
> (7: 492)

Mill agrees that it is legitimate to do this when the hypothesis in question has effectively been shown, by eliminative reasoning, to be the only one consistent with the facts. He allows various other cases of apparently purely hypothetical reasoning which are, in his view, genuinely inductive.

When all such cases have been taken into account, we are left with pure cases of the Hypothetical Method, in which the causes postulated are not directly observable, and not simply because they are assumed to operate – in accordance with known laws, inductively established – in regions of time or space too distant to observe. What are we to say of such hypotheses? For example of the 'emission' theory, or the 'undulatory' theory of light? They cannot be accepted as inductively established truths, not even as probable ones:

> an hypothesis of this kind is not to be received as probably true because it accounts for all the known phenomena; since this is a condition sometimes fulfilled tolerably well by two conflicting hypotheses; while there are probably many others which are equally possible, but which from want of anything analogous in our experience, our minds are unfitted to conceive.
>
> (7: 500)

Such an hypothesis can suggest fruitful analogies, Mill thinks, but cannot be regarded as yielding a new truth itself. The data do not determine a unique hypothesis: it is this possibility, of underdetermination, which stops him from accepting hypothetical reasoning as an independent method of achieving truth, even though it is a mode of reasoning as spontaneous as enumerative induction.

In seeing the difficulty Mill is certainly on sound ground. What he does not see, however, is how much must be torn from the fabric of our belief if inductivism is applied strictly. Thus, for example, while his case for empiricism about logic and mathematics is very strong, it is his methodology of science which then forces him to hold that we know basic logical and mathematical principles only by an enumerative induction. And that is desperately implausible.

So it is an important question whether the difficulty can be resolved – and whether it can be resolved within a naturalistic frame-work, which does not yield to idealism. If naturalism can endorse the hypothetical method, it can develop a more plausible empiricism about logic and mathematics than Mill's. But the ramifications of his inductivism are even wider, as becomes apparent if we turn to his general metaphysics.

❧ THE DOCTRINE OF THE RELATIVITY OF ❧ KNOWLEDGE

Mill sets this out in his *Examination of Sir William Hamilton's Philosophy* (1865). Sir William Hamilton (1791–1856) was a Scotsman who sought to moderate the views of Reid and Kant. He was a philosopher of subtlety and erudition (or even pedantry), the last eminent representative of the school of Scottish common sense, and a ferocious controversialist. Mill deemed him a pillar of the right-thinking intellectual establishment, ripe for demolition. But by the time the *Examination* appeared Hamilton's death had made it impossible for him to reply – a fact which predictably caused Mill some regret. For the present-day reader, however, what is more regrettable is that Mill's discussion of general metaphysical issues should be cast in so polemical a form. It means that important issues, particularly on the nature of logic and thought, remain shrouded in obscurity. Mill does however give himself space to develop his view of our knowledge of the external world.

He begins by expounding a doctrine which he rightly takes to be generally accepted (in his time) on all sides. It affirms

> that all the attributes which we ascribe to objects, consist in their having the power of exciting one or another variety of sensation in our minds; that an object is to us nothing else than that which affects our senses in a certain manner; that even an imaginary object is but a conception, such as we are able to form, of something which would affect our senses in some new way; so that our knowledge of objects; and even our fancies about objects, consist of nothing but the sensations which they excite, or which we imagine them exciting, in ourselves.
>
> (9: 6)

This is 'the doctrine of the Relativity of Knowledge to the knowing mind'. But there are two forms in which it may be held.

> According to one of the forms, the sensations which, in common parlance, we are said to receive from objects, are not only all that we can possibly know of the objects, but are all that we have any ground for believing to exist. What we term an object is but a complex conception made up by the laws of association, out of the ideas of various sensations which we are accustomed to receive simultaneously. There is nothing real in the process but these sensations.
>
> (9: 6)

According to the other,

> there is a real universe of 'Things in Themselves,' and . . . whenever there is an impression on our senses, there is a 'Thing in itself,' which is behind the phaenomenon, and is the cause of it. But as to what this Thing *is* 'in itself,' we, having no organs except our senses for communicating with it, can only know what our senses tell us; and as they tell us nothing but the impression which the thing makes upon *us*, we do not know what it is *in itself* at all. We suppose (at least these philosophers suppose) that it must be something 'in itself', but all that we know it to be is merely relative to us, consisting in the power of affecting us in certain ways.
>
> (9: 7)

The first form (omitting from it the appeal to laws of association) corresponds to what is meant by 'phenomenalism' as the term is often used by philosophers today – though it was not so used in Mill's time.

Reid's point, that sensations are not representative mental images but states of mind, does not contradict the doctrine of the Relativity of Knowledge, any more than his thesis that we perceive physical objects does. For on his account sensations, states of sensory consciousness, do mediate between the objects that excite them and the beliefs about those objects which are prompted by them – they are themselves distinct from both the objects and the beliefs. I cannot perceive without sensing. But I can sense without perceiving. For example I may have a visual sensation which prompts me to believe that I am seeing a red triangle on a green field. It is then apparently true to say, in an obvious and legitimate sense, that what I am immediately aware or conscious of is my visual sensation. That remains true even if I am perceiving no red triangle because no red triangle exists. Or, if one objects to talk of consciousness *of* a state of consciousness, one may simply say that my

immediate visual consciousness is of a red triangle on a green field –
in a sense in which that can be true though there is no such triangle.

This is already enough to make epistemology, in Mill's phrase, the
'Interpretation of Consciousness'. The very fact of consciousness seems
to impose the doctrine of the Relativity of Knowledge. To escape it,
something more counter-intuitive would be required than the sensible
points Reid makes about perception and sensation. It is notoriously
difficult to pin down what that might be. Perhaps what is needed is
nothing less than a denial that sensation is a category ontologically
distinct from that of judgement and dispositions to judge: there is no
irreducible category of Pure Experience. But Mill, at any rate, questions
the irreducible status of sensation no more than Reid did. And he
thinks it must follow that – whether or not we *actually* make an
inductive inference from sensations to objects beyond sensation – such
an inference is, epistemologically speaking, *required*.

Is this too hasty? Is it dogmatism on Reid's part simply to point
out that we do form particular beliefs prompted by particular sensations, beliefs which we just do regard as rational? Cannot these
specific cognitive dispositions be defended naturalistically, if the general
disposition to make enumerative inductions can? But there is a difference. If we are immediately conscious only of states of affairs of one
kind (our own sensory states) and on that basis form beliefs about
states of affairs of a *quite distinct* kind (states of external physical
objects) then some warrant is required. Reid needs to show why such
a warrant does not have to rely on inductive inference – even though
it licenses a belief in a state of affairs on the basis of immediate
consciousness of a *quite distinct* state of affairs. He must call on warrants which are neither deductive nor inductive. And this requires
support from ideas in the theory of meaning which had not yet been
formed. We shall return to the point.

❧ MATTER AND MIND ❧

Mill sets about the notion of an 'external' object in great style:

> What is it we mean, or what is it which leads us to say, that the
> objects we perceive are external to us, and not a part of our
> own thoughts? We mean, that there is concerned in our
> perceptions something which exists when we are not thinking
> of it; which existed before we had ever thought of it, and would
> exist if we were annihilated; and further, that there exist things
> which we never saw, touched, or otherwise perceived, and
> things which have never been perceived by man. This idea of

something which is distinguished from our fleeting impressions by what, in Kantian language, is called Perdurability; something which is fixed and the same, while our impressions vary; something which exists whether we are aware of it or not, and which is always square (or of some other given figure) whether it appears to us square or round – constitutes altogether our idea of external substance. Whoever can assign an origin to this complex conception, has accounted for what we mean by the belief in matter.

(9: 178–9)

To assign this origin Mill postulates

that after having had actual sensations, we are capable of forming the conception of Possible sensations; sensations which we are not feeling at the present moment, but which we might feel, and should feel if certain conditions were present, the nature of which conditions we have, in many cases, learnt by experience.

(9: 177)

These various possibilities are the important thing to me in the world. My present sensations are generally of little importance, and are moreover fugitive: the possibilities, on the contrary, are permanent, which is the character that mainly distinguishes our idea of Substance or Matter from our notion of sensation. These possibilities, which are conditional certainties, need a special name to distinguish them from mere vague possibilities, which experience gives no warrant for reckoning upon. Now, as soon as a distinguishing name is given, though it be only to the same thing regarded in a different aspect, one of the most familiar experiences of our mental nature teaches us, that the different name comes to be considered as the name of a different thing.

(9: 179–80)

We may speak of *sensation conditionals* of the form, 'If such and such sensations were to occur, then such and such other sensations would occur with a given degree of probability'. (It need not always be certainty.) They express Mill's famous 'Permanent Possibilities of Sensation'. 'Permanent' is slightly misleading, for there is of course a change in the 'Permanent' possibilities of sensation whenever there is change in the world. Mill also uses other terms – 'certified', 'guaranteed'.

We regularly find that whole clusters of sensation conditionals are true together, whenever some other sensory condition obtains. Thus whenever we experience that condition, we are justified in forming all the conditional expectations expressed in that cluster of conditionals. Moreover, as well as finding simultaneous correlations between certified possibilities of sensation, that is, between the truth of any sensation conditional in a set and the truth of any other in the set, we also find 'an Order of succession'. Whenever a given cluster of certified possibilities of sensation obtains, then a certain other cluster follows – a certain other set of sensation conditionals *becomes* true. 'Hence our ideas of causation, power, activity... become connected, not with sensations, but with groups of possibilities of sensation' (9: 181).

But even if our reflective concept of matter – as the external cause of sensations – can be explained on psychological principles, it remains open for someone to accept the proposed *origin* for the concept, while also holding that good grounds can be given for thinking it to have instances. He or she will say that a legitimate inference can be made from the existence of the Permanent Possibilities and their correlations to the existence of an external cause of our sensations. It is at just this point that Mill's inductivism comes in. Such an inference would be a case of hypothetical reasoning, to an explanation of experience which transcended all possible data of experience; and that is just what Mill rejects: 'I assume only the tendency, but not the legitimacy of the tendency, to extend all the laws of our own experience to a sphere beyond our experience' (9: 187). So the conclusion that matter is the permanent possibility of sensation follows from the combination of the doctrine of the Relativity of Knowledge and inductivism.

If matter is the permanent possibility of sensation, what is mind? Mill considers that 'our knowledge of mind, like that of matter, is entirely relative'. Can the mind then also be resolved into 'a series of feelings, with a background of possibilities of feeling'? He finds in this view a serious difficulty: to remember or expect a state of consciousness is not simply to believe that it has existed or will exist; it is to believe that *I myself* have experienced or will experience that state of consciousness.

> If, therefore, we speak of the Mind as a series of feelings, we are obliged to complete the statement by calling it a series of feelings which is aware of itself as past and future; and we are reduced to the alternative of believing that the Mind, or Ego, is something different from any series of feelings, or possibilities of them, or of accepting the paradox, that something which *ex hypothesi* is but a series of feelings, can be aware of itself as a series.
>
> (9: 194)

Mill is unwilling to accept 'the common theory of Mind, as a so-called substance': nevertheless, the self-consciousness involved in memory and expectation drives him to 'ascribe a reality to the Ego – to my own Mind – different from that real existence as a Permanent Possibility, which is the only reality I acknowledge in Matter' (9: 208).

If we discount this conscientious uncertainty about what to say of the self, the tendency of Mill's analysis is towards the view that all that exist are experiences in a temporal order. Yet he claims, like others before and after him, that this metaphysics is consistent with common-sense realism about the world. Phenomenalism, he thinks, leaves common sense and science untouched. In particular, minds and experiences are still properly to be seen as a part of the natural order.

But are the experiences referred to, in the phenomenalist's analysis, the very same as those referred to in common sense and scientific talk (call this 'naturalistic' talk)? If they are not, then we have yet to be told *what* they are. Then suppose they are the same. In naturalistic talk, we make reference to subjects and their experiences – and also to physical objects and their properties. Psychology, including Mill's psychology, seeks to establish causal correlations among experiences and their physiological antecedents and consequents.

But if phenomenalism is right, only the experiences are real. Mill thinks we are led to that by the very standards of reasoning recognized in a naturalistic 'science of science', or 'system of logic'. If he is right, then the naturalistic vision of the world, which sees minds as part of a larger causal order, is self-undermining. For if we are led to the conclusion, that only states of consciousness are real, *by an application of naturalism's own standards*, then that conclusion has to be understood *on the same level* as the naturalistic affirmation that states of consciousness are themselves part of a larger causal order external to them – and therefore as inconsistent with it. Causal relations cannot exist between fictional entities which are mere markers for *possibilities* of sensation.

So either naturalism undermines itself or there is something wrong with Mill's inductivist analysis of our natural norms of reasoning, or with his endorsement of the doctrine of the Relativity of Knowledge, or both. It is not our business to diagnose the situation further here. But it should not be assumed that Mill's most fundamental tenet – his naturalistic view of the mind – can be safeguarding solely by rejecting inductivism and endorsing the hypothetical method. The result would be a philosophy which postulates the external world as an inference to an hypothetical explanation of pure experience. Something still fails to ring true in that. More is needed: backing for the view mentioned earlier, a view which may be thought of as in the spirit of Thomas Reid, though he did not give it the necessary backing – the view, namely, that there are norms which are neither inductive nor deductive, but which defeasibly warrant experience-based assertions about the physical world.

❧ MORAL FREEDOM ❧

The necessary backing, showing how such defeasible warrants can obtain, could be provided only by a philosophy which treats concepts, and the meanings of expressions in a language, as constituted by rules of use. This conception of concept and meaning is not present in Mill, though it could be reached by a sound progression from his naturalistic analysis of logic, and his rejection of conceptualism, nominalism and realism. Its growth can probably best be dated to the next generation of philosophers after Mill, and to the agenda of problems which they developed (partly at least in response to and reaction against Mill) at the end of the century; thus, to pragmatism, empirio-criticism, as also in some respects to neo-Kantianism and British idealism. That same conception opens up the possibility of new responses to Mill's problem about the method of inference to the best hypothetical explanation – which was that in cases of genuine hypothesis we cannot be certain that there *is* a single best explanation.

Though the roots of the required conception of concept and meaning date to that period, how best to formulate it is still an open issue. Moreover the most difficult (though not unconnected) question for the naturalist, that of giving an account of reasons, still remains. As we have seen, it stands out as an obstacle for Mill when he needs to account for the authority of fundamental norms of reasoning. And it also stands out when he tries to show how, on the naturalistic view, it is possible for human beings to be morally free.

This was a central issue for Mill. He deals with it as it appears in the classic question of freedom and determinism. His commitment to determinism was complete. But the conclusion drawn by others from that doctrine, that we have (in Mill's phrase) no 'power of *self*-formation', and hence are not responsible, properly speaking, for our character or our actions, would have destroyed the very centre of his moral convictions. Power to determine one's own purposes and hold to them, responsibility for one's actions, are at the heart of Mill's ideal of life. 'Moral freedom', the ability to bring one's desires under the control of a steady rational purpose, is a condition of self-realization, of having a character in the full sense at all.

So he must show how causally conditioned natural objects can also be rationally autonomous agents. The sketch of a compatibilist solution which he provides in the *System of Logic* is brief but penetrating. He thought it the best chapter in the book. It is certainly a worthy contribution to the great empiricist tradition, which dismisses the problem as a perennially tempting confusion, to be dissolved by careful analysis.

To describe determinism as the doctrine of 'Philosophical Necessity' is, Mill thinks, misleading. Not just because of the general empiricist point that causation is not compulsion but for a more subtle reason; because 'in common use' only causes which are *irresistible*, whose operation is 'supposed too powerful to be counteracted at all' are called necessary:

> There are physical sequences which we call necessary, as death for want of food or air; there are others which, though as much cases of causation as the former, are not said to be necessary, as death from poison, which an antidote, or the use of the stomach-pump, will sometimes avert... human actions are in this last predicament: they are never (except in some cases of mania) ruled by any one motive with such absolute sway, that there is no room for the influence of another.
>
> (8: 839)

This is a general distinction, but Mill is right to think it important for the analysis of free action. It can be applied to motives; an action caused by an irresistible motive is plainly not free. Without the distinction between resistible and irresistible causes, determinism turns into fatalism. We lose the sense of our moral freedom, which rests on the conviction that the motives on which we in fact acted were resistible. We fall into the idea that we have no power over our character; no ability to resist motives which we dislike or to choose to act on those which we admire.

Now incompatibilists will concede that changes in our character may result from behaviour which is itself caused by the wish to change our character. But they will not concede that this is a true case of 'self-formation', because they think the wish to change our character is heteronomous: it comes from without. And they think that follows simply from the fact that the wish is determined, ultimately if not proximately, by external circumstances. So Mill has to show that while the wish must indeed be determined, that does not entail heteronomy. It can still be *my* wish.

He cannot answer simply by invoking the distinction between resistible and irresistible motives. For a motive might perfectly well not be irresistible, in that it could be blocked by other motives – yet still be heteronomous. Something has to be added if we are to move from the idea of my motives being resistible, in the sense that they could be trumped by conflicting motives, to the stronger idea that *I* have the power to resist motives. That idea is the idea of rationality: the ability to recognize and respond to reasons. I act freely if I could have resisted the motive on which I in fact acted *had there been good reason to do so*. A motive which impairs my moral freedom is one that cannot be defeated by a cogent reason for not acting on it. The difference between a heteronomous agent, driven by conflicting motives which are capable of checking each other, and an autonomous agent who himself or herself resists the motive, lies in the fact that the latter responds to, and acts on, reasons.

Acting from good reason is still acting from a motive which is causally determining. What matters is how the motive determines: it must be so related to the facts, as they are believed to stand by the agent, as to constitute a good reason and it must also be the case that the agent acts on it *as* a reason. The same holds for the will to alter our character. It must indeed always be caused, and hence caused ultimately by circumstances we cannot help. But it still satisfies the conditions of moral freedom, if it results from our grasping that there is reason to change ourselves, and not, say, from indoctrination or obsession.

Moral freedom for Mill is the ability to act on good reasons, as autonomy is for Kant; though Mill does not highlight the point as Kant rightly does. And of course it is not, for Mill, transcendental. It is something I may have to a greater or less degree. I am more or less free overall, according to the degree to which I can bring my motives under scrutiny and act on the result of that scrutiny, I can *make* myself more free, by shaping my motives or at least by cultivating the strength of will to overcome them

> A person feels morally free who feels that his habits or his temptations are not his masters, but he theirs: who even in yielding to them knows that he could resist; that were he desirous of altogether throwing them off, there would not be required for that purpose a stronger desire than he knows himself to be capable of feeling. . . . we must feel that our wish, if not strong enough to alter our character, is strong enough to conquer our character when the two are brought into conflict in any particular case of conduct. And hence it is said with truth, that none but a person of confirmed virtue is completely free.
>
> (8: 841)

The person of confirmed virtue is the person who can conquer desires, when there is reason to do so, by a virtuous habit of willing. One must be careful not to assume that Mill, because he is an empiricist, is in the Humean tradition which holds reason to be a slave of the passions. We have already emphasized the difference between Hume's scepticism about both theoretical and practical reason, and the naturalistic epistemological stance taken in different ways by Reid and Mill. In the practical as in the theoretical case Mill is best understood not as denying the existence of categorical reasons, in the sceptical style of Hume, but as quietly naturalizing them. He takes it that talk of principles of theoretical and practical reason, and of our recognition of such principles, is justified. But the fact remains that he does not explain how it is justified, if nothing is *a priori*.

He does not dramatize the issue, as Kant's Critical philosophy does. And he does not confront the Critical questions: what is it for a reason to exist, what is it to grasp a reason, how can reason be efficacious? But, on his own showing these questions must be answered, in a fashion compatible with naturalism, if we are to make sense of ordinary categories – reasoning, inferring, deliberating, deciding – categories which involve thinking of agents and reasoners as free followers of rationally given norms. For while inference does seem to be a causal process it yet also appears to be something more than, or incommensurable with, a causal process. It seems to involve the *acausal* consciousness of a rule of reason. Precisely the same can be said for the rationalizing relation between motive or deliberation, and free action or choice.

∾ NATURALIZED EPISTEMOLOGY ∾

This Kantian argument, that naturalism cannot account for the rationality of experience, thought and action, was taken up by Mill's idealist successors in Britain. led by T. H. Green. They elevated Hume, who was held to have perceived it, over Mill, who was felt to have hidden his face from it, or been unable to grasp it. And certainly Mill offers no thoroughgoing examination of what, on his own philosophy, the status of fundamental norms of reason is – how they can have objective authority. He merely takes it that they do. The same applies to Reid. Like Reid, Mill assumes that any cognitive disposition which is 'ultimate', original or spontaneous thereby underpins an objective norm. We have seen this in his treatment of beliefs based on memory, as well as beliefs based on induction, and the same applies to his well-known derivation of what is desirable from what is desired 'in theory and in practice'. The similarity between Reid and Mill, on this fundamental point of naturalistic epistemological method – *the appeal to spontaneous dispositions which survive critical reflection* – is easy to miss. It is obscured by the undeniably important disagreement between them in what they actually place on their respective lists of fundamental principles, as also by the intrusion of the controversy between innatist and associationist psychology. But terms like 'ultimate', 'spontaneous', 'natural', etc. need not mean 'innate' – one must not confuse a phenomenon which is important for epistemological method – that of finding a principle naturally obvious – with a particular psychological explanation of its origin.

The divergence between Hume's sceptical naturalism, together with its Kantian and idealist sequels, and the naturalistic epistemology taken for granted by Reid, Mill and others became a great divide in nineteenth-century philosophy. The most influential philosophers in the heyday of the analytic movement in the twentieth century stand also in the Critical rather than the naturalistic epistemological tradition. More recently, however, that has changed, largely through the influence of Quine. 'Naturalized epistemology' is once more influential. The questions concerning it remain the same. Today, as in Mill's time, one can ask whether there *is* any route open to the naturalist, between Humean scepticism and Kantian idealism.

If there is, it requires a sharper distinction than Mill, or indeed Quine, makes between norms and facts. Mill argued soundly from the naturalistic premiss, that no *factual* statement can be *a priori*. But the same is not true of *normative* statements. For *all* that grounds the objectivity of norms is reflective equilibrium and convergence – as indeed Mill's epistemological method implies. Having recognized this crucial point, one may innocently concede that statements about fundamental norms are – in a way Mill himself could have accepted, that is, a way which requires no transcendental or platonic mystery – *a priori*. Norms constitute the concepts which order our thought. Rationality, grasp of concepts, consists in sensitivity to them; it cannot therefore belong in the realm of the factual, any more than the norms themselves do. If this conception of concept and meaning can be made out, we can endorse Mill's naturalistic view of man.

❧ BIBLIOGRAPHY ❧

Citations of passages from Mill are by volume and page number of the *Collected Works of John Stuart Mill*, ed. J. M. Robson (London and Toronto: University of Toronto Press and Routledge & Kegan Paul, 1963–). The following volumes have been cited:

4.1   VII, VIII, *A System of Logic, Ratiocinative and Inductive: Being a Connected View of the Principles of Evidence and the Methods of Scientific Investigation*, textual editor J. M. Robson; introduction by R. F. McRae, 1973.

4.2   IX, *An Examination of Sir William Hamilton's Philosophy and of the Principal Philosophical Questions discussed in his Writings*, textual editor: J. M. Robson, introduction by A. Ryan, 1979.

See also:

4.3   Ryan, A. *J. S. Mill*, London: Routledge and Kegan Paul, 1974.

4.4   Scarre, G. *Logic and Reality in the Philosophy of John Stuart Mill*, Dordrecht: Kluwer, 1989.

4.5   Skorupski, J. *John Stuart Mill*, London: Routledge, 1989.

CHAPTER 5
Sidgwick
C. A. J. Coady

Unlike John Stuart Mill or Jeremy Bentham, Henry Sidgwick's is hardly a household name in intellectual circles beyond the world of professional philosophy. His standing amongst many contemporary moral philosophers as possibly the greatest nineteenth-century writer on ethics would come as a shock to such householders, as would C. D. Broad's estimate of his book *The Methods of Ethics* as 'one of the English philosophical classics' and 'on the whole the best treatise on moral theory that has ever been written' ([5.15], 143). This high reputation could indeed be disputed, but it is not at all idiosyncratic. It is a reputation that has grown since his own time, and is probably at its peak today, but Sidgwick's intellectual power impressed many of his contemporaries, and immediate successors, as well. 'Pure, white light' was one description offered of his intellectual presence ([5.13], 181), and the adjective 'pure' tells as much about the moral intensity with which he applied his mind to the problems that exercised him as the word 'light' testifies to the clarifying power of his intelligence.

Sidgwick was a typical Victorian in many respects, and, in fact, his life paralleled that of the woman to whom the era owed its name. He was born in the north of England at Skipton on 31 May 1838, less than twelve months after Queen Victoria assumed the throne and he died on 28 August 1900, preceding his monarch by about six months. He was the son of an Anglican clergyman who was the principal of a grammar school in Skipton. His father died when he was three, and a strong influence upon his early life was his second cousin, E. W. Benson, a man who was later to be Archbishop of Canterbury. Benson lived with the Sidgwick family for some years, and eventually (in 1859) married Sidgwick's sister. Benson persuaded Sidgwick's mother to send the boy to Rugby school (where he was himself to be, shortly afterwards, a master) even though Sidgwick's father had been against a public school education for his children. Benson argued that the public schools, and especially Rugby, under the influence of Arnold, no longer had the poor 'moral tone' that Sidgwick senior had feared. Henry Sidgwick later recalled that Benson was ' a great believer in the close and minute study of language that was in his time specially characteristic of Cambridge scholarship' ([5.12], 149) and it is plausible to see this influence at work in Sidgwick's later philosophical writings, though the close attention is not only to language but to the detail of concept and theory. Benson's influence waned after Sidgwick went up to Trinity College, Cambridge in October, 1855. For the first half of his under-graduate career, Sidgwick 'had no other ideal than to be a scholar as like him as possible', but other influences then brought him to doubt many of the moral and, especially, religious certainties that sustained his cousin. These influences included at the global level the writings of Mill, Comte, Spencer, Strauss, Renan, Matthew Arnold, George Eliot and Darwin, and more locally the intense debates that went on amongst the clever young men in the society known as 'the Apostles', which he joined in his second year. Sidgwick described his joining the Apostles as having 'more effect on my intellectual life than any one thing that happened to me afterwards'. He described the spirit of the group as that of 'the pursuit of truth with absolute devotion and unreserve by a group of intimate friends' ([5.30], 134).

❧ THE RELIGIOUS BACKGROUND ❧

Victorian England has been faulted for many things, but moral frivolity is not one of them. In spite of a good deal of hypocrisy about public manners, it was an age that was, in one way or another, obsessed with morality. The leading intellects of the time were particularly concerned with the nature and role of morality in a world in which religion had become problematical. For continental thinkers, like Nietzsche, the crisis in Christianity meant a crisis in morality, but for so many English (indeed British) intellectuals, religious doubts seemed an occasion for consolidating morality, for making it more, not less, firm and central to life. There is a reported comment of George Eliot that puts the matter succinctly. Asked how morality could subsist in the absence of religious faith, she replied that God was 'inconceivable', immortality was 'unbelievable', but duty none the less remained 'peremptory and absolute' ([5.20], 21). In many ways, Sidgwick's philosophical career could be seen as devoted to the securing of this central position for morality by providing it with the requisite intellectual foundations, which he believed to be available within the intellectual tradition of utilitarianism. Certainly he was concerned to maintain the 'peremptory' or demanding power of moral claims over our reasoning on practical matters though he may well have been uncomfortable with Eliot's reference to absolute duty. Under the influence of John Stuart Mill, and Mill's interpretation of Comte, he saw this project as part of a scientific endeavour to bring about a comprehensive reform of social life. He understood that he had set himself no easy task and the personal and intellectual honesty that were amongst his most notable attributes would not allow him to disguise this fact from himself or his readers. As we shall see, this strong and confident commitment to honesty and to reason had certain ironic and sad consequences for his final philosophical conclusions. It also created a personal crisis with regard to his Fellowship at Trinity which he felt obliged to resign in 1869, after ten years as a Fellow, because it required a subscription to the 39 Articles of the Church of England, and to these he could no longer in honesty commit himself. This did not prove vocationally disastrous because the College then appointed him to a position that did not require subscription and when the law about subscription was eventually changed he was reappointed a Fellow.

Sidgwick's honesty, conjoined with his commitment to an ideal of 'strict scientific impartiality' ([5.12], 250), led him not only to a persistent scrutiny of his own religious views and those prevailing in the community but to certain general doubts about Christianity that, whilst being characteristic of the time in many respects, were also distinctively his own. These in turn enlivened his interest in the relation of religion and morality and in the need to establish what would now be called 'the autonomy of ethics', but they also led him to suspect easy attempts to disentangle morals and religion, and to an uncomfortable resolution of the original problem.

It would be a mistake to think of Sidgwick as dismissive of the moral and cognitive claims of Christianity or religion, in the fashion of twentieth-century logical positivists, for example, or in the casual fashion of some of his contemporaries. He was persistently interested in a scientific approach to theology, an interest that extended to the vigorous promotion of the work of the Society for Psychical Research, of which he was the first President. He was also as critical of the confident excesses of those who shared his 'scientific' ideal as he was of more conservative thinkers. This can be seen in his comment on rereading Comte and Spencer: 'Have been reading Comte and Spencer, with all my old admiration for their intellectual force and industry and more than my old amazement at their fatuous self-confidence. It does not seem to me that either of them knows what self-criticism means' ([5.30], 421). Sidgwick could not share this self-confidence, partly because of his highly developed critical sense, and partly because of his sense of the deep complexity, even mysteriousness, of the world we live in. In this connection, he quotes Bagehot approvingly: 'Undeniably, this is an odd world, whether it should have been so or no; and all our speculations upon it should begin with some admission of its strangeness and singularity' ([5.30], 395).

Sidgwick never lost his sense of the central importance of religion in human life though he found it difficult to give an account of what that importance amounted to and what its intellectual credentials could be. The gap he detected between the demands of 'scientific' reason and the requirements of faith made him at times sympathetic to the claims of Roman Catholicism. His early mentor, Benson, had struggled against an attraction to Rome and the figure of Cardinal Newman apparently aroused 'a mixture of alarm and fascination' in Benson ([5.21], 3). Sidgwick's correspondence with Cardinal Newman's nephew, J. R. Mozley, is instructive on this and on his complex, and somewhat convoluted, attitude to Christianity and theism. Written in January 1891, the letters express an admiration for Newman's individuality of thought and expression and the fusion of both, but show a certain distaste for Newman's mode of reasoning which Sidgwick thinks to be somewhat 'feminine, in the old traditional sense'. Sidgwick seems to mean that Newman's 'conclusions have always been primarily influenced by his emotions, and only secondarily by the workings of his subtle and ingenious intellect' ([5.30], 507). Leaving aside this dubious, if hoarily traditional, account of feminine thinking, we may note the way that Sidgwick here makes a sharp separation of reason and emotion, and goes on, in a subsequent letter, to attach the value of religion and specifically Christianity to its emotional appeal, particularly its appeal to a certain attitude of optimism that he regards as 'an indispensable creed – not for every one, but for progressive humanity as a whole'. He thinks that no form of optimism has an adequate rational basis, and so cannot himself endorse it since he 'has taken service with Reason' ([5.30], 508). It is tempting to see in Sidgwick's attitude to religion and Christianity another sign of the tension between reason and utility that emerges in his writings on ethics. This is particularly striking in his discussion of the relations between common-sense morality and utilitarianism and in what I discuss below as 'Sidgwick's paradox'. Just as it may be for the best from the point of view of rational utility that the majority continue to practise ordinary morality as if it were self-sufficiently justified and be kept ignorant of the truth of utilitarianism, so it may be practically desirable that ordinary mortals should adhere to religion without the disturbance of knowing their commitments to be irrational. But more of this later.

❧ PERSONAL CHARACTER AND VIEW OF ❧
PHILOSOPHY

Sidgwick was not a man for disciples. Indeed there was a striking contrast between attendances at his Cambridge lectures and those of his Oxford counterpart, the idealist liberal philosopher T. H. Green, which is not altogether explained by the considerable differences between the place of philosophy in the curricula of the two universities. The economist Alfred Marshall had clashed with Sidgwick in 1884 over what seemed to him the latter's 'mania for over-regulation' and had then written Sidgwick a letter claiming that Sidgwick's career had been spoiled by involvement in administration and his devotion to teaching 'a wretched handful of undergraduates' what they needed to know for the Moral Sciences Tripos exams. He compared Sidgwick's intellectual impact unfavourably with T. H. Green's at Oxford: where Sidgwick's classes were attended by a handful of undergraduates taking down what they regarded as useful for examinations, Green's were attended by 'a hundred men – half of them B.A.'s – ignoring examinations, . . . to hang on the lips of the man who was sincerely anxious to teach them the truth about the universe and human life' ([5.30], 394).

Characteristically, Sidgwick was not offended, but took the opportunity to reflect on what he thought accurate in the criticisms. His reflections help us to locate his view of philosophy and of the intellectual life against some prevailing fashions, and to see where they compare with twentieth-century developments. Sidgwick did not envy Green his audiences because he thought them purchased at a price he was not prepared to pay, namely, the presentation of 'incomplete solutions of the universe . . . as complete and satisfying' ([5.30], 395).[1] His intellectual temperament was inclined to the admission of uncertainty and the patient dissection of problems; he was ill at ease with declamation and heady simplifications. This makes his work congenial to certain strands in modern analytical philosophy, as does his thoroughgoing professionalism, and his emphatic, though qualified, respect for common sense. These things set him apart from those of his contemporaries (like Green) who were enamoured of Hegel. It is interesting that T. H. Green's moral philosophy is today virtually unread, while Sidgwick is probably more influential than ever.

It should not be assumed, however, that Sidgwick thought of philosophy as a purely piecemeal activity, as a set of skills with no particular output other than the therapeutic ('showing the fly the way out of the fly-bottle' in Wittgenstein's phrase). He viewed philosophy as an attempt at systematic understanding of the world, though he was conscious of the inconclusiveness of many of its achievements, and aware that one of its persistent virtues was the turning of elusive philosophical material into more manageable scientific problems. He would have recognised the truth in J. L. Austin's picture of philosophy as a 'seminal and tumultuous' central sun from time to time throwing off some portion of itself to 'take station as a science, a planet, cool and well regulated, progressing steadily towards a distant final state' ([5.11], 180), though Austin's image tends to obscure the facts that there are great differences between the planetary sciences with respect to 'cool and well regulated' progress, and, more importantly, that there remain hot and turbulent philosophical aspects to even the most 'well regulated' of them.

Sidgwick's view of philosophy is spelled out in his posthumously published lectures called *Philosophy: its Scope and Relations*. In this book he tries to distinguish philosophy from other disciplines especially the physical sciences, history and sociology. This he attempts to do partly by insisting on the role of philosophy as providing a systematic overview of reality, drawing upon and interpreting the insights of the particular sciences. It is only by aiming at this traditional goal, he thinks, that philosophy can fulfil its 'germinal function' of creating new sciences. He is also critical of certain developments within the special sciences, some of which are as common (and as dubious) today as they were in Sidgwick's day. His criticisms of the sceptical tendencies of some historical and sociological writings, for instance, illustrate some of the ways in which the special sciences can harbour philosophical confusions. Sidgwick emphasizes the 'contradictory state of mind' of the theorist whose most 'fundamental beliefs in ethics, politics, theology, philosophy ... drop from him' in the face of acquired histori- cal or prehistorical beliefs to which 'he clings with a passionate convic- tion which is in singular contrast to the slenderness of the evidence that it is possible to adduce in their support' ([5.8], 166). In the course of the book, he also makes certain important distinctions, which we cannot here pursue fully, within philosophy itself. The most original and interesting claims made by Sidgwick concern the distinction within philosophy between metaphysics and non-metaphysical philosophy. This distinction is not intended as a total rejection, or even a disparage- ment of metaphysics. He explicitly rejects the idea put forward by 'transcendentalists' that metaphysical speculations such as those about whether the world had a beginning in time are merely 'futile' (or in the later jargon of the logical positivists, 'meaningless') though he agrees that they are distinctive in being beyond empirical verification. He thinks it obvious that such claims must be treated 'realistically' (as we would now say) since they are palpably true or false whether we can determine the matter or not.

On the other hand, it is clear that he thinks some metaphysical claims less defensible than others, and his tone is typical of the commonsensical and analytical tradition of British philosophy, as, for instance, in his comments on Hegel's philosophical account of the tides. Here is Hegel as cited by Sidgwick: 'the moon is the waterless crystal which seeks to complete itself by means of our sea, to quench the thirst of its arid rigidity, and therefore produces ebb and flow' ([5.8], 89). Here is Sidgwick's comment: 'Now I do not propose to discuss the truth of this remarkable contribution to the theory of tides. What I wish to point out is that it appears to be clearly incapable of empirical verification, direct or indirect. The alleged effort of the moon to complete itself and quench its thirst has no connection whatever with any part of the system of laws by which physical science explains the empirical facts of terrestrial and celestial motions' ([5.8], 89). The interest of this passage lies not only in its anticipation of later analytical, pragmatist and logical positivist attitudes to the windy nonsensicalities of Hegelian metaphysics, but in its ironic dryness of tone. Compare William James, writing in 1908, in more direct terms:

> But if Hegel's central thought is easy to catch, his abominable habits of speech make his applications of it to details exceedingly difficult to follow. His passion for the slipshod in the way of sentences, his unprincipled playing fast and loose with terms; his dreadful vocabulary, calling what completes a thing its 'negation', for example; his systematic refusal to let you know whether he is talking logic or physics or psychology, his whole deliberately adopted policy of ambiguity or vagueness, in short: all these things make his present-day readers wish to tear their hair – or his – out in desperation. Like Byron's corsair, he has left a name 'to other times, linked with one virtue and a thousand crimes'.
>
> ([5.22], 513).

Sidgwick would probably have applauded the sentiments, though he could never have brought himself to use so abusive a tone.

Sidgwick wrote extensively in a variety of fields from metaphysics to political economy, and I shall later look briefly at some of these other areas. His historical perspective, learning and broad intellectual sympathies are evident in his *Outlines of the History of Ethics for English Readers*. This began life as a long entry on 'Ethics' for the ninth edition of the *Encyclopaedia Britannica* and was produced as a book in 1886. In spite of its modest title and relatively modest length, it is an absorbing piece of philosophical and intellectual history, and throws light upon Sidgwick's own work in moral philosophy. None the less, it is in ethics itself that his claim to fame securely rests, so we must turn to his masterwork, *The Methods of Ethics*, first published in 1874 and revised extensively throughout six editions. As is customary, I shall treat the final, and posthumous, seventh edition (which is basically the sixth with a few minor editorial amendments) as definitive of his outlook, though there is much in the earlier editions that is instructive for a fully balanced view of the work. The basic aim of the book is the examination of three distinctive methods of approaching ethics – the intuitional, the utilitarian and the egoistic. Sidgwick professes not to be advancing an argument for the best method, but it is apparent that he regards both utilitarianism and egoism as more suited to the task of providing a rational or scientific basis for morality than any traditional form of intuitionism, though, as we shall see, his version of utilitarianism itself contains a strong intuitional dose.

COMMON SENSE, UTILITY, AND INTUITION

It is impossible here to summarize further or comment closely upon so large and dense a work, so I shall instead examine in some detail three central philosophical claims of Sidgwick's that are prominent in it. I have chosen them because they are distinctive of his outlook, arise from the intellectual debate of the time and yet remain important for contemporary moral philosophy. All three involve deep tensions, even conflicts, in moral theorizing, two of which Sidgwick thought he had solved but one of which he confessed himself defeated by. The first concerns the relation between utilitarianism and intuitionism; the second concerns what has been called the publicity principle; and the third concerns the clash between the demands of self-interest and morality.

Sidgwick was a convinced utilitarian but he was not a particularly reformist, and certainly not an iconoclastic, utilitarian. He was inclined to see utilitarianism not as vanquishing other outlooks but as accommodating and explaining what was best in them. Up to a point, he is a strong defender of common sense, and part of the project in *The Methods of Ethics* is to reconcile utilitarianism with what he called common-sense morality. This latter he defined as 'a collection of [such] general rules, as to the validity of which there would be apparent agreement at least among moral persons of our own age and civilisation, and which would cover with approximate completeness the whole of human conduct'. Imposed as a code by the public opinion of a particular community, this would count as that community's positive morality, but 'when regarded as a body of moral truth, warranted to be such by the *consensus* of mankind, – or at least of that portion of mankind which combines adequate intellectual enlightenment with a serious concern for morality – it is more significantly termed the morality of Common Sense' ([5.5], 215). Sidgwick was impressed with the broad adequacy of common-sense morality, though he thought that from an ideal point of view there were certain significant imperfections in it. None the less, he thought that when we reflected on the demands of common-sense morality we would see that various inconsistencies and contradictions within it were eliminable by recourse to the principle of utility whilst, at the same time, the principle made the appeal of the common-sense requirements intelligible and rationally defensible. As he says in the Preface to the sixth edition of *The Methods of Ethics*, 'the reflection on Common Sense Morality which I had gone through, had continually brought home to me its character as a system of rules tending to the promotion of general happiness' ([5.5], xx). Consequently, he asserts that 'The utilitarian must repudiate altogether that temper of rebellion against the established morality, as something purely external and conventional, into which the reflective mind is always apt to fall when it is first convinced that the established rules are not intrinsically reasonable' ([5.5], 475).

He sees much of what he is doing in his writings on ethics as rescuing morality from the charge of irrationality. In this and other of his convictions he is a typical Victorian: unable to believe in traditional, orthodox Christianity and aware that its grip on ordinary people was loosening, he wanted morality detached from religion and made secure by appeal to reason alone. His hope was that the principle of utility would ground ordinary morality in intuitively obvious considerations of rationality. To this end he devotes a considerable part of *The Methods of Ethics* to the justification of traditional virtues on the grounds of their social utility. So, he argues that the various virtues can be grounded in the human goods they characteristically promote, and here he is self-consciously Aristotelian. (He tells us in an autobiographical statement that it was after rereading Aristotle that he decided to emulate his examination of the common morality of his own society.) Some governing moral theory was still needed however because, left entirely to itself, common-sense morality shows a tendency to internal conflict or inconsistency.[2]

Inasmuch as traditional intuitionists like Whewell believed that intuitionism was required to support common-sense morality since basic parts of it would otherwise be undermined by utilitarianism, then Sidgwick's arguments, if successful, seem to make the appeal to intuition against utility unnecessary. None the less, this appearance is, as Sidgwick recognized, somewhat deceptive since there remains the problem of the justification for appealing to the principle of utility in the first place, and here, Sidgwick admits, we must once more have recourse to intuition. Where the intuitionists appealed to a plurality of intuitions to determine the various duties, virtues and prohibitions of traditional morality, Sidgwick claimed to be able to prove their validity on the basis of their contribution to human pleasure over pain, and almost on that basis alone. But this primal duty cannot itself be so recommended and, he concludes, its truth is known by intuition. So Sidgwick's utilitarianism has itself an intuitionist basis. Moreover, I used the qualification 'almost' above in reference to Sidgwick's basing morality upon the principle of utility, and the qualification is necessary because Sidgwick also recognizes as basic certain formal features of morality that are also revealed by intuition. These include for instance such 'axioms' as a principle of universalizability (as it would now be called) and a principle of temporal indifference which dictates that 'a smaller present good is not to be preferred to a greater future good' ([5.5], 381). If you are unhappy with the appeal to intuition, then Sidgwick can offer you a great reduction in its scope, but he cannot eliminate it altogether.

Sidgwick's compromise is not only distinctive but it poses a problem that continues to confront modern moral philosophers. Contemporary utilitarians are not attracted to Sidgwick's solution because, along with many other philosophers, they are uncomfortable with any appeal to intuition, at least if the intuition is taken to be a guarantee of truth or reliability. A fashionable response is to build one's utilitarianism upon a subjective base. This move is reinforced by the appeal to a distinction between meta-ethics and normative ethics. One's analysis of the moral vocabulary, particularly its fundamental but abstract categories, the so-called 'thin' concepts such as good, bad, right and wrong, are allowed to be specified as the individual chooses, constrained only by such formal limits as that they are terms of commendation or denunciation (or 'discommendation'). There is also a constraint of universalizability, but it is usually seen as delivered by logic or conceptual analysis of the moral vocabulary. The utilitarian has decided that the terms will be given normative content by recourse to the utilitarian principle, and, of course, hopes that this recommendation will have broad appeal. If not, there is nothing more to say to those who choose different material content for the moral terminology. One may try accusing them of irrationality, but since this term itself is essentially evaluative, the manoeuvre is easily dismissed by reminding the utilitarian of his or her own subjectivist meta-ethical commitments. Of course it may not be too clear why an appeal to intuition has anything over an appeal to feeling. If someone disagrees with you about a basic moral matter then the insistence that your view is a matter of rational intuition seems no more or less impressive than the assertion that you feel very strongly about the matter. I think that a good deal here turns upon what more can be said about intuition to contrast it with strong feeling and also what the disputants hold about other areas of human thought. If someone thinks (more or less with Hume) that, in the end, most human cognitive procedures turn upon proclivities of human psychology that are non-rational, then they will not be inclined to isolate ethics from natural or social science, or even from mathematics. If ethics is as much (or as little) a matter of rational understanding as natural science then in the face of this (rough) equality it may matter less whether we think of its foundations or principles in terms of powerful feeling, rational insight, or even some other resort, such as Wittgenstein's 'form of life'.

Another aspect of Sidgwick's treatment of common sense that deserves mention concerns the important allegation that common-sense morality is internally inconsistent, and hence needs to be supplemented by a consistent, overarching theory. Since it is dubious that common sense is itself a theory of any sort, it is a little unclear what this could mean, and sometimes Sidgwick seems rather to mean that the theory of intuitionism is inconsistent. For the most part, however, his point seems merely to be that common-sense morality does not provide decision procedures to settle complex problems of what would once have been called casuistry. So, for instance, common-sense morality tells us that lying is wrong, but also tells us that we should do no harm to the innocent, and notoriously there can arise circumstances in which (on certain understandings of them) these duties appear to be in conflict. I am a UN 'peacekeeper' in the former Yugoslavia during the civil wars in the early 1990s that resulted from the demise of communism, and I have confidential information that a Bosnian female child is hiding nearby from a troop of Serbian irregulars, known to practise rape and murder against such as her, and they ask whether I know the where-abouts of any Bosnian civilians in the vicinity. If I tell the truth, she is doomed, if I refuse to answer, their suspicions will be dangerously aroused, but if I lie she has a chance of survival. (For Sidgwick's discussion of common sense and 'unveracity' see [5.5], 448–9.)

❧ SIDGWICK'S PARADOX ❧

The second claim concerns what I shall call 'Sidgwick's paradox' since he referred to it himself as paradoxical. The problem is a specific but very special case of the refinements of utilitarian theory required partly by the condition that it be sensitive to the data of common-sense morality but even more by the adaptation of the utilitarian principle itself to the requirements of human nature and circumstance. One such adaptation leads, for instance, to motive utilitarianism where the primary focus of the utility principle is on motives and other human dispositions that can themselves be argued to maximize utility. On a simple (perhaps simple-minded) act of utilitarian analysis it may be best for a group of discreet sadists to torture an orphan child to death in the privacy of their club cellar with no prospect of the victim's sufferings disturbing others or of word of it getting abroad. Yet this indirect version of utilitarianism could argue that the cultivation or further entrenchment of sadistic dispositions is bound to be productive of worse outcomes for society than could be warranted by the short-term gain in the utility of the group here directly affected by the act of torture. Now it seems to me unlikely that this sort of manoeuvre is, in general, going to succeed in showing that such acts are morally wrong, or, even if it did, in explaining *what* is wrong with them. (There is indeed an air of absurdity in the way the explanation takes us away from the specific wrong done to the child and focuses on some general harms that might be produced by the prevalence of such habits in the perpetrators and others.) None the less, I shall not pursue this debate here; I mention it only to illustrate the path taken by indirect forms of utilitarianism as a preliminary to discussing Sidgwick's paradox. The point to be noted is that the dictates of the utility principle, properly understood, are not always what they might at first blush seem. Certain deeds that do not seem to be utility-maximizing may none the less prove to be so if we think more subtly and widely about the matter, but Sidgwick's paradox, though it incorporates this simple reflection, takes us into far more turbulent waters.

The paradox can be briefly stated as the fact that the truth of the utility principle may require that almost no one accept it as true. If the utility principle is true then (almost) no one should believe it, and if it's not true then no one should believe it, so whatever its status no one (or almost no one) should believe it. Put in terms of rationality, the paradox tells us that the most rational way for lives to be conducted is by the utility principle, but this is only possible if (almost) no one conducts their lives by reference to the principle. This paradoxical outcome of the Sidgwick inquiry is the limit case, so to speak, of a general tendency within the utilitarian enterprise to require the exist-ence of dependable moral rules and accompanying behaviour as a back-ground to the occasional beneficial utilitarian violation of them. Given certain empirically plausible assumptions about human nature and the likely effects of making public the utilitarian basis of all morality, it will then quickly emerge, on utilitarian principles, that the rational necessity for violation is something that should not be generally known. If it were to be known then the broad commitment to morality for its own sake, on which wide conformity to moral norms seems in part to rest, might well be undermined, and the overall effect be disastrous from the utilitarian point of view.

Peter Singer, writing in the spirit of Sidgwick, gives as an example the case in which a professor gives a student a higher grade than his work merits 'on the grounds that the student is so depressed over his work that one more poor grade will lead him to abandon his studies altogether, whereas if he can pull out of his depression he will be capable of reaching a satisfactory standard' ([5.31], 166). Singer concludes that this may be the right action but, if so, it would be wrong for the professor to advocate publicly such behaviour because then 'the student would know that the higher grade was undeserved and – quite apart from encouraging other students to feign depression – the higher grade might cheer the student only if he believes that it is merited' ([5.31], 166). Leaving aside the professor's quandaries when the student continues cheerfully to submit inferior work that he now believes to be adequate, we may note that Singer quotes Sidgwick approvingly here as saying that 'the opinion that secrecy may render an action right which would not otherwise be so, should itself be kept comparatively secret' and he thinks it has an air of paradox to maintain that 'it would be right for an individual to do secretly what it is also right for the public code of ethics to condemn' ([5.31], 166). Singer consoles himself with the thought that the paradox does not belong to the secrecy doctrine itself but to the attempt to state it publicly which will be subversive of the public code that the same doctrine says must be supported. In a surprisingly ebullient fashion he goes on to acknowledge that his own public stating is a piece of wrong-doing, but perhaps the cheerful air with which he makes this confession of wickedness is sustained by the belief that only utilitarians will read the book. In any case, the furtive stance can hardly be quarantined to specific violations of public codes, as Singer seems here to show a tendency to believe. Sidgwick, at any rate, is clear that the general acceptance of utilitarianism as the rationale for morality by ordinary people might be a disaster in utilitarian terms. He is explicit that, granted the assumptions mentioned earlier, the truth of utilitarianism must be kept secret by the elite who have discovered it. So he says: 'And thus a Utilitarian may reasonably desire, on Utilitarian principles, that some of his conclusions should be rejected by mankind generally; or even that the vulgar should keep aloof from his system as a whole, in so far as the inevitable indefiniteness and complexity of its calculations render it likely to lead to bad results in their hands' ([5.5], 490). In Derek Parfit's terminology, utilitarian theory would then be 'self-effacing' ([5.27], 40–3), at least for the vulgar. It would of course be different, according to Sidgwick, in what he calls 'an ideal community of enlightened utilitarians' ([5.5], 490), but he was realistic enough to see this prospect as remote from the real world.

So much for the genesis of the paradox, what about its status? One interesting fact about the puzzle is that it has an interesting formal affinity to a puzzle in epistemology. The traditional epistemologist is interested in whether and how it is rational to trust to the deliverances of our cognitive powers, such as perception, memory and so on. But it is often unclear whose rationality is here at stake. When some complex proof is provided of the rationality of relying upon the senses for knowledge, is the theorist's possession of the proof supposed to show that everyone is rational to trust their senses even if they have never encountered the proof and wouldn't (perhaps) understand it if they did? Or is only the theorist rational to trust the senses or memory?

Perhaps the best thing to say is that the theorist's justification (if correct) shows that the practice is rational but not that the practitioners are rational in following it. There are echoes here of the debates about internalist versus externalist justificatory analyses of knowledge. On an externalist account it is enough to show that the justificatory relation, be it causal relation, reliability connection or whatever, obtains between the practice and what it is supposed to deliver. By contrast, internalist theorists maintain that the putative knower cannot be said to know unless he or she at least has some grip on what the relation is, and perhaps why it justifies the relevant belief. As regards rationality, the externalist can rest content with the discovery that the practice is rationally grounded and the rest of us can get on with doing what we always have done. The internalist is likely to be more missionary about the matter since he or she must be worried by the thought that all the other practitioners are not behaving rationally in trusting their senses, memory or word of others. Their procedures can be rationally justified, but their ignorance of the justification suggests the disturbing thought that *they* are not rationally justified in using them. Yet although the externalist is likely to be less missionary, he or she will have no antipathy to the promulgation of his or her discovery. There is nothing in his or her position that demands that the discovery be withheld from the masses, and it would surely be surprising (to say the least) if this were so. For an externalist, the practitioners may not need an understanding of the rational basis of their cognitive practices in order to be acting rationally but such understanding could hardly make the practitioners' behaviour thereby less rational.

Interesting as this issue is, we have the sense that it doesn't matter a whole lot if the ordinary person has no access to the philosopher's proof, since the ordinary person doesn't usually raise the question of rationality here. From the point of view of the philosopher, it is enough that the rationality of the procedures can be demonstrated. The philosopher is, after all, the one worried about the justificatory question, and he or she, just as much as the ordinary person, has no practical doubts about the general viability of the perceptual and memory practices, nor any alternative to persisting with their use. This is the first point of contrast with morality. The contrast is not perhaps as vast as is often made out, but exists none the less. It is not so vast because ordinary people must use values; they (like the philosopher) must act for this reason or that, and so will not be paralysed by the failure to have some general rationale for their ethical choices. Yet there remains a contrast, because our resort to values is not as constrained and automatic as our resort to perceptual and memory practices. As Sidgwick himself recognizes in the first chapter of his book, 'Men never ask, "Why should I believe what I see to be true?" but they frequently ask, "Why should I do what I see to be right?" ' ([5.5], 5). In putting the question 'How should I live?' at the centre of ethics, Socrates rightly emphasizes that there are deeper level questions about the right way to conduct our lives that every person is free to raise and which present genuine options for action depending upon the answers given. Consequently, the interest of the philosopher's question about the rational justification of our moral practices is inevitably less specialist and confined than the otherwise parallel epistemological questions. When the theorist decides that the utility principle is what justifies the practices, then the answer can hardly be considered irrelevant or unimportant to the questions ordinary people are quite often drawn to ask.

✺ ASSESSING THE PARADOX ✺

None the less, they cannot be told, and we must ask whether this gnostic elitism is logically or morally suspect. Certainly, it violates what, since Kant, has been thought of as a basic requirement of a moral system, namely, the publicity principle. In the second appendix to *Perpetual Peace*, first published in 1795, Kant states this as follows: 'All actions affecting the rights of other human beings are wrong if their maxim is not compatible with being made public' ([5.24], 126). This would clearly rule out Singer's specific case, but also the esoteric secrecy of the utilitarian principle itself which seems to be a maxim for conduct in Kant's sense. If the publicity principle is a logical or conceptual condition for any moral system then this seems fatal to Sidgwickian utilitarianism, but it might be argued that the shoe is on the other foot, since the viability of Sidgwickian utilitarianism shows the publicity principle to be mistaken as such a condition. In any case, attractive as the publicity principle seems to be, there are certain 'local' counterexamples to it. For example, there are good reasons for allowing that the legal authorities should not even bring to prosecution certain cases that qualify as legally severe offences, such as mothers who kill their babies whilst in a state of extreme post-natal depression. But although this may be sound public policy, it may also be sound public policy not to make it public knowledge. Again, it may be good public policy in certain circumstances to deal secretly with terrorist groups, but bad policy to make it known that this is your policy. I am inclined to think that examples like these are acceptable only because they fall under more general maxims that can, and perhaps should, be publicly avowed. I will not try to spell these out here, but principles of mercy and avoidance of futility in punishments are relevant to the first example, and certain broad rules of conflict resolution to the second. What is harder to swallow is precisely what is at issue in the Sidgwick paradox, namely, that the basic principle underpinning the rationality of ethics must itself be kept secret.

One difficulty concerns membership in the elite, and here it is a matter of some astonishment that Sidgwick and other utilitarians seem so little concerned with the consequences of publishing their 'discovery' of the truth of utilitarianism. Sidgwick seems to have lectured and published his views with no concern for their potentially disastrous consequences upon an audience that could hardly be presumed to be as all-wise, prescient and strong-willed as possession of the dangerous truth requires. But if the easy assumption that their audience will constitute 'an ideal community of enlightened utilitarians' is surprising, it only seems to reflect the hubris involved in the assumption that the theorist is personally worthy of the revelation. After all, capacity to achieve philosophical truth need not correlate with high moral development or the intellectual capacities for calculating consequences that the ideal utilitarian should have. There is a certain aptitude to Bernard Williams's characterization of the outlook as that of the colonial administrator ([5.35], 108–10).[3] The easy assumption by utilitarian theorists that they, and a few of their friends, are uniquely capable of the rationality that would be disastrous if employed by the *hoi polloi* is not so much, or not only, a piece of hubris but a requirement of the theory. After all, if we assume that the principle of utility is the truth that makes morality rational, but that it is a dictate of the principle that *no one* should base their actions upon it, then its supposed truth is entirely insignificant. As Williams has noted, we would then face the conclusion that if utilitarianism is true, then it is better that people should not believe in it, and if it is false it is better that people should not believe in it, so either way no one should believe in it ([5.34], 68). Consequently, the commitment to elitism is the only way to preserve any significant content for the claim that utilitarianism provides for the rationality of morality.

Another way of dramatizing the difficulty inherent in the paradox is to consider what happens to humble theorists who begin to suspect that they may not be members of the elite. If the theorist cannot be certain that he or she is worthy of the revelation, it may be for the best that they take steps to expunge it from their memory, if this is at all possible. Certainly, theorists will have considerable trouble making the distinction, in their own case, between utilitarianism as a theory of justification of the practice of morality, and utilitarianism as a theory of the correct motivation for right action. Once they have realized it provides the former, how can they avoid treating it as an answer, for them, to the latter, even where they have reason to think that this will be for the worst.

In any case, let us suppose that the theorist is personally worthy of the truth, and knows it. How (we might wonder) is he or she to prevent this truth becoming more widely known? One way would be to engage energetically in the refutation of utilitarianism, crusading against it in the cultural journals and the popular press, and advocating the truth of intuitionism. This Sidgwick notably failed to do. Indeed, his character seems to have been so significantly non-utilitarian that his commitments to honesty would have prevented this recourse. Donagan has argued plausibly that Sidgwick's resignation of his Fellowship at Trinity College over the religious test issue illustrates this aspect of his character and thought ([5.17], 459–60). As Sidgwick himself said at the time in correspondence on the matter after reviewing certain general arguments for and against resignation: 'After all, it is odd to be finding subtle reasons for an act of mere honesty: but I am reduced to that by the refusal of my friends to recognise it as such' ([5.30], 201). This fact is of more than biographical interest, because it shows that, for the theorist himself or herself, the split between motivational and justificatory outlooks is impossible to maintain, as is the related distinction of which Sidgwick, and later Smart and Singer, make so much between reasons for acting (on the one hand) and reasons for praising and blaming (on the other). When the utilitarian claims that it may be right to do some act but also right to condemn it publicly, then we are entitled to ask what sort of attitude utilitarian agents can take towards their own commitment to such an act. They must stand ready to do such acts in spite of having cultivated a strong tendency to condemn them. The difficulties involved here are unwittingly displayed in one of Sidgwick's own comments. Noting that it may be expedient that divergent codes should exist within a society, Sidgwick writes that 'it may conduce most to the general happiness that A should do a certain act, and at the same time that B, C, D should blame it. The Utilitarian of course cannot really join in the disapproval, but he may think it expedient to leave it unshaken; and at the same time may think it right, if placed in the supposed circumstances, to do the act that is generally disapproved' ([5.5], 491). But the assertion that the utilitarian cannot join in the disapproval is simply wrong if it means that the utilitarian cannot publicly blame the act, though ready to do it himself. After all, that is the point of distinguishing reasons for acting from reasons for blaming. Sidgwick's lapse from the letter of consistency here is a testament to the moral integrity and psychological sanity he possessed but felt obliged by theory to ignore.

There is a related issue here that deserves some attention and it concerns the possible transition from a situation in which the vulgar are incapable of receiving the truth of utilitarianism to one which might qualify as inhabited by an ideal community of enlightened utilitarians. It is unclear in Sidgwick whether this is thought to be a real possibility or not, though several passages suggest that he thought it was. If so, then the set of attitudes involved in the paradox seem to make the transition impossible except by magic. Certainly it is hard to see how it could be effected by reasoning or education.

⚬ THE FINAL PUZZLE ⚬

The third puzzle might itself be called a paradox. It concerns a kind of contradiction that Sidgwick affects to find at the heart of ethics. He establishes to his own satisfaction that basic intuitions deliver the rational self-evidence of the fundamental utilitarian principle that he calls the Principle of Rational Benevolence. As we have seen, this enjoins us to 'aim at the happiness of other human beings generally', but for present purposes I do not want to challenge its utilitarian basis, since the problem Sidgwick poses is to some extent independent of his formulations. Let us just think of the principle as one that enjoins us to aim sometimes at the happiness of others, even where this course of action conflicts with the promotion of one's own narrowly conceived good. Although Sidgwick thinks that it is rational to act on this principle and to base one's ethic and life upon it, he cannot rid himself of the thought that it is *also* rational to base one's life and ethic upon the Principle of Egoism, which requires an agent to choose the course of action that will most promote his or her good (and for Sidgwick this means his or her pleasure). Yet Sidgwick plausibly believes that these two principles are in conflict; they are, in a sense, logically incompatible, but both, he thinks, are self-evidently true. Opinions will vary about how compelling the case is for either of these principles, and certainly the case for a benevolence or an egoism as demanding and far-reaching as Sidgwick intuits seems to me to be fairly weak. None the less there is a strong case for there being some altruistic principle at the heart of ethics and this seems likely to be incompatible with any strong version of egoism, and egoism has a long history of appeal as a basic dictate of rationality. (Despite its popularity and longevity, there are, I suspect, serious difficulties in formulating and defending a version of egoism that is at once coherent and ethically challenging.) Supposing however there to be the clash between the egoist and altruistic principles, however refined in detail, then what of Sidgwick's enterprise? He himself sees it as threatened and sees no way of defusing the problem by recourse to the internal logic of the two positions. In so far as he has a solution it consists in the appeal to what he calls a postulate that is required to save the consistency of ethics as a basic department of human thought. This is the postulate of a benign God who reconciles duty and self-interest, or, more antiseptically, a benign Order to the universe in which the reconciliation is achieved.

Does this work? C. D. Broad objects that the two principles remain inconsistent regardless of the existence of God who cannot alter their self-evidence and hence 'something which appeared self-evident to Sidgwick must have been false'. Broad also points out that the postulate might comfort us by showing that it is a matter of 'practical indifference' which of the principles is false, but thinks that this gives us no 'adequate ground' for making the postulate ([5.15], 253).

There are at least two separate elements in the problem, and in Broad's objection, that need to be separated. Firstly, would the existence of a God with the usual attributes of the Christian theistic tradition, benevolently disposed towards human beings, solve the paradox? Secondly, if the answer is 'yes', is this fact sufficient to accept such a God's existence? On the first point, there is a level of understanding the problem at which the answer may well be 'yes', and at which level Broad seems to have missed the point. Call it level A. This is the level at which we may ask whether the actual maximization of an individual's good is always compatible with the maximization of the good of all; or, if there are problems with the concept of maximization here, whether optimizing the individual good is always compatible with optimizing the good of all. What Sidgwick has in mind here is that the sort of God in question will have so arranged the world that individual and communal well-being ultimately harmonize. If so, then there can be no actual clash between action that really promotes one's own good and action that really promotes the good of others. If people acted to achieve what was really their own good they would in fact be acting for what was really the good of others and vice versa. At this level, what happens to Sidgwick's self-evident principles is not that he is wrong about one of them but it doesn't matter which, but rather that they are both true, and possibly self-evident, and it is the appearance of a contradiction between them that is wrong.[4]

But this reconciliation leaves us with a problem about how to conduct our lives here and now that is reminiscent of the shifting relations between justification and motivation that plagued the discussion of the earlier paradox. For consider the agent who is persuaded of the reconciliation achieved at level A. She knows that acting from self-interest and from altruism are ultimately in harmony, but what is she to do now in a situation in which they appear to clash? At this phenomenological level (call it B) it would surely be wrong to leave her free to choose either course of action on the grounds of the perceived reconciliation at level A. If we say that she should rather choose self-interest, in the cheerful hope of the reconciliation offered by God, we have something like Ayn Rand's picture of ethics, or, at a cruder level still, that of economic rationalism and the 'invisible hand'. If we urge the altruistic road, we have something closer to utilitarianism, but the problem is that neither road is mandated at the motivational level by the reconciliation at the justificatory level. The problem could be resolved if we had a revelation from God that utilitarianism was the way to go, or that common-sense morality embodied (ultimately) the path of reconciliation, but in the absence of this, the problem remains. (Butler, to whom Sidgwick is considerably indebted, seems to have thought that conscience constituted such a revelation.)

Finally, on the second point, Sidgwick does not argue that the Deistic postulate (or some postulate not involving a personal God that serves the same function) should be made because it is comforting, but rather that its viability depends upon certain very general considerations of fundamental epistemology. As he puts it:

> 'Those who hold that the edifice of physical science is really constructed of conclusions logically inferred from self-evident premises, may reasonably demand that any practical judgements claiming philosophic certainty should be based on an equally firm foundation. If on the other hand we find that in our supposed knowledge of the world of nature propositions are commonly taken to be universally true, which yet seem to rest on no other grounds than that we have a strong disposition to accept them, and that they are indispensable to the systematic coherence of our beliefs, – it will be more difficult to reject a similarly supported assumption in ethics, without opening the door to universal scepticism.
>
> ([5.5], 509).

Sidgwick's own employment of self-evidence and intuition, and his general picture of the attempt to produce a 'science of ethics', clearly incline him to the first outlook, but he is well aware of the attractions of the second, and its relevance to the problem he confronts. If what we mean by the rationality of our fundamental cognitive and scientific practices gets back to a deep tendency to accept that they are coherent even where there is no further argument to accept them, then the same grace should be extended to ethics. It is even possible, to return briefly to our earlier reflections on Sidgwick's attitude to religion, that a similar grace could be extended to God.[5]

APPLIED ETHICS

Sidgwick's work in economics is now of principally historical interest, but his political philosophy is more important, though much less influential than his ethics. His views on immigration policy, liberalism and war have all been referred to in recent writings. It is also significant that, although he stands at the beginning of the academic professionalization of philosophy that has been extravagantly praised and equally as extravagantly bewailed in recent years, he saw this as no impediment to involvement, as a philosopher, in issues of broad public concern. The picture of the analytical philosopher as professionally unconcerned with public life and its intellectual problems, and as having nothing distinctive to add to the public debate, was not his. Here he was at odds (as on many other things) with his contemporary F. H. Bradley who proclaimed in 'My Station and its Duties' in 1876 that 'there cannot be a moral philosophy which will tell us what in particular we are to do, and ... it is not the business of philosophy to do so. All philosophy has to do is "to understand what is", and moral philosophy has to understand morals which exist, not to make them or give directions for making them' ([5.14], 193). Sidgwick's view was more nuanced, and would have set him apart from a powerful mood within analytical ethics that really began with G. E. Moore – who once claimed that 'The direct object of Ethics is knowledge and not practice' ([5.25], 20) – and prevailed until the 1970s. Quite apart from his interest in political philosophy and his broad commitment to utilitarianism, he was a member of the Ethical Societies in London and Cambridge which were groups, including academics, professional people and figures in public life, that met regularly to discuss papers read by members on matters of public import. The British groups were modelled on the Societies for Ethical Culture that had been earlier established in the USA and led to the founding of the philosophy journal now known as *Ethics*.

Sidgwick's contributions to these discussions were very much in the spirit of what would now be called 'applied philosophy', and a number of his addresses were collected and published in 1898 (with a second edition in 1909) in the book *Practical Ethics*. In this, Sidgwick discusses specific issues of public concern from a philosophical perspective and also ponders the general question of the appropriate role for philosophy in the discussion of such matters. This is a question that considerably exercises contemporary philosophers and non-philosophers, both those who favour the involvement of philosophers in 'practical ethics' and those who oppose it. Sidgwick's discussion of it is characteristically acute and careful. He states the problem as that of determining 'the proper lines and limits of ethical discussion, having a distinctly practical aim, and carried on among a miscellaneous group of educated persons, who do not belong exclusively to any one religious sect or philosophical school, and possibly may not have gone through any systematic study of philosophy' ([5.9], 5). His suggestion is that such inquiries should avoid attempts to get 'agreement on the first principles of duty or the Summum Bonum' ([5.9], 4), and rather strive to clarify and elucidate that fairly extensive agreement in the details of morality we find already existing 'both among thoughtful persons who profoundly disagree on first principles, and among plain men who do not seriously trouble themselves about first principles' ([5.9], 6). Sidgwick believed that this technique could 'get beyond the platitudes of copybook morality to results which may be really of use in the solution of practical questions' ([5.9], 8). He thought that would lead to the development and refinement of 'middle axioms' of moral thought ([5.9], 8), and, though Sidgwick does not acknowledge that this reference is to a technical term used by late medieval theologians in expounding the nature of the art of casuistry, he later explicitly compares the activity of 'practical ethics' to the work of casuistry, understood as 'the systematic discussion ... of difficult and doubtful cases of morals' ([5.9], 17). This comparison is a striking anticipation of very recent writings on the nature of applied ethics, and Sidgwick goes on to offer a partial defence of the older theological casuists against their seventeenth-century detractors that itself anticipates the work of Jonson and Toulmin one hundred years later. Curiously enough, Jonson and Toulmin, in apparent ignorance of *Practical Ethics*, treat Sidgwick as an outright enemy of casuistry, and the source of many of the difficulties that modern moral philosophers have had in coming to grips with the realities of practical ethics ([5.23], 279–81).

It may of course be that there is some tension between Sidgwick's later views and his enterprise in *The Methods of Ethics*, so it is worth pausing here to wonder at the relevance of Sidgwick's sane comments on the viability of practical ethics to his earlier critique of the inconsistency of common-sense morality. Sidgwick, as we saw, argued in *The Methods of Ethics* that common-sense morality needed somehow to be supplemented by utilitarianism in order to overcome its inconsistencies, at least in the sense that a decision procedure was needed to adjudicate between the differing dictates of ordinary virtues or rules. Yet, it seems that we need no such ultimate appeal for the complex problems confronting practical ethics since casuistic analysis and, at most, reasoned appeal to 'middle axioms' can do the trick. This suggests that the drive in Sidgwick's pure ethics towards a sort of foundationist rationality may well be generated by a non-existent problem, or by the conflating of several different problems. He was right to insist that moral thought and action cannot always rest content with surface instincts and intuitions, whether individual or communal, but the work of reason, though always implicated to some degree in generality and principle, may here be justifiably more piecemeal, pluralistic and circumstantial than the utilitarian model requires. If so, we may also have reason to review the sharp separation of reason and emotion to which the model (and, as we saw, Sidgwick personally) is committed. It is indeed arguable that this might require some adjustment in our understanding of philosophy itself, particularly in relation to the activities of the practical intellect, and here the tension in Sidgwick's thought points towards an area of unresolved current debate.[6]

Several of the other more specific essays in *Practical Ethics* discuss topics that have also recently been subjects of passionate debate amongst contemporary philosophers with an interest in applied philosophy or political ethics. There is an essay on the morality of war ('The Morality of Strife'), on dirty hands in politics ('Public Morality') and on philosophy, science and culture ('The Pursuit of Culture'). Two apparently more remote papers, 'The Ethics of Religious Conformity' and 'Clerical Veracity', in fact canvass issues of professional ethics that are much with us today, and the essay on 'Luxury' is interestingly related to later debates about the role of elites. The final chapter on 'Unreasonable Action' is an excellent discussion in the philosophy of moral psychology of the age-old but currently fashionable topic of akrasia. It is unfortunate that these essays are not better known (*Practical Ethics* has not been reprinted since the early twentieth century) because they are all thought-provoking, and the essays on 'Public Morality', 'The Morality of Strife' and 'Unreasonable Action' are outstandingly good.

In addition to this sort of involvement in public issues, Sidgwick was also energetic in the practical pursuit of various public causes, most notably the higher education of women. He was instrumental in opening up university education at Cambridge for women, and was not only one of the founders of Newnham College (the first women's college established in Cambridge) but contributed a good deal of money to its foundation. He was also heavily involved in university affairs, and served on several government commissions of inquiry.

G. E. Moore attended Sidgwick's lectures and apparently thought them dull, and Sidgwick, on hearing that Moore was producing a book on ethics, said he thought it would be acute, but expressed the view that Moore's '*acumen*- – which is remarkable to a degree – is in excess of his *insight* ' ([5.28], 17).[7] Sidgwick was sharp enough himself, however much his patient capacity to explore every aspect of a question could often inhibit a sparkling style, but above all he craved insight. The aim of his intellectual endeavours had been, he wrote two weeks before his death, 'the solution, or contribution to the solution, of the deepest problems of human life' ([5.30], 33–4). He was disappointed that he had not done more to fulfil it, but his own evaluation of his achievements has proved notably less enthusiastic than posterity's.

❧ NOTES ❧

My thanks to Andrew Alexandra, Will Barrett, Bruce Langtry, Kim Lycos, Mary McCloskey, and Thomas Pogge for helpful discussion of Sidgwick's views (though my gratitude does not always extend to following their suggestions), and to Will Barrett for research assistance with references and bibliography.

1 The quote is actually from Bagehot, but adapted by Sidgwick to express his view of Green's work.
2 The discussion of this issue is bedevilled by a tendency Sidgwick displays to conflate common-sense morality and the philosophical theory of intuitionism; indeed, in his Index to the *Methods of Ethics* the two are explicitly identified. It is better to treat common-sense morality as providing the pre-theoretical data for a theory of morality in the fashion recommended by Rawls and usually followed by Sidgwick. The moral theory should then accommodate the pre-theoretical 'facts', mostly by way of explanatory agreement with them, but sometimes by way of new recommendations that are accompanied by an explaining away of the recalcitrant data.
3 In fact, the influence of the English utilitarians upon colonial policy seems to have been more in the direction of Benthamite and openly interventionist policies of change in local practices, customs and laws. It was not marked by Sidgwick's attitude of cautious, if elitist, conservatism towards existing moral attitudes. For an interesting discussion see Stokes [5.32].
4 Derek Parfit thinks ([5.27], 462) that the problem is real, but can be solved in piecemeal fashion if we recognize that in addition to egoism and benevolence there is a third decision principle that may be used to tip the scales, namely, the principle yielded by what he calls the present-aim theory. Roughly, if it is equally rational to follow the dictates of self-interest and of benevolence, but they don't coincide, and we have a strong present desire to follow either benevolence or self-interest, then we have good reason to follow whichever of the two our coolly considered present aims (desires etc.) favour. The success of this tactic depends on what one thinks of the present-aim theory as a theory of rational action and on how it is distinguished from its competitors, but we cannot enter into this complex question here.
5 C. D. Broad thought that something like this was probably Sidgwick's final position with respect to religious belief ([5.16], 109–10). In support he quotes a letter Sidgwick wrote in 1880 to an old friend, Major Carey, in which after asking, 'What guarantee have you for the fundamental beliefs of science except that they are consistent and harmonious with other beliefs that we find ourselves

naturally impelled to hold?' he adds, 'This is precisely the relation which I find to exist between Theism and the whole system of my moral beliefs. Duty to me is as real as the physical world, though not apprehended in the same way; but all my apparent knowledge of duty falls into chaos if my belief in the moral government of the world is conceived to be overthrown' (109).

6 When discussing the nature of philosophy Sidgwick seems unaware of any such tension and keeps very much to the high ground of abstract rationality. So he writes, in *Philosophy, its Scope and Relations*, 'It is commonly felt that an attempt to work out a complete system of duties would inevitably lead us out of Philosophy into Casuistry: and whether Casuistry is a good or a bad thing, it is certainly not Philosophy' ([5.8], 25–6). In this context, he regards moral philosophy as 'primarily concerned with the general principles and methods of moral reasoning, and only with the details of conduct so far as the discussion of them affords instructive examples of general principles and method' ([5.8], 25). Contemporary philosophers are much less confident about this sort of division in every area of thought. For some contemporary views about the role of philosophy in ethics that are, in different ways, sceptical about the high ground see: Walzer [5.33], Williams [5.35], and Jonson and Toulmin [5.23]. For views still seeking a central role for philosophical reason see Donagan [5.18], Gewirth [5.19] and O'Neill [5.26].

7 Schneewind's book [5.28] is a masterly treatment of the background to Sidgwick's ethical thought, and also gives a careful and sympathetic unravelling of what he understands Sidgwick to be doing in *The Methods of Ethics*.

❦ BIBLIOGRAPHY ❦

Works by Sidgwick

5.1 —— *The Development of European Polity*, London: Macmillan, 1903.

5.2 —— *The Elements of Politics*, 4th edn, London: Macmillan, 1919.

5.3 —— *Lectures on the Ethics of T. H. Green, H. Spencer and J. Martineau*, London: Macmillan, 1902.

5.4 —— *Lectures on the Philosophy of Kant and other Philosophical Lectures and Essays*, London: Macmillan, 1905.

5.5 —— *The Methods of Ethics*, 7th edn, London: Macmillan, 1907.

5.6 —— *Miscellaneous Essays and Addresses*, London: Macmillan, 1904.

5.7 —— *Outlines of the History of Ethics for English Readers*, 5th edn, London: Macmillan, 1902.

5.8 —— *Philosophy, its Scope and Relations: An Introductory Course of Lectures*, London: Macmillan, 1902.

5.9 —— *Practical Ethics: A Collection of Essays and Addresses*, 2nd edn, London: Swan Sonnenschein, 1909.

5.10 —— *The Principles of Political Economy*, 3rd edn, London: Macmillan, 1901.

Other works

5.11 Austin, J. L. *Philosophical Papers,* Oxford: Oxford University Press, 1961.

5.12 Benson, A.C. *The Life of Edward White Benson,* London: Macmillan, 1899.

5.13 Blanshard, B. *Four Reasonable Men: Marcus Aurelius, John Stuart Mill, Ernest Renan, Henry Sidgwick,* Middletown: Wesleyan University Press, 1984.

5.14 Bradley, F. H. *Ethical Studies,* 2nd edn, Oxford: Oxford University Press, 1927. Essay 5: 'My Station and Its Duties'.

5.15 Broad, C. D. *Five Types of Ethical Theory,* London: Routledge & Kegan Paul, 1930.

5.16 —— *Religion, Philosophy and Psychical Research: Selected Essays,* London: Routledge & Kegan Paul, 1953. Essay entitled: 'Henry Sidgwick and Psychical Research'.

5.17 Donagan, A. 'Sidgwick and Whewellian Intuitionism: Some Enigmas', *Canadian Journal of Philosophy* 7 (1977): 447–65.

5.18 —— *The Theory of Morality,* Chicago: University of Chicago Press, 1977 (2nd edn, with corrections, 1979).

5.19 Gewirth, A. *Reason and Morality,* Chicago, University of Chicago Press, 1978.

5.20 Himmelfarb, G. *Marriage and Morals among the Victorians: Essays,* New York: Alfred A. Knopf, 1986.

5.21 James, D. G. *Science and Faith in Victorian England,* Oxford: Oxford University Press, 1970.

5.22 James, W. *The Writings of William James,* ed. J. J. McDermott, New York: Modern Library, 1968.

5.23 Jonson, A. R. and S. Toulmin, *The Abuse of Casuistry: A History of Moral Reasoning,* Berkeley: University of California Press, 1988.

5.24 Kant, I. *Kant's Political Writings,* ed. H. Reiss, Cambridge: Cambridge University Press, 1991.

5.25 Moore, G.E. *Principia Ethica,* Cambridge: Cambridge University Press, 1903.

5.26 O'Neill, *Constructions of Reason: Explorations of Kant's Practical Philosophy,* Cambridge: Cambridge University Press, 1989.

5.27 Parfit, D. *Reasons and Persons,* Oxford: Oxford University Press, 1984.

5.28 Schneewind, J.B. *Sidgwick's Ethics and Victorian Moral Philosophy,* Oxford: Oxford University Press, 1977.

5.29 Schultz, B. (ed.) *Essays on Henry Sidgwick,* Cambridge, Cambridge University Press, 1992.

5.30 Sidgwick, A. and E. M. *Henry Sidgwick: A Memoir,* London, Macmillan, 1906.

5.31 Singer, P. *The Expanding Circles: Ethics and Sociobiology,* Oxford: Oxford University Press, 1981.

5.32 Stokes, E. *The English Utilitarians and India,* Oxford: Oxford University Press, 1959.

5.33 Walzer, M. *Spheres of Justice: A Defense of Pluralism and Equality,* New York: Basic Books, 1983.

5.34 Williams, B. A. O. *Morality: An Introduction to Ethics,* Harmondsworth: Penguin, 1973.

5.35 —— *Ethics and the Limits of Philosophy,* London: Fontana, 1985.

CHAPTER 6

Comte and positivism

Robert Brown

The chief aim of all of Auguste Comte's publications, and the constant mission of his entire working life, was the improvement of human character through the perfecting of human society. He was convinced that the scientific knowledge available in his own lifetime – the first half of the nineteenth century – was rapidly making possible, and in a sense inevitable, the creation of the most suitable society for the 'social regeneration of Western Europe'. Born in Montpellier in 1798, Comte was both literally and intellectually a child of the eighteenth century who became an adult during the Napoleonic aftermath of the French Revolution. In searching for social salvation by means of the application of science to political and economic questions, Comte was a perfectibilist of a sort that he helped to make typical of his period. The set of beliefs about society that perfectibilists of his kind had inherited from the eighteenth century have been well summarized by John Passmore in *The Perfectibility of Man*:

> Man had until that time been a mere child in respect of
> knowledge and, in consequence, of virtue; he was now at last
> in a position, as a result of the development of science, to
> determine how human nature develops and what is the best
> thing for human beings to do; this new knowledge could be
> expressed in a form in which all men would find it intelligible;
> once they knew what it is best to do, men would act accordingly
> and so would constantly improve their moral, political and
> physical condition. Provided only, then, that 'sinister interests'
> did not prevent the communication of knowledge, the
> development of science was bound to carry with it the constant

improvement of the human condition, to a degree which would be, like the growth of science itself, unlimited.

([6.50], 208)

Comte is most often remembered now as an early practitioner of the history of science, and as an advocate of the application of scientific method to the explanation and prediction of social behaviour and its institutions. His own opinion of his contribution to society was rather more ambitious in its claims. The nature and scope of these claims are most briefly revealed in a letter that Comte wrote two months before his death in 1857:

he would in the future sign all his circulars 'Le Fondateur de la religion universelle, Grand Prêtre de l'Humanité,' and he let it be known that his being would become more sacred than the Catholic pontiff's. The Pope was only a minister, but he, Auguste Comte, who had discovered the fundamental laws of human evolution, was the very personification of the Great Being.

([6.43], 267)

Comte's formal qualifications for this role were few. He had spent the years 1814–16 enrolled in the École Polytechnique in Paris, and had absorbed the faith in the power and utility of the current physical sciences which the school's highly distinguished staff were noted for instilling in their students. Expelled as a trouble-maker just before graduation, Comte lived by tutoring in mathematics until he became the secretary and, later, 'adopted son' of Comte Henri de Saint-Simon in 1817, a relationship that lasted until the two men quarrelled and separated a year before Saint-Simon's death in 1825. During those years, and up to early middle age, Comte read omnivorously and was influenced, as he reported, by a group of thinkers – Plato, Montesquieu, Hume, Turgot, Condorcet, Kant, Bonald, De Maistre among others – whose widely different views on many topics he pieced together in the thousands of pages that make up his two major philosophical works, the *Cours de philosophie positive* (1830–42, [6.3]) and *Système de politique positive* (1851–4, [6.1]).

In the last fifteen years of his life Comte read and thought little about the serious philosophical and sociological problems that occupied him earlier. Increasingly detached from scientific friends and philosophic debate by his growing confidence that he was a religious seer, bitter and hostile towards his estranged wife, financially dependent in that period on contributions from French and British well-wishers who included, in England, Sir William Molesworth, John Stuart Mill and George Grote, Comte devoted himself, firstly, to the deification of Clothilde de Vaux, the unhappy woman whom he had befriended and loved during the last year of her life and, secondly, to his detailed proposals in *Catéchisme positiviste* (1852) and the *Politique positive* for creating a society worthy of her character. The one person whose intellectual influence Comte refused to acknowledge was Saint-Simon, the hated collaborator whose ideas Comte had shared and extended, and whose career Comte was destined to duplicate in such unfortunate details as poverty, divorce, mental instability, advocacy of the messianic authoritarianism of a new religion of love and the conviction of being a divinely inspired leader. Of the proposal outlined in the *Politique positive* for the Catholic Church to be replaced by a 'corporate hier-archy' of philosophers with spiritual but not secular power, Mill was highly critical. The proposal required us to rely, he said, 'on this spiritual authority as the only security for good government, the sole bulwark against practical oppression'. The remainder of the book Mill went on to characterize, in a much quoted passage, as

> the completest system of spiritual and temporal despotism which ever yet emanated from a human brain, unless possibly that of Ignatius Loyola: a system by which the yoke of general opinion, wielded by an organized body of spiritual teachers and rulers, would be made supreme over every action, and as far as in human possibility, every thought, of every member of the community, as well in the things which regard only himself, as in those which concern the interests of others.
>
> ([6.49], 221)

How, then, had Comte's attempt to regenerate European society, by the application of the method and results of modern science, reached the stage of evoking such a response from a man who had contributed so greatly to the favourable reception of Comte's ideas in Britain? To answer this question is our major task here.

THE LAW OF THREE STAGES

It is best to begin with the problem that troubled Comte: the dis-harmony he believed to exist between the backward state of the Euro-pean social systems with which he was familiar and the advanced state of the scientific knowledge to which he had been exposed in the École Polytechnique. During this period its staff included Gaspard Monge, the originator of descriptive geometry; Louis Poisson, still one of the most famous of mathematical physicists; Gay-Lussac as the professor of chemistry; Ampère, as a chief contributor to electrodynamics; Cauchy, a creator of the theory of functions among many other achievements; and Fresnel, the pioneer of optical research. These were some of the men whose work, both theoretical and applied, was transforming the intellectual and material culture of Europe and was, in Saint-Simon's and Comte's view, also making obsolete the political systems within which it was being conducted. In his two early essays 'A Brief Appraisal of European History' (1820) and 'Plan of the Scientific Operations Necessary for Reorganizing Society' (1822), Comte suggested that the partnership of Catholicism and feudalism that had ruled Europe from the eleventh century was approaching its end. The prosperity of nations and the organization of their intellectual life no longer needed either a military society or its theological superstructure. The rise of industry and the positive – or experience-based – sciences could, and would, replace war and metaphysics as the unifying forces of the new social order. The development of this order could be encouraged if scientists transformed the pursuit of politics into a theoretical science with practical applications, a science that used historical laws to explain and, above all, predict the course of our social existence.

This was the state of affairs for which Comte believed that he had discovered both the correct analysis and the remedy. In the 'Plan for Reorganizing Society' he wrote:

> The fundamental law which governs the natural progress of civilization rigorously determines the successive states through which the general development of the human race must pass. On the other hand, this law necessarily results from the instinctive tendency of the human race to perfect itself. Consequently it is as completely independent of our control as are the individual instincts the combination of which produces this permanent tendency.
>
> ([6.13], 146)

The 'instinctive tendency' referred to here is the tendency of human beings to make full use of their genetic capacities by means of a social life that they develop in a lawlike fashion, but of whose orderly sequence they are largely unaware. People have reached their natural goals and satisfied their innate desires by evolving, over a long history, a social life in several stages. This conclusion about historical stages is found throughout the eighteenth century. From Vico's description of the necessary course of human history to the later multi-stage views of economic advancement held by Turgot, Quesnay, Mirabeau, Smith, Condorcet and Robertson, interest concerning possible regularities of evolutionary succession in human civilization was intense, and schemes of large-scale historical stages were numerous. By the time that Comte 'discovered' his Law of Three Stages he was familiar with the earlier and similar schemes adapted by Condorcet from Turgot's 'Second Discourse on Universal History' (1751) and by Saint-Simon from

Condorcet. Turgot had discerned three stages in the history of human intellectual development:

> Before men were conversant with the mutual interconnection of physical effects, nothing was more natural than to suppose that these were produced by intelligent beings, invisible and resembling ourselves. Everything that happened ... had its god ...
>
> When the philosophers had recognised the absurdity of these fables ... the idea struck them to explain the causes of phenomena by way of abstract expressions like *essences* and *faculties*: expressions which in fact explained nothing, and about which men reasoned as if they were *beings*, new gods substituted for the old ones. Following these analogies, *faculties* were proliferated in order to provide a cause for each effect.
>
> It was only much later, through observation of the mechanical action which bodies have upon one another, that men derived from this mechanics other hypotheses which mathematics was able to develop and experiment to verify.
>
> ([6.57], 102)

In Comte's version, Turgot's scheme of three stages becomes a 'great fundamental law' that governs by 'invariable necessity' the entire development of human intelligence in its different fields. Comte's law is that each of our principal conceptions, each branch of our knowledge, passes in turn through three different theoretical stages: the theological, or fictitious; the metaphysical, or abstract; the scientific, or positive. These are three distinct and opposed forms of philosophical thinking of which the first is a necessary point of departure, the second merely transitional, and the third fixed and final. In the theological stage, the human mind, enquiring into the inner nature of things – the origin and purpose of the impressions that affect us – supposes these phenomena to be the result of direct and continuous action by supernatural agents. In the metaphysical stage, which for the most part is only a simple modification of the first, the supernatural agents are replaced by abstract forces, personified abstractions, inherent in everything, and conceived of as capable of generating and explaining all observed phenomena by referring each one to a corresponding force. In the positive stage the human mind attempts to discover, by combining reason and observation, the laws of phenomena: that is, their invariable relations of succession and similarity. The explanation of facts is simply the establishment of a connection between particular phenomena and some general facts whose number tends to diminish with the progress of science. The perfection of the positive system, towards which it tends unceasingly, but which it will probably never reach, would be the ability to exhibit all the different observable phenomena as particular cases of a single general fact such as gravitation ([6.8], I, 21–2)

In the *Cours*, Comte advances three kinds of evidence in support of his law. The first is that the positive sciences of the present day still show traces of the two earlier stages. The second is that since the starting point in the education of the individual is the same as that of the species, the principal phases of both are the same, and hence, with respect to the more important ideas, each person is a theologian in childhood, a metaphysician in youth and a scientist in adulthood. The third and most important piece of evidence is that in every age human beings have needed theories with which to connect events, but at the outset of their mental development could not possibly have based their theories on the results of observation. Because a scientific theory must be founded on the observation of phenomena, and they in turn require a theory so that we can notice, connect and retain them, the human mind would have been enclosed in a vicious circle, without any means of escape, if it had not been for the spontaneous development of theological conceptions which provided a primitive solution – a solution that was improved only to a limited extent in the metaphysical era. 'The fundamental character of positive philosophy,' Comte writes, 'is that of regarding all phenomena as subject to invariable natural laws whose accurate detection, and reduction to the smallest number possible, is the goal of all our efforts. Because they are completely inaccessible, it is senseless for us to seek what are called 'causes', whether they be first causes or final causes'. Thus positive philosophy eliminates the useless search for the 'generating causes of phenomena', and tries only 'to analyze exactly the circumstances of their production, connecting one to the other by the normal relations of succession and similarity' ([6.3], I, 25–6)

In objecting to the search for 'generating causes' – or indeed causes in general – Comte is giving a rather limited and special use to the term 'causes'; and he is relying on a simple form of the verification principle with which to exclude such causes. In a genuine science, he says, when we try to explain an obscure fact

> we proceed to form a hypothesis, in agreement, as far as possible, with the whole of the data we are in possession of; and the science, thus left free to develop itself, always ends by disclosing new observable consequences, tending to confirm or invalidate, indisputably, the primitive supposition.

> ([6.11] I, 243)

However, when we go on to speculate about causes that are unobservable in principle, such as 'chimerical fluids causing planetary motions', we are introducing factors that are 'altogether beyond the limit of our faculties' and must always remain so.

> What scientific use can there be in fantastic notions about fluids and imaginary ethers, which are to account for the phenomena of heat, light, electricity and magnetism? . . . These fluids are supposed to be invisible, intangible, even imponderable, and to be inseparable from the substances which they actuate. Their very definition shows them to have no place in real science; for the question of their existence is not a subject for judgment: it can no more be denied than affirmed: our reason has no grasp of them at all.
>
> ([6.11], I, 243)

These unobservable causes explain nothing. To use the idea of an unobservable fluid expanding between molecules as an explanation of the expansion of bodies when heated is to use one mystery to account for another. When we employ such fictitious entities there is a serious risk that sooner or later we shall take them to be real. They are simply examples of the metaphysical forces of whose emptiness we have already been warned ([6.11], 1: 244–5).

❧ THE CHARACTER AND ORGANIZATION ❧ OF THE SCIENCES

Very little of Comte's Law of Three Stages has escaped criticism. In part, Comte encouraged this by his claims concerning its philosophical importance and the major role that he took it to play in his system. True, he emphasized that the different sciences moved through the three stages at different rates and at different times, and that some sciences – mathematics and astronomy, for example – were already in the positive stage whereas physics, chemistry and biology were only on the verge of entering it. Nevertheless, Comte left the status of his law as obscure as had the many previous advocates of such laws of large-scale, inescapable and fixed stages of social evolution. In his later work it became clear that he believed that the law provided the basis of his social reforms: they, after all, were designed to entrench in the new society the methods and outlook of the final, and positivist, stage of intellectual development. It was much less clear whether Comte's law was merely a classification of three types of explanatory theories, and their accompanying social systems, or whether the law was a testable sociological hypothesis about the three historical phases of human thought. The kinds of evidence that Comte himself produced in support of his law, and the fact that he took it to be a truth that he had discovered, indicate that he believed the law to be the most general and basic of all sociological propositions. In this interpretation it has met with many objections. John Stuart Mill produced a number of them in *Auguste Comte and Positivism* (1865). It was unlikely, he thought, that mathematical theorems were ever thought to depend on the intervention of divine or metaphysical forces to make them true. ([6.47], 47) Nor was it necessary for religious belief to be restricted to the theological and metaphysical stages, for a positive scientist can believe that God always rules by means of fixed laws, and this satisfies the chief characteristic of the positivist phase, namely the belief that every event, as part of a 'constant order', is 'the invariable consequent of some antecedent condition'. So Comte might be mistaken in claiming that every event has a purely natural antecedent condition ([6.47], 15). He was certainly mistaken, says Mill, in not recognizing that in every field some conclusions have always been drawn from observation and experience. For that reason, some portion of every discipline must always have been in the positivist phase ([6.47], 51). However, here Mill's complaint is misguided. As early as 1825 Comte had written: 'In truth, man has never been entirely in the theological condition. Some phenomena have always existed, so simple and regular, that, from the first, he could only consider them as subjected to natural laws' ([6.13], 183)

Later critics have rejected the very conception of a law of social or intellectual evolution. Karl Popper, for example, has argued that all such 'laws' are simply trends based on past experience and then projected, unjustifiably, into the future. They are summaries of previous events but offer no basis for reliable prediction. Because these 'laws' are actually trends, and thus not accompanied by qualifications that identify the conditions under which the generalizations can be applied, unexpected changes in local conditions can alter the trends and make them inapplicable ([6.53], 105–30) So embarrassing counter-examples need to be warded off by various defences: as being survivals from the past, as having skipped over crucial stages, as having been subject to unusual rates of change. These devices, says Popper, are necessary because the trend-statements themselves can give us no clue as to why the past events to which they refer have ceased to occur; and since the trends are supposed to be the fundamental laws of the system there is no additional law available for explaining why they sometimes do not work. Comte, of course, believed that his law was satisfactory, and he spent a great deal of time and energy in working out what he took to be its ramifications within the various sciences. He also thought that the law made necessary the adoption of certain philosophical principles concerning the nature, organization and application of scientific knowledge. As a result of holding these beliefs, Comte could not agree that the Law of Three Stages was defective without also admitting that its supposed consequences might be mistaken. A large portion of his system would then be exposed to threat.

Attached to Comte's law is a hierarchical classification of the six basic sciences arranged in the order of their decreasing simplicity, generality and abstractness – or in the order of their increasing complexity, specificity and particularity. First is mathematics; it is followed by physics, chemistry, physiology (biology), and last, social physics, for which Comte later invented the name 'sociology'. Each succeeding science relies on some of the conclusions and laws of the earlier sciences, but the later science cannot be derived from them and they are independent of it. It is correct to refer to the sciences as 'earlier' and 'later' because their hierarchical order is the approximate order in which they developed historically. It is also the order of their decreasing precision, and thus of the steps by which human beings advanced from the more precise but simple disciplines to the less precise but increasingly complex fields. More significantly, says Comte, this scheme shows us that there can be no rational scientific education, and hence no great improvement of scientific knowledge, until each science is studied with a knowledge of all the sciences on which it is dependent.

> Physical philosophers cannot understand Physics without at least a general knowledge of Astronomy; nor Chemists without Physics and Astronomy; nor Physiologists, without Chemistry, Physics, and Astronomy; nor, above all, the students of Social philosophy, without a general knowledge of all the anterior sciences.
>
> ([6.11], 1: 32)

Moreover, the various sciences must be studied in their proper order. Otherwise, the student will not be able to use the indispensable methods and results of the simpler discipline in attempting to master the succeeding and more complex science. For this reason the practice of sociology will require the longest, most arduous, preparation and the outstanding ability, and disinterestedness, needed to make use of it.

Comte was by nature and practice an inveterate and indefatigable classifier. Nevertheless, he gives two rational grounds for producing his scheme of classification. One is that by exhibiting the objectives, methods and limits of the different sciences, and their interrelations, we can improve the organization of scientific research. For new work, especially that requiring several disciplines, will be suggested by various features of the general scheme and be fitted into it appropriately. We shall not, for example, waste energy in grappling with topics such as psychology for which there is, and can be, no positive science. The other ground is that the scheme aids us to renovate our system of theoretical education; the student learns the general concepts, procedures and conclusions that belong to the scientific method itself while also learning how they are exemplified in the various sciences. For until 'a certain number of general ideas can be acknowledged as a rallying point of social doctrine, the nations will remain in a revolutionary state'. But once 'first principles' are agreed upon, 'appropriate institutions will issue from them ... for the causes of disorder will have been arrested by the mere fact of agreement' and a 'normal state of society' will ensue. ([6.11], 1: 16). The disorder to which Comte refers was that marked both by the July revolution of 1830 in which the French king, Charles X, was forced to abdicate in the face of middle-class opposition, and by the proletarian riots during the turbulent years of his successor, Louis Philippe, until he abdicated during the February revolution of 1848.

The sociological significance of Comte's law is that he took each of its three stages to be closely intertwined – for he could not have said causally connected – with the three phases into which he divided European history, phases characterized by the relative strength during each period of the temporal and spiritual (religious or philosophical) authorities. Society in the first phase, dominated from the fourth to the fifteenth century by Catholicism and feudalism, was organized, in its economic structure, for war, and in its intellectual structure for the need of a priestly caste, with its theological knowledge, to share power with the nobles of a military court. The latter demanded 'passive obedience' from the common people, and the former required their 'mental submission'. In the second or metaphysical phase, the Protestant subversion of Papal authority replaced blind faith with a limited degree of intellectual freedom and political authority for the educated or the wealthy. At the same time, free cities, the bourgeoisie and science began their development and interacted with the effects of the Protestant Reformation. In consequence, we are now in the modern phase of industrialism, positive science and political revolutionaries seeking legislative, administrative and social power. Our technological and scientific advances must be matched, therefore, by new forms of social and political authority. These new forms are what Comte believes that he, and perhaps he alone, can offer. He does so in his second major work, the *Système de politique positive*, after having described in the *Cours* the scientific method and knowledge that are to culminate in the positivist society.

However, Comte devoted only two introductory chapters (or lessons), and one later chapter, of the entire sixty in the *Cours* to basic problems in the philosophy of science. These include the scientific status of psychology, the nature of scientific explanation and, of course, the character, scope and application of the Law of Three Stages. Comte rejected the study of psychology because he took it to rely on unverifiable introspection of the intellectual processes and the passions. To this he objected that 'there can be nothing like scientific observation of the passions, except from without, as the stir of the emotions disturbs the observing faculties more or less'. Nor can there be an 'intellectual observation of intellectual processes. The observing and observed organ are here the same, and its action cannot be pure and natural'. The reason, for this, he thinks, is that 'In order to observe, your intellect must pause from activity; yet it is this very activity that you want to observe'. Unless your intellect can pause, it cannot observe. But if it does pause, there is nothing left to observe ([6.11], 1: 12). Of this argument John Stuart Mill complained, many years after his initial enthusiasm for Comte's views had waned, that it is 'a fallacy respecting which the only wonder is that it should impose on anyone'. For if we can learn about the mental life of other people only by observing their behaviour, how can we ever interpret it unless we are allowed to use our knowledge of our own feelings and thoughts? We cannot obtain that knowledge merely by observing our own behaviour. In fact, we obtain self-knowledge both by memory and by our ability to attend to 'a considerable number of impressions at once'. Comte's wish to replace introspection with observation of behaviour, including physiological reactions, neglects the impossibility of then correlating that behaviour with what on his own view is our inaccessible mental life.

Mill recognizes that Comte believes that all mental states are produced by – invariably succeed – states of the brain, and hence that the regularities of succession among mental states necessarily depend upon similar regularities among brain states. Nevertheless, even if this is correct, Mill argues, mental regularities cannot be deduced at present from physiological regularities. We are able to investigate the latter only because we have a better knowledge of the former ([6.47], 63–4). Mill could have added what he also knew: that for all Comte's argument shows, the actual relation between mental states and brain states is the reverse of what Comte believes, and that the latter invariably follow on the former. In any case, the fact that one invariably follows on the other does nothing to make the later regularity either impossible to observe or in some way fictitious. The temporal relation, if any, between the two kinds of regularity is irrelevant to their observability – except that if one of them were unobservable in principle we should find it difficult to establish the temporal relationship.

Comte's dismissal of psychology as a genuine science was not based on the scientific evidence available to him, and the rejection led him to neglect describing what Mill did describe in Book VI of *A System of Logic* (1843), the nature of the relationship between psychological and sociological phenomena – between 'the operations of mental life' and the genuine, or irreducible, laws of society of which Comte was the tireless herald. Comte did assert that the explanation of individual human actions could not be logically derived from supposed 'laws of individual life', whether these laws were psychological or otherwise. For individual actions are the outcome of combined biological and social factors that accumulate over time, and thus create the societies to which all actions of individual people owe their existence. Because such factors underlie and produce the psychological features of every person, it is only the fundamental sociological laws that permit us to explain those features. The laws do so by explaining the character, origin and changes of particular types of societies and of civilization taken as a whole. These conclusions, popular throughout the nineteenth century, were one answer to the widespread demand by thoughtful people during that period for a new scientific certainty to replace their lost religious beliefs. Certainly, the interest of both Comte and Mill in social reform and laws of social change was motivated by their common need to be assured that civilization was proceeding at a reasonable pace on a worthwhile journey. But Mill disagreed with Comte in two important respects: firstly, in believing that psychological laws were a necessary, though not sufficient, condition for the explanation of social phenomena; and secondly, in being convinced that there was not, and could not be, one ultimate law of nature concerning the development of civilization. On this latter point Mill wrote that it is a misconception to suppose

> that the order of succession which we may be able to trace among the different states of society ... could ever amount to a law of nature ... The succession of states of the human mind and human society cannot have an independent law of its own; it must depend on the psychological and ethological laws [of character formation] which govern the action of circumstances on men and of men on circumstances. ([6.48], 2: 914)

In objecting to Comte's belief that there can be a law of social evolution, and that he had formulated it in his Law of Three Stages, F. A. Hayek complained that it is 'a curious feature of the Comtean system that this same law which is supposed to prove the necessity of the new science is at the same time its main and almost sole result' ([6.34], 179) This verdict is somewhat harsh. It is true that Comte formulated few, if any, testable social laws – ordinary laws of the constant concomitance, whether of coexistence or succession, between identifiable social factors. That was not his aim. Instead, he was trying to describe the need for a scientific study of social life, the ways in which the methods of the natural sciences could be used to establish a social science, and the general form that its empirical laws would take as the result of genuinely scientific investigation. Comte did not, and could not correctly, claim to be practising empirical sociology, for that discipline had yet to be created. He believed that the task of the sociologist of the future would be to discover social laws that presupposed the existence of biological laws without being derivable from them – social laws that implied various regularities of national and individual character, including those of mental life. Such laws, he reiterated in the last three volumes (lessons 46–60) of the *Cours*, would take account of two facts: the cumulative effect on people's behaviour of social factors over time; and the way in which social institutions and customs are always parts of a social system and operate as an 'ensemble' of interrelated factors in much the same fashion as do the organs of an animal's body.

Each law of observed phenomena offers us an explanation because every such law connects together under one heading a variety of otherwise disparate facts. Thus the theory of gravitation explains planetary 'attraction' by showing that it conforms to 'the ordinary phenomena which gravity continually produces on the surface of our globe'. The theory brings together

> under one head the whole immense variety of astronomical facts; exhibiting the constant tendency of atoms towards each other in direct proportion to the squares of their distances; whilst the general fact itself is a mere extension of one which is perfectly familiar to us, and which we therefore say that we know; the weight of bodies on the surface of the earth. As to what weight and attraction are, we have nothing to do with that, for it is not a matter of knowledge at all. Theologians and metaphysicians may imagine and refine about such questions; but positive philosophy rejects them.
>
> ([6.11], 1: 6)

The reason they are rejected, says Comte, is that the greatest minds have been able to define the two properties only in terms of each other, so that terrestrial attraction is only weight and weight is nothing more or less than terrestrial attraction. Thus, according to Comte, phenomena are observed facts, and facts can be either specific events and processes or general laws. Since weight and attraction are not directly observable, they are not verifiable scientific facts; they are to be classified with ether and heat-fluid as imaginary causes. However, Comte does not make this complaint of the Newtonian theory that atoms attract each other as the squares of their distances. Nor does he make it when discussing indirect observations of the earth's size. His failure to do so reveals the difficulties that he creates for his system by not distinguishing between things that are observable only in principle and those that are observable in practice. As a result, he has to rely on common sense for deciding which events and processes are observable in any given field of science. For this reason, he has trouble in distinguishing between metaphysical and scientific entities, and hence between questions that can be given a scientific answer and those for which this is impossible. So his reliance on the possibility of future verification to discriminate scientific hypotheses from metaphysical ones is unsupported, for he gives no developed account of any criterion of scientific verifiability except, as we shall see, to admit entailments that are unobservable but lead to observable consequences. He leaves unanswered the question 'what is to count as an observation in science?' Yet his Law of Three Stages assumes that he can discriminate between the stage of metaphysical explanation and that of positive scientific explanation.

These problems are both a result and a source of Comte's ideas about causes. As early as 1840, William Whewell pointed out that hypotheses about unobservable causes were often essential in scientific enquiry. How, for example, he asked, 'could the phenomena of polarization have been conceived or reasoned upon, except by imagining a polar arrangement of particles, or transverse vibrations, or some equivalent hypothesis?' Causes could not simply be metaphysical entities ([6.59], 2: 268). Mill's criticism of Comte on causes was rather different. Comte overlooked the difference, Mill complained, between conditional and unconditional regularities of phenomena. The alternation of night and day is an apparently invariable sequence but it is not a natural law, for it is merely the result of a genuinely invariable regularity, or unconditional sequence, that of the earth's rotation around the sun.

> The succession of night and day is as much an invariable sequence, as the alternate exposure of opposite sides of the earth to the sun. Yet day and night are not the causes of one another; why? Because their sequence, invariable in our experience, is not unconditionally so: those facts only succeed each other, provided that the presence and absence of the sun succeed each other.

> ([6.47], 57–8)

Unconditional regularities, ones in which the antecedent always will be followed by the consequent 'as long as the present constitution of things endures', are laws of causation. Conditional regularities are those in which, as a mere fact of our experience, 'the antecedent always *has* been followed by the consequent'. They are Comte's laws or regularities of phenomena. They simply record what has happened to date, and thus offer no basis for the explanation, prediction and control of phenomena that is so highly valued in Comte's system ([6.47], 57–8).

❧ HYPOTHESES AND SOCIAL LAWS ❧

Despite his difficulties with the notions of observation, cause, verification and law of nature, Comte was one of the earliest social thinkers to stress the indispensability in social scientific work of the appropriate use of theories and hypotheses. In his essay 'Philosophical Considerations on the Sciences and Savants' (1825), he wrote:

> Unless man connects facts with some explanation, he is naturally incapable not merely of combining and making deductions from them, but even of observing and recollecting them. In a word, it is as impossible to make continuous observations without a theory of some kind, as to construct a positive theory without continuous observations.
>
> ([6.13], 185)

Some years later, in the *Cours*, Comte expanded on this view. He suggested that without the help of conjectures (or imaginative hypothesis) we could use neither deduction nor induction:

> Neither of these methods would help us, even in regard to the simplest phenomena, if we did not begin by anticipating the results, by making a provisional supposition, altogether conjectural in the first instance, with regard to some of the very notions which are the object of the inquiry. Hence the necessary introduction of hypotheses into natural philosophy. The method of approximation employed by geometers first suggested the idea; and without it all discovery of natural laws would be impossible in cases of any degree of complexity; and in all, very slow.
>
> ([6.11], 1: 241)

Comte's belief in the importance of hypotheses and theories in scientific work leads him to comment on the relatively small role that observation plays in some astronomical investigation:

> The few incoherent sensations concerned would be, of themselves, very insignificant; they could not teach us the figure of the earth, nor the path of a planet. They are combined and rendered serviceable by long-drawn and complex reasonings; so that we might truly say that the phenomena, however real, are constructed by our understanding.
>
> ([6.11], 1: 151)

So in contrast to his own simpler ideas about the limits of observation, Comte here recognizes the need both for direct observations and for their unobservable entailments, concluding that 'the perpetual necessity of deducing from a small number of direct measures, whether angular or horary, quantities which are not themselves immediately observable, renders the use of abstract mathematics indispensable' ([6.11], 1: 151). Of course, this recognition of the necessity of using unobservable quantities makes the exclusion of unobservable metaphysical causes more difficult, for a general criterion that distinguishes one from the other has now to be found. This was the task undertaken much later by the logical positivists of the Vienna Circle, and in England by A. J. Ayer, in the form of a search for a reliable principle of verification that would separate sense from nonsense, and separate theoretically necessary, but fictional, entities from unobservable but actual ones.

'All sciences,' Comte wrote, 'aim at prevision. For the laws established by the observation of phenomena are generally employed to foretell their succession.' This is as true of sociology as it is of chemistry and physics. All sciences use verified conjectures to predict, explain and thus control phenomena ([6.13], 167). However, in the case of sociology Comte qualifies this view in two respects. The first is that the content of such laws, in sociology as in the other sciences, is to be restricted to the succession and co-existence of observable phenomena, whether direct or indirect – to telling us, in the form of an accurate description, how an event or process takes place, but not why it does. We cannot explain why a particular sequence occurs even though we can describe how it takes place. This distinction between the explanatory 'why?' and the descriptive 'how?' is found in the work of a long line of eighteenth-century philosophers, including Berkeley, Hume, Thomas Reid, Dugald Stewart, Thomas Brown, and also in that of the Sicilian physicist Ruggiero Boscovich. At the end of the nineteenth century the distinction featured prominently in the writings of Ernst Mach, the Austrian physicist who was an early advocate of logical positivism. In this group, Comte was forthright in claiming that laws of phenomena give us genuine explanations because all that we can sensibly want to know is how, and not why, something happened.

The other qualification that Comte applies to the laws of sociology is that they must concern large-scale collective events and processes, for it is the general features of an entire society or form of government or economic system, and the types to which they belong, that are the operative factors in the historical growth of human faculties and achievements. 'It is clear,' he says, 'that the social evolution must be more inevitably subject to natural laws, the more compound are the phenomena, and the less perceptible therefore the irregularities which arise from individual instances.' A closely related point is 'that the laws of social dynamics are most recognizable when they relate to the largest societies, in which secondary disturbances have the smallest effect'. As a civilization develops, 'the social movement becomes more distinct and certain with every conquest over accidental influences'. The result, according to Comte, is that 'these fundamental laws become the more irresistible, and therefore the more appreciable, in proportion to the advancement of the civilization upon which they operate' ([6.11], 2: 231).

In describing this qualification, one of central importance in his system, Comte is led astray, as he often is, by not distinguishing more clearly between a general law and the effects of its operation in any given instance. Thus what is more recognizable, if it is, than the effect produced by a social law operating in a small society is the effect of the law's operation in a large society. Again, it is not the fundamental laws themselves that become more 'irresistible' but their effects in the fields in which they operate. That is, the nature, or content, of the laws does not change; it is the changes in the fields in which they operate that make the laws more recognizable and 'irresistible'. For Comte, the significance for scientific procedure of the distinction between large-scale collective events and 'secondary disturbances' is considerable. 'Astronomers,' he writes,' in commencing their study of the laws of the planetary movements omitted all consideration of the perturbations. After these laws had been discovered, the modifications could be determined' and brought within the scope of the law that applied to the chief movements. But if we had begun by trying 'to account for the irregularities, it is plain that no precise theory could ever have been constructed'.

Comte's conclusion, then, is that, in order to examine the secondary disturbances that affect the rate of social change but do not fundamentally alter it, sociologists must first find the general laws that chiefly control social progress. The counter-influences exerted by secondary factors can then be reduced to the fundamental laws. But how, in Comte's view, do we discover at the beginning which is the 'principal movement' and which the secondary, or accidental, influences? What makes a sociological conjecture a plausible one? To this query Comte offers no response, believing, as he did, that the question has no informative answer other than what he has already said about scientific, and thus sociological, procedure in general: a plausible conjecture is one that not only meets the procedural criteria but takes account of the current state of knowledge within the field. We can only say what makes a particular hypothesis plausible, not what makes hypotheses in general plausible. True, we can exclude certain types. That does not, however, give us a useful characterization of the remainder.

Comte's emphasis on the importance of mass phenomena in sociology largely contributed to a major difficulty in his account of the structure of sociological laws. The difficulty arises from his assumption that, for the most part, sociological laws of the future will be direct generalizations from various sorts of aggregates and collective events. It is to assume, for example, that because the Great Depression of the 1930s was a collective event, each singular causal statement about its causes must imply a generalization about the economic and social causes of depressions in general. Yet this is obviously not true. The fact that our palm tree has been torn up by the roots in a hurricane does not imply that there must be a physical law to the effect that all similar trees are torn up in similar hurricanes. What we are committed to by our singular causal statement is simply this: there are generalizations from which, given appropriate statements of initial conditions, our singular statement is derivable, for these generalizations are physical laws that we can use to explain the effects of certain physical forces, such as hurricanes of a given intensity, on specific types of objects under specifiable conditions. Such laws can be applied to many kinds of situations, and that of our palm tree is merely one of them. Comte thought that the future laws of sociology would be direct generalizations about forms of government, armed forces, rebellions, nations and all other collectivities whose operations could in some sense be observed directly, or indirectly. Yet it has often been remarked that the operations and composition of such aggregates are the joint outcome of highly varied influences and causes. Hence, if there are any sociological laws to be found concerning these collectivities, whether observable or not, the laws must be quite general and abstract.

～ THE SOCIAL REFORMER ～

On the first page of the preface to his second multi-volume work, the *Système de politique positive* (1851–4), Comte says that his philosophical career has been 'homogeneous throughout; the end being clearly aimed at from the first'. He is referring here to his lifelong project to reform the intellectual, social and economic life of European society, and to his intention from the beginning of his career, as his earliest writings show, to develop a social science that would both explain the unhappy state of that society and prescribe the appropriate remedies to eliminate its anarchic condition. Many of the early readers of the *Cours*, such as Mill, Littré and Whewell, were unprepared for the kinds of social prescriptions that Comte issued more and more freely and at ever greater length in his succeeding publications. Comte's history of science and his discussion of its methodology had won their professional admiration; and his claims of the benefits that applied science could bestow on a rejuvenated society, one that embraced the positivist Religion of Humanity, had stirred their religious yearnings for individual fulfilment through the pursuit of a worthy common goal, that of a rejuvenated and unified society. In his 'Introductory Remarks' to the first volume of the *Système* or *System of Positive Polity* Comte makes his project of social regeneration quite explicit:

> it becomes every day more evident how hopeless is the task of reconstructing political institutions without the previous remodelling of opinion and of life. To form then a satisfactory synthesis of all human conceptions is the most evident of our social wants: and it is needed equally for the sake of Order and of Progress. During the gradual accomplishment of this great philosophical work, a new moral power will arise spontaneously throughout the West, which, as its influence increases, will lay down a definite basis for the re-organisation of society. It will offer a general system of education for the adoption of all civilised nations, and by this means will supply in every department of public and private life fixed principles of judgment and conduct. Thus the intellectual movement and the social crisis will be brought continually into close connection with each other. Both will combine to prepare the advanced portion of humanity for the acceptance of a true spiritual power. ([6.6], 1:2)

In the fourth and final volume of the *Système* Comte outlines the nature of social reconstruction and true spiritual power, having used the other three volumes to qualify and amplify the argument of the *Cours*. It is in this last volume that Comte advances his belief that the cultivation and use of the benevolent emotions produces the fullest happiness; that the only moral actions are those performed entirely for the good of other people, and that self-gratifying actions are morally worthless and to be eliminated; that all scientific enquiry is to be pursued and valued only in so far as it fulfils human needs and desires of a practical kind, for disinterested investigation, especially of abstract topics, is morally unwholesome for most people; that useless plants and animals should be destroyed along with the major portion of existing printed material; that the practice of art is the most suitable occupation for human beings since it stimulates their worthwhile emotions; and that these views can best be realized by the concerted action of the working classes and the intellectuals, the latter of whom will later form a priesthood that will lead and maintain the public worship of the Religion of Humanity – that is, the worship of the great and valued dead for their past contributions to human happiness. This priesthood will also be in charge of the educational system that will support the detailed arrangements which Comte laid down for the social and economic tasks to which the various classes of citizens will be assigned according to their ability and qualifications. In brief, the reorganized society will have a theoretical class and a practical class: the former will provide the principles and system of general ideas needed for the guidance of the society; the latter will carry out the administrative and practical measures, such as the distribution of authority and the arrangement of institutions that are needed to fulfil the general plan.

In the early essay, 'Plan for Reorganizing Society', Comte remarked on the long span of time that a scientific or social revolution displayed between the announcement of its basic principles and their embodiment in practice. It required a century, he says, for the conception of the elastic force of steam to find a use in machinery, and five centuries for the 'triumph of Christian doctrines' to develop into the Catholic–feudal system of western Europe – the system upon which his own proposed two classes are modelled. Hence, the rate of social change depends both on the adoption of clear, well understood policies or principles and on the amount of effort put into carrying them out over a long period. This shows us 'the absurdity of attempting to improvise a complete plan for reorganizing society down to its smallest details' ([6.13], 122). Yet this absurdity is what Comte embraces late in the *Système*. There he proposes that school 'instruction will occupy seven years, during which each pupil remains throughout under the same teacher, teaching, be it added, both sexes, though in separate classes'. Every school will need seven priests and three vicars. Each professor will give two lectures a week for ten months, in addition to a month of examinations. 'Every school is annexed to the temple of the district, as is the presbytery, the residences of the ten members of the sacerdotal college and of their families'. The upshot of these arrangements is 'that the spiritual wants of the West may be duly met by a corporation of twenty thousand philosophers, of whom France would have the fourth' ([6.6], 4: 223). It is true that Comte warns us that these numerals will be corrected when better data become available. However, many of the other details will remain, and throughout the volume Comte provides a very large number of fixed and highly specific recommendations.

The philosophical interest of these utopian schemes is slight, but their presence clearly reveals that the dominant impulse in Comte's thought is social reform. For him, philosophical discussions are just a necessary stage in that regenerative process. For that reason, they often form part of his grand system without themselves being systematic or thorough, and often without being advanced or defended by argument. If the distinctive feature of philosophy is, in John Passmore's phrase, 'its being a critical discussion *of* critical discussion', then Comte is a philosopher only on rare occasions. Moreover, he often proceeds to his conclusions without either first- or second-order critical discussion. For instance, in his treatment of astronomy in the *Cours* he begins by asserting that 'astronomical phenomena are the most general, simple, and abstract of all' and that the study of science must begin with them ([6.11], 1: 28). However, this claim depends upon the truth of Comte's later and additional belief that in the case of the planets 'we may determine their forms, their distances, their bulk, and their motions, but we can never know anything of their chemical or mineralogical structure; and much less of organized beings living on their surface'. Not only can we 'never learn their internal constitution', and the amount of heat absorbed by their atmospheres, but their mean temperatures are 'for ever excluded from our recognition'. The laws of astronomy must therefore be the laws solely of the geometrical and mechanical features of the heavenly bodies ([6.11], 1: 148–9) It is this limitation achieved by tendentious definition that makes astronomical phenomena most general, or simple, and abstract; for knowledge, such as we now have, of the chemical and physical structure of astronomical bodies would convert portions of astronomy into 'celestial' physics and chemistry, thus destroying, for Comte, its generality and abstractness.

Again, in his discussion of intellectual progress Comte says of truth,

> our doctrines never represent the outer world with exact fidelity. Nor is it needful that they should. Truth, in any given case, social or individual, means the degree of exactness in representation possible at the time. For positive logic is but the construction of the simplest hypothesis that will explain the whole of the ascertained facts.
>
> Any superfluous complication, besides causing a waste of labour, would be a downright error, even though a fuller acquaintance of facts might at a later time justify it. In fact, without this rule subjectivity runs wild, and the mind tends toward madness ... But in proportion as our observations are extended, we are forced to adopt more complicated theories in order adequately to represent facts. ([6.6], 3: 19)

There are two points of immediate interest here. The first is that the notion of 'exactness in representation' is ill prepared to stand unsupported as it does. For Comte, representation or enunciation of facts – whether the facts are statements of observation or statements of a lawlike kind – can have meaning, and thus be scientific, only if they are testable. The construction of simple explanatory hypotheses is an essential part of the process of confirmation that establishes the claim of factual statements to have meaning. But what makes a testable representation, of varying degrees of exactness, a true one rather than merely a meaningful one? On this point Comte is unhelpful. On the second point he is little better. Permitting undue complication of hypotheses has often been criticized for leading us away from the truth, but seldom for allowing, or perhaps encouraging, the wilder flights of imagination. It is true that unduly complicated hypotheses are sometimes the expression of unchecked imagination although, as Comte himself points out, complex hypotheses are often required. However, what injunctions of simplicity, such as Occam's Razor, are designed to do is to smooth the path to adequate hypotheses, not to constrain imaginative and complex conjectures. Whether they are unnecessarily complex is often impossible to determine until simpler testable ones become available, and even then the nature of the criterion of simplicity may itself be open to debate.

Against such defects in Comte's architectonic method must be set his achievements, near-achievements and fertile errors. His outline of sociology as a new science of social systems, one using empirical data and testable laws to study collective behaviour, combines all three of these characteristics. Before Comte, many writers had advocated the creation of a natural science of politics, but it was Comte who produced a detailed description of its future structure, subject-matter, the scientific procedures appropriate to its topics and the relationship of sociology both to the other sciences in the hierarchy of scientific knowledge and to political action. Social behaviour in the form of interconnected practices, systems and institutions is the cumulative outcome of the historical development of a society in its conformity to the Law of Three Stages, each stage bearing within itself the seeds of the next one. In the case of Europe, Comte thought that each of these intellectual stages was correlated with a distinct type of social system: the theological stage with a theological–military system; the metaphysical stage with a metaphysical–legal system; and the positive stage with a scientific–industrial system. A large portion of the second half of the *Cours*, and also volume three of the *Système*, are devoted to the characteristics, historical development and geographical location of the three systems and their correlated stages. Comte's procedure was to begin with what he took to be the basic general properties of the systems – their types of religion, government, commerce, industry and art, for example – and then to account for either their maintenance or their changes by means of reference to more specific factors and local conditions. He did this because he believed that our knowledge of the three stages and their associated systems was superior to our knowledge of particular institutions and customs. Knowing the Law of Three Stages and their systems we know both the past and present of civilization better than we know the sub-sections that they so strongly influence.

In a general way, we can predict, explain, and thus control, aggregate social behaviour whereas we often cannot do this in cases of individual or sectional or local behaviour and beliefs. Our knowledge of the laws of social wholes, and our ability to observe them, is primary; our information about small-scale phenomena is derivative from that we have on large-scale ones. 'All political action,' Comte says, 'is followed by a real and durable result, when it is exerted in the same direction as the force of civilization, and aims at producing changes which the latter necessitates. On every other hypothesis it exerts no influence or a merely ephemeral one' ([6.13], 148). The phrase 'force of civilization' refers to the Law of Three Stages that 'rigorously determines the successive states through which the general development of the human race must pass'. Because 'this law necessarily results from the instinctive tendency of the human race to perfect itself ... it is as completely independent of our control as are the individual instincts the combination of which produces this permanent tendency' ([6.13], 146). One of the obvious benefits of our knowledge of this rigorous succession, according to Comte, is this:

> When in tracing an institution and a social idea, or a system of institutions and a complete doctrine, from their birth to their present stage, we find that, from a given epoch, their influence has always been either diminishing or increasing, we can foretell with complete certainty the destiny which awaits them ... The period of their fall or triumph may even be calculated, within narrow limits, from the extent and rapidity of the variations observed.
>
> ([6.13], 151)

Claims to foreknowledge of the pattern of social history held special appeal for an educated, and largely Christian, audience in the nineteenth century. Many people agreed with Comte – and with such groups as the British Chartists, the young Hegelians and later the Marxists – that industrial capitalism was in an economic, social and moral crisis. An explanation of its sources and 'prevision' of its outcome were constantly called for, and equally often supplied either as a supplement to, or substitute for, Christian eschatology, these various considerations emerge very clearly in Harriet Martineau's preface to her translation into English in 1853 of the *Cours*. 'We are living in a remarkable time,' she wrote, 'when the conflict of opinions renders a firm foundation of knowledge indispensable.' She thought that 'for want of an anchorage for their convictions' a great number of people are now 'alienated for ever from the kind of faith which sufficed for all in an organic period which has passed away'. No new firm and clear conviction had taken its place, and although 'The moral dangers of such a state of fluctuation are fearful in the extreme', Comte's work, she believed, was 'unquestionably the greatest single effort to obviate this kind of danger' ([6.11], 1: xxiii-xxiv). For in his work 'We find ourselves living, not under capricious and arbitrary conditions... but under great, general, invariable laws, which operate on us as a part of the whole'. Martineau concluded that despite Comte's singular and wearisome style with its 'constant repetition' and overloaded sentences, positive philosophy opened boundless prospects. It had established, among many other 'noble truths', that 'The law of progress is conspicuously at work throughout human history' ([6.11], 1: xxx).

∾ COMTE'S INFLUENCE ∾

After Comte's death, when positivism had to make its own way without the guidance of its first 'High Priest of the Religion of Humanity', it exerted influence in several ways. The first, and least significant, was by doctrinal descendants and proselytizing enthusiasts, and by friendly critics. Prominent in the last group was Emile Littré, editor of the *Journal des savants*, and a decade later of the highly regarded *Dictionnaire de la langue française*. In the former two groups were Pierre Lafitte, a mathematics teacher not favoured by Comte as his successor but who afterwards was the Professor of History of Science at the Collège de France, and an English band consisting, among others, of Edward Beasly, Professor of History, University College, London; Frederick Harrison, the lawyer, philosopher and prolific author; F.S. Marvin, historian and author of *Comte: the Founder of Sociology* (1936); and the Anglican clergyman, and former Oxford tutor, Richard Congreve, who in 1867 founded the London Positivist Society and wrote that 'Positivism is the one idea of my life' ([6.56], 49). Both the British and the French societies founded journals that lasted for several decades, and both societies underwent a long series of internal quarrels and schisms. Nevertheless, the various positivist societies with their small number of members, and a Parisian lending library, kept up a programme of meetings, lectures and courses, in addition to their doctrinal rivalry, until the First World War. They strongly agitated for, and gave firm support to, the establishment of both sociology and the history of science as academic fields of study, and they also campaigned, with some success in France, for a scientific and secular education in schools. However, their more ambitious hopes of arousing popular support for the future Religion of Humanity were never fulfilled.

A second, and more important, influence exerted by positivism on the intellectual life of the nineteenth century was independent of both the organized piety of the positivist societies and the messianic aspirations of Comte himself. Through the early enthusiasm of Mill, a number of eminent and able people in Britain came to read and appreciate the *Cours*. They included not only Grote, Whewell and Molesworth, but also G. H. Lewes, consort of George Eliot, and author of *The Biographical History of Philosophy* (1845–6) which favoured positivism, and of *Comte's Philosophy of the Sciences* (1853); George Eliot herself who was impressed by religious positivism; Henry Sidgwick, the Cambridge philosopher, who later criticized Comte's views; John Morley, editor, biographer of Gladstone and highly successful politician; and John Austin, one of the most influential jurists of the nineteenth century. Of these people only Mill and Lewes were ever substantially influenced by Comte in their work, but the earlier editions of Mill's *A System of Logic* (1843) owed much to Comte's methodology and the later Mill still defended the Law of Three Stages. In France, the historian of science Paul Tannery, an editor of the standard edition of Descartes' *Works* (1897–1910), was said to have believed that Comte's influence on him was stronger than that of any other thinker ([6.56], 133). The philosopher of science Emile Meyerson was a friendly critic of Comte, and in *Identity and Reality* (1908) respectfully criticized Comte's ideas on cause, scientific laws, psychology and physics. Claude Bernard, famous as a physiologist and for his book *An Introduction to the Study of Experimental Medicine* (1865), was thought to have been a disciple of Comte until middle age; after 1865 he became a resolute anti-positivist ([6.56], 15). These three men are merely a small sample of Comte's serious readers in France during the half-century after his death. They, like many other philosophers, scientists and historians, took the reading and study of the *Cours* for granted. They absorbed from it the conceptions that seemed to them valuable and discarded or ignored the remainder. Hardly any of the eminent ones among them, however sympathetic to some of Comte's views, could be described as disciples. In that respect they would have bitterly disappointed Comte's expectations for the future success of his system.

Another and most important way in which Comte's influence made itself prominent was through the young Emile Durkheim, the man who in 1887 was the first person appointed to lecture on sociology in a French university. For a few years Durkheim was a discriminating enthusiast for Comte's conception of the nature of sociology; he adopted much of Comte's belief in the significance of the collective mind in society as the creator and sustainer of religious and moral attitudes, the guarantor of social stability, and the chief bulwark against the loss of self-esteem by the members and their accompanying alienation from common values. However, even though Durkheim's second book, *The Rules of Sociological Method* (1895), attacks positivist claims on many issues, he later reiterated his debt to Comte and 'continued to recommend the *Cours* as the best possible initiation into the study of sociology' ([6.56], 147). Other sociologists of this period, such as Gabriel Tarde, were similarly both critical and appreciative of Comte's work. Much of their kind of discussion was incorporated into the academic teaching of sociology and anthropology throughout Europe and America, and in that form has continued to influence social science until the present day.

In its devotion to major social reform, positivism found a responsive audience among the early Fabians. Like Durkheim, they rejected the anarchic, irrational, inefficient individualism that they took to be the hallmark of materialistic capitalism. Like Saint-Simon and Comte, they wished to create a scientifically organized society in which, to use Gertrude Himmelfarb's words,

> the parts were arranged, ordered, regulated, planned, so as to make for the most efficient and equitable whole. Such a society could come about only through the conscious effort of intellectuals and 'scientists' ... who were prepared to dedicate themselves to the public good and bring their superior reason to bear upon the reorganization of the public order.
>
> ([6.35], 359–60)

The Fabian collectivist society of the future would be led and presided over, as were the utopias of Comte and Saint-Simon, by a theoretical class devoted to the social good and the elimination of competitiveness. It would be ascetic and non-materialistic as was positivism, and yet evolutionary rather than revolutionary – and so anti-Marxist. These Fabians were not, of course, religious positivists, but as socialists they claimed the politically conservative Comte as one of their own. Five of the seven authors of *Fabian Essays* (1889) were positivist sympathizers:

> Beatrice Webb (then Beatrice Potter) had been familiar with Comte from her schoolgirl reading of Mill, Harrison, and George Eliot; by 1884 her diary contained frequent references to Comte and excerpts from his writings. Long before he met her, Sidney Webb had heard about Comte at the Zetetical Society and later at the London Positivist Society. He and his friends Sydney Olivier, a fellow clerk in the Colonial Office, and Graham Wallas, a young schoolmaster, were so taken with Comte that they embarked upon a systematic reading of all his works.
>
> ([6.35], 358–9)

These four were not the only Fabians who were sympathetic to positivism. Its project of individual moral reform produced by social regeneration, the latter itself the result of the application of scientific knowledge and method to a sick society, had widespread appeal in the late nineteenth century. It is an appeal which – however viciously distorted by various communist regimes in the twentieth century – is still with us today.

❦ BIBLIOGRAPHY ❦

Works – French editions

6.1 *Système de politique positive*, 4 vols, Paris, 1851–4; reprint Osnabrück: O. Zeller, 1967.

6.2 *Oeuvres*, 12 vols, reprint Paris: Editions Anthropos, 1968

6.3 *Cours de philosophie positive*, ed. M. Serres et al., 2 vols, Paris: Hermann, 1975.

6.4 *Lettres d'Auguste Comte à John Stuart Mill, 1841–1846*, Paris: E. Leroux, Paris: 1877.

6.5 *Correspondance Générale et Confessions*, ed. P. Berredo Carneiro and P. Arnaud, 8 vols, Paris: Mouton, and J. Vrin, 1923–90.

English translations

6.6 *System of Positive Polity*, trans. J. H. Bridges, Frederic Harrison et al., 4 vols, London: 1875: reprint New York: Burt & Franklin, 1966.

6.7 *A General View of Postivism*, trans. J. H. Bridges of *Discours sur l'ensemble du positivisme* (1848), London: W. Reeves, 1880.

6.8 *Appeal to the Conservatives*, trans. T. C. Donkin and R. Congreve of *Appel aux Conservateurs d'ordre et progrès* (1855); London: Trübner, 1889.

6.9 *Religion of Humanity . . . Subjective Synthesis*, vol. I, trans. R. Congreve of *Synthèse subjective* (1856), London: Trübner, 1891.

6.10 *The Catechism of Positive Religion*, trans. R. Congreve of *Catéchisme positiviste* (1852), London: Kegan Paul, 1891; reprint Clifton, N.J.: Augustus Kelley, 1973.

6.11 *The Positive Philosophy*, trans. and condensed by H. Martineau, 3 vols (1853), from *Cours de Philosophie positive* (1830–42), London: George Bell, 1896.

6.12 *Confessions and Testament of Auguste Comte and his Correspondence with Clothilde de Vaux*, trans. A. Crompton of *Testament d'Auguste Comte et correspondance avec Clothilde de Vaux* (1884), Liverpool: H. Young & Sons, 1910.

6.13 *The Crisis of Industrial Civilization: The Early Essays of Auguste Comte*, London: Heinemann, 1974; reprint of general appendix, vol. 4, *System of Positive Polity*.

Discussions

6.14 Acton, H. B. 'Comte's Positivism and the Science of Society', *Philosophy*, 26 (99) (1951): 291–310.

6.15 Annan, N. *The Curious Strength of Positivism in English Thought*, London: Oxford University Press, 1959.

6.16 Arnaud, P. *Sociologie de Comte*, Paris: Presses Universitaires de France, 1969.

6.17 Aron, R. *Main Currents in Sociological Thought*, trans. R. Howard and H. Weaver, 2 vols, vol. 1, London: Weidenfeld and Nicolson, 1965.

6.18 Bréhier É. *The Nineteenth Century: Period of Systems, 1800–1850* (1932), trans. W. Baskin, Chicago: University of Chicago Press, 1968.

6.19 Brown, R. *The Nature of Social Laws*, Cambridge: Cambridge University Press, 1984.

6.20 Caird, E. *The Social Philosophy and Religion of Comte*, Glasgow: James Maclehose, 1885.

6.21 Charlton, D. G. *Positivist Thought in France*, Oxford: Clarendon Press, 1959.

6.22 Ducassé, P. *Méthode et Intuition chez Auguste Comte*, Paris: Félix Alcan, 1939.

6.23 Dumas, G. *Psychologie de Deux Messies, Positivistes Saint-Simon et Auguste Comte*, Paris: Félix Alcan, 1905.

6.24 Durkheim, E. *The Rules of Sociological Method* (1895), trans. S. A. Solovay and J. H. Mueller, New York: Free Press, 1964.

6.25 —— *Socialism and Saint-Simon* (1928), trans. C. Sattler, London: Routledge, 1959.

6.26 Eisen, S. 'Herbert Spencer and the Spectre of Comte', *The Journal of British Studies*, 7 (1967): 48–67.

6.27 Evans-Pritchard, E. E. *The Sociology of Comte: An Appreciation*, Manchester: Manchester University Press, 1970.

6.28 Fletcher, R. *Auguste Comte and the Making of Sociology*, London: Athlone Press, 1966.

6.29 Flint, R. *Historical Philosophy in France*, Edinburgh: William Blackwood, 1893.

6.30 Gouhier, H. G. *La Jeunesse d'Auguste Comte et la formation du positivisme*, 3 vols, Paris: J. Vrin, 1933–41.

6.31 —— *La Vie d'Auguste Comte*, Paris: J. Vrin, 1965.

6.32 Hawkins, R. L. *Auguste Comte and the United States*, Cambridge, Mass.: Harvard University Press, 1936.

6.33 —— *Positivism in the United States (1853–1861)*, Cambridge, Mass.: Harvard University Press, 1938.

6.34 Hayek, F. A. *The Counter-Revolution of Science*, Glencoe, Ill.: Free Press, 1955.

6.35 Himmelfarb, G. *Poverty and Compassion*, New York: Knopf, 1991.

6.36 Höffding, H. *A History of Modern Philosophy*, 2 vols, vol. 2, New York: Dover reprint, 1955.

6.37 Kremer-Marietti, A. *Auguste Comte et la théorie sociale du positivisme*, Paris: Seghers, 1970.

6.38 Laudan, L. 'Towards a Reassessment of Comte's "Méthode Positive" ', *Philosophy of Science*, 37 (1971): 35–53.

6.39 Lévy-Bruhl, L. *The Philosophy of Auguste Comte*, trans. K. de Beaumont-Klein, London: Swan Sonnenschein, 1903.

6.40 Lewes, G. H. *The History of Philosophy, From Thales to Comte*, 4th edn, 2 vols, vol. 2, London: Longmans, 1781.

6.41 Littré, E. *Auguste Comte et la philosophie positive*, Paris: Hachette, 1863; reprint Westmead, Gregg, 1971.

6.42 Manuel, F. E. *The New World of Henri Saint-Simon*, Cambridge, Mass.: Harvard University Press, 1956.

6.43 —— *The Prophets of Paris*, Cambridge, Mass.: Harvard University Press, 1962.

6.44 Marvin, F. S. *Comte, The Founder of Sociology*, reprint, New York: Russell & Russell, 1965.

6.45 Meyerson, E. *Identity and Reality* (1908), trans. K. Lowenberg, London: Allen & Unwin, 1930.

6.46 Michel, U. *La Théorie du savoir dans la philosophie d'Auguste Comte*, Paris: Félix Alcan, 1928.

6.47 Mill, J. S. *Auguste Comte and Positivism* (1865), 2nd edn, London: Trübner, 1866.

6.48 —— *A System of Logic*, 2 vols, Toronto and London: University of Toronto Press and Routledge, 1974.

6.49 —— *Autobiography and Literary Essays*, Toronto and London: University of Toronto Press and Routledge, 1981.

6.50 Passmore, J. *The Perfectibility of Man*, London: Duckworth, 1970.

6.51 Pickering, M. 'Comte and German Philosophy', *Journal of the History of Ideas*, 50 (3)(1989): 443–63.

6.52 Plamenatz, J. *Man and Society*, 2 vols, vol. 2, London: Longmans, 1963.

6.53 Popper, K. *The Poverty of Historicism*, London: Routledge, 1957.

6.54 Scharff, R. C. 'Mill's Misreading of Comte on "Interior Observation" ', *Journal of the History of Philosophy*, 27 (4) (1989): 559–72.

6.55 —— 'Positivism, Philosophy of Science, and Self-Understanding in Comte and Mill', *American Philosophical Quarterly*, 26 (4) (1989): 253–68.

6.56 Simon, W. M. *European Positivism in the Nineteenth Century*, Ithaca: Cornell University Press, 1963.

6.57 Turgot, A. *On Progress, Sociology and Economics*, trans. and ed. R. L. Meek, Cambridge: Cambridge University Press, 1973.

6.58 Vernon, R. 'Auguste Comte and the Withering-Away of the State', *Journal of the History of Ideas*, 45 (4) (1984): 549–66.

6.59 Whewell, W. *The Philosophy of the Inductive Sciences*, 2 vols, London: Parker, 1840.

6.60 Whittaker, T. *Comte and Mill*, London: Constable, 1908.

6.61 —— *Reason: A Philosophical Essay*, Cambridge: Cambridge University Press, 1934.

6.62 Wright, T. R. *The Religion of Humanity*, Cambridge: Cambridge University Press, 1986.

CHAPTER 7

Nietzsche
Robin Small

Friedrich Wilhelm Nietzsche (1844–1900) is one of those thinkers whose personalities cannot easily be separated from their achievements in philosophy. This is not because his life was an unusually eventful one in outer respects. Rather, it is due to the intensely personal engagement in thinking that is evident throughout his writings. Franz Rosenzweig's description of Nietzsche as 'the first real human being among the philosophers' is a striking testimony to this characteristic; though Rosenzweig was less justified in dismissing the content of Nietzsche's thinking as irrelevant to his real importance.

Nietzsche was born in 1844 in Röcken, a village in Saxony, the son of a Lutheran minister. After the death of his father four years later, the family moved to Naumburg, where Nietzsche attended the local Gymnasium before being sent as a boarder to the famous Pforta school. He emerged as a classical scholar of great promise, moving on to the universities of Bonn and Leipzig, where he attracted the sponsorship of the influential Ritschl. With his assistance, Nietzsche was appointed at the early age of twenty-four to a chair in classical philology at the University of Basel. His early promise in scholarship was soon overshadowed by new developments. Making the acquaintance of Richard Wagner, Nietzsche was drawn into the Wagner circle, which turned his talents to its own purposes. His first book, *The Birth of Tragedy*, published in 1872, created a storm of controversy. It gave great offence to professional colleagues for its championing of the Wagnerian 'artwork of the future', as well for its unconventional approach to scholarship. But Nietzsche had by now largely lost interest in philology; his writings over the next few years, published under the general title *Untimely Meditations*, are essays in cultural criticism, often stimulating and sometimes brilliant, yet marred by a Wagnerian mixture of pomposity and abrasiveness.

Several events now brought about decisive changes in Nietzsche's life. A breakdown in his health led to a temporary separation from the university; a year's leave was spent in Sorrento, working on a new book, *Human, All-Too-Human*. A break with Wagner followed, brought about primarily by Nietzsche's negative reaction to the 1876 Bayreuth festival and to Wagner's new opera *Parsifal*, whose religiosity aroused Nietzsche's lasting hostility. Two years later, renewed illness led to permanent retirement from the university on a modest pension. From this time onward, Nietzsche was a man seemingly always on the move. He established a regular routine: summers spent in Germany or eastern Switzerland, reading widely and making extensive notes which, during winters on the Italian and French Riviera, were turned into a succession of books. After *Human, All Too Human*, the works in which Nietzsche's mature style is confidently established followed at regular intervals: *Mixed Opinions and Maxims*, *The Wanderer and His Shadow*, *Daybreak* and *The Gay Science*.

This pattern was to last for a decade. Although restless, Nietzsche was at the same time a man of regular habits. Apart from one not very successful trip to Sicily, he tended to return to the same places, neither cultural centres nor tourist spots but smaller cities in which he lived in inexpensive boarding houses. Always intensely health-conscious, Nietzsche suffered from a variety of illnesses, despite a healthy regime of frugal eating and long walks. Although often alone, he was not a recluse but made friends and joined in social activities. Indeed, he retained a certain Naumburg bourgeois character, which surfaces from time to time in his opinions. Nietzsche the person was no bohemian: conventional in dress and manner, he was also courteous and forbearing in responding to sometimes obtuse correspondents, reserving his polemical skills for his writings. As one observer reported after an 1884 encounter in Nice, 'He was extremely friendly, and there is no trace of false pathos or of the prophet about him, as I had rather feared from the recent works'.

The question of Nietzsche's relations with women has excited and frustrated biographers. He always retained unusually close links with his mother and younger sister, despite a few periods of estrangement. Apart from this, there is evidence for only one significant attachment. After his Sicilian expedition of 1882, Nietzsche visited Rome with his friend Paul Rée, a writer on moral psychology. There he met a young Russian girl, Lou von Salomé. An intense emotional period followed, during which the two men conducted a fierce, but unacknowledged, rivalry for Lou's loyalty. The outcome was an estrangement, incited by the hostility of Nietzsche's conservative sister Elisabeth, though also due, in part, to Nietzsche's own conventional side. A disillusioned Nietzsche returned to the Italian Riviera and began work on a new kind of writing, *Thus Spoke Zarathustra*. The successively published parts of this, his best known work, occupied him for several years.

In 1886 Nietzsche returned to the format of *The Gay Science* with his most accomplished book, *Beyond Good and Evil*. The subsequent year produced a bold exploration of moral concepts, *The Genealogy of Morals*. During the autumn of 1888, Nietzsche's letters and writing took on an ominous tone of exaltation, as he worked on a series of works in rapid succession: *Nietzsche Contra Wagner*, a summary of his long campaign against his former friend; *The Antichrist*, a polemic against Christianity; and a remarkable autobiographical essay, *Ecce Homo*. In the early days of 1889, Nietzsche suffered a sudden mental collapse in the streets of Turin, where he was spending the winter. Brought back to Germany by a friend, he was treated in a Jena asylum, but without improvement, and afterwards nursed at home by his mother and sister. Nietzsche never regained mental clarity, and underwent a steady physical decline until his death in 1900. The cause of the catastrophe is unconfirmed, but the initial diagnosis of syphilis seems the likeliest explanation.

～ WORKS AND STYLES ～

Nietzsche's style of writing is very varied: hardly two of his books can be put in a given category. Works such as *Human, All Too Human* and *Daybreak* are often described as 'aphoristic', though they are really composed of short essays, often carefully arranged in an overall progression of thought. One philosophical style hardly ever used by Nietzsche is that of extended argument. He gave an indication of his strategy when he wrote: 'I approach deep problems like cold baths: quickly into them and quickly out again' (*The Gay Science*, section 381). Yet Nietzsche returns to these problems again and again, and one can often see patterns in his ways of approaching them: not only continuities, but variations on a theme, developments of a line of thinking, reactions against former approaches, ideas gained from other thinkers, and ventures into new alternatives. The consistencies over the twenty years of his writing life are of style rather than doctrine.

Particularly striking is Nietzsche's use of the aphorism, which serves, as he puts it, 'to say in a few words what other writers say in a book – or do *not* say in a book'. We can take, as a typical example, section 126 of *The Gay Science*: '*Mystical explanations*. Mystical explanations are considered deep. The truth is that they are not even superficial.' Setting aside its superfluous title, this is a genuine aphorism, a self-contained thought which nevertheless lends itself to interpretation and elaboration. The 'mystical' is anything that refers to something higher, as when some experience is explained as the voice of God. The 'superficial' is the surface of things, the qualities experienced through the senses. Thus, the opposition invoked is that between appearance and reality. In the metaphysical tradition of Plato, appearance is devalued as in need of explanation by reference to a truer reality. But Nietzsche, who called his thinking an 'inverted Platonism', wants a greater respect for appearance. Science, he suggests, has advanced only in so far as the senses have been trusted; and so we do not need to flee from appearance, but to engage more closely with both inner and outer phenomena; and metaphysical explanations merely distract us from that task. Typically, however, Nietzsche elsewhere takes a different line, praising the courage of those who have repudiated the evidence of the senses, like Parmenides and Plato in metaphysics, and Copernicus in natural science.

Putting Nietzsche's thought into traditional philosophical categories, such as idealism or materialism, rationalism or irrationalism, is a vain exercise. Sometimes he is included in the assortment of thinkers labelled 'existentialists'. This is an arbitrary and in some ways misleading categorization which, with a greater appreciation of Nietzsche's thought, has now gone out of use. One can at most specify certain recognizable philosophical principles for which Nietzsche often expresses support: the idea that the world is one of becoming, not of being, and as a consequence of this, an opposition to any doctrine that posits a reality over and above the world of appearance. An important corollary is the rejection of traditional religion, not only as a metaphysical doctrine but also in its implications for moral concepts. These points are closely linked with Nietzsche's professed admiration of Heraclitus; in his own words:

> The affirmation of passing away *and destroying*, which is the decisive feature of a Dionysian philosophy; saying Yes in opposition and war; *becoming*, along with a radical repudiation of the very concept of *being* – all this is clearly more closely related to me than anything else thought to date. The doctrine of the 'eternal recurrence' that is, of the unconditional and infinitely related circular course of all things – this doctrine of Zarathustra might in the end have been taught already by Heraclitus.
>
> (*Ecce Homo*, 'The Birth of Tragedy', 3)

Nietzsche wants to be an affirmative thinker, a 'yes-sayer'. But the possibility of such an affirmation depends on overcoming a system of concepts that have dominated human thinking. Hence he is, in practice, a critical thinker – indeed, one of the most destructive in the history of philosophy. Nietzsche provides a critique of knowledge, and its concept of truth and objectivity; of morality, and its concepts of good and evil; of philosophy, and its concept of being or reality; and of religion, and its concept of God. In each case, Nietzsche champions the concepts rejected by these systems: he affirms the value of lies, of fate, of semblance and becoming. But his critiques are not external ones; he argues that the highest values *devalue themselves*. To take an example: the will to truth is something we owe to the Christian tradition, which judged the world of appearance as one of untruth, and so posed the task of finding genuine truth. But the determination to follow a line of thought to its end – not a natural human trait, but a capacity acquired with great difficulty – has led to the downfall of those beliefs. We now recognize that our knowledge is based on metaphors; and a metaphor, because it asserts the identity of what is not identical, is really a lie. It is these lies that human beings need to create a world of stable and regular objects, within which they can live.

In his early sketches, Nietzsche supports this view of knowledge by using a vocabulary of rhetoric rather than logic. The basic operation of thought is not unconscious inference, as suggested by some neo-Kantians. Rather, figures of speech provide the model for all thinking: in particular, metonymy and metaphor are its crucial operations. Language, Nietzsche suggests, consists entirely of metaphors; and metaphor, which equates the unequal, is a lie, or perhaps a riddle.

> What, then, is truth? A mobile army of metaphors, metonyms, and anthropomorphisms – in short, a sum of human relations, which have been enhanced, transposed, and embellished poetically and rhetorically, and which after long use seem firm, canonical, and obligatory to a people: truths are illusions about which one has forgotten that this is what they are; metaphors which are worn out and without sensuous power; coins which have lost their pictures and now matter only as metal, no longer as coins.
>
> ('On Truth and Lie in an Extra-Moral Sense')

These ideas about knowledge suit the Heraclitean concept of absolute becoming which, as Nietzsche understands it, implies a process which has no beginning or end, and contains no pauses. 'If there were just one moment of being in the strict sense,' he writes, 'there could be no further becoming.' Yet that is not how we ordinarily understand the world. Our organs of perception are geared to the conditions of our survival, and they allow us to apprehend only a minute fraction of what happens. Hence we suppose that there are discontinuities and separate things: even the most fleeting process, such as a flash of lightning, is imagined as the activity *of* something. Our language contains philosophical assumptions: 'Every word is a prejudice' (*The Wanderer and His Shadow*, section 55). Because the Indo-European languages contain the distinction between subject and activity, they determine our conceptual bias towards belief in permanent or at least enduring beings, and lead inevitably to belief in the soul and in material substance. The line of thought here is akin to the more recent hypotheses concerning the determining influence of language structure on our ways of seeing the world. But our conditions of life demand such illusions; for absolute becoming makes the world ungraspable. Hence we invent fictions which enable us to make sense of the world, such as things, and hence numbers and formulae. Nietzsche is not proposing any move to a new language: even Zarathustra, who proclaims a 'new speech', still uses German. It seems that we must go on using the only language available to us, while acknowledging that its concepts are inadequate to reality.

❧ INFLUENCES AND REACTIONS ❧

A search for direct influences on Nietzsche is not very rewarding. He did speak of a supposed group of 'new philosophers'; but in reality, Nietzsche had no philosophical associates. Schopenhauer and Wagner are often mentioned as early influences. Nietzsche gained much from both – as thinkers he could react against, primarily in ethical and aesthetic concepts respectively. Schopenhauer was an early passion, and the subject of an 'untimely meditation' which makes no mention of transcendental idealism, pessimism and the doctrine of the will as essence of the world; instead, Schopenhauer's independence and hatred of philosophical obscurantism are celebrated. Emerson was an influence for similar reasons. His essay form, flexible and loosely structured, was very congenial to Nietzsche. Again, the doctrines are hardly important, and the idea of an 'over-soul' common to all thinkers is the opposite of Nietzsche's view. Yet he retained a high opinion of Emerson, and an essay such as 'Self-Reliance', with its forthright rejection of any consistency in belief or action, has a very Nietzschean ring: 'Speak what you think now in hard words; and tomorrow speak what tomorrow thinks in hard words again, even though it contradict everything you said today'. Moreover, the Emersonian emphasis on the will has a direct relation to Nietzsche's later idea of the will to power.

Among philosophers of a more academic kind, Nietzsche's reading was largely in contemporary writers, some not much known even in their day, let alone a century later. Two figures worth attention are the idealists Friedrich Albert Lange and Gustav Teichmüller. In *Beyond*

Good and Evil, Nietzsche pays a generous tribute to both thinkers for the courage of their metaphysical thinking – at the same time as he rejects their principal theses. Nietzsche studied Lange's important *History of Materialism* shortly after its publication in 1865, and often returned to it later. It was a fortunate encounter, for the book provides a comprehensive survey of materialist thought, from Democritus to the nineteenth century. Just as valuable is Lange's responsible and fair-minded approach, which gives full credit to the contributions of the materialist philosophy, while in the end rejecting it in favour of a neo-Kantian idealism. Lange characterises materialism as a conservative force in science, emphasizing facts at the expense of ideas, hypotheses and theories. He recommends a more speculative approach, raising even paradoxical questions. Materialism 'trusts the senses', Lange says, and it pictures the world accordingly. Yet the scientific investigations that arise on this basis undermine philosophical realism. Lange's treatment of perception is like that of Hermann von Helmholtz: when we understand how information received by the senses is transformed by our sensory apparatus, we must conclude that the world as we perceive it is really a product of our organization. This includes our own sense organs, since their status as objects of perception is no different from other things. Nietzsche rejects Lange's argument as incoherent: 'But then our organs would be – the work of our organs! It seems to me that this is a complete *reductio ad absurdum*' (*Beyond Good and Evil*, section 15.) In contrast, he suggests that 'Today we possess science precisely to the extent to which we have learned to *accept* the testimony of the senses – to the extent to which we sharpen them further, arm them, and have learned to think them through to the end.' (*Twilight of the Idols*, ' "Reason" in Philosophy', section 2.) This is not realism, but 'sensualism', an affirmation of appearance in its own right, however unstable and contradictory it may be.

In 1882 Nietzsche read a newly published book entitled *Die wirkliche und die scheinbare Welt* (*The Real and the Apparent World*), by a former Basel colleague, Gustav Teichmüller. From this work he gathered several concepts of great use for his subsequent thinking. Central to Teichmüller's metaphysical system is the idea of 'perspective'. The defect of dogmatism in all its forms is, he argues, its failure to appreciate that all philosophies are 'projective' or 'perspectival' images of reality from a certain standpoint. The same is true of the knowledge of everyday life, in which we rely on what Teichmüller terms 'semiotic' knowledge, that is, a translation of phenomena into the vocabulary of a particular sense. Even our own mental states are known in this way alone. Each sense has its own 'sign language', and philosophy has been dominated by a bias in favour of sight; we need to overthrow this dictatorship and establish a kind of democracy of the senses and their corresponding concepts. Treating space and time as perspectival concepts, Teichmüller arrives at a conventionalist account, according to which questions about infinity reduce to arbitrary decisions about measurement. Materialism and idealism are alike inadequate, because they remain within their limited perspectives. Teichmüller's own system posits an intellectual intuition of the real self, a timeless subject which, transcending all perspectives, is their ultimate source.

With the exception of this last point, Nietzsche's own view of knowledge takes up many of Teichmüller's themes. His most striking idea is usually referred to as 'perspectivism', though in fact Nietzsche uses the word *Perspektivismus* not for a certain doctrine but for the property of being perspectival, that is, for 'perspectivity'. The assertion that there are only perspectives, without the underpinning supplied by either things-in-themselves or by a 'real' self, implies an opposition to objectivity, or at least to one version of objectivity. Nietzsche says that we need to control our drives 'so that one knows how to employ a *variety* of perspectives and affective interpretations in the service of knowledge'. This leads to a truer conception of objectivity: 'There is *only* a perspective seeing, *only* a perspective "knowing"; and the *more* affects we allow to speak about one thing, the *more* eyes, different eyes, we can use to observe one thing, the more complete will our "concept" of this thing, our "objectivity" be' (*The Genealogy of Morals*, Third Essay, section 12). Nietzsche often asserts that we are prisoners of our human perspectives, forever unable to see 'around our corner'. Yet he also suggests that artists have the ability to provide us with otherwise unavailable perspectives; and he claims for himself a special talent for 'reversing' perspectives. A condition of this genuine objectivity is an avoidance of 'convictions', that is, of beliefs purporting to possess certainty. 'Convictions are more dangerous enemies of truth than lies,' Nietzsche writes (*Human, All Too Human*, section 483). Avoiding convictions does not imply an ironic withdrawal from engagement and commitment: on the contrary, we should 'live dangerously' in the quest for knowledge, risking ourselves in following an hypothesis as far as it can be taken.

These concerns are crucial in Nietzsche's attitude towards science. Cut off from primary scientific sources by his lack of mathematics, Nietzsche browsed widely among popular science and *Naturphilosophie*, and was aware of current debates – for instance, over the implications of the second law of thermodynamics. Many of these authors were what one might term vulgar Leibnizians, writers opposed to mechanism for its supposed superficiality and soullessness, and often willing to suggest a close link between materialism and the English national character. Nietzsche's approach is free of this tone, and his assessment of materialism is of far more interest.

For Nietzsche, mechanism is first and foremost a *methodology*. Its ideal, he says, is 'to explain, i.e. put into formulae, as much as possible with as little as possible.' ([7.5], 7/3. 158). The best theory is the one which uses the fewest concepts, while encompassing the most natural phenomena. This idea is well known in Ernst Mach's formulation of the 'principle of economy'. But Nietzsche links it with a main theme of his own: the will to power. Scientific theory enables us to exert more control over our environment. More importantly, however, scientific theory is itself a form of power. Mechanism is the most advanced and successful form of science, just because it embodies this scientific imperative in its purest form, nowhere seen more than in *reductionism*, its essential strategy and the key to its greatest successes.

Nietzsche's complaint against materialism is that it has not pushed its own programme far enough. He took the dynamic physics of Boscovich to represent a further step. Whereas Copernicus overcame the belief in the stability of the earth, Boscovich opposed an equally deep prejudice: the notion of material substance. The outcome is a theory in which solid material atoms are replaced with unextended 'points of matter' (in the terminology of Faraday, 'centres of force') whose spatial fields produce all the familiar modes of interaction with other centres: repulsion, cohesion and mutual impenetrability. Boscovich thus eliminates not only the distinction between matter and force but also the distinctions between kinds of force.

Another concept to be eliminated is, Nietzsche considers, that of causality. Materialism eliminates teleology, and uses only causal explanation; yet Nietzsche suggests that efficient causes are not alternatives to final causes, but only disguised versions of them. Scientific formulae establish quantitative equalities (in terms of energy or mass) between states of affairs, which make no mention of cause and effect. Thus, Nietzsche argues, science should give up any pretence to provide *explanations* of phenomena, and content itself with an accurate description of them. If explanation is turning the unfamiliar into the familiar, then it appeals to what we take to be familiar, the everyday experience of what can be seen and felt, and the even more familiar processes of our own minds, thinking, willing, and so on. However, the seeming certainty of these phenomena is an illusion. Even the simplest experience, the 'I think', turns out on closer examination to contain a number of assumptions, such as the distinctness of the subject from the process of thinking. Summarizing these critiques, Nietzsche writes:

> When I think of my philosophical genealogy, I feel in agreement with the anti-teleological, i.e. Spinozistic movement of our time, but with this difference, that I hold even the 'aim' and 'will' *within us* to be an illusion: similarly with the mechanistic

movement (tracing all moral and aesthetic questions back to physiological ones, all physiological to chemical ones, all chemical to mechanical ones) but with this difference, that I do not believe in 'matter' and hold Boscovich to be one of the great turning-points, like Copernicus.

([7.5], 7/2: 164)

Also unusual in Nietzsche's approach to science is his refusal to separate scientific thought from the personality of the scientist. The original founders of science, the materialist thinkers of ancient Greece, were free spirits. Modern scientists are less admirable: unlike the poet Lucretius, they are prosaic minds, who turn science into a routine procedure, relying on measuring and calculating to ensure security. Their materialism is taken as a doctrine, when it should be a provisional hypothesis, allowing us to run ahead of our present knowledge into unknown areas. With this in mind, we cannot separate these ideas from Nietzsche's more obviously imaginative and speculative writings.

❧ THUS SPOKE ZARATHUSTRA ❧

Nietzsche regarded *Thus Spoke Zarathustra* as his most important achievement. The work's subtitle, 'A Book for Everyone and No one', conveys its mixture of accessibility and inaccessibility. In style, it is most obviously modelled on the Bible; and Nietzsche may have gained a hint of the possibilities of Biblical pastiche from Mark Twain's satirical description of the Mormon scriptures. Although the name 'Zarathustra' is borrowed from the ancient Iranian figure, there is no particular relation between Nietzsche's protagonist and the historical Zarathustra. Rather, Nietzsche has chosen a format which allows a dramatic and poetic presentation of ideas which could hardly be expressed in a more conventional manner. Although he had been preparing and making notes for the composition for some time, the actual writing of each instalment was done in a few weeks. This may account for the spontaneity of many passages, but it cannot be denied that the level is uneven. Zarathustra is forceful, poetic, thoughtful and satirical; he can also be rambling and querulous or, worse still, as sentimental as his all-too-legitimate descendant, Kahlil Gibran's best-selling 'Prophet'. Especially in Part Three, the careful organization of Nietzsche's earlier books is lacking; and the turn to a kind of satirical burlesque in Part Four, while it has some admirers, is seen by most (including, perhaps, its author) as failing to achieve its intentions. Martin Heidegger advised that we ought to read *Thus Spoke Zarathustra* just as rigorously as we read a work of Aristotle – though he added that this does not mean in precisely the same way ([7.40], 70). There is much in this, even though, knowing something of Nietzsche's personal life, we recognize various allusions in the text.

In Part One Zarathustra is introduced as a sage who, weary of his solitary possession of wisdom, descends from a mountain retreat to bring it as a gift to humanity. In a marketplace he announces to an unreceptive audience his message of self-overcoming, the process of transforming oneself into something higher through turning passions into 'virtues'. The aim in this process is what Zarathustra calls the *Übermensch*. (Since some readers are distracted by the overtones of English words like 'superman', recent practice has been to leave the term untranslated.) This idea has often been misinterpreted: it has nothing to do with any evolution of the human species towards a more 'advanced' form. Even taking it as the development of a single person is too literal, since Zarathustra's further discourses specify the problem in terms of forces or impulses *within* the individual. We have no literal vocabulary for these, it seems, and so need to personify them. The *Übermensch* is thus a symbol for higher states of being, as when Nietzsche speaks of 'the invention of gods, heroes, and *Übermenschen* of all kinds' (*The Gay Science*, section 143).

The relation between soul and body is a main theme in Part One. Zarathustra insists that the soul is not separate from and superior to the body. On the contrary, the soul is an instrument of the body, and its characteristics express the state of the body – where 'body' is to be understood as a collection of impulses and drives. Our virtues arise from the body, and are indissolubly linked with the passions that morality usually condemns. Hence those who seek refuge in a world 'beyond' are enemies of life, whose assertions are only symptoms of their own sickness and weariness of life. Zarathustra's scorn for these 'preachers of death' is expressed in a series of fierce denunciations.

Part Two is more poetic, and we now catch glimpses of the higher state, as important themes emerge with greater emphasis. Zarathustra states his task as the 'overcoming of revenge': 'For *that man may be delivered from revenge*, that is for me the bridge to the highest hope, and a rainbow after long storms'. The key to this liberation is the creative will, which, as a 'will to power', is identified as the essence of life itself. Yet Zarathustra notes that one obstacle stands in the way of this otherwise omnipotent power: its own past.

> But now learn this too: the will itself is still a prisoner. Willing liberates; but what is it that puts even the liberator himself in fetters? 'It was' – that is the name of the will's gnashing of teeth and most secret melancholy. Powerless against what has been done, he is an angry spectator of all that is past. The will cannot

will backwards; and that he cannot break time and time's covetousness, that is the will's loneliest melancholy.

(*Thus Spake Zarathustra*, Second Part, 'On Redemption')

Because the will cannot will backwards, it suffers from frustration and anger, and *revenge* is its attempt to escape from the predicament. Revenge can be understood at various levels. As a common pattern of social behaviour, it expresses a mixture of motives, ranging from immediate self-preservation to a maintenance of social prestige (*The Wanderer and His Shadow*, section 33). In a narrower sense, revenge is an attempt to redirect one's own pain on to others, under the pretext that their 'guilt' requires them to suffer. From that rationalization in turn derives the whole apparatus of moral thinking and, for that matter, the concept of the individual subject as bearer of moral responsibility. Ultimately, however, revenge is concerned with time: 'This, indeed this alone, is what revenge is: the will's ill-will against time and its "It was" '. It is this alone that accounts for the extraordinary prevalence of revenge, or rather of its intellectual form, the 'spirit of revenge', across the range of human thinking.

Just what is it that makes the past a problem here? Not, it seems, its factual content, but simply its pastness. In that case, whether the events and acts of the past were good or bad, pleasurable or painful, is irrelevant. So is the distinction between actions and mere happenings: one's own past actions, having become past, are as far removed from the power of the will as anything else that has taken place. The past is thus an undifferentiated totality. The solution, if there is one, to the problem of the past must enable us to *affirm* the past as a whole, not just with its pains but with its trivial and meaningless elements. There must, Zarathustra hints, be a way of transforming 'It was' into 'Thus I willed it' and, in turn, into 'Thus I will it; thus shall I will it'. The thought of eternal recurrence, to be considered below, must be seen in that light.

In Part Three of *Thus Spoke Zarathustra*, Nietzsche enters into deeper themes. Peaceful episodes of exalted mystical feeling alternate with stormy scenes of confrontation and struggle, as Zarathustra comes slowly and reluctantly to accept his role as teacher of the eternal recurrence. It is clear that this thought, more than any other, is only for those few who are ready to let it gain power over them. A fourth part of the work changes direction again, with Zarathustra's encounters with the 'higher men' who, in different ways, illustrate the pitfalls in the way of self-overcoming. The intended tone is satirical – but modelled on the ancient satyr plays which followed performances of Greek tragedy. Nietzsche himself was apparently dissatisfied with Part Four since, after having copies privately printed, he withdrew it from circulation. Whether *Thus Spoke Zarathustra* can be regarded as a completed work is doubtful. Certainly, many of its themes are left unresolved, not least the one that Nietzsche called the 'fundamental conception' of the book, the thought of eternal return.

❧ ETERNAL RECURRENCE ❧

On his own account, the idea of the eternal return came to Nietzsche quite suddenly, during his summer residence in Switzerland in August 1881. Yet his notebooks of the time reveal a wide reading in popular science and philosophy of nature, including discussions of the idea of recurrence. From the beginning, the idea is sketched out by Nietzsche in several forms. In his notebooks, though not in published works, he sketches an argument using the vocabulary of science. The key to this line of thought is Nietzsche's finitism. He takes the world to be a finite amount of energy, within a space which is also finite although unbounded. If the world consists of a finite number of 'centres of force', and any state of affairs consists in some configuration of these elements, then the number of possible states of affairs must be finite; or so Nietzsche supposes: critics have pointed out that this is a *non sequitur*, supposing space to be a continuum. But the time within which changes occur is infinite. Nietzsche insists on an infinitude of past time, since a beginning for the world would raise the question of its cause, and perhaps invite a theistic answer. Therefore, after a long but finite period of time, the whole range of possible situations must be exhausted, and some past state will reappear. Such a recurrence of a single total state will lead to the recurrence of the whole sequence of states, in exactly the same order, leading to another complete cycle, and so on into infinity.

This is not a wholly original argument: something similar can be found in earlier philosophers, going back at least as far as Lucretius. With the required premises, it has the look of a valid demonstration. If we suppose that whatever is possible must occur in an infinite time, that past time is infinite, and that the present state of affairs is a possible one, it follows that this state must already have occurred in the past, not just once but infinitely many times. Similarly, it must occur again infinitely many times in the future. Once a principle of causal determination is added, it follows that the whole course of events leading up to this moment, as well as that following from it, must recur eternally in the same sequence.

As a line of thought, all this is somewhat inconsistent with Nietzsche's expressed views. A vocabulary of static 'states' is at odds with his support of a Heraclitean doctrine of absolute becoming, which allows no standstill, even the most momentary one. Further, the argument relies on a causal determinism stated in terms of necessary relations between 'total states' of the universe. Elsewhere Nietzsche maintains that reality consists not of momentary states related by cause and effect but rather of extended processes which are somehow 'intertwined' or 'entangled' with one another. Causality cannot explain why there should be any change at all, or why change should occupy some finite amount of time, instead of being instantaneous. Nietzsche proposes to explain the finite duration of processes by an inner conflict of forces, a conception bound up with the idea that the will to power is found in physical as well as psychical processes.

In these sketches, the theory of eternal recurrence is arrived at by eliminating two other accounts of the world. The view that becoming continues endlessly into new states of affairs is, Nietzsche argues, excluded by the finitude of the universe. On the other hand, the idea of a final state, one in which all change comes to an end, is refuted by immediate experience. Given an infinitude of past time, such an ending would already have been reached; and, if reached, it would never have given rise to further development, assuming no divine intervention. Since our thinking shows that becoming has not come to an end, a final state must be impossible. This leaves only one possibility: that the same states are repeated again and again, infinitely many times. Now this procedure is not very consistent with Nietzsche's programme for scientific thinking: a theory arrived at by elimination is not a daring hypothesis, or even a particularly imaginative conception. In any case, a scientific theory of eternal recurrence, however valid, does not account for anything in our experience, and so has no value for scientific explanation; it is just a final consequence of premises already accepted. We could see all this as an *ad hominem* strategy, arguing with science on its own grounds, and using its own principles of thought. Arguing ideas to their final consequences, even to the point of absurdity is, after all, valued by Nietzsche as a mark of integrity.

In Nietzsche's published works, the idea of eternal recurrence is always presented in a dramatic context of confrontation and challenge. This is especially true of the striking section of *The Gay Science* in which the idea is first introduced:

> What, if some day or night a demon were to steal after you into
> your loneliest loneliness and say to you: 'this life as you now live
> it and have lived it, you will have to live once more and
> innumerable times more; and there will be nothing new in it,
> but every pain and every joy and every thought and sigh and
> everything unutterably small and great in your life will have
> to return to you, all in the same succession and sequence – even

this spider and this moonlight between the trees, and even this moment and I myself. The eternal hourglass of existence is turned upside down again and again, and you with it, speck of dust!'

Would you not throw yourself down and gnash your teeth and curse the demon who spoke thus? Or have you once experienced a tremendous moment when you would have answered him: 'You are a god and never have I heard anything more divine.' If this thought gained possession of you, it would change you as you are and perhaps crush you. The question in each and every thing, 'Do you desire this once more and innumerable times more?' would lie upon your actions as the greatest weight. Or how well disposed would you have to become to yourself and to life *to crave nothing more fervently* than this ultimate eternal confirmation and seal?

(The Gay Science, section 341)

Here the thought of recurrence is announced, not demonstrated. There is no question of a debate, or even of a choice between acceptance and rejection. Each of us will presumably respond according to the sort of person we are. One possible reaction is a complete collapse. In this respect, the thought is something like the doctrine of eternal punishment; in fact, Nietzsche's depiction of this outcome owes much, surprisingly, to English accounts of Methodist preaching. But the thought is also presented as a power for transformation into a higher state, in which one is able to affirm 'each and every thing' as having a status which is a kind of approach to eternal being, without an imagined escape from the course of becoming.

The element of challenge is just as evident in a powerful chapter of *Thus Spoke Zarathustra* (Third Part, 'On the Vision and the Riddle'). Zarathustra describes an episode in which he confronts his enemy, the dwarflike 'spirit of gravity', and initiates a contest of riddles. He points out a gateway which stands between two lanes, stretching forwards and backwards into an infinite distance. The gateway, at which they come into conflict, has a name: 'Moment'. Zarathustra poses a question: do the lanes contradict one another eternally? The dwarf answers that 'time itself is a circle' – implying that any conflict between past and future is a mere semblance. Angered by the evasion, Zarathustra retorts with a direct statement of the thought of recurrence: must not everything that runs on these lanes do so again and again? The dwarf, apparently unable to confront this idea, disappears from the scene. A new turn follows, as Zarathustra describes a vision which is also a riddle. A young shepherd is choking on a 'heavy black snake' which has crawled into his throat. The shepherd bites the head off the snake, and leaps up, transfigured: 'one changed, radiant, *laughing*!' What does this mean? The question remains unanswered. Perhaps Nietzsche is unwilling to eliminate the tension and enigmatic character of this situation, or alert to Emerson's suggestion that 'The answer to a riddle is another riddle'.

Some aspects of the theme of eternal recurrence are shared by another main idea of Nietzsche, the 'death of God', first announced in section 125 of *The Gay Science*:

> Have you not heard of that madman who lit a lantern in the bright morning hours, ran to the market place, and cried incessantly, 'I seek God! I seek God!' As many of those who do not believe in God were standing around just then, he provoked much laughter. Why, did he get lost? said one. Did he lose his way like a child? said another. Or is he in hiding? Is he afraid of us? Has he gone on a voyage? or emigrated? Thus they yelled and laughed. The madman jumped into their midst and pierced them with his glances.
>
> 'Whither is God' he cried. 'I shall tell you. *We have killed him* – you and I. All of us are his murderers ... God is dead. God remains dead. And we have killed him. ... Is not the greatness of this deed too great for us? Must we not ourselves become gods simply to seem worthy of it? There has never been a greater deed; and whoever will be born after us – for the sake of this deed he will be part of a higher history than all history hitherto.'

As in *Thus Spoke Zarathustra*, the message is not received by the marketplace crowd; and the 'madman' acknowledges the failure of his mission. He has come too early, he says.

> This tremendous event is still on its way, still wandering – it has not yet reached the ears of man. Lightning and thunder require time, the light of the stars requires time, deeds require time even after they are done, before they can be seen and heard. This deed is still more distant from them than the most distant stars – *and yet they have done it themselves*.

It must be noted that the message of the death of God is addressed not to believers but to 'those who do not believe in God'. The assumption is that there are no believers in the modern world, or at least in the marketplace, symbol of mass society. When Zarathustra encounters one believer, a hermit who lives apart from society, he refrains from revealing that God is dead; the message is only for those who have brought it about. The hermit is 'untimely' too, and would appear as absurd in the marketplace as the madman. There, support for Christianity is not an error, Nietzsche alleges in *The Antichrist*, but a deliberate lie. 'Everyone knows this, *and yet everything continues as before.*' Nietzsche's target here is those who have abandoned traditional religion yet who assume that morality can be continued in the same way. 'They are rid of the Christian God and now believe all the more firmly that they must cling to Christian morality ... Christianity is a system, a *whole* view of things thought out together. By breaking one concept out of it, the faith in God, one breaks the whole: nothing necessary remains in one's hands.' Nietzsche is insisting on understanding the full implications of disbelief. It puts in doubt not just the explicit content of old beliefs but the standards of knowledge and morality whose foundations they supplied. The madman expresses this as the predicament he and his listeners are in, whether they realize it or not.

As with the thought of eternal recurrence, Nietzsche's emphasis is on the consequences of the idea, rather than on reasons for supporting it. His atheism does not arise from any critique of arguments for the existence of God. Once we have a psychological account of the origin of belief in God, he argues, 'a counter-proof that there is no God thereby becomes superfluous' (*Daybreak*, section 95). Elsewhere his atheism seems to be not a reasoned view but a stipulation. Zarathustra says: '*If* there were gods, how could I endure not to be a god? *Hence* there are no gods.' His real objection is to the *concept* of God, as a denial of life and, in turn, a symptom of a lack of creative power within individuals and groups.

In this way, the 'death of God' is part of a wider theme: what Nietzsche, in his last years of work, termed 'nihilism'. The collapse of all values, even that of truth, has led to a historical situation of hopelessness. 'One interpretation has collapsed; but because it was considered *the* interpretation it now seems as if there were no meaning at all in existence, as if everything were in vain' (*The Will to Power*, section 55). Within philosophy, scepticism and pessimism fit into this picture, as symptoms of decline – ultimately, Nietzsche suggests, owing to physiological causes. But he makes an important distinction between two kinds of nihilism. *Active* nihilism is an expression of strength, while *passive* nihilism is a sign of weakness. Active nihilism finds satisfaction in destroying old illusions, and the will to pursue ideas through 'to their ultimate consequences', even to absurdity. This is just the truthfulness that leads to a paradox, by putting the question of its own origin and value, and thus undermining its own validity. Affirmative nihilism represents a preparation for a new phase of creativity. In the symbolic language of *Thus Spoke Zarathustra*, it is the strength of the lion, courageous and defiant, who destroys the authority of every 'Thou shalt' and assumes the lonely task of setting up his own values.

✿ NIETZSCHE AS PSYCHOLOGIST ✿

Nietzsche often called himself a 'psychologist' rather than a 'philosopher'. What he meant has little to do with any science of behaviour modelling itself on the physical sciences. In the first section of *Human, All Too Human*, he uses the metaphor of 'sublimation', taken from physical chemistry, to express the transformation of lower into higher impulses. (Borrowed by Freud, this expression has become common.) Moral and religious sentiments do not have a higher origin, or give access to any realm of values; their difference from lower impulses is one of degree, not of kind. Crucial to this picture is a rejection of the unity of personality. The self is, in fact, a plurality of forces – Nietzsche says 'personlike' forces, whose relation to one another is a sort of political structure. A healthy and strong personality is one which has a well organized structure amongst its drives and impulses. Despite his talk of the 'will to power', Nietzsche regards the will in its usual sense as a fiction. When we analyse the typical 'act of will' we find a mixture of various elements: sensations of the 'before' and 'after' states, of the movement, of the thinking, and above all of the 'affect of superiority' associated with an inner commanding. This last is close to synonymous with the will to power. But where that concept comes to the fore is in biology, where it allows Nietzsche to oppose Darwinism, or at least what he takes to be the Darwinist emphasis on the will to live: 'The physiologists should take heed before they assume self-preservation as the cardinal drive of an organic being. Above all, a living being wants to discharge its energy: life as such is will to power. Self-preservation is only one of its indirect and most frequent consequences' (*Beyond Good and Evil*, section 13).

For many philosophical questions, it is difficult to separate psychological and metaphysical components in Nietzsche's approach. His critique of pessimism is an example. Nietzsche argues that it is absurd to make any judgement about the value of the world as a whole, simply because there can be no external measure by which to assess it. If pessimism means that there is more pain than pleasure in life, it implies a hedonism which Nietzsche regards as a superficial psychology. Pleasure and pain are not 'facts of consciousness', phenomena whose nature is self-evident, but themselves interpretations, and therefore dependent on context for their meaning. Accordingly, Nietzsche attacks utilitarianism for its uncritical view of pleasure and pain, as well as its appeal to quantitative calculation: 'What can be counted is worth little'.

Similarly, valuing oneself is entirely dependent on what sort of self this is; despising oneself may represent a higher state. The egoism that Nietzsche advocates is unlike the common version, in that it involves no solicitude for the existing self; that is a sign of weakness, not strength, and a failure in the important task of self-overcoming. Further, the 'self' that such importance is placed upon is a very secondary phenomenon, often merely the product of others' expectations. The personality that we are aware of in our everyday lives is only the surface of what we are, and the thoughts and motives we attribute to ourselves are only the end-products of the real processes going on within us. A genuine egoism must direct our attention towards the real self, and bring about a transformation of the person. It must be an affirmation of becoming, implying not just change but conflict, contradiction and even destruction. Conflict has to be seen as a positive and creative process, in the spirit of Heraclitus's statement that 'War is the father of all things'. Becoming is not just a philosophical concept but something to be affirmed in our lives, by committing ourselves to the process of self-transformation. As Emerson said, 'Power ceases in the instant of repose'. Affirming becoming means affirming conflict, between individuals and groups of individuals, but also within ourselves.

A constant theme in Nietzsche's writing, from its earliest period, is his rejection of the freedom of the will and endorsement of a fatalist view of becoming, for which 'Event and necessary event is a tautology'. But Nietzsche opposes what he calls 'Turkish fatalism', which separates human beings from circumstances, and sees them as the passive victims of impersonal, incomprehensible forces. We must realize that we are ourselves a part of nature, and exert as much influence over what is to come as does any other factor. On the assumption that all things are connected with one another, even our most trivial acts make a difference to the whole course of later events. This notion of *ego fatum* is closely related to another: *amor fati*, often invoked in enthusiastic tones, as Nietzsche asserts that we must not merely accept fate but love it: 'My formula for greatness in a human being is *amor fati*: that one wants nothing to be different, not forward, not backward, not in all eternity' (*Ecce Homo*, 'Why I am So Clever', section 10). Fatalism is not a crushing weight if we 'incorporate' it, so that the force of past and present circumstances is balanced by the same force within ourselves. That there are no goals beyond the process of becoming, no reality above the world of appearance, is to be experienced as a precondition for true freedom.

> For what is freedom? That one has the will to assume
> responsibility for oneself. That one maintains the distance
> which separates us. That one becomes more indifferent to
> difficulties, hardships, privation, even to life itself. That one is

prepared to sacrifice human beings for one's cause, not excluding oneself.

> (*Twilight of the Idols*, 'Skirmishes of An Untimely Man',
> section 38)

This responsibility for oneself has nothing in common with the moral responsibility which is a pretext for assigning blame and justifying punishment. It is a function of the strength of will whose typical expression is the ability to make and keep promises – primarily to oneself, not to others. To this 'free spirit', Nietzsche poses the demand: 'Become what you are!' This may suggest a Kantian or Schopenhauerian concept of intelligible character; yet Nietzsche has no belief in an intelligible self, located beyond the realm of becoming.

❧ A REVALUATION OF VALUES ❧

A constant theme in Nietzsche's thought is a radical revaluation of moral conceptions. In *Human, All Too Human*, he introduces a crucial distinction between two kinds of morality. One, the earliest source of these concepts, is the creation of ruling groups and individuals. 'Good and bad is for a long time the same thing as noble and base, master and slave. On the other hand, one does not regard the enemy as evil: he can requite. In Homer the Trojan and Greek are both good. It is not he who does us harm but who is contemptible who counts as bad' (*Human, All Too Human*, section 45). The second kind is that of the subjected and the powerless, the system of moral concepts that rational-izes their lack of power. Nietzsche returns to this theme in *Beyond Good and Evil*; but it is in *The Genealogy of Morals* – the last work he published, and one of his most daring – that the theory is fully elaborated. Each of its three long essays develops a central moral theme in terms of the concept of the will to power. There are two types of morality, 'master morality' and 'slave morality', though Nietzsche adds that 'at times they occur directly alongside each other – even in the same human being, within a *single* soul' (*Beyond Good and Evil*, section 260). In the first case, a ruling group posits its own sense of nobility and superiority as valuable and good. Here 'good' means 'noble', whereas 'bad' means 'common'. In the second case, the weak establish their own values, in which strength is regarded as 'evil'. At the most fundamental level, the distinction is a 'physiological' one, between active impulses, spontaneous expressions of one's own energy, and the 'reactive' impulses, which by their nature are directed *against* some-thing, an external danger. In fact, the noble are really not much interested in the ignoble; but the weak are preoccupied with the strong.

Nietzsche uses the French word *ressentiment* for their attitude. 'The slave revolt in morality begins when *ressentiment* itself becomes creative and gives birth to values: the *ressentiment* of natures that are denied the true reaction, that of action, and compensate themselves with an imaginary revenge.' Christian morality is the most successful instance of such a system. But since the weak lack the power to take revenge directly, their revenge has to be mediated by a long and indirect process of deceitful conceptual manipulation which induces the strong to value respect and pity for the weak, and to condemn their own virtues.

Having laid out this schema, Nietzsche goes on to discuss the concept of responsibility, proposing a prehistory of harsh discipline out of which human beings have acquired the ability to maintain a commitment. Moral conscience is an internalized product of social custom. But like so much of morality, this turns against itself – for its final product is the person whose independence extends to the choice of goals. A further discussion of asceticism brings out the ambiguity which so often appears in Nietzsche's interpretation of moral phenomena. Asceticism can mean either of two very different things. Poverty, humility and chastity can be found in the lives of the great creative spirits; but here they are not valued for their own sakes, only as conditions enabling their activities to flourish most advantageously. This is very different from the attitude of the 'ascetic priest' who is really hostile towards life itself.

Nietzsche's thinking about society is really an extension of his attack on morality. He always emphasizes distinctions and 'order of rank'. He is hostile to socialism, as he understands it, understood as a levelling phenomenon, based on *ressentiment*. It must be remembered that his prototype of the socialist was not Karl Marx but rather Eugen Dühring – ironically, remembered later only as the target of Friedrich Engels's polemical work *Anti-Dühring*. Dühring traces the concept of justice back to the impulse towards revenge. He argues that revenge is given an impersonal and universal form by society, which establishes its own monopoly and takes vengeance out of the hands of individuals. Dühring was also a leading anti-Semite; and Nietzsche perceptively attributes this ideology ('the socialism of fools', as August Bebel called it) to the same underlying impulse. In one way, Nietzsche agrees with Dühring: that a formalist approach cannot account for the concept of justice. But he objects that Dühring has overlooked another class of drives: the active and creative ones. Systems of law are not set up by the weak for their common protection against the strong, or in order to satisfy their reactive feelings. Rather, they are instituted by individuals or groups who are 'active, strong, spontaneous, aggressive.'

❧ CULTURE, ART AND MUSIC ❧

Although its scholarship plays a secondary role to intuition, *The Birth of Tragedy* has been influential for its distinction between the 'Apollonian' and 'Dionysian' strains in Greek culture. Nietzsche wanted to get away from the classical stereotype of Greek culture, to point to a darker, more violent and uncontrolled side. He traces the origins of tragedy to the trancelike state of the devotees of Dionysus, the god of death and rebirth. In their drunken ecstasies, the distinction between individual and world is eliminated; the truth of existence as a never-ending process of creation and destruction is revealed. The original performers of tragedy, Nietzsche suggests, are the chorus, who translate this insight into the visible forms of the Apollonian style, modelled on dream images. The downfall of ancient tragedy, Nietzsche goes on to argue, was brought about by the ascendancy of rationalism, as represented in the figure of Socrates. Access to the sources of tragic wisdom is now blocked, and so the fruitful interaction of the Dionysian and Apollonian becomes impossible.

Having reached this conclusion, *The Birth of Tragedy* turns into an exercise in special pleading for the Wagnerian 'artwork of the future' as a vehicle for national revival. Nietzsche's ideas on aesthetics cannot be separated from the history of his involvement with Richard Wagner. By the time Nietzsche knew him, Wagner's early admiration for the humanistic materialism of Ludwig Feuerbach had given way to a Schopenhauerian pessimism, clearly visible in the operas of his *Ring* cycle, as in *The Birth of Tragedy*. Much of Wagner's influence was bad, especially a pompous tone and indulgence in personal polemic, both of which Nietzsche soon outgrew. In later years, Nietzsche clearly missed the camaraderie he had enjoyed in the Wagner circle, and wistful references to a group of 'new philosophers' appear in such later writings as *Beyond Good and Evil*. Wagner had argued for an art based on *pathos* rather than *ethos*, claiming Beethoven as both the paradigm case and his own immediate precursor. Many of Nietzsche's later reflections on style take the form of attacks on Wagner and a critique of the Wagnerian musical style which is often just a reaction against it. Music remained a preoccupation for Nietzsche, extending to several ventures in musical composition; in comparison, attention to the visual arts is notable by its absence. Perhaps surprisingly, Nietzsche took no interest in the operas of another winter resident of Genoa, Giuseppe Verdi; instead, he expressed admiration for Bizet's *Carmen*, much to the disgust of one reader, the unrepentant Wagnerian Bernard Shaw. Whether Nietzsche would have welcomed the *verismo* of the 1890s is unclear; his hostility to literary naturalism suggests not, and yet the abrupt termination of his development leaves such questions open.

More importantly, however, Nietzsche wanted to become known as a poet. His published works contain not only some light satirical verse but also more serious poetry, so-called 'dithyrambs', a term suggesting the choral hymns of Greek drama; *Thus Spoke Zarathustra* contains many instances of such a poetic prose.

Nietzsche wanted to be thought of as a 'good European', like Goethe, standing above national divisions. He often made derogatory comments about German culture, arguing that the political and military victories of the Prussian Empire had been achieved at the expense of its cultural values, and professing to think more highly of French culture for its *esprit*. The light style of French aphorists such as La Rochefoucauld and Chamfort appealed to him as a model which he emulated with some success. As a humorist he is less skilful, but *The Wagner Case* is a true satire, which conveys serious ideas with a light touch.

❧ INTERPRETATIONS OF NIETZSCHE ❧

Although his books sold poorly when first published, Nietzsche had become a well-known writer by the time he died. His unpublished writings, which included several completed works and a large collection of notebooks, remained under the control of his sister until her death in 1935. The history of their publication is a dramatic and in part scandalous story. Extensive notes from the last years of his work were brought out under the name *The Will to Power*, one of the many titles for works that Nietzsche projected. Whether he would ever have issued anything resembling this book is very doubtful indeed. The value of Nietzsche's notebooks has been the subject of a somewhat sterile controversy amongst commentators, with opinions ranging from summary dismissal to the equally exaggerated view that Nietzsche deliberately withheld his most important ideas. The sudden ending of his working life makes any claim as to what he would have later published speculative.

The control of Nietzsche's writings by his sister, until her death in 1935, had unfortunate effects. Nietzsche's reputation has suffered from her admiration for Adolf Hitler, an honoured guest at the Nietzsche Archiv in Weimar, where he was photographed contemplating a bust of the philosopher. More significantly, the works themselves were often tampered with, passages being removed or even altered to suit the purposes of Elisabeth Förster-Nietzsche. A scholarly edition, begun in the 1930s, was interrupted by the Second World War before it had progressed beyond the earliest writings; not until the 1960s was a collected edition of Nietzsche's writings begun again, under the editorship of two Italian scholars, Giorgio Colli and Mazzino Montinari. This work has continued steadily, to the great benefit of scholarship.

Nietzsche's influence has been strong on artists. Composers such as Richard Strauss and Delius set passages of *Thus Spoke Zarathustra* to music, and Nietzsche's life has inspired such works of fiction as Thomas Mann's *Doctor Faustus*, and was even the subject of a 1977 film entitled *Beyond Good and Evil*, described by one reviewer as 'somewhat disturbingly unpleasant'. In English-speaking countries, appreciation of Nietzsche was slow to come. His admirers were often eccentrics of an intellectual fringe, attracted by his scornful remarks about democracy, socialism and feminism. James Joyce's story 'A Painful Case' gives a cruelly accurate picture of the 'Nietzschean' of this period. A collected English edition of Nietzsche's published works was brought out by these enthusiasts shortly after his death. The translations are of variable quality, with *Thus Spoke Zarathustra* dutifully rendered in a distractingly pseudo-Biblical style. The later translations of Walter Kaufmann and R. J. Hollingdale, covering the same range, are far superior in both reliability and readability.

The 1960s saw a renewal of interest in Nietzsche and, in a slightly arbitrary way, three important works of that time, appearing in different languages yet in close succession, may be singled out. Martin Heidegger's two-volume *Nietzsche* (1961) was really the text of lectures delivered twenty years earlier. Nietzsche is here a figure of historical importance: the last western philosopher of the tradition beginning with Plato, who brings the glorification of the human will to its most explicit form, and whose conception of nihilism captures accurately the essence of our own historical situation. Gilles Deleuze's *Nietzsche et philosophie* (1962, [7.34]) presents Nietzsche, in a version suited to the French philosophical scene of the time, as an opponent of Hegelian dialectical thought, a philosopher who replaces opposition and contradiction with difference. In Arthur Danto's *Nietzsche as Philosopher* (1965, [7.33]), Nietzsche is something of an analytic philosopher, interested in the problems that have concerned such philosophers: about truth and knowledge, morality and religion. More recently, the 'postmodern movement' in particular is strongly influenced by Nietzsche, as a radical thinker who subverts all established norms. Alexander Nehamas's widely read *Nietzsche: Life as Literature* (1985, [7.50]) is less unorthodox, yet it offers an original interpretation. Nehamas argues that Nietzsche recommends treating one's own life as something like a work of art. By reinterpreting the past, we can overcome the angry frustration of the will confronting the 'stone it cannot move'. All these versions of Nietzsche find support in his writings, as do yet other lines of interpretation. The days when Nietzsche could be put under the 'existentialist' heading are gone.

❧ CONCLUSION ❧

Few philosophers have been as little read during their working lifetimes as Nietzsche. During the century since the ending of his life as a thinker, his reputation has increased steadily. In many ways he seems a twentieth-century rather than nineteenth-century thinker, a prophet of modernism, and even of the social and political changes that began in 1914. He has also remained a source of controversy. Nietzsche has always aroused strong opinions, and been both praised and condemned for the wrong reasons. He was never an academic philosopher, and the entry of his thought into that philosophical sphere has good and bad aspects. Nietzsche would have welcomed the resulting attention, and especially the careful and scrupulous reading of his works. He would have been less pleased at contributing to the academic publishing industry, and at becoming something of an intellectual fashion in some circles. Yet the accessibility of his works ensures that a co-option is not to be looked for. Nietzsche remains the untimely thinker that he wanted to be.

❧ BIBLIOGRAPHY ❧

Original language editions

7.1 Förster-Nietzsche, E. et al., eds, *Werke (Grossoktavausgabe)*, 2nd edn, 19 vols, Leipzig: Kröner, 1901–13.

7.2 Oehler, M. and R. Oehler, eds, *Gesammelte Werke (Musarionausgabe)*, 23 vols, München: Musarion Verlag, 1920–9.

7.3 Mette, H. J. and K. Schlechta eds, *Historisch-Kritische Gesamtausgabe: Werke*, 5 vols, München: C. H. Beck'sche Verlagsbuchhandlung, 1933–42.

7.4 Schlechta, K. ed., *Werke in drei Bänden*, 4 vols (inc. Index-Band), München: Carl Hanser Verlag, 1954–6.

7.5 Colli, G. and M. Montinari eds, *Kritische Gesamtausgabe: Werke*, Berlin and New York: Walter de Gruyter, 1973– .

7.6 —— eds, *Kritische Gesamtausgabe: Briefwechsel*, Berlin and New York: Walter de Gruyter, 1975– .

English translations

Complete and selected writings

7.7 *The Complete Works of Friedrich Nietzsche*, ed. O. Levy, 18 vols, Edinburgh and London: T. N. Foulis, 1909–13; reprint, New York: Russell and Russell, 1964.

7.8   *The Portable Nietzsche*, ed. and trans. W. Kaufmann, New York: Viking Press, 1954.

7.9   *Basic Writings of Nietzsche*, ed. and trans. W. Kaufmann, New York: Modern Library, 1966.

7.10 *A Nietzsche Reader*, ed. and trans. R. J. Hollingdale, Harmondsworth: Penguin 1977.

7.11 *Philosophy and Truth: Selections From Nietzsche's Notebooks of the Early 1870's*, ed. and trans. D. Breazeale, Atlantic Highlands, NJ: Humanities 1979.

7.12 *The Will to Power*, ed. W. Kaufmann, trans. W. Kaufmann and R. J. Hollingdale, New York: Random House, 1967.

7.13 *Selected Letters of Friedrich Nietzsche*, ed. and trans. C. Middleton, Chicago and London, Chicago University Press, 1969.

Separate works

7.14 *Beyond Good and Evil*, trans. M. Cowan, Chicago: Henry Regnery Company, 1955; trans. W. Kaufmann, New York: Random House, 1966; trans. R. J. Hollingdale, Harmondsworth: Penguin, 1973.

7.15 *The Birth of Tragedy and The Case of Wagner*, trans. W. Kaufmann, New York: Random House, 1967.

7.16 *The Birth of Tragedy and The Genealogy of Morals*, trans. F. Golffing, Garden City, NY: Doubleday Anchor Books, 1956.

7.17 *Daybreak*, trans. R. J. Hollingdale, Cambridge: Cambridge University Press, 1982.

7.18 *Dithyrambs of Dionysus*, trans. R. J. Hollingdale, London: Anvil Press, 1984.

7.19 *Ecce Homo*, trans. R. J. Hollingdale, Harmondsworth: Penguin Books, 1979.

7.20 *The Gay Science*, trans. W. Kaufmann, New York: Random House, 1974.

7.21 *Human, All Too Human*, trans. M. Faber and S. Lehmann, Lincoln, Nebr.: University of Nebraska Press, 1984; trans. R. J. Hollingdale, Cambridge: Cambridge University Press, 1986.

7.22 *On the Genealogy of Morals and Ecce Homo*, trans. W. Kaufmann and R. J. Hollingdale, New York: Random House, 1967.

7.23 *Philosophy in the Tragic Age of the Greeks*, trans. M. Cowan, South Bend, Ind.: Gateway Editions, 1962.

7.24 *Thus Spoke Zarathustra*, trans. R. J. Hollingdale, Harmondsworth: Penguin Books, 1961; trans. W. Kaufmann, New York: Random House, 1966.

7.25 *Twilight of the Idols and The Anti-Christ*, trans. R. J. Hollingdale, Harmondsworth: Penguin Books, 1968.

7.26 *Untimely Meditations*, trans. R. J. Hollingdale, Cambridge: Cambridge University Press, 1983.

Bibliographies

7.27 Reichert, H. W. and K. Schlechta, *International Nietzsche Bibliography*, Chapel Hill: University of North Carolina Press, 1968.

7.28 Hilliard, B. B. *Nietzsche Scholarship in English: A Bibliography 1968–1992*, Urbana, Ill.: North American Nietzsche Society, 1992.

The philosophy of Nietzsche: general

7.29 Allison, D. B. ed., *The New Nietzsche: Contemporary Styles of Interpretation*, New York: Dell, 1977.

7.30 Ackermann, R. J. *Nietzsche: A Frenzied Look*, Amherst: University of Massachusetts Press, 1990.

7.31 Blondel, E. *Nietzsche: The Body and Culture*, trans. S. Hand, Stanford: Stanford University Press, 1991.

7.32 Clark, M. *Nietzsche on Truth and Philosophy*, Cambridge: Cambridge University Press, 1990.

7.33 Danto, A. C. *Nietzsche as Philosopher*, New York: Macmillan, 1965.

7.34 Deleuze, G. *Nietzsche and Philosophy*, trans. H. Tomlinson, London: Athlone, 1983.

7.35 Derrida, J. *Spurs: Nietzsche's Styles*, trans. B. Harlow, Chicago: Chicago University Press, 1979.

7.36 Fink, E. *Nietzsches Philosophie*, Stuttgart: Kohlhammer, 1960.

7.37 Gillespie, M. A. and T. B. Strong, eds., *Nietzsche's New Seas*, Chicago: Chicago University Press, 1988.

7.38 Grimm, R. H. *Nietzsche's Theory of Knowledge*, Berlin and New York: Walter de Gruyter, 1977.

7.39 Heidegger, M. *Nietzsche*, trans. D. F. Krell, 4 vols, San Francisco: Harper and Row, 1981–7.

7.40 —— *What is Called Thinking?*, trans. F. D. Wieck and J. G. Gray, New York: Harper and Row, 1968.

7.41 Hollingdale, R. J. *Nietzsche*, London and Boston: Routledge and Kegan Paul, 1973.

7.42 Jaspers, K. *Nietzsche: An Introduction to the Understanding of his Philosophical Activity*, trans. C. F. Wallraff and F. J. Schmidt, Chicago: Henry Regnery, 1965.

7.43 Kaufmann, W. *Nietzsche: Philosopher, Psychologist, Antichrist*, Princeton: Princeton University Press, 1950.

7.44 Klossowski, P. *Nietzsche et le cercle vicieux*, Paris: Mercure de France, 1969.

7.45 Krell, D. F. *Postponements: Woman, Sensuality, and Death in Nietzsche*, Bloomington: Indiana University Press, 1986.

7.46 Krell, D. F. and D. Wood, eds., *Exceedingly Nietzsche*, London: Routledge, 1988.

7.47 Magnus, B. *Nietzsche's Existential Imperative*, Bloomington and London, Indiana University Press, 1978.

7.48 Moles, A. *Nietzsche's Philosophy of Nature and Cosmology*, New York: Peter Lang, 1990.

7.49 Müller-Lauter, W. *Nietzsche: Seine Philosophie der Gegensätze und die Gegensätze seiner Philosophie*, Berlin and New York: Walter de Gruyter, 1971.

7.50 Nehamas, A. *Nietzsche: Life as Literature*, Cambridge, Mass.: Harvard University Press, 1985.

7.51 O'Hara, D. T. ed., *Why Nietzsche Now?*, Bloomington: Indiana University Press, 1985.

7.52 Schacht, R. *Nietzsche*, London, Routledge and Kegan Paul, 1983.

7.53 Schutte, O. *Beyond Nihilism: Nietzsche Without Masks*, Chicago and London: Chicago University Press, 1988.

7.54 Schrift, A. D. *Nietzsche and the Question of Interpretation*, New York and London: Routledge, 1990.

7.55 Shapiro, G. *Nietzschean Narratives*, Bloomington and Indianapolis: Indiana University Press, 1989.

7.56 Solomon, R. C. ed., *Nietzsche: A Collection of Critical Essays*, New York: Anchor Books, 1973.

7.57 Solomon, R. C. and K. M. Higgins, eds, *Reading Nietzsche*, New York and Oxford: Oxford University Press, 1988.

7.58 Spiekermann, K. *Naturwissenschaft als subjektlose Macht? Nietzsches kritik physikalischer Grundkonzepte*, Berlin and New York: Walter de Gruyter, 1992.

7.59 Stambaugh, J. *Nietzsche's Thought of Eternal Return*, Baltimore and London: Johns Hopkins University Press, 1972.

7.60 —— *The Problem of Time in Nietzsche*, trans. J. F. Humphrey, Lewisburg: Bucknell University Press, 1987.

7.61 Stern, J. P. *Nietzsche*, London, Fontana Modern Masters, 1978.

7.62 Strong, T. B. *Friedrich Nietzsche and the Politics of Transfiguration*, Berkeley: University of California Press, 1975; 2nd edn, 1988.

7.63 White, A. *Within Nietzsche's Labyrinth*, New York and London: Routledge, 1990.

7.64 Wilcox, J. T. *Truth and Value in Nietzsche*, Ann Arbor: University of Michigan Press, 1974.

7.65 Young, J. *Nietzsche's Philosophy of Art*, Cambridge: Cambridge University Press, 1992.

Studies of Thus Spoke Zarathustra

7.66 Alderman, H. *Nietzsche's Gift*, Athens, Ohio: Ohio University Press, 1977.

7.67 Higgins, K. M. *Nietzsche's Zarathustra*, Philadelphia: Temple University Press, 1987.

7.68 Lampert, L. *Nietzsche's Teaching*, New Haven: Yale University Press, 1986.

7.69 Whitlock, G. *Returning to Sils-Maria: A Commentary to Nietzsche's 'Also Sprach Zarathustra'*, New York: Peter Lang, 1990.

Studies of Nietzsche in relation to other thinkers

7.70 Ansell-Pearson, K., ed., *Nietzsche and Modern German Thought*, London and New York, Routledge, 1991.

7.71 Hollinrake, R. *Nietzsche, Wagner, and the Philosophy of Pessimism*, London: George Allen and Unwin, 1982.

7.72 Houlgate, S. *Hegel, Nietzsche and the Criticism of Metaphysics*, Cambridge: Cambridge University Press, 1986.

7.73 Megill, A. *Prophets of Extremity: Nietzsche, Heidegger, Foucault, Derrida*, Berkeley: University of California Press, 1985.

7.74 Simmel G. *Schopenhauer and Nietzsche*, trans. H. Loiskandl, D. Weinstein and M. Weinstein, Amherst: University of Massachusetts Press, 1986.

7.75 Stack, G. J. , *Lange and Nietzsche*, Berlin and New York: Walter de Gruyter, 1983.

7.76 —— *Emerson and Nietzsche: An Elective Affinity*, Athens, Ohio: Ohio University Press, 1992.

7.77 Williams, W. D. *Nietzsche and the French*, Oxford: Clarendon Press, 1952.

Biographical studies

7.78 Gilman, S. L., ed., *Conversations with Nietzsche*, trans. D. J. Parent, New York and Oxford: Oxford University Press, 1987.

7.79 Hayman, R. *Nietzsche: A Critical Life*, Harmondsworth: Penguin, 1980.

7.80 Hollingdale, R. J. *Nietzsche: The Man and his Philosophy*, London and Baton Rouge: Louisiana State University Press, 1965.

7.81 Janz, C. P. *Friedrich Nietzsche: Biographie*, 3 vols, München and Wien, Carl Hanser, 1978.

7.82 Pletsch, C. *Young Nietzsche: Becoming a Genius*, New York: Free Press, 1991.

CHAPTER 8

Dilthey
Michael Lessnoff

ᵒᵍ INTRODUCTION ᵍᵒ

Wilhelm Dilthey was born in 1833 near Wiesbaden, and thus lived through the period of Bismarck's creation of a unified German Empire by 'blood and iron'. These turbulent events, however, scarcely perturbed his career, which was wholly that of academic and scholar. For almost forty years he was to hold, successively, four university chairs of philosophy, the first as early as 1866, and culminating (from 1882 to 1905) in that of Berlin. Crucial to Dilthey's philosophical achievement, however, is the fact that he was not a philosopher only, but was equally interested, and distinguished, in the fields of cultural history and biography. Small wonder, then, that Dilthey is famous as the philosopher of the '*Geisteswissenschaften*' – the 'sciences of mind' or (as the term is often translated), the human sciences, or the human studies.

Indeed, the human mind and its products are the beginning and end, the alpha and omega, of Dilthey's philosophy; so much so that it is hardly possible, from his perspective, to draw a definite line between philosophy and psychology. Dilthey's philosophy is above all an epistemology, or theory of knowledge, and human knowledge arises in the human mind. Dilthey's viewpoint here can be interestingly compared with that of Hume. 'It is evident' wrote Hume in the Introduction to his great *Treatise*, 'that all sciences have a relation, greater or less, to human nature [and] are in some measure dependent on the science of MAN; since they lie under the cognisance of men, and are judged of by their powers and faculties'. With this proposition Dilthey was in full agreement, but thereafter the two philosophers sharply part company. Hume, starting from the premiss that all knowledge is a judgement of the human mind, and deducing therefrom the need to understand the operations of the human mind, ended up, somewhat

206

paradoxically, with an account of the mind based on, and assimilated to, our (or its) knowledge of external nature, or natural science. Dilthey arrived at the opposite position. For him the mind is an autonomous realm, with its own principles of operation: correspondingly, knowledge of the mind is the discovery of these inherent principles, not a reading back of the way we know external nature, or natural science. The latter, indeed, are to be understood in a sense derivatively, as the mind's response to the non-mental: to nature as it impinges on human consciousness, and is grasped from the perspective of human life. Dilthey, who, it seems, took the primacy of the human mind more seriously than did Hume, was led by it to a philosophical and epistemological dualism, encapsulated by his famous distinction between two kinds of 'science' (knowledge): the *Geisteswissenschaften* (sciences of the mind, or of the human) and the *Naturwissenschaften* (sciences of nature).

Dilthey fully shared Hume's resolutely *empirical* epistemology (as Hume puts it, none of the sciences can go beyond experience). But he found many reasons to reject the Humean analysis of that experience – to reject, in other words, Hume's psychology, which was accepted by British empiricism generally. In this empiricism, the mind is viewed as the passive recipient of 'impressions' (which it copies in the form of 'ideas'), and as governed by mechanical laws of association of such ideas. To Dilthey (here, doubtless, the heir of Romanticism), this passive and mechanical picture of the mind is false: false, not only of human life as a whole, but even of the 'knowing subject'. (In a well known passage, Dilthey charged that 'no real blood' flows in the veins of the knowing subject 'fabricated' by Locke and Hume – and also Kant.) 'The core of what we call life is instinct, feeling, passions and volitions'; and this 'whole man' must be taken 'as the basis for exploring knowledge and its concepts' ([8.32], 13). Knowledge arises not just in the mind but in 'life' – the life of a feeling, willing, passionate human being. Indeed, the German words *erleben* and *Erlebnis*, used by Dilthey to express the idea of experience in the sense he considered fundamental, are derivatives of the word for life (*das Leben*). In order to bring out the importance of this for Dilthey, *Erlebnis* is often translated into English as 'lived experience'.

As we saw, Dilthey's epistemology is dualistic, which means that there are two kinds of human experience – external and internal. The difference between them is fundamental. Internal knowledge is the subject's knowledge of itself – of its volitions and cognitions, its reasonings, decisions, values and goals, its mental states and acts in general. In the very having of these states, we are conscious of them, and know them *directly and immediately*. External knowledge also depends on the subjective states and acts of our minds, but it is not knowledge of them. Rather, we experience the external world in relation to our will, and especially in the frustration of our will, or as resistance. As Dilthey put it: 'In the experiences of frustration and resistance the presence of a force is given' – an external force, 'a force [that] is acting upon me' ([8.71], 58). Out of such experiences we construct our picture of the external world. This world, however, is known to us only by inference, not directly, our knowledge of the external world is thus a construction only. We do not know it as we know ourselves, it is fundamentally alien to us. In a way, Dilthey's view of our external knowledge is similar to Kant's: we cannot know things 'in themselves', but only as they appear to us. But he is more radically subjectivist than Kant – Dilthey refused to admit any *a priori* element in our knowledge of external appearances, ascribing it wholly to experience. And his view of our internal knowledge, our knowledge of our minds, is totally un-Kantian, for he held that in this realm we have direct knowledge, by experience, of a reality, of mental things-in-themselves. Kant's distinction between the noumenal (things in themselves) and the phenomenal (things as they appear to us) is replaced by a distinction between internal and external knowledge. It is obvious that this distinction is the root of Dilthey's famous distinction between two kinds of sciences – *Geisteswissenschaften* (sciences of mind or human sciences), and *Naturwissenschaften* (sciences of nature).

Dilthey's interest, as we saw, was primarily in the *Geisteswissenschaften*: he was interested in the *Naturwissenschaften* mainly for the sake of showing that, and how, the *Geisteswissenschaften* must differ from them. What then is the character of the natural sciences? The most fundamental point is that they deal with a world that is, as we have seen, external and alien to us – a world which impinges on our experience, to be sure, but of whose ultimate, elemental nature we perforce remain ignorant because it is beyond our experience. In Dilthey's own words: our idea of nature is 'a mere shadow cast by a reality which remains hidden from us' ([8.32], 73). The picture of reality constructed by natural science therefore remains always 'hypothetical' – Dilthey referred, in this connection, to the 'groping' towards an adequate theory of nature which was initiated by the philosophers of ancient Greece (and is still continued by physics today) but which can never fully succeed, for 'it is not possible to demonstrate a definite inner objective structure of reality, such that remaining possible structures are excluded' ([8.32], 318). This does not mean, however, that Dilthey considered natural science to be useless or invalid. On the contrary, it is a highly appropriate and fruitful way of conceiving of external nature, from a human standpoint. Science conceptualizes nature in such a way as to facilitate its description in terms of precise, quantitative causal laws. It is thus concerned, in relation to all phenomena, with their typical and quantifiable aspects. In this sense, it is an abstraction from reality, but (in part due to the development of the experimental method) a hugely successful one, giving man mastery over nature: 'Once the causes of change in nature become accessible to our will we can produce the effects we want ... A limitless prospect of extending our power over nature has opened up' ([8.36], 110). But Dilthey insisted on the distinction between mastery over nature and knowledge of nature-as-such:

> if one ... investigates nature insofar as it is the object of
> intelligence or insofar as it is interwoven with the will as end or
> means, it remains for the mind only what it is in the mind;
> whatever it might be in itself is entirely a matter of indifference
> here. It is enough that the mind can count on nature's lawfulness
> for the mind's activities in whatever way it encounters nature.
>
> ([8.32], 88)

But scientific laws of nature are also hypothetical, at best probable, never provable by experience; causal necessity (as Hume showed) is likewise a construction beyond experience. In a rather extreme formulation of his position, referring to the scientific world-picture of particles or atoms interacting with one another according to laws, Dilthey commented: 'neither atoms nor laws are real' ([8.32], 319).

Dilthey's conception of the natural sciences is based rather directly on his conception of external knowledge: his conception of the human sciences is based on his conception of internal knowledge, but less directly. Direct, internal knowledge is introspective knowledge, given in the experience of each individual person, of his or her own mental states and acts. Such knowledge is insufficient to constitute the human sciences in general: the latter depend on the presumption of a world of 'other minds' with basically similar contents to our own, revealed in words, deeds, and artefacts. In Dilthey's view, we make this presumption quite unproblematically, and he himself never treated it as a problem. The human world and its doings and makings (what Dilthey called the 'mind-affected world') indubitably exists, and provides the subject-matter of the human sciences. One should perhaps stress the phrase 'mind-*affected* world', in order to avoid misunderstanding of Dilthey's term *Geisteswissenschaften*. Human beings are, as Dilthey often put it, psycho-physical complexes, not pure minds; and the human sciences deal with what he called *objectifications* of mind (sometimes he used the Hegelian phrase 'objective mind', though not with Hegel's meaning), i.e. the material world as formed by mental activity. Nevertheless the mental aspect is crucial.

The fundamental difference between the *Geisteswissenschaften* and the *Naturwissenschaften* is that, whereas in the latter we construct hypotheses about a world alien to us, in the former we deal with our own world, which we know directly. Thus, Dilthey thought, we can attain to a certainty in our knowledge which is beyond the reach of natural science, and which more than compensates for the much superior precision and generality of scientific laws. The latter can, in a sense, explain (*erklären*) but in a deeper sense the material world must always remain incomprehensible to us. But the human sciences deal with what we can and do understand (*verstehen*). Dilthey's starting-point here is the individual's understanding of his or her own mental life, of the connections, for example, between one's desires, beliefs and actions. By analogy with this directly understood connection, one can understand the actions of others, as 'expressions' of mind. As Dilthey put it, we understand the mental life of others by re-living or re-experiencing (*nach-erleben*) that experience. Actions are the most direct but not, Dilthey ultimately believed, the most important expressions of mind from the standpoint of the human sciences: most important are the permanent or lasting expressions – social institutions such as law and religion, human artefacts like the great cathedrals, and – perhaps most important of all – writings and works of art.

Dilthey insisted on a number of crucial differences between the human and natural, or mental and physical worlds. The human world is not a world of strict causal determinism, but one in which individuals are free (within limits) to pursue chosen ends: not a dead and meaningless world, but one in which values are created and recognized; a *historical* world which develops new forms through time, a creative world. Some of these differences are brought out in this graphic contrast of Dilthey's, between a waterfall (a natural phenomenon) and human speech:

> The waterfall is composed of homogeneous falling particles of water; but a single sentence, which is but a noise in the mouth, shakes the whole living society of a continent through a play of motives in absolutely individual units, none of which is comparable with the rest; so different is the ideal motive from any other kind of cause.

([8.71, 165)

Clearly, Dilthey implies that, if the sentence were treated as nothing more than a noise or succession of noises (which, from the standpoint of natural science, is precisely what it is), the effects produced would be utterly incomprehensible. To understand them, a completely different framework is necessary. Hence the need for a distinctive group of disciplines – the human sciences.

Dilthey's view of the relation between these disciplines differed at different stages of his career. At one, relatively early, stage he considered psychology to be fundamental (not, of course, a psychology modelled on natural science – on this, more below). Later, he came to the view that psychology is not self-sufficient but is as dependent on other human sciences as they are on it: in particular, he was inclined to stress the importance, for all the human studies, of the interdependence of psychology and history. This, presumably, follows from the element of freedom and creativity which, Dilthey insisted, characterizes human life, making historical development an essential component of it, so that only in history are the potentialities of human psychology – of human nature – revealed. Similarly Dilthey points to a like interdependence between what he calls the two great classes of the human sciences, the historical and the systematic (or generalizing) sciences. Clearly, it was no part of Dilthey's intention to confine the human studies to particularities, and not infrequently he even referred to their discovery of laws (e.g. Grimm's Law in linguistics). Presumably, however, these laws or generalizations do not have the strict deterministic status that Dilthey attributed to the laws of natural science. Indeed, notwithstanding the generalizing aspect of the human sciences, Dilthey regarded their historical aspect as so fundamental that he referred to the epistemology of the human sciences which he sought to develop as a 'critique of historical reason'.

The idea of a 'critique of historical reason', with its obvious Kantian echoes, occurs in a work published in 1883, the *Einleitung in die Geisteswissenschaften* (*Introduction to the Human Sciences*), and Dilthey's attempt to formulate it in a fully satisfactory form was to preoccupy him for the rest of his life. That much remained constant, but there are notable inconsistencies in the views Dilthey expressed over the years, and even in a single work. In the *Einleitung*, for example, the distinction between historical and systematic (generalizing) sciences is made, but it is doubtful whether it is actually used in Dilthey's survey and classification of the various 'special' human sciences. This is as follows. First, and most basic, are the sciences that deal with individual human beings – psychology and biography. (But biography is really an aspect of psychology – its historical aspect. It is also, in Dilthey's view, a main component of history proper.) In addition there are two kinds of social science (as we would now call them): sciences of systems of culture, and sciences of external organization of society. By 'systems of culture', Dilthey means complexes of interdependent actions devoted to some particular human purpose (examples are economics, religion and art); by 'external organization of society' he refers to the state and other associations, communities and relations of dominance and dependence (we might call these formal and informal social structures). Both types, Dilthey believed when he wrote the *Einleitung*, are dependent on psychology: their fundamental concepts are psychological concepts. Examples are the concepts of 'need, economy [i.e.

thrift], work, value and the like', which are the foundation of political economy; or the 'instinct for sociability' which, Dilthey says, underlies human communal organization. Dilthey says that these concepts are, from the psychological point of view, 'second-rank concepts', i.e. non-basic; but he does not mean by this that they are simply deducible from the basic concepts and laws of individual psychology, as might have been asserted by, for example, John Stuart Mill – rather, they are concepts having to do with *interaction* between individuals, rather than concepts relating to individuals as such. (Dilthey is not very forthcoming about the precise nature of this relationship, which he describes as 'complicated', but he is emphatic that the attempt to eluci-date it in terms of deduction and induction is useless – it rests on a wholly inappropriate model borrowed from natural science.)

The above schema may seem to be consistent with Dilthey's dis-tinction between historical and generalizing sciences, but this is actually doubtful, for in the *Einleitung* Dilthey gives prominence to – he repeats it several times – a different schema of classification involving not two but three elements, and which are said to distinguish not different types of human sciences but different types of *assertion* made within the human sciences generally. The three types of assertion are the particular or historical, the generalizing or theoretical, and – thirdly – the value-judging or prescriptive. It is clear that Dilthey considers that a single human science can, or should, contain all three. Perhaps the difference between historical versus generalizing sciences, and historical versus generalizing elements within a science, is a relatively minor discrepancy. However, the addition of evaluation or prescription is of the greatest importance. Dilthey was, indeed, insistent on the impossibility of separ-ating factual statements and value-judgements in the historical and human sciences – though it is not clear in exactly what sense he believed the value-judgements involved to be scientific. On this puzzling aspect of Dilthey's thinking more will be said below. At any rate, it illustrates an important point, namely, that Dilthey's conception of the range of the human sciences is much wider than the word 'science' might suggest to English speakers. Thus, a list (in a later work by Dilthey) includes not only history, economics, jurisprudence, politics and psychology but also the study of religion, literature, poetry, architecture, music and 'philosophic world views and systems' ([8.36], 170). The earlier *Einlei-tung* mentions three 'special human sciences' which deserve some com-ment – philosophy, aesthetics and ethics.

Ethics, Dilthey insists, is one of the 'sciences of systems of cul-ture', it is the study of social morality, rather than an 'imperative of personal life', or a 'theory of the righteous life' separate from sociology, a view of ethics that Dilthey attributes to Herbert Spencer. Dilthey's own view appears to be an example – even the most important example

– of his general belief in the inseparability of fact and value in the human sciences. In the present case, it makes him an ethical empiricist. Put slightly differently, his view is that values, like knowledge, arise within the context of human life, in experience. We experience them in ourselves, and attribute them to others, as motives and as grounds of judgement. Dilthey rejects the notion of any 'transcendent' ground of moral judgement, higher than human life itself. Nor, it seems, does he wish to make any sharp, qualitative distinction between the 'third person' value-judgements that the human scientist may discover in his subject-matter, and 'first person' value-judgements that he makes *qua* human scientist. When we discuss (below) Dilthey's view of history and the great variability of historical forms, we shall see that his view of ethics gives rise to a serious problem of relativism.

Aesthetics and philosophy are said by Dilthey to be sciences that study, respectively, art and science. The two cases are of interest for different reasons. The case of aesthetics illustrates, again, Dilthey's contention that, in the human sciences, knowledge and evaluation are inseparable and equally indispensable elements. (Some scholars, indeed, believe that Dilthey's whole conception of the human sciences is rooted in his conception of aesthetics.) Equally important, art – especially literature – is for Dilthey itself an expression of the attempt to understand human life. Great art – great literature – by definition abounds in such understanding. This does not mean that art or literature is itself one of the human sciences, because it is not expressed in the systematic form of a science. Nevertheless, art and the human sciences have in a sense a similar task. The human sciences have much to learn from the arts: 'None of us would possess more than a meagre part of our present understanding of human conditions, if we had not become used to seeing through the poet's eyes' ([8.71], 233). Furthermore, aesthetics must have a special status among the human sciences, being the attempt to understand attempts to understand human life, or expressions thereof taking a particular form. It is not surprising, therefore, that Dilthey attached so much importance to aesthetics, and indeed contributed largely to it.

To call philosophy a human science, as Dilthey does, may seem surprising: it may seem that philosophy has as its subject-matter all reality, not only human activity. Consistently with this, there can of course be historical and other study of human philosophizing (again a field in which Dilthey was himself prominent) – but that is something different. The notion of philosophy as a human science is itself the staking out of a philosophical position, and follows from Dilthey's oft-repeated, fundamental standpoint, the primacy of *life* (that is, human life). 'Thought cannot go behind life.' All speculation about reality, therefore, must actually concern itself with the way in which reality manifests itself in, or appears to, human life. In other words, genuine and valid philosophy must be epistemology or theory of knowledge. It is the attempt to achieve 'universally valid knowledge' about human knowing. 'As such a theory of knowledge it is a science' ([8.36], 125). Dilthey's own philosophy certainly takes this form – so it is after all perhaps not so surprising to find him placing philosophy among the human sciences.

Implicit (and explicit) in Dilthey's philosophical stance is a repudiation of rival philosophical positions. Dilthey's is an embattled philosophy, and two of his main enemies are metaphysics and positivism. By metaphysics, Dilthey means abstract, schematic doctrines that claim to grasp the structure or essence of reality. Such doctrines he rejects as false to experience, over-simplifications that cannot capture reality's variety and complexity, manifested especially in history. They are attempts to grasp the meaning of existence, but premature, one-sided attempts. On these grounds Dilthey repudiates, in the *Einleitung*, what he calls the philosophy of history as 'not a true science'; he is here referring to theories which see history as the unfolding of some master-plan, aiming at some pre-given *telos*, and interpret historical particulars in the light of, hence in subordination to, the supposed plan or *telos*. To Dilthey this is a distortion that fails to take empirical history sufficiently seriously, in all its particularity and multiplicity. An obvious exemplar of this style of theorizing, which Dilthey repudiates, is Hegel. Another is Comte, who from Dilthey's point of view is a double sinner, author of a metaphysical schematization of history (the Law of the Three Stages), and a metaphysic that is positivist to boot, that is, which sees the application of the positivist method of natural science to all disciplines, including the human sciences, as the historical *telos* (or at least the *telos* of human thought).

Another way in which Dilthey characterizes a metaphysical system is as a *Weltanschauung* or world-view taking, or claiming to take, philosophical form: 'When a world-view has been raised to a level at which it is grasped and grounded conceptually and thus claims universal validity, we call it metaphysics' ([8.32], 29). Hegel and Comte, in fact, can stand as exemplars of two of the three great 'pure types' of *Weltanschauungen* that, Dilthey maintained, have constantly recurred in the history of human thought and culture, namely naturalism (or materialism), and objective idealism. These are two opposed monistic views of the world, the one interpreting everything in terms of matter, the other in terms of mind or spirit. Dilthey's third pure type of *Weltanschauung*, what he calls the idealism of freedom, is dualistic, seeing the mind as independent of physical causality (and superior to it). Dilthey himself might well appear to be an exponent of this third, dualistic *Weltanschauung*, but this categorization could hardly be acceptable to him, given his view that all the *Weltanschauungen* (including, explicitly, the idealism of freedom) are partial, incomplete views of reality, bound to encounter problems they cannot solve. However, metaphysical philosophy is only one of three spheres in which, Dilthey says, *Weltanschauungen* manifest themselves – the others are religion and art, especially 'poetry' (a term which for Dilthey applies to literature generally). Dilthey's view of the historical relation between religious and metaphysical *Weltanschauungen* is reminiscent of Comte: 'The mental law that general ideas can be completed only in conceptual thought . . . forces the religious *Weltanschauung* to become philosophical' wrote Dilthey in *Das Wesen der Philosophie (The Essence of Philosophy*, 1907) ([8.30, 51]) But of course he did not agree that Comte himself, in his positivistic philosophy, had got beyond metaphysics.

Dilthey's famous typology of world-views can stand as an exemplification of his own prescriptions for the carrying on of the human sciences. It results from a wide-ranging historical survey (in this case, of intellectual and cultural history); and it shows forth, in Dilthey's opinion, a constant of human psychology – for the drive to formulate world-views, in the attempt to make sense of the universe, is, he thinks, precisely that. It thus returns us to the twin premises of Dilthey's philosophy of the human sciences – psychology and history. We must now examine his views on both of these in more detail.

❧ DILTHEY'S VIEW OF PSYCHOLOGY ❧

Dilthey's 'Ideas Concerning a Descriptive and Analytical Psychology' (*Ideen über eine Beschreibende und Zergliedende Psychologie*) was published in 1894. It is a major element of his *oeuvre*, and a major source of his views on the subject, but by no means the only one. It must be supplemented by later writings, including some not published in his lifetime.

In developing his ideas on psychology, Dilthey had to fight a war on three fronts, against Comtean positivism, British empiricism and German neo-Kantianism. Comte's positivism simply denied the validity of any independent science of psychology whatever, on the grounds of its unamenability to investigation by what Comte took to be the necessary method of all science, the 'positive' method of external observation. The neo-Kantians, such as Heinrich Rickert (their most prominent spokesman), drew a sharp distinction between the historical or cultural sciences, which focus on the particular, and natural sciences, which seek general laws. They placed psychology in the latter category, at the same time denying that it could give knowledge of the transcendent 'noumenal' self, or of the realm of *Geist* or spirit. As for the British empiricists, they took psychology to be a natural science like any other – on this point they agreed with the neo-Kantians, but differed as to whether there is some deeper spiritual reality undiscoverable by natural scientific method. Dilthey took psychology to be a science, but not a natural science, a science precisely of *Geist*.

In the *Ideen*, Dilthey offers two somewhat different arguments against a psychology based on natural scientific method, a project which he often refers to as 'explanatory psychology'. Natural science is hypothetical. More precisely, it breaks reality down into hypothetical elements, postulates laws connecting them and thus explains phenomena. Such a manner of explanation is called by Dilthey 'constructive' – it constructs a picture of reality out of hypothetical elements linked by hypothetical relations. This method works very well in certain areas, notably those dealing with phenomena that are precisely measurable and subject to controlled experiment. Neither of these conditions obtains in psychology. The result is a chaos of competing theories: 'To each group of hypotheses is opposed yet a dozen more ... One sees absolutely nothing which can decide the issue of the struggle' ([8.31], 26). Nor can one hope to improve matters by recourse to areas where the natural scientific method is applicable, such as physiology: 'Consciousness cannot go behind itself' ([8.31], 75): in other words, the conscious cannot be explained by the non-conscious. Thus, Dilthey concludes, 'Explanatory psychology is not only now unable, but will never be able to elaborate an objective knowledge of the nexus of psychic phenomena'. It is, Dilthey says, 'bankrupt' ([8.31], 49). Fortunately, however, there is no need, in psychology, to postulate hypothetical entities governed by hypothetical laws, and then construct a picture of reality – for in psychology knowledge of reality is given to us directly. Such a psychology will, however, not be explanatory and constructive, but descriptive and analytic.

What exactly does Dilthey mean by a descriptive and analytic psychology? The crucial point, stressed over and over again by Dilthey, is that apprehension of the psychological is the directly lived inner cognition of systematically connected elements constituting a functional unity or whole. It is not simply the individual elements but equally their unity and connectedness that are directly given to us. To designate this unity or connectedness Dilthey used the word *Zusammenhang* (literally, a hanging-together). The word is important, for two reasons: firstly, because it is perhaps the most characteristic and frequently used term in all of Dilthey's writings; secondly, because its translation into English is neither straightforward nor uniform, since it may refer either to a totality of parts (whole, structure) or to connections between elements. This ambiguity is of some consequence in Dilthey's thinking, and can be illustrated by considering the following passages in the

'*Ideen*' which show how the term functions in his concept of a descriptive and analytic psychology:

> Hypotheses do not at all play the same role in psychology as in the study of nature. In the latter, all connectedness [*Zusammenhang*] is obtained by means of the formation of hypotheses; in psychology it is precisely the connectedness which is originally given in lived experience.
>
> ([8.31], 28)

> By descriptive psychology I understand the presentation of the components and continua which one finds uniformly throughout all developed modes of human psychic life, where the components form a unique nexus which is neither added nor deduced, but rather is concretely lived. This psychology is thus the description and analysis of a nexus which is originally given as life itself ... Every connection [*Zusammenhang*] utilized by it can be verified unequivocally by inner perception, and from the fact that each such ensemble can be shown to be a member of a larger whole, not as a result of deduction, but as given originally in life.
>
> ([8.31], 35)

> For psychology the functional system [*Zusammenhang*] is *given from within* by lived experience. Every particular psychological cognition is only an *analysis* of this nexus ... Psychic life is a functional system [whose] component parts ... exist within individual systems of a particular kind, [which are the source of] problems to psychology. These problems can be resolved only by means of analysis: descriptive psychology must be at the same time an analytic psychology ... Analysis separates the component parts which are united in reality.
>
> ([8.31], 56–7; emphases in original)

In brief, Dilthey, in the course of these three passages, moves from asserting the experienced connectedness of psychological items, to asserting that these connections constitute larger wholes or systems, also directly experienced (and the word *Zusammenhang*, translated in the first passage as connectedness, refers in the third passage to the total functional system). Thus Dilthey arrives at his conclusion that psychology should take the form of analysing the elements of given psychic wholes.

The ambiguity of the word *Zusammenhang* is significant primarily because of its bearing on two concepts that are central to Dilthey's philosophy of the human sciences, namely understanding (*Verstehen*) and meaning (*Sinn, Bedeutung*). Do 'understanding' and 'meaning' turn on relations between connected elements or on relations between parts and wholes? Dilthey gives both answers, and the importance of this will become apparent for the philosophy of social science as elaborated in his later work. But the point is already prefigured in his writing on psychology. Here is one account given by Dilthey of his favoured method of psychological analysis. A state of human consciousness characteristically involves, he says, three elements or modes, namely, representations (of the world), feelings and volitions. Dilthey stresses the interrelation of all three, but especially the role of volitions, in producing action. Analysis, then, must 'define the concepts of goal-positing, motive, relation between ends and means, choice and preference and unravel the relations which exist among these' ([8.31], 70). It is, in other words, a process of relating actions and their outcomes to the motives, goals and volitions which produce them – and corresponds to the (or a) definition of *Verstehen* (understanding) later given by Dilthey: 'Understanding penetrates the observable facts of human history to reach what is not accessible to the senses and yet affects external facts' – for example, values and purposes ([8.36], 172–3) But more often, in the *Ideen*, Dilthey relates *Verstehen* not to such connections but to the grasping of wholes. For example:

> The processes *of the whole psyche* operate together in [lived] experience ... In the lived experience a particular occurrence is supported by the totality of psychic life, and the whole of psychic life belongs to immediate experience. The latter already determines the nature of our *understanding (Verstehen)* of ourselves and others ... In understanding we proceed from the coherent whole which is livingly given to us in order to make the particular intelligible to us [emphases in original] ...
> Precisely the fact that we live with the consciousness of the coherent whole, makes it possible for us to understand a particular sentence, gesture, or action. All psychological thought preserves this fundamental feature, that the apprehension of the whole makes possible and determines the interpretation of particulars.
>
> ([8.31], 55)

What exactly does Dilthey have in mind when he refers to a psychological (psychic) whole? The answer is twofold, but both aspects relate to the life of the human individual. One is what might be called the individual's personality-structure (*Zusammenhang des Seelenlebens*); the individual is a psychic unity or (in another of Dilthey's phrases) *erworbener seelischer Zusammenhang* (translatable as 'acquired psychic nexus'). This phrase implies the unification of an individual's experience, representations, feelings, purposes and values into a whole that makes one the person one is, and makes one pursue the goals that one pursues. Thus, when Dilthey talks of a 'descriptive and analytic' psychology, he means the description, analysis and classification of such structures. Such a study should cover the entire range of human life, 'from its more humble to its highest possibilities'. But Dilthey was especially interested in the latter – in 'religious genius, historical heroes, creative artists'. Since such outstanding figures are 'motive forces in history and society', psychology 'will become the instrument of the historian, the economist, the politician' ([8.31], 40–1).

In referring to the acquired psychic nexus, Dilthey refers to the enduring values, habits of will, and dominant goals that make it up. But values and goals generate action, and therefore change. Thus the psychic structure is inherently dynamic. It develops over an individual's life. And the individual life is also, according to Dilthey, a systematically connected whole – one that develops through time, and can be understood. The writing of a biography is the attempt at such a coherent understanding of an individual life (autobiography is the individual's attempt at such understanding of his or her own life). Dilthey frequently applies the concept of *meaning* to this understanding of human life; but an ambiguity is detectable, similar to that mentioned above in relation to understanding itself. Is this 'meaning' the relation between an action and its purpose, goal or motive? or does it lie in the coherent relation of parts of a whole (life)? Again, Dilthey gives (or at least suggests) both answers. Thus, his remark that the meaning of a life is the relation between its outer events and 'something inner' ([8.35], 91) suggests the former. But predominantly the latter interpretation is stressed, as in this typical passage:

> What is it that, in the contemplation of one's life, links the parts
> into a whole and thus makes it comprehensible? It is the fact
> that understanding involves ... the categories of ... value,
> purpose and meaning ... Looking back at the past in memory
> we see, in terms of the category of meaning, how the parts of a
> life are linked together.
>
> ([8.35], 103)

Despite the importance of the concepts of value and purpose, 'only the category of meaning', Dilthey insists, expresses 'the connectedness of life' ([8.35], 104). Again the grasping of meaning is the grasping of a *Zusammenhang*.

The quotation above is also significant for another reason, namely, the reference to memory, for this relates to one of the most characteristic and suggestive, and possibly influential, elements in all of Dilthey's work, namely, the *temporality* of life. To say that a human life is lived through a duration of time may seem banal; but Dilthey was at pains to stress the difference between *lived* time and the abstract time of (say) the physical scientist. Lived time 'is not just a line consisting of parts of equal value... Nowhere [in such a linear continuum] is there anything which "is" '. Indeed, the character of lived time is paradoxical, in that we live *always* in the present, but the present *includes* the past, through memory, and the future, through our plans, hopes and fears.

> Concrete time consists... of the uninterrupted progress of the present, what was present becoming the past and the future becoming the present, [that is], the becoming present of that which a moment ago we still expected, wanted or feared... this is the character of real time... The present is always where we live, strive and remember: in brief, experience the fullness of our reality, [but] the continued effectiveness of the past as a power in the present, gives to what is remembered a peculiar characteristic of 'being present'.
>
> ([8.35], 98–9)

In these passages, where human life is characterized as a continually moving present which contains a (likewise continually moving) past and future, Dilthey is referring to the structure of the life of an individual: but he could equally well be referring to his view of history.

❧ PSYCHOLOGY, HISTORY AND THE ❧ HUMAN SCIENCES

Many commentators on Dilthey have remarked on a pronounced change in his thinking about the human sciences in the years after he wrote the *Ideen*, and especially in the last period of his life. In brief, the change discerned is a down-grading of individual psychology, and a corresponding turn to emphasizing the importance of concrete, objective manifestations ('expressions') of mind in history and society, and the interpretation of such expressions. Michael Ermarth, for example, in his *Wilhelm Dilthey: The Critique of Historical Reason*, speaks of Dilthey's thought moving away from subjective acts of experience to intersubjective and mediated contexts of experience, or in other words from the psychological to the cultural and historical ([8.65], 232). There is undeniably much truth in this perception of the trend of Dilthey's thought. He certainly abandoned his view of psychology as the very foundation of the human sciences, and he at least wavered of one of the cornerstones of his early thinking, namely the certainty of the knowledge afforded by introspection of lived experience. On the other hand, the continuities between the earlier and later phases of his thinking should not be overlooked. For example, already in the *Ideen*, Dilthey clearly stated the need to study not just the individual psyche but all of human history and culture, in order to arrive at a full description, classification and analysis of the mental. The following passage in the *Ideen* puts the point quite bluntly: 'Man does not apprehend what he is by musing over himself, nor by doing psychological experiments, but rather by history' ([8.31], 62). To understand human psychology, also, we must study the mind's *creations* – in literature and art, but also 'in language, myth, religious ritual, customs, law, and in the external organization of society' – in brief, in all historical processes which are products of the human mind. Recourse to 'the objective products of psychic life' must supplement perception of inner states, is indeed, Dilthey says, of the greatest importance: 'it is an inestimable advantage to have before us stable and enduring formations, to which observation and analysis can always return' ([8.31],81). As for methods, we learn about 'inner processes' of mental life by recourse to such evidence as diaries and letters, the reports of poets on poetical creation and the lives of religious geniuses, such as St Francis, St Bernard and Luther.

It is clear, then, that the theory of mental expressions – certainly the most celebrated idea in Dilthey's 'critique of historical reason', and probably his most admired contribution to philosophy – was already present *in nuce* at a relatively early stage, even if it had to await its fullest and most systematic formulation till much later. And the references (above) to Sts Francis and Bernard, and to Martin Luther, serve as a reminder of another continuity between the earlier and the later work, namely, the pivotal role of biography. Biographies are both source and subject-matter for psychology and history equally. Biography and history, of course, cannot be simply equated, as Dilthey was well aware – he never reduced history to the doings of 'great men', however much he stressed their historical importance. Rather, the point is what might be called the structural homology between history and biography. The individual human life, Dilthey says, is the 'germinal cell' of history, in which 'the specific historical categories arise' ([8.35], 73). The individual life, as we noted above, 'is present in the memory' of the individual; thus 'the sequence of a life is held together by the consciousness of identity … the discrete is linked into continuity'. Likewise, history

is only possible … through the reconstruction of the course of events in a memory which reproduces … the system of connections and the stages of its development. What memory accomplishes when it surveys the course of a life is achieved in history by linking together the expressions of life which have become part of the objective mind, according to their temporal and dynamic relationships. This is history.

([8.35], 89)

Just as the individual life is lived always in the present, but a present which includes (memories of) the past, so the present of collective humanity also includes its past – is historical:

> We are hourly surrounded by the products of history. Whatever characteristics the mind puts into expressions of life are tomorrow, if they persist, history. As time marches on we are surrounded by Roman ruins, cathedrals, and the summer castles of autocrats. History is not something separated from life or divided from the present by distance in time.

([8.35], 124)

And in another striking passage, Dilthey suggests that the role played by memory in the life of the individual is played, in that of 'nations, communities, of mankind itself' by the historian. But for his efforts, their past would mean as little to them as would his to a person without a memory. 'The ruins, the remnants of things past, the expressions of mind in deeds, words, sounds and pictures, of souls who have long since ceased to be' surround us but are in themselves dead and meaningless. The historian 'stands in the midst' of these things: his task is to 'conjure up' the past, by 'interpretation of the remnants that remain' ([8.35], 139). He provides human communities with an essential part of human life.

It may seem from the above quotations as if Dilthey, *qua* historian, was a believer in what could be called 'collective minds' of human communities such as nations. This, however, is at best an oversimplification, at worst misleading. Certainly he accepted the reality of peoples or nations (*Völker*) as significant social and historical entities: this is explicit, for example, in the *Introduction to the Human Sciences* ([8.32], 100). But in that book he immediately went on to reject as mystical any suggestion that these entities are supra-individual organisms, or possess a supra-individual 'folk soul' or 'folk spirit' (*Volksgeist*). Such notions were unacceptable from Dilthey's fundamentally empirical standpoint: empirically, the only bearer of mind is the individual. The relation between the individual and collective entities like nations was therefore a problem that Dilthey took seriously. He later posed it as follows:

> The question now arises, how can a system which is not produced as such in one mind, and which is therefore not directly experienced nor can be reduced to the lived experience of one person, take shape as a system in the historian's mind

from the expressions of persons and statements about them? This presupposes that logical subjects can be formed which are not psychological subjects. There must be a means of delimiting them, there must be a justification for conceiving them as units ... And here arises the great problem.

([8.71], 289)

Dilthey's solution to the problem was to identify the nation or people with the national consciousness of individuals: 'It is ... the consciousness of belonging together, of nationality and national feeling, on which the unity of the subject finally rests.' This consciousness is firmly rooted by Dilthey in individual psychology: 'The consciousness of belonging together is conditioned by the same elements that assert themselves in the individual's consciousness of himself' ([8.35], 152–3). Yet the consciousness of belonging together creates a collective entity, which in turn influences the consciousness of individuals: 'The common experiences of a nation, common purposes and memories are real. They are the source of the communally determined purposes of individuals.' It is a commonplace, Dilthey says, that only individuals can experience the satisfaction of realized purposes: yet such satisfaction may come from identification with one's nation. 'An individual wills national ends as his own, experiences the nation's experiences as his own, has memories of such experiences as belonging to himself, is filled with them and carried along by them' ([8.71], 294). A nation, therefore, is not only a reality but a distinctive unity: 'Nations are often relatively self-contained and because of this have their own horizon' ([8.35], 130). By this Dilthey means that they have a characteristic conception of reality and system of values. They are not only (through, for example, state organization) historical agents, but appropriate contexts for the interpretation of individual acts and expressions, which they condition. In this, non-metaphysical sense, the term *Volksgeist* can be accepted.

Much the same may be said about the term *Zeitgeist* (or *Geist des Zeitalters*). The *Zeitalter* (epoch, era or historical period) is in Dilthey's thought an important and undoubted reality, often indeed referred to alongside, and in similar terms to, the people or nation, as a 'structural system' or 'unit of the world of mind'. Dilthey puts it thus:

The common practices of an epoch become the norm for the activities of individuals who live in it. The society of an epoch has a pattern of interactions which has uniform features. There is an inner affinity in the comprehension of objects. The ways of feeling, the emotions and the impulses which arise from them, are similar to each other. The will, too, chooses uniform goals, strives for related goods ... It is the task of historical analysis to discover the consensus which governs the concrete purposes, values and ways of thought of a period.

([8.36], 198)

The *Zeitgeist* is, once again, an appropriate context for the understanding of such expressions, and vice versa. Thus (to cite an example given by Dilthey), the historian can use the civil law of the 'age of Frederick' to 'understand the spirit of that age; he goes back from the laws to the intentions of the legislature and from there back to the spirit from which they arose', or in other words 'the social values, purposes [etc.] present at a certain time and place and which [thus] expressed themselves' ([8.35], 76). Another example, developed at some length by Dilthey, is Teutonic society in the time of Caesar and Tacitus:

> Here, as in every later period, we find economic life, state and law linked to language, myth, religiousness and poetry... Thus heroic poetry arose from the warlike spirit in the Teutonic age of Tacitus, and this poetry invigorated the warlike spirit. From this same warlike spirit inhumanity arose in the religious sphere, as in the sacrifice of prisoners and the hanging up of their corpses in sacred places. The same spirit then affected the position of the god of war in the world of the gods.

([8.35], 150–1)

It must be stressed, once again, that for Dilthey the *Zeitgeist* is an empirical generalization, not a deterministic force – for if it were the latter there would, presumably, be no change – no history. Yet historicity is, as we know, central to Dilthey's vision of human life. Thus every 'historical configuration' is 'ephemeral'. But historical change is of course neither random nor total. According to Dilthey it arises (in part at least) from the perceived imperfection inevitable in every age, from man's 'unfulfilled longing' (due, for example, to the social inequalities – 'impoverishment of existence' and 'servitude' – said by Dilthey to spring from the power relations that are inseparable from human social life). Thus successive ages are linked in the following way:

> Every age refers back to the preceding one, for the forces developed in the latter continue to be active in it; at the same time it already contains the strivings and creative activities which prepare for the succeeding age. As it arose from the insufficiency of the preceding one so it bears in itself the limits, tension, sufferings, which prepare for the next age.

([8.35], 156)

Thus Dilthey integrates his conception of the *Zeitgeist* into his conception of historical change in a way that allows for individual freedom and creativity. Although we quoted Dilthey (above) on the historian's task of discovering 'the consensus which governs' the values and conceptions of an epoch, 'governs' is really too strong a word; for almost at once Dilthey adds that the historian must assess 'what the individual has achieved within this context, *and how far his vision and activity may have extended beyond it*' ([8.36], 198, emphases added). History is not a realm governed by scientific causality but of 'action and reaction'. The coherences and structures that the historian seeks and discovers are real but 'can never bind or determine what is new, or may appear in the future'. Historical events and changes can be understood after the event, but not predicted in advance. As Dilthey sums it up, 'History does not cause, it creates'. He adds: 'It creates because the structure of life is at work in the acts of knowing, evaluating, setting of goals, and striving for ends' ([8.65], 308). The concepts of all the human sciences (not only history) reflect this fact. Despite the limits placed on human freedom by the causal necessities of nature (within which humanity exists), the freedom due to the human element is real:

> Surrounded though it is by that structure of objective necessity which nature consists of, freedom flashes forth at innumerable points ... Here the actions of the will – in contrast with the mechanical processes of change in nature (which already contains from the start everything which ensues later) – really produce something and achieve true development both in the individual and in humanity as a whole.
>
> ([8.32], 79)

❧ DILTHEY'S HERMENEUTIC TURN ❧

In only the last decade or so of his life, Dilthey elaborated what is probably now the most celebrated aspect of his philosophy of the human sciences, or critique of historical reason – namely, hermeneutics. Not that hermeneutics was by any means a new interest for Dilthey – his first major work, indeed, was a notable biography of Schleiermacher (the 'father of modern hermeneutics'), so that the late 'turn to hermeneutics' was for Dilthey a return to scholarly beginnings. Nevertheless, the innovation was marked, for only in his late phase did hermeneutics become for Dilthey the centre of his philosophy rather than an object of historical study.

Dilthey defined hermeneutics as the 'science' of 'the interpretation of the written records of human existence' ([8.36], 228). Thus, his hermeneutic methodology of the human sciences gives pride of place to a science of linguistic interpretation. This is not to say that Dilthey wished these sciences to take as their object of study only written documents: the latter are only one (though very important) category of the 'expressions of mind' which form their subject-matter. Nevertheless, the hermeneutic emphasis does put a particular slant on the mode of interpreting these expressions: they are to be interpreted, so to say, 'as if' they were verbal expressions. This has significant implications for some of the central concepts of Dilthey's philosophy of the human sciences – notably understanding (*Verstehen*) and meaning (*Sinn, Bedeutung*).

Some of these implications emerge from a consideration of the two typical concerns of hermeneutic technique as it developed prior to Schleiermacher and Dilthey (according to the Dilthey scholar Ilse Bulhoff). One (dubbed 'philological') was concerned to restore corrupt texts (e.g. classical texts) in which errors had accumulated through repeated copying. Another (called 'theological') aimed at grasping the 'true meaning' of Biblical texts ([8.60], 56). Different though these are, both make sense only given a presumption of *unity* or *coherence* in the texts handled. Errors in corrupt texts become apparent through their failure to 'fit', to 'make sense', in terms of the text as a whole – correction restores the 'fit'; similarly, the exegesis of biblical texts proceeded on the assumption that they are mutually coherent and consistent – it might be described as the enterprise of demonstrating their coherence or unity. Dilthey's hermeneutic methodology of the human sciences bears the marks of this ancestry, in its preoccupation with relations of coherence between *wholes* and *parts*. To be sure, we have already seen a similar preoccupation in Dilthey's earlier work; however, some problematic aspects thereof are thrown into relief by the later hermeneutic emphasis.

Perhaps the best-known element of hermeneutic methodology is the so-called 'hermeneutic circle'. Here is how Dilthey at one point defined it: 'The general difficulty of all interpretation [is that] the whole of a work must be understood from individual words and their combinations, but full understanding of an individual part presupposes understanding of the whole' ([8.36], 259). Another passage elaborates the point. In hermeneutics,

> understanding must try to link words into meaning and the
> meaning of the parts into the structure of the whole given in
> the sequence of words. Every word is both determined and
> undetermined. It contains a range of [possible] meanings ... In
> the same way ... the whole, which is made up of sentences, is
> ambiguous within limits, and must be determined from the
> whole [*sic* – error for parts?]. This determining of

determinate–indeterminate particulars is characteristic of hermeneutics.

([8.36], 231)

In brief, hermeneutics is a procedure in which the parts and whole of a text mutually clarify each other, on the presumption that the whole is a meaningfully coherent relation of parts.

To repeat, this is the *model* for Dilthey's late philosophy of the human sciences which, however, embraces not just texts but also non-linguistic expressions of the human mind. Thus extended, the analogy gives rise to certain problems (or at least issues), of which three sources may be mentioned. (1) Not all 'expressions' express meanings in the same sense as do words and texts; (2) Dilthey applies (or seems to apply) the hermeneutic methodology to a range of expressions much wider than the purely linguistic, but not to *all* expressions; (3) in applying the hermeneutic analogy to the human sciences generally, rather than the exegesis of texts narrowly, Dilthey greatly expands the range of 'wholes' (and parts) relevant to interpretation, understanding and the elucidation of meaning.

Regarding the first of the three points above, Dilthey himself explicitly distinguished several different sorts of 'expressions' relevant to the human sciences. Particularly germane is the distinction between *actions* and so-called *Erlebnisausdrücke* ('expressions of experience'), which are verbal, usually written, accounts. The former are 'expressions' in the sense that they reflect purposes, the pursuit of goals etc., and are in this sense meaningful or have a meaning ([8.97], 65–6). Verbal utterances are no doubt likewise purposeful acts, but they also have a meaning in another sense, that is, words conventionally signify some semantic content. It therefore seems as if the fundamental, or most general, sense in which expressions of mind have a meaning which can be grasped or understood is not the same as the straightforwardly hermeneutic sense. This introduces some ambiguities into Dilthey's terminology in that, alongside the hermeneutic version of meaning and understanding, he continued to make use of the 'pre-hermeneutic' sense. Thus, he remarks on 'the fact that inner states find outward expressions, and that the latter can be understood by going back to the former' (this is the business of the human sciences) ([8.35], 75). But he adds that there are two ways in which 'an outer manifestation is the expression of an inner state, namely, 'by means of an artificial convention' [e.g. as in language], or 'by a natural relationship between expression and what is expressed' (as in non-linguistic expressions such as actions which express, and can be understood as expressing, a purpose). It seems that Dilthey is reluctant to make any sharp distinction between the two cases.

It is arguable that the blurring of this distinction encouraged Dilthey to apply his hermeneutic methodology to a wider range of 'expressions' than may be justified. But how widely did he wish to apply it? It appears (though it is difficult to be certain on this point) that the hermeneutic methodology is *not* coextensive with all acts of understanding of expressions. Dilthey makes a distinction between 'elementary' and 'higher' understanding. The distinction is not particularly clear, but one aspect of it seems to be that 'elementary' understanding is understanding of a *single* expression, such as 'picking up an object, letting a hammer drop, cutting wood with a saw' – actions which 'indicate the presence of certain purposes' ([8.36], 220). All that is involved in this understanding is 'to spell out the mental content' which constitutes the goal of the action. The implication is that 'higher understanding' goes beyond this, and involves the placing of actions in a wider context. It appears to be Dilthey's view that the hermeneutic methodology is a means to 'higher understanding', and is required, or appropriate, where the understanding of expressions is not straightforward but problematic ([8.97], 101). Clearly this is liable to be the case in relation to textual records emanating from distant periods or cultures; but it is equally likely to be true wherever 'understanding' has to go beyond the everyday intercourse of participants in a common culture – in other words, to embrace the understanding required of historians and social scientists. It looks, therefore, as if Dilthey considered the range of the hermeneutic methodology to be more or less coextensive with that of the human sciences. It is to apply, that is, to actions (as studied by historians and social scientists), as well as to written material.

From Dilthey's assimilation of these different kinds of expressions arise some problematic implications. One is that he is led, quite explicitly, to detach the understanding of expressions, and their meaning, from the goals and intentions of agents ([8.35], 163). For this there seem to be two slightly different reasons, both however derived from the hermeneutic perspective. One is that the meaning of language (which is the focus of hermeneutic interpretation) is a matter of public conventions, rather than the intentions of language users. The other is that, as we saw, the fundamental tool of hermeneutic interpretation is the 'hermeneutic circle', which rests understanding and the grasping of meaning on the part–whole relation, on the presumption that one is dealing with a coherent whole made up of consistently related parts. Dilthey applies this idea (or analogy) quite universally to the categories of understanding and meaning in the human sciences. For example: 'Meaning means nothing except belonging to a whole' ([8.36], 233); 'The category of meaning designates the relationship, inherent in life, of parts of a life to the whole' ([8.36], 235). Dilthey makes it clear that these definitions follow from an analogy between linguistic meaning and the understanding of life in passages such as the following:

> As words have a meaning (*Bedeutung*) by which they designate something ... so on the basis of the determined–undetermined (*bestimmt–unbestimmten*) meaning of the parts of life, its structure (*Zusammenhang*) can be figured out. Meaning is the special kind of relationship which the parts of life have to life as a whole.
>
> ([8.60], 121)

In detaching the meaning and understanding of expressions from the intentions of agents, Dilthey appears to risk an incoherence in his philosophy. For he never abandoned his original insight, on which he based his distinction between natural and human sciences, namely that we understand others, their doings and their products in fundamentally the same way as we understand our own. Thus:

> we cannot understand ourselves and others except by projecting what we have actually experienced into every expression of our own and others' lives. So man becomes the subject-matter of the human studies only when we relate experience, expression and understanding to each other.
>
> ([8.36], 176)

This concept of understanding surely cannot be detached from agents' goals and intentions – rather it seems to require our empathizing with them.

Displacement of understanding of actions and their meaning from agents' intentions to the place of the action in a larger whole raises another problem: how to specify the relevant whole. In the strictly or narrowly hermeneutic case, this problem may not appear to be insoluble; but when a hermeneutic approach is applied to history and the human sciences in general, it becomes acute. We have already taken note (above) of Dilthey's predilection for treating the individual human life as a meaningful unity, in terms of which the meanings of its parts are to be discerned. A similar approach is applied to historical events. But as we shall now see, this – and especially the latter – appears to introduce an intrinsic uncertainty or relativism into Dilthey's central concept of meaning (and hence of understanding, which is the grasping of meaning). Dilthey writes:

> The category of meaning designates the relationship, inherent in life, of parts of a life to the whole. The connections are only established by memory, through which we survey our past ...
> But in what does the particular kind of relationship of parts to

a whole in life consist? It is a relationship which is never quite complete. One would have to wait for the end of a life, for only at the hour of death could one survey the whole from which the relationship between the parts could be ascertained. One would have to wait for the end of history to have all the material necessary to determine its meaning ... Our view of the meaning of life changes constantly. Every plan for your life expresses a view of the meaning of life.

([8.36], 235–6)

Some obvious problems arise from this passage. So far as the individual life is concerned, Dilthey vacillates between two points of view: namely, that a human life is a natural unity stretching from birth to death, from which the meaning of its parts derives; and that it is a continually developing and changing unity, with corresponding change in the meaning of parts. Something similar applies to history. 'One would have to wait for the end of history to have all the material necessary to determine its meaning.' But Dilthey elsewhere has explicitly stated that history as a whole has no single meaning, no over-arching *telos* or goal ([8.71], 303). Where then can the historian find the unity needed to discern meaning and permit understanding? Does he or she need to find such a unity? Undoubtedly, historical development continually reveals new connections (as Dilthey might have put it, *Zusammenhänge*) which call for reinterpretation of past events, and the historian's function is a continual analysis and re-analysis of these connections. But a *Zusammenhang*, in the sense of structured connection, is not a definable *whole* made up of definable parts. Or to put it another way, to ask the historian to convert a pattern of connections into a meaning-conferring whole seems to give him or her a great deal of latitude in the assignment of meaning. One has to wonder if this is any longer 'science'.

❧ HISTORICISM AND THE PROBLEM OF ❧ RELATIVISM: DILTHEY'S SOLUTION

There is one answer given by Dilthey to this problem of the definition of historical wholes, which is of particular interest because, in so far as it does help to solve that particular problem, it immediately raises another. We noted above the importance attached by Dilthey to the concept of the historical period (*Zeitalter*) and its unifying 'spirit': we must now note his view that this constitutes a whole that confers meaning on its parts:

Everything in an age derives its meaning from the energy which

gives it its fundamental tendency ... All the expressions of the
energy which determines the age are akin to each other. The task
of analysis is to find the unity of valuation and purpose in
different expressions of life ... The context forms the horizon
of the age and through it, finally, the meaning of every part in
the system of the age is determined.

([8.35], 156)

For the sake of argument, let us suppose that this particular kind
of unity is a more or less objective fact that can be discovered by the
scientific historian. If so, we have solved one problem only to raise
another – one of which Dilthey was acutely aware, indeed it concerned
him deeply. Each age takes its own values, its own world-view, as
unproblematically valid – this is even the necessary condition of its
creativity – but historiography shows such assumptions to be naive and
untenable. The historical study of human life reveals – this indeed is
its point, and its glory – the immense variety of expressions of that
life, including values and world-views. But the obverse of this is the
problem of historical relativism:

Historical comparison reveals the relativity of all historical
convictions. They are all conditioned by ... circumstances ...
Historical consciousness increasingly proves the relativity of
every metaphysical or religious doctrine which has emerged in
the course of the Ages.

([8.36], 112)

The same applies to 'values, obligations, norms and goods'. Dilthey
writes:

History does indeed know the positing of something
unconditional as value, norm, or good ... But historical
experience knows only the process of positing ... and nothing
of their universal validity. By tracing the course of development
of such unconditional values, goods or norms, it notices that life
has produced different ones and that the unconditional positing
itself becomes possible only because the horizon of the age is
limited ... It notices the unsettled conflict among the
unconditional positings.

([8.35], 165)

This state of affairs Dilthey called 'the wound brought about by the
knife of historical relativism' ([8.60], 21).

Is the wound so fatal? Does the 'chaos' of conflicting world-views
and values mean that none of them can be objectively true, or – worse
– that there is no such thing as objective truth in these realms? It might

well seem that such sceptical and unsettling conclusions do *not* follow from any amount of historical evidence. But here we must remind ourselves of Dilthey's philosophy of values, which like everything else in his philosophy rests finally on the bedrock of 'life' – values arise *in life*, and there is nothing 'behind' life to which we can appeal. The relativist implications of Dilthey's combination of ethical subjectivism and historicism seem inescapable.

Yet Dilthey sought to escape them, and to assert at least some universal values – even to deduce them as implications of his philosophy of history and the human sciences. These are values of individualism, freedom and creativity. According to Dilthey 'the dignity and value of every individual' is an unconditional value ([8.35], 74); 'the individual is an intrinsic value [which] we can ascertain beyond doubt' ([8.36], 224). Why so? Because says Dilthey, the individual is the ultimate 'subject-matter of understanding'. 'Understanding has always an individual for its object' ([8.71], 276). A philosophy of human sciences which proposes to understand mental life must presuppose the value of the bearer of mental life, the human individual.

Furthermore, Dilthey's philosophy of the human sciences is posited on a conception of mankind as being (unlike nature) free and genuinely creative. A historiography which reveals a multiplicity of values and world-views is a revelation of this freedom and creativity. Revelation of this truth is liberating. Historicism, therefore, continues and even completes the increasing realization of man's potential for freedom and creativity that was earlier carried forward by such episodes as the Renaissance, the Reformation and the Enlightenment:

> The historical consciousness of the finitude of every historical phenomenon ... and of the relativity of every kind of faith, is the last step towards the liberation of mankind. With it man achieves the sovereignty to enjoy every experience to the full and surrender himself to it unencumbered, as if there were no system of philosophy or faith to tie him down ... The mind becomes sovereign over the cobwebs of dogmatic thought ... And in contrast to relativity, the continuity of creative forces asserts itself as the central historical fact.
>
> ([8.35], 167)

Alas, this resolution of the problem hardly seems satisfactory. Dilthey seems to oscillate uneasily between spelling out what he takes to be the moral implications of a humanistic science, and extracting a historicist ethic from its findings. This latter kind of argument hardly seems open to him, given his denial that history has any necessary *telos* or goal. We surely do not want to put the values of individuality, freedom and creativity at the mercy of unpredictable historical trends.

The last quotation cited above bristles with problems. How can Dilthey predict with such confidence the liberating effects of the 'historical consciousness', given his view that history is inherently unpredictable? And suppose his prediction is right – is it really desirable that people become free 'to enjoy *every* experience to the full'? The problem of liberty and its proper limits cannot be solved by invoking history in this way. A historicist ethic is liable to end up with either an arbitrary interpretation of history, or an undiscriminating endorsement of whatever happens. Dilthey, unhappily, falls into the latter trap. Let us fill in some gaps left in the last quotation above. 'The mind' writes Dilthey 'becomes sovereign over the cobwebs of dogmatic thought'. He continues:

> Everything beautiful, everything holy, every sacrifice relived and interpreted, opens perspectives which disclose some part of reality. And equally, we accept the evil, horrible and ugly, as filling a place in the world, as containing some reality which must be justified in the system of things.

Do we? Must it? Surely not.

➤ DILTHEY'S HUMANISM ➤

Dilthey's attempts to solve the problem of relativism led him to an unacceptable conclusion; however, the problem itself is, in part, the obverse of what is perhaps most attractive in his philosophy, namely what may be called his humanism – his passion to understand all the varied and multifarious expressions of the human spirit. Dilthey stressed equally the enormous variety of these expressions, and the fundamental unity of human nature from which they spring. As he put it in a famous remark, for interpretation of the expressions of human life to be necessary – to be a science – there must be something alien about them, something puzzling that sets us a problem of understanding: on the other hand, if they were utterly alien, interpretation and understanding would be impossible. His entire enterprise therefore presupposes a fundamental unity of the human race.

➤ DILTHEY'S INFLUENCE ➤

Dilthey's influence on later thought has undoubtedly been significant, in both philosophy and the social sciences. So far as philosophy is concerned, a recent discussion underlines his relevance to the shaping 'of the dominant Continental movements of phenomenology, existentialism, and hermeneutic philosophy' ([8.87], vii). In Dilthey's relations with Edmund Husserl (the chief creator of phenomenological philosophy) influences in fact ran in both directions. The two men met in the winter of 1905/6, and, according to Husserl's own testimony, thereafter 'the problems pertaining to phenomenology as a human science ... occupied me more than almost all other problems' ([8.87], ix-x). There is no doubting the influence of Dilthey's 'philosophy of life' on Husserl's central concept of the 'life world'. Equally clear is the kinship between some of Dilthey's ideas and those of the existentialism of Martin Heidegger – for example, the key role of time and memory in human life, the conception of man as essentially free and creative, and the corresponding relativity of values. Another existentialist philosopher, Karl Jaspers, explicitly acknowledged Dilthey's influence on his thinking (in his *Allgemeine Psychopathologie*, a work of psychiatry rather than philosophy – nevertheless the influence is likely to have been more general). Dilthey's importance for the hermeneutic movement in philosophy is almost too obvious to mention (a recent review in the *Times Literary Supplement*, 24 July 1992, p. 7, refers to him simply as 'the founder of modern hermeneutics'). But it is perhaps worth pointing out, in this connection, that (for example) Hans-Georg Gadamer's well-known concept of the 'fusion of horizons' seems clearly to be a response to Dilthey's references to the 'closed horizon' of the historical period (*Zeitalter*). Equally obviously, Jürgen Habermas, leading contemporary representative of the 'critical theory' of the Franfurt School, is indebted to Dilthey for his categorization of human knowledge – or rather for two-thirds of it, since Habermas has turned Dilthey's dichotomy into a trichotomy. However, Habermas's category of 'historical-hermeneutic sciences' has an unmistakable Diltheyan ring, while his category of 'empirical-analytic sciences' stemming from a human interest in technical control of nature has much in common with Dilthey's conception of the *Naturwissenschaften*.

Even more important, perhaps, has been Dilthey's influence on social science and psychology, or rather on those within these 'human sciences' who resist their assimilation to the natural sciences. In anglophone psychology Dilthey's influence has not been great (it has been swamped by the behaviourists and Freudians) but in the German-speaking world it has given birth to a movement known as *verstehende Psychologie* and has been influential with a number of psychiatrists, such as Heinz Hartmann and Ludwig Binswanger ([8.60], 160). Cultural anthropology is another field in which significant influence has been attributed to Dilthey – Franz Boas attended his lectures in Berlin, while Ruth Benedict explicitly invokes Dilthey in her *Patterns of Culture* ([8.60], 175). But if Dilthey has been influential within the social sciences, it has been above all by influencing one of the most influential of all social scientists, Max Weber. Marianne Weber, in her famous biography of her husband, informs us that Dilthey was a frequent visitor to the Weber household in Berlin ([8.111], 39) and confirms that Weber based his own concept of *Verstehen*, so central to his sociology, on that of Dilthey ([8.111], 312). Another central concept of Weberian sociology – that of meaning and the meaningful – likewise looks to have a Diltheyan ancestry. However, some care is needed here, and it is perhaps as important to point to the differences as to the similarities in the conceptual schemes of the two men. According to Weber, the subject-matter of the social sciences is 'social action', and by 'action' he means 'all human behaviour when and insofar as the acting individual attaches a subjective meaning to it' ([8.112], 88) In other words, for Weber, the meaning of an action is defined by the agent's motives and intentions: understanding is grasping these motives and intentions. Weber's concept of understanding or *Verstehen*, therefore, seems to derive from the earlier, pre-hermeneutic phase of Dilthey's thought – the later, hermeneutic phase had no influence on him. Nor did Weber (unlike Dilthey) see any incompatibility between understanding (*Verstehen*) and causal explanation (*Erklären*) – in his view of the social sciences the two must go hand in hand.

❧ BIBLIOGRAPHY ❧

Original language editions

Only a fraction of Dilthey's work was published in his lifetime. Since his death, his students and followers have undertaken a multi-volume publication in German of his entire *oeuvre*, the *Gesammelte Schriften* (Collected Works). The undertaking, not yet complete, projects a total of thirty-two volumes. So far, twenty volumes have been published. The first twelve volumes were published jointly by B. G. Teubner of Stuttgart, and Vandenhoeck & Ruprecht of Göttingen; subsequent volumes by Vandenhoeck & Ruprecht alone. The titles, editors and original publication dates of individual volumes are as follows:

8.1   Vol. 1: *Einleitung in die Geisteswissenschaften: Versuch einer Grundlegung für das Studium der Gesellschaft und der Geschichte*, ed. B. Groethuysen, 1922.

8.2   Vol. 2: *Weltanschauung und Analyse der Menschen seit Renaissance und Reformation*, ed. G. Misch, 1914.

8.3   Vol. 3: *Studien zur Geschichte des deutschen Geistes*, ed. P. Ritter, 1921.

8.4   Vol. 4: *Die Jugendgeschichte Hegels und andere Abhandlungen zur Geschichte des deutschen Idealismus*, ed. H. Nohl, 1921.

8.5   Vol. 5: *Die geistige Welt: Einleitung in die Philosophie des Lebens. Erste Hälfte: Abhandlungen zur Grundlegung der Geisteswissenschaften*, ed. G. Misch, 1924.

8.6   Vol 6: *Die geistige Welt: Einleitung in die Philosophie des Lebens. Zweite Hälfte: Abhandlungen zur Poetik, Ethik und Pädagogik,* ed. G. Misch, 1924.

8.7   Vol. 7: *Der Aufbau der geschichtlichen Welt in den Geisteswissenschaften,* ed. B. Groethuysen, 1927.

8.8.   Vol. 8: *Weltanschauungslehre: Abhandlungen zur Philosophie der Philosophie,* ed. B. Groethuysen, 1931.

8.9   Vol. 9: *Pädagogik: Geschichte und Grundlinien des Systems,* ed. O. F. Bollnow, 1934.

8.10   Vol. 10: *System der Ethik,* ed. H. Nohl, 1958.

8.11   Vol. 11: *Vom Aufgang des geschichtlichen Bewusstseins: Jugendaufsätze und Erinnerungen,* ed. E. Weniger, 1936.

8.12   Vol. 12: *Zur preussischen Geschichte,* ed. E. Weniger, 1936.

8.13   Vol. 13: *Leben Schleiermachers, Erster Band* (in two half-volumes), ed. M. Redeker, third edn 1970.

8.14   Vol. 14: *Leben Schleiermachers, Zweiter Band* (in two half-volumes), ed. M. Redeker, 1966.

8.15–17 Vols. 15–17: *Zur Geistesgeschichte des 19. Jahrhunderts,* ed. U. Herrmann, 1970–4.

8.18   Vol.18: *Die Wissenschaften vom Menschen, der Gesellschaft und der Geschichte: Vorarbeiten zur Einleitung in die Geisteswissenschaften,* ed. H. Johach and F. Rodi, 1977.

8.19   Vol.19: *Grundlegung der Wissenschaften vom Menschen, der Gesellschaft und der Geschichte: Ausarbeitungen und Entwürfe zum zweiten Band der Einleitung in die Geisteswissenschaften,* ed. H. Johach and F. Rodi, 1982.

8.20   Vol. 20: *Logik und System der philosophischen Wissenschaften,* ed. H. Lessing and F. Rodi, 1990.

N.B. Rickman 1976 [8.36], contains (pp. 264–6) an extremely useful English translation of the table of contents of each volume of the *Gesammelte Schriften* up to vol. 17.

Other works by Dilthey, not yet included in the Gesammelte Schriften

8.21   *Das Erlebnis und die Dichtung: Lessing, Goethe, Novalis, Hölderlin,* first published 1906, and frequently reprinted, e.g. Göttingen: Vandenhoeck & Ruprecht, 1970.

8.22   *Mozart: Figaro, Don Juan, die Zauberflöte,* Tiessen, 1986.

8.23   Gadamer, H. G. ed., *Grundriss der allgemeinen Geschichte der Philosophie,* Frankfurt am Main: Klostermann, 1949.

8.24   Nohl, H., ed., *Die grosse Phantasiedichtung und andere Studien zur vergleichende Literaturgeschichte,* Göttingen: Vandenhoeck & Ruprecht, 1954.

8.25   Nohl, H. and G. Misch, eds, *Von deutscher Dichtung und Musik: Aus den Studien zur Geschichte des deutschen Geistes,* first published 1932, 2nd edn, Stuttgart: B. G. Teubner; Göttingen: Vandenhoeck & Ruprecht, 1957.

Letters and diaries

8.26 Misch, C. ed., *Der junge Dilthey: Ein Lebensbild in Briefen und Tagebüchern, 1852–70*, first published 1933, 2nd edn, Stuttgart, B. G. Teubner; Göttingen: Vandenhoeck & Ruprecht, 1960.

8.27 Schulenburg, S. v.d. ed., *Briefwechsel zwischen Wilhelm Dilthey und dem Grafen Paul Yorck v. Wartenburg 1877–1897*, Halle: Max Niemeyer, 1923.

8.28 'Der Briefwechsel Dilthey–Husserl' (with introduction by W. Biemel), *Man and World*, 1 (1968): 428–46. (English translation in P. McCormick and F. Elliston, eds., *Husserl: Shorter Works*, Notre Dame, Indiana, Notre Dame University Press, 1981.)

English translations

8.29 *Dilthey's Philosophy of Existence: Introduction to Weltanschauungslehre*, trans. W. Kluback and M. Weinbaum, London: Vision, 1960.

8.30 *The Essence of Philosophy*, trans. S. A. Emery and W. T. Emery, New York: AMS, 1969.

8.31 *Descriptive Psychology and Historical Understanding*, The Hague: Martinus Nijhoff, 1977. Contains 'Ideas Concerning a Descriptive and Analytic Psychology', trans. R. M. Zaner, and 'The Understanding of Other Persons and their Expressions of Life', trans. K. Heiges. There is a lengthy introduction by R. A. Makkreel.

8.32 *Introduction to the Human Sciences*, trans. R. J. Betanzos, London: Harvester Wheatsheaf and Wayne State University Press, 1988.

8.33 Makkreel, R. A. and F. Rodi, eds., *Poetry and Experience*, Princeton: Princeton University Press, 1985. (This is vol. 5 of a projected *Selected Works* in six volumes.)

8.34 Makkreel, R. A. and F. Rodi, eds., *Introduction to the Human Sciences*, Princeton: Princeton University Press, 1989. (Vol. 1 of the *Selected Works*.)

8.35 Rickman, H. P., ed., *Meaning in History: W. Dilthey's Thoughts on History and Society*, London: Allen & Unwin, 1961. Contains selections from vol. 7 of the *Gesammelte Schriften*, with commentaries.

8.36 Rickman, H. P., ed., *Dilthey: Selected Writings*, Cambridge: Cambridge University Press, 1976.

8.37 Hodges, H. A. *Wilhelm Dilthey: An Introduction*, London, Routledge & Kegan Paul, 1944. Contains some fifty pages of selections in translation.

8.38 'The Dream', trans. W. Kluback, in his *Wilhelm Dilthey's Philosophy of History*, New York: Columbia University Press, 1956.

8.39   'The Understanding of Other Persons and Their Life-Expression', trans.
        J. J. Kuehl, in P. Gardiner, ed., *Theories of History*, New York: Free
        Press, 1959.

8.40   'The Rise of Hermeneutics', trans. F. Jameson, in *New Literary History*, 3
        (1972): 229–44.

8.41   'The Eighteenth Century and the Historical World', trans. J. W. Moore, in
        P. Gay and G. J. Cavanaugh, eds., *Historian at Work*, vol. 4, New
        York and London: Harper & Row, 1975.

Bibliographies

8.42   Diaz de Cerio, F. 'Bibliografia de W. Dilthey', *Pensamiento*, 24 (1968):
        196–223.

8.43   Herrmann, U. *Bibliographie Wilhelm Diltheys*, Weinheim: Julius Beltz, 1969.

8.44   Weniger, E. 'Verzeichnis der Schriften Wilhelm Diltheys von den Anfägen
        bis zur Einleitung in die Geisteswissenschaften', in *Gesammelte Schrif-
        ten*, 22: 208–13.

8.45   The *Dilthey-Jahrbuch für Philosophie und Geschichte der Geisteswissenschaf-
        ten*, Göttingen: Vandenhoeck & Ruprecht (first published in 1983),
        regularly includes bibliographical supplements on Dilthey.

Commentaries and other relevant literature

8.46   Abel, T. 'The Operation Called *Verstehen*', in H. Feigl and M. Brodbeck,
        eds., *Readings in the Philosophy of Science*, New York: Appleton-
        Century-Crofts, 1953.

8.47   Antoni, C. *From History to Sociology*, trans. H. V. White, Detroit: Wayne
        State University Press, 1959.

8.48   Apel, K. O. *Analytic Philosophy of Language and the 'Geisteswissenschaften'*,
        Dordrecht: Reidel, 1967.

8.49   Aron, R. *La Philosophie critique de l'histoire: Essai sur une théorie allemande
        de l'histoire*, Paris: J. Vrin, 1950 (originally published in 1938 as *Essai
        sur la théorie de l'histoire dans l'Allemagne contemporaine*).

8.50   Bambach, C. R. *The Crisis of Historicism: Neo-Kantian Philosophy of History
        and Wilhelm Dilthey's Hermeneutics*, Ann Arbor: University of Michi-
        gan, 1987.

8.51   Bauman, Z. *Hermeneutics and Social Science*, London: Hutchinson, 1978.

8.52   Bergstraesser, A. 'Wilhelm Dilthey and Max Weber', *Ethics*, 62 (1947):
        92–110.

8.53   Betti, E. *Die Hermeneutik als allgemeine Methodik der Geisteswissenschaften*,
        Tübingen: Mohr, 1962.

8.54   —— *Allgemeine Auslegungslehre als Methodik der Geisteswissenschaften*,
        Tübingen: Mohr, 1967.

8.55   Binswanger, L. *Grundformen und Erkenntnis menschlichen Daseins*, 4th edn,
        Munich and Basel: Ernst Reinhardt, 1964.

8.56 Bollnow, O. F. *Das Verstehen: Drei Aufsätze zur Theorie der Geisteswissen-schaften*, Mainz: Kirchheim, 1949.

8.57 —— *Dilthey: Eine Einführung in seine Philosophie*, Stuttgart: Kohlhammer, 1955.

8.58 —— *Die Lebensphilosophie*, Berlin: Springer-Verlag, 1958.

8.59 Brown, D. K. 'Interpretive Historical Sociology: Discordances of Weber, Dilthey and Others', *Journal of Historical Sociology*, 3 (1990): 166–91.

8.60 Bulhoff, I. N. *Wilhelm Dilthey: a Hermeneutic Approach to the Study of History and Culture*, The Hague, Boston and London: Martinus Nijhoff, 1980.

8.61 Choi, J.-U. *Die geistig gesellschaftliche Krise des 19. Jahrhunderts und die Aufgaben der Diltheyschen 'Kritik der historischen Vernunft'*, 1987.

8.62 de Mul, J. 'Dilthey's Narrative Model of Human Development: Necessary Reconsiderations after the philosophical Hermeneutics of Heidegger and Gadamer', *Man and World*, 24 (1991): 409–26.

8.63 Donoso, A. 'Wilhelm Dilthey's Contribution to the Philosophy of History', *Philosophy Today*, 12 (1968): 151–63.

8.64 Ebbinghaus, H. 'Über Erklärende und Beschreibende Psychologie', *Zeitschrift für Psychologie und Physiologie*, 9 (1895): 161–205.

8.65 Ermarth, M. *Wilhelm Dilthey: The Critique of Historical Reason*, Chicago: University of Chicago Press, 1978.

8.66 Friess, H. L. 'Wilhelm Dilthey: a Review of his Collected Works as an Introduction to a Phase of Contemporary German Philosophy', *Journal of Philosophy*, 26 (1929): 5–25.

8.67 Gadamer, H. G. *Truth and Method*, trans. G. Burden and J. Cumming, New York: Sheed & Ward, 1975.

8.68 Habermas, J. *Knowledge and Human Interests*, trans. J. J. Shapiro, Boston: Beacon Press, 1971.

8.69 Herva, S. 'The Genesis of Max Weber's Verstehende Soziologie', *Acta Sociologica*, 31 (1988): 143–56.

8.70 Heinen, M. *Die Konstitution der Ästhetik in Wilhelm Diltheys Philosophie*, Bonn, Bouvier, 1974.

8.71 Hodges, H. A. *The Philosophy of Wilhelm Dilthey*, London: Routledge & Kegan Paul, 1952.

8.72 Holborn, H. 'Wilhelm Dilthey and the Critique of Historical Reason', *Journal of the History of Ideas*, 11 (1950): 93–118.

8.73 Horkheimer, M. 'The Relation between Psychology and Sociology in the Work of Wilhelm Dilthey', *Studies in Philosophy and Social Science*, 8 (1939): 430–43.

8.74 Hughes, H. S. *Consciousness and Society: The Reorientation of European Social Thought 1890–1930*, New York: Alfred A. Knopf, 1958.

8.75 Iggers, G. G. *The German Conception of History*, Middletown, Conn.: Wesleyan University Press, 1975.

8.76 Ineichen, H. *Erkenntnistheorie und geschichtlich-gesellschaftliche Welt: Diltheys Logik der Geisteswissenschaften*, Frankfurt: Klostermann, 1975.

8.77 Jalbert, J. E. 'Husserl's Position between Dilthey and the Windelband-

Rickert School of Neo-Kantianism', *Journal of the History of Philosophy*, 26 (1988): 279–96.

8.78 Jaspers, K. *General Psychopathology*, trans. J. Hoenig and M. W. Hamikon, Chicago: University of Chicago Press, 1963.

8.79 Johach, H. *Handlender Mensch und Objektiver Geist: Zur Theorie der Geisteswissenschaften bei Wilhelm Dilthey*, Meisenheim am Glan: Anton Hain, 1974.

8.80 Kluback, W. *Wilhelm Dilthey's Philosophy of History*, New York: Columbia University Press, 1956.

8.81 Knüppel, R. *Diltheys erkenntnistheoretische Logik*, Fink, 1991.

8.82 Krausser, P. *Kritik der endlichen Vernunft: Diltheys Revolution der Allgemeinen Wissenschafts- und Handlungstheorie*, Frankfurt am Main: Suhrkamp, 1968.

8.83 Linge, D. E. 'Dilthey and Gadamer: Two Theories of Historical Understanding', *Journal of the American Academy of Religion*, 41 (1973): 536–53.

8.84 Makkreel, R. A. *Dilthey: Philosopher of the Human Studies*, Princeton: Princeton University Press, 1975.

8.85 —— 'Husserl, Dilthey and the Relation of the Life-World to History', *Research in Phenomenology*, 12 (1982): 39–59.

8.86 —— 'Traditional Historicism, Contemporary Interpretation of Historicity, and the History of Philosophy', *New Literary History*, 21 (1990): 977–91.

8.87 Makkreel, R. A. and J. Scanlon, eds., *Dilthey and Phenomenology*, Washington, DC: Centre for Advanced Research in Phenomenology and University Press of America, 1987.

8.88 Masur, G. 'Wilhelm Dilthey and the History of Ideas', *Journal of the History of Ideas*, 13 (1952): 94–107.

8.89 Misch, G. *Lebensphilosophie und Phänomenologie: Eine Auseinandersetzung der Diltheyschen Richtung mit Heidegger und Husserl*, 3rd edn, Darmstadt: Wissenschaftliche Buchgesellschaft, 1967.

8.90 —— *Vom Lebens- und Gedankenkreis Wilhelm Diltheys*, Frankfurt am Main: G. Schulte-Bulmke, 1947.

8.91 Morgan, G. A. 'Wilhelm Dilthey', *Philosophical Review*, 42 (1933): 351–80.

8.92 Müller-Vollumer, K. *Towards a Phenomenological Theory of Literature: a Study of Wilhelm Dilthey's Poetik*, The Hague: Mouton, 1963.

8.93 Nenon, T. 'Dilthey's Inductive Method and the Nature of Philosophy', *South-Western Philosophical Review*, 5 (1989): 121–34.

8.94 Ortega y Gasset, J. 'A Chapter from the History of Ideas – Wilhelm Dilthey and the Idea of Life', trans. H. Weyl, in *Concord and Liberty*, New York: Norton, 1963.

8.95 Orth, E. W., ed. *Dilthey und die Philosophie der Gegenwart*, Freiburg: Alber, 1985.

8.96 Palmer, R. E. *Hermeneutics: Interpretation Theory in Schleiermacher, Dilthey, Heidegger, and Gadamer*, Evanston: Northwestern University Press, 1969.

8.97 Plantinga, T. *Historical Understanding in the Thought of Wilhelm Dilthey*, Toronto: University of Toronto Press, 1980.

9.98 Rickman, H. P. *Understanding and the Human Studies*, London: Heinemann, 1967.

8.99 —— *Wilhelm Dilthey – Pioneer of the Human Studies*, Stanford: University of California Press, 1979.

8.100 —— *Dilthey To-day*, New York: Greenwood, 1988.

8.101 Rand, C. G. 'Two Meanings of Historicism in the Writings of Dilthey, Troeltsch and Meinecke', *Journal of the History of Ideas*, 25 (1964): 503–18.

8.102 Ricoeur, P. 'The Model of the Text: Meaningful Action considered as a Text', *Social Research*, 38 (1971): 529–62.

8.103 Rodi, F. *Morphologie und Hermeneutik: Zur Methode von Diltheys Aesthetik*, Stuttgart: Kohlhammer, 1969.

8.104 Sauerland, *Dilthey's Erlebnisbegriff: Entstehung, Glanzzeit und Verkümmerung eines literaturhistorischen Begriffs*, Berlin: de Gruyter, 1972.

8.105 Spranger, E. *Lebensformen: Geisteswissenschaftliche Psychologie und Ethik der Persönlichkeit*, 5th edn, Halle (Saale): Max Niemeyer, 1925.

8.106 Tapper, B. 'Dilthey's Methodology of the *Geisteswissenschaften*', *Philosophical Review* 34 (1925): 333–49.

8.107 Taylor, C. 'Interpretation and the Sciences of Man', *Review of Metaphysics*, 25 (1971): 3–51.

8.108 Tuttle, H. N. *Wilhelm Dilthey's Philosophy of Historical Understanding: A Critical Analysis*, Leiden: Brill, 1969.

8.109 Wach, J. *Die Typenlehre Trendelenburgs und ihr Einfluss auf Dilthey*, Tübingen: Mohr, 1926.

8.110 —— *Das Verstehen: Grundzüge einer Geschichte der hermeneutischen Theorie im 19. Jahrhundert*, 3 vols, Tübingen: Mohr, 1926–33.

8.111 Weber, Marianne *Max Weber: A Biography*, New Brunswick, NJ: Transaction, 1988.

8.112 Weber, Max *The Theory of Social and Economic Organization*, Glencoe: Free Press, 1964.

8.113 Weiss, G. 'Dilthey's Conception of Objectivity in the Human Studies: a Reply to Gadamer', *Man and World*, 24 (1991): 471–86.

8.114 Wellek, R. 'Wilhelm Dilthey's Poetics and Literary Theory' in *Wächter und Hüter, Festschrift für Hermann J. Weigand*, New Haven: Yale University Press, 1957.

8.115 Wilson, B. A. *Hermeneutical Studies: Dilthey, Sophocles and Plato*, Leviston: Mellen Press, 1990.

8.116 Zöckler, C. *Dilthey und die Hermeneutik: Diltheys Begründung der Hermeneutik als 'Praxiswissenschaft' und die Geschichte ihrer Rezeption*, Stuttgart: Metzlersche, 1975.

See also editorial introductions to works listed under *English translations*.

CHAPTER 9

Logic and the philosophy of mathematics in the nineteenth century
John Stillwell

➤➤ INTRODUCTION ➤➤

In its history of over two thousand years, mathematics has seldom been disturbed by philosophical disputes. Ever since Plato, who is said to have put the slogan 'Let no one who is not a geometer enter here' over the door of his academy, mathematics has been the standard of exact truth against which other philosophical discourse is measured. Descartes' *Discourse on Method* grew out of his *Geometry*. Spinoza wrote his *Ethics* in the style of Euclid's *Elements*. And Leibniz dreamed of a *Characteristica Universalis* by means of which 'we should be able to reason in metaphysics and morals in much the same way as in geometry and analysis'.

Mathematics is not only supremely logical, it is also astonishingly powerful. Here is how it struck Thomas Hobbes, according to Aubrey's *Brief Lives*:

> He was 40 yeares old before he looked on Geometry; which happened accidentally. Being in a Gentleman's Library, Euclid's Elements lay open, and 'twas the 47 *El. libri* I. He read the Proposition. *By G——*, sayd he (he would now and then sweare an emphaticall Oath by way of emphasis) *this is impossible*! So he reads the Demonstration of it, which referred him back to such a Proposition; which proposition he read. That referred him back to another, which he also read ... that at last he was demonstratively convinced of that trueth. This made him in love with Geometry.

> ([9.1], 230)

It was this power of mathematics to draw unexpected conclusions, to solve difficult problems, that overcame the occasional philosophical doubts about the validity of its methods.

Up until 1800 the main doubts about mathematics centred on the following issues: the existence of irrational numbers; the use of numbers in geometry; the existence of imaginary numbers; infinite objects and processes.

Irrational numbers were a thorn in the side of the Pythagoreans (*c.* 500 BC), who believed that the natural numbers 1, 2, 3 . . . were the key to understanding the universe. They found, for example, that musical harmony involved simple natural numbers – halving the length of a vibrating string raised its pitch an octave, reducing its length to 2/3 raised its pitch a fifth, and so on. However, they also found the theorem of Pythagoras, which implies that the diagonal of the unit square is the square root of 2, $\sqrt{2}$, and then were horrified to discover that $\sqrt{2}$ is *not* a ratio of natural numbers. In their view, this meant $\sqrt{2}$ was not a number at all, and hence numbers were not an adequate measure of geometric quantities.

Rather than abandon geometry, the Greeks developed a geometric system parallel to arithmetic in which lengths were added and multiplied like numbers. It was also possible to *compare* a length such as $\sqrt{2}$ with ratios of natural numbers (rational numbers). That is, one could say whether $m/n < \sqrt{2}$ or $m/n > \sqrt{2}$ for any natural numbers m, n. The geometric meaning of $m/n < \sqrt{2}$ can be seen from the equivalent relation $m < n\sqrt{2}$, which says that the line segment consisting of m units of length is contained in the line segment consisting of n copies of $\sqrt{2}$. This occurs just in case $m^2 < 2n^2$. Thus the geometric relation $m/n < \sqrt{2}$ is in fact equivalent to the natural number relation $m^2 < 2n^2$.

Eudoxus (*c.* 350 BC) realised that to know the position (> or <) of a length ℓ relative to *arbitrary* rational numbers m/n is to know ℓ with complete precision. Hence calculations in the world of lengths are just as exact as those in the world of natural numbers. If $m/n < \ell$ and $m'/n' < \ell'$, for example, then one can conclude that $m/n + m'/n' < \ell + \ell'$, and in this way one knows all rational numbers less than $\ell + \ell'$. By such arguments, Eudoxus was able to develop a system of calculating with lengths and comparing them with (ratios of) natural numbers. It was preserved in Book V of Euclid's *Elements* and became known as the *theory of proportion*.

Eudoxus also developed a more general method for reasoning about geometric quantities called the *method of exhaustion*. Just as the theory of proportion captures an irrational by comparing it with arbitrary rationals, the method of exhaustion captures a figure of unknown magnitude by comparing it with known ones. Typically, a curve will be compared with polygons, and this may enable the exact determination of areas and volumes of curved figures when the corresponding polygonal ones are known.

For example, Archimedes showed that the area A of the parabolic segment (Figure 1) is 4/3 that of the inscribed triangle $\triangle 1$ by showing

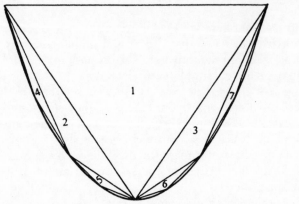

Figure 1

(1) A can be approximated arbitrarily closely by a finite sum of inscribed triangles $\triangle_1, \ldots, \triangle_n$ (indicated by their subscripts in Figure 1).

(2) $4\triangle_1/3$ is also approximated arbitrarily closely by such finite sums.

It follows that $A = 4\triangle_1/3$ because any value of A unequal to $4\triangle_1/3$ can be refuted by summing sufficiently many triangles $\triangle_1, \ldots, \triangle_n$. The method 'exhausts all possibilities' except $A = 4\triangle_1/3$ and, more importantly, each incorrect possibility is eliminated by reasoning about the *finite* sum of $\triangle_1, \ldots, \triangle_n$.

The theory of proportions and the method of exhaustion enabled mathematicians to sidestep their first encounter with infinity. It was not necessary to sum infinitely many triangles to determine A, for example; the sum of $\triangle_1, \ldots, \triangle_n$ was sufficient, *provided n was arbitrary*. One might say that infinity is present in the arbitrariness of n, but only 'potentially' so. The Greeks (and most mathematicians until the nineteenth century) drew a sharp distinction between the *potential infinity* which supplies natural numbers one by one, and the *actual infinity* which delivers them all at once. The concept of natural number is in fact potential infinity in a nutshell; the process of beginning with 0 and adding 1 'indefinitely' is what the natural numbers are all about. The idea that this process could ever be completed seems at first as unnatural and uncalled for as a last natural number.

However, the distinction between potential and actual infinity is not so easy to maintain in other cases. Consider the following example. To travel a distance of one kilometer, say, one first has to reach the 0.9 kilometer mark, then the 0.99 kilometer mark, then the 0.999 kilometer mark . . . , and in general the $1-1/10^n$ kilometer mark for each n. One seemingly cannot complete the journey without also completing the infinity of values $1-1/10^n$. A similar example is discussed in Aristotle's *Physics*, 239b, 14, under the name of Zeno's paradox of Achilles and the tortoise. Aristotle refutes it by appealing to the (potentially) infinite divisibility of space and time. The kilometer can be subdivided at 0.9, 0.99, 0.999, . . . and the time interval required for the journey can be subdivided similarly, so completion of the journey involves only the *potential* infinity of subdivisions.

We do not know the purpose of Zeno (c. 450 BC) in formulating his paradoxes, since they are known to us only through Aristotle, who wished to debunk them. Nevertheless, Zeno does seem to have put the fear of infinity into Greek mathematics. It is otherwise hard to understand the rejection of irrational numbers, and the restriction to potential infinity even in cases where actual infinity seems harmless. We now know, in fact, that Archimedes used actual infinity to discover his results on areas and volumes. His original methods were uncovered only in 1906, thanks to some extraordinary detective work by Heiberg ([9.26], 5). By then, it was too late for them to have any effect on mathematical practice.

After the classical era, the next major encounter with infinity was in the seventeenth century. The occasion was the invention of the calculus, a resurgence of Archimedes' theory of curved figures powered by the new algebraic geometry of Fermat and Descartes. Algebra made an enormous difference to geometry. Whereas Archimedes had to make an ingenious new approach to each new figure – for example, the approach to the parabolic segment using specially placed triangles – calculus dealt with a great variety of figures in the same way, via their equations. That was the whole point. Calculus was a method of *calculating* results, rather than proving them. If pressed, mathematicians could justify their calculations by the method of exhaustion, but it seemed impractical if not unnecessary to do so. Even before the stream of new results reached full flood with Newton and Leibniz (from 1665 onward) Huygens had warned:

> Mathematicians will never have enough time to read all the discoveries in Geometry (a quantity which is increasing from day to day and seems likely in this scientific age to develop to enormous proportions) if they continue to be presented in a rigorous form according to the manner of the ancients.

([9.30], 337)

In fact, Huygens was probably the only major mathematician who stuck to the 'methods of the ancients'. The methods of calculus were so much more powerful and efficient that rigour became secondary. Hobbes and Berkeley wrote scathing attacks on the illogical language of 'infinitesimals' used by mathematicians as a substitute for exhaustion, but they could not deny that it got results. And what results! By the middle of the eighteenth century, calculus had solved almost all the problems of classical geometry, and new ones the ancients had not dreamed of. It had also revealed the secrets of the heavens, explaining the motions of the moons and planets with uncanny precision. Apart from a few marginal controversies over such things as the infinite series $1 - 1 + 1 - 1 + \ldots$, all the results of calculus stood up to rigorous scrutiny.

The confidence inspired by the success of calculus was infectious. During the eighteenth century, mathematicians pushed their luck even further, using some concepts they did *not* know how to justify. They freely used $\sqrt{-1}$ while calling it 'imaginary' or 'impossible'. They assumed that arbitrary continuous functions were expressible as infinite sums of sine waves. And once again their faith was rewarded, with an avalanche of new discoveries in mathematics and physics by d'Alembert, the Bernoullis, Euler and Lagrange. With this much success, mathematicians could afford to ignore philosophical questions about the meaning and rigour of their work. Only a direct contradiction in the heart of mathematics could give them pause. When it came, all the forgotten fears of irrationality and infinity would come back to the surface.

➳ THE CRISIS IN GEOMETRY ➳

Before 1800, geometry was thought to be part of physics. Its simplest elements – straight lines and circles – were idealizations of the simplest physical curves, constructed by the simplest drawing instruments, the straight edge and compasses. However, what set geometry apart from the rest of physics was its logical structure. It appeared that all properties of straight lines and circles (in the plane) were logical consequences of five axioms postulated by Euclid in his *Elements* (c. 300 BC):

Let the following be postulated
1. To draw a straight line from any point to any point.
2. To produce a finite straight line continuously in a straight line.
3. To describe a circle with any centre and distance.

4. That all right angles are equal to one another.
5. That, if a straight line falling on two straight lines make the interior angles on the same side less than two right angles, the lines, if produced indefinitely, meet on that side on which are the angles less than the two right angles.

([9.27], 154)

Euclid's axioms were physically plausible, at least within the limits of measurement possible before 1800, though of course the fifth axiom could not be tested properly with finite lines. What was more import-ant, in the opinion of most mathematicians and philosophers, was that no alternatives to Euclid's axioms could be *imagined*.

In particular, it seemed impossible to imagine either of the following alternatives to axiom 5:

5$^+$. Two straight lines, if produced indefinitely, meet on *both* sides.
5$^-$. There are straight lines which fail to meet even though a straight line falling on them makes interior angles on the same side less than two right angles. (Or the following logical equivalent: given a line L and point P not on L there is more than one line through P not meeting L.)

The strongest statement of the *a priori* nature of geometry was made by Kant in his *Critique of Pure Reason*. Kant believed that the fact that we cannot imagine alternatives such as 5$^+$ and 5$^-$ made Euclid's geometry the only one logically possible or meaningful:

It is therefore, solely from the human standpoint that we can speak of space, of extended things, etc. If we depart from the subjective condition under which alone we can have outer intuition, namely, liability to be affected by objects, the representation of space stands for nothing whatsoever.

([9.31], 71)

Kant's philosophy was the high-water mark of intuitive geometry. The tide turned during the nineteenth century when mathematicians became increasingly absorbed with the construction of geometries contradicting Euclid, and later with the reconstruction of Euclidean geometry itself.

These investigations stemmed from dissatisfaction with Euclid's axiom 5, the so-called *parallel axiom*. Gauss, Bolyai and Lobachevsky realized that it was impossible to confirm the parallel axiom by physical experiment, and in fact conceivable that one could *refute* it. This was because the parallel axiom has the consequence that the angle sum (in radians) of any triangle is π. Since perfectly accurate measurement is impossible, one could never be sure that an angle sum measured to be

π was in fact equal to π; and conceivably a triangle could be found with angle sum definitely *not* equal to π, i.e. differing from π by more than experimental error. While no physical refutation of the parallel axiom succeeded at the time (success was not achieved until 1919, as part of the confirmation of general relativity theory) its very possibility was enough to encourage Gauss, Bolyai and Lobachevsky to explore an alternative to Euclidean geometry. Their investigations were made independently, roughly between 1800 and 1830, and reached similar conclusions.

Each of them studied the replacement of the parallel axiom by the axiom 5⁻. The geometry that results from this replacement is now called *hyperbolic geometry*. It is in some ways more complicated than Euclidean geometry. For example, there are no similar figures of different sizes. There are no squares. Equilateral triangles of different sizes have different angles (always less than the angle $\pi/3$ of a Euclidean equilateral triangle). However, in other ways hyperbolic geometry is extremely elegant and convenient. The fact that equilateral triangles of different sizes have different angles yields an *absolute unit of length*. One could define the unit to be, say, the side of the equilateral triangle with angle $\pi/4$, since there is only one size of equilateral triangle with this angle. Likewise, the fact that the angle sum of a triangle is less than π makes it possible to show that the area of a triangle is proportional to the difference between π and the triangle's angle sum. Thus, in hyperbolic geometry, area can be measured by angles.

These beautiful consequences of axiom 5⁻, and the non-appearance of any contradictory consequences, convinced Gauss, Bolyai and Lobachevsky that hyperbolic geometry was meaningful and worth pursuing. However, there was no immediate threat to the authority of Euclid and Kant. Gauss was too afraid of controversy to publish his results. Bolyai gave up soon after publication of his work in 1832, discouraged by the lack of response from other mathematicians and troubled by the possibility that contradictions might yet emerge. Lobachevsky published doggedly from the obscurity of Kazan from 1829 until 1856, the year of his death, without any encouragement from the outside world. (Gauss in fact admired Lobachevsky's work, but communicated his feelings only to his friend Schumacher in a letter [9.24].

But in 1855 Gauss died, and his interest in hyperbolic geometry became known to the mathematical world through the release of his unpublished papers. This led to a more widespread interest in hyperbolic geometry, particularly in the light of *differential geometry*, a field also pioneered by Gauss with his book on curved surfaces [9.23], and invigorated by the ideas of Riemann [9.38] on curved space of arbitrary dimensions.

On any smooth surface there are curves called *geodesics* which are 'as straight as possible' and hence can be regarded as the 'lines' of a 'geometry'. On the sphere, for example, the geodesics are the great circles, because a great circle gives the shortest distance between any two points on the sphere. The corresponding 'geometry' is *spherical geometry*, which studies such things as spherical triangles. Spherical geometry had in fact been studied since ancient times because of its applications to astronomy and navigation, but the idea of its being a 'geometry' with theorems contrary to those of Euclidean geometry had not come up, perhaps because its 'lines' are manifestly finite and closed.

However, the curved 'lines' on the sphere can be made straight by projecting the sphere from its centre on to a tangent plane (Figure 2). Admittedly, only half of each spherical 'line' can be seen at a time this way, and spherical distance becomes distorted. However, it does make spherical geometry look like a geometry of genuine lines, and it raises an interesting question. For which surfaces is there a map to the plane carrying geodesics to straight lines?

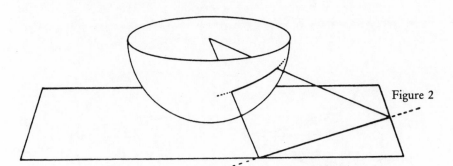

Figure 2

Beltrami [9.2] found the answer in terms of the *curvature* of the surface, a concept introduced in Gauss [9.22]. The surfaces whose geodesics can be mapped to straight lines are precisely those of *constant* curvature. The plane itself is of zero curvature, a sphere has constant positive curvature – which explained the known examples – but there are also surfaces of constant *negative* curvature. The first of these to be discovered was the *pseudosphere*, a trumpet-shaped surface (Figure 3) whose geometry had been investigated by Gauss's student Minding in 1840. Minding even made the pregnant discovery that its triangles are governed by formulas like those for spherical triangles, but with the circular functions sine and cosine replaced by their hyperbolic analogues sinh and cosh (hence the name 'pseudosphere'). The same formulas had already been found to hold in hyperbolic geometry by Lobachevsky [9.34].

Unfortunately the pseudosphere cannot be regarded as a complete

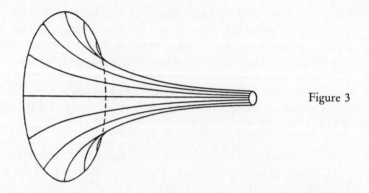

Figure 3

realization of hyperbolic geometry, because 'lines' on the pseudosphere do not extend indefinitely. The rim of the trumpet is an impassable boundary, beyond which the pseudosphere cannot be extended because its curvature becomes undefined there. In 1868 Beltrami [9.3] saw a way round this difficulty with his mapping of geodesics to straight lines. The pseudosphere is mapped on to a portion of the disc (Figure 4) and the line segments representing its geodesics have a natural exten-

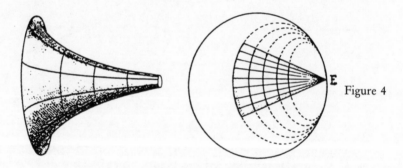

Figure 4

sion to the whole interior of the disc. (The boundary of the disc is infinitely far away, in the sense of distance on the pseudosphere. In particular, the point E represents the infinitely distant end of the trumpet.) Thus the whole interior of the disc has a geometry, inherited from the pseudosphere, and it is the *complete* hyperbolic geometry of Gauss, Bolyai and Lobachevsky. The validity of the hyperbolic parallel axiom 5^- is particularly clear, as Figure 5 shows.

Beltrami had found what we now call a *model* of hyperbolic geometry – an interpretation of the terms 'point', 'line', etc. within Euclidean geometry under which the axioms 1, 2, 3, 4, 5^- are satisfied.

It follows that the Gauss-Bolyai-Lobachevsky axioms *cannot lead to a contradiction*, unless there is a contradiction in Euclidean geometry

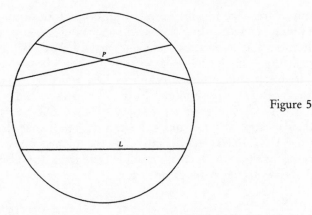

Figure 5

itself. This was Beltrami's great contribution to the philosophy of geometry. As he put it (rather modestly) in his 1868 paper:

> In recent times the mathematical public has begun to take an interest in some new concepts which seem destined, if they prevail, to change profoundly the whole complexion of classical geometry.
>
> These concepts are not particularly recent. The master Gauss grasped them at the beginning of his scientific career, and although his writings do not contain an explicit exposition, his letters confirm that he had always cultivated them and attest to his full support for the doctrine of *Lobachevsky*.
>
> ... we have sought, to the extent of our ability, to convince ourselves of the results of *Lobachevsky*'s doctrine; then, following the tradition of scientific research, we have tried to find a real substrate for this doctrine, rather than admit the necessity for a new order of entities and concepts. We believe we have attained this goal for the planar part of the doctrine.
>
> (Beltrami 1868 in [9.17], 533)

Beltrami's model showed that Euclid's axioms 1, 2, 3, 4, 5 are not the only logical possibility. It was therefore admissible to doubt that they were true of physical space.

If Euclid's geometry was not about physical space, what *was* it about?

❧ ARITHMETIZATION ❧

With the discovery of non-Euclidean geometry the nature and existence of geometric objects was called into question. It was time to take up an option which had been available for two centuries, but held back out of respect for the Greek tradition of separating the concepts of number and length – the *arithmetization* of geometry. Around 1630, Fermat and Descartes independently discovered the method of co-ordinates which makes it possible to describe curves by equations in variables x and y. Given two lines OX and OY in the plane (Figure 6), any point P is determined by its distances x and y from them. (It is convenient, though not necessary, to take OX and OY to be perpendicular, and to let y and x be the perpendicular distances from P to them.) As P traverses a curve in the plane, x and y enter a certain relationship, which Fermat and Descartes found they could easily describe in many important cases.

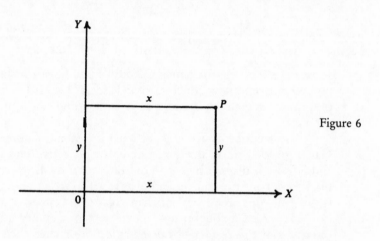

Figure 6

For example, if P describes the straight line passing through O and equidistant from OX and OY, then $y = x$. More generally, any straight line is described by an equation of the form

$ax + by + c = 0$ where a, b, c are constants,

and which we now call a *linear* equation for that reason. Conversely, any such equation (provided a, b are not both zero) represents a straight line, so there is a correspondence between lines and linear equations.

Linear equations are recognizable algebraically as those in which x and y occur to the first power. The next simplest equations, called *quadratic*, include terms in x^2, y^2 and xy as well as linear terms. Fermat and Descartes discovered that the curves described by quadratic equations are precisely the *conic sections* (ellipses, parabolas, hyperbolas), which had been studied by the Greeks, particularly by Apollonius, c. 200 BC. Apollonius even knew the relationship between x and y for a conic section, but he expressed it in words (taking about half a page!) and not as an equation. Lacking algebraic notation, the Greeks could hardly form the idea of equations, let alone manipulate them so as to be able to recognize the curves they described.

Fermat and Descartes had the advantage of a well developed notation and technique for algebra, thanks to the efforts of their compatriot Viète (1540–1603) and the Italians del Ferro, Tartaglia, Cardano, Ferrari and Bombelli in the sixteenth century. In turn, Descartes' *Geometry* (1637, [9.15]) made a big impression on Newton, who carried the analysis of equations beyond the range of classical geometry with a classification of *cubic* curves [9.37]. Thus by the end of the seventeenth century it was well established that curves could be studied by algebra, at least the curves expressed by *polynomial* equations, i.e. equations formed by applying arithmetic operations to x and y.

However, these developments did not prompt any reassessment of the nature of curves. No one said that curves were equations. Moreover, the variables x and y were regarded as lengths rather than numbers. Thanks to Eudoxus' theory of proportions (see Introduction above), x and y could be regarded as lengths while only arithmetic operations were applied to them, so the Greek segregation of geometry from number remained in force. The inadequacies of the theory of proportions (and indeed the theory of numbers) were not exposed until questions about *curves in general* began to be asked in the eighteenth century. Perhaps the turning point was Gauss's proof of the fundamental theorem of algebra [9.22].

The exact statement proved by Gauss does not concern us here (the modern equivalent is that any polynomial equation has a solution in the complex numbers). The point of interest is the following statement *assumed* by Gauss in his proof. If K_1 and K_2 are curves inside a circle, and the endpoints A_1, B_1 of K_1 separate the endpoints A_2, B_2 of K_2 on the circle (Figure 7), then K_1 and K_2 have a common point. The only justification Gauss offered for this statement was that 'no one, to my knowledge, has ever doubted it'. This was probably true, but

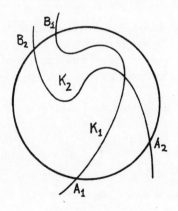

Figure 7

nevertheless a poor excuse, particularly since Gauss was well aware of gaps in previous attempts to prove the fundamental theorem, and at pains to point them out. Quite likely, the only reason the statement had never been doubted is that it had never previously been used in a mathematical proof. Gauss's proof was probably the first *existence proof* in the history of mathematics – one where the existence of a point was proved without a means of constructing it – and probably the first to use *topological* reasoning. The basic concept of topology, namely *continuity*, had not even been defined in 1799, and Gauss's claim is not easy to prove even when the notion of continuous curve has been made clear.

It seems that Gauss realised the seriousness of the gap in his proof, because in 1816 he offered another proof of the fundamental theorem of algebra in which the role of continuity was minimized. In his second proof he assumed only that if $p(x)$ is a polynomial such that $p(a) < 0 < p(b)$ for some real numbers a and b then $p(c) = 0$ for some c between a and b. This assumption, known as the *intermediate value theorem* (for polynomials) can be viewed as a special case of the assumption in the first proof, namely, where K_1 is part of OX and K_2 is part of the curve $y = p(x)$ (Figure 8).

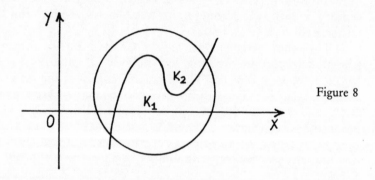

Figure 8

The intermediate value theorem is needed even to show the existence of $\sqrt[n]{2}$, which is the value for which $p(x) = x^n - 2$ becomes zero between, say, $x = 1$ and $x = 2$. Thus any proof of the fundamental theorem of algebra involves the intermediate value theorem, at least implicitly.

This point was recognized by Bolzano in 1817 [9.5], immediately after the appearance of Gauss's proof. Bolzano gave a proof of the continuity of polynomial curves $y = p(x)$, and attempted a proof of the intermediate value theorem for arbitrary continuous curves $y = f(x)$. His definition of continuity was essentially the modern one:

a function fx varies according to the law of continuity for all values of x inside or outside certain limits means just that: if x is some such value, the difference $f(x+\omega) - fx$ can be made smaller than any given quantity provided ω can be taken as small as we please.

(Bolzano 1817 in [9.17], 565)

However, his proof of the intermediate value theorem assumes the following *least upper bound* property of real numbers:

whenever a certain property M belongs to all values of a variable quantity i which are smaller than a given value and yet not for all values in general, then there is always some *greatest* value u, for which it can be asserted that all $i < u$ possess property M

([9.17], 565)

Actually, the value u is *greatest lower bound* of the values *not* having property M. It is now more usual to consider the equivalent least upper bound property: every bounded set of real numbers has a least upper bound. Bolzano was unable to prove this property rigorously because he did not have a definition of real number. Nevertheless, identifying the property was an important step. It set a requirement that any future definition of real number would have to meet, and was the first indication that further clarification of geometric concepts would depend on clarification of the concept of number.

❦ WHAT IS A REAL NUMBER? ❦

In 1858, the last student of Gauss, Richard Dedekind, found himself teaching elementary calculus at the Polytechnic School in Zurich. He later wrote:

In discussing the notion of the approach of a variable magnitude to a fixed limiting value, and especially in proving the theorem that every magnitude which grows continually, but not beyond all limits, must approach a limiting value, I had recourse to geometric evidences. Even now such resort to geometric intuition... I regard as exceedingly useful... But that this form of introduction into the differential calculus can make no claim to being scientific, no one will deny.

([9.14], 1)

Dedekind, too, had glimpsed the elusive least upper bound property. He was determined to capture it.

I made the fixed resolve to keep meditating on the question until I should find a purely arithmetic and perfectly rigorous foundation for the principles of infinitesimal analysis. The statement is so frequently made that the differential calculus deals with continuous magnitude, and yet an explanation of this continuity is nowhere given; even the most rigorous expositions of the differential calculus do not base their proofs on continuity ... they either appeal to geometric notions ... or depend upon theorems which are never established in a purely arithmetic manner. Among these, for example, belongs the above-mentioned theorem, and a more careful investigation convinced me that this theorem, or any one equivalent to it, can be regarded in some way as a sufficient basis for infinitesimal analysis

([9.14], 7)

Having seen clearly what the difficulty was: 'It then only remained to discover its true origin in the elements of arithmetic and thus at the same time to secure a real definition of the essence of continuity. I succeeded Nov. 24, 1858' ([9.14], 2).

What then was Dedekind's definition that captured the essence of continuity? In a nutshell, it was what Eudoxus would have said if he had believed in actual infinity. Like Eudoxus, Dedekind determined a length by comparison with rational numbers, but, unlike Eudoxus, Dedekind considered the totality of rational numbers to be an actual object – a *set* – and he declared the length being determined to be a *number*.

The length $\sqrt{2}$, for example, is greater than a positive rational m/n if and only if $2n^2 > m^2$, as we observed in the Introduction above. This gives a numerical *process* for comparing m/n with $\sqrt{2}$, essentially Eudoxus' theory of proportions. Dedekind sought a numerical *object* he could identify with $\sqrt{2}$, and found it in the *completed outcome* of the comparison process, namely the pair of sets of positive rationals $\{m/n : 2n^2 < m^2\}$ and $\{m/n : 2n^2 > m^2\}$.

In general, Dedekind defined a *real number* to be a partition of the rationals into two sets A_1, A_2 such that each member of A_1 is less than every member of A_2. He called such a partition a *cut*. Each rational number r itself produces a cut, or rather two cuts (one with r the maximum member of A_1, the other with r the minimum member of A_2), so the rationals are naturally absorbed into this more comprehensive concept of number. The real numbers also inherit natural operations of sum, product, etc. from the rational numbers. For example, if α is the cut (A_1, A_2) and β is the cut (B_1, B_2) then $\alpha + \beta$ is the cut (C_1, C_2), where C_1 is the set of sums $a_1 + b_1$ where a_1 is in A_1 (i.e. $a_1 < \alpha$) and b_1 is in B_1 (i.e. $b_1 < \beta$), and C_2 consists of the rationals not in C_1.

In this way it becomes possible to prove results such as $\sqrt{2}\sqrt{3}$

$= \sqrt{6}$, which Dedekind believed had not been proved rigorously before. (It would, however, have been possible to prove $\sqrt{2}\sqrt{3} = \sqrt{6}$ rigorously for *lengths* $\sqrt{2}$, $\sqrt{3}$, $\sqrt{6}$ by the theory of proportions.)

Finally, it was easy to prove the least upper bound property. If a real quantity α grows continually but not beyond a limit β say, consider the set L_1 of all rationals belonging to lower sets A_1 of values of α. Then if L_2 is the set of rationals not in L_1 (in particular L_2 includes the rationals greater than β) it is easily seen that (L_1, L_2) is a cut and it is the least upper bound of the variable quantity α.

The least upper bound property is one of several equivalent statements of what Dedekind called the *continuity* of the real numbers (nowadays called the *completeness* of the real numbers). Another is that there is *no gap*, that is, no partition of the real numbers into sets A_1, A_2 with each member of A_1 less than every member of A_2, no maximum member of A_1 and no minimum member of A_2. This property is an almost immediate consequence of Dedekind's definition, which essentially *fills* each gap in the rational numbers by a real number.

As Dedekind pointed out, the continuity of the real numbers enables them to serve as a model of points on the line. Thus the key step in the arithmetization of geometry was finally achieved. With the *line* defined as the set of real numbers x, it is natural to define the *plane* as the set of ordered pairs of real numbers, (x, y), and then curves can be defined by equations in x and y. This programme was completed in the *Grundlagen der Geometrie* of Hilbert (1899, [9.26]). Incidentally, the pair (x, y) is also used as a concrete representative of the complex number $x + y\sqrt{-1}$, thus giving a meaning to 'imaginary' numbers (see Introduction above).

In the meantime, several other definitions of real number had been proposed, notably by Meray [9.32], Weierstrass [9.29] and Cantor [9.9]. Weierstrass [9.37] also gave the first rigorous proofs of the fundamental theorems on continuous functions, in particular the intermediate value theorem anticipated by Bolzano [9.5]. Meray, Weierstrass and Cantor all defined real numbers as sets of convergent infinite sequences – definitely a more complicated approach than Dedekind's, but one more suited to modern analysis, where convergent sequences (of objects which are not necessarily numbers) are the stock in trade. All these definitions are equivalent, as it happens, so it does not matter which one is used to define the line.

The important question is whether it is necessary to accept completed infinities to arithmetize the concept of line. With hindsight, one can see how the cut defining $\sqrt{2}$, say, might be explained away as a potential infinity (see the next section). But can the infinity of real numbers be regarded as merely potential? This was one of the profound questions answered by Cantor in the next episode of our story – the development of set theory.

❧ SETS ❧

Cantor, like Dedekind, was drawn into accepting actual infinities in order to clarify the meaning of points on the line. In Cantor's case the problem was more technical (though with a pedigree going back to the Pythagorean investigation of vibrating strings), concerning the points of discontinuity of infinite sums of sine waves [9.9]. He found that such a set of points could be very complicated. So complicated, in fact, that an operation he used to 'thin' the set could be repeated infinitely often without removing all of it. He therefore decided to apply his thinning operation 'more than an infinite number of times', or rather, to continue applying it after the first infinity of applications was complete. The implication was, of course, that this infinity of operations was *actual*.

To count the number of applications of the thinning operation, Cantor [9.11] introduced *ordinal numbers*, a generalization of natural numbers to infinity and beyond. The first infinite ordinal number, following the complete series 0, 1, 2, 3, . . . , is called ω. It is followed by $\omega + 1$, $\omega + 2$, $\omega + 3$, . . . , and this second infinity of ordinal numbers is followed by a number called $\omega \cdot 2$. Any ordinal number α, like a natural number, has a successor $\alpha + 1$. Cantor [9.11] called this the 'first principle of generation' of ordinal numbers. He also introduced a second principle, which generates, ω, $\omega \cdot 2$ and further ordinals by wholesale actualization of infinities:

> If any definite succession of defined whole real [i.e. ordinal]
> numbers exists, for which there is no largest, then a new
> number is created, by means of this second principle of
> generation, which is thought of as the *limit* of these numbers,
> i.e. it is defined as the next number larger than all of them.
>
> ([9.11], 196)

In calling his ordinal numbers whole *real* numbers Cantor wished to stress their reality, i.e. the reality of infinite sets, rather than any analogy with the real numbers (which is *reell* in German and not the word *real* used by Cantor). There is a much better analogy with the natural numbers, of course, though it is striking that the ordinals share the least upper bound property with the real numbers. The relationship between the ordinals and the real numbers was in fact an unsolved problem of Cantor's set theory, the *continuum problem*, and it remains today one of the great mysteries of mathematics. As will become clearer below, the real numbers are generated by a principle which is possibly even more powerful than Cantor's second principle of generation for ordinal numbers.

Cantor's investigation of sets of real numbers led him to another generalization of the concept of natural number, the concept of *cardinal number*. Two sets A and B are said to have the *same* cardinal number if there is a *one-to-one correspondence* or *pairing* between the members of A and the members of B. The cardinal number of a finite set A is simply the (natural) number of members of A, because if A has, say, seventeen members then any set B whose members can be paired with the members of A will also have seventeen members. The set of all natural numbers has an infinite cardinal number which Cantor called $\aleph_0$.

Cantor found that many seemingly 'larger' × sets can be put in one-to-one correspondence with the natural numbers, and hence also have cardinal number $\aleph_0$. One such set is the rational numbers. Another, as Cantor [9.10], found, is the *algebraic numbers*. A number is called algebraic if it is the solution of an equation

$$(*)\ a_n x^n + a_{n-1} x^{n-1} + \cdots + a_1 x + a_0 = 0$$

where $a_0, a_1, \ldots, a_n$ are integers. Cantor observed that if each such equation is assigned the 'height'

$$h = |a_0| + |a_1| + \cdots + |a_n| + n$$

then there are only finitely many equations with height h less than a given natural number i. It is therefore possible to make a (potentially infinite) list consisting of all equations of height ≤ 1, then all equations of height ≤ 2, then all equations of height $\leq 3 \ldots$, thus obtaining a list of all equations (*), in which each equation has some natural number position j. This puts the equations (*) in one-to-one correspondence with the natural numbers j. Finally, if each equation is replaced by the (finite) list of its solutions we get a list of all algebraic numbers, on which each algebraic number appears at some natural number position k.

The listing of the algebraic numbers is a very strong result, since it includes listings of many other sets, in particular the integers and the rational numbers. It follows that all these sets have cardinal number $\aleph_0$. However, it does not follow that the set of all real numbers has cardinal number $\aleph_0$. It was already known, from the work of Liouville [9.33], that certain real numbers are not algebraic. Cantor [9.10] discovered the more dramatic result that *almost all* real numbers are not algebraic. He showed that the cardinal number of the reals is not $\aleph_0$, by showing that the reals cannot be paired with the natural numbers.

This result is known as the *non-denumerability* or *uncountability* of the set of real numbers.

Non-denumerability was so unprecedented that Cantor initially attempted to downplay it as far as possible, calling his paper 'On a Property of the Collection of All Real Algebraic Numbers' and using non-denumerability only to give a new proof of Liouville's result. (The algebraic numbers have cardinal number $\aleph_0$, the reals do not, so not all reals are algebraic, QED.) He soon realized, however, that non-denumerability was the gateway to a new world. It revealed the existence of cardinal numbers beyond $\aleph_0$, so mathematics was able to distinguish different kinds of infinity. It also showed that the real numbers could not be explained away as a potential infinity. For what is a potential infinity but one whose members can be paired with the natural numbers?

As pointed out in the Introduction above, the natural numbers 0, 1, 2, ... are the epitome of a potential infinity – a list which includes any given member, if carried sufficiently far. The non-denumerability of the reals means that any proposed listing of real numbers is doomed to incompleteness – certain numbers (depending on the list, of course) will never appear on it, no matter how long the list is continued.

In 1891 [9.12] Cantor gave a second proof of non-denumerability which makes the futility of listing real numbers crystal clear. Suppose that $x_1, x_2, x_3, \ldots$ is a list of real numbers, and let x_i be expanded as a decimal up to and including the ith decimal place. For example, the list may begin like this: $x_1 = 17.7\ldots, x_2 = 0.16\ldots, x_3 = 2.131\ldots, x_4 = 0.7474\ldots, x_5 = 11.11312\ldots$ No matter how the list continues, a number x *not on it* may be constructed by making x different from x_1 in the first decimal place, different from x_2 in the second decimal place, different from x_3 in the third decimal place ... , and so on. An explicit way to do this (which avoids getting an expansion which is ultimately all 9s or all 0s, and hence expressible in two ways) is to let the ith decimal place of x be 1 if the ith decimal place of x_i is *not* 1, and otherwise let it be 2. Thus no list includes all the real numbers.

Since the number x is constructed from the sequence of digits along the diagonal of the list, this technique came to be known as the *diagonal argument*. It was actually used before Cantor by du Bois Reymond [9.16], though in a less transparent way. Cantor [9.12] was the first to see that the diagonal argument was not simply a trick with numbers but actually a fundamental insight into the relationship between sets and their subsets, showing that *any set has more subsets than members*. This yields the astonishing conclusion that *there is no largest set*.

To apply the diagonal argument in the general case let S be any set, and let S_x be a sub-set paired with element x. (You may like to think of S_x laid out in a 'row' beside element x, which is in a 'column' of the members of S.) Then one sub-set of S which is not among the sets S_x is the 'diagonal sub-set' D defined as follows:

x belongs to D if and only if x does not belong to S_x.

This ensures that D is different from each S_x, with respect to the element x in fact, and hence there are more sub-sets of S than members of S. The operation of forming all sub-sets of a given set is called the *power set* operation. This is the operation, mentioned above, which is possibly more powerful than the second principle of generation of ordinal numbers. While the generation of ordinal numbers admits a larger number only when there is some way of 'approaching' it, the power set operation creates a new set without offering any means of approach.

In the case where S is the set of natural numbers it is easy to show (though a little technical) that the power set of S has the same cardinal number as the set of real numbers. Thus the continuum problem, which asks how big an ordinal number is required to count the real numbers, is about the size of the power set of the natural members.

❧ WHAT IS A NATURAL NUMBER? ❧

With the help of the set concept, Dedekind had reduced the concept of real number to the concept of rational number, as explained on pp. 255–7. Since relations between rational numbers are equivalent to relations between natural numbers, this meant that all the concepts of geometry and analysis were definable in terms of sets and the natural numbers 0, 1, 2, 3, ... Most mathematicians felt that this was as solid a foundation as it was necessary or possible to have. After all, statements about the natural numbers were not contested (the way the parallel axiom, or the intermediate value theorem had been, for example) and no simpler concept than natural number seemed likely as a basis for mathematics.

In taking this view, mathematicians tended to overlook the fact that the foundation was not just the natural numbers, but natural numbers *and* sets. Sets were unavoidable, as experience with the real numbers made clear, so if there was a simpler basis for mathematics than natural numbers and sets it had to be just sets.

The first to grasp this possibility was Gottlob Frege, who developed a definition of natural numbers in terms of sets, or more precisely in terms of *properties*, in his 1884 book *Die Grundlagen der Arithmetik* [9.19]. There is a subtle but important difference between sets and properties (or *concepts*, as Frege called them). Corresponding to each set S there is the property of belonging to S, and for each property P there is the *extension of P*, consisting of all things with property P (or of all things *which fall under concept P*, as Frege put it). However, the extension of a property can have paradoxical behaviour if one assumes it to be a set (see pp. 266–8). This was not known in 1884, so there is no distinction between sets and extensions of properties in the *Grundlagen*. To make a distinction possible, and at the same time to give a concise description of Frege's original idea, we shall use the term *class* for the extension of a property.

Frege began with a highly entertaining demolition of previous attempts to define the notion of number, then opened his own investigation by defining what it means for two classes to have the same number. Like Cantor, he said that this is the case when there is a one-to-one correspondence between their members, though he pointed out that for finite classes this criterion had already been given by Hume (*A Treatise of Human Nature*, Book I, part III, section I). Note that it is not necessary to use the number 1 to define one-to-one correspondence. A relation $\phi(x, y)$ between the elements x of a class X and the elements y of a class Y is a one-to-one correspondence if

for each x in X there is a y in Y such that $\phi(x, y)$,
for each y in Y there is an x in X such that $\phi(x, y)$,
if $x \neq x'$ and $\phi(x, y)$ and $\phi(x', y')$ then $y \neq y'$,
if $y \neq y'$ and $\phi(x, y)$ and $\phi(x', y')$ then $x \neq x'$.

The *number of a class X* may then be defined as the property of admitting a one-to-one correspondence with X, i.e. the class of all classes that admit a one-to-one correspondence with X ([9.19], 79).

Frege spent some time discussing the numbers 0 and 1. Any contradictory property serves to define a class with number 0, and Frege used the property 'not identical with itself'. Thus 0 is the class of classes admitting a one-to-one correspondence with the (empty) class of things not identical with themselves. The concept of the empty class was novel, and Frege felt he would have to overcome some resistance to the idea:

Some may find it shocking that I should speak of a concept in this connection. They will object, very likely, that it contains a contradiction and is reminiscent of our old friends the square circle and the wooden iron. Now I believe that these old friends are not so black as they are painted. To be of any use is, I admit, the last thing we should expect of them; but at the same time, they cannot do any harm, if only we do not assume that there is anything that falls under them.

([9.19], 87).

Frege proceeded to show that the empty class is not only harmless, but wonderfully fertile, by pulling the natural numbers out of it, one by one. First

> 1 is the number which belongs to the concept 'identical with 0'.

([9.19], 90)

That is, 1 is the class of classes which admit one-to-one correspondence with the class whose member is 0. Then to define $n + 1$,

> we shall choose the concept 'number of the series of natural numbers ending with n'.

([9.19], 92)

That is, $n + 1$ is the class of classes which admit one-to-one correspondence with the class whose members are 0, 1, . . . , n. Admittedly, there is something to be proved before we know that 'the series of natural numbers ending with n' is well defined. However, this was a matter of pure logic, which Frege already understood. As we shall see in the next section, he had laid the foundations of mathematical logic in 1879.

Thus Frege's work in 1884 was essentially the last step in a reduction of mathematics to pure logic, the previous steps being the definition of the real numbers in terms of rationals and the arithmetization of geometry and analysis. This stunning achievement went unnoticed at the time, even by Frege himself. Strange as it may seem, Frege rejected the arithmetization of geometry, so he missed the opportunity to extend his ideas beyond the field of number. When Hilbert's *Grundlagen der Geometrie* [9.28] appeared in 1899, Frege wrote him several long letters ([9.20], 34) protesting against Hilbert's definitions of 'point' and 'line' and insisting on spatial intuition as the source of geometric axioms. He seemed oblivious to all that had happened in geometry since Kant. The opportunity Frege missed was taken up by Bertrand Russell (with due credit to Frege) only after the turn of the century.

∿ WHAT IS LOGIC? ∿

Logic has been a part of mathematics since ancient times, but until the nineteenth century it was the least understood part. In mathematics there was no 'theory' of logic the way there was a theory of numbers, for example, no attempt to analyse the content of logic and to describe it completely. It is true that Leibniz and others had dreamed of making logic as exact and mechanical as calculation, but little progress resulted from these speculations. The proper understanding of logic arose from the attempt to understand the foundations of mathematics, and eventually encompassed it.

The first important, though small, step was taken by George Boole. In his *Mathematical Analysis of Logic* (1847, [9.6]) and *The Laws of Thought* (1854, [9.7]) he introduced a logic of classes which is now known as Boolean algebra. In a deliberate imitation of algebraic notation, he used $x, y, z, \ldots$ to denote classes, and let xy, $x + y$ and $x - y$ denote intersection, union and relative complement respectively. Since a thing belongs to

xy if and only if it belongs to x *and* to y,
to $x + y$ if and only if it belongs to x *or* to y,
to $x - y$ if and only if it belongs to x *and not* to y,

the algebra of Boole's product, sum and difference reflects the logic of 'and', 'or' and 'not', or *propositional logic* as it is now called. This algebra is not exactly the same as ordinary algebra – for example, $x^2 = x$ for any class x – but it was near enough for Boole to venture the opinion that

> There is not only a close analogy between the operations of the mind in general reasoning and its operations in the particular science of Algebra, but there is to a considerable extent an exact agreement in the laws by which the two classes of operations are conducted.

([9.7], 6)

He was correct in thinking that his algebra was similar to ordinary algebra in its operations and laws, but quite mistaken in thinking that such an algebra could reflect 'general reasoning'. If thought was really as simple as Boole's algebra we should not be able to grasp very much mathematics, not even the concept of number, as Frege realized in 1879. By reflecting on this difficulty, Frege was able to discover a vastly more powerful system of logic.

The difference between Boole and Frege was that Boole was looking for a mathematics of logic, whereas Frege was looking for a logic of mathematics. Boole's search was less fruitful, because the mathematics of his time contained a reflection of only a small part of logic – the logic of 'and', 'or' and 'not'. We can now see that Frege made a better choice, but still it is astounding that he was able to succeed so completely at his first attempt.

Frege's logical system came to life fully grown in his *Begriffsschrift* (*Concept Writing*) of 1879 [9.18]. Unlike the *Grundlagen* of 1884, the *Begriffsschrift* is not a masterpiece of clear and persuasive writing; in particular, most of its logical content is expressed in a strange, labyrinthine symbolism of Frege's own invention. Frege believed that the structure of deduction is best revealed by displaying it in a two-dimensional, treelike form. He managed to overcome his printer's objections to this typographical nightmare, but apparently forgot that readers, too, prefer symbols to follow one another in a sequence. Fortunately it is now possible to translate the *Begriffsschrift* into a widely accepted notation, and I shall do so in what follows.

The first difference one sees between Frege and Boole is that Frege regards the laws of logic not as algebraic identities but as *theorems* derivable from *axioms* by certain *rules of inference*. In the part of Frege's logic that coincides with Boole's, namely propositional logic, the difference shows itself as follows. Instead of Boole's 'and', 'or' and 'not', Frege uses 'if . . . then' and 'not', which we shall denote by $\rightarrow$ and $\sim$ respectively. This difference is not really important, since 'and', 'or', 'not' are expressible in terms of 'if . . . then', 'not' and vice versa, but 'if . . . then' and 'not' more naturally reflect the processes of deduction. In terms of $\rightarrow$, $\sim$, Frege's axioms are:

1 $a \rightarrow (b \rightarrow a)$.
2 $(c \rightarrow (b \rightarrow a)) \rightarrow ((c \rightarrow b) \rightarrow (c \rightarrow a))$.
3 $(d \rightarrow (b \rightarrow a)) \rightarrow (b \rightarrow (d \rightarrow a))$.
4 $(b \rightarrow a) \rightarrow ((\sim a) \rightarrow (\sim b))$.
5 $(\sim\sim a) \rightarrow a$.
6 $a \rightarrow (\sim\sim a)$.

It is one of the expository defects of the *Begriffsschrift* that Frege does not announce his axioms. He does say, at the beginning of his section II, that 'a small number of laws' (the axioms) 'contain all of them' (the theorems), but the reader finds the axioms only by searching through a long series of sample derivations. His rules of inference have to be found the same way; they are

Modus ponens: from theorems B and $B \rightarrow A$ derive the theorem A (for any formulae A, B).
Substitution: from theorem A derive the result of substituting, for each occurrence of a variable x in A, a formula $\phi(x)$.

Since it is very easy to confuse a rule of inference with a theorem of logic – for example, *modus ponens* can be confused with the theorem $b \rightarrow ((b \rightarrow a) \rightarrow a)$ – Frege let his readers down badly by not making these rules explicit in section II. It seems clear that he did understand the difference between a theorem and a rule of inference. In his section I he discusses the idea of a 'mode of inference' and mentions *modus ponens* in particular. However, this was not clear enough for the logicians of his time, and they were still confused thirty years later (see, for example, the indiscriminate mixture of axioms, rules of inference and rules for the construction of formulae in Whitehead and Russell's *Principia Mathematica*, vol. I, part I, section A*1 [9.41]).

Frege offers no explanation for his claim that all laws of logic are consequences of his axioms. In fact for propositional logic this is not difficult to prove, though proofs did not appear until around 1920. The claim is much more remarkable for his system as a whole, which is a logic of properties and relations now known as *predicate logic*. (Here 'predicate' is used as a synonym for 'relation', and a property is a special case of a relation.) The consideration of relations is the second, and major, difference between Frege and Boole.

As we know from his analysis of the concept of number (pp. 261–3 above), Frege recognized that reasoning about properties and relations was fundamental to mathematics. He therefore decided to build the formulae of his logic from atomic formulae such as

$P(x)$ 'x has property P'
$R(x, y)$ 'x and y are in relation R'

etc. All mathematical statements can be built from such atomic formulae with the help of the equality sign, $=$, the universal quantifiers, $\forall x$ ('for all x'), $\forall y$ ('for all y'), etc., and the connectives $\rightarrow$, $\sim$ of propositional logic. The task then was to find all the laws of this logic. Frege claimed that they could be obtained as theorems from the propositional axioms 1–6, plus the following rules and axioms specific to predicate logic.

$\forall$ *introduction rules*: from theorem $A(x)$ derive $\forall x A(x)$; from theorem $B \rightarrow A(x)$ derive $B \rightarrow \forall x A(x)$ (when x does not occur in B).
Axioms:
7 $(c = d) \rightarrow (f(c) \rightarrow f(d))$, where f is any formula
8 $c = c$
9 $\forall x f(x) \rightarrow f(c)$, where c is any letter not in f.

Quite amazingly, he was right! However, this is a deep theorem, first proved by Gödel [9.25], and it is doubtful that Frege fully understood the meaning of his claim, let alone knew why it was true. It was enough that he had captured logic in a system, of axioms and rules of inference – proving theorems *about* such a system was a task for a later generation of logicians.

❧ A FEW CLOUDS ON THE HORIZON ❧

In the last decades of the nineteenth century, mathematicians enjoyed a period of satisfaction with the foundations of their discipline, rather like that enjoyed by their colleagues in physics (before the discovery of relativistic and quantum effects). Geometry and analysis had been reduced to the theory of real numbers, the real numbers had been reduced to sets of natural numbers, and nearly everybody was satisfied with the natural numbers. If Frege's work had been generally known the satisfaction could have been even greater (despite Frege's personal objection to the arithmetization of geometry), because everything was wrapped up in his logic of classes. However, few were granted a glimpse of this mathematical heaven, because Frege remained in obscurity until the turn of the century. Then his logic became generally known only because Bertrand Russell found something wrong with it.

The background to Russell's discovery was this. In 1891 [9.12] Cantor introduced the general diagonal argument which shows that any set S has more sub-sets than members, as we saw on pp. 257–61 above. This obviously implies that there is no largest set, but it has a more serious implication: *there is no set of all sets*. If there were, it would be the largest set, by definition, yet the set of its sub-sets would be larger. Thus it is contradictory to suppose that the class of all sets is itself a set. This was the first of the so-called 'paradoxes' of set theory. A similar paradox, involving the class of all ordinal numbers, was published by Burali-Forti in 1897 [9.8]. Cantor did not discuss the paradoxes in print, but he suggested a possible resolution of them in a letter to Dedekind in 1899.

> a multiplicity can be such that the assumption that *all* of its elements 'are together' leads to a contradiction . . . If on the other hand the totality of elements of a multiplicity can be thought of without contradiction as 'being together', so that they can be gathered together into '*one* thing', I call it a *consistent multiplicity* or a 'set'.
>
> ([9.13], 14).

In other words, to avoid contradictions, some classes should not be regarded as sets. This in fact is the solution favoured today, but at the time it was not clear how to recognize the inconsistent sets. Russell's contribution was an analysis of the 'set of all sets' which made its inconsistency more obvious.

Recall from pp. 257–61 how the diagonal construction is applied to a set S, with members x and sub-sets S_x paired with the members. One constructs the diagonal sub-set D of members x such that x does not belong to S_x. Then D differs from each S_x with respect to x.

Now if S is the set of *all* sets x, then each subset y of S is also a member of S and we can pair y (as a sub-set) with *itself* (as a member). The diagonal set D then consists of all sets y such that y does not belong to y. Consequently, D differs from each set y with respect to the member y: y belongs to D if and only if y does not belong to y.

But D is itself a member y of the set S of all sets, so D has the contradictory property of being different from itself.

This is how Russell came to discover the inconsistency of the set D whose members are the sets that do not belong to themselves. Of course, its inconsistency is obvious once one has thought of it. Each of the two possibilities

(1) D belongs to D,
(2) D does not belong to D,

implies the other. However, it is not easy to see how to prevent logic from being infected by such inconsistencies, and for this reason Russell's discovery was a severe blow to Frege (see Russell [9.39], Frege [9.21]). Most of the classes Frege used to define numbers were inconsistent when regarded as sets, but if the logic of sets did not apply to them, what did? Evidently logic would have to be overhauled, taking the properties of sets into account, if inconsistencies were to be avoided.

Even if the paradoxical sets were successfully excluded, how could one be sure that inconsistencies would not later arise in 'indispensable' parts of mathematics, such as arithmetic and analysis? In view of the trouble arising from the diagonal construction, one had to be suspicious of any field in which it was applicable, such as the theory of real numbers.

Drastic cures for these ills were proposed by several mathematicians, especially those who had not gone along with set theory in the first place. Kronecker refused to accept completed infinities, and even denied the existence of irrational numbers. Poincaré and Borel opposed the use of 'self-referential' definitions. However, Hilbert probably spoke for the majority when he urged the construction of foundations to save as much as possible of set-theoretic mathematics. In 1900 [9.29] he presented a list of twenty-three problems to the mathematical community as tasks for the coming century. The first two were concerned with foundations, and focused on the real numbers:

   1 *The continuum problem*: decide whether each infinite set of real numbers admits a one-to-one correspondence either with the set of natural numbers, or with the set of all real numbers.
   2 *The consistency of arithmetic*: prove that no contradiction can arise from the axioms of arithmetic. (These axioms are essentially the basic properties of +, × and < normally assumed for real numbers, together with the least upper bound property.)

These two problems effectively exposed the two greatest difficulties in the nineteenth-century reduction of mathematics to logic. Firstly, the set concept was not clear. Between the simplest infinite set (the set of natural numbers) and the set of all its sub-sets (equivalently, the set of real numbers) was a gulf whose size and general nature was not understood. Secondly, it was not clear that mathematical concepts were correctly captured by axioms. The consequences of a given set of axioms were difficult to foresee and they could conceivably include contradictions.

The answers to Hilbert's problems 1 and 2 obtained so far do not boil down to a simple yes or no. They reveal many aspects of the foundations of mathematics not anticipated in the nineteenth century. The picture is no longer as simple as it once seemed, nevertheless the general outline remains intact.

∾ BIBLIOGRAPHY ∾

9.1 Aubrey, J. *Aubrey's Brief Lives*, Harmondsworth: Penguin, 1982.

9.2 Beltrami, E. 'Risoluzione del problema: "Riportare i punti di una superficie sopra un piano in modo che le linee geodetiche vengano rappresentate da linee rette" ', *Opere Matematiche*, Milan, 1865: 1 262–80.

9.3 —— 'Saggio di interpretazione della geometria non-euclidea', *Opere Matematiche*, Milan, 1868, 1: 374–405.

9.4 Bolyai, J. *Scientiam spatii absolute veram exhibens*, Appendix to W. Bolyai, *Tentamen*, Marosvásárhely 1832. English translation in R. Bonola, *Non-euclidean geometry*, New York: Dover, 1955.

9.5 Bolzano, B. *Rein analytischer Beweis des Lehrsatzes dass zwischen je zwey Werthen, die ein entgegengesetzes Resultat gewähren, wenigstens eine reelle Wurzel der Gleichung liege* (1817), Ostwalds Klassiker, vol. 153, Leipzig: Engelmann, 1905.

9.6 Boole, G. *The Mathematical Analysis of Logic*, London and Cambridge, 1847.

9.7 —— *An Investigation of the Laws of Thought*, London, 1854.

9.8 Burali-Forti, C. 'Una questione sui numeri tranfiniti', *Rendiconti del Circolo matematico di Palermo*, 11 (1897): 154–64. English translation in *From Frege to Gödel*, ed. J. van Heijenoort, Cambridge, Mass.: Harvard University Press, 1967: 104–11.

9.9 Cantor, G. 'Über die Ausdehnung eines Satzes aus der Theorie der trigonometrischen Reihen', *Mathematische Annalen*, 5 (1872): 123–32.

9.10 —— 'Über eine Eigenschaft des Inbegriffes aller reellen algebraischen Zahlen', *Journal für Mathematik* 77 (1874): 258–62.

9.11 —— *Grundlagen einer allgemeinen Mannigfaltigkeitslehre*, Leipzig, 1883.

9.12 —— *Über eine elementare Frage der Mannigfaltigkeitslehre*, Jahresbericht der Deutsch. Math. Vereinigung 1 (1891): 75–8.

9.13 —— Letter to Dedekind, 28 July 1899, in *From Frege to Gödel*, ed. J. van Heijenoort, Cambridge, Mass.: Harvard University Press, 1967: 113–17.

9.14 Dedekind, R. *Stetigkeit und die Irrationalzahlen*, Braunschweig, 1872, English translation in *Essays on the Theory of Numbers*, Chicago: Open Court 1901.

9.15 Descartes, R. *La Géométrie*, Leyden, 1637, English translation, *The Geometry*, New York: New York, 1954.

9.16 du Bois Reymond, P. 'Über asymptotische Werthe, infinitäre Approximationen und infinitäre Auflösungen von Gleichungen', *Mathematische Annalen*, 7 (1874): 363–7.

9.17 Fauvel, J. and Gray, J., eds, *The History of Mathematics: a Reader*, Basingstoke, Macmillan, 1987.

9.18 Frege, G. *Begriffsschrift*, Halle 1879. English translation in *From Frege to Gödel*, ed. J. van Heijenoort, Cambridge, Mass.: Harvard University Press, 1967: 5–82.

9.19 —— *Die Grundlagen der Arithmetik*, Breslau, 1884. English translation, *The Foundations of Arithmetic*, Oxford: Basil Blackwell 1953.

9.20 —— Letter to Hilbert, 27 December 1899, in *Philosophical and Mathematical Correspondence*, Oxford: Basil Blackwell, 1980.

9.21 —— Letter to Russell, 22 June 1902, in *From Frege to Gödel*, ed. J. van Heijenoort, Cambridge, Mass.: Harvard University Press, 1967: 127–8.

9.22 Gauss, C. F. 'Demonstratio nova theorematis omnem functionem algebraicum rationalem integram unius variabilis in factores reales primi vel secundi gradus resolvi posse', *Werke*, Göttingen, 1799, 3: 1–30.

9.23 —— *Disquisitiones generales circa superficies curvas*, Göttingen, 1827.

9.24 —— Letter to Schumacher, 28 November 1846, *Briefwechsel mit H. C. Schumacher*, Hildesheim, Georg Olms Verlag, 1975 3: 246–7.

9.25 Gödel, K. 'Die Vollständigkeit der Axiome des logischen Funktionenkalküls', *Monatshefte für Mathematik und Physik*, 37 (1930):349–60. English translation in *From Frege to Gödel*, ed. J. van Heijenoort, Cambridge, Mass.: Harvard University Press, 1967: 582–91.

9.26 Heath, T. L., ed., *The Method of Archimedes*, Cambridge: Cambridge University Press, 1912.

9.27 —— *The Thirteen Books of Euclid's Elements*, vol. 1, Cambridge, Cambridge University Press, 1925.

9.28 Hilbert, D. *Grundlagen der Geometrie*, Leipzig: Teubner, 1899.

9.29 —— *Mathematische Probleme*, Göttinger Nachrichten, 1900: 253–97.

9.30 Huygens, C. 'Fourth part of a treatise on quadrature', *Oeuvres complètes*, La Haye, 1659, 14: 337.

9.31 Kant, I. *Critique of Pure Reason*, trans. N. K. Smith, London and Basingstoke, Macmillan, 1929.

9.32 Kossak, E. *Die Elemente der Arithmetik*, Berlin: Programm Friedrichs-Werder. Gymn., 1872.

9.33 Liouville, J. 'Nouvelle démonstration d'un théorème sur les irrationelles algébriques', *Comptes rendus de l'Acad. Sci. Paris*, 18 (1844): 910–11.

9.34 Lobachevsky, N. I. 'Géométrie imaginaire,' *Journal für die reine und angewandte Mathematik*, 17 (1837): 295–320.

9.35 Meray, C. 'Remarques sur la nature des quantités définies par la condition de servir de limites à des variables données,' *Revue des soc. savantes, sci. math. phys. nat.*, 4 (1869): 280–9.

9.36 Minding, F. 'Beiträge zur Theorie der kürzesten Linien auf krummen Flächen', *Journal für die reine und angewandte Mathematik*, 20(1840): 323–7.

9.37 Newton, I. 'Enumeratio linearum tertii ordinis', *Mathematical Papers*, Cambridge, 1695, 7: 588–645.

9.38 Riemann, G. F. B. 'Über die Hypothesen, welche der Geometrie zu Grunde liegen', *Werke*, Leipzig, 1854, 2nd edn: 272–87.

9.39 Russell, B. Letter to Frege, 16 June 1902, in *From Frege to Gödel*, ed. J. van Heijenoort, Cambridge, Mass.: Harvard University Press, 1967: 124–5.

9.40 Weierstrass, K. *Einleitung in die Theorie der analytischen Funktionen*, Göttingen: Mathematische Institut der Universität Göttingen, 1874.

9.41 Whitehead, A. N. and B. Russell, *Principia Mathematica*, vol. 1, Cambridge: Cambridge University Press, 1910.

CHAPTER 10

Philosophy of biology in the nineteenth century
Jagdish Hattiangadi

⮞⮞ THE PHILOSOPHY OF BIOLOGY ⮜⮜

The emergence of biology as a unified subject

Students of history and of biology share a common delight: as they study the details of any subject, they find a fascinating diversity of cases which far exceeds any preconceived expectations. But that is not their sole delight. Some will also see unifying themes therein, with coincidences that beg for explanation and leitmotifs which please the aesthete. Some scholars choose to stress the diversity, perhaps even the perversity, to be found in events in history (or, in biology, of living forms). Other scholars may feel happier following the motto *e pluribus unum*.

There is no right or wrong to it, that one is a unifier and another a divider of forms. We ascribe these differences in scientific or philosophical temperament to individual style or taste: some like a tidy story and others prefer a wealth of detail. Nor is this a matter of respect or lack of it for detailed facts. A grand unifier may study facts painstakingly while trying to unify (perhaps bending the facts, or perhaps ruefully admitting failure) while the person with a predilection for detail may believe in it only in principle, leaving it to others to dig them up and record them. Those who grant that details are important may do so either to prove that they fit into a grand scheme or to disprove that very point.

This difference is, perhaps not unsurprisingly, more than a matter of style. It is also an issue of substance in the nineteenth century, both in history and in biology. It became a topical question whether there is meaning in unfolding events: whether history exhibits fundamental laws, and whether there is a grand design to explain adaptation among living things. Do some things just happen, or is everything determined by a deep plan? Philosophers and scientists alike were on both sides of this celebrated debate, and on each side there are examples of intellectuals of both temperaments. But the issue of substance was not merely a matter of temperament, it was a matter of doctrine, of theory and of the future direction of thought.

The main issue of substance which animates the philosophy of biology in the nineteenth century has its root in the seventeenth, in the difficulties faced by Galileo's mechanical conception of the universe. This conception of a world ruled by mathematical laws of motion, or mechanics, became the central feature of the so-called scientific revolution of the seventeenth century. It was proposed by Galileo consciously in opposition to the Scholastic conception of the universe, which was dismissed with Ptolemaic astronomy as false. Galileo proposed that it was superseded by the new Copernican solar system, and proposed his new mechanics to replace the older physics of the scholastics.

The subsequent success of the mechanical conception of the universe cannot be equated with the success of any one of the mechanical systems proposed to describe motion. Galileo's laws were followed in turn by those of Descartes, Huygens, Newton, d'Alembert, Euler, Lagrange, Poisson, Laplace, Fresnel, Hamilton, Maxwell. At the end of the period we are studying there followed entirely new mechanical systems from Einstein (relativistic laws of motion) and Schrödinger and others (quantum mechanics). The accepted laws of motion keep changing, sometimes in matters of detail and at others in more fundamental ways, but the general idea of a mechanical universe conjoins consistently with any of them.

What is common to all the mechanical conceptions of the universe following Galileo is what they seemed to exclude: certain aspects of the universe which were readily understood as far back as in Aristotle's or even in Plato's accounts of the world seemed to be incomprehensible within a thoroughgoing mechanistic scheme. The existence of forms, the prevalence of purposes and the realm of morality seemed to lie entirely beyond the mechanical conception of the universe. If we regard mechanics as forming the basis of a new comprehensive philosophy to rival the old Scholastic philosophies (as modified from those of Plato and Aristotle), then form, purpose and morality had to be understood somehow as part of the new mechanical conception. But how? There is no ready explanation for the existence of any of these three. To resolve this difficulty there were two basic ways to proceed: with ingenuity we could develop mechanical models to reproduce the effect of forms, purposes and morality artificially; or we could devise a conception of the world in which form, purpose and morality are quite real, and wherein mechanics has a diminished role to play in our understanding.

A thoroughgoing mechanist could dismiss forms as residing in the eye of the beholder, or (invoking the medieval doctrine of nominalism) as residing in the act of naming. Purposes could be denied to all animals, and restricted to the human psyche, within which can also be located the free will, allowing us the luxury as moral beings, apparently denied to animals, of being naughty (domesticated animals being interesting exceptions). In this convoluted way the problems posed by forms, by purposes and by morality can be reduced to the mystery of the human mind. But having done so, we have only artificially isolated the recalcitrant Scholastic phenomena without having thus made any attempt at solving the problems posed for mechanists. The thoroughgoing mechanist such as Descartes who throws all recalcitrant Scholastic phenomena into the category of mind is no better off as a mechanist than the one who, like La Mettrie, regards all these phenomena as external, and explicable in material terms, without saying exactly how.

Interaction between two substances is ruled out by Spinoza's powerful argument that a substance is by definition autonomous, and hence cannot be affected by anything which is independent of it. The mechanical conception of the universe seemed to leave us with no option but to adopt one of these two alternatives: some form of materialism, or some form of idealism; we have either to seek an extension of mechanism to model and recreate the effect of the recalcitrant Scholastic phenomena or to subsume all material phenomena under the realm of ideas in a modified form.

A titanic debate was touched off between Newton and Leibniz just prior to the latter's death, which is found recorded in the Leibniz–Clarke correspondence [10.1]. Clarke, as Newton's voice, describes a material world which is governed by mathematical laws, but which has many physical features for which there are no mathematical laws governing them. Newton's own view was that God acted upon the world from time to time to preserve it in its required form (the solar system, for instance, was unstable according to Newton, and continues without signs of collapse because God holds the planets constantly within their orbits). Leibniz, on the other hand, proposed a fully rationalist conception of the universe, in which everything and every event is determined by the Principle of Sufficient Reason. The world according to Leibniz consists of a community of spirits (monads) each of which is completely determined in itself by its own nature. Each interacts successfully with other monads (or appears to do so, since any monad's experiences of other monads are completely predetermined by its own nature) only because of the pre-established harmony by which God has established an order among all things (monads).

If we neglect the references to God, either because we no longer believe in any, or for those who still continue to do so because we want to restrict ourselves to natural phenomena, then the choice for us lies between these two schemes: Firstly, a world in which some things just exist and some events just happen without natural cause, and they have no natural explanation (Newton). Secondly, a world which is fully determined in its smallest detail, and in which everything and every event within it is determined by a Grand Design which pre-establishes an otherwise inexplicable harmony (Leibniz).

These two points of view – one materialist and the other idealist, one indeterministic and the other deterministic, one antithetical to Scholasticism and the other friendly to some of its features, one seeking to understand what can be understood only in terms of the laws of matter and motion, and the other seeking to understand everything in terms of a pre-established rational order – are not the only two possible ways to approach the subject. But they did seem to many to offer the two most reasonable alternatives. In biology in the nineteenth century, however, are to be found some new ideas which cut across these extremes. They resolved some of the difficulties which were raised within Galileo's mechanical conception of the universe.

Thoroughgoing mechanists who avoided the relegation of all recalcitrant Scholastic phenomena to the mind, but accepted instead that forms and purposes were to be found among the phenomena (in short, materialists), had to find a way to understand form, purpose and morality in a material world governed by mechanical laws. A lively discussion between materialists and their opponents characterizes what we may identify in retrospect as the condition of biology as it coalesced into a subject in the nineteenth century.

Biology or the science of life arose as a unified subject among the discussions between French materialists and their opponents in the last years of the eighteenth century. Buffon, La Mettrie, Lamarck and their free-thinking contemporaries conceived a unified science of life, or of biology. Such was the need for recognizing this new subject that it was quickly taken up by many scholars of different persuasion across the scientific world. There is no doubt of course that the unity of biology was strengthened by the remarkable but later developments in cytology, genetics and evolutionary theory all of which cut across earlier divisions within the previously known sciences of living things. The prior unification of the sciences of life depends on this: form and purpose are to be found among all living things on earth, and barely outside of them. The need for a unified science of life arises out of the need to find mechanical models for these two categories of recalcitrant Scholastic phenomena, all of which seem to be found in and about living things. These issues are central to 'Modern Philosophy' as this is taught in universities to this day. If we take that as our cue, we may say confidently that the unification of biology was a philosophical attempt to solve some central problems of modern philosophy.

On mechanism and vitalism

The schism in modern thought between the thoroughgoing mechanists and those who sought to put mechanism in its proper (and diminished) place in the grand idealist scheme begins with the clash between Newton and Leibniz. Unlike the seventeenth century, the eighteenth marks a deepening separation between natural philosophy and moral philosophy. By the nineteenth century this division became established. The word 'philosopher' came to be reserved for an apologist for idealism or perhaps an opponent of thoroughgoing mechanism in any form, and the expression 'scientist' came into use for the thoroughgoing mechanist who followed the experimental method of investigation. These two professions came to inhabit different parts of the university, and came to adopt different curricula, and thus and only so were able to keep the peace.

The mechanists adhered to three things: some form of the laws of motion to understand everything in the world; a conception of scientific method as experimental and inductive; and a healthy scepticism about Scholastic issues which were dismissed as superstitious.

It is an unfortunate fact that heated debates between scientists on the question of how to accommodate form and purpose within mechanism often led them to accuse one another of becoming unscientific. Two schools of thought exist within the group of thoroughgoing mechanists early in the nineteenth century concerning how to accommodate purpose in nature. One group sought to explain it by a special life force (attached to a kind of fluid, vital matter); another group hoped to explain it entirely in terms of other known forms of matter and force, such as the magnetic, the electric, the chemical, etc. The first sought to identify all living forms by an ingredient common to them, and the other sought to understand life in terms of organization (of the organism) from ordinary or inert matter. In principle either of these ploys might have been true (or of course neither might be true). As it happens, by the end of the nineteenth century the odds had swung in favour of the latter point of view, and in the twentieth century, whatever a scientist accepts she will regard vitalism as an intellectual oddity. Nevertheless, in the nineteenth century it would be premature to describe vitalism as unscientific as is done all too often today.

One of the unfortunate terminological ambiguities of this debate lies in the description of the opponents of vitalism as 'mechanists'. In a certain sense, a vitalist is also a mechanist who happens to believe in an additional element with a force much like magnetic or electric forces as they were conceived at the end of the eighteenth century. The mechanists were, therefore, not necessarily the only mechanists in that conflict of opinion, if by mechanics we mean the well known laws of motion accepted at the time as governing all matter.

Galvani's experimental and theoretical contributions were regarded as unscientific by Volta late in the eighteenth century, but we may wish to differ in our assessment today. Perhaps Galvani was not correct in arguing that since the severed leg of a frog had been separated from its organisation (i.e. within the previously live frog) its twitching when probed by two metal prongs shows that there resides in the severed limb of the frog the principle of living matter. Perhaps Volta was right that this was not even a credible argument. But if it had not been for Galvani's argument, would Volta have sought to show that the twitch in the severed leg of a frog arose from the ordinary metals separated by the ordinary acidic fluid therein? Would he have otherwise looked for an apparatus to duplicate his model of a schematic form of a frog's leg being probed by two metal prongs, by inventing the voltaic pile? And would we have discovered current electricity, or the decomposition of water by electrolysis, or any of those remarkable things in physics and chemistry which followed Volta's invention of the pile and the discovery of the electric current?

Moreover, the methods used by vitalists could be and often were thoroughly experimental. Bichat made an excellent case for vitalism by conducting detailed studies of anatomical phenomena. Perhaps it is this more than anything else which led Claude Bernard, the great physiologist and methodologist, to recognize some fifty years later that while the experimental method needs preconceived ideas, it needs also a healthy scepticism (see pp. 292–5 below). Between the time of Bichat and Bernard, the tide seem to have swung against vitalism in physiology, though the full demise of vitalism had to await the twentieth century. The debate between vitalists and mechanists is a fine example of a thoroughly scientific controversy, in which experimental results and good arguments played an important role in the eventual outcome. As the difficulties for vitalism mounted and those for mechanists diminished, the tide of opinion swung against the vitalists. It is frequently but not invariably true that predominance of opinion among experts is a good gauge of the strength of the case made for and against the opinion, and in this instance the correlation seems to be quite good.

The factors which led to the decline of vitalism in the nineteenth century lay both within and without biology. In physics, there was an eighteenth-century consensus that the various forces of nature were distinct, and that each of them emanated from a characteristic and distinct type of matter. For example, physicists thought they had discovered electric fluids which supported electric forces, and magnetic fluids which supported magnetic forces, and caloric, which induced heat. This is quite compatible with a living material supporting a life force. But in the nineteenth century the growing experimental confirmation of the interchangeability of forces (or the unity of all force, later redefined and identified as 'energy') came to undermine the vitalist idea of a special force shared by all and only living things. Within biology, arguments leading to the demise of mechanism had much to do with the rise and predominance of physiology as opposed to anatomy in the study of form. The close connection between physiological function and evolution in Darwin's account eventually made vitalism an outsider to science as Darwin's views, and their improved descendants, came to occupy centre stage in biology.

Although vitalism had its share of friends and opponents in the nineteenth century, it was only after Darwin's conception of evolution by natural selection was grasped that vitalism came to fall in favour very generally. The heated debate over the merits of Darwin's theory of evolution by natural selection, however, was not between two versions of mechanism as was the case between the vitalists and the so-called mechanists. The issue debated by Darwin was the very different one philosophers had raised as the problem of design. He provided us with a mechanistic alternative to a grand design, or a pre-established harmony, or to some form of idealism. If we regard the French materialists' location of forms and purposes in matter as basically correct (in contradistinction to interactionists who find them in the mind), then we may say that Darwin's theory of evolution by natural selection solves the mind–matter problem (or the mind–body problem) of the Cartesian philosopher.

On biology as a development of the science of Galileo

When Leibniz proposed his idea of a divinely pre-established harmony, he had in mind the extraordinary coincidence that two monads which 'interact' have complementary experiences. In his account, two monads have two aspects of the same world. Each monad determines its own inner nature, and two 'interacting' monads might well have not been co-ordinated, and thus they may fail to 'interact' at all. (They may not possess aspects of the *same* world.) But in creating the universe, God created the best of all possible universes, and thus created a universe in which everything which exists and every event within each monad is there for a reason: were anything other than as it is, this would have been a different possible universe and therefore a universe inferior to this one. This being the best of all possible universes it determines for us what there is in every minutest detail – a determinism as complete as can be imagined – based on the assumption that anything else would not have sufficient reason to exist.

It is a remarkable fact of the history of ideas that Leibniz, the author of modern determinism (i.e. the Law of Sufficient Reason), was forgotten as its true author by the early part of the nineteenth century. Instead, the determinism invented by Leibniz is attributed to Newtonian mechanics. Perhaps it is not so surprising that this is so, after all. As Koyré expresses it:

> the world-clock made by the Divine Artifex was much better than Newton had thought it could be. Every progress of Newtonian science brought new force for Leibniz's contention: the moving force of the universe, its *vis viva* did not decrease; the world-clock needed neither rewinding nor mending.
>
> The Divine Artifex had therefore less and less to do in the world. He did not even need to conserve it, as the world, more and more, became able to dispense with this service.
>
> Thus the energetic God of Newton who actually 'ran' the universe according to his free will and decision, became in quick succession, a conservative power, an *intelligentia supermundana*, a 'Dieu fainéant'.
>
> Laplace, who, a hundred years after Newton, brought the New Cosmology to its final perfection, told Napoleon, who asked him about the role of God in his *System of the World*: 'Sire, je n'ai pas eu besoin de cette hypothèse.' But it was not Laplace's *System*, it was the world described in it that no longer needed the hypothesis God.
>
> ([10.4], 276)

But if Leibniz's determinism had taken over the Newtonian system of the world, it was not by providing mechanism with a new pre-established harmony. Laplace's determinism is one in which the particles at a given time, with their positions and momenta, determine once and for all the future and past states of the world; but this is not any explanation for the existence of forms or purposes (real or apparent) other than in the form of an unencashable promissory note.

The positions taken on these issues by scientists in the nineteenth century are varied and complex. The variety spans many intermediate forms between the two extremes which are represented here as mechanism and teleology. In the nineteenth century, both philosophers and scientists had become determinists. Only the form of determinism separated the two. The mechanists had come to adopt *physical determinism*, a determinism by mechanical forces alone, whereas the philosopher followed Leibniz in seeing in the system (or harmony) of the world such things as forms, their essences, purposes and purposeful beings (spirits). All of these were found by the philosopher in a simple 'common-sense' examination of the world. The pre-established harmony that was once postulated between minds or monads was now postulated to explain the adaptation of life forms. In this manner the pre-established harmony came to be regarded as a grand design in which physical organisms were adapted one to another. Even the description of development in an organism, in the work of von Baer, for instance, shows allegiance to both a mechanical perspective and a teleological perspective, tempting some modern commentators to call it 'teleomechanism', though this term would also apply to theologically inclined strict mechanists of the period as well (e.g. the geologist Hutton).

William Paley likened a living organism to a watch: if we were accidentally to find a watch, would we not postulate a watchmaker? The wonderful way in which all of the parts of the watch fit together allows us to infer that there must have been a watchmaker. In much the same way, the extraordinary manner in which living forms are adapted to their very particular surroundings, and often unable to survive in certain very slightly changed surroundings, suggests a designer. But it is not the existence of a designer which is the problem, but of a design or a plan. Many mechanists were faithful believers. They might still find a pre-established harmony to be unpalatable, given the success of modern mechanical science.

The existence of forms on earth had thus taken a particular twist late in the eighteenth and early in the nineteenth century: the fact that Scholastic forms are evident among phenomena is embarrassing enough for modern science. But the extraordinary coincidence that the various forms were uniquely fitted or adapted to their surroundings made them a double embarrassment to a mechanist. In order to respond to this challenge, Lamarck proposed his theory of evolution, in which all living forms metamorphose into other forms as they strive to make best use of the environment. Over the ages, thus, the various forms come to fit their surroundings with all the appearance of design, without a designer. (Other precursors of evolutionary theory and/or metamorphosis, include David Hume, Erasmus Darwin and Goethe.)

There were two difficulties with Lamarckian evolution: the concept of 'striving' was still a difficulty for a thoroughgoing mechanist. But this was not such a difficulty if one were also the kind of thoroughgoing mechanist who might be called a 'vitalist'. A more fundamental difficulty than that was a methodological flaw which arose in the usual defence of its main thesis. We turn to this difficulty of the theory of evolution, which was solved by Darwin.

Darwin's reconciliation of scientific metaphysics and method

Newtonian mechanism was not merely a set of ever-changing math-ematical laws of motion; it came also with a distinctive method. Newton espoused an experimental method, which was both championed and practised with great success in many fields of science, old and new. The success of modern science was attributed to the adoption of Newton's experimental method, which enjoined a close study of the facts and a repudiation of all hypotheses. If we study the great debate between evolutionists before Darwin and their opponents concerning evolution, we find however that it is their opponents who were clearly scientific in their treatment of phenomena.

The celebrated debate in 1830 in the French Academy between Geoffrey St Hilaire, who defended Lamarck, and Cuvier, who ridiculed evolutionary theory, was a clear defeat for the evolutionists. Cuvier was a remarkable comparative anatomist. He had minutely studied the skeletal structure of a great many animals. On the basis of measure-ments he was able to establish ratios between skeletal limbs of a great variety of species. The minute and exhaustive studies of bones allowed him to reconstruct entire skeletons from a few fossil bones, sometimes from a single bone. Cuvier came to be regarded as the Newton of comparative anatomy, for such were his accomplishments in that subject.

In 1812, Cuvier had come forward boldly to assert that a study of the fossil record for different ages revealed that the earth had entirely different species from time to time inhabiting it. This evidence, he claimed, was compatible only with the catastrophic destruction of spe-cies and subsequent creation of a new collection of living forms during successive ages on earth. The facts he collected left him no other choice that he could imagine but cycles of destruction and special creation.

The evolutionists (e.g. Lamarck or his follower Geoffrey St Hilaire) could not challenge Cuvier's claims about the existence of these very different species in successive ages on earth. Cuvier's scientific method was too rigorous to allow that counter-attack. His techniques continue to be useful in palaeontology and comparative anatomy even today.

The best that an evolutionist could do was to suggest a possible mapping between species in one age and the next to show how one set of species might have metamorphosed into an entirely different one in the intervening period between two fossilizations. But so far apart were the species in different ages that the suggested pathway from one form extant in one age to one extant in another was sometimes fantastic. Evolutionists seemed to be dreaming up their models of change, where the hard-nosed scientist who studied the established facts would be fully on the side of Cuvier, the consummate observer of minute and detailed facts about anatomy in different species.

For a philosopher of biology this debate is instructive not only because we now admire an idea that was once regarded as an unscientific speculation. It is also instructive because it is a clash of opinion between an ingenious metaphysical solution to a dilemma of Newtonian mechanics and a rigorous application of Newtonian method. The facts are, as they were then known, clearly investigated by Cuvier in a scientific manner. The evolutionist, on the contrary, appears to be a dreamer, a myth maker. The Lamarckian hypothesis defended by Geoffrey St Hilaire seems to be methodologically flawed, because it is an hypothesis (of the kind that Newton would not feign), and not an experimentally established statement, such as Cuvier's.

This clash of opinion is of seminal importance. Lyell formulated a 'uniformitarian' geology in contradistinction to Cuvier's catastrophic theory of the history of the earth. This clash changed the way in which uniformitarians and evolutionists approached their subject. The vicious attack on evolutionism on methodological grounds made subsequent uniformitarians and evolutionists nervous for decades about proposing hypotheses.

Darwin would not publish until he had investigated a great many particulars, perhaps more than absolutely necessary for the purpose of promulgating or defending their views. Darwin himself, whose evolutionary theory was of a different kind altogether, nevertheless immersed himself in the study of minute details of living things before coming forward with his views, which made his work both immensely richer and much less accessible to contemporaries than it might have been. Some controversies following Darwin's writing may be attributed to a lack of understanding of its main features, which were sometimes not clear to everyone, so great was the mountain of factual evidence in which it was lost. But an echo of Cuvier's earlier critique remains to this day: the fossil record, they say, is too incomplete to warrant evolutionary theory. The case for evolution cannot be made with so many gaps in the evidence. In the methodological developments of the nineteenth century it became evident that this demand is too great to make of any theory. Suffice it to say that the fossil record cannot support Cuvier's view either. If evolution is fantastic, then repeated extinction and creation are equally fantastic, without further evidence.

The critical feature of the evolutionary theory of Geoffrey St Hilaire and Lamarck which made it unsatisfactory is that this form of evolution did not allow for the extinction of species. Darwin's theory of evolution by natural selection does. The fossil record from one age to the next may be very different; and it may be futile to seek a one-to-one correlation between a species in one age and its descendants in another. Darwin suggests that even if most species in an age become extinct, a few which survive will produce all the variations which populate the next age. To take a popular example, it would be futile to look for an evolved successor today to every dinosaur which once roamed the earth. But there may well be one form (*archaeopteryx*) from which have evolved all the birds of today. Cuvier believed in mass extinction during the ice ages, and Lamarck in no extinction but only evolution. Darwin's theory is successful because it allows for almost complete extinction, and for evolution as well. Darwin's theory of evolution by natural selection postulates that there is a large amount of small variation in offspring. His proposal of blind variation combined with natural selection resolved the scientific and metaphysical issue of how form and purpose may arise – or may seem to do so – in a material and mechanistic universe.

In one theory, he was able to defend the mechanistic conception of the world in a manner which was compatible with detailed study of fact. Newtonian method and Newtonian metaphysics were reconciled, and a major philosophical problem for Galileo's science was solved.

There is nowadays some confusion about the form of gradualism which is necessarily entailed by Darwin's theory and a form of catastrophism which is compatible with it: Darwin's theory is often described as gradualist in the sense that there are no catastrophes in the history of the earth. This form of gradualism is not appropriately attributed to Darwinian theory. The hypothesis that the extinction of a very large number of dinosaur species in a very short period of time by the catastrophic event of a meteor striking the earth is certainly not a critique of Darwinian theory. But the evolution of subsequent life-forms would be described by a Darwinian as descent from the surviving life-forms then extant, and this evolution would be gradual in the specific sense that the evolution would depend on small variation within species and their differential advantages. Whereas Lyell's geology denied the assumption that there are regular catastrophes, Darwin's theory describes how to do without periodic bursts of creation *de novo*. On Darwin's account, the evolution of species does not show leaps of creation, though it may well undergo rapid destruction of species in what may be described as catastrophes.

Two of the three Scholastic phenomena which could not be fitted into mechanistic theory were reconciled with it in Darwin's model. Forms (species) were described as mutable, but apparent at a given time; and the appearance of a great purpose or a grand design was also feigned in nature by the almost adaptive character of living forms which had been naturally selected in their environment in competition with variations which become extinct.

Continuing issues in the philosophy of biology

After Darwin successfully promulgated his theory of evolution by natural selection, an entirely new set of issues in the philosophy of biology came to light which were only dimly realized before.

Form and species

One of these issues concerns the classical idea of form. There may be a certain sense in which the mechanical conception of the universe challenged the idea of forms as the basis of all knowledge. Certainly, in some subjects in which mechanics was successful, forms ceased to play an important role. Many were the subjects, however, which resisted the advent of mechanical theories. The study of form in animals, plants and minerals (particularly crystals) left forms as a fundamental category for our knowledge.

In classifying species of plants, for instance, Linnaeus and Buffon provided rival schemata. Buffon's nominalist scheme was more general and philosophical, whereas that of Linnaeus, which stressed the essential qualities of species, was found much more useful in the practice of classification. Whichever system of classification one adopts, it is necessary for the practising natural historian, in order to classify things according to their form, to presuppose that each species *has* a characteristic form, which may be captured in a typical specimen. Abnormal individuals may be found, of course, but the natural historian had to guard against choosing one of them as a specimen, which difficulty prompted Buffon's doubts about essential properties. An elaborate methodology had been developed to pursue natural history to respond to these concerns, the recounting of which falls outside the scope of this essay.

Darwin's theory of evolution by natural selection undermines the theoretical basis for this enterprise. Species, according to Darwin are not fixed but constantly changing. The normal situation is an abundance of variety in offspring. Thus in any species the characteristic form is not one but a multiplicity. Are there such things as species at all? (This is not quite the traditional problem of natural kinds and realism, though perhaps related to it.)

Darwin did not deny that an examination of the flora and fauna around the earth would yield a knowledge of identifiably different species. As a young man he delighted in collecting beetles. He did not need to be reminded that identifying forms is what makes the practice of natural history possible. His claim is a historical one: Darwin envisaged living organisms as belonging to a single tree. As the branches fanned out, some lines would come to an end (the forms would become extinct) but some would continue to flourish and would produce numerous varieties. Given a cross section of time the tree would project on a plane the characteristic grouping together of living things into species, genera, etc. as we find these in our records. But there are two provisos: Firstly, there are always some variations, and these are the source of evolutionary change. Secondly, over time, we recognize that species are mutable, and organisms from one species will be seen to have a common ancestry (and therefore share formal similarity) with the most remote of living organisms if only we are willing to go back far enough on the tree of life.

Darwin's theory eats its cake and has it, too. Species have characteristic properties more often than not, because the process of natural selection may well isolate a form of life as a species. This is what makes Linnaean natural history possible. But within any species there are many small variations, which will, in the course of time, speciate. Because species change in this manner, each existing variation has equal right to be regarded as characteristic of the species – or better still, it is the variety which characterizes the species. So Buffon is perhaps right after all in denying the existence of essences to living forms.

This conception of mutability challenged the idea of 'sorts' or 'kinds' as fundamental to our understanding of living organisms. In the theory of collections or aggregates or classes, it is possible to take any aggregate and regard it as a class. If any collection is a class, is there anything special about a species considered as a class? Is there some way in which it is natural, and not artificial?

From the old conception of morphology, it is only their form which binds similar organisms into a species. But when we consider Darwinian evolution, a species must be understood as a class of organisms which share the ability to generate common offspring. Thus we find in Darwinian theory a criterion for describing a class, when it is a species, as a natural kind. There are no doubt difficulties with this. For one thing, inability to generate offspring may be due to separation in time or by geography, which leaves it an open question whether two separated groups belong to the same species when they do not generate common offspring, even though we may suppose that they could. On the other hand some combinations of animals may have only sterile offspring, or have offspring which are sterile after one or two or more generations. For all these and still more reasons the notion of a species has become both richer and more troublesome since Darwin. The criterion of form or essence to identify specimens, however practical and useful, is usually undermined by the existence of variety, and has been seriously undermined as a fundamental tool of biological thought.

Quite recently, this issue has been raised again under the slogan 'species as individuals', i.e. the idea that any one species is not a class of objects similar in some respect but an organic unity. This twentieth-century discussion seems to contribute little to what Darwin had already considered apart from obscuring the perfectly good notions of class and of individual. The theory of classes allows any collection to be also considered as an individual if we so wish; one might even wish to say that that is its whole point. Considering a species as an organic unity does not deprive it of its status as a class of organisms, any more than the class of cells within an organism is denied status as a class because they are all part of one organism. In both cases the defining property of the relevant class may be a historical one. All (or almost all) the living cells in the body of Georg Cantor have the property of having descended from one fertilized egg from his parents. They form a class none the less, as defined by that property, and Georg Cantor was an individual all the same.

History and determinism

Another fundamental issue of interest to philosophers to emerge from evolutionary theory is the conception of an 'open' history. Darwin's account of evolution included an idea of small variation in great abundance which has been variously described as 'blind' and 'random'. The inability of the environment, or of the organism, to direct the variation in the offspring is a very fundamental feature of Darwinian evolutionary theory. In order to distinguish the first view which was proposed by Darwin from a theory which allows organisms to have offspring which inherit the good acquired characteristics of the parent, the latter is often called 'Lamarckian'. Darwin himself vacillated between giving Lamarckian and what we may wish to call Darwinian accounts of adaptation. Climate-induced or environment-induced variation would be a third variety, which we may wish to call Lyellian evolution, to commemorate Lyell's views on it in his *Principles of Geology*.

What is interesting from a philosophical perspective about Darwin's distinctive theory (even if he sometimes used other theories also) is that in his account there is an element of chance in the evolution of species which cannot be eliminated. A chance event here and now could have a profound influence upon the course of the future history of life on earth. Indeed, the entire history of life is a history of many chance events which produce the appearance of a pre-established harmony (or what is more neutrally called 'adaptation').

It may seem at first that this is a peculiarity of biology that it raises chance to such an important level of fundamental principle, though we have seen it repeated latterly in thermodynamics and quantum mechanics. Although Darwin was not technically a statistician, his conception of the biosphere was a fundamentally statistical one. His theory gave the statistical view, itself adumbrated earlier in the nineteenth century, considerable scope for development, although this development had to await the 'new synthesis' of Darwinian theory of selective fitness with Mendel's theory of genetic inheritance, and Waismann's theory of the eternal or at any rate long-living germ line.

Among nineteenth-century philosophers, Peirce is perhaps the only philosopher to adopt this indeterminist consequence of Darwinian evolution. There are many philosophical problems concerning indeterminism, statistics and probability, and chance that are of interest to a philosopher of biology, though only in forms evident in the twentieth century.

Methodology

When Darwin wrote his *Origin of Species*, there was almost universal agreement that any scientific theory, to be successful, must describe the world as fully deterministic. The indeterministic theory of Darwin with a prominent place for chance within it creates a methodological difficulty. Whether it is a methodologically satisfactory theory or not can be asked while assuming that a theory must fit the model of theories in physics as then conceived. In the nineteenth century this was not as great an enigma as it became in the twentieth, when methodologists frequently worried about the methodological status and explication of Darwinian evolutionary theory.

In the nineteenth century, and indeed to this day, the central methodological difficulty raised about Darwin's theory of evolution by natural selection is that the record of facts (i.e. fossils) is incomplete. Darwin's theory may be described for that reason as unfounded, or poorly founded. Alternatively we may dismiss the methodology which demands so much of Darwinian theory or of any other, for that matter, as an unrealistic methodology to adopt.

Compared to methodologies propounded in the nineteenth century, theories of method in the twentieth are much more varied and much less demanding. Foundationalism is in doubt today more than ever. It would be a mistake, however, to think that Darwin's theory had a great deal to do with this change. All the evidence seems to suggest, rather, that methodology has developed more in response to problems in mathematics and in physics, and less in response to those in biology, even though the present scepticism concerning foundations fits Darwinian science extremely well.

Although the influence on methodology of reflections upon the development of evolutionary theory is minimal, the same is not true for reflections on the content of evolutionary theory. Darwin was among those who realized that his theory implied that all life including human life has evolutionary origins. In his *Evolution of the Emotions in Animals and Man*, Darwin sought to extend his theory explicitly to human feeling. We also know from his diaries that he regarded human intelligence and some critical ideas to have been inherited, too. In fact a case can be made that Darwin was a follower of Whewell until he became a Darwinian in 1839 when he realized that a substitute for what Whewell had called fundamental ideas (which are not derived from experience) could be understood as having been inherited from our simian ancestry [10.3]. An evolutionary epistemology promises to be one of the most fundamental and profound philosophical consequences of Darwinian evolutionary theory, though what it is exactly remains undecided.

Morality

The mechanical conception of the universe still fails to accommodate one class of Scholastic phenomena, concerning morality. Where evolutionary epistemology is clearly an interesting subject with much to teach us, evolutionary morality is, like a mechanistic conception of purposes in the seventeenth century, still enigmatic. Whereas Darwin's account shows how to do without a grand design, and how to explain the existence of forms among living organisms, there is in evolutionary theory as yet no satisfactory theory of the existence of morality.

There is of course ample room to account for the fact of the existence of mores among groups of people. Just as we can study different animals to study their mating, nesting or feeding behaviour, so too we can observe humans in different groups and study them moralizing. This might lead us to think that we have an evolutionary understanding of morality if we have some explanations of how they come to acquire their moralizing habits, but that would be a mistake. The characteristic feature of morality is not that we behave in some way, or moralize in some way, but that we regard some behaviour as immoral or wrong even as we practise it. What needs to be understood is how it comes about that some things are wrong, or immoral, and not just why we so regard them.

The understanding of morality from an evolutionary perspective certainly had a controversial and well publicized attempt in the nineteenth century. One of Darwin's most ardent admirers, Herbert Spencer, proposed a doctrine called Social Darwinism. In this doctrine the lesson for us from competing living forms as Nature evolves (red in tooth and claw), is that the fittest survive, and the weak perish. Applied to the social sphere it led to what was roundly attacked as an amoral and callous view of human society. Its popularity with some despicable political movements in the twentieth century (e.g. with the National

Socialists, or Nazis) has left many intellectuals with a horror of social theoretical biologists.

But the issue of morality is squarely one which remains unresolved within the Galilean revolution, and, however distasteful and misguided Spencer's Social Darwinism, one must give him and other intellectuals of the nineteenth century credit for recognizing this as a fundamental difficulty of modern science which needs to be addressed. Indeed it is because an entire society under the Nazis, in the name of their entire society, espousing Social Darwinist slogans, was so immoral as to practise systematic murder and genocide that we have to ask not only how individual immorality is possible but also how collective immorality is possible. No account of how actual mores are acquired or propagated can explain this.

As opposed to Spencer, who tried to extract a morality from the natural course of events as he interpreted them, G. E. Moore argued early in the twentieth century that any attempt to derive a claim that something must be so based on the claim that it is so, is a fallacy (what he called the Naturalistic Fallacy). His argument is that of whatever is described as a fact we may still ask meaningfully whether it is good that it is so. Since we can always meaningfully ask that question, we cannot identify the meaning of 'good' with what is the case. Moore's argument purports to make the realm of morality (and of norms and prescriptions generally according to later philosophers) independent of the realm of nature. How it may have come about that these realms are independent is a difficulty for naturalists.

The situation at the turn of the twentieth century was that naturalism in ethics was opposed to normativism, and the matter was unresolved, and so it remains to this day.

∾ METHODOLOGY OF BIOLOGY ∾

Origins of the subject and of some terms

Whether there was any philosophy of biology in the nineteenth century is debatable: there is as good reason to deny it as to assert it. The expressions 'philosophy of science' and 'philosophy of biology' were invented in the nineteenth century by William Whewell. Were we to rely on that alone we would have to allow that there is such a subject by 1840. But if we were to seek practising philosophers of biology, none comes to mind, at least none who would self-consciously describe any of their work as belonging to such a field. The name invented by Whewell for this field came to designate something which clearly exists only in the latter half of the twentieth century, with some writings of

T. Goudge and J. H. Woodger. Later, the writings of D. Hull, still later followed by a host of interesting writers on the subject (Ghiselin, Ruse, Wimsatt, Sober), all of whom would be happy to describe their relevant works as belonging to the philosophy of biology.

To a modern historian of the philosophy of biology in the nineteenth century this creates an interesting question of choice: lacking a clearly defined field in the nineteenth century, one could dismiss it as non-existent. This implies that there is no philosophy of biology until concerns arising out of logical empiricism (a unique intellectual movement of the twentieth century) led to the birth of this subject. But this would belie the fact that many of the issues taken up today did arise earlier, as we have seen, however different the context in which they arose in the nineteenth century.

The strategy which suggests itself is to pick out issues in the philosophy of biology today and to seek to present these very issues as they once emerged or developed in the nineteenth century. This is the strategy which has been adopted in this chapter. The obvious difficulty with this strategy is that it may be prone to anachronism: how do we prevent our criteria of choice of issue from imposing our own concerns for those of the past? To a certain extent this is unavoidable. In writing a history of philosophy in the nineteenth century, or in writing a history of the subject of history, there would be a generally accepted sense *at the time in the period being studied* that some things were within the field, even if today they were to be classified as belonging elsewhere. Issues in psychology or in sociology, for instance, which arose in the early part of the nineteenth century would have to be classified as part of philosophy because they were so regarded then. In this sense we cannot find a bench mark or a criterion of what would have been part of the philosophy of biology in the nineteenth century as seen by a contemporary then. But to be forewarned was to be forearmed.

The issues of the philosophy of biology may be divided into two kinds: methodological, and substantive. There is, as I shall soon suggest, an overlap there as well.

The substantive questions within nineteenth-century biology which are of concern to philosophers of biology today may be classified into three categories: those connected with problems of evolutionary theory and related developments; those connected with the problem of reduction of life sciences to physics and chemistry; and those related to the understanding of human beings in the light of modern biology. There are of course a host of issues which may fit within or across these categories. All these issues were already controversial in the latter part of the eighteenth century and continue to attract interest to the present day, and some of them have been sketched in the first section above.

In studying the methodology of biology in the nineteenth century one could include the commentators on science (Whewell, Bernard) or those involved in the practice of scientific research who exhibit or are obliged to pronounce upon method (Cuvier, Pasteur, Darwin): the discussion of methodology in the practice of scientific research is generally a sign of a clash between defenders of different theoretical perspectives, all of whom attempt to use methodological considerations to buttress their respective cases.

The second kind of methodological pronouncement is usually controversial, because it is made in the interests of controversy. The substantive issues in biology which stand out today as worth discussing are just those that were once the subject of controversy. Practical methodology is therefore closely bound up with the same substantive issues that we have identified as part of the philosophy of biology in the nineteenth century.

There may also be a connection between the writings of abstract methodology and the controversies of the nineteenth century: Whewell's work may be related to the controversies arising from substantive issues in physics (empiricism versus *a priori* knowledge, for instance) and Bernard's from those in medicine (anatomical as opposed to physiological considerations in medical research). Nevertheless, the form of these self-consciously written methodological tracts differs from the others: the former must be taken literally as methodologies. The others are more casual and less systematic remarks uttered in the interests of other argumentation. We may sometimes disregard the methodological apologia and prefer instead to analyse the science in action. For this reason there has been included, in the section below, a brief account of two methodological treatises of the nineteenth century of particular interest to the philosophy of biology.

Since the unification of biology is an important part of the story recounted here, perhaps some comments are in order about each of the subjects of history, philosophy and biology as they are found in the nineteenth century. The first two of these subjects trace their origin to an era which is at least as early as that of the ancient Greeks – Herodotus and Socrates respectively being cited as their originators. (The words were invented then, but it is always possible to suggest that there were predecessors in or around ancient Greece, or in another civilization prior to the Socratic invention of the word.) Philosophical history, a particularly influential conception of time and events in human history, seems to be an especially noteworthy product of the nineteenth century (Hegel, Comte, Marx). It is an open question which will not be taken up here what direct or indirect influence philosophical history might have had on biology.

Unlike philosophy and history, biology is a comparative beginner. It is recognized as a unitary and integral subject worthy of a separate designation for the first time only late in the eighteenth century. Many of the fields which are now part of biology as we understand it have a hoary history: zoology, botany, physiology, anatomy, as well as hosts of sub-disciplines like ornithology, entomology. They were well developed subjects for a long time before they came to be regarded as component parts of a single subject identified as the science of life, or of biology. It is an interesting fact about this new subject, biology, that there is a philosophy of it according to us. In contrast, we would find a philosophy of entomology or of botany to be unnecessary without further argument. It seems that there is a unity to biology which warrants a philosophy of it. Perhaps the thesis that the unity of biology is a unity of philosophical approach, prompted by the fundamental problems of modern philosophy, is not the whole story. But if it is part of the story, it still makes philosophy much more central to the development of biology, and vice versa, than is generally supposed.

Two important methodological treatises

The origin of the expression 'philosophy of science' may be traced to Whewell, who proposed it in his book *Philosophy of the Inductive Sciences, Founded upon Their History* (1840). Book IX is entitled 'The Philosophy of Biology', which is part of the philosophy of science.

> The advances which have, during these last three centuries, been made in the physical sciences; – in Astronomy, in Physics, in Chemistry, in Natural History, in Physiology; – these are allowed to be real, to be great, to be striking: may it not be then that these steps of progress have in them something alike? – that in each advancing movement there is some common process, some common principle?

Then a little later he says, 'if we can, by attending to the past history of science, discover something of this common element and common process in all discoveries, we shall have a *Philosophy of Science*' ([10.5], vi). In the opening section of Book I, philosophy of science is said to offer nothing less than a complete insight into 'the essence and conditions of all knowledge, and an exposition of the best methods of the discovery of all truths'.

It is evident that a philosophy of science would include at least a methodology, and an informed analysis of the history of science to exhibit that methodology. In addition it would have to exhibit an insight into all real knowledge – a tall order indeed. Whewell's own writings are remarkable for the insight he exhibits into diverse subjects and their history, which few have matched.

But when we turn to his account of the philosophy of biology, the reading is disappointing (but no more than Mill, Comte or Spencer). There he lists five schools of biological thought, and a cursory account of some developments in physiology. We do not find any especially remarkable insight into the essence and conditions of biological knowledge, or even of the particular methods which may have made them successful. Instead, we find that when he can he applies the paraphernalia of a philosophy arrived at from the study of physics and mathematics to biology – his conception of a fundamental idea not derived from experience, for instance, is inspired by Kant's conception of *a priori* synthetic judgement, introduced to show how mathematical knowledge is possible.

Searching for a nineteenth-century figure who actually studied what Whewell may have called the essence and conditions of biological knowledge and who reflected upon the process of discovery to extract some insight from it, we find only one book which merits our attention, Claude Bernard's classic, *An Introduction to the Study of Experimental Medicine* (1865).

Claude Bernard was one of the great physiologists of his day. His most memorable achievement perhaps was the discovery of the internal environment of animals, which allows for an explanation of the comparative autonomy of some animals even though they remain in constant interaction with environment. He had also made numerous and brilliant discoveries in physiology before that, such as the function of the pancreas, animal glycogenesis, experimental production of diabetes, the existence of vasomotor nerves, which are mentioned among other discoveries in Paul Bert's introductory eulogy ([10.2], v–xii).

Claude Bernard's work does not address biology as an integral subject. He deals exclusively with physiology, and mentions anatomy. But his work is so centrally in philosophy of biology as we now understand it that it cannot be left out of account.

Bernard argues forcefully for the need to study not just form as in comparative anatomy but function as well. And he suggests that in order to do so it is necessary not just to observe organisms but to experiment with them. What, we may ask, is the difference between observation and experiment?

Bernard provides us with one of the most lucid and brilliant accounts of experimentation and experimental reasoning ever given. He begins by distinguishing the process of experimentation from that of observation. We take observation to be a passive gathering of facts, where in experiments there is an intervention into the process being studied, 'a variation or disturbance that an investigator brings into the conditions of natural phenomena' ([10.2], 5). But in distinguishing an observation from an experiment and both from experimental reasoning, he notes that the objective of an experiment is to understand a phenomenon from a perspective under our own control. 'to reason experimentally, we must usually have an idea and afterwards induce or produce facts, i.e. observations, to control our preconceived idea'. ([10.2], 20).

Bernard's account of the experimental method in observations as well as in experimentation is anything but passive. 'Of necessity, we experiment with a preconceived idea. An experimenter's mind must be active, i.e. it must question nature, and must put all manner of queries to it according to the various hypotheses which suggest themselves.' And his account of the experimental method is this:

> the metaphysician, the scholastic, and the experimenter all work
> with an *a priori* idea. The difference is that the scholastic
> imposes his idea as the absolute truth which he has found, and
> from which he then deduces consequences by logic alone. The
> more modest experimenter, on the other hand, states an idea as
> a question, as an interpretative, more or less probable
> anticipation of nature, from which he deduces consequences
> which, moment by moment, he confronts with reality by means
> of experiment.
>
> ([10.2], 27)

Bernard's brief for a study of experimental medicine is an attempt to bring science to bear on a subject which he saw then as

> still in the shades of empiricism and suffers the consequences of
> its backward condition. We see it still more or less mingled with
> religion and with the supernatural. Superstition and the
> marvellous play a great part in it. Sorcerers, somnambulists,
> healers by some virtue of a gift from Heaven, are held as the
> equal of physicians. Medical personality is held above science
> by the physicians themselves; they seek their authority in
> tradition, in doctrines or in medical tact. This is the clearest of
> proofs that the experimental method has by no means come into
> its own in medicine.
>
> ([10.2], 45)

The conception of experimental medicine proposed by Bernard suggests that experimentation has exactly the same character whether we experiment on inorganic chemicals or on living tissue. Thus he argues that there is just one method for the study of all living and non-living things, which is in direct contrast to the claims of some vitalists that living organisms provide exception to the general rules governing the study of dead (non-living) matter.

While Bernard argued forcefully and lucidly for the unity of experimental method, he also pointed out that living objects must be treated differently from inorganic things.

> So far we have been explaining experimental conditions
> applicable to both living and inorganic bodies; for living bodies
> the difference consists merely in the greater complexity of the
> phenomena.... But in the behaviour of living bodies we must
> call the reader's attention to their very special interdependence;
> in the study of vital functions, if we neglected the physiological
> point of view, even if we experimented most skilfully, we should
> be led to most false ideas and the most erroneous deductions.
>
> ([10.2], 87)

Living organisms must be treated as a harmonious whole. And in this manner he argues for the need to do not only comparative anatomy but experimental medicine as well.

The greatness of Bernard's suggestions lies not only in the profound changes that he foresaw and helped advance in the profession of theoretical medicine but also his genuine contributions to methodology, or to the philosophy of science as this subject had been conceived by Whewell. Bernard's analysis of the sceptical doubt which is used by the experimenter without letting it get out of control, his defence of the need for preconceived ideas together with the injunction that we must be ready to abandon them as soon as nature turns recalcitrant – all these are so remarkable in capturing the essence of scientific method that it is one of the few books on methodology which continues to be read as profitably now as when it was first printed.

Compared to Bernard's brilliant work, there is nothing else of interest in the nineteenth century, and perhaps even since then, in the form of a sustained methodological treatise on the topic of experimental method in biology.

⮞⮞ NOTE ⮜⮜

My thanks to Professor Margaret Schabas and Mr David Clingingsmith for their comments and assistance with the paper; the errors which remain are of course my own.

❧ BIBLIOGRAPHY ❧

10.1 Alexander, H. G., ed., *The Leibniz–Clarke Correspondence*, Manchester: Manchester University Press, 1956.

10.2 Bernard, C. *An Introduction to the Study of Experimental Medicine*, 1865, trans. from the French by H. C. Greene, 1927, reprint New York: Dover, 1957.

10.3 Curtis, R. *Charles Darwin and the Refutation of Whewellian Metascience: How The Philosophy of Science Learned from the History of Science*, Ph.D. Dissertation, York University, 1982.

10.4 Koyré, A. *From the Closed World to the Infinite Universe*, Baltimore: Johns Hopkins University Press, 1957.

10.5 Whewell, W. *Philosophy of the Inductive Sciences*, 2nd edn, 1847, reprint London: Frank Cass, 1967.

CHAPTER 11

The separation of psychology from philosophy
Studies in the sciences of mind 1815–1879
Edward S. Reed

> An age which demands free inquiry, pushed without fear or compromise to its legitimate conclusions, turns up an Epicurus or a Hobbes. In one which likes to put up at a half-way house, there will be no lack of a Dugald Stewart or a Mackintosh, to provide it with comfortable entertainment.
>
> Thomas Love Peacock, 'The epicier' (1836)

❧ THE IMPOSSIBLE SCIENCE ❧

Traditional metaphysics

The consensus of European opinion during and immediately after the Napoleonic era was that psychology as a science was impossible. This was not the position of a few retrograde thinkers but was the thoughtfully articulated opinion of the best placed academic thinkers. Much of what we now think of as psychology and philosophy emerged from attempts to overcome these well developed arguments against the possibilities of a scientific psychology.

There is an important terminological shift during this time as well. In Locke's day, the English terms 'natural philosophy' and 'moral philosophy' were used in parallel to mean, roughly, what we would now call natural science as versus social science. By the middle of the eighteenth century a host of other terms were being used to denote all or part of 'moral philosophy', such as the Latin 'psychologia' (both empirical and rational) and the pseudo-Greek 'pneumatology'. Within

Scottish philosophy the phrases 'intellectual powers' and 'active powers' of the mind gained some currency. By the turn of the century, however, the word 'metaphysics' was increasingly used to denote much of what we would now call psychology (although terms like 'moral philosophy' were still common as well). Around 1815, the linguistically sophisticated poet Shelley wrote that 'Metaphysics is a word which has been so long applied to denote an inquiry into the phenomena of mind that it would justly be presumptuous to employ another [although] etymologically considered it is very ill adapted to express the science of mind' (Shelley also spoke of Kant as a 'psychologist'). At about this time Maine de Biran and Schopenhauer were using this term in a similar way, and a generation later one finds the young Charles Darwin also using 'metaphysics' to refer to psychological inquiry.

As Napoleon swept across Europe academic theorists increasingly argued that 'metaphysics' (psychology) was not a science, or at least that it could not be an empirical science in the same way that physics or chemistry could. The two most important sources of this broad consensus were literally situated at opposite ends of the continent: Immanuel Kant in East Prussia and Thomas Reid in Scotland. It is no exaggeration to say that these were the two most influential psychologists between the French Revolutions of 1789 and 1830. Their views on psychology were widely taught, analysed and discussed. I shall call the position that emerged under this influence 'traditional European metaphysics'. Ironically, traditional metaphysics is *not* a position to which either Reid or Kant would have subscribed; nevertheless, it is a set of views which arose in large part because of the influence of Reidian and Kantian arguments.

Neither Kant nor Reid was against the study of psychology – on the contrary, both were acute practitioners of this discipline. Nevertheless, they both had strong reasons for attacking any pretensions put forward for treating psychology as a science. Kant and Reid took Newtonian mechanics to be the model empirical science; arguing that explanations in terms of patterns of efficient causality conforming to empirically determinable laws are essential to real science. Both Kant and Reid presumed such laws would be expressed mathematically, and that controlled experimentation (perhaps mixed with observational modelling as in astronomy) was the proper method for deriving the laws.

Kant argued that the various claims about the nature of the human mind or soul are impossible to evaluate in this scientific manner. He attacked the 'rational psychology' then popular in Germany for claiming to be able to prove such propositions as 'the soul is unitary and simple'. Instead, as Kant showed in the antinomies of his first *Critique*, diametrically opposing views of the soul could be sustained with equal rational force. In his 'anthropology' Kant endorsed a kind of natural historical model for psychology, using observational techniques to illustrate how different people(s) have developed, and how they react in diverse situations. Kant's 'critique' was a novel discipline, or method, intended to undercut all pretensions to a science of metaphysics beyond this sort of observational procedure.

Reid's attack on psychology as science had a different origin from Kant's, but ended up in much the same place. Responding to what he called the 'way of ideas' – and in particular to what we would see as Lockean psychology – Reid objected to what he saw as an inadequate appreciation of the difficulties of accounting for intentional psychological states on the basis of sensory data. Reid argued that psychological capacities, such as the ability to perceive external objects (which Reid saw as central to all mental powers), could not be explained as causal outcomes of physical stimuli affecting the mind or the body. He tried to show that all such accounts either violated the concept of efficient causality, or were not explanatory, or both. The causal effects of, for example, light on the retina are one thing, and the sensory awareness of light (visual sensations) another thing, and the visual perception of objects yet a third thing. The widespread claim, originating in Descartes and running through Locke, the *philosophes* and beyond, that the first caused the second which caused the third, were simply what we would now call category errors – because physical stimuli cannot be the efficient causes of mental states, nor can sensory (non-intentional) states be the causes of perceptual (intentional) states. Reid occasionally flirted with Berkeleian semiotic explanations of the stimulus-to-sensation transition, and also dabbled with occasionalist interpretations of the sensation-to-perception transition. But, in his mature works on *The Intellectual Powers* and *The Active Powers*, he most often argued that these transitions cannot be causal and simply do not fit available models of explanation.

Reid did not argue against the distinctions among the concepts of stimulus, sensation and perception; on the contrary, it was Reid who sharpened these three concepts into modern form – thus setting the stage for many a nineteenth-century dispute. However, Reid strongly stated that explanation of the causal interrelationships among these three kinds of events was not possible, and he objected to claims that such interrelationships had to conform to patterns of cause and effect. For Reid the ultimate fact in psychology was teleological: God had so arranged our bodies and minds that upon receipt of a certain stimulus, our bodies felt a given sensation, and our minds conceived a particular perceptual belief. In an intriguing parallel with Kant's *Critique of Judgement*, Reid argued that the relationships among the various animal and conscious properties of ourselves is a part–whole relationship, contrived by a deity with the purpose of adapting us to the rest of his creation. Like Kant, Reid argued the need for a descriptive psychology, to elucidate the modes of this adaptation of self to world, but denied even the possibility of an experimental, causally based psychological science.

Both Reid and Kant left open a path to what we nowadays call, often disparagingly, a faculty psychology. Through natural history, anthropological observation, intuitive introspection, and other sciences' knowledge of creation, a descriptive psychology might be developed. Such a psychology would provide a taxonomy of mental capacities ('faculties'). This taxonomy could be correlated with medical or physiological knowledge of our bodies' capacities, although no causal explanation of the linkage could be given. Both Kant and Reid were willing to say, for example, that vision begins in the eye, but neither was willing to characterize the events in the eye or brain as efficient causes of vision. Although Reid and Kant left open the possibility of a faculty psychology, neither of them argued for such a psychology. In fact, both Reid and Kant were careful to warn against reifying descriptions of phenomena into substances or forms. None the less, and perhaps because Reid and Kant had left little for psychologically minded inquirers to *do*, their followers did often move in the direction of reifying psychological phenomena into faculties.

Victor Cousin: exemplary traditional metaphysician

The career of Victor Cousin (1792–1867) illustrates many of the features of what I am labelling the traditional European metaphysics of the first part of the nineteenth century. A proponent of an increasingly modified 'Scottish common-sense philosophy', Cousin was influential across the entire continent, and in America as well, especially through his writings in the history of philosophy. Alternately stymied and helped by political events in post-Napoleonic France, Cousin ultimately became the Minister of Education under Thiers in 1840, exerting a direct and powerful influence on higher education in France for the next generation.

Cousin taught primarily at the École Normale, where he began his lecturing career in 1813. In 1815, the premier exponent of Scottish philosophy in France, Royer-Collard, chose Cousin as his substitute, a post he held until 1820. During this period, Cousin became interested in German idealism, especially the work of Schelling and Hegel, and he visited Hegel and others in the German-speaking countries. Thus was begun what Cousin called his 'eclecticism' – a philosophy which proposed to integrate the best of all previous philosophies. (It is an interesting and unsolved question why Cousin eagerly sought connections between Scottish philosophy and Hegel's ideas, whereas Dugald Stewart at the same time professed to be completely baffled by Hegel.)

Cousin attacked the French Lockeans, from Condillac down to the ideologues, in a way reminiscent of Reid's critique. Reid argued that the Lockean (really Cartesian, but Cousin downplayed this) 'way of ideas' led to materialism. That is, argued Cousin, the notion that mental states are 'ideas' which are the effects of physical causes (stimuli and the impressions they make on our bodies and brains) makes no sense except on the kind of materialist interpretation given to it by Diderot or, worse, d'Holbach.

Cousin promoted these ideas in his lectures on eighteenth-century philosophy, and also in a separate volume, *The Elements of Psychology*, an immensely popular chapter-by-chapter duel with Locke's *Essay*. Although Cousin here endorsed Reid's critique of Locke, he was unable to articulate a complete and coherent version of Reid's alternative to Lockean epistemology. In particular, Cousin's account of Reid's theory of perception as direct (not based on either ideas or sensations) was very muddled, in ways that prefigure William Hamilton's disastrous version of Scottish philosophy. Most importantly, Cousin (who was followed in this by Hamilton, Mansel and others) tied Reid's everyday concept of perception into an almost mystical concept of intuitions of realities. Responding to Locke's attack on enthusiasm (*Essay*, IV, xix) Cousin endorsed what he took the Scottish school to be saying as a 'spontaneous intuition of truth by reason, as independent as possible of the personality and of the senses, of induction and demonstration'. Thus the common sense of the Scottish enlightenment became the enthusiastic intuition of nineteenth-century orthodoxy. What for Reid had been tied into the senses, based on experience, and not on reason, Cousin twisted into a quasi-mystical access to truth, with an eye towards religious and moral orthodoxy. It was to be his greatest contribution.

The success of traditional metaphysics – what Kant and Reid saw as an impossible science – was really quite impressive. Fichte and many others in German-speaking countries developed post-Kantian taxonomies of powers of the soul, and began to speculate about the mechanics of the soul as well. In France Reid's influence on Royer-Collard and Kant's on Maine de Biran defeated Lockean psychology even before Napoleon had met his Waterloo. Dugald Stewart's influence in Scotland (and around the continent as well) at this time was immense. In *The Encyclopaedia Britannica* of the 1820s, in the curriculum of faraway Harvard College, and all around Europe, in Paris, Naples, Vienna and elsewhere something like this metaphysical or faculty psychology was at the centre of the philosophy curriculum. The concert of European ideas about the mind was every bit as broad and strong as the concert of reactionary powers that ruled the European nations rigidly from 1815 to 1830. After 1830 the unity of support for traditional metaphysics began to erode, under the influence of new philosophical positions, and especially with developments in physiological and experimental analyses of neural and mental phenomena. Nevertheless, thanks to Cousin's eclecticism, traditional metaphysics was still very much alive up to 1848. Although disagreeing about much else, the French-speaking, German-speaking and English-speaking proponents of traditional metaphysics increasingly endorsed psychological theories which made room for Cousin's intuitionism, a kind of sanctimonious transcendentalism which would have disturbed Kant and Reid. Nevertheless, this kind of intuitive psychology found a home in a broad array of writers: the right Hegelians, Cousin and his French followers, Whewell in England, Hamilton and his followers throughout Britain and the United States. Indeed, it is almost impossible to find a textbook of 'moral philosophy' or 'metaphysics' from this period that does not promulgate something akin to Cousin's intuitionism. James Mill's *Analysis* is a conspicuous and important exception to this rule, but it is probably not completely representative of the views of those who opposed traditional metaphysics, as I shall now explain.

Frankenstein's science: an alternative psychology

Try as they might, Metternich and his allies in reaction could not completely eradicate progressive thinking. Similarly, although the set curriculum of most academic institutions and texts followed a kind of popularized Reidian or Kantian psychology, there was at the same time a widespread, if non-academically-based, alternative psychology. To a great degree this oppositionist psychology was what might be dubbed a 'fluid materialist' position. This psychology had its roots in Franklin's two-fluid theory of electricity, and its branches in Mesmer's animal magnetism, Galvani's and Volta's exciting work on electric phenomena in animal tissues, and in Boscovich's reconceptualization of physical force. Increasingly, some thinkers were led to speculate that an understanding of electricity – or perhaps some other, subtler, fluid within the nerves – would unlock the secrets of life and mind.

Priestley was perhaps the earliest proponent of this materialist psychology – and was soundly attacked first by Kant and then by a mob organized by the British authorities to drive him out of the country. Above all it was Priestley who placed associationism (derived from Hartley) at the centre of materialist psychology, launching a tradition of psychologists and physiologists looking for associations among neural processes and pathways. Priestley however shied away from serious neurophysiological analysis of the mind (and called Hartley's attempt at such an analysis a failure). Thus it was Erasmus Darwin's *Zoonomia* (many editions and translations from 1792 to 1812) that properly launched a fluid materialist psychology. This text, which appears to have been widely influential across Europe, treated sensory impressions as the fluidic activity of nerves when impressed by stimuli, and went on to develop an elaborate associationist mechanism for psychological processes. In addition, Darwin here and elsewhere speculated about the possibility that electricity is the key to understanding not only neural processes but even life itself. For example, he reported on the experiments of Aldini (Galvani's nephew) in which dead flesh is 'reanimated' by the use of electricity.

A glimpse of the ideas involved in this oppositionist psychology is afforded by Mary Shelley's novel *Frankenstein*. First published in 1818, this novel emerged from Shelley's attempts to think through the implications of Darwin's psychology. Victor Frankenstein is a scientist in the mould of the elder Darwin: 'I was led to examine,' this character says, 'the cause and progress of th[e] decay [of living tissue]' and such studies helped him succeed 'in discovering the cause of generation and life'. But not only is life science capable of being studied causally, so is psychology. Mary Shelley follows Hartley and Darwin carefully in her description of how Frankenstein's android, abandoned by its creator, would develop psychologically. In the creature's original state, 'no distinct ideas occupied my mind; all was confused'. What confused the creature was a bewildering array of sensations. But some of the sensations were more pleasurable than others, and these captivated the creature's mind. The most powerful feelings were elicited by the creature's witnessing scenes of social intercourse among the family members upon whom it is spying: seeing the ageing father playing music for his daughter, the creature 'felt sensations of a peculiar and overpowering nature: they were a mixture of pain and pleasure, such as I had never before experienced'.

Shelley follows the materialist psychology of her day in seeing both language and morals as emerging from the association of weaker feelings with these powerfully strong sensations of social origin. 'I perceived,' says the android, 'that the words they spoke sometimes produced pleasure or pain, smiles or sadness, in the minds and countenances of the hearers. This was indeed a godlike science, and I ardently desired to become acquainted with it.' Such acquaintance is made by the creature's straining to associate names of familiar objects and people with their referents. Like her mentors, Hartley and Darwin, Mary Shelley did not try to explain how a creature limited in its experience to sensations could come to perceive the significance of such a thing as a pained countenance. She understood that even simple objects can have multiple names (such as the boy in the family being called alternately 'Felix, brother, or son') but was able to convince herself that the bewildering associations of sound and sense could nevertheless be worked out by a naive listener. But some associations are not so simple: the android discovers that it can hear the sounds of some words, even though it does not grasp their reference, words 'such as good, dearest, unhappy'.

To understand such words, the materialist psychologists argued, required experience with people and their ways. Here is the beginning of the great nineteenth-century conflict between an experiential, or empiricist, psychology and a nativist one. The standard metaphysics asserted that knowledge of good and evil, right and wrong was not based on experience, and certainly not based on the sensations of pain and pleasure; on the contrary, writers like Fichte, de Biran and Stewart held that we each have a kind of direct intuitive apprehension of right and wrong. Reid had warned that the Hutchesonian concept of 'moral sense' was incoherent – that an apprehension of good and evil could never be obtained by mere sensation. Reid's own response to this was to argue that morals were empirical (he spoke of moral judgements and moral perceptions, based on experience and intuitive – God-given – standards of conduct). Although this view influenced American thinkers, especially Thomas Jefferson, it appears to have been abandoned in nineteenth-century Europe even by followers of the 'Scottish school'. In its place was substituted the traditional metaphysicians' assertion of an innate, intuitive, apprehension of right and wrong.

The metaphysical mainstream shied away from Reid's empirical ethics for reasons well understood by the materialists, and well illustrated in the narrative of *Frankenstein*. If moral evaluation derives from experience, then certain repeated patterns of association might generate moral monsters: people who get pleasure from and justify acts which the rest of us judge to be evil. At first, when his experience derives primarily from reading history, the android 'felt the greatest ardour for virtue arising within me, and abhorrence for vice' but these terms, as the android explains, should be understood only as 'relative ... to pleasure and pain alone'. Hence, when it emerges that human beings cannot stand even to look at him, and that even his creator finds him horrific, the android develops an inverted morals: what destroys humans will destroy all his greatest pains, and is therefore the greatest good.

Contemporary critics detested this point of Shelley's book, and attacked her for promulgating a false morals, or an amoral position. 'Our taste and our judgment alike revolt at this kind of writing' said the *Quarterly Review*, 'and the greater the ability with which it may be executed the worse it is – it inculcates no lesson of conduct, manners or morality.' A psychology that treated humans as natural objects, that did not assume that humans were creatures with a transcendent soul – as did the traditional metaphysics – would end up offering a scenario of mental and moral development that looked frighteningly like the one in Shelley's novel. To make psychology into a science could threaten the moral fibre of society.

The suppression of psychology as a natural science

In evaluating the conflict between traditional metaphysics and the materialist psychological tradition, the modern reader should keep in mind that this battle often went well beyond the realm of ideas. Especially after the defeat of Napoleon, State and religious authorities (often the same people, and almost always the same bureaucracies) exerted enormous efforts to prevent dissemination of ideas like those of Erasmus Darwin and Mary Shelley. Censorship, the use of informers and highly active secret police forces were the norm in all European countries from 1815 to 1830. The authorities were on the lookout for fluidic psychology, in order to crush what they saw as 'pantheism', 'atheism' and 'materialism' – all assumed to be enemies of the status quo. A number of historians have argued that it was the emerging sciences of phrenology and mesmerism that were specifically under attack. I would argue that proponents of these ideas were attacked only in so far as they were seen as overlapping with the fluidic materialists. Once the second generation of Mesmerists gave up Mesmer's claims concerning the physical force supposedly at the root of mesmeric phenomena, once the second generation of phrenologists adopted a moderate nativism (especially in Calvinist Scotland), they were widely accepted.

In contrast to mesmerists or phrenologists, those who propounded the idea of studying life and mind within the framework of natural science were zealously prosecuted, even in the most 'liberal' of European states at this time, Great Britain. One of the most important cases of such repression is that of William Lawrence (1783–1867), a distinguished but radical surgeon (soon to be an editor of the insurgent medical periodical *The Lancet*, and later Surgeon to Queen Victoria). Lawrence was a follower of Bichat who believed that research on electricity and other physical forces would ultimately reveal the connection between neural structure and mental function, giving us a kind of natural science of the soul. Doctors should rejoice in this, Lawrence believed, because it means that insanity is not a disease of the soul (only treatable, if at all, by moral suasion) but a physiological disorder, perhaps curable by medicine. In 1819 Lawrence prepared to publish a work explaining these ideas, his *Lectures on Physiology, Zoology, and the Natural History of Man*. After a brief period of publication, there was an orchestrated campaign against this book for blasphemy. Leading figures in the medical establishment asked the Royal College of Surgeons to force Lawrence to expunge the blasphemies and to desist from lecturing. Lawrence withdrew the book and lost his lectureship.

One of William Lawrence's patients, the husband of the author of Frankenstein, had even worse problems with State suppression of his philosophical and psychological ideas. In 1813 Percy Shelley had 250 copies printed of the first of his great dramatic poems, *Queen Mab*. Directly influenced by Erasmus Darwin's poetry as well as his theories, this poem included extensive prose notes, amounting to a series of essays on such forbidden topics as republicanism, atheism and materialist psychology. Shelley was explicit in his psychology in these essays, where Mary in her novel could only be implicit. He argued explicitly for treating humans as part of nature, and for seeing psychology, morals and politics, as sciences seeking causal laws: 'Were the doctrine of necessity false, the human mind would no longer be a legitimate object of science; from like causes it would be vain that we should expect like effects', but this is never true. A true psychology would see motives as nothing more than complex causes, and lawful patterns of cause and effect would then be discerned. Where we seem to see action without causes, he said, 'these are the effects of causes with which we are unacquainted.' This psychology would 'introduce a great change into established notions of morality ... there is neither good nor evil in the universe, otherwise than as the events to which we apply these epithets have relation to our own mode of being'.

Shelley was always acute at seeing the implications of his philosophical ideas. One implication he took pleasure in emphasizing was that this new moral psychology would desanctify marriage, and legitimate divorce – an implication chosen to annoy his orthodox readers. Marriages, far from being made in heaven, are natural relationships, 'the worthiness [of which should be] estimated by the quantity of pleasurable sensation it is calculated to produce.... the connection of the sexes is so long sacred [only] as it contributes to the comfort of the parties, and is naturally dissolved when its evils are greater than its benefits'. Much of Shelley's more serious discussions of the implications of his psychology revolved around his vegetarianism, expounded at great length in the notes to the poem. Like Feuerbach and then the German materialists of forty years later, Shelley argued that the intake of food was a key ingredient in a person's constitution, and that proper diet was a basis not only for good physical and mental health but for the formation of progressive characters, capable of educating and reforming the world. Historians of philosophy have often noted, usually with scorn, Feuerbach's extreme materialist phase, with his claim that 'man ist was man isst' (people are what they eat) – but historians would be better advised to try to explain the widespread appeal of this doctrine throughout the middle of the nineteenth century than to make fun of it.

Shelley was attacked for both seditious and blasphemous libel, and his book banned. This was one of a series of events, which included the use of government spies to follow him and his friends and to read his correspondence, that ultimately led to Shelley's self-imposed exile from what he saw as a ruthless and tyrannical government. Shelley tried in various ways to have the ideas in this book, or even parts of the book, published and/or reviewed with varying success. Finally, again, several pirated editions began appearing, including one from Richard Carlile, an important 'working-class' publisher and fighter for a free press. Bans and trials continued to be stimulated by this book, but the text was out of the bag. *Queen Mab* quickly became known as 'the Chartist's Bible'. Many a cobbler and cordwainer cut their philosophical teeth on Shelley's ideas, and his quotations from d'Holbach, Voltaire, Drummond, E. Darwin and Spinoza.

The battle between traditional metaphysics and psychology as a natural science was thus not an even one. The former had access to publication, pulpit and professorships; the latter risked prosecution, imprisonment, loss of positions and banishment. The rapid success and proliferation of materialist ideas across Europe in the wake of 1848 suggests that ideas like the first Darwin's and Shelley's were much more widely known and discussed than the printed records – especially the printed records of philosophical works which tended to be academically and ecclesiastically respectable publications – might suggest. Historians of philosophy need to know much more about what radical surgeons and poets were thinking and saying. It will not be easy to find out what these heterodox thinkers were saying because of the widespread use of police spies and informers, which inhibited people even in private correspondence, much less in publication. It is imperative that historians recognize that the decades following Waterloo imposed the tightest censorship ever seen across most of the European continent.

Here is one example of the mischief this severe censorship has caused to historians of ideas. It is widely believed that Spinozist ideas – especially those relating to pantheism and to psychophysical isomorphism – arose from theological discussions sparked by such 'left Hegelians' as Feuerbach and Strauss in the 1830s and 1840s. Supposedly the first 'serious' writing on Spinoza in nineteenth century England was G. H. Lewes's in the early 1840s, followed by the unpublished translation of *The Ethics* by Marian Evans (later 'George Eliot' and Lewes's spouse). But Lewes acknowledged hearing of Spinoza from discussions with Leigh Hunt in the 1830s. Leigh Hunt was one of Shelley's key literary contacts, and probably knew of Shelley's translation of Spinoza's *Tractatus*. Perhaps Spinoza's ideas, interpreted through the lens of a materialist psychology, influenced philosophical opinion in London well before reaching the 'broad reading public' or the conservatives in Oxford and Cambridge. (A similar story could be told of the dissemination of Spinoza's ideas in France in part via the writings of the radical poet Heinrich Heine.)

The iron grip of the concert of Europe began to be loosened in the 1830s. As we shall see in the next section, there was a corresponding increase in objections to traditional metaphysics in the years between 1830 and 1848. It is possible that some of these ideas were previously censored ones finally seeing the light of day, and it is also possible that some of these ideas were genuinely novel. Without extensive and careful research that includes examination of unpublished documents, and information about non-academic circles (such as working-class reading groups which were common in all the major British cities, and even in some continental cities as well, from 1820 on), it will be difficult to determine the path taken by novel ideas at this time.

✷ THE BREAKDOWN OF THE CONCERT ✷ OF EUROPEAN IDEAS

Emergent naturalism

Despite its widespread popularity, and despite the very real boost it received from the authorities, secular and sacred, traditional metaphysics was a relatively unstable theory for psychology. It is one thing to state that the analysis of the soul goes beyond the boundaries of the natural world, for the soul is a transcendental entity – but it is another thing to produce various analyses of psychological states, all the while protesting that certain modes of explanation do not apply. For example, Reid's denial that sensory impressions can or should be treated as the causes and sensory states as the effects of a single process simply had to strike any independent-minded physiologist as wrongheaded.

The rise of associationist psychological theories after 1820 should be seen in the context of attempts to naturalize aspects of traditional metaphysics. In particular, the associationists were dissatisfied with what they saw as overly general statements about 'laws' and 'dispositions' of the human mind. They wanted these replaced by what we would now call psychological mechanisms. This conflict is well illustrated in the different estimations of the state of psychology offered by Dugald Stewart and his erstwhile student, James Mill. Stewart's

Dissertation exhibiting a general view of the Progress of Metaphysical, Ethical, and Political Philosophy since the revival of letters in Europe (which was prefaced to the fourth edition of the *Encyclopaedia Britannica* in 1819) offered a strong defence of traditional metaphysics. For example, in writing about John Gregory's essay of advice to physicians, Stewart explained that Gregory correctly emphasizes 'the laws of the union of the mind and the body and the mutual influence they have upon one another'. Stewart went on to caution, however, that

> it is only the *laws* which regulate the union between mind and body ... which are here pointed out as proper objects of philosophical curiosity; for as to any *hypothesis* concerning the *manner* in which the union is carried on, this most sagacious writer was well aware, that they are not more unfavorable to the improvement of logic and of ethics, than to a skilful and judicious exercise of the healing art. (425)

Making a sense

One of the specific ways in which traditional metaphysics responded to the Kantian and Reidian arguments against scientific psychology was to invent a new sense. What Kant termed the 'scandal of philosophy' – and it is important to remember that by 'philosophy' he meant something closer to what we mean by 'science' than modern philosophy – was the inability to prove the existence of the external world. Reid was content to avoid proof in this matter, and merely to assert the plausibility of the existence of objects as an assumption on which science should be based. Here Kant went well beyond Reid and investigated how such a proof might be developed, ultimately offering his transcendental arguments to make such a proof. The empirical world of causal interactions, of space and time, Kant asserted, could be proved to exist only if one assumed that the human soul *qua* transcendental creature participated in the construction of these phenomena. Thus Kant was what he chose to call a transcendental idealist but an empirical realist. The phenomenal world could be proved to be real, but only by hypothesizing a transcendentally active mind.

Naturally Kant's conclusions were resisted by many thinkers (whether his arguments were understood by these thinkers is a separate question). Just as Kant chose to make causality, space and time the central test issues of his work, so did the traditional metaphysicians who resisted Kant's transcendental idealism. In the first three decades of the nineteenth century several non-transcendental schematisms were offered to explain how knowledge of causality and space and time might be veridical. One group of arguments revolved around refining and extending the previously inchoate notion of a 'movement' or 'muscle sense'. A second group of arguments revolved around a novel idea of a 'sense of effort' or some sort of direct intuition of personal activity. Maine de Biran and Schopenhauer are the most important thinkers of the second group (some might put Fichte in this group as well). Destutt de Tracy and some of his followers in France, along with Thomas Brown, James Mill and their followers in Britain, make up the important members of the first group. (And there is some reason to suspect that Brown was heavily influenced by de Tracy.) It was the promoters of this new sense who did the most to set the stage for mid-nineteenth-century associationism.

What both these groups of thinkers held in common was the notion that non-transcendental forms of mental activity could be invoked to prove that our knowledge of the external world is reasonably veridical. The crudest form of their idea is the doctrine of 'resistance': that children learn the difference between themselves and the world by coming up against things that resist their actions as they move around. (Berkeley actually anticipated this part of the argument in several passages of his *Three Dialogues*.) Whether this resistance is detected through sense inputs deriving from muscular activity or from something preventing the proper carrying out of an action as willed, the cognitive result might be the same: knowledge of something that is external to, and undetermined by, myself.

Where the two groups of theorists diverge most sharply is on the nature of causation. The second group of theorists offers a kind of output-based theory, by emphasis in the mental output causing action. In contrast to the input-based theorists of muscle sense, these output theorists typically suggested that the human mind has a kind of direct, intuitive knowledge of its own causal power. Both Maine de Biran and Schopenhauer make this supposed intuition central to their metaphysics, arguing that it is through knowledge of our causal powers that we know ourselves as Kantian noumena, not merely as phenomena. Neither a transcendental schematism nor empirical associations need be invoked, these theorists claimed, to explain how we know this one species of causality, because it is known via a special kind of direct access.

This very dichotomy between input- and output-based theorizing raised the question as to what, exactly, is a sense? Could one call the direct intuition of personal causal powers a sense? Even Locke had decided to call such mental facts 'reflection' as opposed to sense experience. In reflection there is no sense organ, aside from the cerebrum, and perhaps not even the brain is necessary for a person to detect his or her own mental activity, or so de Biran seems to have argued on occasion, unlike Schopenhauer. The idea of a muscle or a movement sense also raised a host of questions about what should count as a sense. If there is a separate sense based on our capacity to detect changes of tension in muscles, then how does one distinguish this sense from touch? E. H. Weber, in his seminal experiments on somesthesis in the early 1830s, argued that the only proper way to draw the distinction was to study touch in a completely passive hand or body part. But as early as the 1810s physiologists like Steinbuch in Germany, Bichat in France and Charles Bell in Scotland were exploring the possibility that muscles themselves, as well as skin, were sensitive organs.

In contrast to Weber, Charles Bell in his Bridgewater treatise on *The Hand* emphasized the co-ordination between movement and perception (as, later, did Weber's student, Lotze). It is striking that Bell's early concept of a nervous circle and complex co-ordination between activity and perception was among his least influential ideas. For nearly a century after Bell and Weber, research on touch meant research on the sensitivity of immobilized skin (in which the normal exploratory processes of touch are eliminated), and research on action meant studies of reflex functioning (in which the normal sensory adjustments of bodily parts are eliminated). The contrast between the widely accepted conception of the senses as passive channels of impressions and the natural activity of animals and people is still a fundamental tension in psychological theory.

While the output theorists offered a strong challenge to Kant's claim that noumena are unknowable, the input theorists' challenge was to Kant's doctrine of perception as resting on a transcendental schematism. In particular, associationist psychologists tried to develop intricate models of how sensitivity to muscular motion might provide them with the 'missing information' – just what they needed to explain how external objects are perceived in space and time. The model for how to do this was supplied by a Scottish traditional metaphysician who broke explicitly from Reid, and exerted enormous influence on the Mills and later associationists, Thomas Brown.

Thomas Brown (1778–1820) was the successor to Dugald Stewart in the Chair of Moral Philosophy in Edinburgh. He made his name as a young scholar by defending Hume's theory of causation when Hume was still a bogeyman in Scotland, and by attacking Erasmus Darwin's materialist psychology, and, a little later, phrenology. Brown's lectures on *The Philosophy of the Human Mind* (1820) were exactly that, his lecture notes, published posthumously and widely disseminated in Great Britain, France and the United States. (Brown preferred to spend his energies in the composition of bad poetry.) Although typically categorized as a follower of Reid, Brown was not, and explicitly acknowledged his deviations from Reid's philosophical positions. Brown did not think, as did Reid, that what we perceive are the external objects themselves.

> It is evident, that ... the real object of sense is not the distant object, but that which acts immediately upon the organs, – the light itself, not the sun which beams it on us. ... The reference to the distant sun ... is the effect of another principle of our intellectual nature [than perception], – the principle of association, or suggestion ... without which, indeed, our mere transient sensations would be comparatively of little value.
>
> (1.242)

For Reid the object of sense is always the distant object, and our sensations are different things entirely than our perceptions, so no amount of suggestion or association could turn them into perceptions.

One implication of Brown's sensationalism is that the young child will have to learn to distinguish self from non-self based only on sensations. A Reidian might acknowledge that learning is involved here, but the learning would be based on the Reidian assumption that even babies perceive external objects. It was Brown, above all others, who bequeathed to nineteenth century-century psychology one of its central problems: how can an infant come to perceive objects as external from and independent of itself, and how can it do so on the basis merely of sensations? 'There will be, in the first momentary state,' Brown explains, 'no separation of self and the sensation, – no little proposition formed in the mind, I feel, or I am conscious of a feeling; but the feeling and the sentient I, will, for the moment, be the same.' As Brown understood, once one accepts sensationalism, it is clear that in a childhood state 'we know as little of our bodily frame, as of th[e] material universe.' Luckily 'our muscular frame, is not merely a part of the living machinery of motion, but is also truly an organ of sense. When I move my arm, without resistance, I am conscious of a certain feeling; when the motion is impeded, by the presence of an external body, I am conscious of a different feeling' which arises only in part from touch. The other component of this difference in feeling is muscular, and it is from this that we get sensations of solidity – without muscle sense, touch would be nothing more than painful or pleasant feelings.

Having abandoned Reidian perception of real objects for sensationalism, Brown added this important new sensation: the feeling of solidity. It is from this, through intricate patterns of association, that he and his many associationist descendants chose to explain the origin of our perception of the external world. But in addition to a new sensation, Brown also brought in a new faculty, memory. To explain how feelings of solidity begin to be associated into perceptions of externality, Brown appealed to the infants' knowledge of a succession – 'a feeling which necessarily, involves the notion of divisibility or series of parts, that is so essential a constituent of our more complex notion of matter [which notion is] that which has parts, and that which resists our efforts to grasp it'. Brown then elaborated this idea by imagining what sensations would be available to a baby feeling any object. There would be simultaneous feelings if more than one finger or body part touched the object. There would also be successive feelings as the hands moved over objects. And the pleasant or unpleasant feelings of touch would be correlated with different feelings of solidity, again both successively and simultaneously. Out of this successive series of feelings of hardness, Brown carefully constructed the idea of length, and from this he then constructed the idea of space. The infant, at first feeling its own fingers as they move, will come to associate the sensation of contact between fingertip and, say, palm, with a sequence of muscular feelings (this example comes from Hartley). This will be perceived, Brown claimed, as a certain distance. The next finger movement and contact, or the next hand movement and contact with a body part will be a different distance, and so on. Variants of this model of the perception of the external world are found in numerous thinkers over the next century. Brown's was a crude theory, with many obvious difficulties. For example, if succession – time – can be detected at birth, why not space? Or, another example, how can babies decide that the feelings of solidity underneath their bottoms come from objects different from those in their fingers or hands, since the former are always co-present with the latter? Despite its crudeness, Brown's associationist empiricism had enormous popularity and influence – indeed, variants of this theory are still taught today.

Motor theories of mind

In addition to his important role in bringing associationism, sensationism and empiricism together, Brown also adumbrated a theory of perception that was widely influential, even among non-empiricists. Although he did not use this term (it is a twentieth-century neologism), Brown's 'motor theory of perception' was the basis for much later thinking about spatial perception and cognition. Reid had argued that perception (of external objects) was a fundamentally different psychological process from sensation (awareness of states of feeling). Following Brown, most nineteenth-century thinkers made a very different use of Reid's distinction between sensation and perception: sensations were to be turned into perceptions, via processes of association, memory and, later, judgement. Indeed, Brown asserted that 'Perception ... is only another name ... for the result of certain associations and inferences that flow from more general principles of the mind.' Brown essentially wanted to eliminate 'perception' as referring to either a special class of mental states or a specifiable psychological process, beyond that of association among sensations, a position that John Stuart Mill was to adopt without acknowledgement.

Brown is very explicit about his rejection of Reid's distinction, and his belief that sensations of muscular movement are the basis of all our knowledge of the external world.

> [I]n that state of acquired knowledge, long after the first
> elementary feelings in infancy, in which modified state alone,
> the phenomena of the mind can become to us objects of reflective
> analysis, certain feelings are referred by us to an external
> material cause. The feelings themselves, as primarily excited, are
> termed sensations, and when followed by the reference to an
> external cause, receive the name perceptions, which marks
> nothing more in addition to the primary sensations than this
> very reference. But what is the reference itself, in consequence
> of which the new name is given? It is the suggestion of some
> extended resisting object, the presence of which had before been
> found to be attended with that particular sensation, which is
> now again referred to it. (353)

Brown goes on to make it clear that this 'suggestion' involves the association of any sensation (visual, tactile, auditory, etc.) with a muscular sensation – the feeling of resistance to our action – so that perception as such (knowledge of external objects) would be impossible without the muscular sense. 'In all but one class of our sensations, then, it is evident that what Dr Reid calls perception, as the operation of a peculiar mental faculty, is nothing more than a suggestion of memory or association.' Furthermore, Brown argues that even feelings of resistance are not so much perceptions in Reid's sense as a kind of 'intuitive belief' in the externality of the causes of our feelings of muscular motion.

James Mill codified, organized, and extended Brown's theory. (In explaining Brown's ideas I have doubtless given the impression that Brown's theory was clear and organized, but in fact it is buried amidst hundreds of pages of rather turgid prose.) Mill enunciated what he considered to be several principles of association, and importantly introduced the concept of a *fused* sensation. By this he meant an association of two or more sensations that, through repetition and/or intensity, comes to be felt as a single sensation. This concept of a fused sensation he applied to many cases of our perception of external objects, arguing that our apparently visual awareness of external things, for example, is based upon a fusion of visual with muscular and tactile sensations.

What is most striking about these muscular sensations is that we never seem to be conscious of them. Unlike smells and sights, we never appear to have the kind of feelings hypothesized by Brown and the elder Mill. James Mill suggests that feelings of rest, discomfort and stretching might be instances of muscle sensations, but he is aware that 'there are some muscles of the body in constant and vehement action, as the heart, of the feelings attendant upon the action of which we seem to have no cognisance at all'. Still, 'this is no argument' against their existence, and the lack of consciousness can be explained by habitual inattention. As late as 1869, when he was editing his father's book for republication, Stuart Mill spoke of this as 'the paradox . . . of . . . feelings which are not felt'. And, indeed, Stuart Mill realized this important inconsistency within associationist sensationalism. Supposedly all our knowledge derives from sensations, and supposedly sensations are the simplest modes of feeling, and supposedly feelings are simple mental (conscious) states. But associationist accounts of how sensations become perceptions all require that many of our sensations go unnoticed. This applies to vision and other sense modalities as well as to muscular sense; for example, we are rarely conscious (if ever) of the changing hues of visible objects as we change position with respect to them and the light source, although these sensations are supposedly the basis of our seeing the colour of the objects in the first place.

Alexander Bain (1818–1903) is typically treated as an associationist follower of the Mills, who developed a more empirically based account of perception and volition. However, Bain in fact modified Brown's and the Mills' theory into something much closer to a modern motor theory of perception. Recognizing some of the problems of the sensory associationism found in Brown and James Mill, Bain emphasized not so much muscle sense as motor activity. Bain focused his thinking on the spontaneous activity of animals and infants, not on their receptivity to impressions, muscular and otherwise. He was perhaps the first scientist after Whytt to emphasize the importance of overall muscle tone and the permanent closure of sphincter muscles as evidence of a psychologically important fact.

Bain's is thus the first true motor theory of perception, emphasizing that perception itself is dependent upon prior motor activities. It is only as a consequence of our activity that muscular feelings arise, and it is only because of these muscular feelings that we perceive external objects. To use another anachronistic term, muscular sensations are, for Bain, 'response-produced sensations'. In addition to Brown's notion that muscle sense gave us information about resistance, Bain claimed two more kinds of information for muscular feelings: feelings of effort (as in effort of attention), and feelings of the rate of muscular contraction (a kind of effort of bodily attention). From his motor theory of perception, Bain derived his conception of what a belief is. A belief is not only a mental state for Bain but also a state of preparedness to act. In fact, what a belief is is that upon which one is prepared to act.

Another important motor theorist of the mind was William Carpenter (1813–85). A distinguished comparative anatomist and student of the 'Philosophical Anatomist' Robert Grant, Carpenter was turned down for the Chair of Medicine at Edinburgh in 1842 for his Unitarian beliefs. In 1844 he was so widely suspected of having penned *The Vestiges of Creation* – an infamous evolutionist tract – that he had to issue a denial. (Later he befriended the true author of that work, Robert Chambers, the Scots polymath.) Carpenter explicitly saw his work in neuropsychology as modernizing and improving upon Gall's conception of brain and mental science. Like most serious phrenologists, Carpenter was a strong moral crusader (Carpenter was especially associated with the crusade against drinking alcohol) but, unlike the phrenologists, Carpenter followed Hartley (the Unitarian hero) and not the Scots philosophers (the Presbyterian heroes).

Whereas earlier writers (like Erasmus Darwin and James Mill) had emphasized the need to bring Hartley's associationism up to date, Carpenter attempted to bring Hartley's approach to volition and to moral judgement into mid-nineteenth-century science. His most important writing on the mind is his *Mental Physiology* (1874), which grew out of a large section on the topic in his earlier (and very influential) *Human Physiology*, which went through a number of editions in the 1840s and 1850s. In many ways, Carpenter was a transitional figure. Carpenter even called his work 'physiological metaphysics' on occasion, and his emphasis on 'character' and its formation as central to psychology echoes the writings of Gall, Spurzheim and Combe as well as the ideas of Hartley.

Whereas Bain used the motor theory of mind epistemologically, Carpenter tended to use it ontologically. He regarded 'all the physical forces of the universe as the direct manifestation of the Mental force of the Deity'. Just as Lotze made an analogy between God's creation of the cosmos and our soul's ordering of the mental 'microcosmos', so Carpenter found the idea that our notion of power derives from something like Bain's motor sense an interesting parallel to his speculations on the 'correlation of natural forces'. 'It is to me very interesting to find the two lines of argument – the one starting from the correlation of the Physical, Vital, and Mental forces ... the other from our own subjective consciousness' as running together.

In particular, Carpenter found one important parallel between the Deity and our souls in his concept of volition. Although God receives information from the entire universe, and must act (if she is truly omniscient) on the basis of all the relevant information, her acts are not constrained by this information. The same is true with our souls or wills, which receive all relevant information, but may act in independence of incoming impressions. Like Bain, Carpenter saw that any activity would produce new impressions, but, unlike Bain, Carpenter distinguished between impressions that simply activated nerve channels in the spine or brain in a reflex-like fashion and impressions that required conscious deliberation prior to action. These latter were cases of free action, Carpenter insisted. Despite this emphasis on free action, he also noted that a great deal of habitual action did not require such deliberation, and could be handled 'automatically' (Hartley's 'secondary involuntary acts'). Just as God designed the universe to act on its own most of the time, so our minds are capable of allowing our bodies to act automatically in many instances, on the basis of what Carpenter dubbed 'unconscious cerebration'. This concept of 'unconscious cerebration' requires there to be reflex-like mechanisms that are both cerebral and unconscious which Carpenter called 'cerebral reflexes'.

Carpenter's application of this concept of cerebral reflex (a concept he credited to Thomas Laycock) was unusual and important: he used it to explain Braid's results with hypnosis, and other examples of what are now called 'dissociated states'. If hypnotists can distract a person's conscious attention, or cause them to relax that conscious attention, then hypnotists may be able to engage habitual cerebral reflexes that otherwise would not be activated. For example, a hypnotist might arrange for a person to believe that the solid tennis-ball-sized object in front of him or her was an apple, when in reality it was an onion. And, if their automatism were truly activated, the person might well bite into the 'apple' even though they would never do so when normally conscious. In other words, Carpenter distinguished two forms of 'ideo-motor action'. In the first, one's idea is conscious and freely deliberated, which is ordinary voluntary behaviour; in the second, the idea arrives from some source other than deliberation, nevertheless setting off the 'cerebral reflexes' so that an action follows. Carpenter suggested that this second kind of ideo-motor activity might be invoked to explain many of the 'spiritualist' phenomena then in vogue, such as messages on Ouija boards. Thus Brown's 'suggestion' was transmogrified into Carpenter's concept of 'suggestibility': that some people are especially susceptible to this second kind of ideo-motor action, and that they themselves can act out an unconscious idea, or be made to act out such an idea by a properly trained hypnotist. This theory of suggestibility was to have a great impact on the classical era of psychoanalysis, through Charcot and Binet to Breuer and Freud.

❧ THE BRIEF LIFE OF NATURAL ❧ METAPHYSICS

The traditional metaphysics which reigned throughout the Western world between 1815 and 1830 did not give way all of a sudden to one or even a few different theories. Instead, thinkers chipped away at a number of exposed places on the edifice of the traditional theory. If those who invoked a new sense – whether muscular-based or inner-vation-based – were right, then many of the traditional claims about the possibility of proving the validity of our knowledge of the external world could be shown to be wrong, based as they were on an inade-quate inventory of our sensory experience. Similarly, many of the traditionalists' critiques of associationism could be shown to miss the mark, if associations could include associations to sensations of muscular effort. These various assaults on traditional metaphysics chal-lenged its epistemological and/or psychological assumptions.

Alternatively, some thinkers challenged the traditional views on ontological grounds. This was decidedly riskier, because the challenger could always be accused of materialism or atheism. As a matter of fact, several of these challengers were so attacked, and many of them were also criticized for being 'Spinozists' (a term that still connoted material-ist atheism to the orthodox, and usually warranted the attentions of the secret police). Nevertheless, it was clear to many that the traditional view was highly susceptible at just this point: once one has assembled sufficient facts to map out laws relating psychological and bodily states, it would seem appropriate to suggest hypotheses relating these two realms of phenomena, despite the ban on such suggestions from the orthodox.

To illustrate some of the more important ontological critiques of traditional metaphysics, I have chosen three of the more important early challengers. The first, Schopenhauer, is typically classified as a philosopher; the second, Johannes Müller, as a physiologist; and the third, Fechner, as a psychologist. Each of these thinkers, in his own way, challenged the traditional metaphysical consensus, and offered an alternative ontology in its place.

Arthur Schopenhauer (1788–1860) was the heir of a well-to-do merchant family of Danzig (Gdansk), and the son of a well known woman novelist with whom he was unable to get along. All his life he was an ardent Anglophile (he read the London *Times* daily) and was almost certainly better informed about English-language philosophical trends than any of his German contemporaries. Although aware of some of the British attempts to rectify Kant's epistemology 'by dint of muscle', Schopenhauer chose to improve upon Kant (perhaps the only modern philosopher for whom Schopenhauer showed real respect) in a completely different way.

Unlike Kant, Schopenhauer resolutely refused to supernaturalize noumena. He treated our consciousness of self as direct access to the real, noumenal self. What writers like Erasmus Darwin and Brown vaguely referred to as a sense of effort Schopenhauer saw not as a form of sensory experience but as a direct knowledge of our noumenal being. Although direct and personal, this knowledge is limited primarily to the fact that the noumenon exists. This self or noumenal existence Schopenhauer labelled 'will', although he acknowledged that it bears only a metaphorical resemblance to the phenomenal will as experienced in our activity. Indeed, in his major work, *The World as Will and Representation* (1819 and later editions) Schopenhauer was quite explicit that one cannot even be certain whether your will and mine are two things or one, or whether there is any more than one 'will' in the entire universe.

Although our direct experience of the will is limited, our experience of the phenomenal world which reflects will is not, and offers Schopenhauer many insights into the distribution and nature of will. In his *The Will in Nature* (1836) Schopenhauer noted that evidences of will can be seen in both the anatomy and the behaviour of plants and animals. He considered the emphasis of Linnaean botany on the sexual organs of flowers to be consistent with the idea that the noumenal will of beings like plants can manifest itself in specifically different anatomies. And Schopenhauer considered many forms of behaviour, especially aggressive and sexual behaviour, as phenomenal representations of a noumenal will. Instead of being attacked for his heterodox ideas, Schopenhauer was simply ignored for most of his life, despite the great vigour and clarity with which he wrote. It was only in 1852 that Fortlage devoted some space to Schopenhauer in his history of German philosophy, which led to a discussion of Schopenhauer in *The Westminster Review* of 1853. (At that time this periodical was edited by Marian Evans, not yet 'George Eliot', but already a close friend of both Spencer and Lewes.) From all accounts, this British publication of 1853 put Schopenhauer on the intellectual map, and his uniquely pessimistic ontology became as important in the 1850s and 1860s as Hegel's objective idealism had been in the preceding two decades.

Despite the suddenness and intensity of the new-found interest in Schopenhauer, his was a philosophy to be condemned by all but a very few. Not even the thoughtful reviewer of the *Westminster* could resist attacking Schopenhauer's beliefs. The same reviewer who understood and was willing to state that '[a]ccording to the consistent Kantis[t], physical theology, with its high priests Durham and Paley, is but an amiable absurdity, based on an illegitimate extension of the law of cause and effect to an object which lies beyond its jurisdiction' – was by no means willing to consider Schopenhauer's main ideas with equanimity. The review ends with a strong caveat: 'those who construe any of our remarks into an acceptance of such a system of ultra-pessimism have totally misapprehended our meaning'. Schopenhauer is labelled 'genial, eccentric, audacious, and, let us add, terrible' and 'We only wish we could see among the philosophers of modern Germany a writer of equal power, comprehensiveness, ingenuity, and erudition, ranged on a side more in harmony with our own feelings and conviction than that adopted by this misanthropic sage of Frankfort'. Many writers were to attempt to fit this request, most especially those associated with the rise of modern psychology, such as Helmholtz and Wundt.

Not all critics of traditional metaphysics were as outspoken as Schopenhauer. One of the most effective and influential critics of early nineteenth-century thought, Johannes Müller (1801–58) has long been seen as a conservative. This view of Müller is an inheritance from his students' time. Müller perhaps has had the oddest misfortune of any scientist: to be so eclipsed by his students (among them Helmholtz and Du Bois Reymond) that his views are rarely evaluated on their own.

Müller's physiology was a unique combination of the best of German *Naturphilosophie* with Müller's own interpretation of Spinoza. Although he explicitly renounced Spinoza's metaphysics, it is unclear whether he genuinely meant to distance himself from Spinoza or from the troubles associated with being a Spinozist. In any event, much of Müller's philosophy in his tremendously influential *Handbuch der Physiologie des Menschen* (*Elements of Human Physiology*) (1834–40) reflects a careful assimilation of specific doctrines of Spinoza's *Ethics* into nineteenth-century life science.

For psychology, Müller's most important contribution was his doctrine of specific nerve energies: that each sensory nerve produces its own unique sensory (subjective) quality. Müller considered this doctrine an updating of Spinoza's notion that our perceptual ideas are, literally, mental reflections of states of our bodies. It is only because our nerves are material, and set into motion by other material causes, that the specific ideas we get from them can constitute experience of the world:

> The immediate objects of the perception of our senses are merely
> particular states induced in the nerves and felt as sensations . . .
> but inasmuch as the nerves . . . are material bodies . . . they make
> known to the sensorium, by virtue of changes produced in
> them by external causes, not merely their own condition, but
> also properties and changes of condition of external bodies.
> The information thus obtained by the senses concerning external

nature, varies in each sense, having a relation to the qualities or energies of the nerve.

Müller, like Shelley (whom he never read) and Spinoza (whom both read), believed that every natural occurrence exists as an effect of a series of causes, and that one can 'work backwards' from effect to cause, given enough knowledge. Our nervous systems, Müller claimed, are built with such knowledge that when they feel their own states they also learn something of the external world. The former (internally oriented) aspect of feeling is sensation (in Reid's sense) and embodies Müller's specific energies hypothesis; the latter (externally oriented) aspect of feeling is perception, which Müller saw as based on the former.

Unlike Reid and Kant, Müller argued that it is possible to explain how perception emerges from sensation. Once we know what kinds of changes occur in each sensory nerve we can offer hypotheses as to how these changes can be interpreted as the effects of specific causes, and thus how knowledge of the changes constitutes knowledge of the causes. This is strikingly like the theory found in Schopenhauer's *Fourfold Root* (1817) and Descartes' *Optics* (1637) for that matter, although it is unclear whether Müller was directly influenced by those works.

Where Müller differed from both Schopenhauer and Descartes was in his insistence that the nervous system – and all animate matter – embodied a non-physical force, a vital principle. This vital principle, Müller believed, acted differently from ordinary physical matter, and could in fact cause ordinary physical matter to behave in ways inexplicable by the laws of physics or chemistry.

It is instructive to note that traditional metaphysics would have had a considerable basis on which to criticize Müller. Take, for example, his well known account of voluntary action: 'The primitive fibres of all the voluntary nerves being at their central extremity spread out in the brain to receive the influence of the will, we may compare them, as they lay side by side in the organ of the mind, to the keys of a pianoforte on which our thoughts play or strike'. Both Kant and Reid would have blanched at the calm with which Müller proposed to spatialize the mind, and to locate it within a particular region of space as well.

With Johannes Müller we have a scientist whose particular conceptual innovations – the specific nerve energies hypothesis and the motor keyboard – dominated later thinking long after his ontological views were in disrepute. This can be contrasted with Schopenhauer, whose own knowledge of botany and zoology is now obviously woefully out of date but whose metaphysical views keep resurfacing around different areas of modern science. Gustav Fechner (1801–87) offers a third prospect: someone whose main work is almost totally unknown, and who is nowadays revered for an innovation he himself considered a rather minor incident in a busy career.

Fechner, like Müller, offered a kind of Spinozist metaphysics. But, whereas Müller emphasized Spinoza's quasi-pantheism, Fechner emphasized Spinoza's views on substance, in particular his 'dual aspect' theory of mind and body. Fechner combined this dual aspect metaphysics with a kind of generalized atomism, in which he claimed to be able to show in particular how both electricity and mental force were constituted atomically. Fechner argued that the modern physical world view showed only one side of the universe, the mechanistic side, the interplay of the atoms according to laws of physical mechanism. But another side of the universe existed, the subjective, living side, the mental atoms. Fechner went so far as to speak of a 'day view' (which acknowledged life and mind) and a 'night view' (which did not).

Fechner had come to his atomistic views as a professor of physics in Leipzig. The atomism and invocation of hypothetical forces found throughout the works of such figures as Müller, Fechner and Lotze was very much of a piece with contemporary trends in the physical sciences. When the new generation of physical theorists emerged – with Helmholtz, Hertz and Du Bois Reymond at their head, much of what counted as 'scientific positivism' was aimed at eliminating these hypothetical atomistic and dynamic concepts, in psychology as well as in physics. Wundt and other early self-styled experimental psychologists did not abandon Fechner's dual aspect theory – on the contrary, they built upon it. However, the first generation of self-styled experimental psychologists wanted nothing to do with the *ontological* theories of their predecessors. The dynamical and atomistic theories of Hartley, Erasmus Darwin, Herbart, Fechner and Lotze were strongly opposed. Thus, two opposite trends began to emerge: psychological theorists began increasingly to postulate unconscious processes (see pp. 328–35 below) and yet these same theorists claimed to want a psychological science that clung close to phenomena, and criticized earlier psychologists for their unfounded ontological assertions.

In Fechner's case, his psychology was intimately tied to his ontological theorizing. Fechner's protracted experimentation on subjective after-images in vision damaged his eyes in 1839 and led to what appears to have been an hysterical illness, including some sort of psychosomatic blindness, which forced him to resign his position. In 1843 Fechner regained his ability to see while walking in his garden, and claimed to have seen the souls of the plants there, according to his book of that title (1848). Three years later he published his account of the differences between the day-view and night-view, and also his theory of life after death in his *Zend-Avesta*, the appendix to which inaugurated psychophysics as a sub-discipline of psychology.

Basing his speculation on Helmholtz's recent account of the conservation of forces, Fechner argued that both physical and mental forces must be conserved in the universe. In particular, if physical force was to be conserved, then there would have to be a lawful relation between psychological and physical states. This study of the quantitative relationship between stimulus energy and sensations Fechner derived by generalizing Weber's work and called 'outer psychophysics'. Of more interest to Fechner was 'inner psychophysics', which would be the study of the relation between mental events (sensation) and their neurophysiological correlates – but Fechner's claims to be able to analyse these relations were almost universally dismissed as mere speculation, in contrast to his psychophysical techniques which were both emulated and modified.

Fechner argued that physical laws were of linear form, whereas the psychophysical laws were not, but few nineteenth-century thinkers were wiling to accept non-linear relationships as 'simple' enough to be lawful. The difference between the souls of animals and plants is that the former have brain structures that allow more complex psychophysical interrelations. And not only are plants ensouled according to Fechner, but so is the earth – a sort of nineteenth-century 'Gaia' hypothesis. The earth responds to physical stimuli with the most intricate vibrations and adjustments conceivable, Fechner noted, although it lacks a brain and hence lacks some of the more complex psychophysical relationships. However, we who live upon the earth are part of it, and we contribute to its life and mind as if we were its sense organs, at least as long as we live. Moreover, when we die, our perceptions and memories do not die with us but find some echo in the myriad subtle adjustments of the earth to physical stimuli, and so there is a form of life after death. It is 'inner psychophysics' which explains these relationships among physical states (neural or earthly) and mental states – and it is Fechner's inner psychophysics which had no life after his death.

R. H. Lotze: last of the traditional metaphysicians?

Traditional metaphysics died out for two reasons. Firstly, it was institutionally ill-adapted for the increasingly professionalized and specialized academia that emerged all around Europe at first slowly after 1848, and then more rapidly after 1871. Secondly, as professionalization increased so did secularization, and appeals to either authority or intuition, which both tacitly and explicitly had guided the work of Cousin, Stewart and others, could no longer succeed. Ultimately, agnosticism replaced transcendentalism among professional elites, and traditional metaphysics was replaced by what was typically called scientific positivism. This scientific positivism in its purest forms always maintained that the true nature of either matter, the soul or the deity were unknowable. In this regard scientific positivism should be distinguished from Comtean positivism, and even from Spencerian positivism, as both of those thinkers imagined that they had more knowledge of the transcendental – of what Spencer chose inconsistently to call 'the unknowable' – than was allowed by the agnostics.

The success of scientific positivism in the latter part of the nineteenth century may be attributed to its allowing for extended scientific activity without provoking any direct conflict with religious doctrine. Thus it was an ideology well suited to developments in a Europe increasingly reliant upon scientific advances. However, scientific positivism was far better suited to maintaining rapprochement between physical science and religious orthodoxy than between biological or, especially, psychological science and mainstream religious beliefs. It is one thing for a Mach or a Hertz to deny that physics can understand what matter or forces are, beyond describing the laws of their phenomena; it is quite another for psychologists to limit their science to mapping mental phenomena, and to proscribe the search for how the brain is the mind.

The parallel with Darwin is here very striking. The scientific positivists (including Darwin's 'bulldog' Huxley) argued that Darwinian results spoke neither for nor against belief in God. They took this to be just another instance of their agnosticism. How can one know, they argued, that the causes and effects lumped into the term 'natural selection' do not have, as some sort of hidden or transcendent cause, a deity? Darwin repeatedly resisted this sort of argument, and for good reason. One of the key rationales for his theory was a critique of teleological biology, of the argument from design. In numerous ways Darwin showed that the hypothesis of design might be treated as a scientific hypothesis, and that many facts undermined it as a scientific hypothesis; facts that were better explained by Darwin's theory of natural selection. Perhaps the best known instance of this sort of discussion in Darwin is the conclusion to his *Variation of Animals and Plants Under Domestication*. Here Darwin was confronting the well developed design arguments of the noted botanist (and good friend of Darwin) Asa Gray. Gray proposed that even though evolution proceeded by natural selection, divine design might play a role through the biasing or channelling of genetic variation. Instead of chance, a deity might guide variation in certain directions, so as to pre-adapt animals and species to the rigours of new environments. Neither Darwin nor Gray argued that such an hypothesis was unacceptable because it touched on the actions of the unknowable deity. On the contrary, they examined the implications of this 'guided variation' hypothesis, and Darwin was able to show that none of the predictions which followed from this hypothesis were borne out.

Like Darwin, many psychologists of this era were inclined to try and specify how brain states caused mental states, or the reverse. For example, Johannes Müller unabashedly suggested that the soul plays on the motor cortex as if it were a piano keyboard. But does it? Darwin was able to show that God does not design animals as people design clocks. Could a psychologist show that the soul does not move the body the way people move objects? An attempt at doing just this was made by R. H. Lotze (1817–81), one of Müller's most cogent critics. Although Lotze criticizes Müller, he cannot bring himself completely to abandon teleological thinking in psychology, or even a deity acting in the world. In many ways Lotze is a transitional figure, illustrating a way out of traditional metaphysics that was never to be completed.

Lotze is transitional in a second sense. He was not a specialist, although he did become a professional academic. Trained originally in medicine, he studied with both founders of psychophysics, Weber and Fechner, at Leipzig (where they taught physics). Indeed, while he was teaching medicine and philosophy at Leipzig in the early 1840s he also acted as Fechner's physician. In 1844 Lotze was called to take Herbart's chair of philosophy at Göttingen, and in 1881 he was called to the prestigious Philosophy Chair in Berlin, but died soon thereafter. He made his name in the 1840s with physiological works attacking Müllerian vitalism, but then proceeded in the 1850s to attack the emerging materialism from a position strikingly at variance with that of the ultimately more succesful dual aspect theorists.

Lotze's attack on vitalism was very straightforward. The idea of special powers or forces could be used to prevent inquiry and to encourage sloppy thinking. Lotze here relied on Weber and Fechner's concept of a science (based on physics): science as the establishment of quantitative laws relating phenomena. There is no 'life force' but there are special and interesting phenomena of life, which must be analyzed and reduced to lawful arrangements.

Up to this point Lotze's arguments were not particularly unique, although he was among the earliest to make them against Müller and what he saw as Schellingian or Romantic biology. Where Lotze's own views set him apart is in the next stage of his thinking, summarized in his *Medizinische Psychologie* (*Medical Psychology*) of 1852. Lotze now argued that the mind/body problem was resolvable through his view of science. Both mind and matter could be treated as phenomena emanating from a single set of forces (not substances). Lotze pointed out that it is changes in forces acting upon us that make us believe in matter (resistance) and, he claimed, it is changes in a certain kind of force that make us believe in mental states as well. Later, in his *Metaphysic*, Lotze went so far as to claim that

> We might ... speak of the soul as a definite mass at every moment when it produces an effect measurable by the movement of a corporeal mass. And in doing so we should be taking none of its immateriality from it; for with bodies also it is not the case that they are first masses and then ... produce effects; but according to the degree of their effects they are called masses of a certain magnitude.
>
> (Book III, chapter 5)

While Lotze's theory of the soul as possessing equivocal mass did not catch on, one of the implications he drew from this theory did indeed catch on and continues to influence psychological theorizing. This was Lotze's theory of 'local signs.' From his theory of the soul, Lotze argued that the soul cannot be influenced by the spatial layout of the nervous system but only by its intensity of activity at any given point. Following Müller's early localizationism, Lotze argued that cerebral activity in different locations did, as Müller suggested, produce different mental states (for example, activity in one region of cortex generates visual sensations, in another region auditory sensations). But all the soul could know of this activity was its intensity, the locus of that intensity, and changes in intensity at that locus. The soul could not directly intuit layouts of varied intensity in the nervous system. Knowledge of the locus of activity was the 'local sign' of a mental state, which would co-exist with knowledge of the intensity of that state, and all changes in intensity of that state. Associationists like Steinbuch in Germany and Brown or James Mill in Scotland had made somewhat similar arguments, claiming that the soul's activation of muscles would provide it with information about bodily loci that would be correlated with sensory input, but Lotze's theory was not associationistic (except in the sense that it invoked an innate association) and focuses on central activity, not a response-produces-sensory-activity cycle. Lotze also emphasized that the mental processes involved here are unconscious, thus blocking introspective analyses of these ideas, and promoting his kind of speculative physiology.

Lotze's 'local signs' theory in various forms (some much more associationist and empiricist than his) has exerted considerable influence in sensory physiology ever since its enunciation. Interestingly, Lotze's other critique of Müller, also based on his theory of the soul, has been rather influential but much less well acknowledged. In his *magnum opus*, *Microcosmos*, Lotze took on the teleological view of the soul, although he did not completely eliminate it. He argued:

> We deceive ourselves, when with a favourite simile we compare the body to a ship – the soul to its steersman. For the latter knows, or at least may know, the construction of that which he directs ... Far from possessing this comparatively perfect insight into the working of the machine, the soul, on the contrary, is like a subordinate workman, who knows indeed how to turn one end of a winch ... but understands nothing whatever of the internal transference of movements by means of which a completed product is turned out.

Explicitly attacking Müller's analogy of the motor cortex to piano keyboard, Lotze added that the soul simply would not know what the notes were, nor where they were. The soul 'is ignorant of the relative situation of these notes, it knows not that this and not another note corresponds to the particular movement which it intends to make'. Astonishingly, this important argument remained essentially unheard for nearly a century, although it has recently been taken up in discussions of motor control.

Lotze followed this argument up by asking what sort of information the soul might have about movement, and in doing so he anticipated James's theory that the willing of movements derives from memories of movements. 'We bend our arm, not by giving a particular impetus to each of its several nerves, but by renewing in ourselves the image of the feeling which we experienced in a similar position'. Thus for Lotze the soul can act within itself, calling up a memory, or noticing a local sign, but it cannot act on the body. Instead, the soul's internal actions simply cause correlated bodily movements. There is an appeal here to something halfway between Leibniz's pre-established harmony and James's doctrine of ideo-motor action. Somehow the soul's own actions lead to appropriate bodily actions, and the way this happens is that an idea of action causes the bodily effects. The soul 'does not itself carry out the operation, but in a manner unknown to it the vital mechanism executes it commands'. Thanks to the doctrine of local signs the soul can also learn about the body's pattern of responses to stimuli: even when the body is acting on its own, the soul can keep apprised of changes of activity at different loci and register the feelings involved in particular actions.

Lotze thus stands as the source of two very different developments in psychological science. On the one hand, students of motor and sensory physiology began at this time their quest for locating pathways and correlations of local activity, without concern for the question as to what the soul was willing or perceiving in those activities. Studies of how localized stimulation of cortex generate specific movement patterns are good examples of trying to examine how the 'vital mechanism' translates mental cause into bodily effect. The *assumption* that the central activity is tantamount to a 'command' of the soul was, following Lotze, still made, even though there could now be no question of mental content in that command. What would be the mental content of an efferent pattern exciting contraction in a muscle unknown to the mover? On the other hand, students of ideo-motor behavior could analyse patterns of mental activity, asking questions about cause and effect among ideas (for example, what causes an *idée fixe* and/ or its accompanying obsessive behaviour?) without concern for the neurophysiological substrate of this activity. Lotze's influence among practising psychologists and neurophysiologists, although not acknowledged, seems to have been considerable.

❧ THE THREE UNCONSCIOUSNESSES AND ❧ HOW THEY GREW

From the study of mind to the analysis of the unconscious

The idea of unconscious mental processes, or even of *the* unconscious as some sort of an entity, was by no means original with Freud. On the contrary, many thinkers at the turn of the nineteenth century were pondering the nature of the unconscious. However, the unconscious of the 'romantics' – especially that of Schelling and *Naturphilosophie*, which so influenced German literature – was as much ontological as psychological. In a theory so inchoate as to defy easy description, many of these Romanticists equated the physical forces (fluids?) of electricity and magnetism with irrational urges and vague feelings, some of oneness with nature, others of a far less ethereal longing for oneness. Despite his loathing for Schelling and Fichte, it is clear that Schopenhauer's very carnal will emerged as a coherent ontological response to the irrationalism these writers were parading as a successor philosophy to the Kantian critique. (Probably Maine de Biran's metaphysics has a similar background.)

With philosophers, speculative physicists, Brunonian doctors, mesmerists and animal magnetizers claiming to have an analysis of the unconscious and its role in human life, is it any wonder that the Church-vetted professors of philosophy blanched at the idea of a scientific psychology? Traditional metaphysics's repeated emphasis on introspection as the sole safe method of proceeding in the philosophy of mind or moral philosophy was an attempt to create a boundary between what they saw as sober science and unsafe speculation. The use of physiological methodologies – which we now see as a harbinger of a true, progressive psychology – was equated with these worrisomely unsafe ideas about the irrational nature of the human soul.

Mainstream psychological theory 1815–30 was thus committed to the existence of an individual soul, from which all mental phenomena were to be derived. Evidence of the existence and nature of mental and moral phenomena was to be based on introspection. Nevertheless, even introspection raised some difficult questions about how wisely and well God had made our souls. The phenomena of sleep and drunkenness showed obvious ways in which the mind could be made to wander down dark pathways. And the claims of the mesmerists to produce a kind of 'magnetic sleep' were also worrisome: could physical agencies produce trance-like states? And, if *physical* agencies were uninvolved in mesmerism, then did that mean that some *psychological* force – ultimately to be called 'suggestion' – was operative?

At least three separate strands emerged at this time for the understanding of what we would now call unconscious mental states. In the first line of thought, the unconscious continued to be treated ontologically, and was associated with Kant's noumena. I call this the *supernatural unconscious*. On this theory, actions that people make without consciousness, or against their conscious ideas, are treated as being caused by forces that cannot be observed (are not phenomenal but noumenal). Others refused to treat the unconscious as qualitatively different from other natural mental phenomena. (Although some were willing to invent hypothetical natural forces as explanations, such as the Odilic force theory of the 1840s.)

There were two kinds of theories of what I shall call the *natural unconscious*. The first form of the natural unconscious theory focused on the concept of unconscious ideas or mental states: inferring from introspection that a particular mental state 'had to' have occurred even though introspection did not reveal the idea. The second form of this natural unconscious theory postulated the existence of a whole unconscious mind, separated off from the conscious one. The contrast is important. Herbart, for example, hypothesized unconscious ideas and to a large degree invented the modern concept of a threshold to explain when ideas 'came into consciousness'. But Herbart emphasized ideas only, he did not speculate on the existence of an entire unconscious mind, or part of the mind.

The third kind of theory of the unconscious was the most radically different from its predecessors. Whereas something like the notion of unconscious ideas can be found in Leibniz, and whereas Stahlians and others (like Whytt) had been willing to postulate parts of the soul not easily accessible to rational consciousness, all these prior theories of the unconscious had treated it as in opposition to the conscious soul. In particular, these theorists tended to treat the conscious soul as the rational soul of Christian dogmatics, and the unconscious as irrational, and certainly as incapable of rational thought. Indeed, where theorists had been inclined to see rational activity of an unconscious sort, they had unanimously attributed it to *God's mind*, not to the individuals. For example, Whytt had argued that the 'sensitive soul' in the spinal cord was capable of feeling noxious stimuli and acting in whatever way would remove the potential danger to the organism (he had in mind the capacity of a spinal frog to wipe away an acid-soaked tissue placed on its skin). But Whytt emphasized the great difference between this and the rational soul we know through consciousness, which can feel and think many different things. All Whytt's sensitive soul can do is whatever God has arranged for it to do to preserve our bodies and maintain a harmony among the parts of our organism. Prior to Whytt, Malebranche had argued that such phenomena are in fact instances of *God's* thinking, not of our thinking. What Whytt had seen as a God-given ability of the spinal cord to relate stimuli lawfully to responses via a kind of unconscious feeling Malebranche saw as an instance of God's feeling and acting to enable us to preserve our bodies.

As of 1830, the unconscious was considered to be either a super-natural or a natural source of irrational forces; if and when rational but non-conscious acts occurred, they were attributed not to the individual but to his or her maker. John Stuart Mill changed all this by hypothesizing a rational unconscious mind. He had to make such an unusual hypothesis in order to save the associationist psychology which his father had championed, and which he hoped to make the basis of all social thought.

A logical unconscious

The nineteenth century thus saw the rise of what appears to be a radically novel concept of the unconscious, which I shall call the *logical unconscious*. In this conception, there are non-conscious mental processes which are identical with, or at least resemble, the process of drawing inferences and making judgements. The logical unconscious emerged in the writings of John Stuart Mill as he engaged simultaneously in defending and improving his father's associationism and developing a general logical theory consistent with this new improved psychology. Although historians have tended to locate the doctrine of 'unconscious inference' in the 1850s and 1860s in Germany (especially in the work of Helmholtz and his erstwhile assistant Wundt), Mill's *Logic* is probably the source of this doctrine, and we know that it was read and used by these and other prominent German psychologists. (It is also possible that Mill's defences of associationism against Bailey, published in 1842–3 and reprinted in 1859, were utilized by these German thinkers.)

The proponents of the logical unconscious often appealed to earlier ideas, especially Leibniz's notion of *petites perceptions,* as inspiring their thinking. But the resemblance is superficial, as it does not take into account the difference between the already accepted notion of an irrational unconscious and this newer unusual idea of a rational unconscious. These differences will be clarified after I outline Mill's important innovation and its influence.

In working on what was to become his *System of Logic,* John Stuart Mill faced a set of problems that had yet to be addressed within the kind of associationistic psychology championed by James Mill. In particular, the epistemological context of the younger Mill's work made it imperative for him to identify the sources of our knowledge of truths. One of the passages in the *Logic* known to have been written near the outset of John Stuart Mill's work, and which remained essentially unchanged through eight editions, is the following comment from section 4 of the Introduction: 'Truths are known to us in two ways: some are known directly, and of themselves; some through the medium of other truths. The former are the subject of Intuition or Consciousness; the latter, of Inference.' By focusing on the nature of how truths are known, Mill changed the status of sensations in associationistic epistemology. For Hartley, Condillac, James Mill and others, what we call sensations formed the basis of all knowledge, including knowledge of truths, but no sharp line was drawn between sensations as a truth of consciousness and other truths, called inferences by the younger Mill.

The consequences of Mill's distinction here are of profound importance for psychology. If Mill's distinction is taken as a basis for theorizing, then the first step in any account of a psychological process is to discover what are the intuitions available to subjects. Once a complete list of these intuitions is made, then any other putative knowledge must be inferential – either false or true inference. There are foreshadowings of Mill's distinction in Berkeley's concept of minimum sensibles, and in Hume's basic impressions – but neither in these nor in other cases was the issue one of truth or inference, as Mill made it to be. Logic, for Mill, is the study of the inferences we make from truths already known (as he says at the end of this section of the introduction). This is the source of Mill's psychologism, his belief that logic cannot be distinguished as a special science without the results of a special branch of psychology: the psychology of sensations.

John Stuart Mill's careful attempt to distinguish between sensations and inferences comes in response to the Scottish common-sense psychologists and their emphasis on intuition, or what many of them preferred to call 'consciousness' (a term which the younger Mill used, perhaps grudgingly, in a similar way). But there is an important inversion here: in Thomas Reid's epistemology the truths of intuition are not identical with sensations. On the contrary, Reid invented the modern distinction between sensation and perception largely so that he might attribute truth to *perceptions*. Put simply, Reid was less interested in whether or not my sensation of the colour red is true than in whether my perception of this rose as an existing object (which happens to be red) is true. Reid argued that what are true in consciousness are things like my perception of the rose as well as any sensations of colour or scent I might have. This distinction between two aspects of consciousness – sensation and perception – was considerably muddled by the 1830s, when Mill was working on his *Logic*. As was shown above, Thomas Brown essentially subverted Reid's distinction, resulting in a theory that relied entirely on sensations and associations. William Hamilton, the last great proponent of 'Scottish philosophy' also never understood Reid on this point, and obfuscated the matter greatly with a number of secondary and subsidiary definitions about sub-species of sensation and perception (see his *Notes* to his edition of Reid). Stuart Mill's confusion concerning what should count as a truth of consciousness is thus understandable, as he may have been attempting to contrast Hamilton's (or Thomas Brown's) thinking with the associationist views of James Mill.

In this context, the younger Mill's attack on Samuel Bailey's critique of Berkeley is very significant. Mill wrote his essays on Bailey just as the *Logic* was being completed (1842–3), and he clearly welcomed the opportunity to rethink these basic issues about consciousness and inference. Yet Bailey, unlike other nineteenth-century 'common-sense' philosophers, *did* understand Reid's distinction between sensation and perception (although Bailey used different terminology from Reid's). Therefore it ought to be interesting to see how Mill replied to a Reidian attack on some of Mill's fundamental assumptions. Bailey, like Reid, argued that 'the perception of outness is a component part of the sensation' (of vision or touch) (p. 31); Bailey also argued that 'we cannot explain . . . why . . . these tactual and muscular sensations are not felt without a perception of different distances' just as Reid argued that we could never explain why perceptions (beliefs in objects) accompanied sensations.

Starting from this Reidian basis, Bailey proceeded to demolish Berkeley's theory of vision, as interpreted by associationists like Condillac and James Mill. In that theory, visual sensations are supposed to become associated with tactile sensations in such a way that the perception of distance is achieved, or appears to the subject to be achieved, by means of sight. Bailey's argument is straightforward: firstly, if one assumes that no sensations (visual, tactile or other) contain information about outness, then outness can never be the result of the association of these sensations. In particular, Bailey pointed out that when we touch objects at different distances we have a variety of tactile sensations as well as perceptions of outness; yet, when we see things at different distances, no matter how hard we try, none of these tactile sensations comes to consciousness. Secondly, if one assumes, as Berkeley did, that touch contains information about depth and outness, and that touch 'teaches' vision, what is to stop Bailey from arguing that vision itself contains information about outness (as James later did)? Once again, when we look around we do not become conscious of tactile sensations suggesting outness or associating with visual ones, we simply see out-ness, a psychological fact, encompassing both visual sensation and per-ception.

Mill's critique of Bailey started with an attack on the sensation–perception distinction. Following Brown and James Mill, Stuart Mill argued that 'The sense of sight informs us of nothing originally, except light and colours, and a certain arrangement of light and colours'. Mill needed to start here, because these lights and colours (visual sensations) are the intuitive truths on which all knowledge, for Mill, was based. Yet Bailey had already anticipated this line of attack, noting that there was no empirical evidence for this claim about what we 'originally see' (or what might better be called our visual sensations). As Bailey put it, 'it is certainly true that we see by means of rays directed endwise to the eye, but it is equally true that we do not see the rays themselves either endwise or sideway: we simply see the object'. The evidence for Mill's claim about basic intuitive truths in sight comes from his analysis of the physiological optics of the eye, not from the evidence of con-sciousness nor from empirical evidence about what people see – at best, only geometers and opticians see rays of light.

Once one accepts Mill's starting place, then the rest of his argu-ment follows: that there are 'two powers' of vision, original (intuitive) and acquired (inferential). From here it is a short step to Mill's theory of perception, with its striking echo of his *Logic* in Stuart Mill's edition of James Mill's *Analysis and Sensations*:

> [T]he information obtained through the eye consists of two
> things – sensations, and inferences from those sensations: that
> the sensations are merely colours variously arranged, and changes
> of colour; that all else is inference, the work of the intellect,
> not of the eye; or if, in compliance with common usage, we
> ascribe it to the eye, we must say that the eye does it not by
> an original, but by an acquired power – a power which the eye
> exercises, through, and by means of, the reasoning or inferring
> faculty.

The familiarity of Mill's theory of perception should not be allowed to obscure the novelty and strangeness of his argument: the original powers of the eye, according to Mill, are such as cannot be known through consciousness, because we never do see only light, colours and their changes. Thus, the original powers of a perceptual system are supposed to do two contradictory things: firstly, they are supposed to provide one with the basic intuitive truths on which to build knowledge of the world; and, secondly, they are supposed to be inaccessible to intuition, because of their involvement with complex associations and inferences. For Bailey and other Reidians, the very definition of a sensation or an intuitive truth was something that could be known through intuition or consciousness. Mill had seemed to adopt this definition at the outset of his *Logic*. But, when pushed into justifying his theory of perception, Mill abandoned this basic tenet, suggesting instead that sensations can be known only through inference. Later, in his *Examination of William Hamilton's Philosophy*, Mill adopted Carpenter's term 'unconscious cerebration' and also made explicit his reliance on physiological 'facts' for specifying the basic sensations of vision and the other sensory modalities. (Peirce read this as a licence to cut free from introspective psychology altogether, and combined it with Bain's definition of belief as whatever we are prepared to act on – consciously or not – and invented pragmatism.)

It is amusing to see Mill criticizing Bailey for carelessness in distinguishing between 'what the eye tells us directly, and what it teaches by way of inference'. If Mill were right, then the eye could tell us nothing directly, because it is only through inference that we can know our basic visual intuitions. The rest of Mill's attack on Bailey consisted in trying to show that Bailey had begged the question by using a word like 'perception' when he should have said 'judgement' or 'inference'. But of course it was Mill who begged the question here, refusing to allow Bailey the very distinction on which he built his theory. Bailey repeatedly looked for evidence in consciousness – as Mill told him he should – of the visual and tactile sensations out of which Brown, and the Mills, claimed depth perception was built. Finding no such evidence, Bailey concluded that their theory was wrong.

Mill responded that the evidence of consciousness is irrelevant: after all, the original intuitions of both touch and vision can be unavailable to consciousness, at least on Mill's definitions. This is where Bailey's second argument comes into play. Bailey repeatedly asked how the association of a tactile sensation with a visual sensation can yield information about outness if neither of the sensations contain such information. Mill actually agreed with this point, but hastened to add that the process involved is more like that of an inference or a judgement than that of mere association. Mill used his chemical analogy to good effect here, arguing that the 'association' of several chemicals often yields a distinctively new entity. In addition to unconscious intuitions, Mill was willing to postulate unconscious inferences.

Prior to the 1830s the idea of unconscious intuitions or sensations was a rarity, and the idea of an unconscious inference was unheard of. The interaction of Scottish philosophy with Millian associationism produced a greater precision of language in reference to sensations and perceptions, and introduced a whole series of concepts that soon became ubiquitous in nineteenth-century psychology: original powers of perception, as versus acquired; concept of basic sensations; the concept of unconscious sensory states; the concept of unconscious judgements. Reid's attack on the concept of the association of ideas led to a progressive clarity among associationists, up to and including the elder Mill, who clearly meant association of *sensations* to be the basic law of his system, even when his language slipped into older terminology. The younger Mill, in attempting to extend associationism into logic and epistemology, was careful to distinguish sensations from perceptions, and took the radical step of divorcing sensations from introspective psychology. Henceforth, sensations could be 'analysed' by inference from physiological data about what 'must be' the basic sensory qualities of a given system. Once this decompositional analysis was accomplished, then an analysis of the inferences needed to get knowledge of the world from this sensory basis could proceed.

Epistemology was cut free from introspection – because, after Mill, the elements of introspective awareness ('sensations') were to be analysed in the first place physiologically and, only after this, psychologically. What had begun as the younger Mill's attempt to defend and extend his father's introspective associationist psychology now placed 'the evidence of consciousness' a distant second in importance. The Frankenstein psychology with its explanation of all of the mind in terms of sensation-based associative processses feared by early nineteenth-century orthodoxy now took a central place in the middle of the century – but as an unconscious, not a conscious process. Mill believed in a psychologistic programme of building 'logic' (epistemology and theory of science) on the foundations of physiological psychology. This approach was to reach its high point in the work of Hermann von Helmholtz, who saw his work in physiological optics and acoustics as prolegomena to any future epistemologies.

❧ INTERLUDE: 1848 AND ALL THAT ❧

The remarkable increase of interest in scientific psychology in the 1850s and 1860s has been almost universally interpreted as the emergence of an experimentally oriented, scientifically grounded discipline of psychology out of what had been a more philosophical psychology. Turner expresses this consensus well when he writes that, in German universities,

> [U]ntil the last half of the nineteenth century psychology did not exist as an independent discipline, but rather as a subfield of general philosophy. The philosophers who offered lectures in the field readily incorporated experimental physiological results that came to their attention, but they normally developed their psychological views and systems mainly through logical, metaphysical, introspective, or purely experiential considerations.... Beginning in the late 1850s ... the older tradition of philosophical psychology began to give place to a new tradition that stressed experimental results and physiological considerations.

As with all myths, there is some element of truth here. In Germany, 'professors of philosophy' often worked extensively in psychology. Herbart, Fries and Lotze are three important examples. But the odd thing about these thinkers is that they do not really fit our twentieth-century conception of a philosopher. As a consequence, they figure far more prominently in histories of psychology than in histories of philosophy. We should not be fooled by the label 'philosophy' applied to these thinkers' professorial positions, because there is no reason to assume that that word meant in the 1830s and 1840s what it means now. Indeed, the Philosophy Chair at Göttingen was held successively by Herbart, Lotze and G. E. Müller. No one would even attempt to make the case that the last-named ranks as a philosopher in the modern sense of the term, and the case for the first two is not much better. Modern historians are nearly unanimous in agreeing that not a single major philosopher of this period was to be found teaching philosophy in an academic position with the conspicuous exception of Hegel. Nor should it be forgotten that many of the most important contributions to scientific psychology came from academics who held chairs in physics, like Fechner and the Webers, or in medicine and physiology, like Johannes Müller.

Although intellectuals based in academia had to conform to the ideological standards of Church and State or risk loss of their livelihoods, this was of course not true of independent intellectuals like medical doctors, industrialists, mechanics or parsons. Thus the pressure of arguments from heterodox psychologies became increasingly great until, with the significant social and political changes wrought by 1848, the whole structure of traditional metaphysics was exploded. It no longer became possible to write about the mind in complete ignorance of current physiology and experimentation; or, to be more precise, any pretensions to scientific status in discussions of the mind required acknowledgement of the 'Frankenstein' psychology which had heretofore largely been excluded from the polite company of academic discourse. The ritualistic denunciations of materialism and atheism that pepper the works of traditional metaphysicians (especially their textbooks) became replaced by argumentation. The unthinkable was being thought: metaphysicians were questioning what the role of embodiment might be in psychology. Far from being a marginal doctrine – one that stigmatized its professor as an atheist – Spinoza's dual aspect theory gradually began to win adherents from many different intellectual backgrounds until, by 1880, it had become the dominant position among scientists concerned with the nervous system and the mind.

Attacks upon materialism are common throughout psychological writings in the 1850s and 1860s, from the popular essays of Helmholtz to the positivistic quasi-idealism of the late John Stuart Mill. The flavour of many of these attacks is captured in some remarks in a lecture given by Oliver Wendell Holmes, Sr (the doctor) to the Harvard Phi Beta Kappa Graduates in 1870. The lecture began with a statement that simply could not have been uttered at Harvard a decade earlier: 'The flow of thought is, like breathing, essentially mechanical and necessary, but incidentally capable of being modified to a greater or lesser extent by conscious effort.' Such Shelleyan determinism and apparent materialism would have horrified earlier audiences at such an institution had they been allowed to be spoken. (And, in all probability, Holmes's comments did cause some stir.) But Holmes is no materialist and he repeatedly made clear in his lecture that medical science can and should be indifferent to the conflict between 'materialism' and 'spiritualism'. In other words, the scientific study of the phenomena of thought and action should be divorced from these metaphysical interpretative disagreements. Yet Holmes could not resist showing that he is on the side of the angels, and he ends his lecture making fun of the kind of 'vulgar materialism' promulgated by Büchner and others. Can a human person be reduced to what he or she eats and drinks? No, said the good doctor, 'It is not in this direction that materialism is to be feared: we do not find Hamlet and Faust, right and wrong, the valor of men and the purity of women, by testing for albumen, or examining fibres in microscopes'. After 1848, the bourgeoisie discovered that their morals need not be corrupted by advances in the sciences of human nature – so long as certain 'interpretations' of those sciences were kept at bay.

The 'psychology as a natural science' defended by James had its origins in this spirited demarcation of the transcendental from the natural. The scientists living in a post–1848 world insisted that traditional metaphysics had lost the battle: science had nothing to say about transcendental concerns. 'Systems' as such were now the enemy, because any and all philosophical systems smacked of ideology, and strong ideologies in any form (whether that of the backward-looking peasant or aristocrat or the progressive ideology of the new working class) could upset the status quo. The positivism that swept across Europe was by no means Comte's positivist system but was instead a general anti-systemic bias, which itself proved to be more biased against heterodox than against orthodox ideologies. The defeat of the high orthodoxy of traditional metaphysics was thus used primarily as a cudgel against the heterodox: if science could say nothing of the soul, then it certainly could not affirm the materiality of that transcendental creature. We should thus remain 'agnostic' – to use a term coined by T. H. Huxley to capture just this philosophical suspension of belief.

Kant and Reid had of course tried out their version of agnosticism almost a century earlier, and it proved to be a highly unstable position, as we have seen. Similarly the widely touted scientific agnosticism of the late 1800s also succumbed to its own internal contradictions. On the one hand, psychologists like Wundt could not be constrained from at least formulating hypotheses about the nature of mental activities and states. Wundt offered a form of voluntarism that was a sort of optimistic version of Schopenhauer's world as will. On the other hand, philosophers – and especially the emerging school of neo-Kantians – refused to allow scientists to debar transcendental arguments. The neo-Kantians specialized in turning the agnostic arguments of Helmholtz into a basis for anti-materialist metaphysical theorizing, as the following passage from Lange's extremely influential *History of Materialism* attests:

> this matter, with everything that is formed from it, is only an
> abstraction from [our mental representations.] The struggle
> between Body and Mind is ended in favour of the latter.... For
> while it always remained an insurmountable difficulty for
> materialism to explain how conscious sensations could come
> about from material motion, yet it is, on the other hand, by
> no means difficult to conceive that our whole idea of matter and
> its movements is the result of an organization of purely
> intellectual dispositions to sensations. Accordingly, Helmholtz is
> entirely right when he resolves the activity of sense into a kind
> of inference.

❧ THE DEVELOPMENT OF A POSITIVE ❧ PSYCHOLOGY

Institutional confusion: theoretical convergence

The evaluation of intellectual trends in the decade or two following 1848 is decidedly tricky. This period is one in which modern institutional and disciplinary boundaries began to emerge, so it is ridiculously easy to miss important patterns simply by not knowing where to look. Although academic positions become increasingly important during this period, it is conspicuous that many of the great scientists and philosophers of Europe at this time worked outside of academia. Prussia perhaps led the way into institutionalizing and dividing up intellectual work along more or less modern lines. But even in Prussia in the 1850s and 1860s it is not always easy to see where to look for philosophical and psychological activities. For example, the linguistics of Paul, Steinthal and others emerged as a fully-fledged discipline in these decades, with its own professorships and journals. But this ostensibly specialist discipline of linguistics was to later influence an important professor of philosophy, Wilhelm Wundt, who made historical and comparative studies of language and gesture the entry-way into his brand of empirical social psychology.

There are signs that an historical and comparative approach to psychology was broadly influential across Europe in these decades after the 'springtime of the peoples' and well before the self-consciously historicist arguments of Dilthey and others in the *fin-de-siècle* period. This historicism was less an emulation of Hegelian ideas – which were in ill repute at this time – than an emulation of *Comte's* method. It is not widely appreciated that Comte's attempt to account for all of intellectual activity through a kind of linear growth and reorganization model spawned numerous attempts to deploy such a model in other areas. Moreover, Comte's and positivism's suspicions of hypothetical entities such as forces and atoms was strongly reinforced by developments in physics, which seemed to be pointing away from the usefulness of positing such entities behind the phenomena.

Several powerful thinkers tried to amalgamate this positivistic interpretation of scientific laws as merely patterns in phenomena with an historical method for deriving the data of human behaviour. A number of the contributors to historical linguistics took approaches along these lines. Even more relevant for the present account was the work of two thinkers who self-consciously tried to create a psychology out of historical materials and positivist hubris, Hyppolite Taine (1828–93) and Thomas Henry Buckle (1825–62).

Both Taine and Buckle argued explicitly that psychological laws could be derived only from historical materials, not from experimental methods. History was said to reveal patterns of behaviour across different situations which, when properly analysed, would yield true laws of human nature. In contrast, Taine and Buckle criticized laboratory-based or introspective-based psychology for its narrow foundation, and its inability to generalize its results. Taine's monumental *History of English Literature* (1861) tried to analyse the human mind using evidence from one nation's history and literary productions. In his remarkable preface to this work, Taine justifies this procedure as being one that is still capable of yielding generalizable results. Buckle's maddeningly rambling but often insightful *History of Civilization in England* (1857) is similarly nationalist in intended scope (but Buckle cannot resist a number of continental excursions). Both Taine and Buckle see human nature as a product of nature and culture, a product arrived at through a particular historical progression.

G. H. Lewes

Looking back over a career which involved four decades' study of philosophy and literature, Taine wrote, 'All I have been doing for the past forty years has been psychology, applied or pure.' But what *was* psychology in the 1850s and 1860s when Taine first made a name for himself? In those years no one anywhere in Europe could make a living teaching, studying or researching psychology. Yet serious psychology in these decades was being done by a greater assortment of people than ever before: philosophers and doctors but also physiologists, journalists, literary writers, spiritualists, phrenologists, mesmerists and more. The career of G. H. Lewes (1817–78) is doubly instructive concerning the institutional fluidity of psychology in the two decades following 1848. Firstly, Lewes was an important thinker whose considerable body of work repays careful study. More so than in Bain's much better known writings, Lewes strove to integrate contemporary trends in philosophy, psychology and physiology. He was especially important for showing how contemporary German physiological thought could be integrated with British evolutionism and associationism. Secondly, Lewes was a prolific and effective popularizer. His texts on physiology influenced both Sechenov and Pavlov, as well as countless British scientists. And in his often reprinted biography of Goethe and his equally popular history of philosophy Lewes gave several generations of English-speaking readers their first introduction to recent German and French schools of thought, including both Hegel's and Comte's ideas.

Despite the demonstrably pivotal position he played in mid-nineteenth-century philosophical psychology, Lewes is nowadays almost invisible in the history of philosophy, and a mere footnote to histories of psychology. Boring devotes only a passing mention to Lewes, seeing him as an evolutionary associationist of less influence than Spencer. More recent histories of psychology either echo Boring or remain silent. Spencer himself credited Lewes with arousing his interest in philosophy (and Spencer almost never acknowledged any form of intellectual indebtedness) so it may be useful to pay more attention to his contribution.

One problem with estimating Lewes's importance is the institutional oddness of the intellectual world of 1840–70 when viewed from the confines of modern academe. Lewes was never anything like a professor or a teacher, nor even more than an amateur physiologist (albeit an amateur who had made it a point to do laboratory work with the likes of Liebig – which perhaps doesn't quite fit our idea of an 'amateur' either). Like Spencer, Lewes was primarily a journalist. He was not merely a contributor to the thriving intellectual journals of Victorian Britain but an editor and founder of several important periodicals, including *The Leader, The Westminster Review* and *The Fortnightly Review*. He was also an influential adviser at the birth of both *Nature* and *Mind*, two of the first 'academic' journals of importance in Britain.

Lewes's interests were always broad, and he made real contributions to drama, literature and biography (his biography of Goethe was the first complete one in any language) as well as in science and philosophy. Lewes's career offers an image of an altogether different kind of intellectual world from the one that has developed since the 1870s. This is why his work does not fit straightforwardly into any single disciplinary history. But this is just my point: historians of philosophy and psychology cannot assume that the boundaries of their discipline are or were clear, and they certainly should not impose a contemporary view of those boundaries on to the history of their disciplines.

Lewes was among the first nineteenth-century philosophers to discuss Spinoza and Hegel in Britain. Lewes's interest in Spinoza was kindled in the 1830s through conversations with Leigh Hunt (who had learned about Spinoza's ideas from Shelley twenty years earlier) and perhaps through reading Heine's work. Lewes's article on Spinoza in 1843 (printed in *The Westminster Review* and also as a pamphlet) proclaimed Spinoza to be a pantheist predecessor of Strauss and Feuerbach. Lewes especially emphasized the doctrine of Spinoza's that came to have great influence on psychology – the idea that spirit and body are merely two aspects of one thing, ourselves, and that the soul is our 'idea' of our bodily self.

But it was Lewes's visit to Paris in 1842, where he met both

Cousin and Comte, that stimulated his most fruitful transmission of European ideas to Britain. Within a year Lewes was publishing enthusiastic accounts of positivism, and discussing plans with Bain and Mill to translate Comte's *Cours* (in the event these plans fell through, but Lewes was later influential in arranging Harriet Martineau's edition of Comte a decade later). It was at this time (1842–6) that Mill himself was most under Comte's influence, and considered that his own *Logic* represented something like a positivist philosophy of science. (A spectacular example of how badly our present disciplinary boundaries apply to the last century is the Mill–Comte correspondence of 1842–3, which is dominated by arguments over whether phrenology is a scientific approach to the study of mind.)

Lewes later revisited Comte in 1846, when Comte's great love, Clotilde de Vaux, was dying, and Lewes was probably the first British 'Comtean' to turn away from the man and his increasingly eccentric ideas, focusing instead on a doctrine, ultimately called 'positivism'.

Lewes's *Biographical History of Philosophy* appeared in 1845–6, including substantial discussions of German philosophy, especially that of Spinoza, Kant and Hegel, and ending with what can only be called a paean to Comte (later toned down and changed into a positivist credo). This book was as popular as any philosophy text had ever been in Great Britain and the United States. Thus, despite being widely repeated in histories of the subject, the claims of the Oxford Hegelians that they brought German philosophy to Britain (after Coleridge's failed attempt) are simply false by more than a decade. It is also interesting to see that this popular text championed positivism a few years before 1850.

After 1848, Lewes was heavily involved for a time in political journalism (he founded *The Leader* with Leigh Hunt's son, Thornton) and in promoting the career of Marian Evans ('George Eliot'), his spouse. None the less, he also found time to write his first popular book on physiological psychology, followed by a series of increasingly technical works. His popular writings, especially *The Physiology of Common Life* (1859–60) promoted the kind of everyday materialist physiology found especially in Moleschott and Büchner but eschewed their anti-idealist metaphysics. Instead, Lewes's positivist views allowed him to remain rather agnostic concerning *how* sensations and feelings accompanied such everyday physiological acts as eating and focus on what Lewes saw to be facts: the correlations of feeling with physiological processes and bodily activity. This invention of a half-Spinozist, half-positivist physiology of mind was Lewes's master stroke. Before the century was out this position would come to dominate physiology and psychology all across Europe.

Lewes did not remain satisfied with this agnostic position, however. In his multi-volume and partially posthumous *Problems of Life and Mind* (1874–9) Lewes broke with the positivists' anti-metaphysical stance to suggest what he called a 'metempirical' philosophy – a binding of philosophical inquiry to scientific findings. Variants of this position became the dominant credo among late Victorian scientists like Huxley, Tyndall and Clifford, all of whom were friends of Lewes's.

Problems of Life and Mind is a self-consciously magisterial attempt to survey various lines of thought about psychology, and to offer a particular programme of research as a 'most promising' course to follow. The treatise is in three parts: a general philosophy of science as applied to psychology (*The Foundations of a Creed* in two volumes); a study of mind–brain from a dual aspect point of view, emphasizing the physiology of everyday life (*The Physical Basis of Mind*); and a sketch of a general psychology, describing its scope and limits (*The Study of Psychology* in two volumes). Lewes did not live to finish this last part, and George Eliot put the manuscript through the press – surely the only psychology text ever edited by a major novelist!

Despite its excessive length, there is also much that is not included in *Problems*. Lewes seems to have been unmoved by the rising tide of experimentalism among continental psychologists. He was familiar with Fechner and Wundt but saw them as marginal figures. Here Lewes's book was less prescient than that other great text of 1874, Brentano's *Empirical Psychology*, which acknowledged Wundt's importance, if only to take issue with his concept of inner observation. Lewes (like Lotze) was more of a physiological than an experimental psychologist. He was more at home in his extensive analysis of the reflex functions of the spinal cord than in worrying about Weber fractions, or the differences between introspection and inner observation.

Lewes's work on spinal function (much of it based on his own replications and extensions of experiments by Whytt, Müller, Hall, and others, all of them using amphibians vivisected in his own amateur laboratory) exemplified a crucial transition in psychological thinking. For Lewes, spinal reflexes are part of psychology, and issues relating to sensation and even consciousness within the spinal column must be addressed. Lewes berated Huxley for misconstruing the psychological issues raised by studies on reflexes in the latter's important 'On the Hypothesis that Animals are Automata' (1872–4). Lewes regarded as very wrongheaded this attempt to treat the marvellous adaptive properties of the spinal reflexes as involving absolutely no psychological processes. On the basis of behavioural evidence from many experiments, Lewes concluded that the spinal column mediates many complex and specifically adaptive behaviours, showing striking resemblance to at least some of the behaviour (and consciousness?) of intact animals. According to Lewes, to treat the spinal cord as a reflex mechanism and the brain as a source of mind requires giving exclusive weight to introspective evidence. However, because introspective evidence is, by its nature, not open to public verification and replication, there can be no conclusive test to show the insentience of the spinal cord.

The trend in British neurophysiology was towards viewing the brain as a complex – and psychologically rich – reflex apparatus. This view achieved dominance with David Ferrier and Hughlings Jackson. In contrast, Lewes always insisted in treating spinal processes as including a psychological component (for example of sensation). Whether in the spine or in the brain, Lewes felt that an animate response was not just the mechanical effect of a stimulus but included an irreducible psychological factor, such as we would now describe as information processing steps. This emphasis on the psychologically active, dynamic nature of the lower parts of the central nervous system was submerged in later neurophysiology. Although later neurophysiologists acknowledge the role that muscle stretch receptors play in eliciting reflex responses, they simply do not address the question of what sorts of sensations might be elicited at the same time.

Lewes's work was in many ways outdated by the time it was published. With Lewes's help the journal *Mind* had begun appearing in 1876, and *Brain* a year later. Wundt's laboratory was already active, and psychological laboratories were even beginning to appear in America, where Peirce had begun to study the psychophysics of colour sensations. The study of the physiology (or psychology) of everyday life was being abandoned by specialists who were increasingly focusing on their own pieces in the puzzle of the human mind: experimental psychologists looking at sensations and reaction times, experimental physiologists analysing motor pathways, medical psychologists working with case studies in hysteria, epilepsy and other disorders. Lewes's death helped to increase this trend toward specialization, as he left money to found a studentship in physiology, explicitly on the German model, a bequest which did much to stimulate the improvement of British work in reductionist physiology over the next twenty years. Ironically, the greatest proponent of a non-psychological analysis of spinal function (combined with a dualistic interpretation of the brain/mind), C. S. Sherrington, was one of three Nobel-Prize-winning physiologists whose studies were underwritten by Lewes's bequest. It would take more than half a century for another philosopher to appear with a comparable amount of physiological and psychological expertise and an interest in trying to understand behaviour and mind (Merleau-Ponty).

The positivism that dominated Europe by 1879 was much more Lewesian and Helmholtzian than Comtean. With regard to psychology and the study of mind, most so-called positivists were quasi-Spinozists.

There was a continent-wide embracing of dual aspect theory that began shortly after 1848 and achieved remarkable hegemony by 1879. It is striking that two of the leading British positivists (in the sense of early proponents of Comte), Lewes and Frederic Pollock, were among the earliest to publish extensively on Spinoza in English. Like Helmholtz, Lewes also attacked the remnants of a *Naturphilosophie* that insisted on finding hidden forces behind psychological as well as physical phenomena.

❧ CONCLUSION ❧

The year following Lewes's death, 1879, is often, if somewhat arbitrarily, treated as the year in which psychology as an experimental science was born. In that year, Wundt's laboratory became officially supported and active at Leipzig. Within the decade a host of more flexible and ultimately more influential experimentalists' careers were launched. By 1890 the most important of these scientists' careers were well established: G. E. Müller in Berlin, Alfred Binet in Paris and Francis Galton in England. These three researchers alone spun out streams of studies on a bewildering variety of topics, from sensory processes to reaction times, from individual differences to memory and cognition. William James's *Principles of Psychology* was essentially written over the course of this decade, and published in pieces alongside these experimentalists' work in the many new professional journals that were appearing. James's book represents two watersheds – the last great work strongly claimed by both psychologists and philosophers. Professionalization and separation was winning out.

Typically, the story is told that psychology as a professional discipline emerged from philosophy, as part of this professionalization, but this is only half right. It is equally the case that philosophy emerged from psychology. In the same decade that Galton, Binet and G. E. Müller (among others) were launching experimental psychology, replacing Mill's and Helmholtz's physiological epistemology with a kind of Lewesian positivism wedded to experimental methodologies, the 'neo-Kantians' were attacking 'psychologism' in epistemology, and Frege and Peirce were beginning their struggle to de-psychologize logic.

Psychology thus became a science unlike any other: a science without any ontological commitments, perpetually stuck within the anti-ontological climate of the 1870s. While chemistry and physics went on to mature out of this phase – leading to the great developments of 1900–10 (physical atoms, electrons, photons, the first quantum theory) – psychology maintained a deep aversion to all ontological theorizing. Ultimately, this led to that combination of behaviourism and 'operationalism' which dominated so much thinking about 'the mind' in the twentieth century.

At the same time as psychology abandoned ontology, philosophers abandoned the natural world. Afraid of a psychologism which threatened to eliminate first philosophy as a 'pure' intellectual discipline, a host of philosophical schools rediscovered transcendence, a trend very much in evidence even in the self-proclaimed anti-metaphysical scientists, such as Du Bois Reymond, whose famous 'ignorabimus' neatly carves out a place for the transcendent. Transcendental arguments in epistemology, metaphysics, and above all in logic, were offered to establish a 'pure philosophy' untainted with any odour of quotidian reality. Some transcendentalists saw their salvation in the allegedly pure logical structure of language, others in the transcendental ideal structure at the heart of experience, still others in reviving Kant's method of transcendental argumentation.

The plea offered by James and countless others in the last quarter of the nineteenth century was that we should treat psychology as just another natural science, like chemistry. This plea misses a fundamental point. Unlike chemistry, psychology is about how we think (among other things). And a science of how we think should eventually tell us how to think, at least in the sense that it ought to reveal the laws and causes of good versus bad thinking. Were such a science to emerge it would be, at least in some sense, the queen of the sciences. By century's end, James doubted whether any such science had emerged, as he stated forthrightly at the outset of his *Talks to Teachers*. In contrast to James, Wundt, the self-proclaimed founder of experimental psychology, thus insisted on clearly demarcating the content of such a psychology. One could have an experimental science of sensation and response, but not an experimental science of cognition and thought. The study of cognition and other intentional states could be naturalistic, descriptive, historical and comparative, but never experimental and nomothetic. Wundtian experimental psychology, under the strong influence of the later Mill and the German agnostics, was itself definitely anti-psychologistic! Nevertheless, psychologism, in the sense of a master science telling us how we ought to think, was a strong presence throughout the latter part of the nineteenth century. It required an odd mixture of Platonism (in Frege) and neo-Kantianism (in Peirce and Wittgenstein) to eradicate psychologism in logic. And it required the very different geniuses of Russell and Husserl to eradicate psychologism in early twentieth-century philosophy. The fact that psychologism has returned, in the guise of artificial intelligence and cognitive science, suggests that the Victorian agnostics, like Kant and Reid, were unable to make their anti-metaphysical claims stick. It is intriguing that this oscillation between naturalism and anti-psychologism seems yet again to be producing new disciplines. If history is any guide, this cycle should continue.

❧ ACKNOWLEDGEMENTS ❧

This research was supported by grants from Franklin & Marshall College. I thank my Research Assistant, Sherry Anders, for consistently cheerful and unflagging help. It was at Rob Wozniak's suggestion that I first looked into G. H. Lewes's work seriously, for which I am grateful. Mike Montgomery gave me various prods and pokes of bibliographic and other advice. Stuart Shanker's questions, encouragement and suggestions have all been of great help.

❧ BIBLIOGRAPHY ❧

General reference materials

11.1 Ash, M. 'Reflections on Psychology in History', in W. Woodward and M. Ash, eds, *The Problematic Science: Psychology in Nineteenth Century Thought*, New York: Praeger, 1982.

11.2 Bain, A. 'A Historical View of Theories of the Soul', *Fortnightly Review*, 5 (1866): 47–62.

11.3 Baldwin, J. M. *History of Psychology: A Sketch and an Interpretation*, London: Watts, 1913.

11.4 Blakey, R. *History of the Philosophy of Mind: Embracing the Opinions of all Writers on Mental Science from the Earliest Period to the Present Time*, London: Longmans, Brown, Green, and Longmans, 1850. 4 vols.

11.5 Boring, E. G. *Sensation and Perception in the History of Psychology*, New York: Appleton-Century-Crofts, 1942.

11.6 —— *A History of Experimental Psychology*, 2nd edn, New York: Appleton-Century-Crofts, 1950.

11.7 Chadwick, O. *The Secularization of the European Mind in the Nineteenth Century*, New York: Cambridge University Press, 1975.

11.8 Clarke, E. S. and L. S. Jacyna, *Nineteenth Century Origins of Neuroscientific Concepts*, Berkeley and Los Angeles: University of California Press, 1987.

11.9 Danziger, K. 'The History of Introspection Reconsidered', *Journal of the History of the Behavioral Sciences*, 16 (1980): 241–62.

11.10 Dewey, J. 'The New Psychology', *Andover Review*, 2 (1884): 278–89.

11.11 Fearing, F. *Reflex Action: A Study in the History of Physiological Psychology*, New York: Hafner, 1964.

11.12 Figlio, K. 'Theories of Perception and the Physiology of Mind in the Late Eighteenth Century', *History of Science*, 12 (1975): 177–212.

11.13   Flugel, J. C. and D. West, *A Hundred Years of Psychology*, New York: International Universities Press, 1964.

11.14   Hobsbawm, E. J. *The Age of Revolution: 1789–1848*, New York: New American Library, 1962.

11.15   —— *The Age of Capital: 1848–1875*, New York: New American Library, 1979.

11.16   —— *The Age of Empire: 1875–1914*, New York: Vintage, 1989.

11.17   Jodl, F. 'German Philosophy in the Nineteenth Century', *The Monist*, 1 (1890–1): 263–77.

11.18   Johnston, W. M. *The Austrian Mind: An Intellectual and Social History 1848–1938*, Berkeley and Los Angeles: University of California Press, 1972.

11.19   Kuklick, B. *The Rise of American Philosophy: Cambridge, Massachusetts 1860–1930*, New Haven: Yale University Press, 1977.

11.20   Leary, D. 'The Philosophical Development of the Conception of Psychology in Germany, 1780–1850', *Journal of the History of the Behavioral Sciences*, 14 (1978): 113–21.

11.21   Lévy-Bruhl, L. *History of Modern Philosophy in France*, revised edn, Chicago: Open Court, 1924.

11.22   Lewes, G. H. *Biographical History of Philosophy*, 8th edn, Manchester and New York: Routledge, 1893.

11.23   Mandelbaum, M. *History, Man, and Reason*, Baltimore: Johns Hopkins University Press, 1971.

11.24   Merz, J. T. *European Thought in the Nineteenth Century*, 4 vols, Gloucester, Mass: Peter Smith, 1976.

11.25   Rieber, R. and K. Salzinger, eds, *Psychology: Theoretical–historical perspectives*, New York: Academic, 1980.

11.26   Rothschuh, K. *History of Physiology*, Huntington, NY: Krieger, 1973.

11.27   Schnädelbach, H. *Philosophy in Germany, 1831–1933*, New York: Cambridge University Press, 1984.

11.28   Schneewind, J. B. *Sidgwick's Ethics and Victorian Moral Philosophy*, Oxford: Clarendon Press, 1977.

11.29   Smith, R. 'The Background of Physiological Psychology in Natural Philosophy', *History of Science*, 11 (1973): 75–123.

11.30   Ward, J. *Psychology* (from the *Encyclopedia Britannica*, 9th edn), Washington, DC: University Publications, 1977.

Traditional metaphysics

Primary sources

11.31   Abercrombie, J. *Inquiries Concerning the Intellectual Powers and the Investigation of Truth*, ed. J. Abbott, New York: Collins and Brother, n.d.

11.32   Anonymous, 'Reid and the Philosophy of Common Sense: An Essay-review of William Hamilton's Edition of *The Works of Thomas Reid*', *Blackwood's Edinburgh Magazine*, 62 (1847): 239–58.

11.33 Bell, C. *The Hand: Its Mechanism and Vital Endowments*, Philadelphia: Cary, Lea, & Blanchard, 1835.

11.34 Blumenbach, J. F. *The Elements of Physiology*, London: Longman, Rees, Orme, Brown, & Green, 1828.

11.35 Brown, T. *Observations on the Nature and Tendency of the Doctrine of Mr Hume, Concerning the Relation of Cause and Effect*, 2nd edn, Edinburgh: Mundell & Sons, 1806.

11.36 Combe, G. *The Constitution of Man Considered in Relation to External Objects*, 20th edn, New York: Samuel Wells, 1869.

11.37 Coleridge, S. T. *Biographia Literaria*, New York: Dutton, 1934.

11.38 Cousin, V. *Elements of Psychology*, New York: Gould & Newman, 1838.

11.39 Dods, J. B. *Electrical Psychology*, 2nd edn, New York: Fowler & Wells, 1850.

11.40 Fichte, J. G. *The Vocation of Man*, Indianapolis: Bobbs-Merrill, 1956.

11.41 Hamilton, Sir W. *Lectures on Logic and Metaphysics*, 2 vols, Boston: Gould & Lincoln, 1865.

11.42 Haven, J. *Mental Philosophy: Including the Intellect, Sensibilities, and Will*, Boston: Gould & Lincoln, 1873.

11.43 Henry, C. S. *An Epitome of the History of Philosophy: Being the work Adopted by the University of France for Instruction in the Colleges and High Schools*, New York: Harper & Brothers, 1842.

11.44 Reid, T. *The Works of Thomas Reid, Now fully Collected, with Selections from his Unpublished Letters*, 7th edn, 2 vols, Edinburgh, Maclachlan and Stewart, 1872.

11.45 Roget, P. M. *Treatises on Physiology and Phrenology*, Edinburgh: Black, 1838.

11.46 Schelling, F. W. J. *Ideas for a Philosophy of Nature*, 2nd edn, Cambridge: Cambridge University Press, 1988.

11.47 Spurzheim, J. G. *Phrenology in Connection with the Study of Physiognomy*, Boston:, Marsh, Capon, & Lyon, 1834.

11.48 —— *Phrenology, or the Doctrine of Mental Phenomena*, Boston: Marsh, Capon, & Lyon, 1835.

11.49 —— *The Natural Laws of Man*, New York: Fowler & Wells, n.d.

11.50 Stewart, D. *The Works of Dugald Stewart*, 7 vols, Cambridge: Hilliard & Brown, 1829.

11.51 Wayland, F. *The Elements of Moral Science*, 11th edn, Boston: Gould, Kendall, & Lincoln, 1839.

11.52 Wight, O. *Sir William Hamilton's Philosophy*, New York: Appleton, 1857.

11.53 Winslow, H. *Intellectual Philosophy: Analytical, Synthetical, and Practical*, 8th edn, Boston: Brewer & Tileston, 1864.

Secondary sources

11.54 Gordon-Taylor, Sir G. and E. Walls, *Sir Charles Bell: His Life and Times*, Edinburgh and London: Livingstone, 1958.

11.55 Howe, D. W. *The Unitarian Conscience: Harvard Moral Philosophy, 1805–1861*, Middletown: Wesleyan University Press, 1988.

11.56 Kennedy, E. *Destutt de Tracy and the Origins of 'Ideology'*, Philadelphia: American Philosophical Society, 1978.

11.57 Lenoir, T. 'Kant, Blumenbach, and Vital Materialism in German Biology', *Isis*, 71 (1980): 77–108.

11.58 Mills, J. A. 'Thomas Brown on the Philosophy and Psychology of Perception', *Journal of the History of the Behavioral Sciences*, 23 (1987): 37–49.

11.59 Robinson, D. 'Thomas Reid's Critique of Dugald Stewart', *Journal of the History of Philosophy*, 28 (1989): 405–22.

11.60 Robinson, D. S. *The Story of Scottish Philosophy*, New York: Exposition, 1961.

11.61 Rosen, G. 'The Philosophy of Ideology and the Emergence of Modern Medicine in France', *Bulletin of the History of Medicine*, 20 (1946): 328–39.

11.62 Smith, C. U. M. 'Friedrich Nietzsche's Biological Epistemics', *Journal of Social and Biological Structures*, 9 (1986): 375–88.

11.63 Stirling, H. 'Was Sir William Hamilton a Berkeleian?', *Fortnightly Review*, 6 (1866): 218–28.

11.64 Truman, N. E. *Maine de Biran's Philosophy of Will*, New York: Macmillan, 1904.

11.65 White, A. *Schelling: an Introduction to the System of Freedom*, New Haven and London: Yale University Press, 1983.

Fluid-materialist psychology

11.66 Cantor, G. N. 'A critique of Shapin's Social Interpretation of the Edinburgh Phrenology Debate', *Annals of Science*, 33 (1975): 245–56.

11.67 —— 'The Edinburgh Phrenology Debate: 1803–1828', *Annals of Science*, 32 (1975): 195–218.

11.68 Darwin, E. *Zoonomia*, 2 vols, London: Johnson, 1794–6.

11.69 Goodfield-Toulmin, J. 'Some Aspects of English Physiology: 1780–1840', *Journal of the History of Biology*, 2 (1969): 283–320.

11.70 Holmes, R. *Shelley: the Pursuit*, Harmondsworth: Penguin, 1974.

11.71 King-Hele, D. *Doctor of Revolution: the Life and Genius of Erasmus Darwin*, London: Faber & Faber, 1977.

11.72 McElderry, R. E. *Shelley's Critical Prose*, Lincoln: University of Nebraska Press, 1967.

11.73 Priestley, J. *An Examination of Dr Reid's Inquiry into the Human Mind . . .*, London: Johnson, 1774.

11.74 —— *Disquisitions Relating to Matter and Spirit*, London: Johnson, 1777.

11.75 Shapin, S. 'Phrenological Knowledge and the Social Structure of Early Nineteenth-Century Edinburgh', *Annals of Science*, 32 (1975): 219–43.

11.76 Shelley, M. *Frankenstein: or, the Modern Prometheus*, ed. James Rieger, Chicago: University of Chicago Press, 1982.

11.77 Shelley, P. B. *The Complete Poetical Works of Percy Bysshe Shelley*, Boston: Houghton Mifflin, 1901.

11.78   Staum, M. S. *Cabanis: Enlightenment and Medical Philosophy in the French Revolution*, Princeton: Princeton University Press, 1980.

The suppression of scientific psychology

Social histories of censorship and police activities

11.79   Desmond, A. *The Politics of Evolution: Morphology, Medicine, and Reform in Radical London*, Chicago: University of Chicago Press, 1989.

11.80   Emerson, D. *Metternich and the Political Police: Security and Subversion in the Habsburg Monarchy*, The Hague: Nijhoff, 1968.

11.81   Jacyna, L. S. 'Immanence or Transcendence: Theories of Life and Organization in Britain, 1790–1835', *Isis*, 74 (1983): 311–29.

11.82   Mudford, P. G. 'William Lawrence and *The Natural History of Man*', *Journal of the History of Ideas*, 29 (1968): 430–6.

11.83   Nicolson, H. *The Concert of Vienna*, London: Macmillan, 1946.

11.84   Rigotti, F. 'Biology and Society in the Age of Enlightenment', *Journal of the History of Ideas*, 47 (1986): 215–33.

Social histories of professionalization

11.85   Ben-David, J. 'Social Factors in the Origins of a New Science', in J. Ben-David, ed., *Scientific Growth: Essays on the Organization and Ethos of Science*, Berkeley and Los Angeles: University of California Press, 1991.

11.86   —— 'Universities and Academic Systems in Modern Societies', in J. Ben-David, ed., *Scientific Growth: Essays on the Organization and Ethos of Science*, Berkeley and Los Angeles: University of California Press, 1991.

11.87   Jacyna, J. S. 'Principles of General Physiology: the Comparative Dimension of British Neuroscience in the 1830s and 1840s', *Studies in the History of Biology*, 7 (1984): 47–92.

11.88   —— 'Medical Science and Moral Science: The Cultural Relations of Physiology in Restoration France', *History of Science*, 25 (1987): 111–46.

11.89   Lenoir, T. 'Teleology without Regrets. The Transformation of Physiology in Germany: 1790–1847', *Studies in the History and Philosophy of Science*, 12 (1981): 293–354.

11.90   Lesch, J. E. *Science and Medicine in France: The Emergence of Experimental Physiology*, Cambridge, Mass.: Harvard University Press, 1985.

11.91   Schiller, J. 'Physiology's Struggle for Independence', *History of Science* 7 (1968): 64–89.

11.92   Sheets-Pyenson, S. 'Popular Science Periodicals in Paris and London, 1820–1875', *Annals of Science*, 42 (1985): 549–72.

Emergent naturalism

11.93 Bain, A. *Mind and Body: The Theories of their Relation*, 2nd edn, London: Henry King, 1873.

11.94 Herbart, J. F. *Lehrbuch zur Psychologie*, Königsberg: Unzer, 1834.

11.95 Lenoir, T. 'Kant, Blumenbach, and Vital Materialism in German Biology', *Isis*, 71 (1980): 77–108.

11.96 —— *The Strategy of Life: Teleology and Mechanics in 19th Century German Biology*, Chicago: University of Chicago Press, 1982.

11.97 Müller, J. *The Elements of Physiology*, 2 vols, London: Murray, 1838–40.

11.98 Prochaska, G. 'A Dissertation on the Functions of the Nervous System', in T. Laycock, ed., *Unzer and Prochaska on the Nervous System*, London: Sydenham Society, 1851.

11.99 Unzer, J. A. 'The Principles of Physiology', in T. Laycock, ed., *Unzer and Prochaska on the Nervous System*, London: Sydenham Society, 1851.

Making a sense

11.100 Brown, T. *Lectures on the Philosophy of the Human Mind*, 3 vols, Philadelphia: John Grigg, 1824.

11.101 Bastian, B. C. 'The "Muscular Sense"; Its Nature and Cortical Localisation', *Brain*, 10 (1887): 1–137.

11.102 Carmichael, L. 'Sir Charles Bell: A Contribution to the History of Physiological Psychology', *Psychological Review*, 33 (1926): 188–217.

11.103 de Tracy, D. *Éléments d'idéologie*, 3 vols, Paris: Charles M. Levi, 1824.

11.104 Jones, E. G. 'The Development of the "Muscular Sense" Concept during the Nineteenth Century, and the Work of H. Charlton Bastian', *Journal of the History of Medicine*, 27 (1972): 298–311.

11.105 Mill, James *Analysis of the Phenomena of the Human Mind*, ed. J. S. Mill with the assistance of A. Bain, G. Grotes and A. Findlater, 2nd edn, 2 vols, London: Longmans, Green, Reader, & Dyer, 1869.

Motor theories of mind

11.106 Bain, A. 'The Intellect, Viewed Physiologically', *Fortnightly Review*, 3 (1865): 735–48.

11.107 —— 'The Feelings and the Will, Viewed Physiologically', *Fortnightly Review*, 3 (1865): 575–88.

11.108 Bastian, H. C. 'The Physiology of Thinking', *Fortnightly Review*, 11 (1869): 57–72.

11.109 Bastian, H. C. *The Brain as an Organ of Mind*, New York: D. Appleton, 1880.

11.110 Carpenter, W. B. *Mental Physiology*, New York: D. Appleton, 1874.

11.111 Danziger, K. 'Mid-nineteenth century British Psycho-Physiology: a Neglected Chapter in the History of Psychology', in W. Woodward and M.

Ash, eds, *The Problematic Science: Psychology in Nineteenth Century Thought*, New York: Praeger, 1980.

11.112 Ferrier, D. *The Functions of the Brain*, 2nd edn, London: Smith, Elder, 1886.

11.113 Smith, C. U. M. 'Evolution and the Problem of Mind, Part II: John Hughlings Jackson', *Journal of the History of Biology*, 15 (1982): 241–62.

11.114 Stirling, J. H. 'Kant Refuted by Dint of Muscle', *Fortnightly Review*, 18 (1872): 413–37.

11.115 Talbott, R. E. 'Ferrier, the Synergy Concept, and the Study of Posture and Movement', in R. E. T. and. D. R. Humphrey, eds, *Posture and Movement*, New York: Raven, 1979.

Natural metaphysics

11.116 Anonymous, 'Iconoclasm in German Philosophy', *Westminster Review* 59 (1853): 202–12.

11.117 Anonymous (Robert Chambers). *The Vestiges of the Natural History of Creation*, 10th edn, London: John Churchill, 1853.

11.118 Bernard, W. 'Spinoza's Influence on the Rise of Scientific Psychology: a Neglected Chapter in the History of Psychology', *Journal of the History of the Behavioral Sciences*, 8 (1972): 208–15.

11.119 Carpenter, W. B. *Nature and Man: Essays Scientific and Philosophical*, London: Kegan Paul, Trench, 1888.

11.120 Fechner, G. T. *Zend-Avesta: oder über die Dinge des Himmels und des Jenseits*, Leipzig: Voss, 1851.

11.121 —— *Life after Death*, New York: Pantheon, 1943.

11.122 Fechner, G. T. 'My own Viewpoint on Mental Measurement', *Psychological Research*, 49 (1987): 213–19.

11.123 Kraushaar, O. 'Lotze's Influence on the Psychology of William James', *Psychological Review*, 43 (1936): 235–57.

11.124 —— 'Lotze's Influence on the Pragmatim and Practical Philosophy of William James', *Journal of the History of Ideas*, 1 (1940): 439–58.

11.125 Lewes, G. H. *The Physical Basis of Mind*, Boston: Houghton Mifflin, 1877.

11.126 Lindsay, T. M. 'Rudolf Hermann Lotze', *Mind*, 1 (1876): 363–81.

11.127 Lotze, R. H. *Microcosmus: An Essay Concerning Man and his Relation to the World*, 2nd edn, New York: Scribner & Welford, 1887.

11.128 Magee, B. *The Philosophy of Schopenhauer*, Oxford: Clarendon Press, 1983.

11.129 Porter, N. *The Human Intellect, with an Introduction upon Psychology and the Soul*, 4th edn, New York: Scribner Armstrong, 1877.

11.130 Santayana, G. *Lotze's System of Philosophy*, Bloomington:, Indiana University Press, 1971.

11.131 Schopenhauer, A. 'The Will in Nature', in A. Schopenhauer, ed., *Two Essays by Arthur Schopenhauer*, London: George Bell & Sons, 1907.

11.132 —— *The World as Will and Representation*, 2nd edn, trans. E. F. J. Payne, New York: Dover, 1969.

11.133 —— *The Fourfold Root of the Principle of Sufficient Reason*, 2nd edn, trans. E. F. J. Payne, La Salle: Open Court, 1974.

11.134 Sully, J. *Pessimism*, London, Kegan Paul, 1877.

11.135 Woodward, W. 'Fechner's Panpsychism: a Scientific Solution to the Mind-Body Problem', *Journal of the History of the Behavioral Sciences*, 8 (1972): 367–86.

11.136 Woodward, W. R. 'From Association to Gestalt: the Fate of Hermann Lotze's Theory of Spatial Perception, 1846–1920', *Isis*, 69 (1978): 572–82.

The three unconsciousnesses

11.137 Bailey, S. *A Review of Berkeley's Theory of Vision, Designed to Show the Unsoundness of that Celebrated Speculation*, London: James Ridgeway, 1842.

11.138 Dallas, E. S. *The Gay Science*, 2 vols, London: Chapman & Hall, 1866.

11.139 Hartman, E. von. *Philosophy of the Unconscious*, 3 vols, New York: Harcourt, Brace, 1931.

11.140 Helmholtz, H von. *Treatise on Physiological Optics*, 3rd edn, 3 vols, trans. J. Southall, New York: Dover, 1962.

11.141 Holmes, O. W. 'Mechanism in Thought and Morals: Address to the Phi Beta Kappa Society at Harvard College, June, 1870' in O. W. Holmes, ed., *Pages from an Old Volume of Life: A Collection of Essays 1857–1881*, Boston: Houghton-Mifflin, 1899.

11.142 Mill, J. S. *A System of Logic: Ratiocinative and Inductive*, Toronto and London: University of Toronto Press and Routledge & Kegan Paul, 1973.

11.143 —— 'Bailey on Berkeley's Theory of Vision', in J. Robson, ed., *Essays on Philosophy and the Classics*, Toronto and London: University of Toronto Press and Routledge & Kegan Paul, 1978.

11.144 —— 'Berkeley's Life and Writings', in J. Robson, ed. *Essays on Philosophy and the Classics*, Toronto and London: University of Toronto Press and Routledge & Kegan Paul, 1978.

11.145 —— *An Examination of Sir William Hamilton's Philosophy, and of the Principal Philosophical Questions Discussed in his Writings*, Toronto and London: University of Toronto Press and Routledge & Kegan Paul, 1979.

11.146 Mineka, F. E. *The Earlier Letters of John Stuart Mill*, Toronto and London: University of Toronto Press and Routledge & Kegan Paul, 1963.

11.147 Mineka, F. and D. Lindley, *The Later Letters of John Stuart Mill*, Toronto and London: University of Toronto Press and Routledge & Kegan Paul, 1972.

11.148 Pastore, N. 'Samuel Bailey's Critique of Berkeley's Theory of Vision', *Journal of the History of the Behavioral Sciences*, 1 (1965): 321–37.

11.149 Smith, C. U. M. 'Friedrich Nietzsche's Biological Epistemics', *Journal of Social and Biological Structures*, 9 (1986): 375–88.

11.150 —— ' "Clever Beasts who Invented Knowing": Nietzsche's Evolutionary Biology of Knowledge', *Biology and Philosophy*, 2 (1987): 65–91.

11.151 Turner, R. S. 'Hermann von Helmholtz and the Empiricist Vision', *Journal of the History of the Behavioral Sciences*, 13 (1977): 48–58.

11.152 —— 'Helmholtz, Sensory Physiology, and the Disciplinary Development of German Physiology', in W. Woodward and M. Ash, ed., *The Problematic Science: Psychology in Nineteenth Century Thought*, New York: Praeger, 1982.

11.153 Wilson, F. 'Mill and Comte on the Method of Introspection', *Journal of the History of the Behavioral Sciences*, 27 (1991): 107–29.

11.154 —— *Psychological Analysis and the Philosophy of John Stuart Mill*, Toronto: University of Toronto Press, 1991.

Positivistic tendencies

11.155 Brown, A. W. *The Metaphysical Society: Victorian Minds in Crisis*, New York: Columbia University Press, 1947.

11.156 Buckle, H. T. *History of Civilization in England*, 2nd edn, 2 vols, New York: Appleton-Century, 1939.

11.157 Clifford, W. K. *Lectures and Essays*, 2 vols, London: Macmillan, 1879.

11.158 Haight, G. S. *The Letters of George Eliot*, New Haven: Yale University Press, 1978.

11.159 Lange, F. A. *The History of Materialism and Criticism of its Present Importance*, 2nd edn, 3 vols, Boston, Houghton Mifflin, 1881.

11.160 Lewes, G. H. 'Phrenology in France', *Blackwoods*, 82 (1857): 665–74.

11.161 Lindenfield, D. F. *The Transformation of Positivism: Alexius Meinong and European Thought*, Berkeley and Los Angeles: University of California Press, 1980.

11.162 Pollock, F. *Spinoza: His Life and Philosophy*, London: Kegan Paul, 1880.

11.163 Simon, W. M. *European Positivism in the Nineteenth Century*, Ithaca: Cornell University Press, 1963.

11.164 Taine, H. *Les Philosophes françaises du XIX siècle*, Paris: Hachette, 1857.

11.165 —— *Les Philosophes classiques au xix siècle en France*, 3rd edn, Paris: Hachette, 1868.

11.166 —— *On intelligence*, New York: Holt & Williams, 1872.

11.167 Tyndall, J. *Fragments of Science*, 2 vols, New York: Appleton, 1898.

11.168 Willey, T. E. *Back to Kant: the Revival of Kantianism in German Social and Historical Thought*, Detroit: Wayne State University Press, 1978.

The emergence of experimental psychology

11.169 Danziger, K. 'The History of Introspection Reconsidered', *Journal of the History of the Behavioral Sciences*, 16 (1980): 241–62.

11.170 —— *Constructing the Subject: Historical Origins of Psychological Research*, New York: Cambridge University Press, 1991.

11.171 Forrest, D. W. *Francis Galton: the Life of a Victorian Genius*, London: Elek, 1974.

11.172 Hall, G. S. *Aspects of German Culture*, Boston: James R. Osgood, 1881.

11.173 —— 'The New Psychology', *The Andover Review*, 3 (1885): 120–35, 239–49.

11.174 James, W. *Essays in Psychology*, Cambridge, Mass.: Harvard University Press, 1983.

11.175 —— *Essays, Comments, and Reviews*, Cambridge, Mass.: Harvard University Press, 1987.

11.176 —— *Manuscript Essays and Notes*, Cambridge, Mass.: Harvard University Press, 1988.

11.177 Mercier, D. *The Relation of Experimental Psychology to Philosophy*, New York: Benziger Brothers, 1902.

11.178 Ribot, T. *English Psychology*, London, Henry King, 1873.

11.179 —— *German Psychology Today*, New York: Scribners, 1886.

11.180 Stumpf, C. 'Hermann von Helmholtz and the New Psychology', *Psychological Review*, 2 (1895): 1–12.

11.181 Tansey, E. M. ' "The Science Least Adequately Studied in England": Physiology and the G. H. Lewes Studentship', *Journal of the History of Medicine and Allied Sciences*, 47 (1992): 163–86.

11.182 Wundt, W. *Lectures on Human and Animal Psychology*, 2nd edn, London: Swan Sonnenschein, 1894.

CHAPTER 12

American pragmatism
Peirce
Cheryl Misak

⊷ INTRODUCTION ⊷

Charles Sanders Peirce (1839–1914), one of America's greatest philosophers, mathematicians, and logicians, was a difficult and not altogether pleasant character. That, combined with what the establishment
regarded as moral lapses, resulted in the fact that he was thwarted in
his attempts to obtain a permanent academic post and died a malnour-
ished and impoverished outcast. He was dismissed from his brief stint
at Johns Hopkins University, dismissed from his service with the US
Coast Survey (a job handed to him by his father, its superintendent),
and ostracized by his alma mater – Harvard University.

Despite this grim life, Peirce was the founder of pragmatism,
semiotics, and a theory of truth and knowledge that is still popular
today. He was a serious student of the history of philosophy and of
science and he was generous in acknowledging the influence of others.
One of the most important influences is Kant, of whom the young
Peirce was a 'passionate devotee' ([12.1], 4: 2).[1] It is from Kant, for
instance, that Peirce inherits a quest for the categories, a penchant
for the notion of continuity and a desire to develop an 'architectonic'
system. But there is also a strong gust of medieval philosophy blowing
throughout his work, Duns Scotus in particular. It is from here that
Peirce gets his Scholastic realism, which is set against the nominalism
and individualism of the British empiricists. But there is also a clear
affinity between Peirce and those empiricists. For instance, Peirce
credits Berkeley's arguments that all meaningful language be matched
with sensory experience as the precursor of pragmatism: 'Berkeley on
the whole has more right to be considered the introducer of pragmatism

357

into philosophy than any other one man, though I was more explicit in enunciating it (letter to William James, 1903 ([12.12], 2: 425)).

The volume and breadth of Peirce's work is staggering. But because he was unsuccessful in securing a permanent academic position, most of it went unpublished in his time. It lies in a huge bulk of manuscripts and scraps. His best known papers are those of the 1870s series in *Popular Science Monthly* called 'Illustrations of the Logic of Science'. These include 'How To Make Our Ideas Clear' and 'The Fixation of Belief'. His Lowell Lectures in 1898 and 1903 and his Harvard Pragmatism Lectures in 1903 also contain essential material. But much of what is important is only now being published in the definitive chronological edition.

THE PRAGMATIC MAXIM[2]

The 'spirit' of pragmatism is captured in the following maxim: 'we must look to the upshot of our concepts in order rightly to apprehend them' ([12.1], 5: 4) There is, Peirce argues, a connection between knowing the meaning of a sentence or hypothesis and knowing what to expect if it is true. If a sentence has no consequences (if there isn't anything one could expect would be the case if it were true) then it lacks an important dimension. It lacks a property that we would have had to get right if we were to know what it means. Pragmatism labels such a hypothesis defective. Understanding requires knowledge of consequences and a sentence is legitimate only if it has consequences.

This criterion of legitimacy permeates Peirce's work. Not only does he disparage certain philosophical positions as pragmatically meaningless, but he argues that if we focus on the consequences of 'H is true', 'the probability of H is n', 'x is real', etc., we will adopt the best accounts of truth, probability, reality, etc. So the pragmatic maxim serves as a standard for determining which expressions are 'metaphysical rubbish' or 'gibberish' ([12.1], 8: 191) and it serves as a methodological principle for formulating philosophical theories.

In 'How To Make Our Ideas Clear', Peirce publicly unveils pragmatism and sets out the maxim as follows:

> Consider what effects, which might conceivably have practical bearings, we conceive the object of our conception to have. Then, our conception of these is the whole of our conception of the object.
>
> ([12.2], 3: 266)

Peirce suggests in this paper that knowing the meaning of an expression is exhausted by knowing its 'practical' effects, which he characterizes as 'effects, direct or indirect, upon our senses' ([12.2], 3: 266). These effects can be described by conditionals of the sort: if you were to do *A*, you would observe *B*. He says:

> we come down to what is tangible and practical, as the root of every real distinction of thought, no matter how subtle [*sic*] it may be; and there is no distinction of meaning so fine as to consist in anything but a possible difference of practice.
>
> ([12.2], 3: 265)

As an example of how the pragmatic maxim operates, Peirce examines the meaning of 'this diamond is hard'. He says that it means that if you try to scratch it, you will find that 'it will not be scratched by many other substances'. ([12.2], 3: 266).

Notice that the consequence in this example is formulated as an indicative conditional, as a matter of what *will* happen. Peirce sees that if he formulates consequences in this manner, it makes little sense to describe a diamond which is in fact never scratched as being hard. He seems to be content with this conclusion in 'How To Make Our Ideas Clear'. But when he considers the matter later, he always insists on a subjunctive formulation. He chides himself for making the nominalist suggestion that habits, dispositions or 'would-bes' are not real. A 'Scholastic realism' about dispositions and subjunctive conditionals must be adopted: a disposition is more than the total of its realizations and a subjunctive conditional is determinately correct or incorrect, whether or not the antecedent is fulfilled. The consequences which concern pragmatism are those which would occur under certain conditions, not those which will actually occur. His considered view about the unscratched diamond is that 'it is a real fact that it *would* resist pressure' ([12.1], 8: 208).

This was not Peirce's only amendment to the pragmatic maxim. In his struggle to arrive at a suitable criterion of understanding and meaning, he sometimes suggested one very similar to the criterion we find later in logical positivism. The positivists' criterion effectively restricted knowledge to that which physical science is about; we can have knowledge only of that which is directly observable or verifiable. Anything else – metaphysics, for example – is literally meaningless. But Peirce is concerned with a much broader account of what is involved in linguistic competence and altered his maxim in order to make it more generous.

For one thing, Peirce himself inclined toward metaphysics and he does not want to do away with it altogether. In metaphysics 'one finds those questions that at first seem to offer no handle for reason's clutch, but which readily yield to logical analysis' ([12.1], 6: 463). Metaphysics, 'in its present condition' is 'a puny, rickety, and scrofulous science'

([12.1], 6: 6). But it need not be so, for many of its hypotheses are meaningful and important. It is the job of the pragmatic maxim to sweep 'all metaphysical rubbish out of one's house. Each abstraction is either pronounced to be gibberish or is provided with a plain, practical definition' ([12.1], 8: 191).

Secondly, Peirce frequently claims that the pragmatic maxim captures only *a part* of what it is to know the meaning of an expression. In order to grasp a term, he argues, a threefold competence is required. The interpreter must be able to (1) pick out what objects the term refers to; that is, know Mill's 'denotation', Hamilton's 'extension' or 'breadth'; (2) give a definition of the term; that is, know Mill's 'connotation', Hamilton's 'intention' or 'depth'; (3) know what to expect if hypotheses containing the term are true; that is, know the consequences of hypotheses containing the term.

Whereas his predecessors identified the first two sources of meaning, Peirce thinks that his contribution was to locate the important third source. He takes his three aspects of understanding to spell out completely what someone must be able to do if she grasps a concept or knows the meaning of an expression.

But none the less, the pragmatic maxim is supposed to be a criterion for meaning identity. Peirce argues that a purported difference which makes no practical difference is spurious; if two hypotheses have the same set of subjunctive conditional consequences, then they express the same content. It is pointless to suggest that they differ in denotation or connotation.

Thirdly, Peirce at times tries to divert the pragmatist's gaze from sensory experience. His account of experience is very generous: any belief that is compelling, surprising, impinging, unchosen, involuntary or forceful is a perception. And such beliefs need not arise from the senses.

He takes there to be two kinds of experience – 'ideal' and 'real'. The latter is sensory experience and the former includes experience in which 'operations upon diagrams, whether external or imaginary, take the place of the experiments upon real things that one performs in chemical and physical research' ([12.1], 4: 530).

These diagrammatic experiments or thought experiments figure in mathematical and deductive inquiry. They involve 'experimenting upon [an] image in the imagination, and of observing the result so as to discover unnoticed and hidden relations among the parts' ([12.1], 3: 363). The mathematician, for instance, draws subsidiary lines in geometry or makes transformations in algebraic formulae and then observes the results: 'his hypotheses are creatures of his own imagination; but he discovers in them relations which surprise him sometimes'.

([12.1], 5: 567). Since surprise is the force of experience, the upshot of such reasoning counts as experience.

What this means is that Peirce, unlike his verificationist predecessors (Hume, Comte) and successors (the logical positivists), wants all hypotheses to be exposed to the pragmatic maxim; he does not exempt formal (or what are now called 'analytic') sentences. Logical and mathematical hypotheses can meet the criterion because there is a kind of experience relevant to them. And some metaphysical hypotheses meet the criterion as well. They must have consequences, Peirce argues, for ordinary, everyday, experience, by contrast with experiences in technical experimental contexts and by contrast with experiences in diagrammatic contexts.

⚬ TRUTH AND REALITY ⚬

Peirce applies the pragmatic maxim to the metaphysical debate on the nature of truth and reality. The philosopher must look to our everyday practices and see what account of truth would be best suited for them: 'We must not begin by talking of pure ideas, – vagabond thoughts that tramp the public roads without any human habitation, – but must begin with men and their conversation' ([12.1], 8: 112).

The correspondence theory, he argues, lacks such human habitation. It holds that a true hypothesis is one which is in agreement with an unknowable 'thing-in-itself'. But:

> You only puzzle yourself by talking of this metaphysical 'truth' and metaphysical 'falsity' that you know nothing about. All you have any dealings with are your doubts and beliefs... If your terms 'truth' and 'falsity' are taken in such senses as to be definable in terms of doubt and belief and the course of experience... well and good: in that case, you are only talking about doubt and belief. But if by truth and falsity you mean something not definable in terms of doubt and belief in any way, then you are talking of entities of whose existence you can know nothing, and which Ockham's razor would clean shave off. Your problems would be greatly simplified, if, instead of saying that you want to know the 'Truth', you were simply to say that you want to attain a state of belief unassailable by doubt.
>
> ([12.1], 5: 416).

Peirce's argument here is that if one offered an account of '*H* is true' in terms of its consequences for doubt, belief and perceptual disappointment, one would be offering a pragmatic elucidation of truth.

And that, if it were a correct specification of the consequences, would be a satisfactory account of truth. But a definition of truth which makes no reference to belief, doubt and experience is an empty definition of truth. It is useful only to those who have never encountered the notion.

Peirce sometimes states this objection to the correspondence theory by labelling it a 'transcendental' account of truth ([12.1], 5: 572). Such accounts regard truth 'as the subject of metaphysics exclusively' – spurious metaphysics, not pragmatically legitimate metaphysics. On the correspondence definition, truth transcends experience; it has no consequences for inquiry. He says:

> The *Ding an sich* . . . can neither be indicated nor found. Consequently, no proposition can refer to it, and nothing true or false can be predicated of it. Therefore, all references to it must be thrown out as meaningless surplusage.
>
> ([12.1], 5: 525)

If we look at the experience of inquirers which seems most relevant to truth – the evidence they have for and against hypotheses – the correspondence theory is speechless. For on that account, there is an unbridgeable gap between what we can have evidence for and the inaccessible reality. We could have the best possible evidence for an hypothesis and yet that hypothesis might fail to be true. The correspondence theory does not tell us what we can expect of a true hypothesis and so it is not capable of guiding us in our actions and inquiries. If truth is the aim of inquiry, then on the correspondence construal, enquirers are left completely in the dark as to how they should conduct their investigations. The aim is not, Peirce says, 'readily comprehensible' ([12.1], 1: 578). How could anyone aim for a sort of truth that transcends experience? How could an enquirer develop a means for achieving that aim?

In anticipation of certain kinds of naturalized epistemologies, Peirce focuses on what he thinks the transcendentalist has lost sight of – the link between truth and inquiry. The pragmatic account deals with the common experience that constitutes inquiry, and so it offers a conception of truth that can be a guide for inquiry.

On Peirce's view, 'A true proposition is a proposition belief in which would never lead to . . . disappointment' ([12.1], 5: 569). This is an account of what we can expect from a true belief: if we were to inquire into *H*, we would find that *H* would encounter no recalcitrant experience. We can predict that if we were diligently to inquire about *H*, *H* would not, in the end, be overturned by experience. An alternative way of making the point is to say that we would expect the following: if inquiry with respect to *H* were to be pursued as far as it could fruitfully go (i.e. far enough so that the hypothesis would no longer be improved upon), H would be believed (it would not be doubted). For if H would be believed after such a prolonged inquiry, then H would not have been overturned by experience; it would not have been put into doubt. A true belief is a permanently settled belief.

Peirce's view of reality is connected to his view of truth. The consequence of a thing's being real is that the hypothesis asserting its reality would be, if inquiry relevant to it were pursued, perfectly stable or doubt-resistant. For a consequence of a thing's being real is that, if we were to inquire into issues for which it is relevant, it would in the long run force itself on our attention. The pragmatic view is that reality is the 'object' of true beliefs – it is what true beliefs are about. Reality is what beliefs in the final opinion would fix on.

This account of reality, Peirce argues, fulfils the definition of reality as that which is independent of whatever 'you, I, or any number of men' think. We have seen that Peirce is a realist about subjunctives. What would be believed to be real is thus independent of what is believed to be real at any particular time. The real 'is that which, sooner or later, information and reasoning would result in, and which is therefore independent of the vagaries of you and me' ([12.2], 2: 239) Peirce thinks that this makes reality 'objective'. ([12.2], 3: 29).

He makes the same point about truth. What would be ascertained to be true would be so ascertained whatever anyone here and now thinks. A hypothesis may be believed, then doubted and then believed again, but this does not affect whether it would be believed at the end of a prolonged inquiry. Independently of whatever any 'definite' group of inquirers may think about the truth-value of H, H either would be or would not be a member of the final opinion (12.1], 5: 565). Thus the truth-value of H is an objective matter – it does not depend on what anyone at any particular point happens to think.

❧ SEMIOTICS ❧

Peirce was a pioneer in semiotics. Not only is he responsible for the distinction between type ('human' as a general term) and token ('human' as applied to various objects), but he developed a complex map of signs which covers sixty-six classes, from which sprout 59,049 varieties.

His theory of signs has interpretation at its centre. For Peirce holds that the sign-referent relation is not able, on its own, to uphold a complete account of representation. Representation is triadic: it involves a sign, an object and an interpreter. Each aspect of this representation relation corresponds to one of the elements in Peirce's division of signs into icons, indices and symbols. And in each of these, one or another aspect of linguistic competence is most prominent.

Icons are signs that exhibit their objects by virtue of similarity or resemblance. A portrait is an icon of the person it portrays and a map is an icon of a certain geographical area. Peirce argues that the meaning of iconic signs lies mostly in their connotation; what makes a painting or a map an icon is that its qualities or attributes resemble the qualities or attributes of its object.

Indices are signs that indicate their objects in a causal manner; an index 'signifies its object solely by virtue of being really connected with it' ([12.1], 3: 360). A symptom is an index of a disease and smoke is an index of fire. The essential quality of an index is its ability to compel attention. A pointing finger, a knock on the door or a demonstrative pronoun, such as 'there' or 'that', draws attention to its object by getting the interpreter to focus on the object. So an index, by being object-directed, has its denotation or extension as its 'most prominent feature' ([12.1], 8: 119). An index picks out or indicates its object; it points to 'that, that and that' as its extension.

A symbol is a word, hypothesis or argument which depends on a conventional or habitual rule; a symbol is a sign 'because it is used and understood as such' ([12.1], 2: 307) Symbols have 'principle' or pragmatic meaning; they have 'intellectual purport'.

Peirce contrasts pragmatic meaning with 'internal' meaning (which he relates to icons and connotation) and with 'external' meaning (which he relates to indices and denotation). He suggests that the pragmatic meaning of symbols has to do with a 'purpose' ([12.1], 8: 119). A symbol has pragmatic meaning because if the utterer knows how interpreters habitually interpret a sign, she can use the sign to cause a specific effect in the interpreter. And Peirce calls this effect the 'interpretant' of the sign. If, for instance, I write 'dog', I intend the sign to cause a certain effect in the interpreter (perhaps I want the interpreter to think of a dog) whereas if I write 'odg', I do not, as 'odg' is not a conventional sign. Or if I assert 'That bridge has a loose plank', I might want the interpreter to be careful when crossing the bridge. Peirce characterizes an assertion as the attempt to produce a disposition in an interpreter; it is 'the deliberate exercise, in uttering the proposition, of a force tending to determine a belief in it in the mind of an interpreter' ([12.4], 4: 249).

Notice that if pragmatic meaning is about this sort of practical consequence, it is no longer about 'effects, direct or indirect, upon our senses'. Pragmatic meaning, rather, involves consequences for action or thought. In 1905 we find Peirce offering this version of the pragmatic maxim: 'The entire intellectual purport of any symbol consists in the total of all general modes of rational conduct which, conditionally upon all the possible different circumstances and desires, would ensue upon the acceptance of the symbol' ([12.1], 5: 438). 'Rational conduct', although Peirce thinks that it will eventually manifest itself in a modification of the interpreter's disposition to behave, includes the conduct of one's thought.

This twist in the pragmatic maxim – that the acceptance of a hypothesis must have effects on an interpreter's train of thought – coincides with a development in the early 1900s in Peirce's theory of signs. That development is a theory of interpretants and Peirce at times locates pragmatic meaning within this theory.

He distinguishes three types of interpretants. The 'immediate' interpretant is the fitness of a sign to be understood in a certain way; the 'dynamical' interpretant is the actual effect a sign has on an interpreter, and the 'final' interpretant is the effect which eventually would be decided to be the correct interpretation. Pragmatic meaning, Peirce says, lies in a kind of dynamical interpretant: the 'ultimate logical interpretant'. A sign, Peirce argues, sparks a subsequent sign, or a logical interpretant, in the mind of the interpreter, and since the logical interpretant is itself a sign, an infinite chain of interpretation, development, or thought, is begun. Peirce stops the regress by introducing the notion of an 'ultimate logical interpretant' or a 'habit-change'. He follows Alexander Bain in taking a belief to be a habit or disposition to behave. And so this new habit is a belief or a modification of the interpreter's tendencies towards action. The pragmatic meaning of an expression, according to Peirce's theory of signs, is the action (which includes the action of subsequent thought, and which ends in a disposition to behave) that arises after an interpreter accepts it.

❧ THEORY OF INQUIRY ❧

The notion of inquiry occupies a central place in Peirce's thought. For the most part, his income was from employment in the United States Coast and Geodetic Survey, where he made numerous and significant contributions. Philosophy, he insisted, must get along with other branches of inquiry. The following motto 'deserves to be inscribed upon every wall of the city of philosophy: Do not block the path of inquiry' ([12.1] 1: 135).

Peirce characterizes inquiry as the struggle to rid ourselves of doubt and achieve a state of belief. An inquirer has a body of settled belief; a set of beliefs which are, in fact, not doubted. These beliefs, however, are susceptible to doubt, if it is prompted by some 'positive reason', such as a surprising experience ([12.1], 5: 51). We have seen that Peirce takes experience to be that which impinges upon us –

experience, he says, teaches us 'by practical jokes, mostly cruel' ([12.1], 5: 51). When experience conflicts with an inquirer's belief, doubt is immediately sparked. And doubt 'essentially involves a struggle to escape' ([12.1], 5: 372 n.2). Inquiry is that struggle to regain belief. The path of inquiry is as follows: belief . . . surprise . . . doubt . . . inquiry . . . belief. . . .

Peirce does not take these points to be mere observations about human psychology; he thinks that psychology should be kept out of logic and the theory of inquiry. Doubt and belief, although they do have psychological aspects, such as making the inquirer feel comfortable or uncomfortable, are best thought of in terms of habits. A 'belief-habit' manifests itself in an expectation: if we believe H, then we habitually expect the consequences or the predictions we derive from H to come about when the appropriate occasion arises. Thus inquirers are thrown into doubt when a recalcitrant experience upsets or disrupts a belief or expectation. There are three stances an inquirer may have with respect to a hypothesis: believe it, believe its negation or consider the matter open to inquiry. Only in the third stance are we left without a habit of expectation and thus it is agnosticism which is the undesirable state. That is, doubting whether an hypothesis is true is not equivalent to believing that it is false, rather, it is not knowing what to believe. What is wrong with this state is that it leads to paralysis of action. An inquirer has some end in view, and two different and inconsistent lines of action present themselves, bringing the inquirer to a halt: 'he waits at the fork for an indication, and kicks his heels . . . A true doubt is accordingly a doubt which really interferes with the smooth working of the belief-habit' ([12.1], 5: 510). Doubt arises because of not knowing how to act. And action can include action in diagrammatic and thought experiments.

Peirce's theory of inquiry has a certain kind of empiricism at its core. Inquirers aim for beliefs that fit with experience. When we replace a belief which has come into doubt, that new belief stands up better than the old one. So we accept it, act on it and think that it is true. But we know very well that it eventually might be overthrown and shown to be false by experience. Peirce adds the more contentious claim that what we aim for is permanently settled beliefs. When we have beliefs that would for ever withstand the tests of experience and argument, he holds that there is no point of refusing to confer upon them the title 'true'. Only a spurious desire for transcendental metaphysics will make one want to distinguish perfectly good beliefs from true beliefs.

A problem faces Peirce here. If beliefs could be settled by a religious authority, or by a charismatic guru or by astrology, so that they were permanently resistant to doubt, there seems to be, on his account, no reason for criticizing them. Peirce considers different methods of fixing belief and suggests that it is hard *really* to end the irritation of doubt.

The method of tenacity, or holding on to your beliefs come what may, will not work, Peirce says, because doubt will be sparked when one notices that the opinions of others differ from one's own. Beliefs produced by the method of authority (fixing beliefs according to the dictates of a State, religion, etc.) will similarly be subject to doubt when one notices that those in other States or religions believe different things. Beliefs produced by the *a priori* method (adopting beliefs which are agreeable to reason) will eventually be doubted when it is seen that what the experts take as being agreeable to reason shifts like a pendulum and is really a matter of intellectual taste. None of these methods will produce permanently settled belief because they have a self-destructive design; the beliefs settled by them eventually would be assailed by doubt.

The agent of destruction which Peirce sees in each of the specious methods seems to be a purported fact about our psychological make-up: if an inquirer believes an hypothesis, and notices that other inquirers do not believe it, that first inquirer will be thrown into doubt. This impulse, Peirce says, is 'too strong in man to be suppressed, without danger of destroying the human species' ([12.2], 3: 250). If this psychological hypothesis expresses a universal fact about us, then the unsatisfactory methods will indeed prove unreliable in the long run. They will not produce permanently settled belief and we should refrain from using them.[3]

There are two other cornerstones to Peirce's theory of inquiry: critical commonsensism and fallibilism. Critical commonsensism is a position about how we ought to regard those beliefs which are settled. It holds that there are many things which inquirers do not doubt and that inquiry must start with a background of beliefs which are not doubted. A body of settled belief is presupposed for the operation of inquiry in that there has to be something settled for surprise to stir up.

This doctrine arose as a response to Peirce's conception of Descartes' project – a systematic attempt to bring into doubt all hypotheses about which error is conceivable. Peirce argued that such doubts would be 'paper' doubts. They are not genuine and they cannot motivate inquiry. The mere possibility of being mistaken with respect to what one believes is never a reason to revise those beliefs. Any of our beliefs might be false, but it would be absurd to doubt them all because of this. If we did, we would not possess a body of stable belief by which to judge new evidence and hypotheses, and hence, we would block the path of inquiry. We can doubt one belief and inquire, but we cannot doubt all of our beliefs and inquire. Peirce's point against Descartes is that if we were to set the requirements on knowledge as high as Descartes does, we would have nothing left to go on. He says,

> there is but one state of mind from which you can 'set out', namely, the very state of mind in which you actually find yourself at the time you do 'set out' – a state in which you are laden with an immense mass of cognition already formed, of which you cannot divest yourself if you would ... Do you call it doubting to write down on a piece of paper that you doubt? If so, doubt has nothing to do with any serious business.
>
> ([12.1], 5: 416)

So Peirce is not concerned with sceptical questions about foundations for certainty, and his arguments are not addressed to those who are.

But he is also a 'contrite fallibilist', holding that all our beliefs can be doubted; that is, that none of them are certain. There is a tension here: how can it be that all our beliefs are fallible, or subject to doubt, but, nevertheless, some of our beliefs must not be doubted if inquiry is to be possible?

Peirce's reconciliation of fallibilism with critical commonsensism is made in terms of his notion of truth. He thinks that many of our beliefs are indeed those which would be included in the final opinion, but since we cannot know for any given belief whether or not it would be in that opinion, we cannot know that it is true. That is, we do not know if the antecedent of this subjunctive conditional is fulfilled: 'if inquiry were pursued as far as it could fruitfully go, then H would be believed'. Inquiry may or may not have been pursued far enough with respect to H, and so we cannot have certainty with respect to any belief.

But the uncertainty or fallibility that in principle accompanies every one of our beliefs does not mean that we should doubt our settled beliefs. 'Practically speaking', he says, many things are 'substantially certain' ([12.1], 1: 152); we do not doubt them. While 'it is possible that twice two is not four ... it would be difficult to imagine a greater folly than to attach any serious importance to such a doubt' ([12.1], 7: 108).

But substantial certainty is different from the 'absolute certainty' which would result from knowing that we have permanently settled belief. We may have this settled opinion about many questions, but we must not infer that we 'perfectly know when we know'. Again, we cannot know that any given hypothesis is permanently settled upon or true – we cannot have absolute certainty. Nevertheless, in every state of intellectual development and information, there are things that seem to us sure 'so that even though we tell ourselves that we are not sure, we cannot clearly see how we fail of being so' ([12.1], 4: 64). Practically, we must treat some hypotheses as certain. Settled beliefs must be regarded as infallible, in the sense that the inquirer does not doubt them for the purposes of inquiry; science has 'established truths' to be used as premises in further deliberation ([12.1], 1: 635). In this sense, we do not doubt what we believe, but in another sense, each of our beliefs can, or could, be doubted.

Peirce's theory of inquiry provides the key to understanding his view of the growth of knowledge and the progress of science. His position is that science 'is not standing upon the bedrock of fact. It is walking upon a bog, and can only say, this ground seems to hold for the present. Here I will stay till it begins to give way' ([12.1], 5: 589).

Accepted hypotheses and theories are stable until they are upset by experience. They are as good as they can be, given the state of evidence, technology, argument, etc. Knowledge is rebuilt bit by bit when experience forces inquirers to revise their beliefs. The rebuilding principle requires modification of our beliefs in the light of recalcitrant experience and Peirce argues that we cannot help but adopt this principle. We do have some reason to believe that, in rebuilding, we are in some sense getting closer to the truth. For the new beliefs will get along with experience better than the old ones. True beliefs are those which would, in the end, get along with experience and one explanation of our beliefs achieving more and more fit with experience is that a good number of them are true. A good number of them would be permanently doubt-resistant.

But Peirce's picture is not one of placing indubitable building blocks upon each other as we progress towards the truth. Rather, the picture is one of doubt (recalcitrant experience) forcing us to inquire until we reach another tentative doubt-resistant belief. The ground upon which inquiry walks is tenuous and it is only the danger of losing our footing that makes us go forward. Doubt and uncertainty provide the motive for inquiry. All our beliefs are fallible and when an agent accepts a belief, she does so with the knowledge that it might very well prove to succumb to surprise. But if the agent knows that the belief is the result of a method which takes experience seriously, then she is warranted in accepting it, asserting it and acting upon it.

In addition, Peirce's theory of inquiry invokes two regulative hopes; assumptions, such that, without making them, the participants in a practice could make no sense of that practice. We must, Peirce says, hope or assume that the community will continue indefinitely and we must hope that there would be, if inquiry were pursued far enough, a final settled answer to 'the particular questions with which our inquiries are busied' ([12.1], 6: 610). He says,

a reasonable disputant disputes because he hopes, or at least, goes upon the assumption that the dispute will come to something; that is to say, that both parties will at length find themselves forced to a common belief which will be definitive and final. For otherwise, why dispute?

([12.1], 2: 29)

Inquiry is the asking of questions, and a presupposition of inquiry is that the questioner hopes for an answer. We have, Peirce says, some ground for this hope because all sorts of questions that seemed at one time to be completely resistant to resolution have been resolved.

⬿ LOGIC: DEDUCTION, INDUCTION, ⬿ ABDUCTION

Peirce described himself first and foremost as a logician and despaired that the current state of philosophy in America was such that most found formal logic to be too difficult. He classified inference into three types: deduction, induction and abduction (which he also called retroduction or hypothesis) and made significant contributions to the study of each. Indeed, the very study of abduction, what is today known as inference to the best explanation, is due to Peirce.

Peirce's contributions to deductive logic are very impressive, although today it is Frege, not Peirce, who is regarded as bringing modern logic into the world. Peirce developed a logic of relations and quantifiers independently of, and at roughly the same time as, Frege, discovered the Sheffer Stroke twenty years before Sheffer, and invented a notation (utilizing normal forms) very similar to the one still in use. In mathematics, he anticipated Dedekind on the difference between finite and infinite sets and independently developed arguments about infinity similar to Cantor's. Unfortunately, setting out the background to these developments and adequately characterizing them is beyond the scope of this chapter (See Dauben [12.6], Putnam [12.13] and Dipert [12.7]).

Peirce is also known for his work on induction. Some see in his writing an anticipation of Reichenbach's probabilistic response to Hume's scepticism about induction while others see an anticipation of the Neyman-Pearson confidence interval approach to testing statistical hypotheses (see Ayer [12.5], Lenz [12.9], Levi [12.10] and Hacking [12.8]).

Peirce called the sort of inference which concludes that all *As* are *Bs* because there are no known instances to the contrary 'crude induction'. It assumes that future experience will not be 'utterly at variance' with past experience ([12.1], 7: 756). This is, Peirce says, the only kind of induction in which we are able to infer the truth of a universal generalization. Its flaw is that 'it is liable at any moment to be utterly shattered by a single experience' ([12.1], 7: 157).

The problem of induction, as Hume characterizes it, is about crude induction; it is about the legitimacy of concluding that all As are Bs or the next A will be a B from the fact that all observed As have been Bs. Peirce assumes that Hume's problem is straightforwardly settled by fallibilism and critical commonsensism. We do, and should, believe that, say, the sun will rise tomorrow, yet it is by no means certain that it will. To show that induction is valid, we need not show that we can be certain about the correctness of the conclusion of a crude inductive inference. Fallibilism holds that this is a pipe dream. What we have to show, rather, is that induction is a reliable method in inquiry.

Peirce holds that it is a mistake, anyway, to think that all inductive reasoning is aimed at conclusions which are universal generalizations. The strongest sort of induction is 'quantitative induction' and it deals with statistical ratios. For instance:

Case: These beans have been randomly taken from this bag
Result: Two-thirds of these beans are white
Rule: Therefore two-thirds of the beans in the bag are white

That is, one can argue that if, in a random sampling of some group of Ss, a certain proportion r/n has the character P, the same proportion r/n of the Ss have P. One concludes from an observed relative frequency in a randomly drawn sample a hypothesis about the relative frequency in the population.

Peirce is concerned with how inductive inference forms a part of the scientific method; how inductive inferences can fulfil their role as the testing ground for hypotheses. Quantitative induction can be seen as a kind of experiment. We ask what the probability is that a member of the experimental class of the Ss will have the character P. The experimenter then obtains a fair sample of Ss and draws from it at random. The value of the proportion of Ss sampled that are P approximates the value of the probability in question. When we test, we infer that if a sample passes the test, the entire population would pass the test. Or we infer that if 10 per cent of the sample has a certain feature, then 10 per cent of the population has that feature.

Peirce took the three types of inference to form the scientific method. The role played by induction is to test hypotheses. The job of abductive inference is to provide hypotheses for this testing. Peirce's settled view on abduction is that it is 'where we find some very curious circumstance, which would be explained by the supposition that it was a case of a certain general rule, and thereupon adopt that supposition' ([12.2], 3: 326). The form it takes is:

The surprising fact, C, is observed;

But if A were true, C would be a matter of course.

Hence, there is reason to suspect that A is true.

([12.1], 5: 189)

Peirce argued with Paul Carus about when an explanation is called for. Carus claimed that irregularity demands an explanation and Peirce disagreed. Nobody, he says, is 'surprised that the trees in a forest do not form a regular pattern, or asks for any explanation of such a fact' ([12.1], 189). Peirce suggests that irregularity is 'the overwhelmingly preponderant rule of experience, and regularity only the strange exception'. A mere irregularity, where no definite regularity is expected, he says, creates no surprise; it excites no curiosity. And it is a surprise or an anomaly that throws us into doubt or demands an inquiry to explain the phenomenon. It is an *unexpected* regularity or the breach of an existing regularity that makes a demand for explanation. It is the interruption of a habit of expectation (a belief) that calls for an explanation.

Abduction is 'the process of forming an explanatory hypothesis' ([12.1], 5: 171) for such regularities. These hypotheses, however, are merely conjectures; we must 'hold ourselves ready to throw them overboard at a moment's notice from experience' ([12.1], 1: 634). For an abductive inference 'commits us to nothing. It merely causes a hypothesis to be set down upon our docket of cases to be tried' ([12.1], 5: 602).

So the first stage of inquiry is arriving at a conjecture or an explanatory hypothesis. Peirce argued that abduction and induction are 'ampliative' and deduction is 'explicative'. In explicative inference, the conclusion follows from the premisses necessarily; in ampliative inference, the conclusion amplifies rather than explicates what is stated in the premisses. He argues that ampliative inference is the only kind that can introduce new ideas into our body of belief. Being a form of ampliative inference, abduction allows us to infer, or at least conjecture, from the known to the unknown. We can infer a hypothesis to explain why we observed what we did.

The second stage is to deduce consequences or predictions from the hypothesis. The 'purpose' of deduction is 'that of collecting consequents of the hypothesis'. The third stage is that of 'ascertaining how far those consequents accord with Experience' ([12.3], 841: 44). By induction we test the hypothesis: if it passes, it is added to our body of belief.

Peirce sees that the validity of abductive inference is hard to characterize. Its conclusion is not even asserted to be true, for it is a mere conjecture. He says:

The hypothesis which it problematically concludes is frequently utterly wrong in itself, and even the method need not ever lead to the truth; for it may be that the features of the phenomena which it aims to explain have no rational explanation at all. Its only justification is that its method is the only way in which there can be any hope of attaining a rational explanation.

([12.1], 2: 777)

He argues that the reason we are justified in making abductive inferences is that, if we are to have any knowledge at all, we must make them. A logician, Peirce says, should have two goals – he or she should 'bring out the amount and kind of *security* . . . of each kind of reasoning' and should bring out the 'uberty, or value in productiveness, of each kind'. ([12.1], 8: 384) Abduction is such that 'though its *security* is low, its *uberty* is high'. ([12.1], 8: 388). It is the other two kinds of inference to which the notions of security and validity more aptly apply.

❧ THE CATEGORIES ❧

Peirce expended a great deal of intellectual energy engaging in a project which absorbed Aristotle and Kant – the categories. Peirce's ubiquitous classificatory scheme – the categories of firstness, secondness, and thirdness – is designed to cover any object of thought. It is a classificatory scheme that takes each category to be an 'independent and distinct element of the triune Reality' ([12.1] 5: 431). The doctrine is extremely complex, vague and difficult to understand, and, like pragmatism, it permeates Peirce's work.

Peirce had three methods for arriving at his list of categories. The first and earliest one is found in the 1867 'On a New List of Categories'. The project is a Kantian one – to find out what 'is' or 'has being' by 'reducing the manifold of sense impressions to unity' via an analysis of the proposition. The second method is an argument from phenomenology, which 'ascertains and studies the kinds of elements universally present in the phenomenon' or 'whatever is present at any time to the mind in any way'. ([12.1], 1: 186). Both of these methods aim to show that everything that we experience or identify, i.e. anything that 'is', has an element of each of the three categories in it, and that we do not experience anything that goes beyond the three categories.

Both the Kantian and the phenomenological derivations of the categories rest on the Aristotelian/Scholastic method of analysis of prescission. This method separates or distinguishes different elements of a concept so that, although we cannot imagine a situation in which one of them is actually isolated, we can tell that the elements are distinct. We can 'suppose' one without the other, for we can, by attending to one feature and neglecting others, isolate features of phenomena which are not in fact separable. We can, for instance, suppose space without colour even though colourless space is not imaginable. Prescission, however, is not reciprocal, as it is a matter of discerning a logical priority of notions. Hence, we cannot prescind colour from space – we cannot suppose colour without spatial extension.

With respect to the categories, Peirce argues that we can abstract or prescind certain notions from experience and classify them as belonging to one or another of the categories. We can prescind firstness from secondness and we can prescind both from thirdness, but we cannot prescind in the other direction.

So the categories are designed to describe the general features of each of the classes of elements that come before the mind or are experienced. Each class is distinct, but its members cannot stand in isolation. Each of the categories is present in everything we experience, but there are many cases in which one or the other of the categories is emphasized or predominant: 'although they are so inextricably mixed together that no one can be isolated, yet it is manifest that their characters are quite disparate' ([12.1], 1: 284). And the list of three is all that is needed.

Perhaps the easiest way to set out Peirce's doctrine of categories is to concentrate on his third derivation, that which rests on the logic of relations. (This method, however, is discussed by Peirce as being part of phenomenology.) Here the categories are represented by n-place relations. Peirce argued that all relations fall into one of three fundamental classes: monadic, dyadic and triadic. Each is irreducible to the others, and all predicates with more than three places are reducible to triadic ones. For instance, 'a is red' is monadic, 'a hit b' is dyadic and 'a gives b to c' is triadic. A four-place predicate such as 'a put b between c and d' is reducible to two three-place ones: 'a put b in spot e'; 'spot e is between c and d'. 'Gives', on the other hand, is not reducible to 'a put b down' and 'c picked b up', as the latter set fails to express the intention of a that c should have b.

The results of each of the three ways of inquiring into the ultimate categories merge. Here is a brief description of those results, one which does not undertake the intimidating task of sorting out the relationships between all of the things that supposedly manifest each category.

The third category involves a medium or connecting link between two things; irreducibly triadic action is such that an event A produces an event B as a means to the production of an event C. Thirdness is characteristically manifested in psychological concepts. For instance, Peirce argues that representation is such that an interpreting thought mediates between sign and object. (One route to Peirce's claim that all experience is a matter of thirdness is via his argument that everything that we experience is of the nature of a sign or representation. There is no experience independent of our representation of it.) Similarly, we cannot grasp what it is for *a* to give *b* to *c* without the notion of intention mediating between *a* putting *b* down and *c* picking up *b*. There must be an intention to give on *a*'s part and a realization of that intention on *b*'s part. Peirce also says that law and necessity manifest thirdness. A law, or a necessary connection, mediates between the action of one thing upon another, making it more than an accident that they behaved in the way in which they did. Continuity and generality are other instances of thirdness.

We can cognitively isolate secondness as the duality of action and reaction without any mediating force. It is brute existence and hence is the modality of actuality. It is found (by prescission) most clearly in the notions of struggle, action/reaction, cause/effect, and brute force. The second category is one 'which the rough and tumble of life renders most familiarly prominent. We are continually bumping up against hard fact' ([12.1], 1: 324). For

> We can make no effort where we experience no resistance, no reaction. The sense of effort is a two-sided sense, revealing at once a something within and another something without. There is binarity in the idea of brute force; it is its principal ingredient.
>
> ([12.1], 2: 84)

A First is a simple monadic element. Peirce says that it suggests spontaneity, and it is real 'regardless of anything else'. In virtue of its very nature, it is indescribable; it can only be grasped by prescission:

> It cannot be articulately thought: assert it, and it has already lost its characteristic innocence; for assertion always implies a denial of something else. Stop to think of it, and it has flown! ... that is first, present, immediate, fresh, new, initiative, original, spontaneous, free, vivid, conscious, and evanescent. Only, remember that every description of it must be false to it.
>
> ([12.1], 1: 357)

These 'qualities of feeling' are mere possibilities:

> I do not mean the sense of actually experiencing these feelings ... that is something that involves these qualities as an element of it. But I mean the qualities themselves which, in themselves, are mere may-bes, not necessarily realized.
>
> ([12.1], 1: 287)

So the first category is that of possibility.

One upshot of Peirce's doctrine of categories is that he thinks that reality comes in three grades. He is a 'realist' with respect to all of the categories – possibility, actuality and generality are real. He insists that 'the *will be's*, the actually *is's*, and the *have beens* are not the sum of the reals – they only cover actuality. There are besides *would be's* and *can be's* that are real' ([12.1], 8: 216). And his 'Scholastic realism' has it that laws or thirds are real; they are not mere mental constructions.

Peirce takes nominalism – the doctrine that '*laws* and general *types* are figments of the mind' ([12.1], 1: 16) – to be pernicious. He says, 'the property, the character, the predicate, *hardness*, is not invented by men, as the word is, but is really and truly in the hard things and is one in them all, as a description of habit, disposition, or behavior' ([12.1], 1: 27 n.1).

Peirce thinks that the fact that we can predict things ought to convince us of realism about generals. Realism explains prediction, for, on that theory, laws and dispositions have causal efficacy: 'if there is any *would be* at all, there is more or less causation; for that is all that I mean by causation' ([12.1], 8: 225 n.10). If a prediction has a tendency to be fulfilled, it must be the case that future events have a tendency to conform to a general rule. Peirce concludes that some laws or generals are real. Laws and dispositions mediate between possibility (Firstness) and actuality (Secondness) – it is the law that makes the possible actual, for laws or general patterns cause their instances.

But Peirce does not think that possibilities and generals actually exist; universals or generals are not 'things'. The realm of existence is the second category, and so possibilities and generals are real but not existent.

❧ METAPHYSICS ❧

The doctrine of categories is not Peirce's only metaphysical venture. But the briefest sketch of these metaphysical positions, which seem to be in a different spirit from the inquiry-directed pragmatic epistemology described in the first six sections, is all that space allows.

Peirce was set against determinism or necessitarianism, which he took to be the position that 'every single fact in the universe is precisely determined by law' ([12.1], 6: 36). His 'Tychism', on the other hand, had it that there is absolute chance in the universe – there is spontaneous deviation from the laws of nature. Peirce took a corollory of Tychism to be that physical laws are statistical, something which physics now takes for granted.

Tychism is tied to Peirce's view of evolutionary cosmology, for Tychism has it that there is a tendency toward diversification in the universe. Laws, Peirce argued, evolved from nothing or from 'pure possibility'. The starting point 'was not a state of pure abstract being. On the contrary it was a state of just nothing at all, not even a state of emptiness, for even emptiness is something' ([12.1], 6: 215). He usually says that it was pure Firstness. Recall that spontaneity is paradigmatic of Firstness. It is a state which has no existing things (Secondness), compulsion (Secondness), or law (Thirdness): it is a state of pure chance or possibility.

From this state of possibility came accidental 'flashes' ([12.1], 1: 412) which, again accidentally, reacted with one another. That is, Secondness emerged. And from these reactions arose a habit-taking tendency or Thirdness. Peirce says that it is the nature of habit ever to strengthen itself and, thus, laws came into being. Evolution is the process of growth; the world becomes more and more rational and law-bound.

This view is connected to Peirce's claims that our ultimate aim or *summum bonum* is the perfection of 'concrete reasonableness' (see [12.1], 5: 3). He was fond of saying that ethics is prior to science and that logic is normative. These claims cover a variety of theses, most of which are compatible with the work on logic canvassed above. For instance, sometimes he means the following: 'Logic is a normative science; that is to say, it is a science of what is requisite in order to attain a certain aim' ([12.3], 432: 1) – the aim of getting doubt-resistant beliefs. And sometimes he means that logic is critical and involves self-controlled thought, just as morals involves self-controlled conduct (see [12.3], 453). But sometimes, especially towards the end of his life, he means that logic must rest on an inquiry into the ultimate good. It seems to him 'that the logician ought to recognize what our ultimate aim is. It would seem to be the business of the moralist to find this out, and that the logician has to accept the teaching of ethics in this regard' ([12.1], 1: 611).

As commentators have long noted, the attempt to base logic on an ultimate aim of something like perfect rationality seems to be in contradiction to the bulk of his work on logic. That work attempts to offer a naturalistic, non-psychological account of logic. Logic, on that naturalistic view, is intimately tied to the scientific method and to getting beliefs which would not be overturned by recalcitrant experience.

Another of Peirce's metaphysical doctrines is 'Synechism', which has it that the notion of continuity is the key to philosophy. Sometimes he says that 'Synechism is not an ultimate and absolute metaphysical doctrine; it is a regulative principle of logic prescribing what sort of hypothesis is fit to be entertained and examined' ([12.1, 6: 173). But at other times he presents it as highly metaphysical.

Like Aristotle, Peirce holds that a continuous series is not a collection of discrete points. A continuous series is rather a possibility of endless further determination. A continuum has no existing parts but only a potential for being divided into parts. The infinite number of points on a continuous line are really places at which a point could be located, they are merely possibles or Firsts rather than actuals or Seconds. Continuity itself is an instance of Thirdness; it is a kind of ultimate mediation. For a continuous series is a path where we can always find one thing between two others. Peirce characteristically tries to link up this example of Thirdness with others, most particularly laws and generality.

Another metaphysical debate which Peirce joined is the debate about reality. Sometimes he writes of reality not in the way described above, where reality is the object of perfectly stable beliefs. Instead, he places his view of reality within the idealism–materialism debate and sides for a kind of idealism. Reality, he says, is nothing but 'effete mind' – 'what we call matter is not completely dead, but is merely mind hidebound with habits' ([12.1], 6: 158). It is unclear whether this idealism can be reconciled with the view of reality elucidated within Peirce's account of truth. And it is unclear whether idealism, along with the other metaphysical doctrines touched upon here, can pass the pragmatic test, which requires metaphysical theories to have consequences for practice.[4]

❧ INFLUENCE ❧

The pragmatic theory of truth is very popular these days. Some of the current brands are not the one Peirce himself offered but closer to those of William James and John Dewey, both of whom acknowledged their debt to Peirce. (In the 1900s Peirce renamed his doctrine 'pragmaticism' to distinguish it from the positions of James, Schiller, etc. He thought that this new name was 'ugly enough to be safe from kidnappers' ([12.1], 5: 414).)

Richard Rorty's pragmatism, for instance, while having affinities with Peirce's, has it that the notion of truth is metaphysical and ought to be abandoned. Peirce, on the other hand, thinks that truth is not only a sensible notion, but, given that it is what inquirers aim for, it is essential for inquiry. W. V. O. Quine (in some moods), Hilary Putnam and Jürgen Habermas are more clearly the inheritors of Peircean pragmatism.

Another area where Peirce's influence is still felt is in the field of semiotics, where many of his distinctions, classifications and terminology still reign. He had influence in the field of logic, but he was a

Boolean and that school was eventually edged out of the mainstream by the Fregeans. Schröder adopted Peirce's notation, and some well known results are written in it.[5] And Whitehead seems to have learnt quantification from Peirce. But despite the quantity and quality of his work in formal logic and statistical inference, he is probably best remembered in logic for introducing abductive inference, something which by its very nature cannot be formalized.

Unfortunately, Peirce's lack of success in securing an academic position, his rather abrasive personality and his penchant for cumbersome terminology combined to render his views pretty much inaccessible during his own lifetime. He died penniless and unappreciated. It has been only recently that his work has found the interest it deserves and the excavation it requires.

ᨆ NOTES ᨆ

1 References to Peirce's *Collected Papers*, are by volume and paragraph number; to the new *Chronological Edition* and to *The New Elements of Mathematics*, by volume and page number.

2 Some of the material in this and other sections is taken from my *Truth and the End of Inquiry: A Peircean Account of Truth* [12.11]. It is reproduced here by kind permission of Oxford University Press.

3 The psychological hypothesis, however, seems to be false. My suggestion as to how to resolve the difficulty is that Peirce is best read as holding that being responsive to evidence is one of the 'essentials of belief, without which it would not be belief' ([12.3], 673: 11). Thus, the aim of inquiry is to get beliefs which are not merely fixed, but which are fixed in such a way that they fit with and respond to the evidence. See [12.11].

4 Peirce did argue against some kinds of idealism on pragmatic grounds: 'Very well; an idealist... is lounging down Regent Street... when some drunken fellow unexpectedly... lets fly his fist and knocks him in the eye. What has become of his philosophical reflections now?' ([12.1], 5: 539).

5 For instance, Löwenheim's theorem and Zermelo's axioms: see Putnam [12.13].

ᨆ BIBLIOGRAPHY ᨆ

Works by Peirce

12.1 Peirce, C. S. *Collected Papers of Charles Sanders Peirce*, ed. C. Hartshorne and P. Weiss (1–6) and A. Burks (7 and 8), Cambridge, Mass.: Belknap Press, 1931–58.

12.2 Peirce, C. S. *Writings of Charles S. Peirce: A Chronological Edition*, ed. M. Fisch, Bloomington: Indiana University Press, 1982– .

12.3 Peirce, C. S. *The Charles S. Peirce Papers*, microfilm, Cambridge, Mass.: Harvard University.

12.4 Peirce, C. S. *The New Elements of Mathematics*, ed. C. Eisle, The Hague: Mouton, 1976.

Other works

12.5 Ayer, A. J. *The Origins of Pragmatism*, London: Macmillan, 1968.

12.6 Dauben, J. W. 'Peirce's Place in Mathematics', *Historia Mathematica*, 9 (1982): 311–25.

12.7 Dipert, R. R. 'Peirce's Propositional Logic', *Review of Metaphysics*, 34 (March 1981): 569–95.

12.8 Hacking, I. 'The Theory of Probable Inference: Neyman, Peirce and Braithwaite', in D. H. Mellor, ed., *Science, Belief and Behavior: Essays in Honour of R. B. Braithwaite*, Cambridge: Cambridge University Press, 1980.

12.9 Lenz, J. 'Induction as Self-Corrective', in E. C. Moore and R. Robin, eds, *Studies in the Philosophy of Charles Sanders Peirce*, 2nd series, Amherst: University of Massachusetts Press, 1964.

12.10 Levi, I. 'Induction as Self-Correcting According to Peirce', in D. H. Mellor, ed., *Science, Belief and Behavior: Essays in Honour of R. B. Braithwaite*, Cambridge: Cambridge University Press, 1980.

12.11 Misak, C. J. *Truth and the End of Inquiry: A Peircean Account of Truth*, Oxford: Clarendon Press, 1991.

12.12 Perry, R. B. *The Thought and Character of William James*, Boston: Little, Brown, 1936.

12.13 Putnam, H. 'Peirce the Logician', *Historia Mathematica*, 9 (1982): 290–301.

CHAPTER 13

American pragmatism
James
J. E. Tiles

❧

❧ THE BERKELEY LECTURE ❧

Pragmatism was introduced to society in a lecture given by William James[1] to the Philosophical Union at the University of California in Berkeley on 26 August 1898.[2] In his lecture James acknowledged that this brainchild was that of his friend Charles S. Peirce, and that Peirce had first introduced him to it in the early 1870s ([13.11], 410). The child had not been appropriately christened – James indicated a preference for 'practicalism' – and needed 'to be expressed more broadly than Mr. Peirce expresse[d] it', but it offered 'the clue or compass' by which James believed 'we may keep our feet' on 'the trail of truth' (412).

James began his exposition of the principle with a formulation drawn from an 1878 article, 'How To Make Our Ideas Clear' ([13.36], 5: 388–410) in which Peirce had first allowed his progeny to appear in public, although not under the name 'pragmatism'. To attain clearness in our thoughts about some object we need to consider the effects of 'a conceivably practical kind which the object may involve' and reckon our conception of these effects to be the whole of our conception of the object, 'so far as that conception has positive significance at all' ([13.11], 411). Peirce had formulated his principle with a view to its application in science and in the metaphysics of science and had consequently illustrated its application with the concepts 'hardness,' 'weight', 'force' and 'reality' in his 1878 article. But he had not hesitated to apply the principle also to the theological dispute over transubstantiation ([13.36], 5: 401).

In the Berkeley lecture James drew his illustrations mainly from philosophical theology. Some of the traditional attributes of God –

381

aseity, simplicity, felicity – could be judged by Peirce's principle to be 'meaningless and verbal' ([13.11], 425). 'What the word "God" means is just those passive and active experiences of your life' (428). Compare this to Peirce: 'The idea which the word 'force' excites in our minds has no other function than to affect our actions, and these actions can have no reference to force otherwise than through its effects' ([13.36], 5: 405). And as Peirce had insisted that the dispute over transubstantiation was empty unless it could be referred to a difference in sensible effects, James urged that such disputes as that between monists and pluralists were barren unless definite practical consequences turned on the outcome.

Although James suggested that the principle needed to be 'expressed more broadly' it is not easy to see from his lecture alone how, or how far, he thought it necessary to deviate from Peirce's understanding of the principle. He offered as his preferred formulation, 'the effective meaning of any philosophic proposition can always be brought down to some particular consequence, in our future practical experience, whether active or passive' ([13.11], 412). The important point is not that he shifted the formulation from concepts to propositions – he was not grinding the axe which Frege, Russell and Wittgenstein were about to add to the logician's tool kit – the stress, rather, was to be placed on the word 'particular'.

Peirce had formulated his doctrine in the context of a conception of practice as a complex of habits, that is as *general* patterns of responding to experience. James cited Peirce's doctrine that the function of thinking is to produce habits of action (411), but where for Peirce 'what a thing means is simply what habits it involves', for James the meaning of a proposition had its bearing on conduct through foretelling some particular turn in our experience. Differences in 'sensible effects' were differences in sensory experiences rather than (as for Peirce) differences in habits of response to sensory experience (see [13.36], 5: 494). James glossed his preferred formulation with the words, 'the point lying rather in the fact that the experience must be particular, than in the fact that it must be active' ([13.11], 412). He thereby departed in a significant way from Peirce, who rejected as a candidate for meaning 'any unity among our sensations which has no reference to how we act'. For, having tied meaning to habits, Peirce tied the identity of a habit to 'how it might lead us to act, not merely under such circumstances as are likely to arise, but under such as might possibly occur, no matter how improbable they may be' ([13.36] 5: 400).

How this difference affected the way the two men applied the pragmatist principle can be seen in their respective treatments of the concept of God. Apart from reservations about the wording, Peirce would have endorsed James's claim that, 'the principle of practicalism says that the very meaning of the conception of God lies in those differences which must be made in our experience if the conception be true' ([13.11], 424). James indicated the sort of thing he meant here by 'differences in our experience': 'conversations with the unseen, voices and visions, responses to prayer, changes of heart, deliverances from fear, inflowings of help, assurances of support, whenever certain persons set their own internal attitude in certain appropriate ways' (428). When in 1908 Peirce offered what he called 'A Neglected Argument for the Reality of God' he made it clear that his understanding of 'experience' placed far more stress on what a believer was prepared to do than on what happens to a believer: 'to be deliberately and thoroughly prepared to shape one's conduct into conformity with a proposition is neither more nor less than the state of mind called Believing that proposition' ([13.36], 6: 467).

Another sign that James and Peirce were moving in significantly different directions occurred at the end of James's Berkeley lecture, when he commended Peirce's principle for expressing the 'English spirit in philosophy' and heaped scorn on the 'ponderous artificialities of Kant' ([13.11] 436). James concluded by urging that 'the true line of philosophic progress lies not so much *through* Kant as *round* him to the point where we now stand' (437).[3] Important elements of Peirce's philosophy – his doctrine that a thought has meaning only through its connection to subsequent thoughts ([3.36], 2: 289) and his stress on habits – had taken shape in (come '*through*') a Kantian framework.

In the course of a long review of an edition of the works of Bishop Berkeley published in 1871, Peirce had appealed to what with hindsight may be seen as an early formulation of his principle. 'Do things fulfil the same function practically? Then let them be signified by the same word. Do they not? Then let them be distinguished' ([13.36], 8: 33). The main thrust of this article, however, was to trace the character of British philosophy back to Scotus and Occam and to condemn the nominalism of late Scholasticism, which had persisted and flourished in the works of Hobbes, Locke and Berkeley. Peirce continued to define his position partly through his opposition to nominalism, which he conceived to encompass the main currents of British empiricism, although he acknowledged that in the early 1870s his 'ideas were acquiring an English accent' ([13.36], 5: 13). He could not have been entirely pleased at James's move to enlist his brainchild in the ranks of 'the English-speaking philosophers' ([13.11], 434).

In time Peirce felt constrained to dissociate himself from the movement which was initiated by James's lecture and its subsequent publication and dissemination. He saw James as 'pushing the method to such extremes as must tend to give us pause' ([13.36], 5: 3) and claimed that 'the most prominent parts' of the doctrine James was presenting were 'opposed to sound logic' ([13.36], 6: 482). It was not his child but a changeling which his friend was sponsoring and Peirce moved to rename his doctrine 'pragmaticism' – a name ugly enough, as he put it, to keep it safe from kidnappers ([13.36], 5: 414).

❧ MIND AS GOAL-DIRECTED ❧

The philosophic distance between James and Peirce not only reveals how remarkable was the genuine respect and admiration each expressed for the other,[4] it raises the question of what it was they had in common, which made it possible for James to appropriate anything of philosophic significance from his friend. The answer lies in the conception of mind as goal-directed, which James and Peirce accepted in different forms. This placed both men in opposition to the tradition of conceiving the essence of mind as lying in its capacity to represent objects in such a way that the adequacy of the representation is independent of its capacity to direct our action and help us to anticipate consequences.

In his *Principles of Psychology* James took '*the pursuance of future ends and the choice of means for their attainment* [to be] *the mark and criterion of the presence of mentality* in a phenomenon' ([13.1], I: 8). Consistent with this criterion, a concept for James was 'really nothing but a teleological instrument. *This whole function of conceiving, of fixing, and holding fast to meanings, has no significance apart from the fact that the conceiver is a creature with partial purposes and private ends*' (482). Peirce had advanced his 'pragmatist' principle in 1878 in the context of a doctrine that thought was directed to the attainment of belief, where belief was a form of habit. Both men treated thought as teleological – although they differed over the character of its *telos* – and were thus attracted to the notion that meaning should be explained in functional terms within a framework of goals and instruments.

Their differences over the *telos* of thought turned, we have seen, on the question of whether it should be conceived as particular (sensory experience) or general (habits of response). There were other differences, more concerned with what should be emphasized, which obscured the nature of the conflict between their different metaphysical outlooks. Peirce tended to speak from the standpoint of 'the community of those who enquired' and of its long-term direction. James did not reject this standpoint, although it is not easy to say how far he would have agreed with Peirce about its character or importance, for he tended to speak from the standpoint of individuals and their short-term achievements, a tendency which can be observed already in his early work.

He had, for example, published a version of his views of concepts in 1879, where he contended that essential qualities were nothing more than those of most *worth* 'relative to the temporary interests of the conceiver' ([13.1], 86–8), and he quoted at length from this article in his *Principles of Psychology* ([13.1], II: 335n.). Peirce would have accepted the contention which James added in his 1890 treatment of essential qualities,

> the only reason why *for the chemist* [water] is H-O-H primarily, and only secondarily the other things, is that *for his purpose of deduction and compendious definition* the H-O-H aspect of it is the more useful one to bear in mind. (334n.)

But Peirce would not have been comfortable with the suggestion that the chemist's interest was merely one of many ephemeral human interests with no claim to special privilege.

Science for Peirce was a historical project which works to eliminate what is limited, arbitrary and accidental in the perspectives of individuals, and what is partial in the interests, which drive them to inquire ([13.36], 8: 12). The definition given by chemists is not to be accepted as expressing *the* essence of water, since this definition may require improvement, but it has an authority over definitions which select other properties of water in that it has arisen out of a context of inquiry in which private ends and partial purposes have become – if not completely, at least *more* – public and impartial. James would not have disputed this, but he said little that highlighted it and much that tended to obscure it.

❧ THE ANALYSIS OF TRUTH ❧

This difference in emphasis contributed in large measure to the differences the two men had over the treatment of truth. According to James, applying the pragmatist principle to truth results in the question, 'What concrete difference will its [an idea or belief] being true make in any one's actual life?' ([13.12], 97). The answer was that ideas we call 'true' are those which we can 'assimilate, validate, corroborate and verify'. All of these words were interpreted in conformity with the doctrine that ideas and beliefs function as instruments. Where they do not interfere with the use of existing cognitive resources we are free to assimilate them to our existing stock of ideas. Where they serve to guide our thought and action in a manner which is 'progressive, harmonious, satisfactory', they are treated as validated, corroborated or verified (35). ' "The true", to put it very briefly, is only the expedient in the way of our thinking, just as "the right is only the expedient in the way of our behaving" ' (106). As a consequence truth became a property of an idea or an opinion, belief or statement on the occasion of our determining the instrumental value of an idea, opinion, etc.

By 1907, when James published this treatment of truth in a book titled *Pragmatism*, 'pragmatism' had become the name of a movement, which was stirring up considerable controversy, and the centre of dispute was the application of the pragmatist principle to the concept of truth. James's vivid and robust advocacy attracted attention, and inspired two stalwart allies – F. C. S. Schiller at Oxford and John Dewey at Columbia – as well as numerous hostile critics. But his failure to express himself with sufficient care and precision, left his cause exposed to apparently easy refutation.

The general problem he faced can be appreciated by exploring the analogy with instruments. Instruments prove useful for certain purposes in specified circumstances, and when these purposes are superseded or circumstances change they are set aside. In calling an idea or belief 'true', however, we seem to be making a claim with some kind of finality about its worth, a claim which is independent of purpose and circumstance.

By appealing to a notion of science as an unending progressive enterprise, Peirce had been able to apply his understanding of the pragmatist principle to the concept of truth in such a way as to finesse this difficulty. Truth, Peirce held, was to be found in 'the opinion which is fated to be ultimately agreed to by all who investigate' ([13.36], 5: 407). It is easy enough to recast this formulation to remove the apparent requirement that there be some point in the future where ultimate agreement is reached: to say an idea, belief, etc. is true is to say that no cause for its rejection or substantial modification will arise for as long as investigation might continue. Since reasons for rejecting an idea or belief include the discovery that its worth depends on special circumstances (which can be eliminated from its formulation) or partial purposes (which admit of being enlarged), Peirce's analysis of truth was able at least to address the finality and independence which appear to be implicit in a claim that something is true.

It was, of course, an important part of Peirce's position – his 'fallibilism' – that we would never be in a position to determine whether an idea or belief was true; the most we could ever say would be that so far we have encountered no reason to reject or modify the idea or belief in question. Even before he pushed pragmatism into the limelight, James had characterized this fallibilist outlook as the *'empiricist'* form of dogmatism and contrasted it favourably with 'the *absolutist* way of believing in truth' ([13.3], 12). Absolutists claim to be able not only to attain truth but to know when it has been attained; empiricists claim it is possible for humans to attain truth but not to know infallibly when they have attained it. This meant that in one sense of the word, 'truth' designated an ideal towards which we would have to strive indefinitely, and in *Pragmatism* James explicitly acknowledged that 'truth' did function, as Peirce insisted, as the name of an ideal. 'The 'absolutely' true, meaning what no farther experience will ever alter, is that ideal vanishing-point towards which we imagine that all our temporary truths will some day converge' ([13.12], 106–7). He did not suggest that what we imagine here was a form of delusion or even a pious fancy; he accepted this rather as a satisfactory account of the meaning of 'absolute truth'.

> On the one hand there will stand reality, on the other an account of it which it proves impossible to better or alter. If the impossibility prove permanent, the truth of the account will be absolute. Other content of truth than this I can find nowhere. (120)

But James had little interest in what was not immediate. The second sentence to follow the last but one of the above quotations ([13.12], 106–7) reads, 'Meanwhile we have to live to-day by what truth we can get to-day, and be ready to-morrow to call it falsehood'.

Peirce rejected any suggestion that it might be permissible to speak of truth as mutable ([13.36], 6: 485). To be sure we can and do change our minds about what we take to be true. There are, moreover, ideas and beliefs which, prior to certain dates, were not even entertained by human beings, let alone subjected to verification. This does not, Peirce held, justify saying that beliefs or ideas become true or may cease to be true. One can see, nevertheless, why James wanted to stress what happens today and might happen tomorrow: the long term, even on Peirce's account, is not constituted independently of what is done here and now. (Or, if it should turn out that we are thoroughly benighted in respect to some matter, the long-term truth of that matter is still not independent of what is done at particular times in the future.)

It may, however, have been a tactical mistake to apply the word 'true' and its cognates to what we embrace at particular times, even if that brought a special dignity to what James regarded as crucial to the concept of truth. It might have been wiser to adopt the course which Dewey eventually adopted: cease to use 'truth', following James's preferred gloss, as 'a collective name for [the current results of] the verification-process' ([13.12], 104)[5] and instead allow that 'whatever we will not find reason to correct, so long as we go on enquiring' is an adequate account of what we mean by 'truth'.

James may not have been open to such counsel. He preferred at crucial points to place severe strains on the ordinary meanings of words in order to secure the attention of his audience, even at the risk of being misunderstood. The interpolation made in the quotation in the previous paragraph points to a further example of this. The official statement of James's doctrine held that the truth of an idea (belief, etc.) is 'the process ... of its verifying itself' ([13.12], 97). This is not the way the word 'truth' is commonly used. Events in which ideas, beliefs, etc. are validated by experience are known collectively as 'verification'; 'truth' is applied as a collective noun for whatever can successfully undergo verification. Within a few pages James acknowledged the strain his definition was placing on our habits of usage. We allow to pass as true a great many ideas and beliefs ('the overwhelmingly large number of truths we live by' (99)) which we do not even attempt to verify. These are not 'abortive' truths; indirect verification – evidence that other people expect experience to bear out the utility of these beliefs – allows us to count them as truths. 'Truth lives, in fact, for the most part on a credit system', although 'beliefs verified concretely by *somebody*' are what preserves this cognitive economy from collapse (100).

A few pages further James appropriated the scholastic distinction between habit and act and acknowledged that to be worthy to be counted a 'truth', a belief does not have to be actually (*in actu*) guiding our practice, just as a person does not have to be lifting weights to be reckoned strong. 'All such qualities sink to the status of 'habits' between their times of exercise; and similarly truth becomes a habit of certain of our ideas and beliefs in their intervals of rest from their verifying activities' (106). So why define truth as a process if, within James's pragmatism, truth can have a sense in which it applies not to the process of verification but to what is able to withstand the process? What James appears to be doing with his definition is drawing attention to what he believed to be crucial, just as his frequent use of financial metaphors ('cash basis', 'cash value') called attention to the same need of a practical foundation for our cognitive practices. But calling truth a process made it easier for opponents to suggest that the doctrine was riddled with confusion, just as financial metaphors and words like 'expedient' allowed opponents to insinuate that behind James's doctrine were crass commercial values.[6]

ANTI-REALISM

Although expressing the doctrine of truth with more care might have enabled James to go some distance toward placating Peirce, it is not clear that this would have resolved all of their differences over the concept of truth. There remains James's fondness for the claim that 'Truth is *made*' ([13.12], 104) as opposed to 'discovered' and the evidence that not all of what he meant by this is contained in the claim that truth arises out of the process of verification (and re-verification). Part of this claim appears to have been intended by James to reflect the degrees of freedom which we have in fashioning representations able to function cognitively as instruments. What truths we embrace here and now (and hence in the long run) depend on how we carve out and carve up the objects of our experience in order to fashion representations. And how we do that is a function of our purposes (121, 206).

Having come to his philosophy *through* Kant, Peirce would not have found alien the idea that objects, and our classifications of them, are in important respects the products of our cognitive activity. But this raises the question whether (within whatever constraints might be imposed by our cognitive constitution) we can adopt different systems of representation, systems which would if adopted lead subsequent enquiry in such different directions that we could not plausibly regard them as taking us to the same 'final opinion', the same 'truth'. This is one way to read the implications of James's doctrines that our means of representation are instruments serving concrete purposes and that truth is made. This implication, however, requires that it makes sense to suppose that we are free at one or another stage in our history to adopt one set of purposes, to which one set of cognitive instruments would be well adapted, and eschew another set of purposes, to which a different set of cognitive instruments would be better suited. If the thought of making such a choice is coherent, we would not be able to say that the beliefs framed in one system were more true than those of the other because beliefs in each system would be established as true through serving a different set of purposes.

The issue in other words is how much freedom does a pragmatist doctrine of truth leave us? It needs to be emphasized that no pragmatist suggested that our freedom is in any sense absolute. We are constrained in what we do by what our environment will permit us to do – by what means it affords for realizing our goals. We do not even have absolute mastery over the most immaterial of our cognitive instruments, 'We can no more play fast and loose with these abstract relations than we can do so with our sense-experience. They coerce us; we must treat them consistently, whether or not we like the results' (101). But it remains possible to ask whether it would make sense to say that long-term truth might not be uniquely determined, because at crucial stages we might make choices that would lead to one long-term truth rather another. Did James allow this when he said 'absolute truth will have to be made . . . incidental to the growth of a mass of verification-experience' (107)?

There seems little doubt that Peirce assumed there would be what is now called 'convergence' if scientific enquiry were indefinitely prolonged. Phrased to avoid the implication that there will be a time when scientific enquiry is complete, this means that should there emerge two or more ways of treating a phenomenon scientifically, the task of reconciling and integrating these theories will not remain impossible indefinitely. Does Peirce's assumption that enquiry will converge amount to anything more than an article of faith?

For one important alliance of anti-pragmatists, Peirce's assumption needs no defence. According to the opponents whom James addresses as 'rationalists' (as well as most philosophers who nowadays profess to be 'realists') representations of the world can be advanced independently of, indeed *'have nothing to do with*[,] *our practical interests or personal reasons'* (109). There has to be convergence amongst the descriptions offered by all who seek an adequate representation of *the* world; two representations could not fail to be reconciled unless there were two different worlds. Truth resides in the one ideal representation regardless of whether anyone will ever ascertain it. For James, 'There never was a more exquisite example of an idea abstracted from the concretes of experience and then used to oppose and negate what it was abstracted from' (109). But having tied truth to 'practical interests or personal reasons' did James have any grounds for the expectation that our 'verification-experience' will converge?

Although James did not address this specific question, his instrumentalism does appear to have definite anti-realist implications. His admonition against thinking that reality is 'literally' made of ether, atoms or electrons (103) does not appear to reflect mere caution regarding the ultimate utility of theories phrased in these terms. He claimed that 'The term "energy" doesn't even pretend to stand for anything "objective". It is only a way of measuring the surface of phenomena so as to string their changes on a simple formula' (103). Peirce's response to this is likely to have been that if the concept of energy continues adequately to guide our interactions with what James here calls 'the surface of phenomena' there is no point in denying that the term stands for something objective. Any object represented in an opinion which continues to be accepted by all who investigate is by Peirce's criterion real and objective.

James accepted that in choosing our 'man-made formulas we cannot be capricious with impunity' (104), but, consistent with his sympathy for nominalism, he suggested there was a certain latitude in our choice. This expectation may well have been linked to the way he wanted to tie truth not only to 'practical interests' but also to 'personal reasons'. Dewey viewed this appeal to the personal with some suspicion. He was content if it was to be analysed and defined in biological and ethical (social) terms, but not if it were (as in the humanism of F. C. S. Schiller) treated as 'ultimate and unanalyzable, the metaphysically real', in order to underwrite a 'pluralistic, voluntaristic idealism' ([13.18], 325–6).

Peirce for his part would have accepted the link to practical interests; these were written into the pragmatist principle. Those who enquire are looking for practical guidance for establishing stable habits of action, and realists and rationalists are mistaken in offering an account of truth which pretends otherwise. Peirce, however, would not have included 'personal reasons' alongside 'practical interests'; these generate the limitations and partialities which scientific enquiry is supposed to eliminate from our representations. The purpose of science includes transcending the personal at least in the sense linked to individualism.[7] If convergence involved an article of faith for Peirce, what rested on faith was the belief that it is possible for humans to transcend the personal in this sense. It was not a matter of faith that science should converge; if our enquiries do not converge it will be because we have not conducted our enquiries in the right spirit.

❧ THE RIGHT TO BELIEVE ❧

That one might rest science on faith of this sort – on a set of beliefs regarding the possibility and supreme worth of working towards a common goal, which is specified only schematically – was endorsed by James even before he publicly adopted Peirce's principle as his protégé. In the title essay (first published in 1896) of a collection, *The Will to Believe*, dedicated 'to my old friend Charles Sanders Peirce', James had defended the right[8] to believe in facts where belief might well be something needed to help create the fact ([13.3], 25). The actuality of pragmatism's truth is indeed dependent in this way on the beliefs of those who enquire and the cognitive posture, which pragmatists thus require of scientists, would be scorned by those – James cites (T. H.) Huxley and (W. K.) Clifford – who insist we must not 'believe anything upon insufficient evidence' (7–8). James was not at this point advancing the doctrine that truth is made – 'in our dealings with objective nature we obviously are recorders, not makers, of truth' (20) – but he insisted on the status of truth as an object of common endeavour, 'Our belief in truth itself ... that there is a truth, and that our minds and it are made for each other, – what is it but a passionate affirmation of desire, in which our social system backs us up?' (9). To insist that we as individuals have sufficient grounds for believing in the attainability of truth, before taking steps to attain it, could well, James argued, stand in the way of our attaining it (24–5).

Thus the issue James took with Huxley and Clifford was over their suggestion that a belief system could be based entirely on intellectual grounds without resting at any point on commitment or, as James put it, on our 'passional tendencies and volitions' (11). Not only does 'our passional nature' influence our beliefs, there are cases in which this influence 'must be regarded both as inevitable and as a lawful determinant of our choice' (19). What Huxley and Clifford were doing, James insinuated, was foisting on others the predilections of their own particular 'passional natures' under the pretence of having put all emotional involvement aside.

'The Will to Believe' although pre-pragmatic in some respects was read as a document of the movement.[9] Thus its attack on Clifford contributed to the accusation that pragmatism encouraged people to believe whatever would prove convenient or would lead to success measured in terms of personal satisfaction. For James had quoted Clifford as claiming, 'Belief is desecrated when given to unproved and unquestioned statements for the solace and private pleasure of the believer' (8). And in *Pragmatism* James said a number of things, which taken on their own might also be interpreted as embracing precisely what Clifford condemned.

In the final chapter James declared that 'On pragmatistic principles, if the hypothesis of God works satisfactorily in the widest sense of the word, it is true' ([13.12], 143). Earlier he had quoted from a Christian Science leaflet and said of it, 'beyond doubt such a confession of faith has pragmatically an emotional value' (74). A page later the mystical teachings of Swami Vivekananda were said to be 'a religion which, emotionally considered, has a high pragmatic value'. Clearly 'works satisfactorily in the widest sense' was meant to *include* 'generates emotional security' but if James's audience failed to bring to bear other things which James had said about the constraints operating on belief (to be discussed here shortly) they were likely to carry away the impression that the solace or personal satisfaction offered by a belief were meant to be a sufficient touchstone of its truth.

If James had taken steps to forestall this impression, he might have stressed that the primary consequences by which a belief or idea was to be tested were those bound up in what Dewey referred to as the 'intent of the idea'. What Dewey meant to convey by this phrase was that included in the conventions which determine the commonly accepted meaning of an idea or belief are quite specific conditions for the correct application of the words which are used to convey it. Dewey thereby implied a criticism of James for his illustrative example argued that the fatal consequences of drinking a liquid to test the idea that it is a poison are very good indicators that the idea is true, and it is these consequences which are relevant to the question of its truth, not the bad consequences of a painful death ([13.18], 320). By implication the emotional consequences of believing something were not to be treated as relevant to its truth.

James might well have replied that beliefs function in multiple ways and, while accepting that he should not neglect the 'intent of an idea', he clearly would have resisted excluding the functions of solace and satisfaction in deciding how well they work. The account, which he gave in his Berkeley lecture ([13.11], 415–24) and reproduced verbatim in *Pragmatism* ([13.12], 51–6), of the pragmatic difference between materialism and belief in God, rested entirely on the reassurance which could be derived from the way the notion of God 'guarantees an ideal order that shall be permanently preserved . . . This need of an eternal moral order is one of the deepest needs of our breast', because it sustained hope where the 'materialist' outlook meant 'the cutting off of ultimate hopes' ([13.12], 55). These needs were not universal but present in 'superior minds', while their absence was a sign of 'the more shallow man' (56).

This account of the pragmatic meaning of belief in 'God' was said by James to have been deliberately phrased in terms of future consequences. He argued that if the universe had no future, if this were its absolutely last moment, it might well be that the 'materialist' and the 'spiritualist' hypotheses were equivalent and there be nothing, pragmatically speaking, in the choice between them ([13.11], 414; [13.12], 50). But in referring to future consequences James clearly had in mind our attitudes towards the indefinite future long after any of our actions (perhaps the actions of any human beings) have determinable practical consequences. In response Dewey claimed that this account of the meaning of 'God' involved a considerable departure from what would appear to be sanctioned by Peirce's principle. If consistently applied, Peirce's principle would 'simply abolish the meaning of an antecedent power which will perpetuate eternally some existence' ([13.18], 315). Dewey protested at what he saw as the 'unpragmatic' procedure of determining the (emotional) 'value of a conception whose own inherent significance pragmatism has not first determined' (316).

James, however, read the pragmatist principle as allowing consequences to be spelled out not only in terms of how we act but also in terms of how we feel. This was underscored when later he claimed that almost from the outset he had thought his argument that the spiritualist hypothesis served only to guarantee an ideal order was flawed. This was because, James believed, there would be for people an important difference if they could regard the universe as containing 'a being who will [at every moment does] inwardly recognize them and judge them sympathetically' ([13.12], 269n.). James's retraction here leaves no doubt of the importance of private conscious experience in the system of values by which he intended to judge whether beliefs worked. He reinforced his claim about the need for God's sympathy and recognition of our inner experience by means of a thought experiment involving a soulless robot woman who behaved in a way indistinguishable from 'an animated maiden'. 'Pragmatically ... belief in the automatic sweetheart would not *work*', because such a creature would not satisfy a man's craving for 'inward sympathy and recognition, love and admiration' (ibid.) Our consciousness requires recognition (by God) and men require conscious recognition (by women) of their qualities. Beliefs that fail to satisfy these requirements do not work.

But this is not to say that the satisfaction of such needs was sufficient by itself to underwrite the truths of beliefs. James made it abundantly clear in 'The Will to Believe' that he did not think we could adopt just any belief at will, simply because it offered personal satisfaction or solace. For any historically situated individual only certain hypotheses were 'live' and only certain choices between believing and not believing were in addition sufficiently important and unavoidable to be 'genuine' ([13.3], 2–4)

The point about the need for new beliefs to cohere with existing beliefs, on which James placed considerable stress in his account of truth in *Pragmatism*, was already prominent in this article. Here it indicated how historical and cultural factors, along with empirical and logical constraints, circumscribe the proper sphere of will and emotion in determining belief. We cannot pick and choose beliefs to suit our tastes. We cannot, after all, just by willing, believe that we are well when 'roaring with rheumatism' or that the sum of two one-dollar bills in our pocket is a hundred ([13.3], 5). But the logical and empirical constraints which hold us to one or another of certain complexes of belief should not be expected to determine for us precisely one complex worthy of belief.

Other of James's examples illustrate well the cultural and historical factors which close off some options and open others to the will and emotions – which, in other words, make an hypothesis live and genuine for some people, dead or spurious for others. In the late nineteenth century belief in the Mahdi may have been among the mind's possibilities for an Arab, but not for a North American (2). Whatever the force of the argument known as Pascal's wager, the option to heed or ignore its conclusion, 'take holy water, and have masses said', is not alive for someone, e.g. Turk or Protestant Christian, who has no pre-existing tendency to believe in masses and holy water (6).[10]

❧ PLURALISM ❧

The shadow cast in James's discussion, here and in *Pragmatism*, by the notion of belief systems as to a large degree mutually impermeable cultural entities gives his development of pragmatism a flavour which has become very familiar nearly a century later. There appears to be a tendency in James's discussion towards what is now known as 'pluralism' (identified in some quarters with 'postmodernism'), that is resistance to the principle that we should expect one system of beliefs to prove superior to all others. There may be a number of viable systems no one of which can ever be declared superior to the others. (In more radical versions pluralism merges with relativism: no system of belief can ever be declared superior to any other.)

It is this tendency in James which allows some recent writers to enlist pragmatism in the pluralist ranks. Whether this tendency is actually present in James or is merely a superficial appearance, which would evaporate under careful reading, it is clear that it is not pragmatism as such which brings pluralism in its train. Peirce expected applications of the pragmatist principle, including those to the concepts of truth and settled belief, to generate in due course a single authoritative system. He wrote consistently as though there was a single preferred method of stabilizing belief, directed at a single objective, with a single expected outcome. And there is nothing in this which is inconsistent with his pragmatist principle.

Nevertheless it should be acknowledged that fallibilism (which, although not the whole, is an essential part of pragmatism) and the undermining of 'rationalist' or cognitivist conceptions of truth, together 'create a space for pluralism. If, as James put it ([13.3], 13), we cannot rely on anything to click inside us when we grasp the truth and thus should remain open to the possibility that our most strongly held beliefs may need to be revised, who can (ever) claim to be in possession of the one truth?

If, as the opponents of pragmatism insist, truth is a two-term relation of 'agreement' or 'correspondence' which obtains between our representations (whether these be conceived as physical entities or as mental states) and the world, it is difficult to allow that there might be more than one relation of agreement. Once this 'rationalist' conception is set aside and it is accepted that 'agreement' has to rest on the functional role which a representation plays in some active intervention in the world ([13.12], 95–7, 216–17), what constitutes 'agreement' has to be taken as relative to the ends served by the intervention. Whether or not there is one truth (towards which we all can work) then depends on whether there is a single end to some of our interventions – for example those interventions which constitute our scientific enquiries –

one that gives a special authority to those representations which serve well the unitary end of those particular endeavours.

In other words pragmatists can acknowledge one truth only if they assume (as Peirce assumed) that there is some one end to which (regardless of whatever other ends we might have) our representations (theories) must serve. It is by no means as easy to specify such an end as it might at first appear. Notions in common use nowadays in analytic philosophy of science, such as 'empirical adequacy', do not sufficiently specify an end. What counts as empirically adequate knowledge in different contexts depends on why one wants to know.

Although James characterized himself as a 'pluralist', it is not clear whether he stood so far from Peirce as to have been prepared to embrace pluralism about truth. The difficulty determining where James stood on this matter arises because the monists, against whom James defined his 'pluralism', were not concerned about this sort of question.

James repeatedly took up the issue of 'the one and the many' to illustrate the application of the pragmatist principle.[11] His interest in the question arose from a long-running dispute, which he had with his friend and colleague, the idealist philosopher Josiah Royce. The issue was ostensibly whether the universe was one or many, and in applying the pragmatist solvent, which in this case required spelling out the consequences of the world being one ([13.12], 65–6), James first had to distinguish several senses in which the world could be said to be one. Did this mean spatio-temporally unified, causally unified, subsumed under a single genus, and so on? It was clearly not worth while applying the pragmatist principle to all eight of the possible senses identified in *Pragmatism*, but even for the more interesting cases James concentrated less on what difference it made to say 'one' or 'many' and a good deal more on how we should respond to the issue if we wish to be properly pragmatic about it.

One of the more important issues which James flushed out of the unruly undergrowth disputed by monists and pluralists was 'Does the world have a unity of purpose?' Empirically minded pluralists observe different and often conflicting purposes in the world. The most they would concede, James suggested, was that 'our world is incompletely unified teleologically and is still trying to get its unification better organized' ([13.12], 70). Idealists sought a unification and reconciliation of this manifold in a single 'purpose that every detail of the universe subserves' so that 'all evil in the universe is but instrumental to its greater perfection' (70).

Although James accepted this as a legitimate hypothesis, albeit one which it was risky to dogmatize, he clearly viewed the long-suffering and complacent attitudes towards evil, which it encouraged, with profound distaste. His discussion at this point alludes to an earlier chapter where he castigated as 'a little ghastly ... the satisfaction with which a pure but unreal system will fill a rationalist mind' ([13.12], 18). With a rare display of social concern, James cited personal experiences of oppressed working men, gleaned from a book by a radical ('anarchistic writer'), Morrison I. Swift, as examples of what his friends Royce and F. H. Bradley ('and a whole host of guileless thoroughfed thinkers') treated as conditions of the perfection of the eternal order (21).

But while James could thus ridicule the idea of an already existing unifying purpose to the universe, he did not appear to reject the thought that 'our world is ... still trying to get its unification better organized'. Still less did he reject the idea that human beings should conceive their cognitive efforts as contributing towards a single goal, and suggest instead that they might expect it to fragment into multiple irreconcilable goals. Although in general James resisted antecedently existing unities, he was prepared to tolerate such unities as ends towards which things might move: 'If such an hypothesis were legitimate, total oneness would appear at the end of things rather than at their origin. In other words the notion of the "Absolute" would have to be replaced by that of the "Ultimate" ' ([13.12], 78). This statement implies a far greater tolerance of Peirce's conception of truth as the end of enquiry than is harboured by more recent pluralists.

James's response to another of the issues covered by the 'monism/ pluralism' blanket is also instructive in this connection. Idealist philosophers not only claimed that the Absolute secured for the world a teleological unity, they also claimed that it provided the world with 'an *all-enveloping noetic unity*' (71). In response to this 'hypothesis' James recalled how he had already credited the omniscience of God with the pragmatic value of sustaining conceptually (for the satisfaction of our emotional needs) an eternal moral order. This monist hypothesis was otherwise on a par with that of the pluralist, according to whom 'there is no point of view, no focus of information extant, from which the entire content of the universe is visible at once' (72).

James was clearly prepared to recognize cognitive value (the grasp of some truths) in viewpoints which did not comprehend the whole. Idealists by contrast commonly argued that to grasp the truth of anything one had to appreciate its interrelations to every other truth, and hence truth was accessible only to an infinite all-comprehending intellect. James reckoned it possible for '[e]verything to get known by *some* knower ... but the knowers in the end be irreducibly many, and the greatest knower of them all may yet not know the whole of everything' (72). In this picture-puzzle universe known only through a multitude of overlapping pieces, there is room for the possibility that the pieces might not go together to make one big picture but instead conflict irreconcilably so that the totality would have to be treated as several pictures of distinct realities. And this possibility remains delicately counter-balancing the possibility of an ultimate truth.

❧ PRAGMATIST REALITY ❧

It may well be that this balancing act was the only stable position for James to adopt given what he said about the extent to which truth is made and what he took to be the implications of this for the concept of reality. James expressed the opinion ([13.12], 117) that his British ally, F. C. S. Schiller, had, in advancing 'humanism' (which was Schiller's preferred label for his own philosophic position), pressed to misleading extremes the claim that truth is made. In 'making' our truths, James emphasized, we have to take account of reality in three different aspects. Sensations are forced upon us; certain relations between our sensations (some of them fixed and essential) are facts; and we are also constrained by what we have previously taken as truths (117–18). Within these constraints we still have a certain amount of freedom, for example to attend to some sensations and ignore others, and may 'read the same facts differently' depending on our interests (118).

James happily embraced the doctrine that there is always a human contribution to human knowledge, that is to say our representations of reality will always reflect our interests and limitations – and that representing reality in a way wholly independent of human thinking is at best an 'ideal limit of our minds' (119). If 'humanism' labelled the doctrine that our beliefs about reality will always contain human elements, James was prepared to recognize it as part of pragmatism. We encounter fresh experience with a set of beliefs which determine what we notice. What we notice determines what we do and this in turn determines what we experience. So 'altho the stubborn fact remains that there is a sensible flux, what is true of it seems from first to last to be largely a matter of our own creation' (122). And if we add to this the thought that our actions and descriptions are themselves additions to reality (123), we will come to see ourselves as qualitative growth points in reality itself.

James's rationalist opponents were, as he saw them, committed to a reality 'ready-made and complete from all eternity'. Reality for a pragmatist on the other hand is 'still in the making' awaiting 'part of its complexion from the future' (123). Pragmatists held there was one edition of the universe, unfinished but growing 'especially in places where thinking beings are at work', while the rationalists held out for a universe in many editions, 'one real one, the infinite folio, or édition de luxe, eternally complete' and many finite, distorted error-ridden editions (124). Although the image of one edition as opposed to many pointed numerically in the wrong direction, James saw this as another version of the opposition between the monist (rationalist, many edition) outlook and the pluralist (pragmatist, single edition) outlook. But even here the apparent commitment to unity suggested by the image of a single (growing) pragmatist edition was balanced within a page by an expression of agnosticism: 'For pluralistic pragmatism, truth grows up inside of all the finite experiences. They lean on each other, but the whole of them, *if such a whole there be*, leans on nothing' (125, emphasis added).

James contended (124) that this issue was not entirely a question of the theory of knowledge. The issue indeed turns in part on how we locate human experience and cognition within reality. If these phenomena – together with the events, the outcomes of which depend on the fact that humans think one way rather than another – are treated without qualification as natural events, it is difficult to resist the claim that reality itself is characterized by growth. In practice epistemology is commonly undertaken with one or both of two fundamental Cartesian presuppositions in place, presuppositions which are seldom made consciously or explicitly. Firstly, human experience and cognition, which shape human representations of reality, are treated as transparent, unaffected by history or culture. Secondly, human thinking is treated as something which occurs outside (beyond, at the margin of) natural events. It is because our thought processes are thus on the one hand not part of nature and on the other known introspectively so that those which are clear and distinct may be taken as transparently true, that human thinking is not regarded as a part of what humans aspire to know. It is hardly surprising in the light of these presuppositions that James's contention that our ways of representing reality always reflect our interests and particular perspectives met with hostility and his contention that our efforts to represent the world are themselves developments of the world met with incomprehension.[12]

When disputes touch these presuppositions (as in debates between pragmatists and 'new realists' shortly after James's death as well as in more recent literature),[13] it is claimed that objectivity in knowledge requires us to suspend all our special (i.e. practical) interests just as objectivity requires us to suspend all personal involvement in judging legal and ethical questions. The notion of objective knowledge, moreover, precludes us from claiming knowledge of anything which our own activity affects (interferes with). In aspiring to know, we aspire to represent things as they are in themselves independently of us. The idea that our own activities (let alone the perspectives shaped by our interests) contribute in important ways to the objects which we aspire to know counts as scientific heresy. The humanist claim about the inevitable human influence on our representations and the pragmatist claim about the inevitable influence of our actions on the objects we aspire to know completely undermine, it is argued, objectivity as we understand it.

The Cartesian presuppositions also appear clothed as a preference for logic over psychology. When Bertrand Russell criticized James, he observed how 'Most philosophies are determined by their initial questions and by the facts which habitually fill the imagination of the philosopher' ([13.28], 104). Pragmatists, he contended, were preoccupied with 'psychical facts'. Where the scientifically minded think of the facts and the theologically minded think of God, pragmatists worry about scientific *theories* and about *belief* in God – signs in Russell's view that what filled the imaginations of pragmatists were 'psychological' phenomena (104). This led pragmatists, Russell contended, to confuse what *is* true with what is *thought to be* true (111). It is the former question which, he insisted, should be addressed.

Characterizing one's opponents as preoccupied with psychology came to be a familiar pattern of criticism in the early decades of this century. There were no doubt serious errors which deserved the stigma that was attached by means of the label 'psychologism'. But the stigma also served to silence or marginalize those who, like James, wished to treat human experience as a part of nature. It in effect placed their concerns on the mental side of the familiar body–mind dualism. Interests, satisfactions and perspectives could all be treated as belonging to the way the world appears to subjects, to features of their mental representations of things. Interests, satisfactions and above all the limitations of historically situated perspectives did not consequently need to be located in the natural (physical, material) world. Logic could (and did in the early decades of the twentieth century) divorce itself from all these psychological conditions – as well as eventually from judgement, belief and even inference – and concentrate on how truth could be distributed over the structure of representations, a structure conceived of as abstracted entirely from human thought processes.

To sustain the pursuit of the question 'what is true?' without becoming entangled in the question 'what is thought to be true?' Russell had to insist not only that (as Peirce had insisted) science could pursue a unitary goal of truth but that it could rest its findings on a body of indisputable truths, in respect to which a fallibilist outlook would be unnecessary and inappropriate. Russell clearly operated with a conception of science as seeking a kind of satisfaction – 'theoretic satisfaction' (108) – which was quite independent of any other kind of utility which might be derived from holding a belief. To achieve this satisfaction, he held, the empirical ('inductive') sciences tried to make all their statements agree as far as possible with observed facts.

The 'old inductive philosophy, as exemplified in Mill's logic' pre-supposed 'that there are truths of fact prior to the whole inductive procedure' (104–5). In the empiricist tradition, which Russell repre-sented, the most secure of these truths of fact were given in sense experience. But, as Russell appreciated, James had sought to loosen the tie between truth and facts. Facts are indeed given to us in sense experience, but they are not truths; truths are what we say about facts (106) and, as noted above, James allows there to be latitude in how we respond to what is given in experience. Russell insisted that the meaning of 'truth' (what can be expected to be in the mind of a person employ-ing the word 'truth', [13.28], 109–10) was tied to facts in the same way as the 'theoretic satisfaction' sought in science. Pragmatists would in the end, therefore, be forced to recognize cases of 'plain matters of fact' about which there would simply be no doubt (134) and hence presumably no latitude in how we should respond to them.

Pragmatism, however, had begun as a principle for achieving clar-ity about what we can possibly mean by terms such as 'true' and 'truth'. It recognized no obligation to remain faithful to what ordinary people meant by such terms. Pragmatists could moreover question the soundness of Russell's inference that our ordinary conception of truth would underwrite a class of statements as representing 'plain matters of fact'. To arrive at such a class Russell had to select statements whose implications were severely restricted. Russell's candidates (bare reports of sense data) may well have seemed unquestionably authoritative, but only at the price of being uncommonly powerless to guide our practical affairs. Russell, of course, had professed more interest in what could be regarded as a matter of fact than in what might offer practical guidance, but ordinary people are as much interested in the latter as in the former. If Russell's path to determinate matters of fact led away from anything of practical consequence, it is not clear that ordinary usage would be prepared to follow Russell.

One might apply the pragmatist principle in the fashion of James and inquire what broader consequences turned on the specific dispute between James and Russell over whether certain of 'the facts' of experi-ence could or should be represented as uniquely authoritative 'truths'. Russell's doctrine had the effect of securing, at the crucial point where experience impinges on our minds, a cognitive relationship to reality in which the mind has no alternative but to reflect passively what is given to it. The logical structure of our thought can then be relied upon to determine how the mind must conform if it is to possess a true, more comprehensive representation of reality. Russell thereby indicates the logical–empiricist route to the ready-made reality which James had opposed in the rationalist (idealist) philosophies popular in his day.

By stressing that there are degrees of freedom even at the experiential interface between human minds and the world in which they are situated, James encouraged a picture of the mind as functioning actively rather than passively. He also stood as an obstacle to the total dominance of the conception of reality as something which imposes on us, requiring conformity from our minds and leaving no room for development in which we might play an essential part. Long before he became associated with pragmatism James had rejected any outlook which entailed determinism and denied human beings the capacity to act freely.[14] The libertarian or voluntaristic position which James favoured may not have followed strictly from pragmatic principles, but pragmatism, even when conceived narrowly as a method for gaining clarity through spelling out practical consequences, rests on a conception of human beings as active and of their cognitive activities as making a difference to the world, rather than merely reflecting the way it is.

～ THE FORTUNES OF PRAGMATISM ～

James's reply to Russell ([13.12], 312–19) concentrated on rebutting what James took to be perverse misinterpretations of his position found elsewhere. He did not engage Russell directly over the issue of whether statements we choose to make about sensory experience could or should be treated as 'plain matters of fact'. He did remark on what he saw as the excessive 'abstractionism' in Russell's procedure. These, as it transpired, were the two most prominent features of the philosophy, logical empiricism, which during the 1930s came to eclipse pragmatism. It was accepted (widely, but not universally) that the possibility of empirical knowledge rested on sensory experience, which provided us with a class of statements which expressed 'plain matters of fact'. These were commonly taken to be observation statements reporting particular experiences, and more general statements (including scientific theories) which did not express plain matters of fact had to answer to such 'truths'. They did so through a structure represented abstractly in the new (mathematical) logic, which Russell had helped to shape, and which held out the promise of a sharp distinction between the empirical content of statements (where they rest on indisputable fact) and the conventions governing the uses of words.

In 1951 W. V. O. Quine challenged 'two dogmas of empiricism': one the belief that we can sharply distinguish between synthetic statements, those with determinate empirical content, and analytic statements, those true in virtue of the conventions governing language; and the other the belief that the empirical content of statements could be reduced to (represented entirely in terms of) the observation statements which they entailed. During the reign of these dogmas, pragmatism, although it had able supporters, was avoided by anyone who did not wish to appear out of fashion. Once the hold of the two dogmas had been broken, it became possible to speak without pejorative overtones of the work of Quine and Donald Davidson as continuations of the pragmatist tradition[15] and possible to proclaim a revival of that tradition. But the pragmatism of Peirce, James and Dewey consisted in more than the denial of Quine's two dogmas. It is far from clear yet whether the current modest fashion for pragmatism will lay sufficient stress on mind as goal-directed, on intellectual clarity as tied to practical outcome, on truth as the long-term product of our enquiries and on human experience as a natural phenomenon, for it to count as a continuation of the tradition rather than a transmogrification into something all its founders would have regarded as quite alien.

❧ NOTES ❧

I am grateful to Ron Bontekoe, John Hodges and Mary Tiles for helping me to eliminate infelicities from the penultimate draft of this chapter.

1 Biographical note: William James was born in New York City in 1842, the eldest child of Mary Walsh and Henry James Sr. His independently wealthy father established a reputation as a man of letters and a somewhat eccentric theologian. The oldest of William's three brothers was the novelist Henry James, Jr, and his only sister Alice has recently been acclaimed for the diaries which she left. After considering a career as a painter, James took a medical degree at Harvard in 1869 and in 1872 began a teaching career at Harvard which moved from physiology through psychology (1875) to philosophy (1879). He was appointed professor of philosophy in 1885, retired in 1907 and died in 1910. For a chapter-length account of James's life and career, see [13.25].

2 The lecture, titled 'Philosophical Conceptions and Practical Results', appeared as the lead article in the *University Chronicle* for September 1898 and as a separately published pamphlet circulated by the Philosophical Union and by James himself ([13.19], 285). Within a year James's address had been discussed by Dickinson Miller in the *Philosophical Review* and pragmatism had been the subject of an address (published in *Mind* in October 1900) by William Caldwell at the American Psychological Association ([13.19], 293).

3 It is ironic that critics have detected distinctively Kantian elements in James's thought. Kuklick ([13.22], 273–4) finds that James became more Kantian as his thought developed up to his death twelve years after delivering his lecture at Berkeley. Henri Bergson ([13.15], 257) remarked on the Kantianism of James's doctrines in an introduction to a French translation of James's *Pragmatism* published in 1911.

4 See Peirce ([13.36], 6: 182–4) for a moving tribute to James.

5 Dewey [13.33] recommended 'warranted assertibility' instead of 'truth'.

6 Dewey ([13.18], 330) expressed frustration with this common misunderstanding. 'No misconception of the instrumental logic has been more persistent than the belief that it makes knowledge merely a means to a practical end, or to the satisfaction of practical needs – practical being taken to signify some quite definite utilities of a material or bread-and-butter type.... I again affirm that the term 'pragmatic' means only the rule of referring all thinking, all reflective considerations, to consequences for final meaning and test. Nothing is said about the nature of the consequences; they may be aesthetic, or moral, or political, or religious in quality – anything you please.'

7 Individualism was for Peirce one of the 'daughters of nominalism' ([13.36], 8: 38).

8 James referred to his thesis in terms of 'right' rather than 'will' and in various places expressed regret over his choice of title ([13.12], 124; see note to 124.13 on 164).

9 Russell regarded it as foundation of the pragmatist theory of truth ([13.28], 89–97, 113). Peirce's complaint ([13.36], 5: 3) that James had pushed the pragmatic principle to unwelcome extremes mentioned this article together with the Berkeley lecture.

10 James places this latter claim within an objection to Pascal and to the idea of exercising volitional control over our beliefs. He thus did not immediately endorse it, but he did nothing to rebut the claim that, without a pre-existing tendency, masses and holy water will do nothing to 'stupefy [one's] scruples' as Pascal was quoted as saying ([13.3], 6). Later James credited Pascal's argument with being 'a regular *clincher*, and . . . *the last stroke* needed to make our faith in masses and holy water complete' (11, emphasis added).

11 E.g. in the Berkeley lecture ([13.11], 430ff.), in a chapter of *Pragmatism* ([13.12], 63ff.) and in a chapter of the book *Some Problems of Philosophy*, on which he was at work when he died in 1910 ([13.13], 61ff.).

12 Peirce's earliest published work had begun with a rejection of Cartesianism epistemology and all of those, who subsequently enlisted under the banner of pragmatism, who repudiated Cartesian dualism. For James's doctrine of 'neutral monism', his doctrine of a 'primal stuff' consisting of 'pure experience', see [13.10], chapters 1 and 2.

13 The New Realist manifesto and Dewey's dispute with a representative of the group are reprinted in [13.34]. More recent articulations of the presuppositions are to be found in [13.38], chapter 2 and [13.35], chapters 1, 2, 6 and 8.

14 During the period between receiving his medical degree and beginning his teaching career James suffered from severe depression in which determinism appeared to him a very real threat to his moral interests. His diary for 30 April 1870 records how he was helped over this crisis by reading the French philosopher Charles Renouvier and also records a resolve which sheds light on his doctrine of a will/right to believe, 'My first act of free will shall be to believe in free will' ([13.25], 43).

15 For an example of such a reading of the continuity of the tradition see Murphy, [13.24]. This posthumously published textbook was seen through the press by Richard Rorty, who has been the prime mover behind the respectability which pragmatism has recently re-acquired. See [13.37].

❦ BIBLIOGRAPHY ❦

Major works published by James

13.1 The Principles of Psychology, 2 vols, New York: Henry Holt, 1890; reprint
New York: Dover, 1950.

13.2 Psychology (Briefer Course), New York: Henry Holt, 1892.

13.3 The Will to Believe and Other Essays in Popular Philosophy, New York:
Longmans, Green, 1897; reprint with [13.4] New York: Dover, 1956.

13.4 Human Immortality: Two Supposed Objections to the Doctrine, Boston:
Houghton Mifflin, 1898.

13.5 The Varieties of Religious Experience: A Study in Human Nature, New York:
Longmans, Green, 1902.

13.6 Pragmatism: A New Name for some Old Ways of Thinking, New York:
Longmans, Green, 1907; reprint with [13.7] as [13.12].

13.7 The Meaning of Truth: A Sequel to 'Pragmatism', New York: Longmans
Green, 1909.

13.8 A Pluralistic Universe, New York: Longmans, Green, 1909.

Works by James published posthumously

13.9 Some Problems of Philosophy, edited by Horace M. Kallen, New York: Longmans, Green, 1911, reprint as [13.13].

13.10 Essays in Radical Empiricism, ed. R. B. Perry, New York: Longmans, Green,
1912.

13.11 Collected Essays and Reviews, ed. R. B. Perry, New York: Longmans, Green,
1920.

A complete edition of the works of William James edited by F. Burkhardt, F.
Bowers and I. K. Skrupskelis, Cambridge, Mass.: Harvard University Press,
includes

13.12 Pragmatism and the Meaning of Truth, 1975.

13.13 Some Problems of Philosophy, 1979.

Works about James

13.14 Ayer, A. J. The Origins of Pragmatism, London: Macmillan, 1968.

13.15 Bergson, H. 'On the Pragmatism of William James: Truth and Reality', in
Creative Mind, trans. M. L. Andison, New York: Philosophical
Library, 1946: 246–60.

13.16 Bird, G. William James, London: Routledge & Kegan Paul, 1986.

13.17 Bradley, F. H. 'Truth and Practice', 'Truth and Copying', 'On the Ambiguity
of Pragmatism', 'On Professor James's "Meaning of Truth" ' and 'On
Professor James's "Radical Empiricism" ', in Essays on Truth and
Reality, Oxford: Clarendon Press, 1914: 65–158.

13.18 Dewey, J. 'What Pragmatism Means by Practical', in *Essays in Experimental Logic*, Chicago: University of Chicago Press, 1916: 303–34; reprint New York: Dover, n.d.

13.19 Fisch, M. H. 'American Pragmatism Before and After 1898', *Peirce Semeiotic and Pragmatism*, Bloomington: Indiana University Press, 1986: 283–304.

13.20 Haack, S. 'The Pragmatist Theory of Truth', *British Journal for the Philosophy of Science*, 27 (1976): 231–49.

13.21 —— 'Can James's Theory of Truth be Made More Satisfactory?', *Transactions of the Charles S. Peirce Society*, 20 (3) (1984): 269–78.

13.22 Kuklick, B. *The Rise of American Philosophy*, New Haven: Yale University Press, 1977, chapters 9, 14–17.

13.23 Moore, G. E. 'William James' "Pragmatism" ', in *Philosophical Studies*, London: Kegan Paul, Trench, Trubner, 1922: 97–146.

13.24 Murphy, J. P. *Pragmatism: From Peirce to Davidson*, Boulder: Westview Press, 1990: 39–58.

13.25 Myers, G. E. *William James: His Life and Thought*, New Haven: Yale University Press, 1986.

13.26 Perry, R. B. *The Thought and Character of William James*, 2 vols, Boston: Little, Brown, 1935.

13.27 Royce, J. 'William James and the Philosophy of Life', *The Basic Writings of Josiah Royce*, vol. 1, ed. J. J. McDermott, Chicago: University of Chicago Press, 1969: 205–22.

13.28 Russell, B. 'Pragmatism' and 'William James's Conception of Truth', in *Philosophical Essays*, London: Allen & Unwin, 1910: 87–149.

13.29 Santayana, G. 'William James', *Character and Opinion in the United States*, New York: Charles Scribner's Sons, 1920: 64–96.

13.30 Scheffler, I. *Four Pragmatists*, London: Routledge & Kegan Paul, 1974: 95–146.

13.31 Smith, J. E. *Purpose and Thought: The Meaning of Pragmatism*, New Haven: Yale University Press, 1978.

13.32 Thayer, H. S. *Meaning and Action: A Critical History of Pragmatism*, Indianapolis: Bobbs-Merrill, 1968: 133–59.

Other works cited

13.33 Dewey, J. *Logic: the Theory of Inquiry*, New York: Henry Holt, 1938.

13.34 —— *John Dewey: The Middle Works, 1899–1924*, vol. 6, Carbondale: Southern Illinois University Press, 1978.

13.35 Nagel, T. *The View From Nowhere*, Oxford: Oxford University Press, 1986.

13.36 Peirce, C. S. *Collected Papers of Charles Sanders Peirce*, 8 vols, ed by C. Hartshorne and P. Weiss, vol. 2 (1932), vol. 5 (1934), vol. 6 (1935); and ed. A. W. Burks, vol. 8 (1958), Cambridge, Mass.: Harvard University Press. (References to this edition are given by volume and paragraph number.)

13.37 Rorty, R. *Consequences of Pragmatism*, Minneapolis: University of Minnesota Press, 1982.

13.38 Williams, B. *Descartes: the Project of Pure Inquiry*, Harmondsworth: Penguin Books, 1978.

CHAPTER 14

Green, Bosanquet and the philosophy of coherence

Gerald F. Gaus

➤➤ INTRODUCTION ➤➤

Along with F. H. Bradley (chapter 15), T. H. Green and Bernard Bosanquet were the chief figures in what is commonly called British idealism. Bradley is widely regarded as the most eminent philosopher of the three; his *Ethical Studies*, published in 1876, was the first in-depth presentation of idealist ethics, including an account of the individual's relation to society (Nicholson, [14.45], 6). But after this initial work, Bradley had little more to say about ethics;[1] the development of the moral, and especially the political, philosophy of British idealism was carried on by Green and his followers, particularly Bosanquet.

Though he published little in his lifetime, Green (1836–82) had enormous influence through his teaching at Oxford. Green was appointed tutor in philosophy at Balliol in 1866 and in 1878 became White's Professor of Philosophy, a post he held until his death in 1882. Green's influence on his students apparently stemmed as much from his moral earnestness and the religious implications of idealism as from his philosophy, prompting C. D. Broad's jibe that he turned more undergraduates into prigs than Sidgwick ever made into philosophers ([14.20], 144).[2] As was the case with many of the British idealists, Green was a political and social reformer, being especially influential in educational reform (Gordon and White, [14.33]). Both of his major works were published after his death. Parts of his *Prolegomena to Ethics* were in a final form prior to his death; his main contribution to political philosophy was his *Lectures on the Principles of Political Obligation*, edited by R. L. Nettleship.

Green, while sometimes dismissed as a philosopher, is almost always treated nowadays with sympathy; Bosanquet (1840–1923) cuts a much less sympathetic figure. In his many published works, he presented a more systematic – and apparently much harsher and more Hegelian – version of Green's philosophy. Not only was he more obviously Hegelian, but Bosanquet seemed inevitably attracted to statements of his views that were most likely to outrage traditional English liberals, speaking, for example, of 'the confluence of selves' ([14.16], 107) and insisting that the moral person composing society is more real than what we call individual persons ([14.14], 145). Thus, the most famous attack on Bosanquet, L. T. Hobhouse's *Metaphysical Theory of the State*, charges that Bosanquet's theory is deeply illiberal: it is unable to account for the 'irreducible' separateness of selves and ultimately endorses a sort of State worship ([14.37], 62; Freeden, [14.29], 35). Yet Hobhouse absolves Green from his most serious charges; indeed, Hobhouse claimed that his own theory was the true successor to Green's ([14.38], chapters 7–8; [14.39], chapters 5–6). Whereas Hobhouse can be called a 'Left Greenian', arguing in support of something like a welfare state, Bosanquet can be understood as a 'right Greenian' (Collini, [14.24], 107–8). Bosanquet spent very little of his life inside academia, the most important exception being his tenure as professor of philosophy at St Andrews University from 1903 to 1908. Most of his life was devoted to the Charity Organization Society (COS), which objected to State provision of welfare such as outdoor relief to the poor. Bosanquet and the COS insisted that such 'mechanical' measures are typically failures that produce dependency; in so far as the poor should be assisted, it must be accomplished through charity focusing on the detailed needs of each recipient – thus pointing to the importance of private social work. This separated Bosanquet from the 'new liberals' (who endorsed the welfare state), reinforcing the erroneous perception that Bosanquet was a Tory; throughout his life he was an active political liberal and reformer.[3]

The problem of the relation of Green's and Bosanquet's idealisms to their liberal politics can be resolved into three more specific questions. Firstly, in what ways are the political and moral views of Green and Bosanquet affected by their idealism? Though almost invariably referred to as the 'British idealists', the relation of their philosophy (logic, epistemology and metaphysics) to their moral and political theory remains, I think, obscure. Secondly, are their moral and political views liberal or, as is often charged, statist and illiberal? Thirdly, our answers to these questions should enlighten us on a third: is Bosanquet a *bona fide* follower of Green, or was Hobhouse right that he perverted Green's teachings?

❧ EPISTEMOLOGY AND METAPHYSICS ❧

Philosophy and coherence

Bosanquet called his major work in political philosophy *The Philosophical Theory of the State*; as I have said, Hobhouse's critique was entitled *The Metaphysical Theory of the State*, suggesting that Bosanquet understood philosophy as essentially metaphysics. Yet this is not quite right. In the first paragraph of the *Philosophical Theory of the State*, Bosanquet explains what he means by a 'philosophical theory': 'a philosophical treatment is the study of something as a whole and for its own sake' ([14.14], 1). Later on he tells us that philosophy aims to establish 'degrees of value, degrees of reality, degrees of completeness and coherence' ([14.14], 47). For Bosanquet, as for Green, philosophy in its various guises aims at completion and harmony: epistemology, metaphysics, philosophical ethics and political philosophy are all manifestations of philosophy's search for coherence and completion.

Reason and knowledge

Given this, it is most helpful to start from the perspective of epistemology. Coherence is the basic demand of reason itself. In contrast to, say, Hobbes, reason is not understood as essentially calculative – a matter of 'reckoning, that is, adding and subtracting, of the consequences of general names agreed upon for the marking and signifying of thoughts' (Hobbes, [14.34], 26). The 'inherent nature of reason', argues Bosanquet, is 'the absolute demand for totality and consistency' ([14.11], 8). It cannot be overemphasized that reason is a demand or, as Bosanquet says elsewhere, an 'impulse' ([14.13]: 130). Logic 'is merely the same as the impulse to the whole' ([14.11], 7). That reason is an impulse driving us to expand and systematize our experiences allows us to make sense of Bosanquet's otherwise obscure remark that 'it is a strict fundamental truth that love is the mainspring of logic' ([14.15], 341); both are expressions of the unifying and expanding impulse.[4]

To obtain knowledge, then, is to bring unity to our particular experiences, 'through which phenomena become the connected system called the world of experience' (Green [14.1], 15). We are thus led to a coherence theory of knowledge; to know that *p* is for *p* to be related to, and to cohere with, the rest of one's beliefs or experiences. We need, though, to be careful here, for coherence goes considerably beyond requirements of formal consistency (Bosanquet [14.6], 2, chapter VII). Most importantly, coherence includes connectedness among beliefs and a richness of content ([14.15], 146); one who obtains consistency by compartmentalizing his or her system so that some beliefs are never related to others, or by impoverishing his or her experience (so that there is less that can conflict with the rest) to that extent falls short of the ideal of coherence. The fully coherent system would have to be complete, i.e., contain all true propositions.

Knowers and the known

Except for their insistence on the affective nature of reason, Green's and Bosanquet's epistemology is not terribly different from contemporary coherence theories of knowledge. The great gulf separating classical idealism from contemporary philosophy is the relation of the theory of knowledge to truth.[5] One contemporary view, endorsed by Laurence Bonjour, is to combine a coherence theory of knowledge with a correspondence theory of truth. He writes:

> [O]ur concern is with coherence theories of *empirical justification*
> and not coherence theories *of truth*; the latter hold that truth
> is to be simply *identified* with coherence.... The classical idealist
> proponents of coherence theories in fact generally held views
> of both these sorts and unfortunately failed for the most part to
> distinguish them. And this sort of confusion is abetted by views
> which use the phrase 'theory of truth' to mean a theory of the
> *criteria* of truth, that is, a theory of the standards or rules
> which should be appealed to in deciding or judging whether
> something is true; if, as is virtually always the case, such a
> theory is meant to be an account of the criteria which can be
> used to arrive at a rational or warranted judgment of truth or
> falsity, then a coherence theory of truth in that sense would
> seem to be indiscernible from what is here called a coherence
> theory of justification, and is quite distinct from a coherence
> theory of the very nature or meaning of truth. But if these
> confusions are avoided, it is clear that coherence theories of
> empirical justification are both distinct from and initially a
> good deal more plausible than coherence theories of the very
> nature or meaning of empirical truth and moreover that there
> is no manifest absurdity in combining a coherence theory of
> justification with a *correspondence* theory of truth.
>
> ([14.18], 88)

Now whatever other philosophical errors the classical idealists committed (and no doubt there were many), confusing coherence theories of justification (or, as they might say, understanding) with coherence theories of truth was not one of them. Indeed, it is the apparent implausibility of a Bonjour-like proposal that, for Green, makes it necessary to embrace a coherence theory of truth. In the *Prolegomena*, having analysed our understanding of nature in terms of systematizing the objects of consciousness, Green writes:

> Now that which the understanding thus presents to itself
> consists, as we have seen, in certain relations regarded as
> forming a single system. The next question, then, will be whether
> understanding can be held to 'make nature' in the further sense
> that it is the source, or at any rate a condition, of there being
> these relations. If it cannot, we are left in the awkward position
> of having to suppose that, while the conception of nature on the
> one side, and that of the order itself on the other, are of
> different and independent origin, there is yet some unaccountable
> pre-established harmony through which there comes to be such
> an order corresponding to our conception of it.
>
> ([14.1], 22–3)

For Green, to suppose that our understanding was achieved through coherence but that truth consisted in the correspondence of our beliefs with a pre-existing nature would make it utterly mysterious how pursuit of coherence reveals the truth about nature; only by supposing an established harmony between our reason and nature could this be so, but such a harmony is an implausibly strong assumption. The core idealist conviction is that, having replaced a representational theory of knowledge with a coherence account, this account can be maintained only by characterizing truth itself in terms of coherence.[6] It is not simply that justified belief is a matter of coherence, but the very essence of truth is coherence and completeness. 'The truth is the whole' ([14.6], 2: 204).

Idealism guarantees that the truth – what nature is really like – is the coherent whole since nature is ultimately mind-dependent; nature is constituted by the unifying and completing force of mind. That being so, what the coherent mind knows *is* nature. But, of course, actual individual minds disagree about what nature is like; if each personal mind constituted its own nature, there would be as many natures as there are minds. Moreover, it would be obscure what scientific discovery could amount to; science searches for what exists but is yet not known. To avoid such difficulties reality cannot be dependent upon individual minds; hence we are led from personal idealism to Absolute idealism. Though Green is sometimes called a personal and not an Absolute idealist, this is surely wrong, for Green's idea of an 'Eternal Consciousness' is straightforwardly Hegelian:

That there is one spiritual self-conscious being, of which all that is real is the activity or expression; that we are related to this spiritual being, not merely as parts of the world which is its expression, but as partakers in some inchoate measure of the self-consciousness through which it at once constitutes and distinguishes itself from the world; that this participation is the source of morality and religion; this is what we take as to be the vital truth which Hegel had to teach.

([14.2], 146)[7]

The Eternal Consciousness – which Green identifies with God – is an all-inclusive consciousness; it is the mind upon which reality rests. Green apparently conceives of finite minds as somehow participating in the Eternal Consciousness – coming to consciousness of the relations in the Eternal Consciousness. The growth of our knowledge is, then, our increasing awareness of the Eternal Consciousness ([14.1], 75).

Though much more developed, Bosanquet's theory of the Absolute is not, I think, fundamentally different.[8] For Bosanquet, the Absolute is the perfection of mind's pursuit of coherence; it is the complete and harmonious mind. Or, rather, it is the systematization and completion of finite minds.[9] 'The general formula of the Absolute', Bosanquet wrote, is 'the transmutation and rearrangement of particular experiences, and also the contents of individual minds, by inclusion in a more complete whole of experience' ([14.15], 373). And being the more complete and more harmonious mind, it is ultimate reality, since reality is mind-dependent. A recurring theme in Bosanquet's philosophy is that the more harmonious and complete is the more real, a position that follows easily enough from the coherence view of knowledge combined with Absolute idealism. The upshot of this, of course, is that finite (i.e., personal) minds are incomplete and contradictory, and so less real. Though not as relentless as Bosanquet in insisting on this point, Green's idealism based on the Eternal Consciousness too identifies the real with 'everything' ([14.1], 27).

Idealist metaphysics, ethics and politics

On the account I have sketched, it is misguided to understand Green's and Bosanquet's idealism as primarily a metaphysical theory, i.e., a theory about the nature of reality. Rather, their philosophy is based on (1) a conception of reason as a unifying, affective, force, (2) a coherence theory of knowledge or understanding, according to which knowledge is a system of relations, and so to know something is to relate it to our other beliefs; (3) an Absolute idealism, which was understood as the most plausible concomitant of (1) and (2).[10] None of these elements is fundamental in the sense of being the basic doctrine from which the others are derived. On my account, the epistemological project leads to the metaphysical; that is, I believe that the former is the best way to explain the motivation behind the latter. But certainly the metaphysics in no way derives from the accounts of reason and knowledge (recall here Bonjour's position). All three doctrines are manifestations of the overarching notion of coherence, the real key to understanding the idealism of Green and Bosanquet.

Understanding the philosophy of the British idealists in this way allows us to approach an old question in a new light: do their moral and political philosophies derive from their metaphysics? My answer should not be surprising: talk of 'derivation' is misleading. Their accounts of the self, moral perfection, the common good, general will and the State are all applications of the ideal of coherence. This is not to say they are unrelated to the other elements of their philosophy; the analysis of reason, knowledge and reality lends plausibility to, and helps justify, their moral and political doctrines. In true coherentist fashion, the various doctrines are mutually reinforcing and justifying.[11] It is, then, fruitless to look for any single doctrine from which the rest follow.

❧ THE SELF AND ITS PERFECTION ❧

The self as a system of content

Having stressed that point, it also must be acknowledged that Bosanquet's and Green's analyses of selfhood are applications of their accounts of mind. If 'the peculiarity of mind, for us, is to be a world of experience working itself out towards harmony and completeness' (Bosanquet [14.15], 193), the same applies to selfhood; the self is an organization of content striving for coherence and completion (Bosanquet [14.11], 48; [14.15], 242). To say this is to emphasize that selfhood is not understood as being constituted by an abstract entity or pure ego (Green [14.1], 103–4; Bosanquet [14.10], 55); for Bosanquet and Green the self is not something apart from 'feelings, desires and thoughts' (Green [14.1], 104), but their unification and systematization. Bosanquet made much of the contrast to J. S. Mill, for whom true individuality consisted in the cultivation of 'an inner self, to be cherished by enclosing it' ([14.14], 57). This, Bosanquet admonished, was to get things precisely wrong; it locates individuality in a core of essentially empty privateness rather than an expansion of feelings, interests and experiences. 'Individuality is essentially a positive conception.... Its essence lies in the richness and completeness of a self' ([14.15], 69; [14.10], 89).[12]

On one side, then, Bosanquet and Green rejected 'formal' accounts of the self in terms of an abstract ego. However, they also criticized Humean or associationist accounts, which located the self (or, rather, failed to) in a series of contents. No mere succession of desires, feelings and thoughts could constitute a self; though the self is 'not something apart from feelings, desires and thoughts', it is not just simply them: it is 'that which unites them' (Green [14.1], 104; [14.4], 339-41).[13] This, though, immediately threatens to lead back towards positing a 'mysterious abstract entity which you call the self' ([14.1], 104) that is different from, but unites, the feelings, desires and ideas that form the content of the self. In responding to this problem, I would suggest, Green and Bosanquet display their most important divergence, one which, we shall see, has significant consequences for their ethics and political philosophy.

Green's proposal has two elements. Firstly (and with this Bosanquet agrees), he stresses that the self cannot be a mere succession of thoughts, feelings and desires, but must form an organized system. Here Green's epistemology and metaphysics do come into play. For to understand an experience is to relate it to the rest of one's experiences, and for something to be real is for it to be located in such a web of understanding. This allows Green to turn the tables on Hume:

> If we are told that the Ego or self is an abstraction from the facts of our inner experience – something which we 'accustom ourselves to suppose' as the basis or substratum for these, but which exists only logically, not really, – it is a fair rejoinder, that these so-called facts, our particular feelings, desires, and thoughts, are abstractions, if considered otherwise than as united in an agent who is an object to himself.
>
> ([14.1], 104; see Thomas [14.56], 177)

Green introduces here the second element of his reply: not only must desires, feelings and thoughts be systematized for them to be real and not abstract but the system must be self-conscious – one must be able to be an object to oneself. For Green such consciousness is absolutely fundamental to selfhood; indeed, his account of selfhood is essentially an account of self-consciousness, of an agent who is able to grasp his system of desires as 'an object to himself'.

Though both elements are present in Bosanquet's theory of the self, there is a marked stress on the organizational aspect and a de-emphasising of self-consciousness. Bosanquet too rejects associationist views of the self: 'In mind... the higher stage of association is organization. The characteristic of organization is control by a general scheme, as opposed to juxtaposition of units' ([14.14] 152). In his *Psychology of the Moral Self* Bosanquet developed his account of the organization of the self in depth. 'The psychical elements of the mind are so grouped and interconnected', he wrote, 'as to constitute what are technically known as Appercipient masses or systems' ([14.10], 42).[14] Such a system, Bosanquet writes, is a

> set of ideas, bound together by a common rule or scheme, which dictates the point of view from which perception will take place, so far as the system in question is active. And without some 'apperception', some point of view in the mind which enables the new-comer to be classed, there cannot be perception at all. The eye only sees what it brings with it the power of seeing. . . . A child calls an orange a 'ball'; a Polynesian calls a horse a 'pig'. These are the nearest 'heads' or rules under which the new perception can be brought.
>
> ([14.14], 155)

A person organizes experience in terms of these 'schemes of attention'; as different situations arise, one mass will arise to prominence in consciousness, leaving the others inert ([14.14], 162). The self,[15] then, is a multiplicity of such systems. However, because one appercipient mass forces the others from consciousness, the self is always imperfectly coherent; inconsistencies and contradictions are hidden because different systems do not rise to consciousness at the same time.

Note that, though consciousness is a necessary element of this theory, it does not have the dominant role that Green ascribes to a person who can grasp his system of desires as 'an object to himself'. In contrast to Green, Bosanquet makes a great deal of the extent to which 'an adult mind contains an immense structure of automatic machinery' ([14.15], 181); the automatic, and so unconscious, aspect of selfhood always looms large in Bosanquet's theory. The idea of an 'I' who unites desires into a system is replaced by the theory of appercipient mass. Self-consciousness now seems to be more a recognizer than a forger of unity.[16]

Self-perfection

Perhaps not quite. Bosanquet certainly recognizes that the self strives for greater coherence. Our nature as self-conscious beings is, he says, to strive for harmony and unity ([14.11], 193–4; [14.16], 189). Indeed, he classifies himself and Green as 'Perfectionists' ([14.16], 208ff.). Their account of self-perfection can be analysed into four claims.

The good

Green and Bosanquet accept the Hegelian critique of Kant: his doctrine of the 'Good Will' is 'ultimately an empty abstraction, an idea of nothing in particular to be done' ([14.4], 154). The first step in rectifying this over-formality is an account of the good: the good, says, Green, satisfies desire ([14.1], 178). The argument, though, quickly takes an Aristotelian turn, stressing the pursuit of perfection, or the development of capacities, as the basis of self-satisfaction:

> The reason and will of man have their common ground in that characteristic of being an object to himself.... It is thus that he not merely desires but seeks to satisfy himself in gaining the objects of his desire; presents to himself a certain state of himself, which is the gratification of the desire he seeks to reach; in short wills. It is thus, again, that he has an impulse to make himself what he has the possibility of becoming but actually is not, and hence not merely, like the plant or animal, undergoes a process of development but seeks to, and does, develop himself.
>
> ([14.1], 182)

This impulse to develop, Green goes on to say, is an impulse to realize one's capacities. Thus Green ultimately holds that a person's good is identified with the development of his capacities, especially the intellectual. Both Green and Bosanquet maintain that individuals have natural capacities for intellectual, social and artistic endeavours (including handicrafts),[18] the cultivation of which is the ground of self-perfection.

Self-satisfaction and coherence

Thus far the impulse to develop is not moralized; it is, says Green, 'the source, according to the direction it takes, both of vice and virtue' ([14.1], 183). Some attempts at self-satisfaction are 'self-defeating', as 'is the quest for self-satisfaction in the life of the voluptuary' (183). The self, we have seen, is a system of content, and reason is an impulse towards completion and unity. Applied to the development of our capacities, this leads to the idea that self-satisfaction – as opposed to the satisfaction of discrete desires or capacities – requires the development of our capacities into a coherent whole. 'The state of mind in question ... is that in which the impulse towards self-satisfaction sets itself upon an object which represents the self as a whole, as free from contradiction or at its maximum of being, and triumphs over the alien and partial will, the tendency to narrower tracks of indulgence' ([14.14], 132). Green's view is much the same, though as always he stresses the role of self-consciousness as crucial, in this instance its role in distinguishing mere desires from those that are self-satisfying ([14.4], 304). In any event, this distinction allows Green and Bosanquet to identify capacities as good or evil in terms of their ability to be integrated into a coherent system of developed capacities. A person developing capacities that cannot be integrated into the whole, such as the voluptuary, can satisfy some of his or her desires, but cannot find self-satisfaction.

An obvious rejoinder presents itself: if a self is organized around only voluptuary interests, coherence can be obtained and, it would seem, self-satisfaction too. But this will not do. As we have seen, coherence goes beyond mere consistency to include fullness of content. Consequently, Bosanquet analyses selfishness as an effort to seek coherence through narrowing rather than expanding the self ([14.10], 97). This path to coherence is ultimately self-defeating. Since reason is an impulse to coherence and completion, seeking coherence through narrowing is irrational, or, as Bosanquet says in his sometimes colourful way, it 'involves stupidity' ([14.13], 232).[19] Remember here that reason is an impulse; such stupidity thus seeks to block our rational impulse towards coherence. Consequently, the success of the narrowing strategy is always illusory:

> It is the narrowness of a man's mind that makes him do wrong.
> He desires more than he can deal with; indeed he aspires to be
> self-complete. But what he can make his own, as a set of values
> which do not conflict, is little. And of what is extruded
> something refuses to be suppressed and forms the nucleus of
> rebellion. Thus the good we are able to aim at is narrow and
> distorted, and more than that, the elements of the good which
> our narrowness forces us to reject lie in ambush to conflict with
> the good we recognise, itself poor and narrow and so weakened
> for the struggle.
>
> ([14.13] 107; see also [14.14], 135–7)

This is Bosanquet's description of the 'bad self or evil will'. The 'good will', then, is determined by 'the connected system of values, that is to say, as much of it as we can appreciate' ([14.13], 133). The Kantian concept of the good will is thus transformed into a will determined by reason in the sense of a coherent system of capacities or values.[20]

Diversity

It may appear to follow from this that the impulse towards self-satisfaction would lead to the development of essentially similar selves. We all seem committed to essentially the same project: the harmonization of as many capacities or values as possible. This, though, is precisely the view Green and Bosanquet reject (see Green [14.1], 201). As Bosanquet puts it, 'It takes all sorts to make a world' ([14.15], 37). Individual quests for self-satisfaction lead to the development of diverse personalities, and this for at least three reasons. Firstly, individual natures differ: people are born with different capacities, some excelling in intellectual pursuits, some in the arts, some in crafts and so forth. Given these different starting points, the quest for coherence leads us in different directions.[21] Secondly, Green ([14.2] 3–19; [14.1], 201, 256) and especially Bosanquet recognized that external circumstances can profoundly influence the course of one's self-development. Bosanquet repeatedly stressed that 'The soul or self is formed by the requirements of its surroundings; that is, the universe so far as it has contact with it' ([14.11], 91).[22] Our different circumstances thus lead us to develop our capacities in different directions. Lastly, even apart from differences in individual natures and circumstances, the very richness of human possibilities means that, if we are to cultivate our capacities at all, we must specialize: 'in the development of human nature, which we take to be the ultimate standard of life, no one individual can cover the whole ground' ([14.14], 164).

Our inherent imperfection

If no one individual can cover the full ground of human nature, no one can attain absolute perfection – a coherent self encompassing all values. As Bosanquet would say, our finite nature limits us, absolute perfection is impossible; at one point Bosanquet goes so far as to declare that 'man is a self-contradictory being, in an environment to which he can never be adapted' ([14.12], 300). The best we can accomplish is a narrow, imperfect coherence. And since a narrow coherence is the root of evil, 'evil and suffering must be permanent in the world' (300). In one of his rare criticisms of Green, Bosanquet charges that Green underestimated the gap 'between human experience and perfection' ([14.16], 165). And it is, I think, true that the gap between the human condition and perfection is a much more important theme in Bosanquet than in Green.[23] To be sure, Green is explicit that we cannot have an adequate conception of what perfection would look like, since we have not as yet obtained it: '[o]f what ultimate well-being may be, therefore, we are unable to say anything but that it must be the complete fulfillment of capacities.' Yet Green goes on to insist that 'the idea that there is such an ultimate well-being may be the guiding idea of our lives', and so we judge a particular person's life on the basis of how closely it approaches 'the end in which alone he can find satisfaction for himself' ([14.1], 256).

In all this there is at least a suggestion that we do not fall hopelessly short of perfection. Yet the difference between Green and Bosanquet here is a matter of nuance. Green too accepts that the individual has absolute limitations on the possibility for self-realization; the 'dream' that these can be done away with is 'the frenzy of philosophy' ([14.2], 86). In true idealist fashion Green insists that 'the whole can never be fully seen in the parts' (86). True perfection can exist only in the overall coherent system of values, which no individual life can fully express.

❧ SOCIETY, THE COMMON GOOD AND ❧ THE GENERAL WILL

Society as an organic whole

An individual's pursuit of perfection requires participation in social life. This is obviously true, of course, in the perfectly straightforward sense that society 'supplies all the higher content' to one's conception of oneself, 'all those objects of a man's personal interest, in living for which he lives for his own satisfaction, except such as are derived from his purely animal nature' (Green [14.1], 201). More fundamentally, Green and Bosanquet follow Hegel in insisting that 'it is through the action of society that the individual comes at once to practically conceive his personality – his nature of an object to himself – and to conceive the same personality as belonging to others' (Green [14.1]). It is only through 'some practical recognition of personality by another, of an "I" by a "Thou" and a "Thou" by an "I" ' (Green [14.1], 210) that consciousness of personality arises (see Bosanquet [14.10], 49–50).

All this, though, is commonplace. Of much more interest is that reason – the impulse to coherence – leads us to participate in a more inclusive scheme of value, which covers the ground of human nature more fully than can any single life. One who pursues perfection must, as I have said, develop only some of the many capacities inherent in human nature; no matter how successful one is in doing so, one ultimately realizes that one's perfection is really imperfect, i.e., partial and incomplete. It is here that our impulse to unite values into a coherent scheme leads us into social life. As Bosanquet understands it, 'our imperfection [i.e., partiality] enables us to better stand for something which is to have its due stress in the whole' ([14.11], 61). But the overall system, encompassing these many partial excellences, more closely approaches perfection than any single element. The different partial perfections of others thus complement and complete one's own; the 'ultimate coherence of all excellences' ([14.15, 379) is better manifested in a complex social life that unites and harmonizes the diverse partial excellences of individuals. Consequently, the same principle that unifies the self also explains the unity of the self with others ([14.15], 315).

This allows us to make sense of the much-abused claim that society is an organism. Bosanquet quite clearly did not mean that, just as the end of all the body parts is the survival of the organism, we should all make service to society our end ([14.15], 9). The idea, rather, is that organic unity is a mode of organization based on interlocking and complementary differences, the totality of which is in some way more complete than any of the elements. Often Bosanquet called such a unity a 'world' or a 'cosmos':

> A world or a cosmos is a system of members, such that every member, being *ex hypothesi* distinct, nevertheless contributes to the unity of the whole in virtue of the peculiarities which constitute its distinctness. And the important point for us at present is the distinction between a world and a class. It takes all sorts to make a world; a class is essentially of one sort only.
>
> ([14.11] 37)

So understood, the idea that society is an organism is not illiberal. It stresses that co-operative systems based on diverse individual aims and capacities can accomplish more than can any single individual alone, something a student of the market should not find troubling, at least so long as, in Bosanquet's words, every member remains 'distinct'. It is here, perhaps, that Bosanquet gets into difficulty. Recall that according to Bosanquet's theory of appercipient masses, a self is composed of a number of such systems (pp. 414–16). This suggests a three-level theory of coherence: (1) each appercipient system is unified by a leading idea, and so organizes an aspect of experience or personality; (2) the individual self is an organization of these appercipient systems; and (3) a social group is an organization of individual selves. The problem is that the second level of coherence tends to get squeezed out, leading to an account of social unity in terms of simply (1) and (3). Bosanquet acknowledges that

> in some examples ... there seems little reason to distinguish the correlation of dispositions within one person from the correlation of the same dispositions if dispersed among different persons. If I am my own gardener, or my own critic, or my own doctor, does the relation of the answering dispositions within my being differ absolutely and altogether from what takes place when gardener and master, critic and author, patient and doctor, are different persons? ... If we consider my unity with myself at different times as the limiting case, we shall find it

very hard to establish a difference in principle between the unity of what we call one mind and that of all the 'minds' which enter into a single social experience.

($[14.14]$, 165–6)[24]

Though Bosanquet insists that 'there is no suggestion that selfhood is a trivial or unreal thing' ($[14.15]$, 298), one could well be excused for thinking he may be suggesting just that. The difficulty, at least on the view I have been developing here, is that Bosanquet's theory of the self puts such great weight on the principle of coherence, while relatively so much less on self-consciousness. To the extent selfhood is to be accounted for simply in terms of coherence, there is indeed a pressure for this middle level of coherence (the self) to evaporate as first level unities (the appercipient masses) form larger systems, be they within the same human or across a number of people.

Green avoids these difficulties by always insisting on a person's self-consciousness as the fundamental unifying factor.[25] Green too believes that 'it is human society as a whole that we must look upon as the organism in which the capacities of the human soul are unfolded' ($[14.1]$ 295). And, Green also believes that our excellences are complementary and interlocking (pp. 420–1). However, as we have seen, Green puts great stress on each individual as a centre of self-consciousness. Hence, even while insisting that perfection must occur in an organic society, Green can immediately add that 'Human society is indeed a society of self-determined persons. There can be no progress of society which is not a development of capacities on the part of persons composing it, as ends in themselves' ($[14.1]$, 295). The individual self is in no danger of evaporating in Green's account of the organic whole. This becomes even clearer when we examine his theory of the common good.

Green's theory of the common good

Green begins his section of the *Prolegomena* on 'reason as the source of the idea of a common good' by claiming that a 'distinctive social interest on our part is a primary fact'.

> Now the self of which a man thus forecasts the fulfillment, is not an abstract or empty self. It is a self already affected by manifold interests, among which are interests in other persons. These are not merely interests dependent on other persons for the means to their gratification, but interests in the good of those persons, interests which cannot be satisfied without the consciousness that those other persons are satisfied. The man

cannot contemplate himself as in a better state, or on the way to the best, without contemplating others, not merely as a means to that better state, but as sharing it with him.

([14.1], 210)

It is, Green claims, 'an ultimate fact of human history that out of sympathies of animal origin, through their presence in a self-conscious soul, there arise interests as of a person in persons' ([14.1], 212). Note the contrast to Bosanquet. Though both insist that reason leads us from our own perfection narrowly conceived to a concern with perfection in others, for Green this is crucially an interest in the perfection *of other persons*, not simply in the perfection of the capacities of human nature. It is not trivial that while Bosanquet claims that 'the development of human nature' is 'the ultimate standard of life' ([14.14], 164), Green insists that 'our ultimate standard of worth is an ideal of *personal worth*' ([14.1], 193). For Bosanquet, society is an intermeshing of developed capacities or values; for Green it is an intermeshing development of persons.

Those who uphold Green's liberalism while insisting upon Bosanquet's illiberalism are apt to stress just this point (e.g., Morrow, [14.43], 94). Two problems, however, confront this 'liberal' aspect of Green's theory. Firstly, Green can certainly say, as he does, that '[a]ll values are relative to value for, of, or in a person' in the sense that '[t]o speak of any progress or improvement or development of a nation or society or mankind, except as relative to some greater worth of persons, is to use words without meaning' ([14.1], 193). Yet this worth of persons cannot be 'ultimate'. As Bosanquet was fond of stressing, 'some particular personality becomes important by what it embodies' ([14.15], 22). Our value as persons derives ultimately from our contribution to the overall system of value (and this opens up the rather unsettling possibility that some persons may be in 'surplusage', i.e., those who make no unique contribution to the whole; Bosanquet [14.15], 116). The value must ultimately reside in the whole rather than the parts. To be sure, in contrast to Bosanquet's, in Green's theory the development of *persons* as opposed to capacities or values is essential for perfection of the whole, but this leads to the second problem. In order to extend the principle of coherent, intermeshing, personal development to the social order, Green postulates a distinctive interest of people in each other's perfection: the perfection of personality becomes the crucial value in the overall scheme of things. To the extent that this interest really is claimed to be a 'primary fact', it invites Sidgwick's rejoinder that it is not 'justified by anything we know about the essential sociality of ordinary human beings' (Sidgwick [14.54], 57). In contrast, Bosanquet's theory supposes no additional social impulse; just as reason leads to the systematization of interests and values within a self, it leads to a social organic unity.

According to Green, then, the common good includes the good of all: it is the harmonious realization of all our individual perfections.[26] That which promotes the common good can be willed by all, and so the common good provides the substantive element that was lacking in Kantian ethics. Reason is realized in one's idea of 'self-perfection, by acting as a member of a social organization, in which each contributes to the better well-being of all the rest' ([14.5], 16). In addition, the theory of the common good provides an account of the motivation to be moral; since our good includes the good of others, the pursuit of our own good necessarily involves the common good, and so the good of others. 'The only reason why a man should not be used by other men as a means to their ends is that he should use himself as a means to an end which is really his and theirs at once' ([14.5] 120).

Upon reflection, however, the extent to which Green has provided substance to the Kantian moral ideal may seem fairly modest; a standard criticism is that the idea of the common good is at best vague and at worst empty (see Nicholson [14.45], 71–80). The crux of Green's reply is given in the previous paragraph: we achieve self-perfection by *acting as a member of a social organization*. The cultivation of one's capacities is a social activity not just because it involves the perfection of others but because it relies on the 'institutions of civil life' which give 'reality to these capacities, as enabling them to be really exercised' ([14.5], 16). This leads Green to endorse a theory of one's station and its duties:

> The idea, unexpressed and inexpressible, of some absolute and all-embracing end is, no doubt, the source of ... devotion, but it can only take effect in the fulfillment in which it finds but a restricted utterance. It is in fact only so far as we are members of a society, of which we can conceive the common good as our own, that the idea has any practical hold on us at all, and this very membership implies confinement in our individual realisation of the idea. Each has primarily to fulfill the duties of his station. His capacity for action beyond the range of those duties is definitely bounded, and within it is definitely bounded also his sphere of personal interests, his character, his *realised* possibility.
>
> ([14.1], 192; see also 341–2)

Green thus understands a social order as a harmonious – or at least largely harmonious – integration of social roles, such that each person's roles allow one to organize one's capacities while contributing to the satisfaction of others (Thomas [14.56], 302). This does not commit Green to a rigid conservatism; room remains for adjusting social roles to render them more coherent, which includes making them more inclusive (indeed, as we will see, that is a crucial function of the State; [14.56], 292). But it certainly does mean that one's possibilities for self-perfection are very much sensitive to the social structure and roles available. Moreover, Green is quite clear that, while an actual system of stations and duties is necessary for self-perfection, it also confines avenues for development.

Bosanquet's theory of the general will

Bosanquet endorses both the doctrines of (1) the common good and (2) my station and its duties. 'The individual', said Bosanquet, 'has his nature communicated to him as he is summoned to fit himself for rendering a distinctive service to the common good' ([14.14], 290; see also [14.17], 113). Bosanquet acknowledges that he follows Green very closely on such matters, but believed that his exploration of the psychological foundations of the general will was one his important contributions ([14.14], viii).

Green himself suggested the link between the common good and the general will in his *Lectures on the Principles of Political Obligation*, where he remarked that 'the truth' latent in Rousseau's doctrine of the general will is that 'an interest in the common good is the ground of political society' ([14.5], 70). Following Rousseau, Bosanquet characterizes the general will as the will of the entire society so far as it aims at the common good ([14.14], 99). But just what sort of 'will' can a whole society share? Bosanquet believes that the key to the answer is in Plato's political philosophy:

> The central idea is this: that every class of persons in the community – the statesman, the soldier, the workman – has a certain distinctive type of mind which fits its members for their functions, and that the community essentially consists in the working of these types of mind in their connection with one another, which connection constitutes their subordination to the common good.
>
> ([14.14], 6)

This brings us back to Bosanquet's theory of social unity and appercipient masses. 'Every individual mind, so far as it thinks and acts in definite schemes or contexts, is a structure of appercipient systems or organized dispositions' ([14.14], 161). Now, Bosanquet goes on to argue, those participating in the same social institution or social group – those who share a common life – possess similar appercipient systems;

their minds are similarly organized, and it is this which constitutes their common mind and will ([14.14], 161–2).

> Not only may the systems of appercipient masses be *compared* to organizations of persons; they actually constitute their common mind and will. To say that certain persons have common interests means in this or that respect their minds are similarly organized, that they will react in the same or correlative ways upon given presentations. It is this identity of mental organization which is the psychological justification for the doctrine of the General Will.
>
> ([14.10], 129; see Chapman [14.22], 129–30)

So those who share common interests share similar mental organization, and it is this shared mental organization that is articulated by the general will. Note that at this point Bosanquet depends not simply on coherence – on a fitting together of different minds into a broader unity – but on similarity of organization. 'All mutual intelligence', Bosanquet claims, 'depends upon the fact that individuals cover each other in some degree' ([14.15], 116n.); social organization thus depends on the similarity or repetition of selves. It is not entirely clear how this principle of social life as based on similarity of organization coheres with that of organic unity,[27] but it does at least allow Bosanquet to argue that a general will is necessarily limited to a community sharing a common life. '[T]he common life shared by the members of a community involves a common element in their ideas, not merely in their notions of things about them, though this is very important, but more especially in the dominant or organizing ideas which rule their minds' ([14.16], 260). Consequently, those sharing no common life – such as mankind as a whole – cannot possess a general will ([14.12], 271–301).

The general will, Bosanquet claimed, is our 'real will', which can be contrasted to our 'actual will'. This distinction, which drives most liberals to distraction (e.g., Berlin [14.19], 133; Hobhouse [14.37], 44ff.)[28] follows easily enough from Bosanquet's analyses of self, the common good and reality. The self, we saw, is a system of desires, interests and beliefs, which reason seeks to make harmonious. Of course, actual selves are shot with contradictions 'through and through' ([14.14], 111). As we saw, appercipient systems tend to crowd each other out; that which is conscious displaces the others, making it very difficult to render the entire system coherent.

> In order to obtain a full statement of what we will, what we want at any moment must at least be corrected and amended by what we want at other moments; and this cannot be done without also correcting and amending it so as to harmonize

with what others want, which involves the application of the same process to them. But when any considerable degree of such correction had been gone through, our own will would return to us in a shape in which we should not know it again, although every detail would be a necessary inference from the whole and resolutions which we actually cherish. . . . Such a process of harmonization and adjusting a mass of data to bring them into rational shape is what is meant by criticism.

([14.14], 111)

Thus Bosanquet's first claim is that a fully coherent self and will, which took into account our interest in the common good, would be very different from a self and will that had not undergone this process of rational reconstruction. The second claim, that the former is more real than the latter follows directly from the idealist claim that the criterion of reality is coherence – that with greater coherence is more real.

~ THE STATE ~

Bosanquet: the general will and the state

Most readers share Hobhouse's conviction that Bosanquet's theory of the general will justifies authoritarianism. If (1) the general will is our real will and if (2) the government interprets the general will, then (3) when the government tells us what to do it is really only informing us what we really want to do. And if (4) the government forces us to do as it instructs it is only forcing us to do what we really want to do. 'Thus it is that we can speak, without a contradiction, of being forced to be free' ([14.14], 118–19).[29] But this is to misrepresent Bosanquet's theory; the problem lies in step (2), the idea that the government interprets the general will (see Nicholson [14.45], 214–15).

To be sure the *State* does represent, at least partially, the real will ([14.14], 141). But the State is not the government. The State 'includes the entire hierarchy of institutions by which life is determined, from the family to the trade, and from the trade to the Church and the University' (140). Such institutions are systems of similarly and correlatively organized minds; the State is a system of those systems; its aim is unified coherence among these institutions.

It is plain that unless, on the whole, a working harmony were maintained between the different groups which form society, life could not go on. And it is for this reason that the State, as the widest grouping whose members are effectively united by a common experience [and, so a general will], is necessarily the

427

one community which has absolute power to ensure, by force if need be, at least sufficient adjustment of the claims of all other groups to make life possible. Assuming, indeed, that all the groupings are organs of a single pervading life, we find it impossible that there should ultimately be irreconcilable opposition between them.

([14.14] 158)

But, as should be clear by now, no one individual, indeed no group of individuals, can be conscious of the system of intelligence that constitutes society. That would be for a part to fully know the whole, a claim that runs counter to almost every aspect of Bosanquet's philosophy. Consequently, Bosanquet is suspicious of claims by individuals that they know the general will. He is thus a harsh critic of Rousseau's attempt to uncover the general will through direct democracy; in the end, all Rousseau's method reveals is the 'will of all'.

> [T]he very core of the common good represented by the life of the modern Nation-State is its profound and complex organization, which makes it greater than the conscious momentary will of any individual. By reducing the machinery for the expression of the common good to the isolated and unassisted judgments of the members of the whole body of citizens, Rousseau is ensuring the exact reverse of what he professes to aim at. He is appealing from the organized life, institutions, and selected capacity of a nation to that nation regarded as an aggregate of isolated individuals.

([14.14], 109)

Bosanquet is thus hesitant about endorsing state policies intended to articulate the general will: 'our life is probably more rational than our opinions' ([14.16], 218). This does not mean that Bosanquet opposes the reform of institutions,[30] but it does imply that such reform is best worked out by the participants who engage in the common life that comprises those institutions. Moreover, Bosanquet is very impressed by the way in which inadequate knowledge of institutions and ways of life leads to reforms with deleterious consequences, such as poor relief that produces dependency ([14.7]: 3ff., 45ff.; [14.17], 103–16). To be sure, Bosanquet does not embrace what he calls 'administrative nihilism', i.e., refusal ever to employ conscious policy to further the common good ([14.17], 301; [14.9], 358–83; [14.14], xxxvi). The 'distinctive sphere' of State agency 'is rightly described as the hindrance of hindrances of good life' ([14.14], xxxii). However, Bosanquet was an adamant critic of economic socialism, precisely because it sought to impose a conscious plan on society. In contrast to economic individualism, economic socialism, he charged, seeks to substitute a mechanical, contrived, unity for the organic unity of society. 'I confess that I believe modern Economic Socialism to rest *in part* on this ineradicable confusion. "We want a good life; let us make a law that there shall be a general good life"' ([14.9], 316, 330).

Green's new liberal tendencies

In most respects Bosanquet is a faithful disciple of Green, and this applies to political philosophy. But three thematic differences – differences in emphasis rather than sharp divergences of principle – point their political theories in somewhat different directions.

The stress on individual rights

The first has been emphasized throughout this chapter: Green makes much more of individuals as self-conscious pursuers of their perfection, and puts somewhat less weight on institutions as weaving an only partially conscious unity. Let me stress once again that is a matter of emphasis; Green too believes that the State is a 'society of societies', and that its main task is to adjust the various claims of the societies to produce 'harmonious social relations' ([14.5], 110, 112). But Green's account quickly focuses on the State as 'an institution in which all rights are harmoniously maintained' ([14.5]: 130). Because the self-conscious pursuit of individual perfection looms so large in Green's work, he gives more prominence to a theory of individual rights, reinforcing the view that he is a more devoted liberal. But we need to be cautious here, for Green's conception of individual rights is not particularly close to those prominent in contemporary political theory. For him 'A right is a power claimed and recognized as contributory to a common good' ([14.5], 79).[32] Today readers are apt to think of rights along the lines suggested by Ronald Dworkin, as claims that protect individuals by trumping society's collective goals ([14.28], xi). Green seems to have precisely the opposite view: 'a right against society, as such, is impossible' (110). The core supposition of the Dworkinian theory of rights – that the social and individual good regularly conflict – is precisely the view that Green (and Bosanquet) reject. 'The principle which it is here sought to maintain is that the perfection of human character – a perfection of individuals which is also that of society, and of society which is also that of individuals – is for man the only object of absolute or intrinsic value' (Green [14.1], 266–7).

The criticism of actual States

A State that is to harmonize individual rights must ensure that the structure of rights is such that all are able to contribute to the common good. Now, and here Bosanquet explicitly disagrees ([14.14], ix, 269–70), Green believed that in the States of his time the lower classes were effectively precluded from participating in the common good. The idea of civil society as 'founded on the idea of there being a common good' is, he insists, unrealized 'in relation to the less favoured members of society'; indeed social life is a 'war' ([14.1], 263). Consequently, those at the bottom of the economic order have inadequate opportunity for self-development. Even more fundamentally, Green indicates that class differences themselves prevent common understanding in society ([14.2], 42). For Green, then, the actual States of his era do not adequately articulate the idea of the State as rationalizer (i.e., harmonizer) of rights; of the most defective instances, such as Imperial Russia, he says that we count them as States 'only by a sort of courtesy' ([14.5], 103). This drives Green to a more reformist position than we find in Bosanquet's *political* philosophy.

Consciousness of the common good

Our inability adequately to grasp the common good is not a dominant theme of Green, unlike Bosanquet, and this, of course, opens up more possibilities for State action. To be sure, Green insists that the law cannot make a person moral:

> that the law cannot make men good – that its business is to set them free to make themselves good – I quite agree. The question is, how these truisms are to be applied. I am no advocate of beneficent despotism. No tendency, inconsistent with the recognised principles of English legislation, lurks under my use of the phrases 'constructive Liberals' or 'organic reforms'....
> As instances of what I mean by 'organic social reforms' I should specify compulsory education, restraint on the power of settling real estate and on freedom of contract in certain respects, specially in respect of Game, between Landlord and Tenant, the inspection of dwelling houses, [and] the compulsory provision of them in some cases.
>
> ([14.5], 345n.)[33]

So Green's 'constructive' programme was by no means radical; and he certainly was no socialist ([14.5], 163–78, 313–17). As is well known, both Green and Bosanquet stress that self-development requires private property rights.[34] Still, Green can soundly claim the title of 'constructive

Liberal' as he allows that the State, and especially local government, can have sufficient insight into the common good to justify political reforms (cf. Harris [14.35]). This is the aspect of Green's political theory upon which Hobhouse builds; Hobhouse insists that the State does have the capacity to regulate public life for the better pursuit of the common good.[35] Again, whereas Bosanquet is apt to stress the unconscious nature of the general will, Green consistently gives a greater role to the conscious apprehension of perfection.

∾ CONCLUSION ∾

Bosanquet developed and systematized Green's idealism (Nicholson [14.45], 4). But development and systematization do not mean that he merely repeats what Green says at greater length. Bosanquet carries the principle of coherence and unity further, explaining social unity without appeal to a primary social interest. Moreover, his theory of appercipient mass provides a psychological interpretation of social unity and the general will far more sophisticated than anything we find in Green. Yet it was the theory of appercipient mass and his relentless pursuit of the idealist theme of coherence that yielded his thin account of selfhood. Green is not, as many have said, a Kantian, but his Absolute idealism is not as developed as Bosanquet's; it is perhaps for this very reason that Green has a thicker account of selfhood. It is this difference, rather than ones in their political philosophies or actual political proposals, that grounds the intuition that Green has a stronger claim to a place in the liberal pantheon.

NOTES

This chapter was written during my tenure as a Visiting Scholar at the Social Philosophy and Policy Center at Bowling Green State University. My thanks to the Center for its generous support. I would also like to express my gratitude to Sharon Hayes: I have greatly benefited from her work on T. H. Green. My thanks also to Sterling Burnett and Ken Cust for their research assistance.

1 A second edition of *Ethical Studies* was published after Bradley's death.
2 See further Richter [14.51].
3 For helpful accounts of Bosanquet's relation to the 'new liberals', see Collini [14.24], Clarke [14.23], Freeden [14.29], Gaus [14.31], Vincent and Plant [14.58].
4 For a useful overview of Bosanquet's logic, see Passmore ([14.48], 86–7).
5 If knowledge is justified true belief, it may be argued that a coherence theory of knowledge implies a coherence theory of truth. For a development of this suggestion, see Davidson [14.27]. If one finds this terminology confusing, one

can substitute 'coherence theory of justified belief' for 'coherence theory of knowledge' in what follows.

6 Richard Rorty ([14.53], 299) holds that this was the great mistake of idealism. Having rejected a representational account of knowledge, the idealists still wanted to say that in some sense our understanding of nature was true to nature's understanding of herself, that we were justified in believing not only what coheres with our concepts but that this reveals what is *true*, i.e. what nature is *really* like.

7 See also Quinton [14.50]; Crossley [14.26], Thomas ([14.56], 141–5). Cf. Milne [14.40], chapter V.

8 Cf. John Morrow's claim [14.42] that whereas Green's metaphysics is 'immanentist', Bosanquet's is 'transcendentist'. See also Geoffrey Thomas's argument that Green's theory is a 'personal' idealism, to be contrasted to the social idealism of Bosanquet and Bradley ([14.56], 142).

9 Precisely in what sense the Absolute is 'composed' of finite minds, and whether we can be said to be 'members' of it is problematic. See Bosanquet ([14.16], 98ff.). But note his remark that 'the Absolute needs us and our conduct just as we need it' (222).

10 Admittedly, this judgement of plausibility depends on a certain religious disposition, at which we are apt to smile today. But those smiles fade a bit when we contemplate Rorty's diagnosis [14.53] of *our* epistemological theories about how we know nature as it really is.

11 Consequently, if as Thomas argues (and I believe he is right), Green's ethics does not *require* 'the full-blown metaphysics' ([14.56, 150), it still may be the case that the ethics derives justification from the rest of the system.

12 Bosanquet is referring here to both individuality and originality. I have elsewhere argued that Bosanquet's contrast between his view and J. S. Mill's is overdrawn. See Gaus ([14.31], 15ff.).

13 For an excellent account of Green's criticism of Hume's theory of the self, see Thomas ([14.56], 173ff.).

14 For one of the best accounts of Bosanquet's theory of the apperceptient mass, see Chapman ([14.22], 128ff.).

15 Bosanquet speaks here of 'mind'.

16 'The consciousness in a particular human self of the identity of its own experiences is merely, as I understand the argument, a case of apprehension of the whole' (Bosanquet [14.16], 155). Understood as a gloss on Bosanquet's argument, this seems correct; what is somewhat surprising is that the 'argument' referred to here is Green's, which Bosanquet is intending to explicate.

17 This is an abbreviated account; see Gaus ([14.31], chapters 1 and 2).

18 For this last, see Bosanquet ([14.14], x; [14.13], 219).

19 See his discussion of the aphorism: 'We are not hard enough on stupidity' ([14.13], 213).

20 These are essentially the same. As Bosanquet remarks, 'Value is the power to satisfy' ([14.15], 297).

21 David L. Norton ([14.47], 54–5) disputes this concerning Green. I criticize Norton's interpretation in Gaus [14.31], 20–2.

22 Bosanquet, indeed, makes so much of the way in which the mind is a product

of nature he sometimes gives the impression of being more a materialist than an idealist. See Passmore ([14.48], 88–9).

23 Though, oddly enough, their positions are reversed when analysing the state; Green insists that actual states are further from the ideal. See pp. 429–31 above.

24 As Thomas points out ([14.56], 221), this view has certain similarities to Derek Parfit's.

25 H. A. Prichard ([14.49], 73) argued that Green too denied the distinction between persons. For a criticism of Prichard, see Gaus ([14.31], 61–4), Nicholson ([14.45], 64ff.).

26 For an excellent account of Green's theory of the common good, see Nicholson ([14.45], 54–82.

27 Cf. Bosanquet's insistence that 'Nevertheless, upon a scrutiny of the true operative nature of social unity, we find that repetition and similarity are but superficial characteristics of it. What holds society together, we find, are correlative differences; the relation which expresses itself on a large scale in Aristotle's axiom "No State can be composed of similars" ' ([14.16], 249). See Bosanquet's distinction between an association and an organization ([14.14], chapter VII; [14.16], 261).

28 For an unusually thorough and judicious account of Bosanquet's theory of the general will, and the place of his doctrine of the real will in it, see Nicholson ([14.45], 189–230).

29 In this chapter I have not examined the theory of positive freedom. Compared to other aspects of British idealism, this has received extensive treatment. The best account of Green's theory of freedom is Nicholson ([14.45], 116–31). See also Weinstein [14.59]; Simhony [14.55], Norman ([14.46], 26–53), Milne ([14.41], 146ff.); Roberts [14.52].

30 Again, care is called for here. Bosanquet considered himself a radical, and was prepared to accept social legislation to alleviate evils. (Muirhead [14.44], 48, 134).

31 Not that Bosanquet disagrees ([14.12], 274).

32 On Green's theory of rights, see Cacoullos [14.21], Nicholson ([14.45], 83–95).

33 Letter to W. V. Harcourt, 1973, quoted in Harris and Morrow's notes to Green's 'Liberal Legislation and Freedom of Contract' [14.5]. See also Nicholson ([14.45], 159).

34 See Green ([14.1], 201; [14.5], 163ff.), Bosanquet ([14.14], 281–2; [14.17], 308–18). This has led to Marxist-inspired criticisms of Green, such as Greengarten [14.34]. For a discussion, see Morrow [14.42].

35 For the importance of this theme in the development of the 'new liberalism', see Gaus ([14.32], 21–3). Collini doubts whether Green's idealism actually strongly supported new liberal collectivism ([14.24], 44–6).

❧ BIBLIOGRAPHY ❧

Works by Green

14.1 *Prolegomena to Ethics*, ed. A. C. Bradley, Oxford: Clarendon Press, (1890).

14.2 *Works of Thomas Hill Green*, vol. III, ed. R. L. Nettleship, London: Longman's, Green, 1891.

14.3 *Works of Thomas Hill Green*, vol. II, ed. R. L. Nettleship, London: Longman's, Green, 1893.

14.4 *Works of Thomas Hill Green*, vol. I, ed. R. L. Nettleship, London: Longman's, Green, 1894.

14.5 *Lectures on the Principles of Political Obligation and Other Writings*, ed. Paul Harris and John Morrow, Cambridge: Cambridge University Press, 1986.

Works by Bosanquet

14.6 *Logic, or the Morphology of Knowledge*, 2 vols, Oxford: Clarendon Press, 1888.

14.7 *Essays and Addresses*, 2nd edn, London: Swan Sonnenschein, 1891.

14.8 'Hegel's Theory of the Political Organism', *Mind*, 7 (1898): 1–14

14.9 *The Civilization of Christendom*, London: Swan Sonnenschein, 1899.

14.10 *Psychology of the Moral Self*, London: Macmillan, 1904.

14.11 *The Value and Destiny of the Individual*, London: Macmillan, 1913.

14.12 *Social and International Ideals*, Freeport, NY: Books for Libraries Press, 1917.

14.13 *Some Suggestions in Ethics*, London: Macmillan, 1918.

14.14 *The Philosophical Theory of the State*, 4th edn, London: Macmillan, 1923.

14.15 *The Principle of Individuality and Value*, London: Macmillan, 1927.

14.16 *Science and Philosophy and Other Essays*, London: Allen & Unwin, 1927.

14.17 ed. *Aspects of the Social Problem*, London: Macmillan, 1895.

Other works

14.18 Bonjour, L. *The Structure of Empirical Knowledge*, Cambridge, Mass.: Harvard University Press, 1985.

14.19 Berlin, I. 'Two Concepts of Liberty', in his *Four Essays on Liberty*, Oxford: Oxford University Press, 1969, pp. 120–72.

14.20 Broad, C. D. *Five Types of Ethical Theory*, London: Kegan Paul, Trench & Trubner, 1930.

14.21 Cacoullos, A. R. *Thomas Hill Green: Philosopher of Rights*, New York, Twayne, 1974.

14.22 Chapman, J. W. *Rousseau – Totalitarian or Liberal*, New York: AMS Press, 1968.

14.23 Clarke, P. *Liberals and Social Democrats*, Cambridge: Cambridge University Press, 1978.

14.24 Collini, S. 'Hobhouse, Bosanquet and the State', *Past and Present*, 72 (1976): 86–111.

14.25 —— *Liberalism and Sociology: L.T. Hobhouse and Political Argument in England, 1880–1914*, Cambridge: Cambridge University Press, 1979.

14.26 Crossley, D. 'Self-conscious Agency and the Eternal Consciousness: Ultimate Reality in T.H. Green', *Ultimate Meaning and Reality*, 13 (1990): 3–20.

14.27 Davidson, D. 'A Coherence Theory of Truth and Knowledge', in Alan Malachowski, ed., *Reading Rorty*, London: Blackwell, 1990, 120–38.

14.28 Dworkin, R. *Taking Rights Seriously*, Cambridge, Mass.: Harvard University Press, 1978.

14.29 Freeden, M. *The New Liberalism*, Oxford: Clarendon Press, 1979.

14.30 —— *Liberalism Divided*, Oxford: Clarendon Press, 1986.

14.31 Gaus, G. F. *The Modern Liberal Theory of Man*, London: Croom Helm, 1983.

14.32 —— 'Public and Private Interests in Liberal Political Economy, Old and New', in S. I. Benn and G. F. Gaus, eds, *Public and Private in Social Life*, London: Croom Helm, 1983, 183–221.

14.33 Gordon, P. and J. White. *Philosophers as Educational Reformers: the Influence of British Idealism on British Educational Thought and Practice*, London: Routledge, 1979.

14.34 Greengarten, I. M. *Thomas Hill Green and the Development of Liberal-Democratic Thought*, Toronto: University of Toronto Press, 1981.

14.35 Harris, P. 'Moral Progress and Politics: The Theory of T.H. Green', *Polity*, 21 (1989): 538–62.

14.36 Hobbes, T. *Leviathan*, ed. M. Oakeshott, London: Blackwell, 1948.

14.37 Hobhouse, L. T. *The Metaphysical Theory of the State*, London: Allen & Unwin, 1918.

14.38 —— *The Rational Good*, London: Watts, 1947.

14.39 —— *Liberalism*, Oxford: Oxford University Press, 1964.

14.40 Milne, A. J. M. *The Social Philosophy of English Idealism*, London: Allen & Unwin, 1962.

14.41 —— *Freedom and Rights: A Philosophical Synthesis*, London: Allen & Unwin, 1968.

14.42 Morrow, J. 'Property and Personal Development: An Interpretation of T.H. Green's Political Philosophy', *Politics*, 18 (1983): 84–92.

14.43 —— 'Liberalism and British Idealist Political Philosophy: A Reassessment', *History of Political Thought*, 5 (1984): 91–108.

14.44 Muirhead, J. H., ed., *Bernard Bosanquet and His Friends*, London: Allen & Unwin, 1935.

14.45 Nicholson, P. P. *The Political Philosophy of the British Idealists*, Cambridge: Cambridge University Press, 1990.

14.46 Norman, R. *Free and Equal*, Oxford: Oxford University Press, 1987.

14.47 Norton, D. L. *Personal Destinies: A Philosophy of Ethical Individualism*, Princeton: Princeton University Press, 1976.

14.48 Passmore, J. *A Hundred Years of Philosophy*, Harmondsworth: Penguin, 1978.

14.49 Prichard, H. A. *Moral Obligation and Duty and Interest*, Oxford: Clarendon Press, 1968.

14.50 Quinton, A. 'Absolute Idealism', *Proceedings of the British Academy*, 57 (1971): 303–29.

14.51 Richter, M. *The Politics of Conscience: T.H. Green and his Age*, London: Weidenfeld & Nicolson, 1964.

14.52 Roberts, J. 'T.H. Green', in Z. Pelczynski and J. Gray, eds, *Conceptions of Liberty in Political Philosophy*, New York: St Martin's, 1984, 243–62.

14.53 Rorty, R. *Philosophy and the Mirror of Nature*, Princeton: Princeton University Press, 1979.

14.54 Sidgwick, H. *Lectures on the Ethics of T.H. Green, Mr. Herbert Spencer and J. Martineau*, London: Macmillan, 1902.

14.55 Simhony, A. 'Beyond Negative and Positive Freedom: T.H. Green's View of Freedom', *Political Theory*, 21 (1993): 28–54.

14.56 Thomas, G. *The Moral Philosophy of T.H. Green*, Oxford: Clarendon Press, 1987.

14.57 Vincent, A., ed., *The Philosophy of T.H. Green*, Aldershot: Gower, 1986.

14.58 Vincent, A. and R. Plant. *Philosophy, Politics and Citizenship: The Life and Thought of the British Idealists*, Oxford: Blackwell, 1984.

14.59 Weinstein, W. L. 'The Concept of Liberty in Nineteenth Century Thought', *Political Studies*, 13 (1965): 145–62.

A good bibliography of works relating to Green's moral theory can be found in Thomas [14.56] and concerning Green's political theory in [14.5]; see also the bibliography in Vincent [14.57]. Nicholson [14.45] and Vincent and Plant [14.58] contain useful bibliographies of works relating to British idealism, including both Green and Bosanquet.

CHAPTER 15

Bradley

T. L. S. Sprigge

∾ INTRODUCTORY ∾

F. H. Bradley (1846–1924) was a fellow of Merton College, Oxford, for all his adult life. Though his personality and life are interesting, information about them is not required for an understanding of his philosophy. Suffice it to say that he was widely acknowledged as the most important British philosopher of his time.

His thought represents the climax of the late nineteenth-century reaction in Britain against British empiricism and utilitarianism, and turning towards the great German masters, Kant and more especially Hegel. Bradley's pages are shot through with negative remarks on this tradition, exhibiting a particular hostility to J. S. Mill, contrasting here with the much more balanced criticisms in the work of such other main figures of the absolute idealist reaction against it as T. H. Green (1836–82) and Bernard Bosanquet (1848–1923). Yet Bradley, despite himself, often develops his idealism in ways closer to the British empiricist tradition than do these other thinkers. This was, indeed, a point made against some of his work by Bernard Bosanquet, who mostly held very similar views.

Apart from a number of articles on introspective psychology (included in *Collected Essays*, 1935, posthumously published) Bradley's main works are *Ethical Studies* (1876; second edition 1927, [15.4]); *The Principles of Logic* 1883; second edition 1922, [15.3]); *Appearance and Reality: A Metaphysical Essay* (1893; second edition 1897, [15.1]). In each case the second edition includes important new material. We will give some account of each of these works, respectively on ethics, logic and metaphysics. References will also be made to the important late collection of essays, reprinted from journals, called *Essays in Truth and Reality* (1914, [15.2]).

❧ *ETHICAL STUDIES* ❧

In *Ethical Studies*, his first major work, Bradley speaks as one bringing to a benightedly provincial 'England' the news of a philosophy from overseas possessing a depth of insight largely unfamiliar to his compatriots.

The work is concerned with what it is to be moral and with the character of the ordinary man's moral consciousness. Sometimes Bradley implies that his is only a phenomenological clarification of how ordinary decent people, rightly or wrongly, think and feel. However, he clearly supports the ordinary man against what he considers the distorted accounts of morality of many philosophers. (Bradley, of course, uses 'man' for 'person' like most writers of his time. It seems better, in this exposition of his thought, to follow him here than give him an air of false up-to-date-ness by employing a less sexist terminology.)

The first chapter concerns moral responsibility and free will. Philosophers are divided into two main schools, determinists or necessitarians and free-will-ists. Neither makes sense of the notion of moral responsibility. If it was settled by the causal process of the world, even before I was born, what kind of man I was to be and how I would act, how can I ever be blamed for anything I do? Equally, if what I do is due in part to the exercise of a contra-causal free will, this seems no more than the intervention of sheer chance into the procession of phenomena. I can hardly be held responsible for doing things where there is no explanation of the fact that I acted thus.

Each theory, thinks Bradley, trades on the defects of the other, as the wrongly supposed only alternative to it. (In his treatment of the law of excluded middle in *Principles of Logic* he points out how easy it is to say '*P* or not-*P*', where not-*P*, *as it is being understood*, is not the only alternative to *P*.)

To resolve matters Bradley considers how the ordinary man would react to precise predictions of his own behaviour in some important, situations. He would certainly dislike the idea that some super-scientist might have been able to predict, on the basis of general laws, perhaps in advance of his birth or emergence from infancy, just how he would behave. But he does not dislike the fact that a friend, knowing his character, correctly predicts that he would behave well in an emergency. (And, if his friend predicts correctly that he would behave badly, it is the fact that he is a bad man, and that his friend knows it, which disturbs him, not the fact of prediction as such.) Indeed, the good man would be offended if the decency of his behaviour could not be predicted.

The fact is, argues Bradley, that we do not mind prediction which is based on a knowledge of oneself as a unitary personality. What one objects to is the idea that there could be predictions in which one's own self seems to be bypassed, because appeal is made to general laws of nature, whether physical or distinctively psychological, (for example, laws of the association of ideas or, in our own day, reinforcement theory of a Skinnerian type) couched in impersonal terms which take no account of one's individuality.

Bradley interprets this as showing that the ordinary man conceives himself as what, in the technical language of Hegelian philosophy, may be called a concrete universal. His behaviour, in so far as it really springs from him, is a manifestation of how that universal manifests itself in that particular situation. Increasing familiarity with the character of that universal which constitutes another's self will increase my power to predict his behaviour, but I will not be doing so on the basis of laws which apply to other people, still less to inanimate nature. That, at least, is the opinion of the ordinary man, and Bradley evidently endorses it.

We must pause for some explanation of the concept of a concrete universal, developed by Bradley, Bosanquet and others under the stimulus of Hegel.

An abstract universal is some common feature humans have found in many different things. It is abstract because this common feature is not an independent reality which could exist on its own and because, as an abstraction, it plays no real role in explaining why the things which exemplify it are as they are. You do not explain why a box is of the shape it is simply by pointing out that one can apply the general idea *cube* to it. If the idea of a human being is simply that of an abstract universal, then you cannot really explain anything about an individual human being by reference to it, for it is simply a non-explanatory registration of similarities. Moreover, the thin idea of what a human being is which we reach by dropping everything which individuates one person from another is far from that full idea (whose object is a concrete universal) of what it is to be a human which involves grasping something of the rich and varied potentialities there are in human nature.

A concrete universal is, like an abstract universal, something identically one and the same in a whole lot of particular things or events. But it is such that the specific nature of these things or events is just what it needs to be if the universal is to insert itself into history at that point. Moreover, to conceive a universal as concrete is to grasp something of the rich variety of its possible instances.

The thesis is not really that some universals are abstract, others concrete, but rather that the idea of abstract universals belongs to an inadequate view of the world better replaced by that of concrete universals.

The notion of a concrete universal (so we may feel) possesses rather an excess of 'open texture' so that its use is extended from time to time in ways which suit an author's present enthusiasms. Thus there is a concrete universal where many individuals with a common characteristic (of some complexity, usually) each owe their possession of it, and what is more their possession of some specific determination of it, to their relation to another of its instances. Humanity is a concrete universal because we are each human through being born of humans and owe our particular form of humanity to them in both physical and environmental ways. (A Martian with no blood relationship to us – even if anatomically akin to us – would not be an instance of the same concrete universal.)

On the face of it, humanity conceived in this way as a concrete universal is not a totality made up of human beings but an identical characteristic present in each of us, in a distinctive form, in virtue of the causal relations between its instances. However, proponents of the concrete universal usually take the totality of its instances as itself the universal in question, arguing that it is a kind of whole which is present in each of its parts. Maybe an insistence on such distinctions is an attempt to transform the notion of a concrete universal into something belonging to another conceptual scheme, and we should learn how to play the relevant conceptual tune rather by ear than by analysis.

At any rate for Bradley's plain man the self is a concrete universal and a man is responsible for what he does in so far as his behaviour is a manifestation (however regrettable a one) of that universal which he is. As for why that particular concrete universal has emerged in connection with that particular human organism, we cannot pursue Bradley's not very decisive answer here beyond remarking that it is built up gradually in childhood by the creative response of itself in an undeveloped version to the challenges of life as they occur.

We can now move on to the key questions of the book. Firstly, why should I be moral? Secondly, what is it to be moral?

Firstly, insists Bradley, it would betray morality to suppose that there was some extrinsic reason for being moral. However, we can give sense to the question if we realize that all action is ultimately motivated by an urge to self-realization and that we can properly ask whether moral behaviour is an adequate form of self-realization or is even perhaps identical therewith.

Self-realization is another difficult concept. Put at its most metaphysical, it is the urge of the concrete universal, which is one's self, to be exemplified in as full and rich a fashion as possible in each of its particulars, i.e. each particular psychological state one lives through, and each action one performs. More informally, it is the urge to live so that one can feel as much as possible in everything that one does that one is really being oneself in doing it, hence living in a way such that one can be satisfied with the image of oneself as so living.

Secondly, granted there is good cause to be moral, doing so must realize the self. But what is it to be moral? Bradley now examines a series of representative answers to this question, and tests their adequacy by the test of the extent to which they show how moral life is a form of (or perhaps the same as) self-realization.

The first answer he considers is hedonism: the good life is one in the course of which one achieves as much pleasure as possible (understand henceforth: and minimum of pain, however these two are balanced).

Bradley has a series of objections to this as a human ideal; some deeply metaphysical, some more matter of fact.

(1) (a) Whatever amount of pleasure I achieve in any situation, a bit more, not too painful effort, could have brought me more; so I can never achieve the end of the maximization of pleasure. (b) Or, looked at in another way, whatever amount of pleasure I achieve, I could never have achieved more, for I always did what so far as my insight went (something I cannot determine for myself) would maximize my pleasure. (Bradley assumes that the hedonist's conception of the good life is derived from a hedonistic account of actual motivation.)

(2) I can never say to myself *I have now achieved the maximum of pleasure in my life*, for my success in this is not settled till I die and then I am no longer here to be gratified at my success.

(3) The self as an abiding entity rather than a mere flux wants an abiding satisfaction, a state in which it can say *here am I presently in achievement of my goal*. It is not, of course, that it wants a goal such that, having once reached it, it can simply halt there for ever without further effort, but it does want a state in which it can say *here I am presently in possession of what I looked for, and if am careful, can continue in its enjoyment throughout my life*. But a series of passing pleasures can never constitute such a satisfying state.

Moreover, the concrete universal, which is the self, feels itself to be in some sense *an infinite whole*, not in what Hegel called the bad sense of 'infinite', namely an uncompletable series, but in the sense of something which has a certain sort of completeness from which nothing is missing. (Hegelians would surely have thought the Einsteinian universe infinite in a good sense in contrast to the bad infinite of a Newtonian or Democritean space which stretches on indefinitely.)

But surely the relevant form of hedonism for discussion in the nineteenth century is utilitarianism, in particular as advocated by

J. S. Mill, and it is this which is really the object of Bradley's attack.[1] Here, of course, the goal is the maximization of the pleasure (understand: and minimization of the pain) of all sentient creatures. And surely this is a genuinely moral goal.

But it was worth examining the simpler egoistic form of hedonism, thinks Bradley, for we there find in a simpler form the faults which are, for the most part, still present writ large in utilitarianism with its goal of the maximization of the pleasure of sentients.

(1) (a) Whatever we do we could have produced more pleasure for ourselves and others. (There seems nothing corresponding to (b).
(2) Much the same applies.
(3) If the maximization of pleasure provides no adequate satisfaction for the individual, we should not foist it on the human race, or the animal realm.

Finally, utilitarianism has the peculiar fault of trying to derive its universalistic ethic from a an egoistic hedonistic psychology. But this is a complete *non sequitur*. Because each man desires his own maximal pleasure, and thus finds it good, he should recognize (so Mill seems to argue in chapter IV of *Utilitarianism*) that the maximal pleasure of all is the good of all, and that each should therefore desire this. But this is like arguing that since every pig at a trough 'desires his own food, and somehow as a consequence seems to desire the food of all' that 'by parity of reasoning it should follow that each pig desiring his own pleasure, desires also the pleasure of all' ([15.4], 113).

The main argument against hedonism, whether individualist or universalist, is that trying to maximize pleasures is no proper end for man since no self can find itself realized in having maximized pleasure either for itself or for others. For the pleasures of different times form no real totality, since they never exist together, and can never constitute a state of affairs of which we can say: 'Here I have that which I was seeking.'

Bradley now turns to the sharply opposed moral theory of Kant. This he calls the ideal of duty for duty's sake. Here the good is identified with sheer rationality, in fact, simply with living a life which exemplifies the law of non-contradiction. One is to behave only in a way which one could will universalized without contradiction.

This marks an advance on pleasure for pleasure's sake in its emphasis on the contrast between two aspects of the human being, the good self and the bad self, and the identification of morality with control of the latter by the former. It also rightly conceives the self as a universal rather than as a series of 'perishing particulars'. But it is only an abstract universal with a purely formal purpose, to live without self-contradiction, and this can give no real satisfaction; for our sensuous selves do not enter into the self-realization of the universal but simply remain in sulky opposition to it. Moreover, the injunction to live without self-contradiction is really quite empty and either allows or forbids everything equally. One should keep a promise because promise-breaking universalized would destroy the very institution on which it depends. But so equally would universal charity towards the poor, for it would leave no poverty to be alleviated.

The inadequacies of pleasure for pleasure's sake and of duty for duty's sake show the need for a concept of morality which will provide unitary satisfaction both to sensuous appetite, that is to our nature as a series of particular desires, and to reason, the universal aspect of the personality.

This is provided by the Hegelian notion of morality which Bradley calls the ethic of 'my station and its duties'. Here the community plays the role of concrete universal with individual people as its instances realizing themselves as such. Because the community is historical and concrete, the requirements it puts upon the individual are determined not by some remote logical abstraction with no appeal for flesh and blood but by the needs of a role in the world which provide a satisfying life for the real empirical man. The good self is no longer depicted as at war with the natural man, while the bad self is simply such propensities as need control if one is to enjoy the satisfactions proper to a social being.

Bradley speaks rhapsodically (to a degree for which he himself apologizes) in favour of this social ethic. But in the end he admits that it is not the whole truth. For this there are a number of reasons.

The great recommendation of my station and its duties is that it achieves a reconciliation of the *ought* and the *is*. That is, the *ought* no longer comes as a demand from some other world in which the I of this world can find no satisfaction but as a demand from precisely that in this world which can most satisfy. However, even this ethic does not quite live up to its pretensions.

(1) My community may not be adequate even for my good self, let alone for my bad self. For (*a*) It may be itself in a rotten state and my goodness may involve recognizing this. (*b*) Even the best community cannot be morally adequate throughout. (*c*) There are miseries no absorption in my community can stem. (*d*) My community may demand sacrifices frustrating self-realization.

In short, self-realization in the faithful carrying out of my station and its duties cannot be complete.

(2) Since society is in progress, there is always some call to criticize the demands and practices of one's own community by reference to

some more ultimate human ideal which one dimly feels in contrast to it.

(3) My station and its duties cannot be the whole good for man. There are values which may take us beyond social life in our community for example the development of our artistic and intellectual powers.

These limitations push us on to what Bradley calls ideal morality. The basic injunction here is to realize everywhere the best self, and our idea of our best self, though it must arise from the ideals we learn in the family and in life in the community, may develop beyond it to take account of values learnt from other societies or based on internal criticisms of our own society.

The good self as thus conceived has these main aspects:

1 The ideal self of my currently socially recognized stations and its duties;
2 A social self which goes beyond this and which divides into (*a*) a social self going beyond, or divergent from, my currently recognized station and its duties and (*b*) a non-social self devoted to such ideals as the fullest possible realization through my activity of truth and beauty.

So is morality simply the same as self-realization? No, it is self-realization in respect of our will. External results are not part of morality. Of course, a will which does not express itself in genuine action is nothing, but success or failure as determined by forces outside us may help or hinder our self-realization but not that aspect of it which belongs to morality. Morality is 'the realization of the self as the good will'.

This good self is especially concerned with more or less permanent objects with which it identifies itself, in whose presence or known flourishing it finds itself affirmed – such as my family, my Church, my nation, some great social or cultural enterprise. Such felt self-affirmation in such things is neither natural appetite (the satisfaction of passing bodily needs) nor lust (craving for savoured pleasures).

How can I come to concern myself with anything other than the satisfaction of my own appetites? My ability to do so originates in my identification in childhood with my mother or nurse (or whoever plays these roles). Unwelcome as some of their demands may be, I feel their will not as something alien but as pertaining to my own more stable self. Thus the good self originates as obedience to dear ones in whose satisfaction I feel myself affirmed, develops, as the ideal of conduct thus set before me, matures through the expectations of society and my own criticism of these in the light of the ideal's own promptings, and may continue into self-affirmation through the knowledge that an impersonal goal is being reached, perhaps quite remote from my own private interests.

But what is the origin of the bad self? (For we are born neither good nor bad.) Its material is simply the variety of impulses, appetites and moods which do not fit in with the good self approved by our loved ones. However, you are neither good nor bad till you know both and experience their contradiction. And you can know both only because you feel genuinely affirmed in both. Only the person who knows evil can be good, and only the person who wills evil can know it. But you must not only know both but know their clash, as a universal whose self-consciousness lies in its ability to separate itself from both and choose (but not by indeterministic free will).

As one becomes a genuine moral agent the chaos of impulses opposed to the unified good self becomes a bad self with its own unity (though what unifies them is solely their common negation of the good). Moral responsibility arises when there is both a good self and a bad self in which one can consciously affirm oneself.

And now the final question is broached: Why can I realize myself only properly in the good self, granted I feel myself genuinely affirmed in both good and evil?

The self, being a universal, realizes itself in the good self which is a genuine system or universal. The bad self stands in opposition to this with no principle of unity organizing it except that negative property of being opposed to the good self. Thus the bad self is a mere collection (like the only self acknowledged by pleasure for pleasure's sake) and thus the ultimate self, which is a concrete universal, cannot realize itself therein, and, when it tries to do so, is false to its very essence.

The book ends with 'Concluding Remarks' on the relation between morality and religion. Religion is not the same as morality. Matthew Arnold wrote mere claptrap when he said that religion was morality tinted with emotion – for the emotion has to be religious.

The distinction between morality and religion is that religion asserts that the good self is not merely something we should strive to realize but that somehow the good self alone is ultimately real, is indeed identical with God or the fundamental reality of the universe, while the bad self is somehow unreal and, just for that reason, must be suppressed. And because only the good is ultimately real, the often despairing struggles of morality give way to the calm activity of faith.

Bradley here broaches the absolute idealism he will develop more fully in later works for which we are all aspects of a unitary spiritual Absolute.

If we know the whole, it can only be because the whole knows itself in us, because the whole is self or mind, which is and knows, knows and is, the identity and correlation of subject and object.

([15.4], 324n.)

This idealism is here treated as the essential truth of Christianity. Later Bradley no longer conceives his metaphysical idealism as so close to Christianity, and at times speaks of the Christian religion in a distinctly negative way. This was doubtless partly the result of a change in his metaphysics, but it was probably more due to his increasing sense that Christian tradition, by its emphasis on preparation for a hereafter, detracted from concern with the possibilities of human fulfilment in the present life. (Bradley thought the question of a life after death was of very secondary importance ethically; a bare possibility with little bearing on what really matters, the realization of eternal values, grounded in the Absolute, in our daily life and in society.)

Religion thus interpreted resolves the contradiction endemic to ethics conceived without it. For, so Bradley rather puzzlingly holds, there is something incoherent in the very idea of a good which is not realized. One is inclined to object that there is no incoherence in the proposition that things are not as they ought to be. In *Appearance and Reality* Bradley does, indeed, say that one cannot simply take it for granted that the non-contradictory nature of the real precludes it from being overall and ultimately bad, but, by rather tortuous reasoning, he does in the end reach this conclusion, and seems always to have found it inviting and natural (see [15.1], 132–3). Thus he seems always to have inclined to see a clash between ideals and sense of fact as a source of unease essentially akin to that which we feel in embracing a logical contradiction and which we have the same necessary nisus to remove, not only in practice but in our conception of how things are.

In spite of the Christian language invoked in this rather passionately written chapter, Bradley already distances himself from any commitment to Christian sacraments as anything other than optional aids to morality and spirituality. 'We maintain that neither church-going, meditation, nor prayer, except so far as it reacts on practice and subserves that, is religious at all' ([15.4], 337). In fact, '[y]ou can have true religion without sacraments or public worship, and again both without clergymen' ([15.4], 339).

The object of true Christian faith, then, is a universal will, present as identically the same, though in a state of difference from itself, both in the individual and in the community and, indeed, in the world as a whole and such that all that appears to conflict with it is an unreality which we must grasp as such by overcoming it.

There is some kinship here with the religion of mankind promoted at that time by the Comtian positivists. However no such deification of mankind will do so long as humanity is supposed a mere collection of resembling particulars, rather than as a genuine concrete universal identically yet differently present in us all. 'Unless there is a real identity in men, the Inasmuch as ye did it to the least of these' becomes an absurdity' (original note 2 to [15.4] 334–5). In stressing the common essence present in us all, Bradley's position chimes in somewhat with the ethical thought of Schopenhauer. But, from his more Hegelian perspective, he must have thought that Schopenhauer paid insufficient attention to the difference which is essential to the identity. We must have a sense of the different roles we each have to play in the scheme of things. For the concrete universal of humanity at large is articulated into a system of distinct roles, each grounding partly different duties, as well as those which spring from the sheer identity of the common essence. Moreover, from a religious point of view, it is the ideal self, rather than one's whole chaotic personality, which is identical with the ultimate single reality present in all things. If there is some incoherence in looking at things in this way, that is, none the less, the religious way of experiencing the world ([15.4], 322). Metaphysically, this presumably means that it is only our ideal self which gives us a clue as to how things would look if we could see them as a whole.

❧ *THE PRINCIPLES OF LOGIC* ❧

In *The Principles of Logic* Bradley presents an account of judgement, that is, of what it is to think that something is the case, and a principle of inference, of what it is to move rationally from one judgement to another.

Like *Ethical Studies* much of it is concerned to present an account of these matters which will serve as a corrective to the indigenous empiricist tradition. Yet the work is less Hegelian than the previous one, and (though Bradley was scarcely aware of this) much nearer to his empiricist forebears. He does, however, draw on a range of German thinkers not very familiar, probably, to most British readers.

The biggest contrast with empiricism is Bradley's continued insistence on the reality of universals (*qua* concrete) and the inadequacy of the concept of mere resemblance between particulars to explain that real identity-in-difference between them which is the basis of predication and of inference. A related theme is the unsatisfactory nature of purely psychological accounts of thought and reasoning.

Bradley is sometimes praised, in this connection, as an early opponent of psychologism, that is, of the treatment of judgement, inference, truth, meaning, the laws of logic and so forth as psychological processes to be studied empirically. Gottlob Frege is regarded as the great saviour of modern thought from the errors of such psychologism, and there is a risk that people may suppose that the main merit of *Principles of Logic* is that of a less lucid attack upon the same thing.

That Bradley was in important respects a critic of psychologism is true. Thus he expressly says that in 'England at all events we have lived too long in the psychological attitude' (see [15.3], 2; 197–9). He believed that the empiricist treatment of thought by James Mill, Bain, J. S. Mill, and others was wrongheaded in treating it as a mere succession of empirical events. None the less, for him (as for Edmund Husserl) judgement and inference were activities of conscious minds, though logic is concerned rather with their assertive content and validity than with their empirical occurrence.

Bradley begins his account of judgement by criticizing a number of theories including most of the typically empiricist views. Thus he objects to the Lockean view that judgement is the joining of ideas, on the ground that if all the mind does is join its own ideas it could not think about anything beyond them. The theory also mistakenly assumes that judgement always involves two ideas. This it clearly does not, for example when it simply affirms the existence of something. It is truer to say that there is always just one idea, our total idea of the state of affairs we believe to be real.

Hume thought that belief consisted in vivacious ideas, but such an account is patently inadequate. Imagination, even when recognized by itself as such, can be very vivacious. In general, empiricists, like Berkeley and Hume, identify judgement with the formation of images, failing to explain what it is for the mind to take these images as representations of something beyond.

After criticizing various inadequate views of judgement Bradley moves towards his own account of judgement as the abstraction of a universal (or concept) from the sensory flux of its own contents and ascription of this universal to reality as that exists beyond one's own private experience in a manner inexplicable as any mere manipulation of my own images.

Bradley develops this view by insisting that we distinguish a psychological and a logical sense of the word 'idea'. Ideas in the first sense are unrepeatable events in time; ideas in the second sense are concepts or meanings which can be embodied in successive ideas in the psychological sense but to which much of their character as mental phenomena is irrelevant.

The importance of Bradley's distinction between these two senses of 'idea' has been widely recognized. More likely to be questioned is his particular view about the nature of the logical idea as a repeatable character or universal which is an *abstracted part* of the total character or *whatness* of the mental ideas which embody it, applied as a predicate to a reality beyond itself.

It will be seen that Bradley was really at one with the empiricist tradition in holding that the fullest sort of judgement involves imagery. (He always regarded merely verbal judgements as secondary to ones carried by thought stuff with more sensuous fullness.) The difference, as he saw it, was that he conceives the mind as actively utilizing a repeatable part of the character of the imagery to characterize a world beyond its own ideas. For surely we could not refer our ideas to a reality beyond the contents of our own consciousness if we had no awareness of that reality except through our ideas of it. Conceptual thought presupposes non-conceptual awareness of something other than concepts. Unless we encounter something other than concepts we cannot think of our concepts as applying to anything (see [15.3], 50).

This pre-conceptual awareness cannot be directed on any particular finite reality since, as Bradley sees it, we need concepts to distinguish any distinct part or feature of reality from others. So the pre-conceptual basis of judgement must be a primordial direction of the mind on reality at large, this being the ultimate subject to which all ideas are ascribed as predicates. Certainly, with the aid of our ideas, we can pick out a particular part or feature of reality as the subject of our thought, but as picked out by ideas it belongs strictly to the predicate rather than the subject of judgement. Bradley spoke in his later work on thought of a special subject of judgement, chosen by our ideas as that which is to be characterized more specifically, but the ultimate subject remains reality at large.

But how does the mind manage to direct itself upon a reality not constituted by ideas? It does so because it is intrinsically continuous with, indeed somehow identical with, a larger reality beyond itself and it feels itself as being such. This is not an opinion in the sense of a judgement using ideas or concepts but the necessary pre-conceptual background of conceptual thinking.

Thus at the root of thought is a feeling of continuity with a larger whole of which our present state of mind is just a fragment. Our thoughts are an effort to apply ideas to this whole which will carry us beyond this mere dumb acquaintance. (At the level of ordinary thought and experience this larger whole presents itself to us spatio-temporally as a physical world. As metaphysicians, or in moments of illumination, we may become aware of it in a manner which leads to a more spiritual characterization of its nature.)

Bradley says in his initial statements that it is the reality presented in the perceptual manifold, as experienced immediately quite apart from any ideas we form of it, which is the subject of which we predicate our ideas. But, as he makes clearer in the second edition, it is not presented only by the perceptually given but by anything else thus directly presented or experienced.

There are intriguing similarities and contrasts in Bradley's position here and that of Bertrand Russell, who was influenced by Bradley in his own treatment of definite descriptions (talking of the King of France where Bradley talks of the King of Utopia) as belonging logically to the predicate (and in his related account of existential statements). For Russell propositions which can be grasped without acquaintance with the particulars with which they are ostensibly concerned are parasitic upon propositions about particulars which can be grasped only by those acquainted with them. Bradley is even more insistent that a kind of acquaintance, which goes beyond its specification in terms of universals, is required if we are to think of something. But for him the reality with which we have this pre-conceptual acquaintance is always the same, namely the one sensible reality which we encounter non-conceptually through sense experience. Not that the thought had failed to occur to him that we may have a pre-conceptual encounter with particular bits of reality, which we can refer to by such words as 'this' and 'here'; indeed he makes suggestions in this connection which may well have influenced Russell. But, although thinking of our ability to locate particular bits of reality by our direct pre-conceptual awareness of them is quite useful at a rather superficial level of analysis it will not, as Bradley sees it, ultimately do. In the end it is always simply reality, *tout court*, rather than some particular bit of reality which is the subject of predication (see [15.3], 50).

This account of judgement strongly suggests the view that a judgement is true if and only if the idea (in the logical sense) which functions as its predicate is a universal actually found in the reality to which it ascribes it. For what else can we be doing in ascribing the character we abstract from our imagery to a reality beyond but supposing that it is actually found there as an actual feature of that reality? And in what other sense could our judgement be true than that it is in fact present there?

Such an account of truth is not far off from the Scholastic view that in true thinking an essence *objectively* exemplified in the mind is recognized to be the essence *formally* exemplified by that reality beyond on to which the mind is directed. And, though Bradley never presents this explicitly as his account of truth, it seems to be frequently presupposed in what he has to say as to how various different sorts of judgement must be taken if they are to give genuine truth about reality.

Admittedly such a view of truth could apply only to judgements the content of which is imaginatively realized in a fairly full manner. However, for one who thinks, as Bradley does, in effect, that other judgements are a kind of substitute for these, their truth will consist in the truth of the more imaginatively fulfilled judgements for which they substitute.

This certainly seems to be the view of truth most obviously implied by Bradley's theory of judgement as we have so far considered it. However, while commentators usually allow that there are traces of a correspondence view of truth in the first edition of *Principles of Logic* they usually take him as having rejected this in his later writings in favour of a coherence view. Though *Appearance and Reality* is relevant here, the main sources for Bradley's supposed coherence view of truth are some of the essays collected in *Essays in Truth and Reality*, first published in 1914, consisting largely of essays published in journals (mainly *Mind*) from 1904 to 1911 (though one goes back to 1899). Of these the most important is chapter VII, 'On Truth and Coherence'. He there sets out to argue, as against expressions of the contrary view by G. F. Stout and Russell, that there are no immediately certain facts delivered to us either in perception or in memory and that every such judgement, like all other judgements, is subject to the test of includability within a total system of acceptable beliefs. This test includes not merely coherence but also comprehensiveness ([15.2], 202; 223–6).

These two requirements have, indeed, a common source, according to Bradley, for, he holds, there is always incoherence in any body of thought which stops short of the whole truth. However, in practice we have to treat them as two distinct criteria which our thought must satisfy if it is to be true. Taken together these criteria constitute the notion of membership of a judgement in a system (see [15.2], 241).

Thus if a judgement as to what I am perceiving, or a memory judgement as to what I perceived in the past, cannot fit into the main body of my knowledge (that is, my current system of beliefs) it will be quite proper for me to reject it, and put a different interpretation on my experience.

The standard criticism of coherence as a criterion of truth is that you can have a coherent system of false propositions. But when it is realized that the test was meant to be used, along with that of comprehensiveness, only on judgements which someone is inclined to affirm, the force of the criticism is largely blunted. Thus taken it bids us accept only judgements which cohere with the largest body of other beliefs which will continue to solicit us however encyclopaedic our concerns become.

The difference between Bradley's position and that of the coherence view of textbooks may go deeper still. For he sometimes says that it is not only with other judgements that a judgement must cohere to be true, but also with experience (i.e. or e.g. sense experience). Such, at least, seems to be his meaning when he says that the 'idea of system demands the inclusion of all possible material'.

It must be emphasized, in any case, that the idea that somehow thought can remove itself from its basis in experience and discover how things are in some quite *a priori* fashion is firmly rejected by Bradley (see [15.2], 203). What Bradley denies, then, is (not that our knowledge or belief system arises from experience and is continually subject to testing thereby, but) that it is based on some hard data supplied by perception which cannot be rejected. It has been observed that Bradley's view, especially as developed in this particular essay, has some affinity to currently influential views of W. V. O. Quine's.

Bradley himself was not unaware, it seems, of a conflict in his thought between a view which makes truth a feature of a system of ideas considered in its own right, and one which makes it turn on its relation to something else. For his final answer to the question 'what is truth?' (reached by the intermediate suggestion that truth is what completely satisfies the intellect) seems to be that '[t]ruth is an ideal expression of the Universe' ([15.2], 223) and this seems designed to meet this very difficulty.

Not that the answer is an easy one to grasp. What Bradley seems to mean is that the Absolute, as somehow present in all its parts, is striving within each part to develop itself into the whole, with the result that the thought pertaining to any part has an initial tendency to develop into ideas which capture something of its total character. Since the whole is coherent and comprehensive this urge takes the form of a nisus towards a coherent and comprehensive system of ideas which will reproduce the character of the Absolute to whatever extent it satisfies itself. However, the ideas do not form a completely closed-off world, for the intellectual part of reality to which they pertain is continually fed by experience stemming from the other parts.

However obscure the notion that reality is working itself out within the intellect of each of us may be, it is apparently Bradley's attempt to combine the view that truth consists in ideas which capture something of the essence of the reality of which they are predicated with the view that it consists in the satisfaction of having ideas which are coherent and comprehensive. For if the reality we are thinking about is expressing itself in the way we think of it, then our system of thoughts can best reach a correct characterization of what they are about by satisfying the internal criteria it imposes on itself.

Besides this general account of judgement Bradley provides an interesting account of the different types of judgement, categorical, hypothetical, negative and so forth. However the main topic of *Principles of Logic*, pursued in Books 2 and 3, is the nature of inference. The central thesis is that inference consists in 'ideal experiment' in the form of synthesis and analysis. Typically this consists in synthesizing the ideas we have of things into some more comprehensive idea of a whole to which they must or may belong and finding through analysis that the whole or its constituents, as thereby presented in idea, consequently possess certain characteristics, or relations to each other, which must or would belong to these as they exist in external fact. 'Reasoning thus depends on the identity of a content inside a mental experiment with that content outside' ([15.3], 436).

In his account of judgement Bradley had already insisted that to think of all judgements as subject–predicate in the Aristotelian sense was a misconception which foundered on existential and relational judgements. (Though Russell held that the Bradleyan treatment of relations depends upon that assumption, his own way out of it owes much to Bradley.) This challenge to tradition is continued in his account of inference in an elaborate critique of the doctrine that all reasoning is syllogistic. (He has received some credit for this from modern logicians who would not, however, go along with his associated view that the criteria of valid inference can never be purely formal.)

One of the main themes is the impossibility of reducing all valid inferences to the syllogistic form except perhaps by an act of torture which distorts their significance. Bradley shows carefully how various sorts of inference cannot be thus treated, in particular those which turn on the meaning of relational expressions. Thus inference cannot be reduced to the application of a limited set of standard rules nor can it become such simply by the addition of some extra rules not recognized by traditional logic. Such an aspiration turns on the wholly mistaken view that the validity of inference is determined solely by the form and never by the content of premises and conclusion. Such rules as there are, are only general guides not formulas to be followed mechanically (Bradley associates this with a similar point about moral rules).

There is much that is of continuing importance in Bradley's treatment of inference and of related themes, though it is often clumsy in comparison with the treatment that modern symbolism makes possible.

❧ APPEARANCE AND REALITY ❧

We must now turn to Bradley's metaphysical position as advanced in *Appearance and Reality* and developed further in *Essays in Truth and Reality*.

Bradley sets out in this work to show that all ordinary things are unreal, such as physical things, space, time, causation and even the self (which is treated with distinctly less respect than in *Ethical Studies*).

Though unreal, however, he insists that these things can properly be said to exist.

What can be meant by saying that tables, space, time or ourselves are unreal, though they certainly exist? Bradley, it would seem, has two things in mind which he does not clearly distinguish, though he would probably say that in the end they come to the same. In the first sense, to say of certain things that they exist but are unreal is to say that, though the concept of such things, and the postulation of their existence, is an effective, indeed indispensable, tool through which thought can deal with the world, so that we must go on speaking of there being such things, there is an incoherence in our concept of them, which means that thought which postulates them cannot possess that final truth as to how things really are which metaphysics seeks.

The second sense in which he seems to think of such existing things as unreal is that though they are so to speak *there*, we conceive of them as having a degree of independent existence when they are really only abstractions from a more concrete totality. Common-sense examples of things which exist but are unreal in something like this sense might be shadows and the surfaces of three-dimensional objects and their merely two-dimensional shapes.

While we may listen patiently to an idealist who tells us that the physical world is unreal in the first sense, it is harder for him to persuade us that we, and even our passing thoughts, are so. In the latter case emphasis on the second sense of 'unreal' renders his thought more promising.

However, Bradley himself would say that in so far as a thing is a mere abstraction from some more concrete whole (of whose nature we take inadequate account) what we have in mind when we speak of it as existing is bound to be somewhat incoherent. So the second sense will be a case of the first.

Bradley marshals a large array of arguments to show that the things mentioned are unreal. Physical things are unreal, because we can form no conception of them which distinguishes between those of their 'properties' which genuinely inhere in *them* and those which are a matter of their effects on an observer. Yet the very idea of a physical thing is of something to which this distinction applies. Moreover, the space and time within which they supposedly exist are riddled with paradoxical contradictions which Bradley exhibits with glee. So whatever aspect of reality it is with which we are really dealing when we think of the physical, it cannot in its true nature answer to properly physical predicates. We ourselves are similarly contradictory and unreal. Whatever is doing what is known as 'our' thinking cannot really be a self or person as such thought conceives it, for there are too many incoherences in the idea of a person for this to be so. (These turn particularly on the matter of personal identity over time.)

The detailed contradictions present in all our concepts are largely instances of one very basic contradiction involved in all our thought, a contradiction inherent in the very idea of a world of distinct things standing in distinct relations to each other.

We (that is eventually the Absolute masquerading as ourselves) cannot help thinking in terms of there being lots of individual things in the world. Equally, we cannot help thinking of these individual things as standing in a variety of relations to each other. But the idea of things held together by relations is radically incoherent, essential tool for dealing with the world though it is.

For if the relations between things are themselves things, then they require themselves to be related to the original things, and those relations must again be related to these relations and what they relate, and so on in an endless incoherent regress.

Should we then say that the relations are not things? But if not things, what are they? Unless something can be said about them they had better not claim to figure in any ultimately true account of the world. Perhaps then they are aspects of the things they relate. But if the relation between A and B is an aspect of either A or of B, or separately of each of them, they do nothing to connect A and B. R as in A is just there in A, and has nothing to do with B. Perhaps then they are aspects of AB, the unity of A and B. But if A and B are a unity to which the relation R belongs, then it seems it is not through R that they are brought together.

This is by no means an adequate account of Bradley's famous, and often correctly or incorrectly controverted, argument but gives a hint of his style of reasoning in this connection.

Some of the criticism of it certainly misses the point. It is said that Bradley thinks of relations as things, but that they are not things but how things stand to each other. But this misses the point that Bradley asks us what they can be if they are not things, and claims to dispose of them whether we conceive of them as things in any proper sense or not. But probably critics are right, that Bradley's arguments can be answered if we bring our full conceptual resources to bear on them.

The Bradleyan reply would be that this is not surprising, since our concepts incorporate all sorts of devices for disguising their basic incoherence. They would not work if there were not such devices. But to appeal to these devices is to lose sight of the underlying insight to which these seemingly rather sophistical arguments are trying to lead us.

That fundamental insight is that when we think of a thing first independently of how it stands to other things, and then as an element of a situation in which other things figure, there is really a *gestalt* switch between two incompatible ways of conceiving the situation. They are incompatible because when we envisage something as a detail in a larger whole it takes on not just characteristics additional to those we envisaged it as possessing when we think of it in isolation (or in something closer to isolation) but characteristics incompatible with this. An angel seen as a detail in a large painting looks different from when it is looked at alone. Our friend presents himself differently to us when we learn about his or her family background. These are not merely different ways of registering the world in our mind; they are different conceptions of what is really there.

But we cannot choose either to envisage the thing in comparative isolation or as a detail in a larger situation. For, on the one hand, the very concept of a thing is of something which can be conceived without reference to other things as a separate unit in its own right, while equally we cannot avoid enriching our concept of every individual thing we postulate by envisaging it simply as a detail in some larger whole. (We may be prepared to say that some of our things, like two-dimensional objects, are mere abstractions from some larger whole, but we cannot say it of every single thing, or else we have no proper things left. Yet every single thing, the universe apart, does figure in a larger whole.)

The concept of a relation is that of something which connects things without making them simply aspects of a larger whole in which they lose their separate identities. The proposition 'A is R to B' allows us to take up two incompatible stances, turn and turn about, as suits our convenience: that of A as a thing in its own right and that of A as an abstraction along with B from some larger whole. Since the proposition is thus an attempt to synthesize two incompatible views it cannot be the literal truth about anything.

It should be evident that these reflections lead by inevitable steps to the view that the only real thing is the universe and that everything else is a mere aspect of it. (The only but unthinkable alternative is that real things exist in total isolation from one another; Leibniz tended to this view though incoherently invoking God to provide a semblance of a single cosmos.)

To arrive at his final conclusion that the only reality is the Absolute, and that everything else is a mere abstraction from it, Bradley has to show that the universe merits this title in virtue of its mental or spiritual nature.

This he does by arguing that when we really press the matter there is nothing which we can form any clear idea of as existing apart from some mental process or activity. Either we tacitly envisage it as presented to some mental state, and in effect a component of that state, or as itself a mental state.

So in the end – for reasons quite separate from the argument concerning relations – we can accept only mental realities as genuinely real. The physical world, for example, must be conceived as existing only as presentation to perception or thought, or perhaps as experiencing itself.

But if the only finite realities which can pass this test of clear conceivability are mental, it follows that the universe is a single reality from which the indefinite number of mental states which so to speak supply its stuff are mere abstractions. But the only conceivable thing from which these mental states can be abstractions must be itself some sort of cosmic mental state or form of consciousness. This cannot change through time, but must rather eternally include all those mental states which appear to themselves to pertain to beings living at different times. That it is not changing in time follows from the fact that past and future and present can only appear to be related to each other because they are all abstractions from something embracing all times, and therefore itself timeless.

Critics such as Bertrand Russell and G. E. Moore were long thought to have put paid to Bradley's metaphysical system. (A more insightful critic was William James.) Upon the whole, they missed the real thrust of it and thought that it was rebutted by exhibiting certain confusions or sophistries in its presentation. Anyone who knows anything of the Hindu tradition, especially Vedanta (though Bradley showed no interest in this), will realize that views like Bradley's are not too eccentric to be the basis of a whole culture. Perhaps western philosophy will turn again to an outlook more like Bradley's. It must stand, at the least, as one of the great possible visions of the world open to humanity. Historically, however, it gave way soon after its completion to different styles of philosophizing in which Moore, Russell and Wittgenstein were key figures. A. N. Whitehead, however, continued, to some considerable extent along the path laid out by Bradley (envisioning a world composed solely of experience and unified in God), though he sought to do greater justice to the scientific view of things.

❧ NOTES ❧

1 The thinker who did most to clarify the relations between psychological hedonism, and ethical hedonism in its two versions, egoistic and universalistic, was Henry Sidgwick in his *Methods of Ethics*, London: Macmillan, 1874, with further revised editions. Although in various controversies Bradley exhibits the utmost

contempt for Sidgwick I have to a limited extent made use of Sidgwick's terminology in expounding Bradley.

✦ BIBLIOGRAPHY ✦

Works by Bradley

15.1 *Appearance and Reality: A Metaphysical Essay* (1893), text of 2nd edn, Oxford: Clarendon Press, 1930.

15.2 *Essays in Truth and Reality* (1914), Oxford: Clarendon Press, 1968.

15.3 *The Principles of Logic* (1883), text of 2nd edn, 2 vols, Oxford: Oxford University Press, 1963.

15.4 *Ethical Studies* (1876), text of 2nd edn, Oxford: Clarendon Press, 1927.

Other works

There are not many recent whole books devoted to Bradley's philosophy, though some are known to be in preparation. The main available works are:

15.5 McHenry, L. *Whitehead and Bradley: a Comparative Analysis*, Albany: State University of New York Press, 1992.

15.6 McNiven, D. *Bradley's Moral Psychology*, Lewiston/Queenston: Edwin Mellen Press, 1987.

15.7 Manser, A. *Bradley's Logic*, Oxford: Basil Blackwell, 1983.

15.8 Manser, A. and Guy Stock, eds, *The Philosophy of F. H. Bradley*, Oxford: Clarendon Press, 1984 (collection of essays by various names).

15.9 Sprigge, T. L. S. *James and Bradley: American Truth and British Reality*, Chicago: Open Court, 1993.

15.10 Wollheim, R. *F. H. Bradley*, Harmondsworth: Penguin, 1959.

Recent books with some general relevance include

15.11 Rescher, N. *The Coherence Theory of Truth*, Oxford: Clarendon Press, 1973.

15.12 Sprigge, T. L. S. *The Vindication of Absolute Idealism*, Edinburgh: Edinburgh University Press, 1983.

15.13 Walker, R. C. S. *The Coherence Theory of Truth*, London: Routledge 1989.

Glossary

analytic *and* **synthetic** – an analytic statement is true in virtue of the meanings of the words in it, e.g. 'Bachelors are unmarried males'. A synthetic statement is true not in virtue of the meanings of the words used, e.g. 'Some bachelors are rich'.

a posteriori – based on experience.

a priori – not based on experience.

***cause, efficient** – a translation of *causa efficiens*, a term which was used by medieval philosophers. The term goes back to Aristotle, who stated that an 'efficient' cause is a source of change or of coming to rest (*Physics*, II, 3). So, for example, a man who gives advice is an efficient cause, and a father is the efficient cause of his child.

***cause, final** – a term that renders the Latin *causa finalis*. 'Final' does not mean here last or ultimate, as when one speaks of a 'final curtain'. Rather, a final cause is that *for the sake of which* something is done. The term goes back to Aristotle, who said that a final cause is an end: e.g. health is the final cause of taking a walk (*Physics*, II, 3).

coherence theory of truth – the view that a true statement is that which coheres, or is most consistent, with the system of accepted statements.

deduction – a form of argument in which if the premisses are true then the conclusion must also be true.

definition per genus et differentiam – a form of definition in which a word is defined by locating the thing to which it refers in a class of things (*genus*) sharing some common features, and then by indicating those features which distinguish the thing from others in that class.

***determinism** – a term covering a wide variety of views, which have in common the thesis that every event or every state of affairs belonging to a certain class is determined by certain factors, in the sense that given these factors the event must occur or the state of affairs must hold. In the past philosophers readily accepted the idea that determinism held in the natural world; but many of them were reluctant to believe that it also held in the sphere of human actions. They believed that (whatever might be the case in the natural world) the will was free, in the sense that, whenever a human agent chooses to do something, that agent could always have chosen to do otherwise.

empiricism – the theory that all knowledge is based on experience.

459

*fatalism – a form of determinism (q.v.) according to which what will happen, will happen, and there is nothing that humans can do to alter the course of events. Although all fatalists are determinists, not all determinists are fatalists.

hedonism – the view that pleasure is the only intrinsically valuable thing.

*idealism – there are three main types of philosophical idealism, all of which have in common the thesis that the external world – the world of physical things – is in some way a product of mind. (1) The first historically was Berkeleian idealism. Bishop Berkeley (1685–1753) argued that a material object consists of nothing but ideas, either in the mind of God or in the mind of conscious beings such as ourselves. (2) 'Transcendental idealism' was a term used by Kant (1724–1804) to refer to his view that the spatial and temporal properties of things have no existence apart from our minds. (3) 'Objective' or 'absolute' idealism, first expounded by Hegel (1770–1831), is distinguished by the fact that it is a kind of monism, asserting that everything that exists is a form of the one 'absolute mind'.

*induction – an inductive argument is an argument in which, from the proposition that all observed members of a certain class have a certain property, one proceeds to the conclusion that all members of the class have this property.

law of excluded middle – the principle that every proposition is true or not true.

law of non-contradiction – the principle (sometimes also called the *law of contradiction*) that a proposition and its negation cannot both be true.

libertarian – one who denies the truth of determinism (q.v.), believing that there are some human acts which are not causally determined.

logical positivists – those who subscribe to the verification principle (q.v.).

materialism – the theory that reality is all material. The mind is therefore not something immaterial.

nominalism – the view that general terms are just words applying to particular things.

phenomenalism – the doctrine that a physical object is, as J. S. Mill put it, 'the permanent possibility of sensation'.

reductio ad absurdum – a mode of argument in which a view is shown to have an absurd implication and is therefore to be rejected.

*universals – it has been argued that universal terms, such as 'triangle', can have meaning only if there exist in some way entities which are called 'universals', e.g. the triangle as such, or triangularity.

utilitarianism – the view that a right act is that which maximizes the general happiness.

utility, the principle of – as formulated by J. S. Mill it is the view that 'happiness is desirable, and the only thing desirable as an end; all other things being only desirable as means to that end'.

*verification principle – also called the *principle of verifiability*. This term has two senses. (1) It can refer to a criterion of meaning; according to this, a proposition is factually significant if, and only if, it can be verified in principle. (2) The term can also be applied to a theory of the nature of meaning; this states that the meaning of a proposition is the method of verifying it.

---

* Explanations adapted from *Routledge History of Philosophy*, Vol. IV.

Index